Professional Selling

Professional Selling

Sixth Edition

David L. Kurtz
University of Arkansas

H. Robert Dodge
Eastern Michigan University

IRWIN
Homewood, IL 60430
Boston, MA 02116

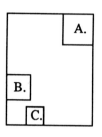

The cover shows 3 categories of selling:

A. Industrial

B. Consumer Goods

C. Services

All photos courtesy of Scott Wanner/Journalism Services

© RICHARD D. IRWIN, INC., 1976, 1979, 1982, 1985, 1988, and 1991

Senior sponsoring editor: Steve Patterson
Developmental editor: Eleanore Snow
Project editor: Karen Smith
Production manager: Bette K. Ittersagen
Designer: Russell Schneck Design
Artist: Alice Thiede
Compositor: Graphic World, Inc.
Typeface: 10/12 Times Roman
Printer: R. R. Donnelley & Sons Company

Library of Congress Cataloging-in-Publication Data

Kurtz, David L.

Professional Selling/David L. Kurtz, H. Robert Dodge.—6th ed.
p.   cm.

Includes bibliographical references.

Includes index.

ISBN 0-256-08725-3

1. Selling.   I. Dodge, H. Robert, 1929-   II. Title.
HF5438.25.K87   1991   90–44067
658.8′5—dc20   CIP

Printed in the United States of America
2   3   4   5   6   7   8   9   0   DOC   7   6   5   4   3   2   1

TO THE IRWIN SALESFORCE . . .
True Sales Professionals!

Preface

The authors are delighted to introduce the sixth edition of *Professional Selling*. When we wrote the first edition back in 1976, we decided to emphasize the professionalism of personal selling. This orientation has been followed in each subsequent revision. The sixth edition is no exception.

Selling is one of society's most important professions in the 1990s. A terrific example of sales professionalism is the textbook representative from Richard D. Irwin, Inc., who presented this book to you.

This new edition continues the strengths of the previous editions. It explains what it is like to be a professional salesperson and explores different types of selling situations—industrial, retail, real estate, and insurance. The core of the text remains its logical presentation of the "nuts and bolts" of the sales process itself. Finally, readers will discover an easy-to-read and example-oriented writing style that has made *Professional Selling* a favorite with the nearly 100,000 students who have already used the book over the years.

Changes in This Edition

The new edition also introduces some changes in *Professional Selling*. In addition to a thorough updating, the following changes will be evident in this revision.

- First, the size of the book has been reduced by a chapter. The material on trends in selling has been moved to Chapter 2 rather than receiving separate chapter coverage as in previous editions.
- The major content change was the complete rewriting of Chapter 7 to reflect the growing competitive importance of establishing a relationship with the customer.
- The most significant pedagogical change is the listing of chapter objectives at the beginning of each chapter. A summary of how each of these objectives has been presented appears later in the chapter.
- The contemporary design introduced in the fifth edition is further enhanced in the sixth edition. The use of color enlivens the textbook and

highlights figures and illustrative materials. Each figure was reviewed and revised where necessary to add clarity and improve understanding. All figures are integrated into the text of the book.

- As with previous editions, the instructor's manual and test bank have been thoroughly revised, and ten additional multiple-choice questions have been added to each chapter.

We hope you like the new edition of *Professional Selling*. We would appreciate hearing your comments and suggestions. Dave Kurtz can be reached at the Department of Marketing and Transportation, University of Arkansas, Fayetteville, AR 72701. Bob Dodge can be reached at the Department of Marketing, Eastern Michigan University, Ypsilanti, MI 48197.

David L. Kurtz
H. Robert Dodge

Acknowledgments

The authors would like to thank the reviewers of the sixth edition of *Professional Selling*. The following individuals provided the candid, insightful reviews that were necessary to keep authors on track:

Robert J. Boewadt, *DePaul University*

Edmund A. Cotta, *California State University–Long Beach*

Elliot B. Gant, *Florida International University*

We would also like to acknowledge these reviewers of previous editions of *Professional Selling*. Their contributions are reflected throughout the current edition.

Ralph M. Davenport, Jr., *University of Dubuque*

Ted Erickson, *Normandale Community College*

Jack E. Forrest, *Middle Tennessee State University*

Jacob Goodman, *Bergen Community College*

Gary M. Grikscheit, *University of Utah*

Thomas Grissom, *Pima College*

Robert E. Harrison, *Northeast Louisiana University*

Janet G. Hibbard, *Eastern Kentucky University*

Nathan Himelstein, *Essex County College*

James C. Kerr, *Phoenix College*

Jerome M. Kinskey, *Sinclair Community College*

Z. W. Koby, *Mississippi State University*

Steven C. Lawlor, *Foothill College*

Harry Moak, *Macomb Community College*

John Mozingo, *University of Wisconsin–Stevens Point*

Henry W. Nash, *Mississippi State University*

Hal Perry, *Northeastern Junior College*

Marion R. Sillah, *Tuskegee Institute*

John B. Southern, *Adams State College*

Ann Squire, *Blackhawk Technical Institute*
William E. Vincent, *Santa Barbara Community College*
Charles Walker, *Harding University*

Finally, the authors would like to specifically note that *Professional Selling* is dedicated to the Irwin salesforce. Ladies and gentlemen, we appreciate your efforts.

D. L. K.
H. R. D.

Contents in Brief

Contents

Professional Selling

PART ONE

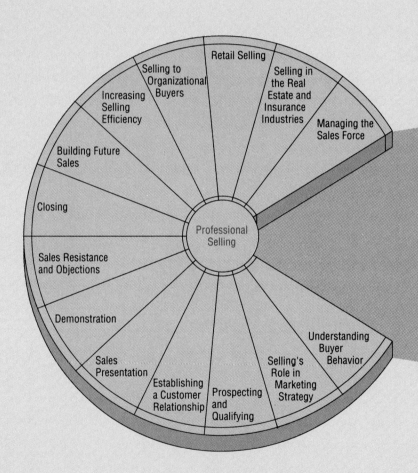

Retail Selling

Selling to Organizational Buyers

Selling in the Real Estate and Insurance Industries

Increasing Selling Efficiency

Managing the Sales Force

Building Future Sales

Closing

Professional Selling

Sales Resistance and Objections

Understanding Buyer Behavior

Demonstration

Selling's Role in Marketing Strategy

Sales Presentation

Establishing a Customer Relationship

Prospecting and Qualifying

Professionalism in Selling

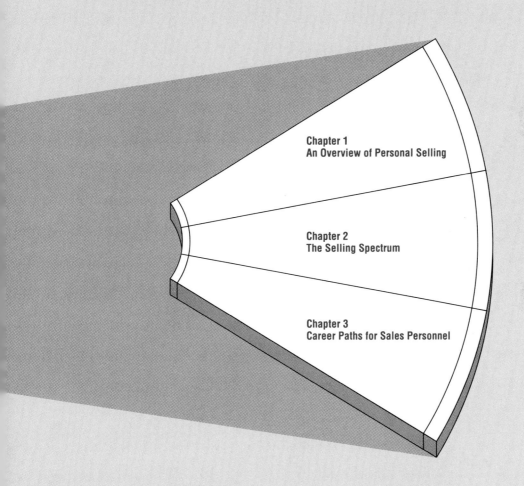

Chapter 1
An Overview of Personal Selling

Chapter 2
The Selling Spectrum

Chapter 3
Career Paths for Sales Personnel

CHAPTER 1

An Overview of Personal Selling

CHAPTER OBJECTIVES

1. To define personal selling.

2. To explain the importance of personal selling.

3. To outline the eras in selling.

4. To differentiate between a seller's market and a buyer's market and to relate these concepts to professional selling.

5. To explain the marketing concept and its effect on personal selling.

6. To list and discuss the primary reasons for studying professional selling.

SALES CAREER PROFILE

ADELE KRAFT
Moore Business Forms

Adele Kraft is a Seattle-based account representative in Moore Business Forms' Systems Division. Kraft, a native of Hawaii, holds a bachelor's degree in business administration from the University of Puget Sound in Tacoma, Washington.

When asked how she got started with Moore, Kraft replied, "I was intrigued by careers in fashion in college, and wanted to be in marketing. After selling in a retail situation and enjoying it, I decided I would pursue a career in selling, but I no longer wanted to work in retail. So I sent out resumés and started interviewing for a position in outside sales.

"I began my career with Moore Business Forms in January 1982. After meeting with the Moore salesperson, I filled out an application and started the interview process. The first step was to interview with the sales supervisor who had the opening. After that, I was interviewed by the district manager and went on a couple of sales calls with one of the sales reps. The final step was an interview with the regional manager. I was really impressed with Moore and felt that it was a good, solid company to work for.

"Moore is the world's largest manufacturer of business forms. It operates internationally and has a good reputation. There is a very thorough initial training school, followed periodically by further training sessions.

"When I started with Moore 5½ years ago, I called on all the accounts in a geographical area with the exception of the major accounts, which were referred to the senior reps. At present, I'm an account representative in the Systems Division, assigned approximately a dozen major accounts.

"Although I work with major accounts, they are mostly companies that Moore has either never done business with or has not worked with for a number of years. I enjoy meeting and working with people to find solutions to their problems.

"We work hard, but the rewards can be great. If we meet our annual objective, for example, the reward is an all-expenses-paid trip. Although the sales reps come from varied backgrounds, there is a real camaraderie among us.

"I feel that I have a good, solid working relationship with my customers. We all have a mutual respect for each other's positions and capabilities.

"In any sales environment, it is imperative to have support from management for the salespeople to do well and the company to succeed. I've always had good managers who have given me assistance, feedback, and encouragement.

"Where do I go from here? I can continue in selling by progressing from sales rep to account rep, then on to account executive, and finally to senior account executive. Another direction leads to management. Many reps have gone from a sales position (sales rep or account rep) into a management position, for example, as a sales supervisor. Some reps have chosen to go "inside" for a few years, in a marketing position. Later, they might return to the field in either a sales or management position. My immediate goal is to become an account executive, which is a natural step after account rep."

Asked why she thought Moore was one of the top 100 U.S. firms to sell for, Kraft commented, "First, Moore has a very extensive training program. The initial training includes knowledge of sales, as well as of the company and the products we offer. The customers I have dealt with over the past five years have changed, and I've been through additional training to help me in my dealings with different types of business environments, products, and systems.

"A compensation plan is another reason Moore is a good firm to work for. Our compensation plan is fair, and we are recognized and rewarded for making our goals.

"We also have a good support system for our products from our research and development department to our manufacturing plants and our marketing and administration staffs."

When asked to define "professional selling," Kraft replied, "Professional selling is to be able to service customers in a manner that gives them a sense of satisfaction for doing business with us. Selling for Moore is not a one-time sale, it's ongoing, so we have to be flexible, to grow and change with the ever-changing demands of our customers."

Asked how important personal selling is to the success of Moore, Kraft remarked: "I think it's very important. We are finding more competition all the time. We need to sell more than just product and price; we need to sell the other services we as a company can provide. We need to know our customers and their businesses, so we can better service their needs. We need to find ways to set ourselves apart from our competition."

Finally, Kraft was asked what advice she would offer students entering a sales career. "They should get a good education. Although it is not a prerequisite in most cases to have a college education to get into a sales career, I know that it has helped me.

"Another point that I feel students should know is that there is no true stereotype of a salesperson. There are many different types of sales jobs, and different types of personalities are the right fit for those positions.

"What it takes to be a good salesperson is a genuine interest in your customers and their businesses. Knowledge of your company and its capabilities, finding answers to questions that arise, and a determination to succeed are key factors in successful selling.

"Two of my most successful sales years with Moore Business Forms were the year that I was pregnant with my daughter and the following year, when I had her. The year that I had her, I was on leave for three months. But I was determined that I would make our achievement club that year, and I did. What I'm saying is that to be a successful salesperson, number one is determination."

While most high-tech companies concentrate on the development of an endless succession of improved products, XA Systems Corp. takes a different tack. The $13 million software firm located in Los Catos, California, concentrates on products costing $40,000 and more, targeted at big data-processing organizations. CEO Lacy Edwards says: "We're not interested in developing stuff that is just neat. People have to want it."

Personal selling is the key ingredient to XA Systems' success. Everything the company does is focused on the sales process, which for XA typically runs 90 days or more. XA's sales process includes an initial appointment, a demonstration, a 30-day trial, and a closing appointment. At least one on-site visit by a sales representative, and probably a technical support person, is required at each stage of the selling process.

Edwards wants his 45-person sales force to close the sale in 3 to 4 months, compared to an industry average of 6 to 12 months. Each rep makes 40 on-site interviews monthly. These interviews are arranged by a nine-person support staff. Edwards and his associates at XA Systems realize that the company's future depends on the effectiveness of their sales effort. This philosophy is highlighted by the earnings of XA's sales force. CEO Edwards remarks, "Sales is this company's dominant, driving force . . . if a few of them (salespersons) aren't earning more than I am, we're in trouble."[1]

The XA Systems' story illustrates the importance that professional selling plays for many organizations. It is often the crucial difference between success and failure.

SOME BASIC OBSERVATIONS ABOUT PERSONAL SELLING

A good way to begin the study of personal selling is to consider some facts about the sales field. Some of these observations are contrary to what many college students believe, yet all are true. Consider the following statements:

- Selling is of vital importance to our economy, our competitive system, and public welfare.
- Salespeople are among the best paid personnel in most companies.
- Successful sales representatives are among the most secure of all participants in the private enterprise system.
- Selling provides meaningful career opportunities for women and minorities.
- Personal selling allows you to apply much of what you have learned in college and other educational experiences.
- Sales is one of the quickest routes to business success.
- Selling is increasingly recognized as a profession.

Selling is a people-oriented activity in which success can be easily and objectively measured. Selling has been the path to success for millions of people over the years. Since people and success are so important in any discussion of personal selling, each chapter in this textbook features case histories of people who have achieved sales success. These individuals teach much about professionalism by their examples.

The difference between success and failure is often very slight. Successful sales personnel are typically those who learn from their failures rather than being overcome by them.

DEFINING PERSONAL SELLING

personal selling

interpersonal persuasive process designed to influence someone's decision

Personal selling is defined as an interpersonal persuasive process designed to influence some person's decision. Sales forces accomplish this objective in a variety of ways. Scott Paper has adopted a sales philosophy called "Stakeholder Alignment" under which its sales representatives attempt to become partners with their customers. Dennis Stewart, Scott's vice president for consumer sales, says, "Our salespeople are already performing the way those of the future will have to. That is, they have more of a business mentality, think more about the customer's profit needs, and know what their strategy is, what they want to do with their shelf space, and what their plans for the future are."[2]

How someone sells depends on a host of factors, such as what is being sold, the customer, and the setting in which the sales interview occurs. Some sales approaches are excellent in one sales situation but wrong in another. Good sales personnel are able to correctly identify the persuasive message that is proper in a given situation. The cost-savings possibilities of a new cutting machine might be demonstrated to a firm that has had cost overruns on recent contracts. Expectant parents might be ideal prospects for a life insurance agent.

Personal selling is dynamic, flexible, and volatile. Traditionally, this persuasive process has been concerned with commercial transactions. But a United Way campaigner, the minister of a local church, a Navy recruiter, a football coach, or a politician could also use this persuasive process. This idea is developed further in the next chapter.

The importance of personal selling derives from three viewpoints: (1) economic contribution, (2) competitive importance, and (3) public contribution. Many of the criticisms about selling advanced over the years stem from ignorance. Understanding the role of selling in modern society corrects this deficiency.

Economic Contribution

Selling improves our standard of living. It generates the revenue on which the business system depends, as well as providing consumers with the goods and services necessary for an improved quality of life. Lyn Andrews, CBS vice president for market development, describes selling this way: "It's the locomotive that drives the train."[3]

Effective selling is important to the economic growth and development of any society. Countries with high standards of living support advanced marketing and distribution systems. New and improved consumer products and better industrial technology are not automatically accepted in the mar-

PROFESSIONAL SELLING IN ACTION

Selling at the Top: The 100 Best Companies to Sell for in America

William J. Birnes and Gary Markmam's book, *Selling at the Top,* is a most interesting discussion of the top 100 firms to sell for in the United States. The authors interviewed companies grouped into four major categories: (1) services, (2) consumer goods, (3) light industry, and (4) heavy industry. The specific industries explored in each of these categories are shown in the table at right.

Birnes and Markmam evaluated the companies in these industries on the basis of four factors: (1) salary, (2) commission paid, (3) company support for field sales representatives, and (4) intangible factors that may favorably or adversely affect sales representatives.

Selling at the Top identifies the five best sales companies in each industry. It also shows their scores on each of the factors previously listed.

Overall, *Selling at the Top* is one of the most comprehensive studies ever made of America's best selling jobs. It is recommended reading for anyone contemplating or currently employed in the field of selling.

Selling at the Top provides the foundation for the

Group 1: Services
1. Advertising
2. Banking
3. Education products
4. Insurance
5. Real estate

Group 2: Consumer Goods
1. Automobiles
2. Book publishing
3. Food
4. Microcomputers
5. Retail

Group 3: Light Industry
1. Mainframe computers
2. Medical equipment
3. Office furniture
4. Pharmaceuticals

Group 4: Heavy Industry
1. Aerospace
2. Building
3. Industrial chemicals
4. Heavy machinery
5. Paper
6. Printing

sales career profiles that begin each chapter of *Professional Selling.* Each of these profiles discusses the sales career of someone who works for one of these top sales companies. Readers can gain invaluable insights into professional sales jobs by studying these profiles carefully.

SOURCE: Used by permission of Harper & Row Publishers, Inc.

ketplace. These innovations have to be sold by professional salespeople. Consider the situation facing IBM and Remington Rand some four decades ago. In 1951, IBM was a marketer of such office products as tabulators and calculators. At the same time, Remington Rand was introducing UNIVAC, the first commercial computer. A year later, IBM entered the computer market. It sought to alleviate customer fears with a highly trained sales force. Service engineers were available to handle any problems that arose. IBM was able to convey an air of confidence, while its competitors explained the technical details of their superior products. IBM's sales-oriented strategy won out. By 1956, IBM had an 85 percent market share.[4] "Big Blue," as IBM is known, remains a leading computer manufacturer and marketer in the 1990s.

Competitive Importance

The importance of selling is self-evident to every business; unless the firm can sell its product, there is no reason for its continued existence. Good production and engineering facilities, an excellent accounting department, and the best staff personnel available are of no significance if the firm's sales force does not move enough volume.

Salespeople are the foot soldiers of marketing. They require accurate intelligence reports (marketing research) and a substantial support effort (advertising, dealer promotions, and public relations), but it is the salespeople who actually move the widgets and zonkles.

Every businessperson knows that new customers are the key to a firm's success. Acquiring new business is usually an impossible goal unless sales personnel are in the field looking for potential new users of their products. A firm can sometimes survive for long periods by servicing an existing group of clients; however, such an organization does not prosper or continue to grow. The development of new business is one of selling's most vital objectives.

Public Contribution

Selling makes an important contribution to the public because it is essential to competition. Aggressive marketing helps prevent collusion in the marketplace. It also aids consumer-oriented objectives, such as pricing and customer services. A freely competitive business environment is an important consumer, safeguard, and selling plays a vital role in ensuring it.

The sales force also makes a public contribution by identifying customer needs. A large portion of new product ideas originates with salespeople who discover unfulfilled needs. Salespeople can also spot legitimate needs unrecognized by industry or consumers and suggest product development that provides solutions.

Another public contribution is selling's role in the marketing of social causes. Selling is as appropriate in a community's United Way campaign as it is in a firm's promotional strategy.

ERAS IN SELLING

Today's sales representative is only a distant cousin to the salesperson who worked in the trade in earlier years. To fully appreciate modern selling sophistication, it is necessary to know something about the history of personal selling.

Selling has gone through four distinct eras, which are characterized as the time of (1) the early traders, (2) the selling revolution, (3) the American peddlers, and (4) professional salespeople. In each era a distinct type of selling was characterized; both selling techniques and sales ethics varied from period to period.

The Early Traders

traders
sales personnel who operated in ancient societies

The earliest sales personnel, usually called **traders,** existed in even the most ancient societies. Numerous historical references describe the traders operating in Greek, Roman, and other early cultures. Some of the earliest city-states based the major portion of their economies on trading with other communities.

Traders typically had an ownership interest in the goods they sold. Generally they or their families had manufactured the products. In most instances, these traders performed other marketing functions, such as transportation and storage, in addition to their selling duties.

caveat emptor
"let the buyer beware"

For the most part, buyers did not hold these early sellers in high regard. Their merchandise was often shoddy, their sales claims exaggerated, and the state-of-selling ethics dismal by today's standards. Early Greek and Roman authors chastised the traders for failing to contribute to society. The public distrusted most salespeople and usually insisted on personally inspecting the goods they bought. **Caveat emptor** (let the buyer beware) was the rule of the marketplace.

This era of personal selling lasted into the Middle Ages. The sales function was mixed with other business tasks, and it was difficult to identify individuals whose primary responsibility was selling.

The Selling Revolution

History books traditionally describe the Industrial Revolution during the mid-1700s as the development of a factory system for manufacturing. Admittedly, industrial output and product quality improved substantially during this period. But expanded production would not have improved the standard of living as it did if an effective sales organization had not developed to move the products from the factory to the consumer. The Industrial Revolution occurred because there was a corresponding "selling revolution." It is unfortunate that most histories of that era fail to show the vital role of personal selling.

bagmen
textile industry sales personnel during the Industrial Revolution

England's Industrial Revolution started in the textile industry, where sales personnel became known as **bagmen.** The fact that the bagmen had selling as their sole responsibility distinguishes them from the traders of earlier years. They sold from samples, which marked a significant switch from the days when consumers insisted on personal inspection. This change suggests that much of the traditional criticism of sales ethics was directed more to product quality than it was to deceptive sales practices.

The American Peddlers

peddlers
self-employed salespeople
in colonial times

The early American sellers were a colorful lot that generated a substantial amount of written folklore. The **peddlers** of colonial times traveled the wilderness of North America to sell their wares to the settlers. Many of these peddlers were immigrants who viewed their job as one of the few available means of getting a fresh start in a new country.

greeters
representatives of
wholesalers and
manufacturers, mid-1800s

drummers
19th century sales reps

Later, when a retail sector emerged, **greeters** represented wholesalers and manufacturers to the retailers during their periodic buying trips to major cities. These greeters became standard fixtures in hotel lobbies. When sales representatives began to call on retailers at their store, they became known as **drummers.** These sellers, who also often sold directly to consumers, were the basis of much American folklore. Toward the end of the 19th century, members of a field sales force were *commercial travelers*—a title still used today in some industries. These travelers typically depended on memorized sales presentations designed to handle all possible customer objections and "ensure" sales. During the first half of the 20th century, salespeople still depended on some type of memorized presentation.

The Professional Salesperson

seller's market
market characterized by a
relative scarcity of goods

buyer's market
market characterized by a
plentiful supply of goods

Professional selling developed shortly after World War II. The economy switched from a **seller's market,** with a relative scarcity of goods, to a **buyer's market,** in which goods were plentiful. Prior to this shift, many companies operated under the philosophy "If we can supply it, the customer will buy it!" A buyer's market occurred when American industry, which had been geared up for the war effort, switched back to the production of consumer goods. Goods had to be marketed because the consumer now had a choice, and selling changed to meet this challenge.

PROFESSIONALISM IN SELLING

marketing concept
organizational philosophy
oriented toward solving
consumer problems and
meeting the needs of the
marketplace

Most marketing experts agree that North American industry has entered the marketing concept era. In the **marketing concept,** all parts of an organization are oriented toward solving consumer problems and meeting the needs of the marketplace. Sales personnel no longer concentrate solely on increasing sales volume; rather, the prospect's real needs become the basis of the marketing plan. Most firms have either adopted the marketing concept or are in the process of doing so. Unfortunately, we can still identify examples of firms and industries that ignore consumers' welfare. If these organizations wish to remain competitive, however, they will have to change quickly in the years ahead.

Companywide acceptance of a consumer orientation requires the sales force to become thoroughly professional in its dealings with prospects and customers. A mark of professionalism in sales is that sellers adopt a problem-solving approach to their work. A professional salesperson does not wonder, "What can I sell this individual?" but instead asks, "How can I best satisfy this person's purchasing goal?" Professional sales forces are service-directed; they identify needs and determine how their customers can best satisfy these needs.

Various trends, such as the wider adoption of the marketing concept and better-informed consumers, indicate that selling will become increasingly professionalized. This fact is an underlying premise of this book. Effective sales personnel today and in the future must be professionals!

Legal and Ethical Constraints in Selling

Professional salespeople and their companies comply with the numerous legal and ethical constraints on selling activity. These laws set the parameters within which sales personnel must operate. At the federal level, for instance, some of the more important laws are:

antitrust legislation
laws that prohibit efforts to monopolize a marketplace

Robinson-Patman Act
prohibition against charging different prices to different customers unless costs differ

Wheeler-Lea Act
ban on deceptive promotional practices

Green River Ordinances
state and local governments' restrictions on door-to-door selling

- **Antitrust legislation**—the Sherman and Clayton Acts prohibit efforts to monopolize a marketplace.
- **Robinson-Patman Act**—prevents the charging of different prices to different customers unless sales costs differ.
- **Wheeler-Lea Act**—bans deceptive promotional practices.

Because state and local governments also regulate selling, professional salespeople must keep abreast of such legal requirements. For example, some communities prohibit, limit, or place restrictions on door-to-door selling. These enactments are known as **Green River Ordinances.**

Professionalism in selling also implies that the sales representatives always act in an ethical manner, even at personal or the company's expense. The essence of ethical selling conduct is contained in the Sales Creed adopted by Sales & Marketing Executives International, a leading professional organization in the field of selling. The Creed, shown in Figure 1–1, clearly outlines many of the salesperson's social responsibilities, as well as appropriate standards of ethical conduct.

REASONS FOR STUDYING PROFESSIONAL SELLING

If one has the interest and basic intelligence necessary for success, the essential concepts of professional selling can be learned just as can any other professional skill. The argument that "Good salespeople are born, not made" is identified with an earlier age in selling. Modern professional sales personnel fully realize the importance of study, practice, and effective sales education.

FIGURE 1–1   The sales creed

Sales Creed

Your pledge of high standards
in serving your company, its
customers & free enterprises

(1) I hereby acknowledge my accountability to the organization for which I work and to society as a whole to improve marketing knowledge and practice and adhere to the highest professional standards in my work and personal relationships.

(2) My concept of marketing includes as its basic principle the sovereignty of all consumers in the marketplace and the necessity for mutual benefit to both buyer and seller in all transactions.

(3) I shall personally maintain the highest standards of ethical and professional conduct in all my business relationships with customers, suppliers, colleagues, competitors, governmental agencies and the public.

(4) I pledge to protect, support and promote the principles of consumer choice, competition and innovation enterprise, consistent with relevant legislative public policy standards.

(5) I shall not knowingly participate in actions, agreements, or marketing policies or practices which may be detrimental to customers, competitors or established community social or economic policies or standards.

(6) I shall strive to ensure that products and services are distributed through such channels and by such methods as will tend to optimize the distributive process by offering maximum customer value and service at minimum cost while providing fair and equitable compensation for all parties.

(7) I shall support efforts to increase productivity or reduce costs of production or marketing through standardization or other methods, provided these methods do not stifle innovation or creativity.

(8) I believe prices should reflect true value in use of the product or service to the customer, including the pricing of goods and services transferred among operating organizations worldwide.

(9) I acknowledge that providing the best economic and social product value consistent with cost also includes:

(A) recognizing the customer's right to expect safe products with clear instructions for their proper use and maintenance

(B) providing easily accessible channels for customer complaints

(C) investigating any customer dissatisfaction objectively and taking prompt and appropriate remedial action

(D) recognizing and supporting proven public policy objectives such as conserving energy and protecting the environment

(10) I pledge my efforts to assure that all marketing research, advertising, and presentations of products, services or concepts are done clearly, truthfully and in good taste so as not to mislead or offend customers. I further pledge to assure that all these activities are conducted in accordance with the highest standards of each profession and generally accepted principles of fair competition.

(11) I pledge to cooperate fully in furthering the efforts of all institutions, media, professional associations and other organizations to publicize this creed as widely as possible throughout the world.

Source: Used by permission of Sales & Marketing Executives International.

There are three primary reasons why every student should learn something about selling:

1. **Selling offers numerous employment opportunities.** Sales occupations are a major segment of the labor force, and projections indicate that there will be substantial employment opportunities for qualified applicants in the future. Figure 1–2 shows some employment projections for selected sales occupations. Qualified sales personnel have several advancement paths from entry-level sales positions. These career paths are outlined in Chapter 3.

2. **Consumers need to know about selling.** As consumers, we all have to deal with various salespeople. It is beneficial to know how salespeople operate—their strategies, tactics, and the like. Consumers should be able to identify sales professionalism so they can deal with sales representatives who exhibit this quality.

3. **Personal selling is important in other facets of everyday life.** The study of personal selling has many related applications, such as communications among friends, relatives, and associates. Effective selling is effective communication. The basic concepts of professional selling apply to various other daily activities.

Many other reasons for exploring the subject of personal selling exist. Selling is an exciting field that requires careful study to understand and appreciate its foundations, principles, and tactics.

| FIGURE 1–2 | Employment projections for selected sales occupations |

Sales Occupation	Recent Employment Figures	Projected Growth to 2000
Insurance agent and brokers	463,000	14–24%
Manufacturer's sales workers	543,000	±4%
Real estate agent and brokers	376,000	35% or higher
Retail sales worker	4,300,000	25–34%
Securities and financial services sales representative	197,000	35% or higher
Services sales representatives	419,000	35% or higher

Source: Bureau of Labor Statistics, *Occupational Outlook Handbook: 1988–89 Edition* (Bulletin 2300), pp. 2, 215–28.

SUMMARY OF CHAPTER OBJECTIVES

1. To define personal selling.

Personal selling can be defined as an interpersonal persuasive process designed to influence some person's decision. Exactly how the salesperson sells depends on a host of factors, such as what is being sold, the type of customer, and the setting in which the sales interview occurs.

2. To explain the importance of personal selling.

Three viewpoints underscore the importance of personal selling: economic contribution, competitive importance, and public contribution. Selling makes a significant economic contribution since it generates the revenue on which businesses depend, as well as providing consumers with the goods and services necessary for an improved quality of life. Selling is one of the primary areas of business competition. Every function in the organization depends upon selling's ability to move goods and services. Selling also makes a significant public contribution because it is essential to the competitive system.

3. To outline the eras in selling.

The four distinct eras in selling are those of: (1) early traders, (2) the selling revolution, (3) American peddlers, and (4) professional salespeople. Each era features a distinct type of selling. Both selling techniques and sales ethics varied from period to period.

4. To differentiate between a seller's market and a buyer's market and to relate these concepts to professional selling.

A seller's market is characterized by a relative scarcity of goods, while goods are plentiful in a buyer's market. The sales philosophy in a seller's market is "If we can supply it, the customer will buy it." By contrast, goods have to be effectively marketed in a buyer's market because consumers have a choice.

5. To explain the marketing concept and its effect on personal selling.

In the marketing concept, all parts of an organization are oriented toward solving consumer problems and meeting the needs of the marketplace. Adoption of the marketing concept requires sales professionalism. A professional salesperson uses a problem-solving approach and always acts in a legal and ethical manner.

6. To list and discuss the primary reasons for studying professional selling.

Chapter 1 concludes with a discussion of why students should learn something about selling: (1) selling offers numerous employment opportunities; (2) consumers need to know about selling; and (3) personal selling is important in other facets of everyday life.

REVIEW QUESTIONS

1. Discuss the definition of selling used in this book. Would you consider it a narrow or a broad definition of personal selling?
2. Review articles and books about selling in your library. Compare the definitions of *personal selling* found in these sources with the one used in this text. What are the similarities? Differences?
3. Explain the importance of personal selling.
4. Trace the different eras in selling.
5. Differentiate among traders, bagmen, peddlers, greeters, drummers, and commercial travelers.
6. Explain the salesperson's role in a seller's market and a buyer's market.
7. What is the marketing concept?
8. Differentiate among the Sherman Act, Clayton Act, Robinson-Patman Act, Wheeler-Lea Act, and Green River Ordinances.
9. Do you agree that good salespeople are born, not made?
10. List three reasons for studying professional selling.

DISCUSSION QUESTIONS AND EXERCISES

1. How would you define *professionalism?* Relate your definition to several occupations with which you are familiar.
2. Explain how students can use the concepts of professional selling in everyday life.
3. Some have argued that the classic *caveat emptor* (let the buyer beware) should now be replaced with *caveat vendor* (let the seller beware). Do you agree with this contention? Explain.
4. Contact a sales manager at a local firm and ask permission to accompany one of the company's sales representatives for a day. Then prepare a brief report on what you observed.
5. Develop your own comprehensive list of reasons why someone should study professional selling. Which of these reasons are most important to you?

SALES DIALOG

Sandra Lewis, a sales representative for Interstate Industries, was enrolled in a history class at a state university in North Carolina. Lewis was an excellent student despite the 10-hour days she had already put in before going to the evening class. Although she planned to get her degree in business administration, Lewis was fascinated with history. One evening, Professor Martin P. Olson was discussing the Industrial Revolution.

OLSON: To summarize, the Industrial Revolution produced significant changes in the way people lived. They became factory workers, and the overall standard of living improved significantly. These advances can be attributed to the more efficient production systems that resulted from the Industrial Revolution. Are there any questions?

LEWIS: Professor Olson, I would be interested in how those early factories marketed the increased output.

OLSON: More efficient manufacturing meant more goods were available for consumers, so the standard of living was higher. I guess the early manufacturers had some salespeople to distribute their output. Is that what you were referring to, Ms. Lewis?

LEWIS: Well, I work full time as a sales representative for a major firm. And I know that our factories could not operate at the level they do unless our sales team was just as efficient. So I was just wondering how they handled it back in those days.

OLSON: To tell you the truth, I have not read much about the point you raise. But maybe you could make it your topic for the term paper that is required in this class.

What do you think the results of this sales dialog will be?

CASE 1–1   STIMMICK OFFICE PRODUCTS

Andrea Martin, a sales representative for Stimmick Office Products of Cleveland, had just completed a sales call on Erie Milling Company. As she sat in her car completing the interview report her employer required for each sales call, Martin wondered if she had handled the interview correctly.

Fred Bornick, the purchasing director of Erie, was definitely in the market to replace some office desks. Martin sensed that Bornick was very sensitive to the price issue, apparently because of a new cost-cutting directive from management. She also knew that her Woodcraft line was comparable to the desks Bornick was replacing, and with which Erie employees were generally satisfied. But Woodcraft sold at a 20 percent premium over her Fall Harvest line.

Martin decided to propose her cheaper line. Her sales presentation centered around the initial cost savings to Erie, even though she knew of data suggesting that total costs would even out over the lives of the lines (Woodcraft was a less fashionable but more durable line). Martin reasoned that Bornick's orders were to minimize acquisition costs, and that is what her sales proposal would do.

Questions
1. Do you think Martin handled the interview correctly?
2. What would you have done if you were in Martin's position?
3. Do you think Martin assessed Bornick's position correctly?

CASE 1–2   MICHIGAN PRODUCTS

Two friends, Monica Calligan and John Colucci, are having coffee in the student union at a state university near Detroit. Both are seniors and their upcoming interviews with several firms are very much on their minds.

CALLIGAN: Do you think I would like the selling job at Michigan Products?

COLUCCI: Oh, I think you can always get into sales with a company. If none of the big positions in marketing like assistant product manager come through, then start thinking about sales.

CALLIGAN: But Professor Reames said that sales is the fastest way to the top.

COLUCCI: I know, but sometimes I think the importance of sales as a stepladder to the top is exaggerated. Sure, some people have made it and some make a lot of money selling, but these people would do well in anything they do.

CALLIGAN: You certainly are negative about selling! The recruiting literature the placement office gave me says that starting salaries in sales are $30,000 and up, plus a car. You also usually get a bonus after you have been with the company a year.

COLUCCI: That's pretty good, but do you feel you can sell industrial machinery?

CALLIGAN: I have always gotten good grades and I can learn to do anything I set out to do.

COLUCCI: I hate to break this up, but we both have class. I'll see you after your interview tomorrow. We can talk after you have found out more about the job and the company.

Questions

1. If you overheard this discussion, how would you respond to Colucci's comments?
2. What information does Calligan need to obtain in her interview with Michigan Products?
3. If you were a representative from Michigan Products, how would you evaluate Calligan's attitude toward selling?

CHAPTER 2

The Selling Spectrum

CHAPTER OBJECTIVES

1. To describe the narrow and broad views of selling.

2. To list the ways of classifying sales jobs.

3. To describe the sales task continuum.

4. To describe the primary duties and responsibilities common to all sales jobs.

5. To examine the major changes taking place in personal selling.

SALES CAREER PROFILE

RAND BARTLE
Altos Computer Systems

Rand Bartle is the western regional sales director for Altos Computer Systems. He is based in San Jose, California. Bartle, in his early thirties, holds a bachelor's degree from Arizona State University.

Bartle explained how he came to Altos: "I was hired on January 4, 1984. I had been working for a customer of Altos for five years prior to coming to Altos and was asked to interview for a position. I did so, was made the offer, and accepted it.

"I selected Altos because of the people more than anything else. I developed a relationship with the company. I thought it was an extremely young, aggressive company that was doing a lot of things right, and that's what really got me involved in it.

"Prior to coming to Altos, I was with a company called Micro Age, which handled a multitude of vendors. I was hardware product manager and had the opportunity to go through a variety of sales training programs. Since coming to Altos I have gone through additional training courses in prospecting and qualifying, the psychological aspects of identifying your customer, the psychological profiles, and so on. The course that stands out the most in my mind is the one that got into the psychology of selling; it taught me to identify which personality traits I am dealing with, and then to direct my sales presentation to hit those.

"My current job is director of sales for the western region in distribution sales. Other jobs I have held in selling include retail computer sales and distribution sales in computers and related products. And then I did some manufacturing sales, so I've kind of gone up the ladder, so to speak, from retail to distributor to manufacturer.

"Currently, my job is basically identical to when I came to Altos. I have more responsibility and more direct reports today than I had initially. I started with two direct reports; today I have seven.

"What I like most about my job is the personal interaction I have with the people at Altos—they really make the company. We have a strong group of people who know how to get the job done. I also enjoy traveling and getting to meet people from different parts of the country, because there are definite geographic patterns. Things occur in one area that don't occur in others.

"I like to feel I have a very strong relationship with a majority of my customers. Coming from that environment—both retail and distribution—I understand their frustrations, and so it makes my job a little easier. I also tend to identify their needs, and to figure out ways to get the job done for them."

When asked which type of people he looked for in hiring new sales personnel, and about some of the problems he encounters, Bartle remarked, "To be a good salesperson you need to be highly aggressive and motivated. In our case, the field sales force is

21

managed remotely, so they need to be self-motivated persons capable of handling basically 90 percent of the work by themselves. Good salespeople have to be money driven. I hate to think of myself as money driven, but when the check gets smaller, I know it bothers me.

"In our industry, there's a lot of turnover. In my opinion, this has created a big pool of qualified people out there looking for jobs in an industry with a smaller number of jobs available because of changes in the last few years. For example, suppose we had a handful of strong competitors that were not IBMs. I firmly believe that strong salespeople will leave one company for another whenever they believe the company they're with has problems or is not competitive. They go to a company they feel better about, and as long as they have that personal belief, then they can go out to their customer bases and get a higher percentage of those—50 percent or greater—to switch with them within a short period—say about six months."

In regard to the qualities needed to be a successful salesperson, Bartle says, "Well, without a doubt, number one is you have to have a strong belief in the product. Second, you need to understand the market you're selling to, and then have a strong belief that you have the product that fits that market. For me personally, I couldn't sell a used car unless it was a used car that I believed in. So I have to have the belief to do it.

"Third, your particular organization needs a business plan that places accountability or responsibility. Any manufacturer, whether it be Altos, Adidas, or whatever, is going to say, here's the market we're attacking, here's how we compete against our competition, and here's your charter or goal. It takes that certain salesperson to go out and do it."

Answering one final question about classifying salespeople, the Altos sales manager responded: "You've got closers and you've got maintainers. For people highly motivated by the competition, going out and getting doors slammed in their faces makes them want to go out the window. Those people are great on the close but they're usually very poor at supporting and maintaining that account. That's why you'll find people who can go out and close a $5 million account and when that relationship ends, that account's taken in only $500,000. Why did it only reach one tenth of its potential? Because the person had given his or her all to close the deal; after the salesperson's motivation and personal gratification were satisfied, that person didn't pay attention to the account. So, we analyzed our sales force, separating them into closers and maintainers. Unless we have everything in place—marketing, communications, engineering, product marketing—unless all those things are all being handled to optimum human level, the account is not going to be satisfied."

In the 1990s, there are countless different types of sales jobs and levels of selling as more and more companies come to the realization that success depends upon how well sales efforts are matched up with targeted markets. Consider how the telephone is now used to sell products that were once thought to be too unique to sell in any way other than face-to-face with the customer. General Electric, for example, views telemarketing as a way to sell whatever they make. As a result, 2,000 employees in 45 telemarketing centers use the phone to sell everything from $1.98 accessories to high-tech energy systems. A few years ago at General Electric, a phone call was received asking about a cogeneration system. Using a scripted guideline, the inquiry was qualified and the relevant information passed on to company sales engineers. The result was a $100 million sale.[1]

DIVERGENT VIEWS OF SELLING

Selling is a universal activity in our society. It has been defined as the conscious practice of a lot of things we already know unconsciously—persuasion, negotiation, and never taking no for an answer.[2]

Indeed, it seems that everyone is involved in selling something at some time or another. The manager of the hardware store sells a riding lawn mower to a person whose son or daughter tries to sell him advertising space in the high school paper. A sales representative from an office products firm calls on the local municipality to demonstrate a new copy machine. An attorney-agent sells the services of professional athletes.

It is obvious that selling is an interpersonal persuasive process designed to influence some person's decision. If everyone sells something at some time, does this mean that everyone is a salesperson? The answer to this question depends on whether we define selling narrowly or broadly.

A Narrow Definition

Traditionally, society has thought of selling and salespeople solely as part of an exchange process or sales transaction. Salespeople promoted products or services with the purpose of making sales at a profit. Although today's sales professional bears little resemblance to the Willy Lomans of the past, the role of selling is essentially the same. The primary task of a salesperson is to present to consumers products or services that will satisfy their needs and wants. Oftentimes, a salesperson is the only contact between a company and its customers.

Many believe that this definition of selling should not be broadened. Selling is still the primary task of salespeople, although the various activities involved in selling have changed dramatically and will continue to change in the years to come. Who is and who is not a salesperson is not a question that concerns most businesses today. The key word now is customer contact. The reasoning is that anyone who comes in contact with a customer can influence a sale and provide customer satisfaction. An emphasis on customer contact by all employees is at least partially responsible for the dramatic turnaround at SAS Airlines. Their operating guidelines are that a customer will come into contact with five employees. Thus, during a year, there are 50 million moments of truth, or opportunities to add to customer satisfaction, for SAS employees.

A Broader Definition

More and more people believe that the definition of selling should be expanded to include nonbusiness activities. Proponents of a broader definition of selling say that all organizations—private or public, profit or nonprofit—must sell. School boards and parent-teacher groups sell school revenue proposals to the public. Political candidates are continuously involved in selling themselves and their ideas. The Armed Forces maintain an all-volunteer military service through their promotional campaign that sells the concept of military careers.

In the broader definition, salespeople may not be called salespeople and selling a particular product or service is not the primary task. Regardless of the definition, everyone does some selling at some time or other. In the words of Charles Schwab: "We are all salespeople every day of our lives. We are selling our ideas, our plans, our enthusiasms to those with whom we come in contact."

TYPES OF SALES JOBS

As stated at the beginning of the chapter, there is not one type of sales job. Rather, there are countless different sales jobs, each with its own list of job-related duties. This fact makes it difficult to compare sales jobs between companies and industries, and even within the same firm. The individual selling injection molding machines for Cincinnati Milacron, Inc., the sales representative for Dart-Kraft, Inc. calling on a supermarket buyer, and the Prudential Insurance Company agent selling life insurance to your next-door neighbor all differ not only in their products and customers, but also in the selling activities they undertake in calling on customers. The following bases can help to sort out various sales jobs:

1. Primary duties and responsibilities (product, customer, geographical area, selling level).
2. Allocation of efforts (sales goals, new and repeat business, service, and selling functions).
3. Types of targeted customers (key accounts, small business).
4. Technical requirements of the products.
5. Extent of customer knowledge.
6. Service and follow-up policies.
7. Overall marketing philosophy of the firm.

It must also be remembered that the activities involved in a salesperson's job or overall task do not remain constant. Sales personnel perform not only a wide variety of activities within the framework of their respective sales jobs, but a varying mix of activities in calling on assigned customers.

CLASSIFYING SALES JOBS

Of the various ways of classifying sales jobs, the most common approaches are: (1) creative/service selling, (2) ultimate consumer/organizational consumer selling, (3) initiate/capture/maintain selling, (4) field sales/administrative sales, and (5) generalists/specialists.

Creative/Service Selling

creative selling

situation in which the salesperson makes prospects aware of needs or wants and convinces them his or her services will solve the procurement problem

The most basic classification divides sales tasks into creative or service functions. In **creative selling,** salespeople search out prospects and qualify them, determining which buying motives are important to their prospects. Next, creative salespeople make their prospects aware of their needs or wants, and convince them of the relevancy of their products or services in solving customers' procurement problems. In other words, creative salespeople respond in creative and often unique ways to evolving needs and wants and, in doing so, generate sales that would not likely have occurred without their selling efforts. By guiding customers, creative sales representatives undertake all of the tasks in the selling process beginning with customer analysis and ending with closing. A good example is the selling of an accounting software package to small businesses.

service selling

situation in which the salesperson assists customer in completing a transaction without influencing the nature of the transaction

At the other extreme is **service selling,** which is defined as assisting customers to complete sales transactions and obtain fulfillment of their expectations without influencing the nature of the transactions. Service salespeople usually function in a passive role as order receivers. An **order receiver,** such as a sales administrator (an in-house account servicer) or trade salesperson, is a salesperson who routinely processes a customer's order. The buyer-seller relationship is known. The order receiver supplies purchase information (such as price, terms, expected delivery dates) and completes the mechanics of the transaction by processing the order forms.

order receiver

a sales administrator or trade salesperson who routinely processes a customer's order

Obviously, a great many salespeople take on both creative and service activities. Sales administrators who function strictly as service salespeople and the developmental salespeople assigned the sole role of securing new business are rarely found in today's business world. Therefore, identifying a particular sales job on the basis of creative/service depends on the actual mix of sales activities in the position.

Ultimate Consumer/Organizational Consumer Selling

Another way of classifying sales jobs is by the selling levels—the ultimate or individual consumer or an organizational consumer. Salespeople in retail sales, insurance, real estate, and telemarketing whose primary job is selling to ultimate consumers are generally classified as service sellers rather than creative sellers. In countless selling situations involving ultimate consumers, sales representatives cannot be anything other than passive and service-oriented. There is, however, growing recognition that this level of selling presents numerous opportunities for creative efforts. In fact, in many instances, salespeople in service areas have been replaced by self-service and telemarketing operations and moved to more creative selling situations. For example, firms selling insurance, heating systems, and security systems use telecomputers with prerecorded phone messages instead of salespeople. The growth of professionalism in selling to the ultimate consumer will see a diminution in service selling with a corresponding increase in creative selling.

trade salespeople
salespeople who sell to retailers

A closer and more continuing buyer-seller relationship exists in selling to either of the two types of organizational consumer. In selling to resellers, salespeople concentrate on those activities that increase the flow of products through the marketing channel to final consumption. In calling on retailers, for instance, sales representatives for Apple Computer, Liz Claiborne, and P&G focus on building relationships that cause greater sales by the reseller. Salespeople who sell to resellers are usually called **trade salespeople.**

Products and services sold to industrial buyers become parts of another product, produce another product, or facilitate the operation of an organization. Salespeople calling on industrial accounts are a vital marketing link and sometimes the seller's only promotional contact with this consumer. Industrial buyers' biggest concern is product quality. Therefore, quality assurance is an absolute must in selling to many firms. Also important are product price and the supplier's reputation for meeting delivery dates, continuity of quality, technical support capabilities, and service policies. In those situations where salespeople must have technical qualifications, they are usually called **sales engineers.**

sales engineer
salesperson with technical qualifications regarding the product

Initiate/Capture/Maintain Selling

A convenient way of classifying sales jobs is by the selling goal the salesperson encounters most often in selling situations. Figure 2–1 illustrates these sales goals. For example, a salesperson has a sales goal of *initiation* when the consumer has not used his or her product or service in satisfying a need or want. In this selling situation, the prospective customer is either using an alternative product or is not satisfying the need or want with any product. The main task for a salesperson in initiating a sale is to develop primary demand for the product by showing how much more satisfaction can be obtained. One way to do this is to compare product types, such as steel versus plastic. Another way is to juxtapose the product type and the unfilled need or want, such as using a computer to prepare periodic cost control reports as contrasted to using no cost control system.

developmental salesperson
generates new customers in initiation or capture selling situations

The salesperson's main task in *capturing* a new customer is to develop a competitive differential between his or her products and those of the competition. This differential may be the product itself, the salesperson's company, or the salesperson himself or herself. At the present time the customer is using a competitor's product to satisfy the need or want. **Developmental salespeople** generate new customers in initiation or capture selling situations.

maintenance selling
situation in which the salesperson is responsible for maintaining or increasing sales volume from existing customers of the firm

In **maintenance selling,** salespeople are responsible for maintaining or increasing sales volume from existing customers of the firm. With the focus on building a long-term buyer-seller relationship, sales representatives attempt to solidify their firm's status by relying more on their service skills than on creative skills. Remembering that satisfied customers are a valuable asset, sales representatives will want to reinforce the original reasons for

FIGURE 2–1   Sales goals

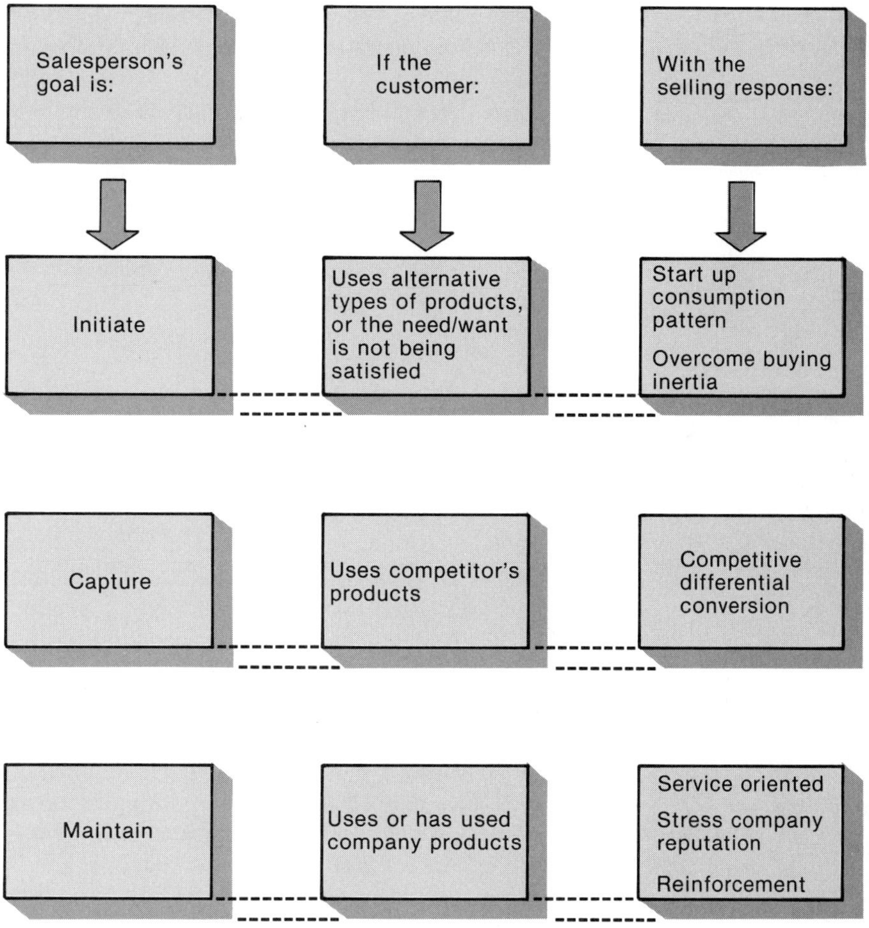

Salesperson's goal is:	If the customer:	With the selling response:
Initiate	Uses alternative types of products, or the need/want is not being satisfied	Start up consumption pattern Overcome buying inertia
Capture	Uses competitor's products	Competitive differential conversion
Maintain	Uses or has used company products	Service oriented Stress company reputation Reinforcement

buying, make sure customers are receiving the necessary service for continued patronage, and continue to offer assistance and problem-solving capabilities to help the customer achieve his or her goals.

Field Sales/Administrative Sales

sales administrator
the customer contact
within the supplier's
organization

A fourth way of classifying salespeople is according to their organizational
location. Field sales personnel do most of their selling outside the company
in the customer's place of business or residence. **Sales administrators** are
customer contacts within the supplier's organization. These two distinct selling tasks are vital for firms marketing products and services to industrial and

resale consumers. Unfortunately, the needed cooperation between field and inside sales personnel is missing in too many firms.

Professional field salespeople recognize the important contributions made by sales administrators who perform vital account-serving functions. These include expediting materials orders so that production can meet promised delivery dates and quality specifications and providing customer information, such as an order status. Professional sales administrators complement, rather than compete with, field salespeople. In situations where there is no field sales force, sales administrators take on more of the selling task.

Generalists/Specialists

Some salespeople are called generalists. They sell all or almost all of a company's product to all categories of customers located within a defined geographical area. Use of such salespeople provides broad market coverage, and the costs of a sales call can be spread over a number of products or product lines. Training costs tend to be lower than with specialists because less is expected of the salesperson in terms of product and/or customer knowledge. Generalists are best suited to selling situations where frequent customer contact is a key ingredient in obtaining sales. Drawbacks to the use of generalists include the tendency to produce a lot of small orders and the lack of selling in depth. Depth in selling refers to the amount of time and the amount of product/customer expertise that can be applied with specialization.

The salesperson who is classified as a specialist is focused on either a class of customer or a type of product. National or key account specialization allows sales representatives the opportunity to single out large and important customers for special consideration. With the increasing concentration in retailing, more and more firms have found it advantageous to go to national account specialization. A good example is P&G. Other specialization options include vertical market or industry specialization, channel of distribution specialization, product or system specialization, and end-use specialization. The trade-off with specialization is increased sales and greater loyalty with increased selling costs. A number of companies have gone to customer specialization from product specialization because of the confusion with the latter when a number of products are sold to the same customer.

THE SALES TASK CONTINUUM

All of the different classification schemes combine into one continuum. This continuum is based on the assumption that sales tasks can be arrayed in a varying mix of creative and service selling activities that are required in particular situations. In Figure 2–2, sales jobs are arrayed on three distinct

---

FIGURE 2–2   A continuum of sales tasks

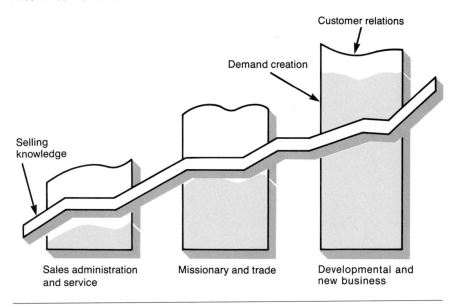

levels; moving from left to right, sales administration and service tasks require a greater proportion of service skills than jobs in each of the other two levels. Sales tasks classified as missionary and trade require about equal amounts of creative and service selling skills. The selling knowledge necessary for a salesperson in performing a particular sales task increases progressively with an increase in creative skills.

These three levels of sales jobs are not mutually exclusive. Salespeople at each level perform some of the same activities required of salespeople at other levels. For example, a developmental salesperson may perform service activities, such as a follow-up on the delivery of an order or a minor repair. Salespeople in sales administration and service, on the other hand, are often in the best position to obtain new business for their firms. At each level, however, the mix of creative and service selling determines the salesperson's major role and the relative allocation of time and selling effort.

To further clarify the many different jobs a salesperson may have, the following section describes typical sales jobs for each of the three levels of the sales task continuum.

Service Representative

Although many would not classify a service representative as a salesperson, IBM Corporation, General Electric Company, and several other large companies do. They have long considered service reps essential to their total

PROFESSIONAL SELLING IN ACTION

National Account Marketing

National account marketing allows marketers to deal with multilocation customers in a coordinated way. The seller focuses on service to the account as a whole rather than piecemeal selling to individual facilities of the one firm. The customers of Petrolite, a specialist in oil field chemicals and services, are the largest oil companies in the world. These businesses make purchasing decisions in the United States for worldwide sites.

Occidental Chemical Corporation, another firm with multinational customers, has adopted a national account strategy for its global programs. The advantage Occidental sees in national accounts is that customers have continuity with a supplier through one-stop shopping.

The government and military are also markets that lend themselves to a national account approach. Both represent markets that have unique and complex needs that cannot be met with a branch-by-branch approach. Johnson Controls, a leading worldwide supplier of con-

trol systems and services, and Xerox are two firms using national account strategies in selling to these types of markets.

National account marketing eliminates territory overlap and the resulting internal conflict. Bio-Ceutie, a marketer of animal pharmaceuticals, biologicals, and insecticides, had as many as five different regional managers serving branches of a national distributor. This led to inconsistent communications and misunderstandings with the distributor. Using a national account strategy, the company centrally administers major distributor accounts. Branches earn benefits based on their contributions to the distributor's overall sales objective.

SOURCE: Kate Bertrand, "National Account Marketing Swings into the Nineties," *Business Marketing*, November 1987, pp. 43–52.

---

service representative

salesperson whose primary duty is to provide after-sale customer service

marketing efforts. The primary duty of **service representatives** is to provide after-sale customer service. This service may involve supplying replacement parts, repairs or delivery, or handling warranties and service contracts, and providing product information. Service adds value to a product by providing whatever the customer needs to use a firm's products efficiently and effectively, thus increasing customer satisfaction.

The basic role of service representatives is to support other salespeople in initiating or capturing new business, and in maintaining customers for the firm. Although service is a support function, it can be crucial not only in maintaining current business, but also in obtaining new business by furnishing new leads.

Service is defined broadly today to include not only repair of a product and on-site service installation, but the development of inventory and problem-solving systems for customers. As competition intensifies and companies augment their products through customer service, the sales role of service representatives will grow.

The actual selling done by service representatives is typically limited to strengthening the company's reputation. Service representatives may also find themselves in situations where they can recommend replacement of a product rather than further servicing or where the addition of accessory equipment may bring added satisfaction from product use.

Sales Administrator

Sales administrators are inside salespeople who usually operate within the seller's organization rather than in the field. As the seller's principal contacts, they provide their customers with information about the status of current open orders, technical information on quality control and product specifications, pricing, and billing.

In companies that have no outside salespeople, sales administrators handle the entire selling process by telephone. The one big difference, however, is that the selling process is usually initiated by the buyer looking for a supplier.

While not as common as it once was, the position of sales administrator may be a stepping-stone to the job of field salesperson. By using the inside sales position as a source of field sales personnel, a firm can be sure that its field salespeople are well-versed in the detailed procedures for making order entries, processing shipping documents, and preparing billing statements and technical specifications. By functioning inside the firm before going into the field, a salesperson also has had opportunities to work with other departments and to develop working relationships with other company personnel.

Technical Specialist

technical specialist
sales rep who deals with the technical details of a buyer-seller relationship

Similar to service people, many do not think of **technical specialists** as being involved in selling. Typically, technical specialists are involved in dealing with customers' requests for specific technical assistance or complaints of a technical nature. This involves developing new applications of the firm's products, altering the firm's products to fit a particular customer's needs, and working with other salespeople to make sure customers get the right product for the right job. None of these activities before or after the sale directly involves selling, yet the role of the technical specialist is of major importance in maintaining current sales and developing new business. Recognizing this, many companies involve technical specialists in sales training courses.

Usually found in companies selling highly technical products or services, technical specialists often develop close working relationships with their technical counterparts in customers' firms. This relationship can be a major factor in promoting customer satisfaction with a firm and its products.

Driver Salesperson and Order Taker

**driver salesperson/
order taker**
sales rep who takes customer orders and provides regular and efficient service

Unfortunately individuals in either of these jobs tend to view their roles too narrowly. **Driver salespeople** and **order takers** must develop professional selling attitudes and begin to think of their respective jobs as critical to their firms' long-run success. PepsiCo, Inc., for example, credits much of its success in take-home sales to the driver salespeople who get the shelf space and cooperation of local retailers. Companies such as L'eggs Products, Inc.

and Abraham & Strauss are investing large sums of money in the training of driver salespeople and salesclerks, respectively. Also, these companies now use entry level positions as one route to management positions.

Although the emphasis in these selling jobs is on taking the customer's order and in providing regular and efficient service, people in these jobs can engage in at least limited creative selling efforts. For instance, driver salespeople for a bakery can promote a new product in their line. Also, a retail salesclerk can suggest other items a customer might want to purchase; the problem for the salesperson is in selecting which items to push.

Trade Salesperson

This job involves selling to market intermediaries such as retailers and wholesalers who, in turn, resell the products to other firms or individuals. Because the product sold by a trade salesperson must be resold at a profit for the intermediary to benefit, the sales task takes on an added dimension. The trade salesperson sells through the intermediary customer by showing what the buyer's customers want and are willing to pay for the products in question. Thus, the trade salesperson must be involved with each customer's marketing program and policies regarding inventory management.

The essential selling activities for the trade salesperson are (1) developing a close working relationship with customers, (2) establishing a reputation as an authority on the marketing of particular products, (3) seeing to it that customers cooperate in the manufacturer's marketing programs, and (4) helping customers merchandise the manufacturer's products. Recognizing the critical importance of trade salespeople, more and more companies have provided them with good market information about their sales territories. These companies also provide strong advertising support for cooperative programs and liberal incentives to do their jobs well. As an example, Wrangler salespeople have portable computers that provide up-to-the-minute, open-to-sell information on thousands of styles, colors, and sizes. As a result, they can make sales presentations on data that is up-to-date. Also, by placing orders immediately, the customer is assured of getting the complete order.

Part-time merchandisers are being used by many companies in the personal and grocery products businesses to help trade salespeople. These part-timers check out shelves, bring merchandise from the back room and stock shelves, and build displays. In some instances part-timers are selling to small stores.[3]

Detail Person

detailer
a sales rep who brings basic product information to the attention of physicians

The task of a salesperson described as a **detailer** is to bring basic product information to the attention of physicians in the hope that they will specify that product in writing prescriptions for their patients. Particularly important in the introduction of new products, detailers distribute product samples, results of research studies, educational materials, and other product information of interest to physicians. Sales representatives for college textbook publishers perform almost the same function as detailers. Sales representatives from publishers call on college professors, who determine which textbooks will be used in courses.

Critics of detailing maintain that these salespeople simply add to the costs of health care and education without providing any benefit to final consumers. This criticism ignores the significant informational role of the detailer. Detailers and direct mail are physicians' two principal sources of information on pharmaceuticals. Sales representatives are by far the major source of textbook information for college professors.

Missionary Salesperson

missionary salesperson
a sales rep who concentrates on the customers of resellers

Salespeople in missionary sales jobs concentrate their efforts on the customers of resellers. "Is there any demand for this product?" is a major question asked by resellers. In attempting to answer this question, **missionary salespeople** make calls on the customers of resellers, hold clinics for customers, and act as demonstrators of products. All of these efforts are focused on producing sales for the reseller. The efforts of missionary salespeople are directed at showing the demand for products and producing long-term increases in sales.

Sales Engineer

A sales engineer is charged with selling highly technical products to industrial consumers. Similar to technical specialists described earlier, sales engineers are able to provide customers with technical information, advice, and assistance. Much of what sales engineers do is before-sale service. Unlike technical specialists, sales engineers' major function is to generate sales.

Many sales engineers sell products or services in accordance with the customer's specifications. In these situations, the sales engineer functions as a technical consultant to the customer. Because of the multiple responsibilities in this job, sales engineers must combine a high level of technical knowledge with creative selling skills. The most likely candidates for the job of sales engineer are graduate engineers, scientists, and technical specialists. A strong sales training program is required to augment the technical skills possessed by these people with sales skills critical to their success.

DUTIES OF THE SALES JOB

Even though sales jobs vary from one company to the next and from one product to the next, certain duties are common. The extent of these duties in each job may vary, but they all are present in every sales position.

Selling Duties

Sales duties include prospecting for customers, qualifying prospects, preparing the sales calls, making sales calls and delivering presentations, demonstrating the product, writing orders, increasing sales to current customers, answering objections, and quoting prices. Each of these activities has a direct impact on current and future sales levels. As part of the selling process, these duties are guided by the goals of the salesperson and the goals of the consumer in making a purchasing decision.

Sales-Support Duties

Although some duties have no direct and immediate impact on sales, they still affect current and future sales levels. Some examples of these duties are handling complaints, providing delivery information, assisting in technical problems, handling special requests, and manning exhibits at trade shows. These service duties support salespeople's sales to consumers.

The extent to which a particular salesperson becomes involved in these activities also varies. In some cases, a salesperson has little to do with these activities because another person in the firm has the primary responsibility for them. On the other hand, the salesperson may have these duties as a primary responsibility. In either case, the professional salesperson must assume responsibility for these activities because, if these jobs are not done well, sales are lost and future business becomes more and more difficult to secure.

Nonselling Duties

All professional salespeople must plan and control their activities. To do this they carefully prepare reports, attend sales meetings and conferences, study and learn, monitor competitive actions, and plan their travel. Without careful attention to these so-called housekeeping duties, a salesperson's performance can be drastically reduced. Professional salespeople know that and see that it does not happen.

RESPONSIBILITIES OF THE SALES JOB

Salespeople have many responsibilities, but two areas of responsibility stand out—their responsibilities to their companies and to customers. Both of these obligations must control every action of a professional salesperson.

In many cases, the salesperson is the only contact a customer has with a company. If the salesperson does not act professionally, the image and performance of the entire firm suffers. The salesperson must also see that sales are made at a profit because without profits, the company will not survive.

Serving and satisfying the purchasing goals of customers are the major responsibilities of salespeople. In the short run, some salespeople may be able to fool or to outwit customers, but in the long run they will lose. Only by sincerely trying to satisfy the particular wants and needs of each customer can salespeople hope to build the kind of customer relationships fostering successful sales careers.

A person who is neither willing nor able to assume these difficult and often conflicting responsibilities is not ready for a career in sales. By the same token, such an individual is not ready to receive the many benefits, both tangible and intangible, that professional salespeople enjoy.

Some of the characteristics of a professional salesperson are:

1. Helps each customer attain his or her purchasing goals.
2. Knows the role of sales in marketing and company operational structures.
3. Knows the problems, differences, and operations for customers as well as the customers' industry.
4. Is enthusiastic not only about the products and company, but also about himself or herself.
5. Demonstrates expertise and an image of credibility.
6. Has an awareness of the continuing need to learn more about customers, products, and competition.
7. Sees the need to upgrade selling skills by doing and by seeking coaching help.
8. Enjoys the constant challenge of selling.
9. Understands the concept of long-term, profitable sales performance.
10. Organizes his or her sales approach around fact-finding and meeting consumer purchasing goals.

Emerging Dimensions in Professional Selling

The relative calm that lasted through the '50s, '60s, and on into the early '70s has been replaced by steadily increasing competitive intensity in most industries that will last through the '90s and into the next century. Maturation of markets and a more sophisticated buyer, coupled with the need for faster response to competitor activities and technologies, means new and innovative approaches to marketing and sales. The firms that cannot meet these challenges will have difficulty surviving.

What the exact philosophy and structure of personal selling will be in the future is unclear, but we do know that major changes are taking place for consumers, the selling function, and the salesperson. All will have a pronounced effect on salespeople in the future. One thing is a certainty—professional selling will not remain static. It will continue to evolve and develop as a result of environmental influences and the actions of those who work in this dynamic field.

CHANGES IN THE CONSUMER

For the most part, modern consumers are better educated and display more confidence in purchasing. As a result, they expect greater professionalism from the salespeople with whom they deal. These factors have greatly influenced the manner in which today's salespeople contact and work with potential and existing buyers of their products and services.

Growing Consumer Importance

As more and more firms become market-driven, their niches in the marketplace begin to reflect a consumer orientation. Products develop niches in the market and are repositioned due to consumers' needs and wants. The sellers evaluate and classify consumers on the basis of potential and link this information to sales efforts. Firm after firm has restricted their marketing attention to those customers with a necessary level of buying power. They spend less time with small accounts and more time with larger ones.

Increasingly, we see buyers, particularly in industrial markets, approaching qualified sellers with definitive needs and a projected product specification. This initiation of the buying process and assumption of what traditionally has been the seller's role has come about possibly by default. More likely, it has come about through increasing purchasing awareness and concerted efforts to improve the purchasing function.

Consumer Education

Modern consumers are better educated and more knowledgeable about the products and services they buy than their predecessors were. Society has begun to recognize the need to improve consumer information and expand its availability. Young people are gaining more awareness of consumer economics through such programs as Junior Achievement, career education starting in the elementary grades, and Distributive Education Clubs of America (DECA). Professional associations such as Sales & Marketing Executives International, the American Marketing Association, and consumer groups have improved the general level of economic literacy and consumer knowledge. There is little doubt that future sales personnel will have to cope with consumers who insist on more detailed, factual, and timely product and service information than in the past.

In addition to being better trained, organizational buyers have a number of sophisticated tools at their fingertips to help them in buying. More and more salespeople see their job as integrating their companies with the buyer's company. Without the best possible products and a comprehensive knowledge of the market, no salesperson can be successful in today's marketplace.

Sales Professionalism

Consumers are placing increasing demands on salespeople. This, in turn, has placed greater and greater emphasis on professionalism. Sales professionalism assumes complete product, market, and competitive knowledge. In today's markets this may necessitate specialization of the sales force. A sales professional is one who treats prospects and customers in a dignified, intelligent manner by attempting to meet their needs rather than selling them anything that is available. The professional salesperson personifies the marketing concept by being consumer oriented, dedicated, sincere, and possessing a long-run outlook.

Increasing Competition and Market Complexity

In today's markets a wide-ranging variety of products exists, each product further differentiated by brands. Consumers are constantly trying to get answers to questions that are extraordinarily complex and interrelated. There is a trend toward collective decision making, an evaluation of the purchasing function, more make-or-buy decisions, and constant pressures to reduce purchasing costs. There will also be increasing emphasis on customer service in line with consumer expectations and as a result of the desire to create competitive differentials. Competition will increase as new products and new companies enter the marketplace, as alternative products seek to satisfy the same need, and as more foreign companies enter markets they have not been in before.

CHANGES IN THE SALES FUNCTION

The personal selling process itself is changing as alterations in various aspects of the marketing system cause modifications in the way companies sell their products. No list of these changes could be complete, but some of them include (1) partnership selling, (2) systems selling, (3) depth selling, (4) computer-assisted selling, and (5) national account selling. It is reasonable to assume that these trends will continue to accelerate during the next decade.

Partnership Selling

Instead of selling to a customer, more and more attention is being directed to having the salesperson develop a partnership with the customer. The basis for this partnership can take two forms. One is enhancement of what is offered to the customer. Sales reps from P&G, Scott Paper, and Liz Claiborne concentrate on helping their customers (retailers) do a better job of selling their respective products. This assistance may take the form of inventory management, promotion, merchandising, and sales training. Frito Lay has been able to attain a position of dominance in supplying small retailers by helping them keep their store shelves filled with fresh snack products.

Partnership selling is also evident in the industrial market, particularly when the buyer is small and lacks expertise in production and/or product development and when selling through distributors. A paper products company, for example, found that their customers needed technical assistance in developing new products. In another marketing situation, a chemical company found it had a competitive edge in supplying help to its major customer, a small fertilizer company. Manufacturers of industrial products find it to their benefit to work with and train distributor salespeople.

The second form of partnership selling is based on confidence and credibility in the sales rep to the extent that he/she is involved in the customer's decision-making process. Where once computer manufacturers tried to sell all of the equipment a customer might need, today the emphasis is on spending enough time with customers to gain acceptance as an unofficial member of the customer's team of decision makers and problem solvers. For both Xerox and IBM this means working with products from other companies, something that was unheard of a few years ago. Regardless of the basis for partnership selling, it will grow in importance as firms seek a competitive edge through customer service.

Systems Selling

systems selling

marketing of a product line or service that satisfies an identifiable need

The basic premise of **systems selling** is that the firm is marketing a product line or service that satisfies an identifiable customer need. A system (or method) of satisfying that need is what the buyer seeks and the seller offers. Systems selling is a logical extension of consumer orientation, which is the foundation of the marketing concept. Various systems include related products, related services, and combinations of products and services.

For example, business forms companies offer to custom design the entire flow of customers' office paperwork. Computer manufacturers offer a complete system of hardware and software to achieve a particular function. Another good example is computer-assisted manufacturing that includes a mainframe, peripheral equipment of various types, robots, and software. Some firms have adopted the concept of systems selling, in which a company markets a complete service or product line rather than individual items. Scott

Paper's Prime System is a complete line of paper goods, soap, containers, dispensers, and other items that is directed toward a food service operation. Andy Wilson, vice president of sales for Commercial Products, says the system makes it easier to sell concepts such as quality. It also allows the seller to better differentiate products competitively and put greater emphasis on value added.[4]

Perhaps the greatest single barrier to the implementation of systems selling is the lack of trained personnel. Salespeople who have been schooled in traditional marketing techniques often have difficulty in adjusting to systems selling. Businesses use thorough orientation and detailed training sessions to introduce systems selling to an existing sales force.

Selling in Depth

Specialization of a sales force by customer type is aimed at increasing revenues from a given customer through the in-depth knowledge of the salesperson. Instead of being stretched out over a number of customers and/or products, the salesperson can concentrate on a specific customer and specific product applications. Mainframe computer sellers were some of the first to use customer specialists because of the high dollar value of an installed sale. Since that time, the benefits of selling in depth have been recognized by other types of firms. H. B. Fuller, for example, a seller of adhesives, switched from territory reps to industry specialization in 1982 and doubled its rate of growth.[5]

National or key account selling are other examples of specialization by customer allowing selling in depth by sales reps. Xerox, for example, has put together a new unit that combines marketing and customer operations in developing complex systems for the federal government and major corporate clients.[6] The growing concentration in retailing has led to greater specialization by companies that sell their products through these channels.

Selling in depth is advantageous when selling new technology. Greater credibility through specialization helps to alleviate adoption inhibitions on the part of the customer. While selling in depth can be advantageous in customer coverage, specialization by customer is costly and limits organizational flexibility.

Sales Force Automation

The use of computers by the sales force should grow for several rather obvious reasons.[7] The first is growing buyer sophistication. Second is the impelling need for faster response to customer inquiries, competitor activities, and unexpected market developments. Key account representatives for Colgate-Palmolive, as an illustration, use shelf-planning software to prepare a model of a product section in a store that in turn suggests options for space allocation and profit potential by optimizing product selection, sizes, and prices. For

PROFESSIONAL SELLING IN ACTION

Changing Operational Modes

Since the turn of the century, sales has undergone three operational modes. The first was consultative selling. With this mode, the salesperson tried to understand the problems of customers and propose innovative solutions. The rep was given very little support to accomplish this job.

Beginning around 1975, the salesperson had PC software to help solve customer problems. For example, customer buying patterns could be simulated to figure out where the right products and services fit into the customer's environment. By 1988 the salesperson had more sophisticated tools that allowed customized solutions for each customer. Currently 25 percent of the management information systems' budget typically goes for support of sales and marketing functions.

With these more powerful tools, the salesperson can serve the customer quicker and more effectively. Also, with desktop publishing software the customer can be presented with more understandable proposals. For example, a Boeing salesperson can now give a device to an airline and tell them, "You can configure the cockpit and the passenger area by pushing these buttons, and we'll come back and give you a proposal in hours instead of months on what it will cost you."

The costs may run from $4,000 to $10,000 per salesperson. These high costs can be justified only if information becomes as important as the product the sales rep is selling. Marketers will have to provide information that will enable the customer to become more profitable. As products become more technical, information on how to use, how to maintain, how to repair, and how to sell will become more critical. Information helps when the product breaks down as well as providing an advantage in selling. In the future, customers and suppliers will be integrated via a common database.

SOURCE: "Selling Will Never Be the Same," *Sales & Marketing Management,* March 1989, pp. 48–54. Reprinted by permission of Sales & Marketing Management, © March 1989.

James River's Towel and Tissue Group, a sales rep is responsible for individual customer profitability. Each customer's order will generate a profit-and-loss statement reflecting a specific combination of James River programs and services. Instead of ordering specific product quantities, the retailer is asked to accept a specific assortment of elements to support its particular strategies.

Laptop computers are used extensively to improve sales force productivity in the areas of call reports and expense reports. Dennis Elsmore, a consultant medical sales rep for G. D. Searle, makes 50 to 60 calls a week. Instead of the tiresome job of writing out reports, he can now plug a laptop into his cigarette lighter, access the call report format, type in the date, name, products discussed, samples left, and any information that might be helpful for the next call.[8]

Other modern technology for the sales force includes software that simulates customer buying patterns and develops customized solutions for each customer, as well as software applications involving cellular phones, voice mail, and artificial intelligence.

marketing information system

computer system designed to produce information relevant to marketing decisions

Computer-based **marketing information systems** (MIS) produce relevant information helpful in making marketing decisions. A marketing information system can be a great help to companies by producing data to facilitate selling decisions. Those considering a career in selling or sales management will need to learn as much as possible about the use of computers in marketing.

National Account Selling

Instead of dealing piecemeal with a customer whose operations are found in several different geographical areas, a firm may consolidate its selling efforts and assign the responsibility to one salesperson. The biggest advantage of so-called **national account selling** (also called *key account selling*) is a coordinated approach toward important customers. Other advantages include the opportunity for specialization by customer, identification of sales responsibility (it eliminates the question of who is responsible—the salesperson who calls on the home office or the one who has a branch in his or her territory), and a promotional opportunity for professional salespersons.

national account selling

assignment of nationwide accounts to just a single salesperson or team

There are several variations on national account selling. In some industrial product companies, industry or product specialists fill the national account sales role. For example, a manufacturer of sophisticated industrial materials has three separate sales forces. These are (1) the regular field sales force assigned to geographic territories; (2) product sales managers assigned to specific products who assist the field sales force with technical and customer application problems for major sales; and (3) marketing managers who develop sales strategies for assigned industries.

CHANGES IN SALESPEOPLE

Salespeople are also changing. The demands of expanded competition, technological innovation, increased government regulation, and rising costs have all played a part in modifying the salesperson's role. Many changes have taken place to enable salespeople to survive in the current business environment. Some of the ways salespeople are changing are:

1. *The salesperson has become more socially responsible*. It is evident that society is requiring all marketers to accept a higher degree of social responsibility, and salespeople are directly involved in this trend. Factual and reliable product information, better customer service, honest and consistent business dealings, and ethical selling conduct are the marks of socially responsible salespeople.

2. *Minority groups are entering sales as a career field*. Blacks, Native Americans, Spanish-speaking Americans, and other minority groups are now taking advantage of equal employment opportunities in sales. Traditional

racial and ethnic barriers have largely disappeared. Selling has become a vehicle for improving the professional and career status of millions of formerly disadvantaged employees. The professionalism of the individual salesperson's approach has become the only criterion for determining his or her effectiveness.

3. *The term salesperson has replaced salesman in the vocabulary of marketing.* Field selling is no longer exclusively a man's world (see Figure 2–3). In the last eight years, the proportion of women in corporate sales jobs has tripled from 7 percent to 18 percent. Women are most visible in real estate (more than 48 percent of the sales jobs), advertising (nearly 48 percent), and securities/financial (nearly 38 percent). Selling offers unlimited possibilities for women who choose this career field. Although women comprise only a little more than 10 percent of the 22,000 agents for Prudential, they won all three major sales awards in a recent year.[9]

4. *Smaller sales forces may be composed of older, more experienced salespeople.* The increased customer load has been offset by customer classification and means other than traditional sales calls.

5. *Salespeople are becoming more involved in territory management.* Salespeople are assuming more of the tasks once performed by the first level of sales management. For example, salespeople will be collecting more market information and making more decisions.

6. *The further professionalization of selling will require the salesperson to continue to change.* An increasingly professionalized sales function will require salespeople to be alert to changes in the way they sell. There seems little doubt that professionalism will be a characteristic of selling endeavors

FIGURE 2–3	Percentage of sales jobs held by women in selected cities

Ft. Lauderdale	16.7%
Norfolk, Va.	16.3%
Pittsburgh	15.6%
Tampa	15.6%
New Orleans	15.3%
Indianapolis	15.2%
Cincinnati	15.0%
Louisville	15.0%
Miami	14.9%
Dallas	14.7%
Philadelphia	14.7%
Nassau, N.Y.	14.5%
Houston	14.4%
Buffalo	14.3%
Cleveland	14.2%

Source: Bureau of Labor Statistics.

in the years ahead. Business can be expected to demand professionalism in selecting the next generation of sales personnel. It has to, if the marketing system is to continue to prosper.

SUMMARY OF CHAPTER OBJECTIVES

1. **To describe the narrow and broad views of selling.**

   Defined narrowly, selling is confined to salespeople and sales transactions. A broad definition would include nonbusiness activities with salespeople not necessarily called salespeople and whose primary task is not selling.

2. **To list the ways of classifying sales jobs.**

   Sales jobs can be classified in terms of whether the job is primarily creative or service oriented; whether the customer is ultimate or organizational; the principal selling goal; whether the salesperson works in the field or inside; and whether the salesperson is a generalist or specialist.

3. **To describe the sales task continuum.**

   The sales task continuum arrays sales jobs in terms of a varying mix of creative and service selling activities. Moving from a mix of more service and correspondingly less creativity to a mix of less service and more creativity, three distinct levels are found. These are: (1) sales administration and service; (2) missionary and trade; and (3) developmental and new business.

4. **To describe the primary duties and responsibilities common to all sales jobs.**

   The primary duties of a salesperson include those related to selling, sales-support, and nonselling. Professional salespeople are responsible to their company and their customers.

5. **To examine the major changes taking place in personal selling.**

   Today's consumer is better educated and more knowledgeable about what he or she is purchasing. The way products and services are sold is changing for many companies. Some of the more noticeable changes are partnership selling, computer-assisted selling, systems selling, depth selling, and national account selling. Salespeople themselves are also changing—they are becoming more socially responsible, minority groups are entering selling as a profession, and more women are exploring careers in sales. There is a trend toward more education and experience, an involvement in territory management, and further professionalization of selling.

REVIEW QUESTIONS

1. Explain how the concept of key target accounts could implement specialist selling by firms.
2. Develop a list of reasons why more and more women are exploring sales careers.
3. Which of the emerging dimensions of professional selling described in Chapter 2 are the most significant? Why?
4. Outline the different ways of classifying sales jobs.
5. Contrast the narrow and broad definitions of selling. Which viewpoint is closest to your own definition? Why?
6. When would you use an inside sales force in addition to a field sales force?
7. Make a list of 10 to 15 sales positions. Then identify each sales job according to the classification scheme outlined in this chapter.
8. Some firms consider a field sales position as a promotion for a successful sales administrator. Evaluate this policy.
9. Is a salesperson responsible only to his or her employer and customers?
10. Interview a salesperson you know. Write a report, based on your interview describing (a) how much this person enjoys the nonselling duties of the job, and (b) how important these duties are to the job.

DISCUSSION QUESTIONS AND EXERCISES

1. Prepare a report on minority hiring for sales positions, and develop a bibliography to accompany your report.
2. Develop a list of reasons why more and more women are exploring sales careers.
3. Do you agree with the statement "Selling is a universal activity in our society"? Why or why not?
4. Prepare a list of examples in which the broadened viewpoint of selling has been applied in your community.
5. Prepare two job descriptions—one for a creative sales position and one for a job in service selling. Compare the descriptions.

SALES DIALOG

George Daehn, a sales engineer with Bremington Electric of Modesto, California, shook hands with Paul Houlihan, the buyer for Willard Engineering, one of Daehn's largest accounts. The receptionist handed Daehn a visitor's pass, and the two men walked back to Houlihan's office near the production floor. Houlihan shared this office with two other people, so it was rather noisy. Daehn and Houlihan sat down and, after some bantering, got down to business.

DAEHN: The first thing is these TRX-14 rejects you called Steve about. (The TRX-14 was a model designation for a transformer core produced by Bremington. Steve was Daehn's inside salesman in the San Diego district office.)

HOULIHAN: Yeah, it looks as though the laminates were simply not stacked properly on them.

DAEHN: Hmmm. That's 18 out of a batch of 500. That's really not too bad, Paul.

HOULIHAN: No, I guess not.

DAEHN: But I'll get the bad ones off your hands and replace them right away. Now, were there any other rejects you ran into?

HOULIHAN: No, that was it, George.

DAEHN: OK, good. Now, you were in a hurry for some of those D-type TRJ-25s . . . You needed 600 out of the total 1,000 on rush order. Did you get those all right?

What do you think the results of this sales dialog will be?

CASE 2–1 CARGWELL, PETERSON & SONS

Cargwell, Peterson & Sons of Phoenix sells a wide range of small appliances to department stores, hardware stores, and appliance stores. Their principal competitors have been General Electric (Black & Decker) and Sunbeam. Thornton Peterson, son of one of the founders and recently appointed vice president of marketing, has decided to install a national account marketing program. To him, national account marketing makes sense because the majority of Cargwell, Peterson's customers operate more than one facility. In fact, most of their key customers have at least 10 outlets. Peterson reasons that a traditional geographical organization would divide the key customers up among several salespeople.

"If Cargwell, Peterson & Sons does not place more emphasis on customers," said Peterson, "we might as well sell out because our competition is moving in that direction." In addition to implementing a more coordinated approach focusing on the account as a whole, Peterson believes that national account marketing would allow more selling time with important customers.

Peterson knows that two steps are necessary to implement a program such as this. The first is getting the support of top management, and the second is deciding which accounts to place under a national account designation.

Questions
1. If you were Peterson, how would you get the support of top management?
2. Should Peterson implement his plan with a few accounts and then slowly add the others?
3. Which criteria should be used in identifying a customer as a national account?

CASE 2–2 EAST COAST AIRLINES, INC.

East Coast Airlines, Inc. is a domestic and international air carrier based in Miami, Florida. The company serves most major cities along the Atlantic seaboard, including Boston, Hartford, New York, Philadelphia, Baltimore, Norfolk, Charleston, Atlanta,

Jacksonville, Orlando, Miami, and Washington, D.C. East Coast also serves major Caribbean Islands, which have become popular vacation spots, and it operates several aircraft for charter travel to points in its service area.

Edward Kronwald is the manager of the firm's Charter Sales Group. Kronwald directs a field force of eight charter sales representatives who maintain liaison with the travel agents in their territories and contact various groups and organizations that use air charters. At a staff meeting, Kronwald suggests that his group implement the concept of systems selling. Here is the way he explains it:

> As you all know, East Coast has recently made two significant acquisitions. First, we bought Funtime Travel, a chain of 13 travel agencies along the Atlantic seacoast. Then only last week we acquired major hotels on three Caribbean Islands, two of which are now served by our regular flights.
>
> This would be an ideal time to introduce the concept of systems selling to the Charter Sales Group. We could develop some vacation packages using these hotels and our regular stops as well as charter flights. Then we could market the packages through Funtime Travel.
>
> It seems to me that the key will be to put together a dynamic, hard-hitting sales presentation. What do you people think?

Questions

1. What is your opinion of Kronwald's idea?
2. Can you cite examples in which systems selling has been used successfully in the travel industry? Have there been any failures?
3. Develop a sample vacation package for East Coast Airlines. Make any necessary assumptions about the location and room rates of the three vacation hotels.
4. Outline a sales presentation to a group or organization interested in charter travel for the package you have developed.

CHAPTER 3

Career Paths for Sales Personnel

CHAPTER OBJECTIVES

1. To identify the career paths available to salespeople.

2. To define the concept of a career path.

3. To describe financial rewards for salespeople.

4. To describe nonfinancial rewards for salespeople.

5. To list the steps in getting a selling job.

SALES CAREER PROFILE

JOAN HITZMAN
Moore Business Forms

Joan Hitzman is a health care sales representative for Moore Business Forms in Chicago. All of her accounts are hospitals. The 25-year-old Hitzman had been hired by Moore only about 18 months prior to this interview. She attended the College of Lake County for two years and then received a bachelor's degree from Northern Illinois University in fashion merchandising.

How did Hitzman end up in selling? She comments, "My career in selling basically started when I was in school, studying fashion merchandising. A lot of my required courses were marketing related and, being involved in marketing, I realized that I really was enjoying those courses even more than my fashion merchandising courses. I think that is what steered me toward sales.

"What made me select Moore as a company, I think, was the fact that I'd dealt with some people at Moore. In addition, I was really impressed and enthused about their job as well as with possibilities that were available for me."

When asked if she knew that one recent book chose Moore as one of the top 100 U.S. firms to sell for, Hitzman replied, "As a matter of fact, I didn't know that. But it's not surprising to me that Moore was chosen as one of the 100 best companies. Moore is a very large corporation that's been in existence for many years—104 years to be exact—and, needless to say, it wouldn't have been around that long if it wasn't a very good company. I do feel that they have given me a lot of support, they gave me a lot of paths to choose from, and overall, Moore treats its employees very well.

"My current job involves dealing with customers, drawing copy for business forms, writing and placing orders, following up on those orders with delivery times, and making sure those orders get to my customers on time."

In describing what she likes most about her job, Hitzman comments, "I would say the variety; I'm not doing the same thing day after day. I'm calling on different customers, I'm working on different projects for them, and I have presentations and proposals to write. I'm not doing the same thing every day. That's probably the most exciting thing about my job—there's always a new challenge."

Hitzman described Moore's sales training program as follows: "My training was basically in the office that I was going to be working out of and I dealt a lot with my immediate supervisor. Together we worked through a series of modules during the first four weeks. It was pretty intense training but very informative; I still refer to that material.

"The first couple of weeks were spent learning about the different products at Moore, how to price those products, and how to draw copy for those forms. I spent the second two weeks learning how to communicate with people. Their videos and cassettes showed me how to sell features and benefits. They really emphasized human interaction, customer needs, and developing relationships. The training was actually very good. I learned a lot from it."

About her customers, Hitzman comments, "I have very, very good relations with them. I haven't run into any circumstances where I wasn't able to accomplish either what I set out to accomplish or what the customer and I were trying to accomplish.

"I try to look at each person's personality and adjust mine accordingly so that we both accomplish what we want. If a customer is very demanding—which I am with myself—I'm willing to give the extra time. Anytime a customer is worried about a product or a little bit hesitant, I go back and spend extra time to build confidence. I never rush through or send in an order without verifying everything and making my customer comfortable. I think my customers find it easy to deal with me."

In describing her feelings about other people in the company, Hitzman said, "I've had very good experience in my office with my sales manager and my supervisor. At this time, I deal mostly with my supervisor. Before his promotion, he used to have my accounts so he's very familiar with them. He knows what I'm talking about when I go into his office. This saves a lot of time. I think because I was fresh out of college, he was very influential in developing my skills. My supervisor spent a lot time trying to mold me into a good sales rep instead of just throwing me out in the field. So we've had a very good relationship.

"Moore is a large corporation so if field salespeople have any questions about a product or something that a customer is inquiring about, they can just pick up the phone and get in touch with someone who has specialized in the area and can provide the necessary support. When I am working on a presentation, there are people I can contact to get flip charts made and get audio equipment. There is also considerable support through the manufacturing plant, in our office, and a lot of support from my peers. Everyone seems to support one another's efforts."

When asked where she will go from here, Hitzman commented, "There are a lot of possibilities, a lot of career paths I could choose. It's basically up to me which one I want to pursue. At this point, I think staying in sales and trying to achieve the next position up the ladder, as an account representative, is where I'm going. From there on out, I've made no decisions or commitments as to which path I'm going to take. I don't feel I want to go into management because I judge my own performance very harshly. In a management position you're counting on other people to make you look good and I don't think I could hold that position without getting ulcers."

Company after company have begun to provide for career growth for sales personnel. At Dow Chemical, for example, there are career paths in field sales, field sales management, and marketing (Figure 3–1). From the entry-level sales representative position, the capable individual moves to sales specialist and from this position to account specialist. After success in field sales assignments, those who demonstrate the ability to lead others may move into field sales management or marketing. At Dow the majority of district sales managers and zone vice presidents were once salespeople. The marketing positions are product manager and marketing manager. Those salespeople who wish to remain in field sales have opportunities as senior account specialist, account/industry manager, and account executive.[1]

FIGURE 3–1   Career paths at Dow Chemical

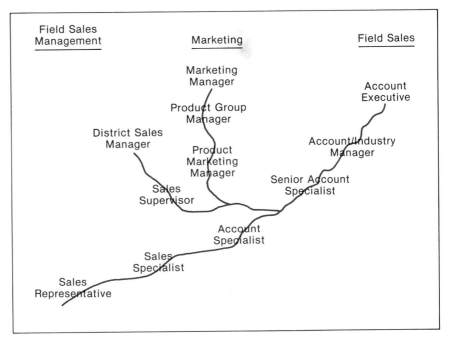

Reproduced with permission of Dow Chemical Company.

Traditionally, promotion for the salesperson has been to a job in sales management or on the marketing staff. Today, however, many firms are offering growth opportunities in field sales. Dow, for example, has an additional three levels in its field sales career path. The Norton Co., a seller of adhesives, abrasives, and grinding wheels, has five levels in its sales career path. One reason for this is that companies such as Dow and Norton feel they cannot afford to lose good salespeople. Another is that the traits inherited in being a successful salesperson do not automatically translate to management skills. Therefore, offering only career paths to management positions may be limiting many people in sales. Still other reasons are that individuals with management potential are not identified in recruiting and no apprentice step has been established between sales and sales management.

ORGANIZATIONAL GROWTH OPPORTUNITIES

Time and time again, research has shown that salespeople cite opportunity for advancement as a primary reason for their career choices. For example, in a recent study of more than 10,000 salespeople and sales managers in automotive sales, 91.3 percent of the salespeople consider a career path important with 70.5 percent indicating it "extremely" or "very important."[2] This reasoning is logical and entirely consistent with the evidence, which indicates that effective salespeople are among the most promotable employees of any firm. Studies over the last 10 years have shown that more chief executive officers have come from sales and marketing than any other area within industry.

The opportunity for advancement may come in several ways: Salespeople can advance to increased sales responsibilities, become a member of sales management, or step up to staff marketing positions in marketing research, product management, or market planning. The possibilities are limitless for the salesperson who achieves a good track record in the field. An advantage the salesperson has is that his or her contributions are easily identified.

The Career Path Concept

Management that realizes the contributions good salespeople make to the organization is likely to move effective performers to areas where they can make the greatest impact on the success of the company. The concept of a **career path** refers to the series of steps or levels employees go through in progressing organizationally through the company with responsibilities and benefits changing with each step.

career path
series of steps employees go through in preparation for advancement

Traditionally, many companies had the idea that sales management is the logical next step for the successful salesperson. This belief—the star salesperson concept—assumes that superior sales performance guarantees effectiveness as a sales manager. Nothing could be further from the truth! Sales and management of a sales force are totally different jobs requiring different skills. What it takes to manage is almost the opposite of what it takes to be a successful salesperson. A common saying is that when you promote star salespeople, the company loses two people—the star salesperson and the manager he or she replaced.

Multiple Career Paths

Management positions, however, are not the only advancement opportunities open to salespeople. Multiple career paths are now widely accepted in industry. Figure 3–2 graphically demonstrates the three primary career paths for sales personnel within a company. Salespeople may be selected to follow sales management careers, professional sales careers, or marketing staff careers.

Companies promote trainees to regular sales positions to gain meaningful field experience before making any career path decisions. The length of the initial job assignment varies according to industry, company, product, and customer requirements. For companies selling packaged groceries, it may be a set period of time, such as 18 months. For other types of companies, it

---

FIGURE 3–2   The multiple career path concept for sales personnel

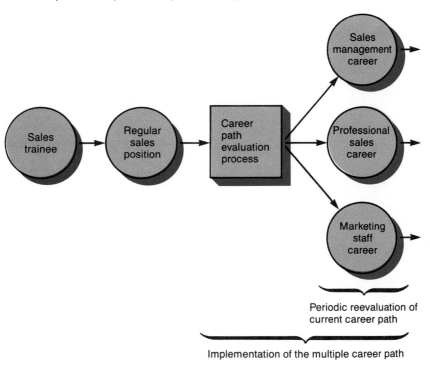

---

will vary according to individual capabilities and organizational needs. The actual career path evaluation process should involve the individual salesperson, the sales manager, and perhaps a staff person skilled in career consultation. The decision that results from this evaluation should be the one that best meets the needs of both the individual involved and the company.

Once an employee has selected a career path, he or she should reevaluate it periodically. A person's career objective is subject to change, and adjustment should be allowed at least in the early stages.

Sales Management Career Track

Salespeople expected to eventually enter sales management should be identified early. One national firm has a policy that salespeople not promoted to sales management in two-and-one-half years are let go. This policy places a decided emphasis on management potential in the initial hiring process. A formal program of job rotation could be set up once adequate field selling experience has been achieved so that the sales management candidate can gain experience in a variety of positions performing short-term projects. This way, he or she better understands the requirements, interrelationships, and responsibilities of a sales management position.

Surprisingly, many firms do little to prepare future sales managers. The manager is often picked from the sales force and assumes the position after only a brief orientation session, perhaps conducted by the outgoing manager. Typically only a small portion of companies have programs to train field sales managers, and many of these programs are informal at best. Examples of firms that provide for the internal development of field sales managers include General Electric, Dow, Georgia-Pacific Corporation, IBM, and the Gillette Company. Both Georgia-Pacific and Gillette have an intermediate step between the salesperson and sales management. At Georgia-Pacific it is called assistant branch manager, while Gillette labels the position assistant district manager.

Professional Sales Careers

Ample professional opportunities should be available to those who follow a sales career path. A sales career such as has been discussed gives salespeople a way of advancing without going into management. Also, by adjusting the sales compensation package, the rewards for staying in sales can be made comparable to those received by managers.

The appropriate philosophy for setting up a professional sales career path is that a salesperson can advance in terms of status, recognition, and pay without moving into management. This career path requires the identification of successive positions, each meeting a different set of responsibilities and/ or dealing with a different group of customers. For example, a salesperson is promoted to what might be called major account representative. This entails selling to only assigned major accounts.

The next step might be industry representative where the salesperson concentrates on making presentations to groups of customers. In setting up a sales career path, the emphasis should be on maintaining initiative and motivation, while at the same time increasing organizational status and rewards.

Marketing Staff Careers

The marketing staff is another career alternative for sales personnel. Many companies regard two to five years of field selling experience as a necessary prerequisite to a marketing staff position. They believe that a person who has not had direct field sales experience cannot function effectively in a sales support area or a corporate staff position such as product manager.

Numerous marketing staff functions are open to people with sales experience. These opportunities are in product management, market research, advertising, distribution, warehousing, customer relations, systems planning,

PROFESSIONAL SELLING IN ACTION

Moving from Management Back to Sales

Promotion to sales management is an established career path and the only one in countless companies. Investigation into why individuals reverse the process and go back into sales helps explain the preference of sales over management. It also reveals some of the problems salespeople have in adjusting to a management job.

Individuals give up sales management jobs and return to selling because it represents something they enjoy doing very much. One former executive in explaining the difference said it this way: "I like management, but I love selling." Another ex-executive described his feelings about selling: "If you really like selling, no matter what you eventually end up doing, you'll always want to get back into the field. I actually like making cold calls and traveling, and I miss that. I felt I was losing touch."

Among the other reasons cited for making the move back to sales were office politics, lack of freedom and the conditions imposed on management, no relationship between efforts and results, and poor preparation for the management job. The limitations placed on management seem to be particularly irritating. A former sales manager did not like office politics, but he also did not like the administrative work, the meetings, the lower salary, and being tied to a schedule. One ex-division manager spent 20 years in administration before returning to sales. The pluses for him in management were in training people, seeing them develop, and seeing his ideas being used. Among the not-so-enjoyable tasks were administration, particularly having to make personnel decisions. Another distasteful part of the job for another executive turned salesperson was the constant overnight travel.

Lack of preparation for management was a problem voiced by another former executive. With little training she was rushed into a job supervising 11 agents, five of whom were new to the firm. In addition to extra meetings, paperwork, and assorted administrative tasks, she had to develop a training program. This took all of her time and left none for selling. She returned to sales after one year because she liked the freedom of selling and the idea of being responsible for herself.

SOURCE: Bill Kelley, "Who Says You Can't Go Home Again?" *Sales & Marketing Management,* September 1989, pp. 38–44. Reprinted by permission of Sales & Marketing Management. © September 1989.

sales analysis, distribution cost analysis, dealer relations, and sales training. People with successful sales experience have proven their worth to the firm, and they are likely candidates for challenging staff positions. Such individuals are in demand, and in many cases staff departments actually bid for their services.

REWARDS FOR SALESPEOPLE: THE NEED FOR AN EVALUATION SYSTEM

Whether moving along a career path or remaining in sales, a salesperson will be eligible for a variety of rewards. Such rewards are broken down into financial incentives and nonfinancial incentives.

The starting point for any reward system is to have a good method of performance appraisal. Rewards need to be planned and allocated systematically rather than given on a haphazard, uncoordinated basis. Salespeople and sales managers alike should perceive the rewards as being fair and should have a clear understanding of the conditions and the rationale supporting them.

In the search for an effective evaluation program that realistically reflects a salesperson's actual performance, Dow Chemical uses what it describes as a "pay for performance" plan. Dow salespeople receive a salary that is adjusted annually according to their respective ratings. Other firms may evaluate on a semiannual, quarterly, or even monthly basis. The key to a good compensation plan is a system of relating compensation (or changes in compensation) to performance. In other words, the salesperson who does the best job receives the greatest reward.

A lack of adequate evaluative measures forces sales managers to rely on subjective opinions about a particular salesperson's worth. In such a situation, salespeople may become disillusioned and discouraged, resulting in excessive turnover of qualified sales personnel. Sales personnel expect to be evaluated on standards they understand and on which they can agree.

FINANCIAL REWARDS

Financial rewards are quite generous in selling; in fact, sales is one of the most lucrative of all career fields. A successful salesperson can earn more than most of his or her contemporaries in other parts of the organization. Unfortunately, the above-average earnings potential tempts some people who are not qualified to enter the field. Such people eventually fail and turn to other occupations for which they are better suited.

High earnings are the reward for qualified personnel willing to invest the time and effort required for success in the field of selling. While actual salaries will vary greatly, the typical sales representative can project a doubling of his or her entry-level salary with experience. How long it takes will depend again on the industry, company, and obviously the performance of the individual. Usually salespeople selling industrial products will earn more than those selling consumer products.

Certainly, salespeople are well rewarded for their efforts. But no one should enter any field simply because of its earnings potential. Nonfinancial rewards for work are also important if one is to be truly content with one's job and lifestyle. Further, all rewards have associated costs, and the financial remuneration of a sales career is no exception. In the case of selling, long hours and sincere, diligent efforts are required for success.

The two major financial rewards are (1) compensation plans and (2) fringe benefits, expense accounts, and sales contests. Both affect the overall level of financial rewards salespeople receive, as well as their motivation.

Compensation Plans

Compensation plans can accomplish a variety of sales management objectives. Two basic objectives are motivation and control. The compensation plan must provide the incentives to sell and at the same time allow sales management to control selling efforts. Other possible objectives are security, market coverage, reduction of turnover, and cost-of-sale reduction. Balance is the key to a compensation plan. Commission sales with no provision for training, expenses, or fringe benefits will not attract and retain good people. Neither will plans that have no incentive.

Compensation Levels. The first basic decision the company must make in establishing a compensation plan is the overall level of payment to be made. Some firms may decide to pay a **competitive wage,** or compensation that is about standard for the industry. Others deliberately pay high salaries (or commissions) that are above those of the competition. Some firms use a high salary level to attract experienced sales personnel from other companies. All good sales personnel should command at least competitive salaries, but many companies fail to review their compensation plans periodically, allowing their compensation scale to slip below a competitive level. Such a situation calls for prompt corrective measures.

competitive wage
compensation plan that is about standard for the industry

Compensation Methods. In addition to its overall level of compensation, the firm also must decide on how sales personnel are paid. There are three basic options: salary, commission, or a combination plan.

Commission or Straight Salary? The original method of compensating salespeople was the **commission plan.** Its primary advantage is that a straight commission links the amount of pay directly to sales productivity. The greater the sales by a salesperson, the higher his or her earnings. Commissions provide maximum sales incentives. Historically, commissions were limited to sales volume, but many firms now try to link them to the relative profitability of the items sold.

commission plan
pay plan that links sales reps' compensation directly to their sales productivity

A **straight-salary plan** is at the opposite end of the compensation continuum. In this plan, salespeople are paid a given amount at specified times. This allows sales management to maintain maximum control over the selling effort. If management decides that sales personnel should allocate greater effort to market research, account servicing, or the like, the salary plan does not penalize the salesperson, as would be the case with a commission plan.

straight-salary plan
compensation plan that pays sales reps a given amount at specified times

Mixed Plans. Between the extremes of straight commission and straight salary are a variety of mixed-compensation plans. These approaches try to achieve the advantages of both sales force control and selling incentives. Mixed-compensation plans include (1) drawing accounts, (2) combination plans, (3) salary plus bonuses, (4) point systems, and (5) the cafeteria approach.

drawing accounts

advances against commissions earned by sales reps

Drawing accounts are advances against commissions earned by the sales representative who draws a set amount each pay period; this advance is charged against the commission account. Then periodically (say, quarterly), the balance of the commissions is paid to the individual. A modification is the **guaranteed draw,** whereby the seller is not liable for repayment if the draw is more than the commissions earned in a given period.

guaranteed draw

compensation plan whereby the sales rep is not liable for repayment if the draw is more than the commission earned in a given time period

A **combination plan** has a set salary as well as a commission component. The exact mix varies from industry to industry. Combination plans are probably the most common mixed-compensation method.

combination plan

compensation plan that has both a set salary and a commission component

Salary plus **bonuses** is another approach to sales compensation. Bonuses differ from commissions in that they are rewards for achievement not directly related to sales. Bonuses might be given for a substantial number of new accounts, feedback on special account servicing efforts, or general overall selling performance. Bonuses usually are paid annually, contrasted to the monthly or quarterly payment of commissions.

bonuses

achievement rewards not directly related to sales

Point systems award points or credits for achievement in a certain area. Salespeople receive points for each level of sales volume garnered, new accounts opened, specific servicing activities, the number of calls made, and the like. Some systems include penalty points as well as credit points; they convert the net point total to a compensation payment on a periodic basis. If each point is equal to 35 cents, then someone who earns 6,400 points in a particular month receives a check for $2,240 (minus deductions).

point system

pay plan that awards points or credits for achievement; the total is then converted to a compensation payment

Another compensation program utilizes the **cafeteria plan,** which allows employees to select the mix of salary, commissions, bonuses, and fringe benefits that best suits their needs. A younger person might elect cash to meet current expenses, while an older salesperson might concentrate on increased insurance or pension payments. Most cafeteria plans have a limited number of options and require that the individual's selections remain set for a given period. These rules cut the costs of administering such a plan. This approach may become a standard feature of future compensation plans.

cafeteria plan

allows employees to select the mix of salary, commissions, bonuses, and fringe benefits that best suits their needs

Fringe Benefits/Expense Accounts/Sales Contests

fringe benefits

financial rewards not directly tied to a firm's compensation plan

Sales personnel also receive financial rewards that are not directly tied to the firm's compensation plan, such as **fringe benefits.** These include automobiles, life insurance, disability insurance, health insurance, vacations, pension plans, and stock options. When salespeople were commission agents, they had a few of these benefits. But times have changed and so has sales compensation. Today's salesperson typically receives a full range of fringe benefits. For example, it is not uncommon for salespeople to participate in stock-purchase plans and various types of retirement plans.

expense accounts

reimbursements to cover legitimate costs of fulfilling the job requirements of selling

Most sales personnel also have **expense accounts** to cover the legitimate

A SALES MANAGEMENT NOTE

Dealing with Senior Salespeople

It is sound management practice to keep senior salespeople in the field where they can make a major contribution. However, they must be assured that they are more valued than their junior counterparts. Some of the ways this can be done are:

1. Make a distinction in job title. Some of the titles that can be used are: major market manager, key account manager, and field vice president.
2. Upgrade company car program.
3. Provide a car phone.
4. Create a field sales council to discuss field marketing conditions with top management.

5. Use senior salespeople as counselors to junior salespeople.
6. Provide single rooms to senior salespeople.
7. Provide outside secretarial support.
8. Publish senior salespeople's success stories.
9. Include senior salespeople in task force assignments.
10. Do not use senior salespeople as trainers.

SOURCE: Jack Falvey, "The Making of a Manager," *Sales & Marketing Management*, March 1989, pp. 42–47, 83. Reprinted by permission of Sales & Marketing Management. © March 1989.

costs of fulfilling their job requirements. An expense account is not a reward for selling, since a salesperson should not make money (or lose it) as a result of an expense account. A good expense account policy is to pay all realistic selling expenses and disallow all those of a personal nature. Legitimate sales expenses include business travel, lodging, meals, and work-related entertainment.

Expense accounts are examined in this chapter because they are a payment to the sales force. However, a company should not allow an expense account to become a type of fringe benefit. Neither should the firm permit the person's expense allowance to dip below the actual costs incurred. A typical example of this failure is an organization that continues to pay 20 cents per mile for automobile travel, even though travel costs are now higher.

Expense accounts can take various forms:

periodic allowance

expense account plan that sets the reimbursement at a given level for a time period

1. **Periodic allowance.** Given a set amount to cover expenses, the salesperson keeps his or her own expense records. A common complaint is that sales management has a tendency to let the allowance fall below the amount actually required. Some salespeople also try to keep a portion of the allowance and thus limit useful sales activities.

unlimited expense account

reimbursement plan that pays all legitimate expenses

2. **Unlimited expense account.** This plan pays all legitimate selling expenses. Salespeople use various reporting systems. Specifically, all lodging expenditures and entertainment costs over $25 require receipts. All expense reports should contain the names and business relationships of persons entertained, dates, and business purpose.

limited allowance

expense account plan that limits reimbursement to a set amount

3. **Limited allowance.** A standard example of this type is a per diem plan that allows salespeople a set amount—say, $100—for each day they are away from home. Similar plans might set weekly limits on various categories of expenses, such as room charges, meals, and entertainment.

Salespeople also participate in special promotions that emphasize a particular line or product. These promotions, usually called sales contests, support the introduction of a new product, stimulate lagging sales, and offset seasonal declines. The objective is to motivate salespeople to market a particular item or product line more aggressively. The prizes used in sales contests include not only money but also items of merchandise, travel, and tickets to sporting events. Some of the most effective promotions are those that involve the family of the salesperson. Travel incentives that involve the salesperson and his or her spouse are used extensively by numerous major firms.

NONFINANCIAL REWARDS

Sales personnel often are the most financially motivated employees in any organization. Any sales motivation effort would be foolish to subordinate the role played by an adequate compensation program, but the nonfinancial rewards associated with a sales career can also be significant motivators in selling.

Perhaps the most important nonfinancial reward is the personal satisfaction a salesperson receives from knowing that he or she is fulfilling a vital need in society. The salesperson satisfies customer needs, participates in the efficient distribution of products, and creates jobs in other segments of the economy, such as manufacturing or the service sector. Salespeople can take pride that their work lubricates the machine of modern economic life. Recognition of a salesperson's efforts by his or her superiors can reinforce these feelings.

Another nonfinancial reward is the salesperson's status within the organization. Because productive firms realize the importance of the seller's efforts in the field, they offer higher average compensation and substantial opportunities for career advancement.

Most salespeople sincerely enjoy the competitiveness of their occupation and regard it as an important nonfinancial reward. Selling is the most competitive activity in any business organization; good sales representatives enjoy the chance to achieve in such an environment. The intense competition quickly separates those who succeed in selling from those who would be advised to seek employment elsewhere.

Freedom of action is one of the most important career advantages cited by professional salespeople, who often say they hate being tied to a desk and really enjoy getting out among customers. The professional salesperson likes the opportunity to meet and interact with people having different personalities, goals, and problems. Salespeople are also able, for the most part, to come and go at will. Because selling is a results-oriented job rather than predicated on routine and procedure, freedom of action is one of the most enticing nonfinancial rewards in this career field.

HOW TO GET A JOB IN SELLING

Up to this point, Chapter 3 has described the rewards and opportunities associated with professional selling. The obvious question then is: How do you get a job in selling? The answer is a plan that begins with self-preparation and ends with closing the employment agreement. Your plan should recognize that getting a job is in itself a selling job because you are competing with other people for the same sales positions.

Step 1: Self-Preparation

The first step in seeking a job is looking the part—take care of all the details in regard to dress and grooming. These are necessary to make the best possible impression. This step might include buying a suit, some shirts, a dress, or taking clothing to the dry cleaners. Your footwear should complement your suit or dress and be in good condition; shined shoes are a must.

Good grooming is also a must for any job applicant. You should ask two questions with regard to grooming: Is my personal appearance appropriate for the selling job I am seeking? Does my appearance project a neat, well-groomed look?

Step 2: Self-Analysis

In the second step, analyze yourself and develop career and monetary objectives. The key is to know not only your strengths and weaknesses but also your aspirations.

The positive personality traits recruiters look for in a job applicant are abilities that can be learned, such as communication, assertiveness, and motivation (see Figure 3–3). Of least importance are age and affiliations in and out of school.

During self-analysis, consider how you can best project positively and honestly those traits that appear most important on your resumé and during job interviews. You might, for example, emphasize previous job experience as evidence of your maturity and motivation. Develop your resumé so that it helps you secure an interview. Remember that employers are looking for people who will work hard and, in the case of selling, work hard without direct supervision.

FIGURE 3–3   Employer ranking of attributes for prospective job candidates

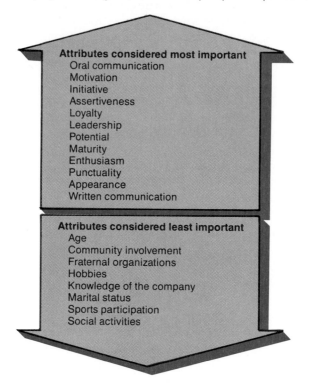

Attributes considered most important
Oral communication
Motivation
Initiative
Assertiveness
Loyalty
Leadership
Potential
Maturity
Enthusiasm
Punctuality
Appearance
Written communication

Attributes considered least important
Age
Community involvement
Fraternal organizations
Hobbies
Knowledge of the company
Marital status
Sports participation
Social activities

Source: John C. Hofer and C. C. Hoth. "Research Finds Students Misinformed on Hiring Criteria," *Marketing News*. Published by the American Marketing Association, July 25, 1980. Used with permission. [Author's note: It is now illegal for recruiters to inquire about marital status.]

The inner drive to succeed—motivation—is all-important no matter which career path you pursue. Therefore, as part of self-analysis, set employment and financial goals. A convenient classification for such goal setting is about 2 years, 4 years, 10 years, and 15 years.

Step 3: Market Research

Job-seeking individuals need to be familiar with all the sources of information about jobs because only 20 percent of the available jobs are public knowledge or publicized in some fashion.

Different sources include newspaper advertisements, college placement offices, professional publications, state employment offices, professional placement firms, and professional organizations such as Sales & Marketing

Executives International and the American Marketing Association. College professors can often provide valuable insights into the job market and specific jobs that might be available in the local area.

Step 4: Contact Strategy

In this step, develop a strategy for contacting prospective employers. Even though direct contact is twice as effective as other techniques, a direct mail approach has to be used with many prospective employers. A well-constructed resumé that highlights your strong points can be the difference between a rejection letter and an interview.

Step 5: Sales Promotion

This step involves contacting and arranging your initial interview with prospective employers. Important points to remember in the interview are:

Project important personal traits.

Obtain vital information about the job and working conditions.

Determine the key contact who makes the hiring decision.

Often, candidates for sales jobs are asked to sell some object on the interviewer's desk to the interviewer. The purpose is to see how job applicants handle themselves in selling situations.

Step 6: Contact

This step involves the interview, or usually interviews, for a position. As a candidate for a position, very likely you will be interviewed by several different people. The first interview is part of the preliminary screening of the individual along with the resumé. Just as a prospect is qualified, employers screen you and other candidates initially to determine:

Your level of interest in the position.

Your qualifications as matched against the job description.

Subsequent interviews provide an opportunity for different people to meet the candidates and develop certain areas in depth. Some of the key factors interviewers are interested in are:

Your motivation. Are you really interested in the job and will you perform well on the job?

Your ability to handle yourself in meeting different people and facing different situations.

Your ability to espouse your strong points.

Your attitudes.

Very likely, you and other candidates will be asked to take tests. The results of the tests along with some form of grading for the interviews determine whether or not you are offered a position.

Step 7: Negotiation

This step corresponds to a sales presentation, as covered in Chapter 8, but in this case the product is yourself. Be sure to discuss salary, expenses, working conditions, fringe benefits, and possibilities for advancement at this time.

Step 8: Closing

Uppermost in this step is knowing this is the job you, the applicant, really want! Getting an offer in writing and confirming in writing are essential. Company policy may dictate a visit to the home office in this step or step six, and you should view such a request positively.

A final word of advice seems appropriate. Once you are hired, do everything possible to learn your job as quickly as possible. Strive to make yourself as valuable as possible to your new employer. When you have learned your job well and are a productive member of the sales organization, start planning the next step in your career path. In short, the personal sales cycle starts all over again. Good luck!

SUMMARY OF CHAPTER OBJECTIVES

1. **To identify the career paths available to salespeople.**

   There are three career paths available to salespeople: field sales management, marketing staff, and sales.

2. **To define the concept of a career path.**

   A career path is a series of steps or levels employees go through in progressing organizationally through the company with responsibilities and benefits changing with each step.

3. **To describe financial rewards for salespeople.**

   The two major financial rewards are (1) compensation plans and (2) fringe benefits, expense accounts, and sales contests. Among the basic compensation plans are straight salary, commission, and mixed plans such as salary plus bonus. The second type of financial reward, which includes fringe benefits, expense accounts, and sales contests, is not directly tied to the compensation plan.

4. To describe nonfinancial rewards for salespeople.

Among the nonfinancial rewards for a salesperson are personal satisfaction in doing an important job, recognition from others, status within the organization, competition, and freedom of action.

5. To list the steps in getting a selling job.

The steps in the job-seeking plan are:
1. Self-preparation.
2. Self-analysis.
3. Market research.
4. Contact strategy.
5. Sales promotion.
6. Contact.
7. Negotiation.
8. Closing.

REVIEW QUESTIONS

1. What is meant by a drawing account? What is a guaranteed draw?
2. Explain how a sales force can effectively use the multiple career path concept. Discuss the various career track options available to a salesperson.
3. Interview some professional salespeople. Ask them to describe the rewards of their particular jobs. Prepare a list of these rewards and present them in a class discussion.
4. Prepare a list of reasons why salespeople typically receive above-average compensation.
5. Describe a cafeteria compensation plan. Which types of compensation would you select?
6. Differentiate between commissions and bonuses.
7. How can a point system be used in a sales compensation program?
8. Discuss the major types of expense accounts.
9. List and discuss the various nonfinancial rewards received by sales personnel.
10. List and discuss the various mixed-compensation plans that have been used in selling.

DISCUSSION QUESTIONS AND EXERCISES

1. Visit a number of companies with sales offices in your community and ask about their career-development programs.
2. Interview a personnel executive at a firm in your area. Ask him or her to describe and contrast the compensation plans used for the following professional occupations: (1) accounting, (2) engineering, and (3) production management. Then prepare a brief report comparing these compensation plans to those used in selling. What are the major differences? Similarities?

3. What are the advantages and disadvantages of commission and salary compensation plans?

4. Jan Vogel, an excellent salesperson, has just turned down a promotion to district sales manager. Here is the reasoning:

The managerial position paid only $2,000 more than I earned last year. And I know of two big accounts I am about to land. When they come through, I'll be making about $4,000–$5,000 in additional commissions every year.

Do you agree with Vogel's reasoning? What does this situation suggest about the firm's compensation plan for sales personnel? For sales managers?

5. Prepare a written plan outlining the steps you would take to get a professional selling job in an industry of your choice.

SALES DIALOG

Carol McMahon has been a senior sales representative for MacBride Enterprises in Fresno, California, for over three years. Senior sales representative is the fourth step in a professional sales career path. Basically, the job is one of making major sales presentations and working with young salespeople who are just out of the training program. James Easterly, the regional sales manager, is her superior.

McMAHON: I would like to change my career path and get into the sales management area.

EASTERLY: Carol, you are only two steps away from national account representative and the top of the ladder. Why don't you stick with it? You do a tremendous job for us as a senior rep.

McMAHON: What I am really doing with young, inexperienced salespeople is management. I think I should be paid and have the status of a sales manager.

EASTERLY: I cannot agree with you on that, and you have absolutely no responsibility as a senior rep. Did you ever think of that? In sales management the manager is accountable for everything that happens in his or her area.

McMAHON: Yes, but managers get paid more and get a chance for the top. That is what I want.

EASTERLY: Another factor is that you would have to go back to being a district manager. That can pay less than you are making now. Another problem may be transferring. The company does not like people jumping around from one career path to the other.

What do you think the results of this sales dialog will be?

CASE 3–1 LEFFINGWELL, LTD.

Janice Moran has been a salesperson for Leffingwell, Ltd. for over five years. After graduating from Eastern States University with a marketing degree, she joined the New England Food Co. as an assistant sales promotion manager. Moran was subsequently promoted to sales manager for Maine, New Hampshire, and Vermont, a job that entailed more selling than managing. After eight years with New England, she resigned to take her present job.

Although the products and customers are entirely different, Moran feels that her performance has been superior at Leffingwell. In fact, she gets more satisfaction from selling material handling equipment to factories than canned food products to grocery supermarkets.

Last month the vice president at Leffingwell, Kevin Tanney, announced the formation of a new marketing group directed toward the designing and marketing of customized, computer-oriented, material handling systems for factories. The group is to include 10 specially trained sales engineers who have marketing interests. The rationale for the new group is that the engineers can explain the technical implications of the system, something present salespeople seem unable to do. Engineers are also in better positions to develop high-level management and engineering contacts.

Questions

1. How do you feel Moran should respond to this change at Leffingwell?

2. In handling the more technically oriented problems that arise, should Leffingwell use a technically oriented salesperson or someone like Moran who has more of a marketing orientation?

3. Discuss the implications of teaching engineers to sell, as opposed to teaching technical material to marketing-oriented personnel such as Moran.

CASE 3–2   FEDERATED INDUSTRIES

Federated Industries, based in Rockford, Illinois, is a medium-sized manufacturer of equipment for the petroleum industry. Its products include lifts, hoists, drills, pumps, pipeline controls, and related items.

Federated sales representatives have always been compensated on a straight-salary basis. Last year, the salary range for field representatives was $37,000–$45,000. Employees with several years' service clustered in the $40,000–$45,000 range, while the range for less-experienced personnel tended to be about $37,000–$39,000. Each of the 30 representatives is evaluated annually, and salaries are adjusted accordingly. Federated granted salary hikes of 6 to 10 percent this past year.

Benton Avery, Federated's executive vice president, has long been concerned about turnover and the relative lack of incentive in the current salary structure. He blames the turnover on the compensation system, which he believes does not adequately recognize superior performance. Recently, Avery was heard to remark:

It's crazy; some of our salespeople have become bureaucrats. They sit around and try to appease their sales manager but do very little real aggressive marketing.

But why should they? The highest earnings are reserved for those with the longest seniority in our sales organization. The reps know that they will get a cost-of-living increase and that any merit plan is based more on internal politics than on sales performance.

Avery has since directed Scott Polner, the national sales manager, to develop a compensation plan that would provide a greater incentive to good sales performance. He

---

EXHIBIT 1   Federated Industries' revised sales compensation plan

Salary Component

0–5 years' experience with Federated	$20,500
6–10 years' experience with Federated	21,500
11–15 years' experience with Federated	22,500
16-20 years' experience with Federated	23,500
Over 20 years' experience with Federated	24,500

Commission Component

All products in the Federated line are classified in commission categories identified A, B, C. Based on gross profits to Federated, A represents the most profitable items and C the least profitable ones.

A commission schedule covers all sales over the assigned sales quota in each category. Initial sales quotas represent 90 percent of the previous year's sales of each product group. The commission schedule is:

Category A = 10% of sales over quota for this category.
Category B = 8.5% of sales over quota for this category.
Category C = 7% of sales over quota for this category.

Bonus Component

Annual performance reviews will continue but concentrate on activities not directly related to sales volume. Attention will focus on customer relations, new accounts, account servicing, cooperation in securing marketing intelligence, and the like.

The district sales manager, with approval of Mr. Polner, may grant annual bonuses of up to $5,000 for a salesperson.

Notes:
1. The salary component will be reviewed every two years and adjusted to reflect changes in the cost of living.
2. The national sales manager estimates that this plan will result in approximately the same level of compensation as currently exists for the salary plan.

---

instructed Polner to increase incentive compensation but still retain enough of a salary base to cover basic living costs.

After several weeks of intense study, Polner and his staff are set to reveal their new sales compensation plan to Avery. An outline of the plan appears in Exhibit 1.

Questions

1. Do you agree with Avery's criticism of the current compensation plan at Federated Industries?

2. How do you believe Avery will react to the proposed revision of the compensation plan? Why?

3. What is your own evaluation of Polner's plan?

4. What changes or modifications (if any) would you make to Polner's plan? Why?

PART TWO

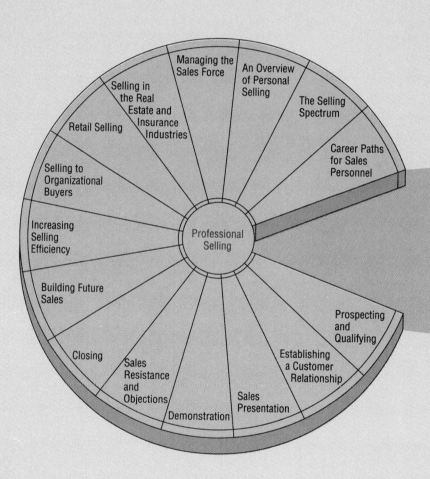

Foundations of Professional Selling

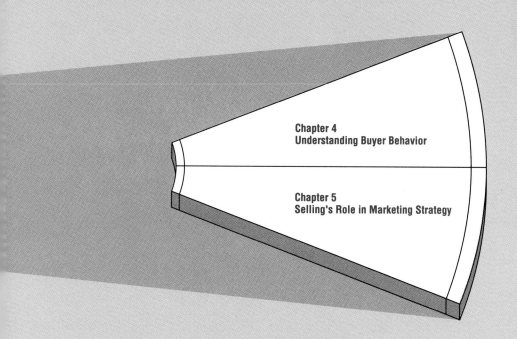

Chapter 4
Understanding Buyer Behavior

Chapter 5
Selling's Role in Marketing Strategy

CHAPTER 4

Understanding Buyer Behavior

CHAPTER OBJECTIVES

1. To define the purchase decision process.

2. To explain the steps in the purchase decision process.

3. To develop the conceptualization of a product or service as features/benefits and choice criteria.

4. To describe how consumers use decision rules in choosing a product or service.

5. To define postpurchase dissonance.

6. To explain the impact of selectivity, knowledge and learning, attitudes and beliefs, and situational influences on the purchase decision.

7. To discuss risk perception.

SALES CAREER PROFILE

JAN LAPPIN
Metropolitan Life

Jan Lappin, a branch manager with Metropolitan Life in Novato, California, holds an associate degree from Santa Fe Community College and a bachelor's degree from the University of Florida. Lappin admits one thing attracted her to selling: "The thing that made me select a career in selling was the money. I saw an ad in the newspaper saying, 'You can earn up to $500 a week.' I wasn't even sure what the job was when I first saw it in the paper. I just knew it was in selling.

"I had no selling experience when I came to Metropolitan. I had been a program director for an association for retarded citizens. I liked the counseling profession, but the money wasn't very good. In the insurance field I can help people and also make money. I have a lot of pride in what I do because I feel I'm really helping people. I am protecting families. Or, I'm showing them how they can protect themselves.

"I do a lot of financial planning. People don't think about what could happen when they die. They don't even think about retirement. Most people in their 20s have never thought about what they're going to do 40 years from now. I bring up all these situations, and I've had a lot of people thank me for doing so.

"People know I'm an insurance salesperson. They think, 'She's just gonna try to sell me something.' Well, yes, I am coming out to try to sell them something, but not just anything. I'm coming to show them something that is going to solve their problems. I'm going to tailor it to their needs. When I leave, people feel good about what they've bought."

Lappin was not surprised that Metropolitan Life was named one of the top 100 U.S. firms to sell for. "To me, it's the only firm to sell for. When I'm in the field, the company speaks for itself. I don't have to go out there and sell Metropolitan; everyone has heard of us. The clients we've had for years are really happy with the company. Basically, I just have to sell myself so people trust me.

"We try to screen, or qualify, our prospects by looking at their ages. For instance, a 17-year-old usually doesn't have or need, or desire life insurance as much as someone who is 35, married, with three dependents.

"Marital status is another factor, although more single people are getting life insurance because they realize they also have a need, especially single parents. Of course, if they can't afford to buy insurance, it's not fair to show them their need and not be able to give them a solution. So income is a qualifying factor.

"I also look at residence and location. I target areas close to me. I prefer to work with people who live in nice neighborhoods and own their homes. Another thing I look at is estates. People with large estates usually have estate tax problems. Another area would be businesses. For instance, in a partnership, there's almost always a need for a buy-sell agreement."

When asked how she assesses prospects' buying behavior, Lappin replied, "I assess prospects' buying behavior by their body language, objections, tone of voice, the way they look at me, look at their spouses, get up, or turn around. I adjust my sales presentation on the basis of this assessment. People frequently have objections and the first thing I have to do is to acknowledge that. Then, I try to find out exactly what their objections are. Sometimes, people will say, 'Well, I want to think about it' or 'I want to talk to my lawyer about it.' By finding out why they're hesitating, what it is that they want to discuss with another person, I can figure out what their actual objections are, and solve them.

"I also find out what they see as the key benefits of insurance—called owner benefits. It might be important for one person to have the house paid off if the spouse were to die. Another person might want to be sure the kids can go to college.

"The whole buying or selling process is pretty basic. I have to do certain things to be able to sell. The first is to create a favorable impression by building up credibility and trust. I want my clients to like me, trust me, and respect my knowledge; they must know that I'm there to help them.

"I spend probably 80 percent of my time showing them their problems, why they need insurance. After that, they'll look at alternative solutions and 99.9 percent of the time they'll go to life insurance because there is no better way to create an immediate estate.

"Next they look at what product best solves their problem. The primary thing in life insurance is the death benefit, an amount of money readily available to the survivors. Frequently, I have people who are more interested in the money they're going to get back later than the death benefit. A lot of people have a feeling of immortality. So, instead of looking at it as the death benefit, they look at it as saving for retirement.

"People also want to know if the product and the company will fit their future needs. For instance, some people know their income will grow substantially, or they're going to buy a bigger house later, or they're going to have more kids, and they'll probably have a need for more insurance.

"Every person is different; the way they look at things is different, their needs are different, their financial situations are different. I do a type of financial planning that Metropolitan calls personal risk management. The final 20 percent of my time is spent offering people a solution tailored to their needs, something that will help them in their particular situation. And then I close."

Selling to medical professionals, many of whom are highly specialized, has always been a tough job. Today it is even tougher because legal requirements specify that a sales representative must tell a doctor not only what a pharmaceutical product can do but also what it cannot do. Merck & Company, one of the nation's most admired corporations, has the top-rated sales force among pharmaceutical companies with high marks in such categories as product/technical knowledge and reputation among customers. In fact, among sales forces from 13 different industries, only DuPont's chemical sales force was given a higher rating score on product knowledge.[1]

Much of the success of Merck salespeople can be attributed to the introductory training program and its heavy emphasis on what might be called customer-related product knowledge. In order that each of the 1,500 salespeople are able to discuss products knowledgeably, they spend a full year learning a lot of what their customers already know—basic anatomy, physiology, and the nature of diseases. This is followed by a period of six months to a year in the field learning how to make effective sales presentation on specific benefits of the products they will be selling. In this phase of training, new salespeople work with experienced representatives. Finally, the new salespeople spend three weeks on medical knowledge, specifically the diseases and conditions where Merck products are used in treatment. In this phase of training, the new representative will make rounds with doctors.

It is the job of the salesperson to respond creatively and uniquely to the needs and wants of the consumers as well as his or her continually changing expectations. Individuals behave differently in purchasing situations depending on (1) their attitudes and needs/wants, (2) product characteristics, and (3) situational factors. Much of the marketing effort is directed toward creating favorable attitudes about products and services as well as the firms and salespeople that sell them. However, consumers must have identified a need or want before these attitudes can be translated into goals for purchasing action. The critical role of a salesperson is to help consumers attain their purchasing goals. Although these purchasing goals are frequently stated as a solution to a problem, they may also involve attainment of an objective or enhancement.

THE PURCHASE DECISION PROCESS

Consumers go through a process or a series of steps in making purchase decisions. Salespeople must study the whole decision-making process as well as their customers' needs and wants if they are to be effective in influencing purchasing decisions. Figure 4–1 illustrates the basic steps in the purchase decision process.

How a particular consumer goes about making a purchase decision depends to a great extent on his or her involvement. **Purchase involvement** is the amount of effort or interest a consumer puts into the decision-making process. Over time and with experience, consumers gain purchasing knowledge that alters the effort they spend on purchasing decisions. The more experience a consumer has in purchasing, the more likely he or she is to develop routine, automatic decision-making processes.

There are three types of decision making: extensive decision making, limited decision making, and routine decision making. The selection of a specific type depends on the level of purchase involvement. **Extensive decision making** entails substantial purchasing effort over an extended period of time to make a complex evaluation of multiple alternatives. Extensive

purchase involvement
amount of effort or interest a consumer puts into the decision-making process

extensive decision making
substantial purchasing effort over an extended period of time to make a complex evaluation of multiple alternatives

FIGURE 4–1   Purchase decision process

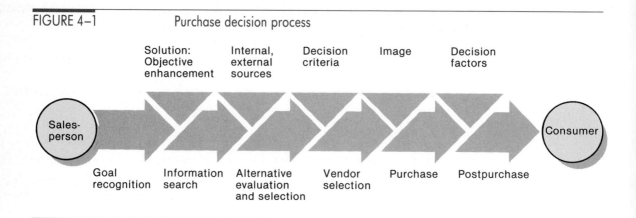

decision making is frequently involved in organizational buying situations. An example of extensive decision making would be the purchase of an overhead crane for a steel mill.

limited decision making

situation involving fewer alternatives and less purchasing effort than extensive decision making

Limited decision making involves fewer alternatives and less purchasing effort than extensive decision making. Limited decision making occurs much more frequently and takes up less time than extensive decision making. Often the purchase is guided by a simple decision rule—take the lowest price or longest warranty. The amount of information sought varies from low to moderate with primary emphasis on internal sources and only limited external search.

routine decision making

purchase that incurs little or no purchasing effort

Routine decision making occurs almost automatically with little or no purchasing effort. Purchasers rely substantially on what they have learned from previous purchase decisions. There are two routine buying situations. In one, purchasers are loyal to a brand and/or the vendor that best serves their interests. In the other, purchasers feel the different brands and vendors are all about the same and so continue to buy a specific brand or patronize a satisfactory vendor.

Goal Recognition

The purchase decision process begins with the activation of goals a consumer wants to achieve or satisfy. This sequence of purposeful actions focuses on a solution to an existing or anticipated problem, attaining an objective, or bringing about an enhancement or added value. The importance of the purchase and, therefore, the amount of purchasing effort, varies in relation to (1) the difference between the present and what is desired, and (2) the importance of the goal to consumers.

How consumers look at their present and desired or needed states depends on their perception of the current situation as well as their needs and attitudes. The role of salespersons is to show the difference between the present and

A SALES MANAGEMENT NOTE

Knowing Your Customers

The customer is a key element in the success of any business. Thus it makes sense that the more you know about your customer, the more likely you will be able to do business with him or her. Traditionally, sales managers have helped build this relationship through customer-record forms and printouts of sales results. Unfortunately, the performance of salespeople in maintaining account records has had no direct relationship to selling performance. Some of the best sales producers will keep very poor records while the opposite holds true for many poor sales producers.

The dilemma is that, although a sales manager wants his or her sales representatives in the field selling with as few distractions as possible, in order to do the best job, sales representatives need as much up-to-date information as possible on their customers. One possible answer is provided by the following steps.

1. As much as possible, transfer administration of account records away from the sales representative in the field. Account records can usually be computerized. Sales representatives can make corrections and additions by phone.

2. Segment customers by importance and require only the most basic data on the 80 percent that produce only 20 percent of the business.

3. Rank your most important customers in a territory (the 20 percent that contribute 80 percent of the business).

4. Pick an important account where the sales representative already has a reasonably good relationship and good information and do an in-depth study.

5. Develop key account and key person profiles for the remainder of the important accounts or at least those you cannot afford to lose.

DO YOU KNOW THEM?

Key Account Profile

[ ] Who is your customer's customer?

[ ] What are the strengths of your customer's product and service?

[ ] How does your customer go to market?

[ ] What are your customer's key events, such as promotional campaigns, trade shows, contract deadlines?

[ ] What are the lead times within which your customer works?

[ ] What is the history of past dealings with your customer?

[ ] Who are the key players in your selling cycle?

[ ] What is the ideal selling cycle to this customer?

[ ] What has the competition been able to do in the past?

[ ] Realistically, what plans do you have for future business? Why?

Key Person Profile

[ ] What is the basic business background of your key person?

[ ] Who does your key person report to?

[ ] What are his business objectives?

[ ] When is his birthday? Where did he go to college? What is his wife's name?

[ ] What is the best transaction you ever had with him?

[ ] What is the worst?

[ ] How does this person like to do business?

[ ] What does he look for most?

[ ] What are the names of his support people?

[ ] When is the ideal time to see them?

[ ] What are their vacation schedules?

SOURCE: Jack Falvey, "Get the Lowdown on Your Customers," *Sales & Marketing Management*, May 1989, pp. 16–17. Reprinted by permission of Sales & Marketing Management. © May 1989.

desired states, thus activating the purchasing decision process. Typically, the wider the gap between the present circumstances and what is needed or desired, the greater the probability of making a sale. For example, a salesperson from an insurance company might show the difference between present and desired states by comparing the prospect's present coverage with what the customer needs to educate his or her children. In selling industrial machinery, a salesperson demonstrates the increased speed of the machinery (more parts produced in a given time period), the increased quality of the parts produced, and the reduction in labor to run the machine (one worker rather than two workers).

In the first example, the importance of insurance to cover college costs will vary by family size, among other factors. In the second example, importance will vary in relation to the state of existing machinery and the urgency of filling existing and anticipated orders.

A salesperson can usually do little to influence the basic needs and wants of an individual consumer or an organization. Along with advertising, salespeople make consumers aware of their needs and wants and show how these needs and wants can be satisfied. Abraham Maslow's categorization of needs can be applied to many marketing situations. These needs are outlined in Figure 4–2. At the lowest level are physiological or basic needs necessary for survival. Next is safety needs expressed as security, stability, and physical safety. At the next higher level is belongingness reflected in acceptance, affiliation, and friendship. Esteem needs include prestige, status, and respect. The highest need level is self-actualization, which involves self-fulfillment and the need to become all we are capable of becoming.

Salespeople can make use of the Maslow categorization in two ways. One is the prioritization of needs. Lower-level needs have priority in any situation because they must be satisfied before higher-level needs are activated. For example, few consumers will purchase status products like a Mercedes when they have not satisfied lower-level needs for belongingness.

Secondly, the number of individuals motivated by needs at a particular level tends to decrease from one level to the next higher level. This is particularly true for the three highest levels of belongingness, esteem, and self-actualization. Salespeople can expect fewer consumers to be motivated by esteem than by belongingness, and fewer still to be motivated by self-actualization.

Information Search

internal search
study of relevant information from memory of past searches, personal experiences, and learning

Once their goals are recognized, consumers begin to search for information. All buyers—consumers or organization buyers—have internal and external sources of information available to them. **Internal search** deals with relevant information based on past searches, personal experiences, and learning. Internal search activates memory about a specific situation. For instance, we

FIGURE 4–2   Classification of products by need levels

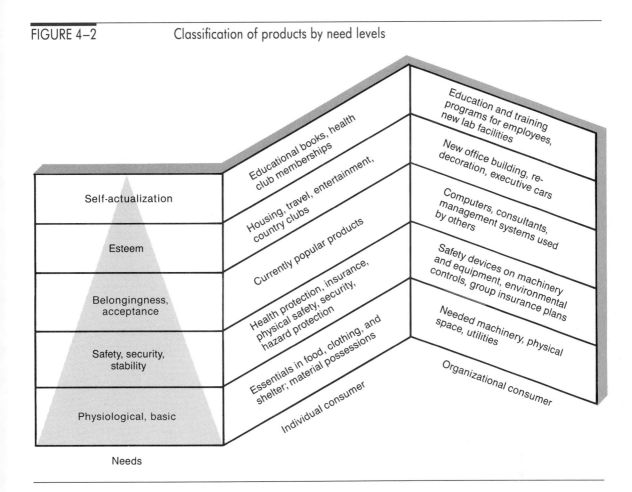

consider field materials as an extension of memory and classify them as internal sources.

By contrast, **external search** relies on outside factors. External search includes:

external search

use of personal, published, seller, and experience sources in the buying decision process

1. Personal sources: friends, family members, and business associates.
2. Published sources: magazines and reports.
3. Seller sources: salespeople and advertising.
4. Experience sources: demonstrations, inspections, and trial use of the product.

Consumers conduct external searches for several reasons. The most obvious is that consumers feel they do not know enough about the product or service in question. As a rule, the newer the product or service, the more limited consumer knowledge. Another reason for an external search is to collect information to substantiate the purchasing decision to others. This frequently occurs in organizational buying situations where there is divided responsibility for purchasing and final approval has to be obtained from a superior or committee.

Consumers look for various types of information in their searches. First, consumers try to determine **choice criteria**, that is, which features or characteristics produce the benefits that have priority in producing customer satisfaction. Choice criteria are what a consumer ends up looking for in a product or service. Figure 4–3 shows features and benefits that may be a possible choice criteria for a riding lawn mower and a small truck.

Consumers do not buy products or services, they buy bundles of features. These **features** as shown for both a riding lawn mower and a small truck are characteristics of a product or service that provide benefits or value to

choice criteria

features/benefits with the most importance or priority in producing customer satisfaction

features

characteristics of a product or service that provide benefits or value to consumers

---

FIGURE 4–3   Possible features/benefits for two products: riding lawn mower and small truck

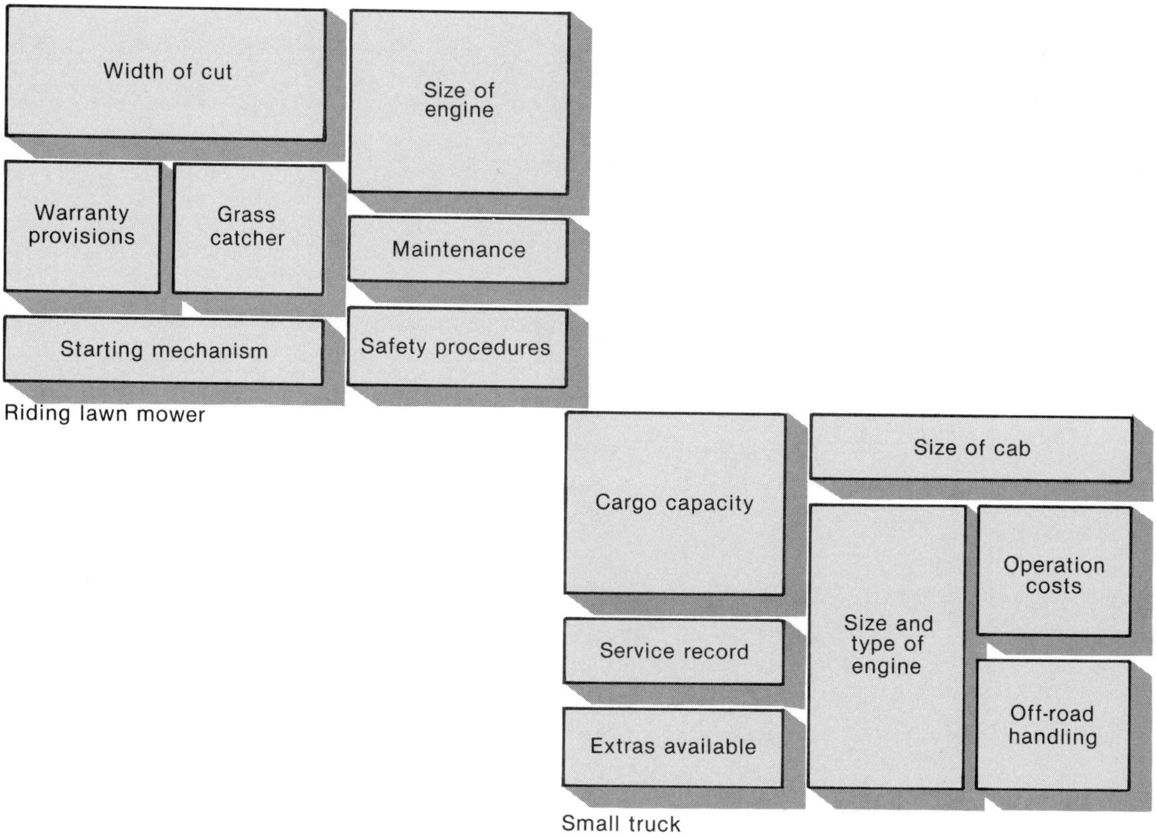

Riding lawn mower

- Width of cut
- Warranty provisions
- Grass catcher
- Starting mechanism
- Size of engine
- Maintenance
- Safety procedures

Small truck

- Cargo capacity
- Size of cab
- Service record
- Size and type of engine
- Operation costs
- Extras available
- Off-road handling

the consumer or his or her organization. Sellers must link product benefits to consumer needs. By keying benefits to needs, the salesperson has a greater probability of success in getting the sale. Without this association, customers or prospects become confused and lose interest.

Whether particular features/benefits become choice criteria depends upon their importance to the consumer. Each consumer will have his or her own set of choice criteria that may or may not coincide with other consumers. The choice criteria may be different for consumers who buy the same product and even for those who buy the same brand of a product. In buying a lawn mower, for example, a home owner's choice might be the starting mechanism, safety features, and the warranty. For a greenskeeper at a local golf course, the choice criteria might be the width of the cut, the size of the engine, and ease of maintenance.

Benefits are often expressed in relative terms such as fewer dollars, less time, lower operating costs, more comfort, and easier handling. As an illustration, cargo capacity of a small truck might translate into larger loads and less time and money spent in hauling materials to a job site or buyer. The off-road handling capabilities might translate into greater adaptability to weather conditions and terrain.

The connection between a feature and a benefit can be thought of as a perceived advantage in using the product or service. To illustrate, let's use a feature of the riding lawn mower.

Feature: Starting mechanism.

Advantage: Quick and effortless starting.

Benefit: Anyone can start and use mower; less time spent in starting.

If the advantage is available on only the riding mower being sold by the salesperson, then the salesperson has a competitive advantage. The job of a salesperson at this point is to get the consumer to select as choice criteria those features or benefits where a competitive advantage that favors his or her products exists.

To help both the salesperson and the consumer, features and benefits can be sorted into three categories. In one category are features and benefits we can label physical/performance. These are the most obvious to the consumer and include the physical identity of the product, the functioning of the product, and the design of the product. The looks of an automobile and the capabilities of a machine tool would fall under this category. Complementary features/benefits, a second category, are the extras, such as warranties, and customer service, that can be added to the basic product. The latter is especially important today as products often become generic in terms of identifiable physical/performance features/benefits. The third category, symbolic features/benefits, pertains to the image of the product and the satisfaction achieved from possession. Among the more common symbolic features/benefits are status, prestige, beauty, quality, health, and reputation.

Consumers seek information on appropriate alternatives and the performance level or characteristic for each choice criterion in an alternative. For example, in searching for information about a truck to be used in delivery, a consumer would probably want to ascertain the dimensions of loading space and the tonnage capacity of each model and/or brand of truck being considered. In organizational buying situations, much of this information is available on specification sheets.

Alternative Evaluation and Selection

Once they have considered the information necessary to make a purchasing decision, buyers can evaluate the alternatives and make a selection. An effective salesperson needs to know the prospect's choice criteria, how they are to be measured or characterized, and the order of their importance. The clearer and more precise the benefit and its measurement, the easier the job of selling. Salespeople will want to emphasize those features and benefits where their product has competitive superiority. Similarity between products or services accentuates price differences. To offset this, salespeople have two tasks: First, they must ensure that their own, as well as their company's reputation, capacity, or guarantee is included as a choice criteria. Second, sales representatives must establish and continually reinforce these characteristics and performance levels during their sales calls. Figure 4–4 shows the importance of this effort. Purchasing agents want reliability and credibility as well as professionalism and integrity from the salespeople that call on them.

Basic decision rules can be used to produce the best alternative or alternatives. Two decision rules reduce the number of alternatives. Using the **minimum standards decision rule**, consumers consider all products or brands that surpass a minimum standard on each evaluation criterion. The **minimum acceptance decision rule** bases acceptance on a product or brand surpassing the minimum standard on any one criterion.

In addition to these decision rules, consumers must use another decision rule to select from the acceptable set. The **best or most important criterion decision rule** requires consumers to arrange relevant choice criteria in order of importance. They select the product or brand that performs best on the most important criterion. In case of a tie, the products and brands are evaluated in relation to the second most important criterion. Suppose, for example, a consumer uses the minimum standards rule to narrow the brands of tires being considered to five. The most important criterion is price, and the next most important is mileage projection. After comparing the prices of the five tire brands, the consumer selects the brand with the lowest price. If the prices of two brands are about the same, the consumer compares the mileage projections for each and selects the one with the highest projection. The logic in using this decision-making process is that the brand finally chosen best fits the decision criteria in a decreasing order of importance. The brand is

minimum standards decision rule

consideration of all products or brands that surpass a minimum standard on each evaluation criterion

minimum acceptance decision rule

consumer acceptance based on a product or brand surpassing the minimum standard on any one criterion

best or most important criterion decision rule

arrangement of relevant choice criteria in order of importance

FIGURE 4–4   Purchasing agents' ratings of salespeople

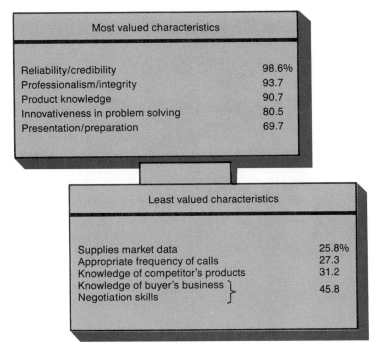

Source: "PAs Examine the People Who Sell to Them," *Sales & Marketing Management,* November 11, 1985, p. 39. Reprinted by permission of Sales & Marketing Management. © November 11, 1985.

chosen by first looking at the criterion of lowest price, and then at the criterion of best mileage at the lowest price, rather than considering all tires at various prices.

best overall decision rule

rating all products or brands on each criterion

The **best overall decision rule** requires rating all the products or brands on each of the criteria. The product selected is the one with the highest total rating. Usually each criterion is weighted according to its importance. If five criteria are evaluated, then a weighting of five could be given to the most important, four to the next most important, and so on. The score for a specific criterion is its weighting times its rating.

Vendor Selection

As mentioned previously, the salesperson must ensure that his or her vendor is a choice criterion. In the selection of any product or service, the choice criteria show a close association between what is offered for sale and who offers it. The association between the product or service and the vendor may be so complex that consumers find it difficult to separate the two. Customer service and warranty protection are two criteria that are more closely associated with vendors than with products.

For both consumers and organizational buyers, image, which includes consumers' perceptions of salespeople, is of major importance in selecting a vendor. There are four reasons for this:

1. Product or service performance levels and characteristics constantly change, while vendors' images remain fairly stable. Consumers feel more confident about their perceptions of vendors than their perceptions of products or services.

2. Product or service performance levels and characteristics are not the only areas of interest to consumers. More often than not consumers make purchasing decisions based on criteria not included in product specification sheets. For example, a consumer might include such aspects as billing method, delivery, service quality, sales personnel, and technical or marketing support.

3. Product or service performance levels and characteristics between competing brands are often undistinguishable. As a result, consumers place greater reliance on the more discernible differences between vendors.

4. Product or service performance levels and characteristics rank lower than vendors' ratings in purchase evaluation. Consumers feel that vendors are more important than look-a-like products.

Purchase

It is critical that salespeople know the key benefits and features of the product or service considered by consumers in reaching their decisions, which key vendor aspects consumers consider in reaching decisions, and how consumers make their decisions. Salespeople do not want consumers making decisions with too little information or too much information. The latter is a particular problem, because too much information only confuses buyers.

Salespeople must learn to recognize which criteria are included in a decision and how they affect evaluation and selection. Then they can reinforce, redefine, and restructure choice criteria if necessary. Salespeople can reduce buyers' confusion by reinforcing or re-emphasizing choice criteria that favor their products or services. Another approach to reducing confusion is for salespeople to help consumers redefine choice criteria, informational sources, and possibly even purchasing goals. Sometimes it may be necessary to help consumers restructure the decision process or parts of the decision process, particularly in the evaluation and selection stages.

Postpurchase

Once the decision has been made, buyers still must decide whether the purchase was a wise choice. Buyers ask, "Did I make the right choice or should I have chosen another product or service?" The doubt related to a

PROFESSIONAL SELLING IN ACTION   Frieda's Finest

How does a small company compete successfully in the wholesale fruit and vegetable business? The answer for Frieda Caplan, chairperson and founder of Frieda's Finest, has been to go after business that mainstream wholesalers of fruits and vegetables have turned away because orders are not big enough. The product line for Frieda's Finest is low-volume specialty produce such as Chinese gooseberries. Her marketing strategy is to position the company as the authority on the subject of specialty produce by showing how to add value from the perspective of both the retailer and the final consumer. The targeted buyer is the produce manager or buyer in the retail supermarket, not the final customer. In fact, if a specialty item such as kiwifruit gains acceptance as it has in the last few years, then the product cannot be called a specialty and Frieda's Finest is at a disadvantage in marketing it because larger competitors are more price competitive on the ensuing larger orders.

The role of the sales force is not just selling specialty items, but advising produce managers and buyers on how to be successful in the retailing of specialty items. Karen Caplan, president of Frieda's Finest and daughter of its founder, wants her salespeople to analyze their customers to learn "what makes them tick." This includes their primary interests as well as their primary buying motives. In addition, Karen Caplan herself conducts retail supermarket seminars critiquing stores and lecturing on produce. The results of developing a marketing niche and modifying the traditional role of the produce salesperson has produced significant results. In the last three-and-one-half years, sales have increased 60 percent.

SOURCE: Erik Larson, "Strange Fruit," *INC.*, November 1989, pp. 80–88.

---

postpurchase dissonance
doubt related to a relatively nonrevocable decision

relatively nonrevocable decision is called **postpurchase dissonance**. The primary reason for postpurchase dissonance is that in making buying decisions consumers have to give up the desirable benefits and features of other alternatives.

Salespeople can help consumers reduce dissonance and, in doing so, build future sales and continued patronage. Consumers are continually learning, and they are not likely to make unwise decisions a second time. One of the biggest reasons for postpurchase dissonance is the difficulty of choosing between alternatives. Salespeople can re-emphasize the key benefits and features of the product or service purchased, make objective comparisons between products or services under consideration, and reduce the alternatives.

Postpurchase dissonance increases with the economic importance of the purchasing decision and a consumer's level of purchase involvement. For example, much more dissonance can be expected with the purchase of hardware and software for a new computer system than with the purchase of sweeping compound for the cleaning of floors. There is virtually no dissonance with routine purchasing and only some with limited decision making, but a considerable amount accompanies extensive decision making. Salespeople can reduce dissonance from this source by building consumers' confidence in the products or services, the vendors, and the salespeople themselves. They should also help in re-evaluation of the purchase decision and keep in contact with customers to supply additional information and check up on how well the product or service is satisfying needs and wants.

INFLUENCES ON THE PURCHASE DECISION

Although each individual consumer and organizational buyer goes through the purchase decision process described earlier, each decision is unique due to both internal and external influences.

Selectivity

selectivity
screening process that affects exposure, perception, and retention

Consumers pay attention to certain parts of sales strategies intended to influence them and exclude other parts. This screening process, which affects exposure, perception, and retention, is called **selectivity**. First, there is selectivity of exposure; consumers only look to certain sources for product information. A dentist, for example, might not think to consult a sales representative from a local dental supply house about remodeling his or her office. An office manager might not consider an office supply salesperson a source of information on computers.

Second, selectivity also occurs in perception. Consumers seek information to help them attain their purchasing goals. They screen out sales messages about products or services unrelated to purchasing goals. A wintertime sales call about air conditioning is not likely to be as effective as a call about heating. Third, consumers are selective in their retention of sales messages. Only small amounts of the information a customer is exposed to are perceived and passed on to memory. Repetition of sales messages is one way to offset the possibility that consumers will not remember the sales message. Also, salespeople may develop sales presentations that consistently emphasize aspects of the company and themselves. These aspects include their company's reputation for service, engineering, or research leadership; reliability; availability of products; and their attention to customers' problems and the importance they place on customers.

selectivity profile
likely reactions of the consumer to the products or services, salesperson, and the vendor company

Regardless of its form, selectivity disrupts communications between sellers and buyers. Selectivity cannot be eliminated because it helps consumers in making purchasing decisions. Therefore, salespeople must anticipate selectivity in planning sales calls and making sales presentations. One way to do this is to set up a selectivity profile for each targeted consumer. This **selectivity profile** describes the consumer's likely reactions to the products or services, salesperson, and the vendor company. Figure 4–5 provides a hypothetical example of selectivity toward a pharmaceutical company as it might be practiced by different physicians.

Profiles such as the two examples in Figure 4–5 can be extremely valuable in determining the how and why of a sales call. Using the two types of medical professional as an illustration, the salesperson must spend

FIGURE 4–5   Hypothetical example of selectivity profiles for two customer targets of a
                             pharmaceutical company

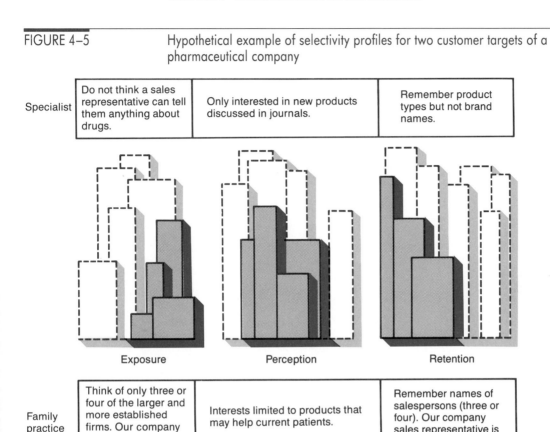

| Specialist | Do not think a sales representative can tell them anything about drugs. | Only interested in new products discussed in journals. | Remember product types but not brand names. |

Exposure   Perception   Retention

| Family practice | Think of only three or four of the larger and more established firms. Our company is not normally included. | Interests limited to products that may help current patients. | Remember names of salespersons (three or four). Our company sales representative is not included. |

a considerable amount of time on developing awareness of himself or herself and his or her company in sales calls on family practice physicians. He or she must also be prepared to discuss any of the company's products because there is no way to predict what will be of interest to the family physician at the time of the sales call. Product knowledge, particularly of new products, is very important in calling on specialists. However, at no time should the salesperson convey the impression of being an authority. Instead, the seller should rely on appropriate published findings.

Knowledge and Learning

In addition to selectivity, the purchasing decision is influenced by the knowledge and learning of the buyer or buyers, and by their attitudes and beliefs. Knowledge and learning is part of the situation in which the purchase is made (Figure 4–6). As consumers engage in the purchasing process, they

FIGURE 4–6   Influences on the purchasing decision process

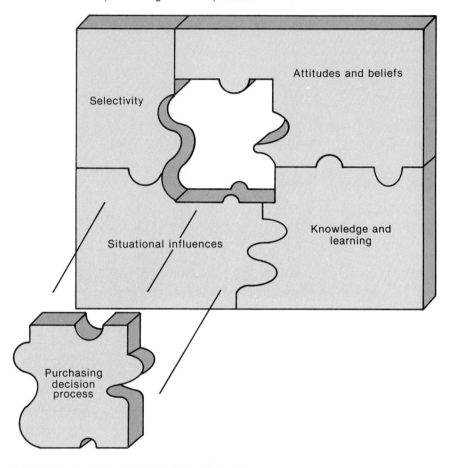

continually acquire knowledge and attach meaning to products, services, salespeople, and vendors. They interpret each aspect of their relevant environment and specific experience in terms of their prior knowledge stored in memory. No two consumers are likely to have the same experience; each draws on different knowledge that produces different meanings. Consumers will also differ because of varying degrees of cognitive resistance. This factor can be particularly important in regard to innovations.

Consumers use knowledge as a composite of meanings to interpret their environment and to make purchasing decisions. If salespeople want to influence and direct the purchasing process, they must understand how consumers use cognitive and emotional meanings to form representations pertaining to specific products or a class of products, services, salespeople, or vendors.

For example, a consumer may form a representation of a specific brand of product or all the brands in a product class. Cognitive meanings are consumers' beliefs about the features and benefits of a product or class of products. Emotional meanings, on the other hand, are feelings about products reflecting their satisfaction from use.

Consider the case of luxury automobiles. Cognitive meanings might include sophisticated engineering, reliability, high quality construction, and the presence of extras such as superior quality sound systems, anti-lock brakes, air bags, and four-wheel drive. Emotional meanings might include comfortable ride, roomy interior, high performance, and the image that driving a particular car might convey about the driver.

Attitudes and Beliefs

attitudes and beliefs
predispositions to react in certain ways in certain situations

Attitudes and beliefs are predispositions to react in certain ways in certain situations. Salespersons must understand that consumers enter into the purchasing process with certain attitudes and beliefs. As a general rule, the more favorable the attitudes and beliefs of consumers toward a product or service, salesperson, and vendor company, the more chance there is that a purchase will take place. This means that salespeople must strengthen the positive attitudes and beliefs of consumers and weaken their negative attitudes and beliefs. Another way for salespeople to change attitudes and beliefs is to add an attitude or belief. This change may come about by an actual change in the product, the method of distribution for the product, or the company selling the product. It is important to give the consumer ample evidence that as a salesperson you are working creatively in their best interests.

Salespeople must understand the attitudes and beliefs of consumers as well as what causes these attitudes and beliefs. In regard to a product or service, for example, consumers are likely to have attitudes and beliefs about features and benefits, and they gain results from use, and value from use, of the product or service. Although consumers' attitudes and beliefs may vary over time, they are determined by (1) individual characteristics such as business objectives, what he or she looks for most in a product, and how the consumer wants to do business; (2) group influences such as who he or she reports to and who the key support people are; and (3) cultural influences such as the consumer's industry and product.

Situational Influences

Situational influences on the purchasing decision process are separate from the products in question and consumers. The three situations include the consumption situation, the purchase situation, and the communication situation.

PROFESSIONAL SELLING IN ACTION

IBM

Spending more time with the customer and learning more about customers are keys to IBM's new marketing strategy. IBM's management believes the strategy will allow the company to compete effectively in an ever-changing marketplace it no longer dominates. It is a marketplace where customers want to purchase system packages including hardware, software, installation, service, and training, and where hardware is becoming more generic. For the IBM sales representative, pleasing the customer is the single most important job responsibility. George Conrades, head of U.S. marketing, has instructed salespeople to "just say yes."

The IBM sales representative is pictured as living with a customer constantly looking for opportunities to help out at a price. To make sure sales representatives concentrate on customers and not sales volume, the commission system based on number of units sold or rented has been replaced by a reward system based on total revenue.

IBM sales representatives must also face the challenges of selling to potential customers heretofore bypassed and dealing with different purchasing practices. A redeployment of technical and staff people has permitted the sales force more time with small customers, 70 percent of whom are estimated not to have a computer. IBM salespersons must also position themselves to sell to customers who are more likely to mix and match brands than buy from a single source.

SOURCE: Joel Dreyfuss, "Reinventing IBM," *Fortune*, August 14, 1989, pp. 30–39.

The consumption situation determines how the product is used. Some of the questions salespeople might ask to clarify the consumption situation include:

- Is the insurance policy for protection or retirement?
- Is the van for delivery or hauling and storing tools?
- Is the computer for inventory control or storing customer information?
- Is the laser printer to be operated by anyone or only specifically designated individuals?

Situational influences on purchases include the physical and social settings, definition of the purchasing task, and time perspectives. Where the purchase takes place, as well as who is involved in the purchase situation, can impact consumers' perceptions and influence the purchasing process. As an illustration, feed sellers found it essential to use a flip chart that fits on top of a fence in selling to farmers raising cattle or hogs. This type of flip chart allows the sales rep to make effective sales presentations without taking the farmer away from his or her work environment. Purchasing situations vary depending on those present in the situation, their respective roles in the decision, and the interactions between them. For instance, a sales rep making a sales call on a purchasing agent experiences a different situation than when three or four members of the engineering staff are involved. And a purchasing situation involving both the husband and wife is different from one where only one spouse is involved.

Definition of the purchasing task also influences the purchasing situation. Consumers may just want to gather information, get prices, or compare sources for products. Whether the purchase is a gift or for personal use can significantly influence the decision process. How much time consumers have to complete the decision process or obtain the product or service is yet another situational influence. Time constraints may cause consumers to purchase certain products or services from vendors they might not otherwise select.

The circumstances under which consumers receive information about a product and a vendor influence the decision process. Consumers may be alone or part of a group, pressed for time or in no hurry, receptive or unreceptive due to prior activities. The degree of receptivity often comes from something or someone affecting the consumer's state of mind immediately prior to a sales call. Although salespeople cannot control such influences, they can use their flexibility to bring about a receptive state. Experienced salespersons may even want to reschedule the sales call.

Risk Perception

The risk consumers perceive in purchasing decisions can also affect the decision process. Risk is what is at stake in a purchase decision. Normally, risk is measured in financial terms, but it may involve breaking with the past and choosing a new product or selecting a new vendor where performance of either is uncertain. The risk consumers foresee in breaking with the past centers on their abilities to make decisions and their possible loss of status as decision makers. Possible fears are personal discomfort with the decision and social ridicule.

Consumers reduce risk by reducing uncertainty through seeking more information or relying on past experience. The latter is done primarily because consumers resist having to seek out more information about a product. Salespeople are in an excellent position to offer consumers additional information. They also can point out to consumers that relying too much on past experiences is self-limiting. Of course, when past experience favors salespeople, they should reinforce loyalties to the product, themselves, and/or the company.

When consumers find they cannot reduce uncertainty, they reduce the amount of risk at stake. This may mean forgoing purchases entirely, causing a loss of sales for salespeople. Since the amount at stake is usually measured in financial terms, salespeople may suggest a small trial purchase, or a purchase-lease option.

SUMMARY OF CHAPTER OBJECTIVES

1. To define the purchase decision process.

Consumers go through a sequence of steps in making a purchase decision. These steps in the order in which they are taken are: (1) goal recognition; (2) information search; (3) alternative evaluation and selection; (4) vendor selection; (5) purchase; and (6) postpurchase.

2. To explain the steps in the purchase decision process.

The six steps in the purchase decision process are:

1. Goal recognition—The consumer begins the purchase decision process with the activation of the goals he or she wants to achieve or satisfy through a product or service. These goals are a solution to an existing or anticipated problem, attainment of an objective, or an enhancement or value addition.
2. Information search—The consumer uses internal and external sources of information on product features/benefits to determine the choice criteria.
3. Alternative evaluation and selection—The consumer uses decision rules to evaluate alternatives and makes a decision based on the information collected on choice criteria.
4. Vendor selection—The consumer, after deciding what to buy, makes a decision on where to buy. Vendor aspects are frequently choice criteria.
5. Purchase—The consumer finalizes the purchase decision and makes the transition to customer.
6. Postpurchase—The consumer, now a customer, is concerned with whether the purchase decision was a wise one. This doubt is called postpurchase dissonance.

3. To develop the conceptualization of a product or service as features/ benefits and choice criteria.

Consumers buy bundles of features, not products or services. Features are characteristics of a product or service that offer a perceived advantage through use or ownership resulting in a benefit. A consumer's set of choice criteria depends upon the relative importance of features/ benefits.

4. To describe how consumers use decision rules in choosing a product or service.

Consumers use decision rules to reduce the number of alternatives and to arrive at the best alternative. Minimum standards and minimum acceptance decision rules reduce the number of alternatives to an acceptable set. The best or most important criteria decision rule and the best overall decision rule are used to reduce the set to one alternative.

5. To define postpurchase dissonance.

Postpurchase dissonance is the doubt related to making a relatively non-revocable decision. It arises when a consumer, in choosing one alternative, has to give up desirable benefits of other alternatives.

6. To explain the impact of selectivity, knowledge and learning, attitudes and beliefs, and situational influences on the purchase decision.

Selectivity—The consumer screens out parts of the sales strategies. This screening affects exposure, perception, and retention.
Knowledge and learning—The consumer uses knowledge to interpret his or her environment and to make purchasing decisions. Knowledge is a composite of cognitive and emotional meanings that form representations of products, salespeople, and vendors.
Attitudes and beliefs—The consumer enters into the purchasing process with certain predispositions to react in certain ways in certain situations.
Situational influences—The consumer's purchasing decision is influenced by how the product is to be used, the purchase situation, and the circumstances in which information is received.

7. To discuss risk perception.

The consumer perceives risk in making a purchase decision. This risk may be financial, performance, personal, and/or social.

REVIEW QUESTIONS

1. Can a single product satisfy more than one of the needs Maslow identified? Explain.
2. How do product features become benefits?
3. When does a salesperson have a competitive advantage?
4. How does a salesperson determine choice criteria?
5. Which questions should a real estate agent ask to learn whether a buyer wants a house to enhance his or her lifestyle or to obtain convenience to schools and shopping?
6. Which four decision rules are useful in selecting alternatives? Describe each of these decision rules.
7. Under which circumstances would a salesperson prefer buyers who use best performance as the most important criterion to buyers who use satisfactory performance?

8. How should an automobile salesperson's presentation to an individual consumer differ from a presentation to an organizational buyer?

9. What is postpurchase dissonance? Give an example based on personal experience.

10. Describe how buyers reduce risk.

DISCUSSION QUESTIONS AND EXERCISES

1. Describe a purchase experience you have had in which the salesperson was sincerely interested in understanding and identifying your purchasing goal. Describe an experience where just the opposite was the case. Which salesperson was more effective? Why?

2. Arrange an interview with an industrial buyer and ask the buyer to describe a recent purchase decision. Try to determine (*a*) which decision factors the buyer considered; (*b*) whether company policies affected the decision; and (*c*) who, besides the buyer, took part in the decision.

3. Select a volunteer, preferably the instructor. The volunteer has to truthfully answer questions the class asks about his or her lifestyle, attitudes, and beliefs, as well as the use of selectivity. (To protect the volunteer's privacy, some questions may be answered with general descriptive statements.) Using only the answers to these questions, the class should try to determine the type of car he or she drives, where he or she buys clothes, and other things about the person's shopping habits.

4. Examine a recent decision you made to go to a particular movie or restaurant. Describe in detail the entire purchase decision process.

5. Select a person to role-play a disgruntled customer returning a toaster to a department store. The toaster burns rather than toasts, and the customer has found the same model costing 10 percent less in a discount store. Let the rest of the class suggest various ways a salesperson might reduce this customer's postpurchase dissonance.

SALES DIALOG

Two computer salespeople were discussing their customers over lunch. Both had been with the company about five years.

FIRST SALESPERSON: All of my customers have computers, usually our brand. This makes it very difficult to sell nowadays.

SECOND SALESPERSON: My territory is about the same, but I have found a number who want to update their equipment.

FIRST SALESPERSON: My customers all have the capacity they need, so there is less need to upgrade.

SECOND SALESPERSON: When I talk about upgrading, I don't mean more capacity. A good number of my customers use computers as a kind of status symbol. By buying one of our newer models, they keep up or get ahead of their competitors.

FIRST SALESPERSON: I don't think the status angle would work with my customers. However, you have given me an idea. Suppose I say that all their competitors are buying more advanced computers that will provide better customer service.

SECOND SALESPERSON: You would need information on competitors and that might be difficult to get. I think you would do better by showing your customers how fast everything is changing in the world of computers. A lot of companies can gain some sort of status by keeping up with change. For some of your bigger accounts, you could bring in the big guns from headquarters. I did that with a university in my territory. We showed them how they can be a technology leader. They placed an order for our most advanced unit and another order for one that is still on the drafting board.

FIRST SALESPERSON: From what you have said, customers will buy computers even though they already have enough capacity. What I have to do is figure out their needs, or should I say, wants.

What do you think the results of this sales dialog will be?

CASE 4–1 THE DYNAFORGE COMPANY

Tom Alves, sales engineer for the Dynaforge Company, has just received a call from Hank Schoof, general manager of the Exacto Corporation plant in Lima, Ohio. Within the next three weeks, Schoof wants to negotiate a contract for 40,000 fan blades.

Exacto buys blades from Dynaforge as titanium forgings and then machines, tests, and inspects the blades before shipping them to its customer, Universal Products. Universal Products installs the blades in jet engines. Dynaforge's position as Exacto's sole source of the blade is in jeopardy because Toronto Corporation, a small forge shop in Fort Wayne, Indiana, has submitted a bid to make the forgings for $39 each. Dynaforge's price is $43.

The largest titanium blade forging Toronto Corporation has ever produced is half the size of this one. Alves estimates that to get the $39 price, Schoof has to agree to pay Toronto Corporation's tooling costs of more than $20,000 and to buy over $100,000 in additional equipment to be installed in Toronto's plant. Schoof has never confirmed or denied this, but he did admit that he had some reservations about Toronto's ability to meet the technical specifications and the delivery requirements because of its inexperience with this size blade. All of Toronto's other work for Exacto has been excellent, however.

Universal Products is Exacto's largest and most important customer, and its most important purchase is the fan blade. Exacto cannot afford to lose the blade to competition.

The Dynaforge Corporation has supplied the fan blade to Exacto for several years, and Schoof is extremely pleased with its performance. Several price reductions due to technological breakthroughs have been passed on to Exacto during this time, and improvements in forging the blade have resulted in economies to Exacto. Schoof has noted this pleasant and rewarding relationship between the two companies on more than one occasion.

Since the fan blade will be produced for several more years, Alves does not want to lose this contract. But he does not want to meet the $39 price if he does not have to because Dynaforge makes very little profit at that price, and his performance is measured on profits, not sales. Further, he knows that recent increases in wages and in the price of titanium will necessitate a price increase to about $45 to maintain the existing profit margin.

Because this is the largest blade contract ever negotiated, Alves feels that Schoof might give some of the business to Toronto. In Alves' opinion, Schoof is a gambler and has made riskier decisions than this before.

Alves' decision will be less difficult if the vice president of marketing, Bob Beamer, insists on a specified profit margin, so he calls him. Beamer says that Alves can meet the $39 price if it is necessary to keep the blade business.

Questions

1. Which factors should Alves consider before deciding on his strategy for negotiations with Schoof?
2. If you were Alves, what would you do?

CASE 4–2   RAVENCROFT CORPORATION

The Ravencroft Corporation is a large furniture manufacturer in High Point, North Carolina. About 15 months ago, Debra Gerak, director of marketing, initiated an extensive dealer training program involving videotapes, audiocassettes, and a training manual. The training program focuses on the consumer as the key to improved sales performance for the furniture dealer. Among the topics covered are the sequence of activities involved in purchasing furniture, classification of customers as to furniture needs and wants, obtaining vital information from customers, and selling skills. The program is divided up into hourly segments with accompanying homework and self-testing on the major points covered in the segment.

To sell the program to dealers, the sales force selected the top 40 dealers in the country and invited them to High Point. Thirty-eight of these dealers came to the conference; after viewing and going through the entire program over a three-day period, all 38 bought the program at a cost of $700 each.

Gerak's problem is that she has been able to sell the program to only 80 additional dealers since the kickoff conference, despite testimonials from all of those using the program as to how it has increased sales and profits. In her visits to many of the 800 dealers handling the Ravencroft line, she has heard a number of negative responses. The most important ones are:

1. Stereotyping customers is not possible because each potential customer is different.
2. The purchasing process is different for each customer; or, there is more than one purchasing process.
3. Dealers have to pay for something that benefits the manufacturer.

Questions

1. If you were Gerak, how would you answer the comments about stereotyping customers?
2. Develop a response to the comment that there is not one purchasing process, but several.
3. Since the $700 price tag barely covers the cost of producing the program, how can Gerak handle the price objection?

CHAPTER 5

Selling's Role in Marketing Strategy

CHAPTER OBJECTIVES

1. To explain the relationships between corporate, marketing, and sales strategies and the salesperson.

2. To describe the customer sales plan.

3. To describe the planning process as applied to customer sales plans.

4. To distinguish between marketing and sales.

5. To distinguish between sales and advertising.

6. To explain the concept of personal selling as communications.

SALES CAREER PROFILE

STEVE SULLIVAN
International Paper Company

Steve Sullivan is the national sales manager of the distribution group of International Paper Company. His sales force sells to paper merchants, who inventory paper in large warehouses and then resell it to the so-called trades. Examples of the distribution group's customers are commercial printers, quick copy shops, and magazines. Steve holds a bachelor's degree in international relations from the University of Florida and a master's degree in systems management from the University of Southern California.

Sullivan joined International Paper after a stint in the military. "What made me select International Paper Company was the individual for whom I was going to work. Coming out of the military not knowing a great deal about business, I recognized that it was important to work for somebody who would be a mentor. I bonded quickly with the individual who interviewed me. So I decided not so much to go to work for International Paper Company as to go to work for this individual.

"I also liked doing things that were measurable. I think the challenge in selling is that I am doing something that is very measurable. At the end of the year, if I haven't met my budget, I haven't succeeded. I equate selling in business with the infantry. Salespeople are the front line troops—it's basically where the action is. The pressure that high-performance companies place on sales personnel makes accomplishment even more rewarding."

Asked if he knew that International Paper was one of the nation's best companies for salespeople, Sullivan responded, "I wasn't aware of that. But I can understand how we would be picked. International Paper Company is now almost a $7 billion organization with our recent acquisition of Hammermill. There are tremendous resources available to a salesperson. The scope at International Paper is great: the challenge of interacting with our different business groups, our mills, the manufacturing side of our business, our marketing people, and trying to sell the massive quantity of product. In my particular area, sales will be in the neighborhood of $800 million next year. We do that with a limited number of people, so each individual has massive responsibility. It's an important industry that has been on top; but, with the influx of imports and some of the things going on in the paper industry, every day is a challenge."

Sullivan travels extensively as a national sales manager. "One of my jobs is to get out and see the key customers on a regular basis. I travel 80 to 90 percent of the time because I think it's important that they hear exactly what International Paper Company's plans are, where we are going. As large as it is, it's basically one family and so it's critical to interact a great deal wtih our customers."

Describing the role the national sales manager plays in shaping overall marketing objectives, Sullivan said, "I think the real focus of the national sales manager should be dealing with the customer. Customers have specific wants, specific needs. And although product-line people or marketing people may identify a particular market that may be moving in a certain direction, the fact of the matter is we rely on our customers to move the products we manufacture. It is the role of the national sales manager, through the regional sales managers, and down to our salespeople, to identify what markets and customer mix should be established to meet an overall sales objective. The regional sales managers then get into more specificity when they deal in their individual markets.

"Each national sales manager, I would think, has a particular focus. I firmly believe that communication is the key to success in business. There's no question that you have to make a quality product and get it to the customer in a timely manner. If you do that but can't communicate to your customers, then you're going to have a shortfall. So over the last several years in this job, my focus has been to ensure that our people are out talking to our customers. What I do in shaping our overall marketing objective is to identify the programs our marketing people want to push and to temper them with some common sense and knowledge of our customers. Once I've distilled that, I give it to our people and give them their instructions to go out into the marketplace, identify the customers we want to do business with, and make the kind of presentations that ultimately will get orders for the products we sell."

Granted that promotion is a key element of International's marketing mix, Sullivan believes personal selling is important in his firm's promotional strategy. "It's the salesperson's responsibility to call on a customer on a regular basis. My focus has been to get our people out calling on accounts with more regularity, becoming highly visible, doing the kinds of things that our customers need to help them sell their products. There is no substitute for salespeople knocking on doors and, as I said, presenting the features, advantages, and benefits of International Paper Company's products.

"One other point is that by having salespeople going out and presenting products, I get feedback. I may think I have something that the market is dying for but, unless I have feedback, I may devise an entire marketing program for a product with no market. One of the critical things about having salespeople calling on accounts is that not only am I able to present the program and the products, but also I'm able to get some feedback from the customers' sales force, merchandising people, and upper management. This feedback helps me refine what I'm trying to do. Once again, salespeople are critical to complete that communication link."

Planning was of critical importance in the successsful turnaround of Black & Decker from a $160 million loss in 1985 to a profit in 1988. Nolan D. Archibald, president and CEO, believes that without a clear plan a firm drifts with changes, and two other ingredients for success—believing in possibilities and a vision—become useless fictions. In his words, "a plan must absolutely cut through the clutter." A plan must also stand up under adversity, be flexible to change, and be expansive rather than limiting. Crucial to the turnaround has been getting the right people to execute plans.[1] Implementation is also important at other large corporations such as Caterpillar and Scott Paper, where planning is an important function of those in field sales.

CORPORATE PLANNING AND THE SALES FORCE

Top-level management devotes considerable effort to determining objectives and goals, developing strategies and programs to attain these ends, and setting up ways to measure accomplishment. Often little is done, however, to see that all of the pieces of the puzzle fit together so that the different parts of the firm function as a team. All parts of the organization must contribute value to meet the competitively superior levels of satisfaction demanded by the customer. A clear-cut task of the sales force is to produce sales volume, but salespeople cannot perform professionally in satisfying the needs and wants of consumers without the efforts of other parts of the firm.

Lacking a clear understanding of what their position in the firm is or how their selling activities fit into the firm's overall marketing and sales strategy, sales reps look at their jobs solely in terms of existing contacts with present customers. Such salespeople are put in a position where all they can say is "I don't really know why I am doing this."

Successful implementation of marketing and sales strategies hinges on the sales force knowing the hows and the whys. The three big questions members of a sales force ask are: (1) "How do I as a salesperson fit into company operations?"; (2) "Why am I called on to do certain selling activities?"; and (3) "Do I have any part in the planning process?".[2] Also, by knowing what is going on, the salesperson feels personally involved and will work harder to make what has been planned happen.

Strategic Marketing and the Sales Force

Fighting to gain market share is a tougher job than ever before because real growth is lessening in many markets and competition overall is intensifying. Recognizing the competitive advantage of having satisfied loyal customers, businesses are developing plans and methods for achieving customer satisfaction goals. Managing a business as a customer-satisfying process has meant not only significant redirection of the company in terms of objectives and goals, but also developing innovative strategies and programs to attain these ends, as well as new ways of measuring accomplishment.

Sales reps for Liz Claiborne, for example, concentrate on creating lasting, long-term relationships with resellers. Instead of trying to sell as much as they can, sales reps place the lines of clothing based on an overall view of the marketplace and the market position of the reseller. The result is that store buyers buy only what they can sell. Further support is given the reseller by a staff of 15 sales trainers. The sales staffs for both P&G and IBM have also seen changes take place. P&G sales reps now treat retailers as partners rather than tough, penny-pinching adversaries. In addition, special teams are assigned to major accounts like Wal-Mart and Kroger to help in improving inventory, distribution, and sales promotion.[3]

PROFESSIONAL SELLING IN ACTION

Metier Management Systems

A systematic sales management philosophy coupled with a rigidly disciplined sales force are credited with bringing success to Metier Management Systems. The company's rapid growth from start-up to $100 million in eight years despite significant obstacles is testimony to business success under any definition. One sales obstacle was that its products were technologically superior to competition for no more than 18 months. Another was the loss of primary markets such as the petrochemical and engineering industries and the necessity of refocusing on new market targets (government and defense). There were also complications in end-use applications that created new sales cycles, customer segments, and problems.

A highly disciplined sales force allowed Metier the flexibility to adjust to market volatility. This discipline is attained by placing a heavy emphasis in both training and the review process on qualifying a prospect and influencing the prospect's buying criteria. Sales reps are heavily rehearsed in qualification procedures, questioning, and listening, as well as influencing skills.

Using team selling enables Metier to build good relationships with potential customers quickly. Team selling with the sales rep as the "point man" provides the opportunities for more people to obtain information and speed up the whole sales process. Technical support personnel who are typically part of the sales teams receive sales training along with anyone else who has significant prospect or customer contact.

Continuous updating and review of selling efforts is done monthly. Sales reps must have the answers to a whole series of crucial questions about prospects and customers and be able to justify current status given to either. In an effort to close as quickly as possible, prospects are given nine months to close. After this time period, they are removed from the forecast of new orders.

SOURCE: William E. Gregory, Jr., "Time to Ask Hard-Nosed Questions," *Sales & Marketing Management*, October 1989, pp. 88–93. Reprinted by permission of Sales & Marketing Management. © October 1989.

More focus on the customer as opposed to the product is also taking place at IBM. Positioning themselves as problem solvers rather than sellers, sales reps for IBM work to become a member of the customer's team. There has also been a shift in customer mix for the IBM sales rep as more emphasis is being placed on smaller businesses, many of which do not have computer facilities.

Translating Marketing and Sales Strategies into Selling Actions

The flow of planning is from the top down (see Figure 5–1). Using Rubbermaid as an example, top management in the person of Stanley C. Gault set the goal for the firm of 15 percent annual growth in sales or a doubling of sales every five years.[4] This growth is to come from internal as well as external sources such as the purchase of small, undervalued companies that are market leaders. For marketing, growth is to be obtained through market positioning, new product development, and an emphasis on quality. Derived sales strategies from a market positioning strategy include specialization by

FIGURE 5–1   Company strategies related to marketing and sales objectives for Rubbermaid, Inc.

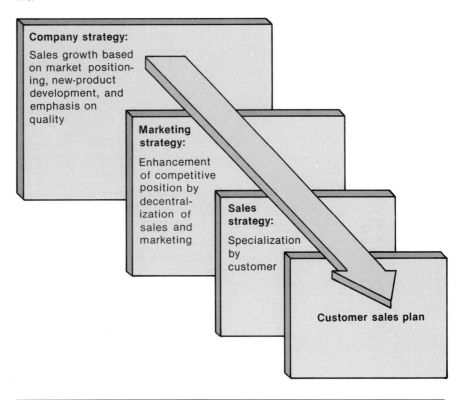

Company strategy:

Sales growth based on market positioning, new-product development, and emphasis on quality

Marketing strategy:

Enhancement of competitive position by decentralization of sales and marketing

Sales strategy:

Specialization by customer

Customer sales plan

customer segment (distribution channel), separation of sales and marketing, and increasing the number of customers (retail outlets).

To take on a marketing approach, all parts of the business organization must contribute value to the customer. The efforts of the salesperson must complement other parts of the company and in turn be complemented by other parts of the company. As an example, the primary reason for new products at Rubbermaid is to identify and develop new product categories that permit the company and its sales representatives to enter new areas and new sections within a retail store. This strengthens sales with present customers and at the same time expands the possibility of adding new customers.

The salesperson is guided in his/her planning efforts as well as his/her actions in selling by the mission or statement of purpose for the company. Obviously, salespeople for Metropolitan Life, Mack Trucks, and Hewlett-Packard will operate differently given their missions or statements of purpose.

Metropolitan Life—"Met Life customers are our first priority; without customers, there is no reason for a business to exist."

Mack Trucks—"We service our customers around the world through the innovative design, engineering, manufacturing, and servicing of trucks and vehicles that meet their needs at low life-cycle cost."

Hewlett-Packard—" . . . to provide products and services of the highest quality and the greatest possible value to our customers, thereby gaining and holding their respect and loyalty."

CUSTOMER SALES PLANNING

Customer sales planning integrates the customer or prospect into the company's marketing and sales programs. A salesperson is in the best possible position to integrate what a customer needs or wants with company goals and strategies. Salespeople analyze the customer, customer requirements, past selling experience (if any), and the competition.

sales plan

contains the sales goal for a given customer as well as sales strategies, analysis of the customer, and specific actions to be taken

A **sales plan** for an individual customer contains a sales goal, and sales strategies applicable to the customer, a rather complete profile of the customer, as well as programs and specific actions to be undertaken. In setting up the plan, salespeople consider the basics of selling to a particular account and then follow this up with a more detailed analysis (see Figure 5–2). The basics of selling to a particular customer include (1) purchasing goals of the customer, (2) purchasing patterns, (3) present product usage, and (4) competition. Following this should be a more detailed look at the customer's product usage and purchasing patterns, including:

- Purchasing levels.
- Purchasing influences (who are they and degree of influence).
- Purchasing decision responsibility (who makes the decision).
- End uses of products.
- Conditions of use (environment, importance to customer, and training of personnel involved with product).
- Customer's interests (competitive pricing, quality and uniformity of product, performance reliability, technical and service support, timeliness of delivery).

On completion of the customer analysis, the next step is deciding on a sales goal (usually expressed as how much product is sold during a specified time) and the specific programs and actions the salesperson will use. At this point, the salesperson considers the purchasing policies of the customer and any characteristics of the customer that may play a vital role in the purchasing decisions. The latter might include the economic situation affecting sales of the customer's products and the philosophy of top management in the customer's firm. Salespeople also need to consider the selling strategies of their

FIGURE 5–2 Customer sales planning

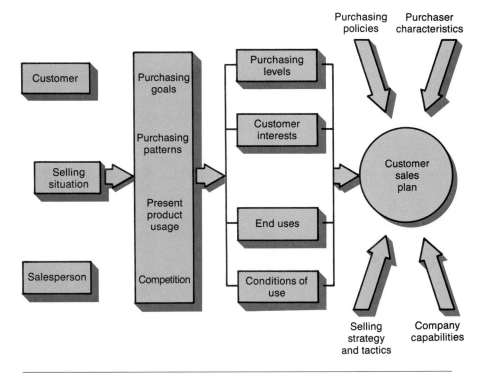

own company as well as their own company's capabilities. The latter would include technical support, after-sale service, the firm's responsiveness in meeting customers' requirements, quality assurance programs, pricing practices, and R&D.

What Is Planning?

Planning can be defined as determining what actions must be taken to attain a certain desired result or situation that is not likely to occur in the future without something being done now in a positive sense. The basic assumption in planning is that taking action now will attain desired future results. This desired result is called an objective by some and a goal by others.

Determination of the objective or goal is the first step in the planning process (see Figure 5–3). For the salesperson, his or her goals will be handed down by sales management. Let's suppose the sales goal is to obtain a 10 percent sales increase from the customer segment served by the sales rep. One means the sales rep might employ in attaining more sales is to identify and concentrate selling efforts on key accounts in his or her sales territory.

A SALES MANAGEMENT NOTE

Maintaining Salesperson Morale during Lengthy Sales Cycles

A problem for many firms and in particular their sales managers is how to keep up the morale of a salesperson when it takes a year or more to make a sale. John Milne, Sales Operations Director for 3M's Traffic Control Materials Division, uses several techniques developed from experience to overcome the sense of giving up that may accompany long, drawn-out selling situations.

1. Sales reps need to be focused on attainable goals in selling reflective materials for pavement markings and road signs.

2. Sales reps need to have a business plan for each account detailing what is supposed to happen and when.

3. Sales reps are required to complete a minimum of 40 hours of formal training a year.

4. Sales reps' selling productivity is stressed (e.g., car phones are provided to each sales rep).

5. Sales reps' compensation plans are substantially fixed income (e.g., 85 percent fixed and 15 percent incentive).

SOURCE: Martin Everett, "This Is the Ultimate in Selling," *Sales & Marketing Management*, August 1989, pp. 28–38. Reprinted by permission of Sales & Marketing Management. © August 1989.

Another way might be to add to the customer base by calling on new accounts. One resource a salesperson has is selling effort measured in terms of sales calls. Another resource is the support the company provides the salesperson. Examples might be new products, sales literature and video presentations, technical support, pricing flexibility, and computer access. With the first alternative, a salesperson will spend more time with key accounts and proportionately less time with smaller accounts. The second alternative will require a salesperson to allocate more time to securing new accounts and spend less time with current customers.

implementation

procedures necessary to carry out a plan

Plans have no value until they are put into action. The third step in planning, **implementation,** involves setting in motion the action directive embodied in the plan. To implement the key account strategy, the accounts of the salesperson must be analyzed, key accounts identified, and adjustments made in sales call frequency. Implementation of a strategy calling for an increase in the customer base requires an analysis of the salesperson's territory to identify potential customers not presently being sold and a reallocation of sales efforts. The final step in planning calls for development of feedback mechanisms to identify opportunities for improvement and the need to make adjustments. Usually, performance indicators are the same for all members of the sales force within a firm. An individual sales rep can develop other means that more clearly measure his or her performance or suggest how existing indicators can be reported on a more timely basis.

FIGURE 5–3   Sequence of steps in planning

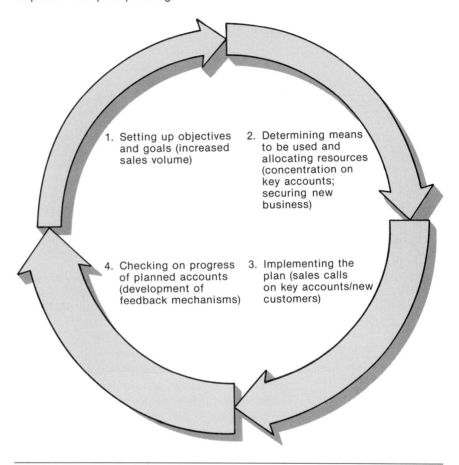

1. Setting up objectives and goals (increased sales volume)

2. Determining means to be used and allocating resources (concentration on key accounts; securing new business)

3. Implementing the plan (sales calls on key accounts/new customers)

4. Checking on progress of planned accounts (development of feedback mechanisms)

Marketing versus Sales

Marketing and sales are not the same, but neither are they in conflict with each other. Marketing, which includes sales, is a long-range process dealing with creating an environment that produces a favorable buying decision on the part of the targeted customer. Market share is the typical goal of marketing. Sales, on the other hand, deals with the execution of the marketing plan and is more short-range in nature. A purchase decision in favor of the salesperson is the goal of sales. Another possible goal of sales is to obtain the best possible distribution scheme of the company's products. What this means is that while sales volume remains important, so too is who is the customer for the product. For example, if the customer is a reseller, the sales rep must make sure that the reseller can in turn sell what is bought, a practice observed by sales reps for Liz Claiborne. If the customer is a user, the sales rep must make sure the product is being used as intended. Quite disastrous is the failure of a customer's product because a component part is used incorrectly.

Marketing and sales strengthen each other. Marketing decisions that have the greatest impact on sales take into account these questions: (1) Which groups of consumers or market segments does the company want to serve?, (2) What is the makeup of the marketing mix?, and (3) What tasks are assigned to the sales force?

Most companies realize that it is not worthwhile to attempt to sell to every potential customer. A more practical approach is to pinpoint a group of consumers or a market segment whose needs or wants can be best served by the company's products. By targeting potential customers, the company focuses its marketing efforts where they can do the most good. Also, by concentrating on a limited number of customer types, the sales force benefits from specialization that leads to improved selling performance through greater customer knowledge and attention, a crucial competitive factor in today's market.

Decisions made about the makeup of the marketing effort determine the emphasis placed on sales. Although most companies recognize the critical importance of sales at the point of customer contact, there is a wide variance in marketing mixes. The type of market served seems to have the greatest impact on the emphasis placed on personal selling or advertising. For instance, manufacturers of industrial products rely primarily on the efforts of salespeople and give little attention to advertising. Oftentimes the role of advertising is limited to securing sales leads.

Advertising does a large part of the marketing job for manufacturers of consumer products and services. For consumer nondurables, as an example, advertising has the major role in creating demand while salespeople are relegated to making sure the product is available on store shelves. Generally, other promotional activities take on greater importance for consumer goods manufacturers as opposed to industrial product sellers. A large number of sales promotion or merchandising incentives are employed to supplement and strengthen sales and advertising efforts of consumer products. Sales promotion varies from samples, coupons, refund offers, premiums, and contests to retailer and wholesaler incentive programs. The best program for a company is the most cost-effective mix of sales, advertising, and sales promotion coordinated by goal, content, sequence of use, and style.

SALES VERSUS ADVERTISING

Before deciding to use either personal selling or advertising, a marketing manager needs to understand the distinguishing characteristics of each and where each fits in most effectively in the firm's marketing plan. Many of

the differences between personal selling and advertising are obvious (see
Figure 5–4). Personal selling is a direct, often face-to-face means of communication. Advertising, on the other hand, is an impersonal, controlled
means of mass communication. Once it is decided upon, a particular advertisement cannot be changed. While presenting their sales messages, salespeople have the flexibility of adjusting to consumer reactions. A salesperson
for a real estate firm, for example, can find out the primary concerns of a
family in selecting a new home and show only those residences that fit their

FIGURE 5–4   General characteristics of personal selling and advertising as promotional
                              methods

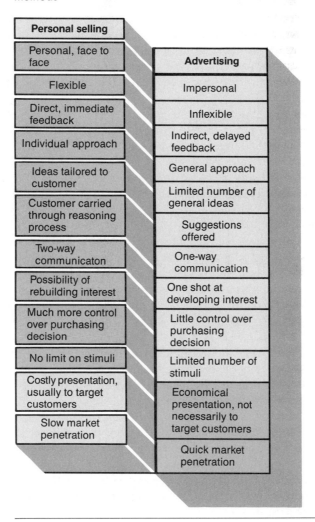

needs. If public schools are a major concern, the salesperson can narrow the choices to houses in areas with good public schools. When price is also a major concern, the salesperson shows only those residences in the desired price range in areas with good public education. This can be contrasted with ads showing various houses for sale and descriptions of each house in print.

Closely allied to flexibility is the individualization of personal selling as contrasted to the generalized nature of advertising. Usually salespeople focus on one customer or a small group of customers. Advertising has the ability to expose the sales message to large groups of prospective customers. Often advertising is likened to a shotgun promotion, whereas personal selling is a rifle shot promotion.

Advertising is advantageous because it is a quick way of exposing sales messages at a low per-prospect cost. A television commercial may reach several million people at a cost of $10 to $17 for every 1,000 viewers. Even though every viewer cannot be considered a prospect for the advertised products, the cost is considerably less than that of a sales call, which now runs approximately $230 or more. Another strength of advertising is its ability to reach prospects unavailable to salespeople on a regular basis.

Image Building

Image building is almost solely the job of advertising. Its ability to get wide exposure at a relatively low per-contact cost makes advertising appropriate for the job of image building. Sales personnel have the responsibility of acting in accordance with the image projected for the company. If, for example, the desired image for a company is technological competence and versatility, its advertising would show a wide range of highly engineered products for an array of technical applications, and sales personnel backed up by technical support should have a high level of technical competence. Emphasizing the firm's image in their sales presentations, salespeople create competitive differentials by stressing the capacities of their entire organizations.

Reinforcement

Advertising has traditionally held a dominant role in strengthening the buyer-seller relationship as a source of satisfaction to the buyer. The principal reason is that advertising can do the job more economically. Realizing that satisfied customers are the best customers, many firms have begun to assign this task to the sales force. These firms, while acknowledging that the main source of satisfaction comes from the products involved, realize how vital it is to maintain market contact with customers after the sale. The four major forms of reinforcement are showing customers that they made the right decision, thanking customers, asking if the firm (salesperson or service department) can be of further assistance, and providing an update in training and service.

PUSH AND PULL STRATEGIES

push strategy
promotional strategy
emphasizing personal
selling

pull strategy
promotional strategy
emphasizing advertising

The use of either a push or pull strategy governs whether emphasis is placed on personal selling or advertising. A **push strategy** places greater emphasis on personal selling to move the product through the marketing channel to the final customer. For instance, a typical pattern for consumer products has the manufacturer's salespeople call on wholesalers who in turn sell to retailers who sell to final customers. At every level, product distribution depends primarily on the efforts of salespeople. Push strategies are also common in the industrial market, particularly when competitive differentials exist between products.

A **pull strategy** is the opposite of a push strategy. Here, advertising to the final customer stimulates demand for the product. This demand moves from the final customer back up the marketing channel to the manufacturer. If the product is sold by retailers, the customer asks the retailer for the product, the retailer asks the wholesaler, and the wholesaler asks the manufacturer. Although advertising generates demand, salespeople see to it that product distribution moves smoothly and efficiently. Another reason for a pull strategy is to overcome reseller resistance. A pull strategy in effect creates a market and a reason for the reseller to carry the product. The products are defined as presold. Pull strategies are most frequently found with consumer products. However, industrial sellers with small sales staffs, such as those in computers and computer-related equipment, are also using the pull strategy with success.

Product Introduction

A low per-prospect cost, rapid market penetration, and the ability to reach difficult prospects are all advantages of advertising in establishing a market position for a new product. This typically translates into a bigger role for advertising and a lesser role for personal selling in product introductions. Figure 5–5 shows the objectives in four market situations. In each situation, the advantages of advertising favor greater emphasis on it as compared to personal selling.

Competitive Marketing

The competitive struggle to increase or protect market share calls for a different set of promotion objectives and new roles for personal selling and advertising (see Figure 5–5). Generally, personal selling takes on a bigger role as competition increases and product preference is sought from the target market. The personalized approach of the salesperson, as well as the possibility of using mutliple stimuli, and the opportunity for immediate action are important in building or maintaining market share. Other aspects of

FIGURE 5–5   Market situations and promotion goals affecting personal selling and advertising

New product situations	Competitive marketing situations

Product type is well established
New product type with new applications/
  functions
New product type replacing product on
  the market
New product type with undefined
  applications
	Increasing sales through increasing
	  market
	Increasing sales through increasing
	  market share
	Protect share of market against direct
	  competitors
	Protect share of market against indirect
	  competitors
	Maintain share in mature or dying market

Personal selling and advertising tasks	Personal selling and advertising tasks

Generate target market sales leads
Obtain recognition of differential
  advantage importance
Increase knowledge of where and how to
  purchase
Generate inquiries
	Increase brand preference
	Increase share of market that knows how
	  and where to purchase
	Generate target market sales leads
	Maintain market share that prefers
	  product over competition

competitive marketing situations that favor personal selling over advertising are the knowledge, helpfulnesss, and courtesy of sales personnel. Advertising can supply sales leads and build awareness of where and how to purchase products. This is particularly important in adding new customers or market segments to the customer base.

Promotion Goals

Although the ultimate objective of any promotion program is to increase sales, the goal of each element of promotion is some type of communication response. Communication responses are typically classified as a sequence of steps or levels that consumers experience during a promotion program. One such classification is awareness, interest, desire, conviction, and action. For example, the goal for publicity might be awareness; however, the goal for advertising is the development of awareness, interest, and desire. The goal for personal selling and sales promotion is desire and action.

Figure 5–6 shows the uses of personal selling and advertising defined by communication response and the status of the customer in the purchasing

FIGURE 5–6   Use of personal sales and advertising in relation to expected communication
                    response and status of customer

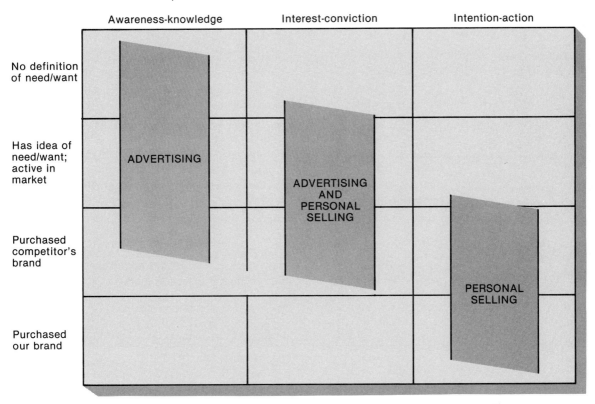

process. For example, if consumers have yet to define their needs or wants, publicity releases for the appropriate media and advertising in selected media would be the most appropriate. As consumers move from learning to attitude change, the elements of advertising and personal selling are assigned tasks of an interest-conviction nature. Continuing on with the progression, consumers move from a situation requiring interest-conviction to one of intention-action. Consumers buy either your brand or the brand of a competitor. In getting action, the promotion focus switches to personal selling.

For those who purchase a competitor's brand, it may be necessary to rebuild interest in the benefits offered by the product and clearly distinguish between brand alternatives. In such a case, an interest-conviction communication response may be called for even though purchase of the product has already taken place. When the consumer has purchased your product, the emphasis shifts to bolstering that purchase through reinforcement and increased usage.

PERSONAL SELLING AS COMMUNICATION

Both personal selling and advertising are based on effective communication. Thus it is essential that a salesperson or advertising copywriter understand the basics of communication to be effective.

communications

the sharing of information between a buyer and a seller

As it relates to personal selling, **communications** is the creation of a relationship between a buyer and a seller through a sharing of information about products, services, and the company employing the salesperson. In communicating with consumers, salespeople inform and persuade them to develop understanding. The communications process consists of a sender or salesperson, the message or sales presentation, and the receiver (consumer or buying influence). Also present is feedback or communication from the receiver back to the sender, and interference that takes the form of any distraction that disrupts or blurs the understanding or reception of the message or feedback (see Figure 5–7).

Sender

As the originator of the sales message, the sender determines its content, modifying it as necessary after feedback from the receiver. The credibility of the sender affects the reception and the acceptance of the sales message.

FIGURE 5–7   Model of direct communications (personal selling)

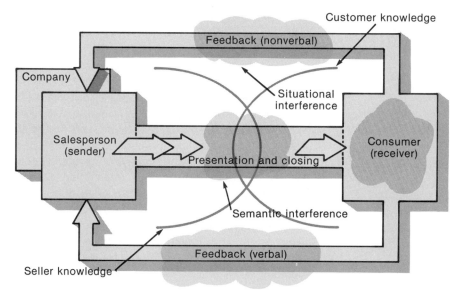

When the receiver distinguishes between the sender and the sender's company, it can add to or detract from the sender's credibility. A sender from a company with a good reputation begins the communications process with an added plus. When the company has less of a reputation or is unknown to the receiver, the sender is in a less advantageous position in starting the communication process. Nevertheless, the sender's perceived credibility is the critical element in communication.

The influence of salespeople in the communications role of senders depends on their competence and selling skills, particularly their ability to persuade. Salespeople demonstrating competence or showing capability can exert influence in delivering their sales messages. Usually this competence is limited to the products handled or a particular application situation. For example, dentists rate the salespeople who call on them as highly knowledgeable about dental supplies and materials. However, dentists question whether dental salespeople are knowledgeable regarding the practice of dentistry. The salesperson's selling skills determine his or her ability to influence. The better the sales presentation, the more willing a customer is to accept a product or service, and the more influential the salesperson will be in the selling situation.

Message

In personal selling, the form of the sales message depends on relevance, meaning, and receptivity. Promotional relevancy is a measure of fit to the consumer. Generally, the effectiveness of the sales message depends on how well product features are translated into customer benefits and choice criteria. The sales presentation is the mutual sharing of information. Feedback in the form of questions and answers plus other nonverbal reactions permits salespeople to make on-the-spot adjustments. The informative and persuasive aspects of sales messages must have common meanings to both salespeople and consumers. If, for example, a consumer refers to rearward movement as "backlash," then the salesperson must use backlash in describing this characteristic of the product.

The sales message can be varied between consumers and intended end-users, according to their interests or responses. In fact, salespeople will want to keep checking to ensure that consumers understand the presentation.

Receiver

If salespeople are to achieve their goals, receivers must be properly identified as purchasers or those influencing purchasing. This means that salespeople need to talk to the right people on an individual basis or in groups. The right persons are those actively involved in the purchasing decision process.

The knowledge, background, and attitudes of receivers filter the meaning of the sales message. Communication breaks down when the meaning given to the sales message differs from the intended meaning of the sender or salesperson.

An active participant in the communications process, the receiver sends as well as receives the messages. This reciprocal process goes on and on until, hopefully, there is a shared meaning between the two parties. Shared meaning can be defined as the overlap of the knowledge fields of both the sender and the receiver. The extent of shared meaning depends on how well the sender (salesperson) adapts the sales message to the behavior of the receiver (consumer).

Feedback

feedback

the receiver's response to a sales message

The response of the receiver to the sender's message is called **feedback.** This immediate feedback gives personal selling a definite edge over advertising. The salesperson modifies subsequent sales messages by introducing or reintroducing stimuli and/or carrying the customer through a reasoning process. Sensitivity to feedback makes the selling process dynamic, as opposed to static.

Feedback may take a verbal or nonverbal form. Although what the receiver says is obviously important, the sender needs to be aware of the receiver's nonverbal signals. Among the more common nonverbal signals are posture, gestures, facial expressions, aspects of the voice, and eye behavior. Other not so obvious signals are the physical setting for the sales presentation and the location of the sender in relation to the receiver.

Such nonverbal feedback affects the spoken messages of the receiver. As an illustration, the same spoken words can have different meanings for the sender if nonverbal signals in one case show the receiver to be interested and, in another, to be bored and impatient.

Interference

interference

distractions that occur in a communications channel. Also called noise.

Interference, sometimes labeled noise, is any distraction that may disrupt the sales message or the feedback during the communication process. Semantic interference is the use of different words to describe product benefits, end-uses, and conditions of sale. Words can produce different meanings and, thus, different thought and behavior patterns. Salespeople need to learn the consumer's vocabulary and the customer's industry or locale.

Situational interferences, such as the mood of a consumer or his or her past experiences with the salesperson's company, can disrupt the receptivity of the sales message and feedback. Competitive sales messages are another common form of situational interference. Salespeople sometimes find that they can only call on customers on certain days and during certain hours. This concentration of communication can have a disruptive effect on a selling situation because of the blurring of sales messages. This same situational interference is undoubtedly present as potential customers move from dealer to dealer in shopping for cars, appliances, furniture, and other large-ticket items.

SUMMARY OF CHAPTER OBJECTIVES

1. **To explain the relationships between corporate, marketing, and sales strategies and the salesperson.**

   The flow of planning is downward. Corporate strategies are translated into marketing strategies and then sales strategies and finally sales plans for customers at the point of contact between the company and the marketplace. Sales plans for customers form the basis for selling actions.

2. **To describe the customer sales plan.**

   A customer sales plan contains a sales goal for a given customer, as well as sales strategies, analysis of product usage and purchasing patterns, and specific actions to be taken.

3. **To describe the planning process as applied to customer sales plans.**

   Planning starts with setting up objectives and goals, which are usually passed down by sales management to the salesperson. Next, the means and resources to attain the objectives or goals are determined. The third step is implementation of the action alternatives. This is followed by setting up checks on planned actions.

4. **To distinguish between marketing and sales.**

   While marketing and sales are not the same, neither are they different. They should strengthen each other. Marketing is long-range in perspective while sales, in dealing with the execution of marketing plans in the marketplace, is necessarily short-range in nature. Marketing decisions having the greatest impact on sales are those relating to customers, marketing mix, and assigned tasks.

5. **To distinguish between sales and advertising.**

   The distinguishing characteristics of personal selling and advertising favor the use of one as opposed to the other in different marketing situations and when different responses are desired. Generally, personal selling is a direct and flexible means of communication. On the other hand, advertising is impersonal and highly controlled with no immediate feedback. The flexibility of the salesperson can be contrasted with a lower relative cost for advertising and the possibility of quicker market penetration.

6. To explain the concept of personal selling as communications.

Communications as it relates to personal selling is the creation of a relationship between a buyer and a seller through sharing of information about products, services, and the company employing the salesperson. The role of the salesperson is to inform and persuade in an effort to develop understanding.

REVIEW QUESTIONS

1. List the reasons why nonverbal feedback is important.
2. Discuss the relationship between means and resources.
3. Why do you think customers make distinctions between companies and their sales representatives?
4. Describe the communication process, and define each of its elements.
5. Contrast semantic interference with situational interference.
6. Why is the communication process thought of as dynamic?
7. Why is it necessary to revert back to interest-conviction when the customer has already bought the product?
8. Can you think of any situation in which advertising would play a greater role than personal selling in product introduction?
9. Comment on the following statement: You don't need a good product, just good salespeople and advertising.
10. Why should selecting a customer target come before determining the market mix?

DISCUSSION QUESTIONS AND EXERCISES

1. Using a company objective of increased profitability, trace the evolution of marketing planning through the marketing and sales level down to the salesperson. Assume a company makes storm windows, and the customer target is building supply stores open to the general public.
2. Pick a product—an automobile, appliance, or major item of clothing—and show the different promotion roles for personal selling and advertising.
3. In buying consumer products for which the same brand is available from several sources, do you feel customers distinguish between the store and the salesperson? Explain your answer.
4. For a very complicated consumer product (possibly a heating or cooling system), discuss the advantages of personal selling as a promotion method.
5. Discuss how a customer could become unsold.

SALES DIALOG

A meeting of the salespeople and sales managers in the Eastern Region of the Salesbury Company, Inc., was underway. The vice president of sales announced that the company had adopted a key account strategy. Each representative received a list of customers identified as key accounts. The reps were also supplied with the information on marginal accounts. At the conclusion of the meeting, two salespeople began talking.

MARGARET AMES: How do you like that? The company develops a sales plan and hands it to us.

STAN THORSEN: Yes, I would have liked having more say-so in the planning operation.

AMES: You know what they did? They gave me some names of accounts I have never called on. They are plants of major companies that have been handled by a national account rep.

THORSEN: I disagree with you. I think that we should have responsibility for every customer in our assigned territories. I know that I have had to service accounts in my territory I don't get credit for. My problem with this new program is that some accounts they marked as key accounts are not really that good in my opinion.

AMES: That could be. I see two of my customers who don't mean very much in sales volume listed as key accounts. Let's see, the definition of a key account is one that contributes three times the average cost of a call in your territory. Contribution is defined as: Gross profit or sales − Cost of goods sold. That means that a key account will vary from one territory to another. It also means that an account that needs two calls a month will have to buy more than one who needs only one call a month.

THORSEN: It may be confusing, but I agree with how they define a key account. If you think about it, a customer's purchases should be an indicator of how much attention we give to an account. What puzzles me is the lack of attention to potential. They have only considered actual sales.

AMES: I know we will have problems with the customers we are to drop. I've called on one account for 10 years, and they give us 60 percent of their purchases. What am I supposed to tell them, we don't need your business?

THORSEN: You didn't listen to the vice president. He said the changeover would be over a year. Maybe that account you mentioned could give us all their business.

What do you think the results of this sales dialog will be?

CASE 5–1   GLADSTONE FURRIERS

Gladstone Furriers of Denver, Colorado, is an old, well-established retailer of fur coats. For the last two years, sales have not been good at any of the four Denver stores. A review of sales revealed that most sales were made at discounted prices during one of Gladstone's promotions.

Dan Livingston, general manager, has developed a proposal to turn Gladstone Furriers into an upscale fur mart selling all products at a set discount. He also envisions a reduction in the variety of styles, shades, type, and designers carried in stock. By concentrating their efforts on such furs as beaver, mink, sable, and lynx, they can offer a standard 30 percent discount.

The sales approach will be entirely different than anything presently attempted in the fur trade. Instead of commissioned sales personnel, Livingston wants to hire people who view their main job as developing rapport with customers and serving their needs after selection. These people would determine customers' desires as well as their capabilities for payment. At each store a staff of technical experts would be available to help sales personnel. Everyone would be paid a fixed salary plus a bonus based on the overall performance of that particular store.

Questions

1. If you were the president of Gladstone Furriers, what would your reaction be to the Livingston plan?
2. What are the advantages and disadvantages of the new sales approach?
3. Outline a training program for the new sales personnel.

CASE 5–2   NUMERICAL MACHINE TOOL COMPANY

Numerical Machine Tool Company is one of the country's largest producers of numerically controlled machine tools. Customers are located across the entire United States although foreign sales are minimal. Most of Numerical's customers are machining companies that do contract machining for other industrial firms. Another large segment of Numerical's market is made up of manufacturing enterprises that buy numerically controlled machine tools for use in their own manufacturing operations.

Numerical's marketing activities are the responsibility of Tom Parsons, a 53-year-old man who had come up through Numerical's sales force. Parsons knew the business inside and out; he knew all of the major officers in all of the major accounts. He knew many of the top executives of Numerical's competitors. "Parsons," as one competitor put it, "is one of the top people in the business. He grew up in the industry and helped make it what it is today. Everyone respects Tom's knowledge and integrity."

Late one Friday afternoon, Parsons was looking over a report he had just received from accounting. He noticed that marketing expenses had gone over budget for the third month in a row. He felt something had to be done. Items included in this line were price lists, trade shows, catalogs, trade press advertising, and technical bulletins.

Parsons was bothered by this problem for two reasons. First, he never had really seen why so much money had to be spent on these items. They seemed to be luxuries; the real focus of his marketing effort—he had always felt—was his experienced, talented sales force. Why so much money had to be spent on these other items, he would never understand. Second, even when he agreed to the budget for these items, he always felt a certain sense of uneasiness over his inability to make the expenditures more productive. He intuitively sensed what had to be done to make the sales force efficient and productive. But the marketing expenses budget was something with which he always had difficulty.

Parsons picked up the phone and asked Dick Levin, his administrative assistant who had direct responsibility for the marketing expenses budget, to come into his office to discuss the matter.

PARSONS: Hi, Dick. Sit down; I want to check the marketing expenses budget with you. We went over budget again. Something's got to be done.

LEVIN: You're not going to suggest we drop these expenses altogether again, are you? I thought we had agreed to burn that bridge behind us.

PARSONS: No, I'm not suggesting we do that. But I do want a report from you justifying each of these expenditures. Why does a company with our reputation and product quality have to spend over 3 percent of sales on advertising? Why do we need exhibits at trade shows? Explain the purpose of technical bulletins, price lists, catalogs, and so forth. Couldn't we handle a lot of this with letters instead of expensive four-color literature?

LEVIN: OK, that seems reasonable. Is there anything else you want the report to cover?

PARSONS: Yes, even more importantly, I want you to show how these items can create a synergy between them and the sales effort. You know how you're always telling me that these expenses more than pay for themselves in terms of reduced selling expenses. Give me several examples of this in your report. Also, show how some of these items work together. That is, show how a synergy is created between, say, catalogs and trade press advertising so that the cost of each is less than if we were to run one without the other. Does that make sense?

LEVIN: Sure, I'll have the report prepared in a month. Soon enough?

PARSONS: No! I need this in two weeks at the latest. With all that you know about this matter, it should be easy. I'll see you tomorrow morning at the first tee.

Questions

1. Can you understand why Tom Parsons feels as he does?
2. If you were Dick Levin, what would you say in your report?

PART THREE

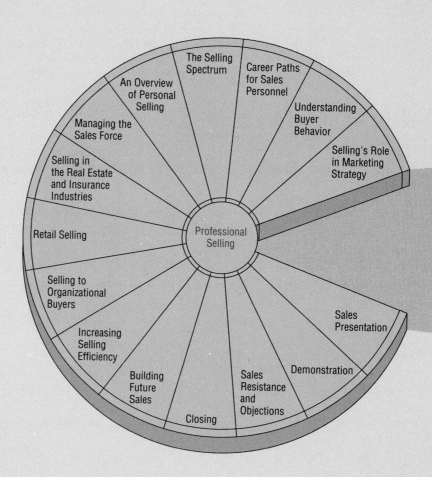

Precall Preparation

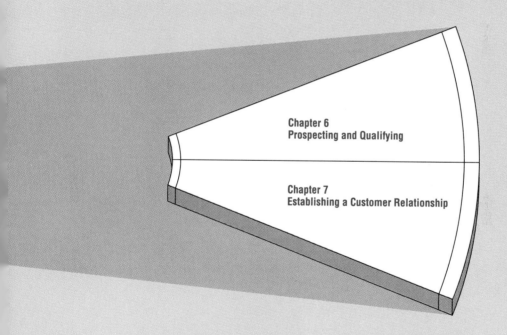

Chapter 6
Prospecting and Qualifying

Chapter 7
Establishing a Customer Relationship

CHAPTER 6

Prospecting and Qualifying

CHAPTER OBJECTIVES

1. To define a sales lead and a prospect.

2. To explain the importance of prospecting.

3. To identify the sources for prospects.

4. To identify the steps in qualifying.

SALES CAREER PROFILE

CHRIS ERTEL
Bowne & Co., Inc.

Chris Ertel, a marketing representative for Bowne & Co., Inc., sells financial printing to attorneys, investment bankers, and corporations. Ertel, who holds a bachelor's degree from Catholic University in Washington, D.C., is a scuba diver, reader, marathon runner, and baseball fan.

Asked why she selected a career in selling, Ertel commented, "I have had several careers and, except for my stint teaching third graders, have always been involved with sales. It was while I was retailing manager at Abraham & Strauss and later at a major investment bank that I became aware of the dichotomy between line and staff personnel. One either made money for the company or was considered "overhead." This philosophy of rewarding the producers made sense to me, so I decided to sell to participate in these rewards.

"I came to Bowne in May 1982. After countless rounds of interviews, it seemed as if I had met everyone in the company. Before I was hired I spent an entire day with Ralph Stoesser, a senior sales rep for Bowne, so I had a general idea of how salespeople at Bowne structure their day. I was impressed with the professional attitude of those who interviewed me. I was also impressed with the single-mindedness of the company, and with the frankness and openness of Ralph Stoesser."

Asked about her experiences in the training program, Ertel replied, "My training program consisted of two phases: time spent in the customer service department, and time spent with an experienced Bowne salesperson.

"The purpose of spending time in Customer Service is twofold: to learn the mechanics of how a job comes together from beginning to end, and to be involved with Bowne's clients from a customer service representative's point of view. Learning the company's capabilities helps sell Bowne's products, which is not only printing but also service. In working with the customer service representatives, you get to understand their concerns, frustrations, and problems, which leads to a stronger team. We who sell can never forget that we are only one part of the team.

"In the second aspect of the training program, we work with an experienced salesperson. It is an invaluable experience, because you become intimate with how this salesperson deals with different types of clients, his or her daily routine, and the joys and frustrations of the job. A by-product is development of a close bond with the salesperson."

Ertel described the uniqueness of her product: "The product is perceived as a commodity but we are truly selling a very high level of service. The primary qualities required to sell financial printing successfully are tenacity and empathy. It can take one to two years to build a relationship of trust. So much depends on the printer's ability to deliver in a timely and accurate manner.

"Selling financial printing is unique because the decision to buy is often made by committee. The company, the investment banker, or the company counsel can choose the printer, or it can be any combination of these. This is one of the few sales situations where the salesperson is not present at the close. Feedback on what happened when the printer was chosen is never firsthand information. It is sometimes difficult to know what made the difference between getting the job and losing it.

"Professionalism is very important in our sales environment because our customers are the top executives of major companies, and the bankers and lawyers who make the money markets move. As deadlines become tight, a professional manner and a level head can save the day."

Ertel went on to describe what she liked best about her job: "I like the freedom I have in selling. The one requirement at Bowne is that when clients are 'in-house' the salesperson must be 'in-house,' too. This goes a long way toward ensuring the clients receive good service. You are judged twice a year when commission checks are distributed. It would be difficult for me to do a job with someone always looking over my shoulder and evaluating me. I would also have great difficulty working at a desk all day. I cherish the freedom to leave the office to call on clients.

"Bowne gives its salespeople superb support. Management, pricing, customer service, accounting, technical and secretarial sales support, the composing and pressrooms—all work to facilitate the printing we are paid to do."

When asked why prospecting is important in her industry, Ertel answered, "The financial printing industry is very competitive. Bidding is standard practice, and lowballing is common. A good salesperson can never assume that clients will buy from her, and must constantly monitor and improve the standard of service she provides. A customer may walk away from you at any time."

Finally, Ertel was asked what prospecting methods work best for her. "First, read the 'morning report.' The 'MR' tells you who was working at Bowne the previous evening. If they were doing SEC work, they are potential clients. This is a very good time to meet and service potential customers since they are a captive audience.

"Second, read the 'green sheet.' The green sheet gives you the names of people working on a deal being printed by Bowne. It is a good way of garnering names of people too senior to be spending time at the printer.

"Third, deliver a 'red box.' A potential customer who is doing SEC work will usually see you if you bring a 'red box' with you. This contains pamphlets detailing the rules and forms of the SEC, which are the bread and butter of anyone doing SEC work.

"Finally, ask people who are pleased with Bowne's services for names of colleagues or friends who also buy printing services. Using a satisfied client's name when calling is often the 'leg up' I need to get through on the phone to a new prospect. Because Bowne has a superb reputation in the marketplace, for the most part buyers are willing to see me."

Huck Manufacturing of Irvine, California, a producer of fastener systems with sales of $125 million, has installed a formal program for handling the nearly 2,600 inquiries it receives during the course of a year. Under the program, inquiries received from advertising and promotions are sent to the advertising and sales promotion department where they are coded by the product group and campaign that generated the lead. After coding, the cards are forwarded to Inquiry Handling Service, a lead management company, who processes the names and mails each prospect the requested materials. Along with the sales literature, each mailing contains a letter signed by Jim Dauw, Huck's manager of advertising and sales promotions, and a reply card asking for more information about the person and company doing the requesting. Figure 6–1 shows a sample of this letter.

At the same time the package is mailed, the prospect's name is forwarded to the salesperson or distributor who covers the territory where the product is located. The lead slip is shown in Figure 6–2. Over the next couple of weeks the salesperson or distributor is to call on the prospect and send an evaluation to Dauw. Experience has shown that the entire process will take about one month. About 10 days later, or 40 days after the original mailing, a follow-up card is sent asking the prospect if he or she received the desired literature and whether he or she needs more information.[1]

SALES LEADS AND PROSPECTS

sales lead

prospective customer the salesperson has identified as needing or desiring a product or service

The above example may be misleading because the typical firm does not have a formal program and in fact may ignore inquiries. This inattention to inquiries is fairly widespread despite studies which show that 20 to 25 percent of the **sales leads** generated will result in sales within a six-month time period.[2] This lack of attention may result from the fact that too many inquiries in the past have not produced results or simply that no effective system has been installed to process inquiries.

The task of prospecting and qualifying starts out with the generation of sales leads. A sales lead is some person or organization that might need or desire the salesperson's product. Sales leads come from many sources— present customers, inside salespeople, inquiries from advertising, direct mail, trade shows, and the like. Many of these sales leads amount to nothing because the persons involved have no need or desire for the product or service. A purchasing agent, for example, may inquire about a product simply for informational purposes. Indeed, in many companies it is policy to maintain a library of product information.

prospect

sales lead that the salesperson or other party has identified as needing or desiring the product or service

A **prospect** is a sales lead that the salesperson or other party has identified as needing or desiring the product or service. The identification of this need converts a sales lead into a prospect. Prospects, then, are potential customers as measured by their need or apparent desire for the item. Once a sales lead is identified as a prospect, the next step is to qualify the prospect's ability and authority to purchase the good or service. The key to qualifying leads is finding out how far along the prospect is in the buying decision process. One company uses 10 questions, the answers to which determine a rating

FIGURE 6–1

We need your opinion!

Several weeks ago we sent product information to you regarding specific Huck Fastening systems. We hope that the package is beneficial and our service satisfactory to you. If not, we need to know how to improve. Please take a moment to complete and return this postage paid questionnaire. You will help us deliver, "The promise that holds."™

1. Did you receive the information package?　☐ Yes　☐ No

2. Was this information complete enough for your needs?　☐ Yes　☐ No

3. What additional information would you like? _____
_____

4. Were you contacted by a Huck representative?　☐ Yes　☐ No

5. If not, would you like to be?　☐ Yes　☐ No

6. What is your phone number　(_____) _____ Ext _____ and when is the best time to contact you? _____

7. Would you like to participate in a product demonstration? (Other people are welcome)　☐ Yes　☐ No

8. If you have purchased or if you plan to purchase a fastening system, please state the manufacturer and type: _____
_____

9. Is your requirement　☐ Immediate　☐ 1-6 months　☐ 6+ months　☐ Longer

10. Do you:　☐ Recommend　☐ Specify　☐ Have final approval　☐ Purchase

11. If you have decided on purchasing, what factors determined your decision? _____
_____

Please refold this form to expose the postage paid address, tape or staple shut and return to us. We welcome any additional comments and appreciate your participation toward improving our service to you.

Sincerely,

James E. Dauw
Corporate Communications Manager

Huck Manufacturing Company
World Headquarters
6 Thomas
Irvine, California 92718
(714) 855-9000

HUCK
A Federal-Mogul Company

FIGURE 6–2   Example of form sent to salesperson on prospect

QUALIFIED LEAD
FOLLOW-UP IMMEDIATELY!
RETURN COMPLETED FORM TO:

Shown below is a **QUALIFIED SALES LEAD** produced from our advertising and publicity efforts. Product information has been sent to the prospect who has responded with the card shown below.

Please follow-up this sales lead immediately. Complete bottom of form and return to the above address.

SALES REPRESENTATIVE: _____

DATE PROCESSED: _____

Please complete and return this card to Huck Manufacturing Company

What type of business is your company in?

☐ Transportation
   Specify: _____

☐ Electronics

☐ Distribution

☐ Construction

☐ Other: _____

Is your project need:

☐ Immediate

☐ 1 to 6 months

☐ More than 6 months

☐ Information only

Do you:

☐ Recommend

☐ Specify

☐ Have final approval

For immediate information:
Huck Manufacturing Company
Industrial Fastener Division
Waco, TX
817-776-2000

What additional information would you like?
_____
_____
_____

What is your application?
_____
_____
_____

Phone Number   Ext   Best time to call

HUCK
A Federal-Mogul Company

FORM HWB 855

Please make necessary changes to prospect's name, address and phone.

DATE CONTACTED: ____/____/____   ☐ IN PERSON   ☐ BY PHONE

LEAD QUALITY: ☐ EXCELLENT   ☐ GOOD   ☐ FAIR   ☐ POOR

PURCHASE POSSIBILITY: ☐ IMMEDIATE   ☐ 3 MONTHS   ☐ 6 MONTHS
                        ☐ LONGER   ☐ SOLD   ☐ NONE

END PRODUCT OR APPLICATION: _____
                            _____

OTHER INTERESTS: _____
                 _____

FOLLOW UP DATE: ____/____/____

COMMENTS: _____
_____
_____
_____
_____
_____
_____

Salesperson: _____

Date: _____

from 15 to minus 10. A "hot" sales lead will have a high rating while a minus score will be given to a lead that has just started the decision process. Some companies use salespeople to qualify while others rely on telemarketing.

qualifying

determining prospect's ability and authority to buy a product

qualified prospect

customer who has the ability and/or the authority to purchase the good or service

By **qualifying** a prospect, the prospect's ability to buy the product being offered is assessed. For example, an executive who may prefer a certain brand of word processor is not a **qualified prospect** because of a corporate-level decision to purchase another brand. Similarly, even though a young couple may aspire to live in a prestigious condominium, their combined income may not qualify them for the mortgage.

Once the salesperson has secured a qualified prospect, the sales process begins. Seven basic steps constitute the normal selling sequence: (1) prospecting and qualifying, (2) preapproach and approach, (3) presentation, (4) demonstration, (5) handling objections, (6) closing, and (7) building future sales. Steps two through seven are the topics of later chapters. The sales process, it is hoped, converts the qualified prospect into a customer. Then, through an effective sales follow-up procedure, a customer who is satisfied with a purchase leads to repeat sales. Figure 6–3 shows this conversion.

Figure 6–3 outlines the sequence from sales leads to repeat customer. As the figure demonstrates, the initial, basic step in obtaining customers is

FIGURE 6–3 An overview of the selling process

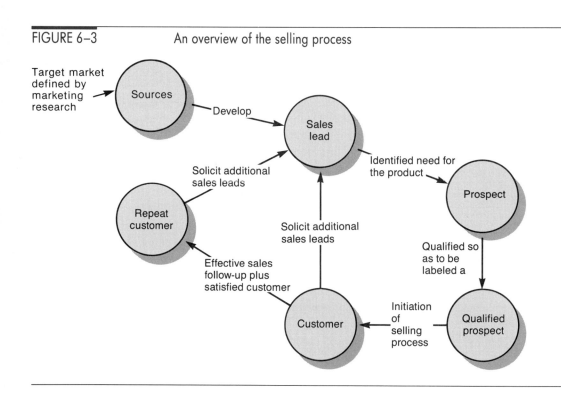

always prospecting and qualifying from targeted sources. This step in the sales process is the subject of this chapter.

THE IMPORTANCE OF PROSPECTING

Systematic, well-planned prospecting is one of the primary building blocks allowing salespeople to get the jump on the competition. This factor often separates high performers from low performers because when you have no leads, you have no sales.

Without an adequate pool of prospects, salespeople eventually fail. Consider the case of Walt, a recent college graduate, who entered the insurance sales field. In his first year, Walt won several awards from the company and realized double the earnings of his classmates. Yet a couple of years later, his friends found him at another job far removed from the field of insurance. They wondered, "What happened to Walt? Why did he give up selling insurance? I thought he was doing extremely well."

Quite likely Walt failed because he ran out of prospects. He began his career with an established pool of prospects: his immediate family, other relatives, friends, and classmates. This select group of prospects provided him with a good start in selling. Walt's downfall began when he failed to add to his starting pool of prospects with new contacts. When his select group of prospects stopped buying, Walt stopped selling!

Prospecting is important to the overall sales effort because existing customers must be replaced periodically. Most estimates of annual customer turnover fall in the 10 to 25 percent range, depending on the source consulted. This means that a significant portion of the firm's customers cease to buy its products every year. Consumers may switch brands, move, decide to shop elsewhere, die, or eliminate certain purchases they have made previously. Industrial customers may change vendors, switch to an alternative product, go bankrupt, or close down the purchasing office in a salesperson's territory.

In addition to maintaining current customers, most companies want to expand sales through new customers. This places even greater importance on prospecting.

SECURING SALES LEADS AND PROSPECTS

Leo Cunningham prospects the old-fashioned way: door to door. Cunningham is a modern Fuller Brush salesperson who contacts about 50 customers each day between 4 P.M. and 7 P.M. Cunningham has remarked, "Only half of them will talk to me, but 90 percent of the time, if they look at the book they'll buy something." He continues, "The hardest thing about this job aside from parking, that is . . . well, that would be keeping my smile. Sometimes

PROFESSIONAL SELLING IN ACTION

Chemical Milling International

Chemical Milling International, with sales of approximately $2.5 million, uses a chemical bath process to reduce the thickness of aluminum sheets for the aerospace industry. In 1975 Adoph Miera, president of the company, decided to circumvent metal forming companies, their original customer, and go directly to aerospace companies. His principal method of prospecting was to go door-to-door. If a purchasing agent told him to check back, this was an excuse for him to reappear. Also, the normal turnover of purchasing personnel made it necessary to re-establish contacts. His first contact was with North American Aviation and resulted from his firm being familiar to purchasing personnel who were experiencing difficulty with regular sources not wanting a small order. In addition to making repeat calls, he also began to send sales letters detailing information about his company.

Today Miera has discarded cold calls. Instead he goes straight to the small business office in each firm and obtains a list of names of buyers who deal with his service. He then calls for appointments with these individuals.

Success for Miera is based on continuous contact with customers and keeping his word about delivery being better than that provided by competitors. The latter is especially important, he feels, even though it costs him money.

SOURCE: Norman Sklarewitz, "Tiny Chemical Milling Wins Them with the Basics," *Sales & Marketing Management,* February 1990, pp. 58–59. Reprinted by permission of Sales & Marketing Management. © February 1990.

when the door slams, it's hard to do that, just to smile and move on over to the next house."[3]

No source list of potential prospects is ever complete. The sources are numerous and diverse; some can be exhausted, others may continue to be fruitful for years. Effective salespeople must be knowledgeable concerning all the possible sources of prospects for a product. Salespeople must be flexible and make use of several sources of prospects if they are to be successful.

These prospect sources include (1) customers; (2) inquiries; (3) company sources; (4) cold canvassing; (5) friends, social contacts, and acquaintances; (6) organizational contacts; (7) spotters; (8) sellers of related products; (9) direct-mail and prospect lists; (10) public information; (11) other prospects; and (12) trade shows, meetings, and demonstrations. The next section discusses these sources.

Customers

Customers who are satisfied with their purchases are probably the best single source of additional sales leads. Satisfied customers will usually agree to suggest friends, relatives, neighbors, or associates as prospects. When customers are pleased with a purchase, the usual tendency is to talk about it to their friends and associates.

referral

prospecting method in which the customer introduces and recommends the seller to prospects

One productive way of soliciting sales is the **referral** method, in which customers are asked to introduce and recommend salespeople to other prospects. Personal and telephone introductions such as the following are extremely effective:

> Hello, Ralph . . . I am going to send a representative from Allied Aluminum Products over to see you this afternoon. I think she might have just the item you are looking for.
>
> Marsha, I'd like you to meet Angie Forsheen from Designs Unlimited. She is the person who solved our decorating problems over at the Brairbush store.
>
> Ellen, I have a fellow sitting in my office who I think has an insurance plan your association will want to consider. We just signed up with him today.

In other cases, satisfied customers may write brief letters of introduction for salespeople who request them to do so. Short notes of introduction written on backs of business cards are traditional practice. The following is an example of such a note:

> Hi, Hal! This will introduce Hewitt Fawson of Consolidated Insurance. Judy and I recently bought a homeowner's policy from him, and we've been pleased with Consolidated. I look forward to seeing you next Thursday.

Referrals are of considerable help to salespeople. They minimize the time spent on prospecting and qualifying and improve the likelihood of friendly receptions for their sales presentations.

Inquiries

Companies routinely receive direct inquiries about their products or services. Some inquiries are solicited through direct mail or advertisements in magazines and newspapers. Others can come in as a result of nonselling contacts with potential customers by company personnel, publicity releases about a firm's product, community involvement programs, or a luncheon speech by a corporate executive.

The first of two ways to qualify inquiries is to forward the inquiries to the salesperson serving the particular territory where the inquirer is located. That salesperson can then complete the qualifying process. Another, and perhaps the preferred way, is to do the qualifying at the home office or with an outside firm and send only qualified prospects to salespeople.

Company Sources

Salespeople can often obtain sales leads from other people within their own companies and should build relationships with them. For example, the service department may pass on word of someone whose present equipment is old and constantly in need of repair. Marketing staff personnel may have contacts who are prospects. Sales managers usually refer leads to salespeople, and sellers of other product lines in the organization may also prove helpful.

The two most obvious internal sources are the sales administrators and the service department. Inside salespeople are in continuous contact with customers as well as individuals who call the firm in regard to a product. Service departments provide valuable information about the current status of the customer.

Internal sources can sometimes be prolific providers of quality sales leads. Successful salespeople should do everything possible to nurture and cultivate productive internal sources of prospect information. For instance, a daily visit to the firm's service department can pay substantial dividends. Payment for a lead that turns into a sale is another.

Cold Canvassing

cold canvassing

securing prospects through unsolicited contacts by the sales force

Cold canvassing is the time-honored sales tradition of securing prospects through unsolicited contacts by the sales force. This is accomplished either through personal, face-to-face contact or by telephone canvassing. When Tandy Corporation decided to set up a field sales force, it subjected 500 sales applicants to a week of training highlighted by cold canvassing in person and by phone. Tandy was able to eliminate a third of the candidates by the end of the week.[4] Cold canvassing is uniformly resisted by most salespeople.

Cold canvassing is based on the idea that salespeople contact every person or firm in a given area. Sellers of industrial equipment may blanket an area in an effort to uncover sales leads. They call on purchasing agents in every plant within an area looking for potential customers. Obviously, cold canvassing increases the cost of prospecting, since it is often difficult to obtain good sales leads through unsolicited visits or calls. However, cold canvassing does allow salespeople to completely cover a given sector of the market which in turn may reveal a previously untapped market segment. Cold canvassing can also fill in "down time" when salespeople are not actively selling or prospecting through other means.

Beginning salespeople may often be assigned the job of cold canvassing as one of their first duties. When this is the case, the new salesperson will probably secure sales leads, identify them as prospects, and qualify. The results will then be turned over to experienced salespeople for initiation of the selling process.

Telephone canvassing is another common technique for obtaining sales leads. The objectives and strategy are similar to those in personal-contact cold canvassing. Unsolicited sales calls—particularly those placed via automatic dialing devices—have become a major public issue in recent years. Because people resist these intrusions on their privacy, many states have taken steps to restrict unsolicited calls in cold canvassing efforts.

Friends, Social Contacts, and Acquaintances

A rich source of leads is the salesperson's own friends, social contacts, and acquaintances. Because of their close association with the salesperson, they usually are helpful in providing the names of potential prospects. The referral technique is often used to reach sales leads provided by this source.

key-influence method
prospecting method that uses people who command respect within their social, work, or professional groups

The **key-influence method** is frequently used in connection with this source of prospects. Many people who are influential within their social, work, or professional groups can be solicited for sales leads in a very candid manner. For example, stockbrokers sometimes use this approach.

One important note of caution should be sounded. Friends, social contacts, and acquaintances tend to disappear if they are valued strictly as a source of sales leads. There are limits to how much a salesperson can impose on any source of leads. An effective prospector should be careful not to cross this barrier.

Organizational Contacts

Salespeople join the same civic and professional organizations as their prospects. Many professional associations openly encourage them to do so, because it provides an opportunity for the group's members to keep up-to-date on the latest products and services available. However, salespeople must draw the line against "excessive commercialism." Salespersons should belong to professional associations of clients because they are sincerely interested in the advancement of the profession. If a product can serve a particular segment of the profession, then the salesperson has an obligation to demonstrate its usefulness. But a representative does not have the ethical right to use a membership to sell "anything to everybody." Those who do so are usually soon labeled as hustlers and effectively excluded from further transactions with the group's members.

Membership in civic organizations is also important. In addition to being a rich source of sales leads, civic organizations allow salespeople to keep attuned to activities and current opinion in the communities in which they work. The value of civic club memberships goes beyond their contributions to a salesperson's prospecting effort. Here too, however, a salesperson must avoid excessive commercialism; the representative should join a civic organization because he or she believes in the goals and objectives of the club—not for business or social reasons alone.

Spotters

spotters
people who make specialized surveys or canvasses to assess prospects' needs

Spotters—sometimes referred to as bird dogs—are people who make specialized surveys or canvasses to assess the needs of prospects. Spotters allow experienced salespeople to concentrate their specialized sales knowledge on bona fide prospects. This practice makes the best use of the salesperson's

PROFESSIONAL SELLING IN ACTION

Henry Baldwin Hyde

Henry Baldwin Hyde founded Equitable Life in 1859. Starting with just two agents, the sales force expanded to 200 in the next five years and today is one of the largest in the industry. Hyde kept in touch with his sales force by circulating motivational articles. The following are excerpts from an article on prospecting that is as relevant today as it was in the 19th century when it was written.

1. Remember that your biggest problem will be getting new clients.

2. Getting access to a potential customer can be difficult and so will getting his or her undivided attention.

3. Extend your circle of acquaintances. Through those you know, endeavor to seek those you don't know.

4. Serve every client so well that he or she will be glad to introduce you to people with whom he or she has influence.

5. Join social, business, and religious organizations.

6. Use mailings to reach people you don't know. Make sure you make it easy to reply.

7. Don't forget women. Many insure for the protection of their children.

working time. Sellers of automobiles, major appliances, home improvements, and housewares often utilize this method of prospecting. Typically, spotters are part-time employees who prospect in conjunction with other daily activities or on a temporary basis.

Sellers of Related Products

Sellers of related products are another source of prospects. Service station operators and mechanics can provide valuable tips to new car sellers. A bartender, barber, or waitress is also likely to know who has been discussing the purchase of recreational property, for example. Contractors, real estate agents, consultants, accountants, and lawyers may be able to suggest leads for various sellers.

In some cases, sellers of related products provide prospect information gratis. In other cases, they can receive a finder's fee if the prospect actually buys the item from the salesperson. In one modification of this approach, present customers are asked to provide names of prospects and then are compensated for the information if those prospects buy within a certain time.

Direct Mail and Prospect Lists

Salespeople sometimes use direct mail advertisements to develop prospect lists. Vacation home developers use direct mail to invite leads to a dinner and slide presentation about the property or to actually spend a minivacation at the site. Stockbrokers and investment counselors send out direct mail invitations to attend investment seminars. Direct mail prospecting has proved very effective for many sellers of industrial goods.

list brokers
firms that sell mailing (or prospect) lists

Companies obtain mailing (or prospect) lists from many sources. Some firms develop their own lists; others purchase them from **list brokers** that provide lists of virtually any segment of the population. All sales personnel, however, should also develop their own lists of prospects.

Public Information

Many public records are open for inspection by sales personnel. The list of current building permits can provide good leads for building supply houses, exterminators, and furniture stores. Tax rolls can be helpful in developing lists of people in certain financial brackets and thus in selling automobiles and other big-ticket items. A list of new residents is another source.

Various publications, such as magazines, newspapers, and the trade press, provide many sales leads. Insurance sellers look for newspaper accounts of accidents, burglaries, and births. Jewelry and dinnerware sales representatives closely follow engagement announcements. A trade press account of a new plant opening can be an important lead for many industrial sales representatives in that area.

Representatives use telephone calls, direct mail, and personal contacts to determine whether these leads are good prospects for particular products. Since in these cases the need is already apparent, salespeople should at least mail or personally present their business cards. This helps keep the seller's name in front of the prospect while the prospect is contemplating a purchase.

Other Prospects

Prospects themselves can often generate other sales leads. Many salespeople make prospecting for sales leads a regular part of each sales interview. Thus they are able to maintain a continuous pool of potential buyers. Simple questions such as the following can be quite effective in obtaining sales leads.

> Do you know anyone else who might be interested in this unique set of cookware?
>
> Are there other dentists in your association who currently handle their own accounting records?
>
> Is any other family on the block considering listing their home?

chain of prospects
situation where a seller tries to get one or more additional prospects from each person interviewed

A technique commonly used to generate additional prospects is the **chain of prospects** method, which is valuable in any sales interview situation. Salespeople use this method to get one or more prospects for each prospect to whom they talk. The chain is typically used by sellers of insurance, household wares, real estate, and many other products. Often the prospect is offered an incentive such as additional merchandise for names of other prospects.

Trade Shows, Meetings, and Demonstrations

Trade shows, professional meetings, exhibitions, clinics, fairs, and demonstrations are excellent sources of sales leads. In fact, prospecting is the primary reason for any company to participate in such activities. Publishers display new textbooks at a state teachers' meeting; automobile dealers display their new models at an auto show; furniture makers have booths at trade shows and marts; the fashion industry displays the latest styles at seasonal showings. Trade shows, exhibitions, and demonstrations are excellent methods of finding prospects for new products and aid in identifying previously unexplored markets for established products.

Localized clinics given by national manufacturers are another way of obtaining prospects. These clinics may focus on a particular problem area (waste disposal), a type of installation (mezzanine shelving), or some item of equipment (log splitter). Clinics are used extensively where it is not possible or practical to transport the product or service from one customer or prospect to another.

THE IMPORTANCE OF QUALIFYING A PROSPECT

Qualifying a prospect saves time and improves selling efficiency. Although a prospect may identify a need for a product, only a qualified prospect is able to make such a purchase. Many salespeople launch into a sales presentation as soon as they establish that the prospect has a demonstrated need for the product. This approach may be adequate for low-value consumer goods that nearly everyone is able to purchase. In most other cases, however, a prospect should be qualified to determine ability to buy and product suitability.

Salespeople who do not take time to qualify prospects are less efficient than they otherwise might be. Too often salespeople waste their valuable selling time on unqualified prospects. This means that the salesperson should set up a formalized procedure for qualifying. If their home offices or some other agency does the qualifying, salespeople should make sure they understand how the process is implemented.

HOW TO QUALIFY A PROSPECT

There are three essential steps in qualifying a prospect:

1. Delineate the factors on which a prospect should be qualified.
2. Determine whether the prospect possesses these qualifications.
3. Decide whether or not to approach the prospect.

The first step in the qualifying process is to define which factors or characteristics are important to the purchase decision. Age, income, occupation, place of residence, and marital status may be important to many consumer decisions. Credit ratings are considered in nearly all attempts to qualify a prospect. Type of business, input into the buying decision (does the individual specify or recommend?), and the final approval on the purchase are critical factors in qualifying industrial prospects. Also important are end-use, quantity of purchase, and timing of purchase. The last refers to whether the need is immediate or in the future. Other factors might include the advertising responded to, previous inquiries, and past sales record, as is the case with the form shown in Figure 6–4.

| FIGURE 6–4 | Example of a form used in qualifying prospects for a financial firm |

Reprinted by permission of LCS industries.

It is not always easy to delineate the characteristics relevant to qualifying a buyer. A variety of purchasing influences exists at each stage of the purchase decision. For instance, a child may initiate the acquisition of a new bicycle, but key buying influences such as parents, grandparents, and other children may alter the final purchase decision.

In the second step in qualifying a prospect, the salesperson must determine whether a particular prospect possesses the relevant qualifications. If the prospect fails this test, the salesperson is probably best advised to concentrate his or her efforts in other directions. Salespeople use various techniques to qualify particular prospects. In some sales situations, it is necessary only to qualify the prospect with regard to one variable, such as credit rating. Other sellers use simple checklists to qualify their prospects, possibly using a scoring system to differentiate between prospects.

Finally, each seller has to decide whether to pursue a particular prospect. This should be a totally rational, economic decision. There are some cases in which a seller is justified in not pursuing a qualified prospect. The key to this decision is whether the prospect would be a profitable account. Unfortunately, sales organizations have traditionally been very volume-conscious, even at the expense of profitability. The truth is that some sales are not profitable, either because of an uneconomical order size or the modest margin that is involved. A common occurrence is the small-order problem, in which a purchaser buys in such small quantities that it is currently unprofitable to supply the account. The seller's eventual decision has to be balanced by an assessment of the likelihood of a larger (and profitable) account in the future, as well as the legal and ethical considerations involved. A complete periodic analysis of all accounts is useful in making this decision.

MAINTAINING A FILE ON QUALIFIED PROSPECTS

After qualifying a prospect, it is essential that the salesperson maintain a file about the prospect's particular problems, operating methods, professional and emotional needs, and buying characteristics. Such a file allows the salesperson to plan future approaches and presentations more effectively. These records are crucial to the salesperson's future success.

Some sales personnel just record information on index cards for their own reference. Other firms have set up established procedures for analyzing this important sales data, such as a customer sales plan. The development of an information file on prospects should be part of the sales force's overall objectives. Professional salespeople know the relevant market information about every prospect.

Many companies have now computerized their prospect files. This permits them to maintain more comprehensive data on potential buyers, and allows ready access for both sales personnel and sales management.

SUMMARY OF CHAPTER OBJECTIVES

1. To define a sales lead and a prospect.

A sales lead is some person or organization that might need or desire the salesperson's product. A prospect is a sales lead that the salesperson or other party has identified as needing or desiring the product or service.

2. To explain the importance of prospecting.

Without an adequate pool of prospects, the salesperson soon fails. Prospecting is important to the overall sales effort because existing customers have to be replaced periodically, and new prospects are necessary for any sales expansion.

3. To identify the sources for prospects.

The sources of prospects are:
1. Customers.
2. Inquiries.
3. Company personnel.
4. Cold canvassing.
5. Friends, social contacts, and acquaintances.
6. Organizational contacts.
7. Spotters.
8. Sellers of related products.
9. Direct mail and prospect lists.
10. Public information.
11. Other prospects.
12. Trade shows, meetings, and demonstrations.

4. To identify the steps in qualifying.

The steps are: (1) delineate the factors on which the prospect should be qualified, (2) determine whether the prospect possesses these qualifications, and (3) decide whether to approach the prospect.

REVIEW QUESTIONS

1. Differentiate between a sales lead and a prospect.
2. Contrast the chain of prospects, referral, and key influence methods of obtaining prospects.
3. Without an adequate pool of prospects, sales personnel eventually fail. Discuss this statement.

4. Outside firms specializing in prospecting are helpful in some selling situations. Identify sellers that might benefit from the use of such organizations. Why do you think this would be a useful approach for these firms?

5. Why do some salespeople prefer to canvass via telephone, rather than through personal contacts? Do you think sales leads uncovered by telephone contacts are as useful as those uncovered by personal contacts?

6. Salespeople should forget prospects who do not qualify at the present time. Comment on this statement.

7. Discuss the steps a salesperson should go through in qualifying a prospect. How can the salesperson's company help?

8. Develop a prospecting plan for new business majors at your college.

9. How can inquiries be shown to be valuable to a salesperson?

10. Discuss the differences between a trade show and an advertisement as sources of inquiries.

DISCUSSION QUESTIONS AND EXERCISES

1. Assume that you are a salesperson for the following firms. How would you go about prospecting for a:
   a. Producer of aluminum siding.
   b. Specialty steel manufacturer.
   c. High-price, quality furniture store.
   d. Lawn care firm.

2. What information should a salesperson collect about qualified prospects for:
   a. A uniformed guard service.
   b. Replacement tires for automobile fleets.
   c. A large book bindery.

3. How would you go about prospecting for funding sources in these nonbusiness efforts:
   a. A local Little League program.
   b. United Way.
   c. Second Chance House (a drug rehabilitation center supported by private funds).
   d. Catholic Social Services.

4. How would you go about qualifying a prospect for the following items:
   a. The trust services of a bank.
   b. A portable sewing machine.
   c. An African safari.
   d. A complete line of office supplies.
   e. A line of gourmet dog food (to buyers from grocery store chains).

5. Contact several experienced salespeople in different lines of business. Ask them how they prospect for new customers. Compile their responses in a brief three- to five-page report.

SALES DIALOG

Margaret Thayer is a new stockbroker in Rapid City, South Dakota. She is on the telephone with Gail Fredericks, a longtime acquaintance.

THAYER: Well, I am glad to hear that things are going well for you and Charlie. It sounds like you guys are really enjoying life.

FREDERICKS: Yes, we are . . . but we are also spending every dime both of us make.

THAYER: Gail, that is one of the reasons I called today. I would like to see you and Charlie start a regular investment program where you buy good quality stocks that pay dividends and have the potential for considerable appreciation in the future. Our firm has a list of suggested stocks. How does that sound to you?

FREDERICKS: Charlie and I would like to start investing, but to tell you the truth . . . we even wiped out our savings account with that last trip to Southern California. Maybe we could discuss this subject again in three or four months . . . once our savings account is replenished.

THAYER: Fine, let's plan a lunch about the time of the arts and crafts festival. In the meantime, do you know of anyone else who might be interested in investing?

FREDERICKS: As a matter of fact, I was talking to a woman at the racquetball club just the other evening . . . .

What do you think the results of this sales dialog will be?

CASE 6–1   WESTLEY SERVICES

For over 20 years, Westley Services has provided janitorial and maintenance products and services to a variety of commercial establishments in the New York metropolitan area. Peter Williamson, together with his newly hired marketing manager, Janus Whitmore, recently decided to reposition the firm to serve large accounts in New York and two new markets, Philadelphia and Washington, D.C. Response to an extensive advertising campaign plus calls placed to an 800 number have exceeded expectations.

The sales force, which Westley expanded from 36 to 45, has increased sales and produced more new customers. However, the number of large accounts has not increased and average customer size has declined, along with profits. After traveling with salespeople, Whitmore discovered that a telephone inquiry furnishes the salespeople with nothing more than a name and an address. The typical approach taken by the salesperson is to make a cold call on those who have inquired after sorting the inquiries by geographical location. When a salesperson is in a particular area, he or she also makes calls on other accounts that appear to have potential.

Questions
1. What is the problem with inquiries?
2. How would you change the salesperson's approach to selling products and services for Westley?
3. Should the selling approach be different for Philadelphia and Washington, D.C.? Explain.

CASE 6–2   VALLEY STEEL CORPORATION

Valley Steel Corporation of Yakima, Washington, has sold industrial shelving through a nationwide network of distributors for over 40 years. Although not the largest or best known in the industry, Valley Steel Corporation has grown at a rapid rate, particularly in the last five years. This recent growth parallels a decision to advertise extensively in trade publications primarily. The president of the corporation, Keith Diamond, feels advertising is the only way for a small firm relying on distributor salespeople to become known.

The problem Diamond sees is that even though growth has been adequate, sales leads coming from advertising are typically ignored by members of the distributors' sales forces. A study revealed that a typical salesperson made use of no more than 25 percent of the sales leads supplied. Lori Dewell, a salesperson for one of the largest distributors, is a case in point. She feels that sales leads have very little value in comparison with other forms of prospecting. In her words, "advertising inquiries are a poor substitute for knowing your territory and who is and is not a potential customer for industrial shelving." She goes on to add that a lot of shelving is purchased by her present customers. New customers will contact her.

Questions

1. Since Lori Dewell sells more shelving than anyone else in the country, is the generation of inquiries really important?

2. Should inquiries be forwarded directly to the distributor or should Valley Steel Corporation do the qualifying?

3. Assuming advertising inquiries are valuable, how would you suggest Valley Steel Corporation go about increasing use?

CHAPTER 7

Establishing a Customer Relationship

CHAPTER OBJECTIVES

1. To explain what a salesperson must do to establish the desired customer relationship.

2. To define preapproach and approach.

3. To list and explain the advantages of preparation.

4. To identify the critical elements in making a sales presentation.

5. To classify customers in making the presentation.

6. To define the levels of aggressiveness in selling.

7. To explain the effect of the product life cycle on the product/customer knowledge mix.

SALES CAREER PROFILE

CHRIS M. SCOTTO
CIGNA Financial Services

Forty-one-year-old Chris Scotto is a financial consultant with CIGNA Financial Services in Allentown, Pennsylvania. He has been with CIGNA for only six years and currently earns over $300,000 annually.

Scotto holds a bachelor's degree from Seton Hall University. He selected a career in selling because he enjoys meeting people and evaluating their financial alternatives. "During my college years, I sold men's clothing in a department store and progressed to management. From there, I went to the Keebler Biscuit Company as a field sales rep. I was soon promoted to divisional manager. I then went to the Bemis Company in Minneapolis; Bemis sells plastic packaging to corporations and small businesses. I stayed there for five years until the opportunity at CIGNA came along.

"What I like most about my job is the opportunity to run my own business and choose the clients with whom I want to work. This job gives me the chance to express myself, my beliefs, and to structure my business in a manner I feel will be successful."

In discussing his relationship with his customers, Scotto said, "I call them my clients and my friends. My relationship with them is based on the long-standing philosophy of the CIGNA Corporation, the 'serve first' philosophy. I recognize that a fine line between friendship and the business relationship must be maintained. And I am sure never to cross that line."

As for the future, Scotto said, "Many people ask if I will go on my own eventually. That really depends. However, I do feel very comfortable in saying that the support the staff and the financial division provide to consultants is extremely valuable. I question whether I would want to cut the ties with the CIGNA office since I would lose the daily support that has assisted me in being so successful up to this point."

When asked how he prepares, manages, and opens a sales interview, Scotto commented extensively on the preapproach and approach: "I believe it is very important that I know as much as I can about my potential client. It's impressive to show the client some preliminary investigative work. If it's a referral, I ask the referrer all about the potential clients, their work life, their personal life, and why my client is referring them to me. I am sure to have a sample fee-based, financial plan available, as well as a current client list so potential clients can see those individuals and corporations I have worked with in the past. I also have a list of our staff and their credentials. Before I get in front of the client, I want to be sure I am utilizing the three Bs: be positive, be relaxed, be prepared.

"I don't let my mouth flow when I'm in front of a client. Many times as salespeople we sell ourselves out of a sale, instead of listening. It's our responsibility to get the clients to talk, so we know where we stand during our approach.

147

"Let's set the scene. I'm about to enter a meeting. I do a final check and remember that I'm an entrepreneur and a showman, not an orator who gives a speech. I must consider myself a conversationalist who enjoys disturbing people about their problems, getting myself totally involved in their lives, so that I can understand what they are experiencing.

"Next is show time. Once in front of the client, I'm at that approach door. And, most important, I have to state my agenda. Who am I? Who is CIGNA Financial Services? Who are my staff? What about an advisory relationship? Very important: ask questions. I converse with the client to determine whether or not our services are applicable and, if so, to what degree. I always have an aggressive icebreaker comment. This lets the client know that I'm not there to sell something like every other salesperson in the world. I'm there to discuss the service that CIGNA provides. It is important to gain the client's confidence and respect so that I have their attention.

"Appearance and body language play a very important role in whether or not clients want to associate with salespeople and place their confidence in us. Think about it. Would you rather portray a casual look or the look of a successful banker? In other words, would I, if I were the client, buy from the CIGNA consultant sitting before me?

"I don't give the impression to the potential client that it is a do-or-die situation that I secure his or her business. Let the potential client know that this is an opportunity for each of us to evaluate the other. For a referred call, I utilize the strength of the referrer: 'I am quite sure, John, that if Jack did not think I would be of assistance to you he would not have referred me to you. The fact that I'm here means that he has confidence in me, so please ask questions so that we can evaluate how applicable our services are for you.'

"It is very important to get potential clients to talk, talk, and talk. However, I also remember to disturb, disturb, and disturb to motivate clients to think and to want to solve their problems. It's very important to use open-ended questions that get clients to elaborate and talk about their situations.

"Now let me comment on the best way to get a sales interview. I believe that the success I have attained is a direct result of the fact that I have recognized that one must secure good, qualified referrals.

"Looking back, my average income during the five years before coming with CIGNA was $32,000 a year along with an expense account and a company car. Today, I am earning over 10 times my earnings of six years ago; I feel this is quite an achievement, and I also know that there are no limits or boundaries on my future earnings."

For years the sales representative's responsibility to a furniture manufacturer such as Bassett was quite simple: sell as much furniture as possible. Today it is not that simple. Sales representatives have to contend with greater demands from both factories and retailers, while having fewer opportunities to sell. Another change is that distribution has become more selective. Where once a sales representative had 100 accounts, he or she now has 20 accounts who may produce greater sales, but require much more service than the previous 100 accounts. Obviously, mere effort on the part of the sales representative may not be enough. He or she must have knowledge of the finer points of marketing, advertising, and service that make the difference in making a sale or not making a sale. Joe Meadows, senior vice president at Bassett Furniture, points out some of the differences. "Today's sales representatives have to be more professional, more sophisticated, a id he or she must be a better businessperson. You don't see any more of the slap-them-on-the-back, get-the-order, and see-them-later routine. The sales representative must be a better detail person, a better marketing person, and he or she has to dedicate himself or herself to service to the dealer." [1]

DEVELOPING A CUSTOMER RELATIONSHIP

The professional salesperson concentrates on customer satisfaction. This is a demanding task made all the more difficult by the seemingly endless changes in the marketplace that are beyond the control of the salesperson or his or her company. The most obvious changes are with the customer, but there are also changes occurring with the company employing the salesperson as well as the competition. An effective salesperson must concentrate on establishing a strong relationship with the customer as opposed to selling propositions or "packaged deals."

A salesperson who makes a cold call on a small business to sell an accounting software package and a representative from a securities firm who makes a phone call to someone he or she does not know to offer tax-free bonds both make the same mistake. Namely, they have failed to establish a relationship with the customer where both parties, the seller and the buyer, work together to attain each other's purchasing goals on a long-term basis.

It is clearly the responsibility of the salesperson to establish the customer relationship. First, the salesperson must position himself or herself in relation to the customer. The salesperson must build trust and believability while at the same time determining how to educate the customer and gain the individual's interest. Some customers will want more, some less from the salesperson. Nevertheless, it will be necessary for the salesperson to determine the expectations and goals of each customer. The salesperson must remember that the purpose of his or her efforts is not to sell, but to get customers to buy.

The salesperson must also ask the right questions in order to know the customer's requirements and to reaffirm the signals the customer verbally and nonverbally provides. This allows the salesperson to focus on those products in his or her line that best suits the customer's requirements and those features/benefits that are the most important to the buyer in a particular purchasing situation. It also provides information that allows the salesperson to relate effectively with the customer and get valuable feedback.

Third, the salesperson must be a good listener as well as a good observer of nonverbal signals given by customers during a selling/buying situation. We already know that the selling/buying situation is a purposeful interaction. We also know that the customer would not be a party to the situation without purchasing goals. The salesperson must listen and look for signals from the customer, knowing that the information provided is not always perfect.

The salesperson must also be in control of himself or herself and the selling/buying situation at all times. The salesperson must lead the way step by step, providing information to ensure complete understanding on the part of the customer. The context of words and the balance in the approach to the customer is important. The salesperson is not an adversary and should not try to put the customer in a position where he or she feels defeated.

Finally, the salesperson must back up what he or she says by showing how the product fulfills the purchasing goals of the customer better than does that of the competition. In establishing a competitive edge, the salesperson has the responsibility of offering proof that his or her product has more value, saves money, saves time, is more saleable, and so forth.

Considerations in Building a Customer Relationship

The process of selling begins with the preapproach and approach steps. The **preapproach** is the salesperson's preparation for sales calls on specific customers. The **approach** is opening the sale and setting the stage for the sales presentation.

preapproach
preparation for a sales call

approach
opening of a sales interview with the right person

repurchase
continued purchases at the present level or increases in purchase volume

Sellers regard the preapproach and approach steps differently, depending on the status of the customer. If the salesperson is making a first call on a qualified prospect, the preapproach and the approach are important building blocks in gaining a customer for the company. They are crucial because the seller in all likelihood will get only one chance with this particular customer.

When the customer is already an active account, the preapproach and approach focus on repurchase. **Repurchase** can involve either continued purchases at the present level or an increase in purchase volume. Salespeople can increase purchase volume by persuading customers to buy more of the items they are already buying or to buy other products. Repurchase is also concerned with not losing accounts when customers for some reason cannot get what they want when they want it.

Frequently, inactive customers can be successfully approached. Several firms have found it profitable to have inside salespeople contact inactive customers. They can either try to sell over the phone or make arrangements for a sales call. Insurance firms are beginning to call on older customers to show how policies presently owned can be used to purchase increased insurance coverage.

Although unique approaches have worked for various salespeople in particular situations, most salespeople concentrate on specific goals during these steps:

1. Establish or reinforce a customer relationship.
2. Gain or retain a customer for the firm as opposed to making a sale.
3. Gather and provide information.

PREAPPROACH

By preparing for a sales call, the sales representative becomes doubly effective. The individual is able to react to the particular demands of the situation and at the same time be prepared to talk about specific and appropriate product benefits that may satisfy a customer's needs or wants. By preparing for a sales call, the salesperson can also anticipate possible objections the customer might have. Preparation also helps the salesperson know the prospect's:

- Position in the decision-making structure.
- Primary concern (price, service, product quality).
- Personal interests and hobbies.
- Receptivity to sales presentations.

Another advantage of preparation is the effect it has on the salesperson. A prepared sales representative has more personal confidence and is not as likely to make mistakes that lose the customer's respect. The salesperson also tends to be more enthusiastic.

The starting point is the customer sales plan. The salesperson considers four aspects of the anticipated selling situation. The first is what will be said, or the content of the sales presentation. Next, the salesperson has to consider the prospect and that person's role in the purchasing decision. This in turn affects the content of the sales message. Third, the salesperson must consider how to give the presentation, which can be thought of as the selling technique. Finally, there is the question of balance between imparting product knowledge and customer knowledge.

Contents of the Presentation

All any customer really wants to hear from any salesperson is how the individual can satisfy a particular purchasing goal. The most commonly voiced complaint about industrial sales personnel concerns their lack of product knowledge. Survey after survey shows that buyers feel the salespeople who call on them do not know enough about their respective products, do not present or demonstrate what they are selling, and rely primarily on price. Seemingly, salespeople can not translate product benefits into specific customer satisfactions. Buyers are inclined to feel that salespeople do not know enough about customer's problems, processes, or products. Buyers want solutions, not products.

Sales representatives, in introducing a new food product to a buyer for a grocery chain, should focus on how putting this product on the store shelves can make money for the retailer. Points of emphasis would include research on the target market, production quality, and the marketing support program.

PROFESSIONAL SELLING IN ACTION

LeCroy Corp.

For the first 20 years of its 25-year existence, LeCroy Corp. sold electronic testing equipment to a narrow market target, principally universities and labs. Five years ago, in an effort to grow faster, the firm introduced oscilloscopes priced from $10,000 to $25,000. With this change in product came a change in market target. Now the customer is the industrial buyer who is normally a buying group composed of purchasing agent, engineer, and project director. This is a dramatic change for the 46-member sales force, all of whom have technical backgrounds more suited to the previous market target.

The approach LeCroy takes is to find custo-mers through advertising in trade publications. Inquiries are followed up by scheduling demos with the customer. The philosophy of LeCroy is that if they can interest someone enough for a demo, their chances of selling the product are pretty good. A lingering problem for the company is adjustment of the sales force to the new customer.

SOURCE: Bill Kelley, "When Your Customer Base Changes," *Sales & Marketing Management*, February 1990, pp. 72–74. Reprinted by permission of Sales & Marketing Management. Copyright February 1990.

A salesperson who talks about product benefits for a particular customer will sell more than one who talks about product features. Customers do not want to hear about products; they want to know what the product can do for them. What determines a sale is more often customer knowledge than product knowledge. Professional salespeople do not tell customers, they sell customers.

A list of product features becomes the guide salespeople use to translate product benefits into customer satisfactions. The first step is to select features of particular interest to that customer. Reducing the number of features is logical because no customer is equally interested in all of them. With only a limited time to make the presentation, the seller must concentrate on what is most important to the customer or what are called choice criteria.

The salesperson who calls on a customer regularly has a reasonably good idea of the customer's primary interests; but when the seller makes the first call on a customer, the job of selecting appropriate product features is more formidable. Nevertheless, the representative should not let the apparent lack of information about the customer prevent the identification of important product features. Several sources of information are available about a new customer: (1) other customers, (2) published articles and directories, (3) annual reports, and (4) marketing research. The seller can often wait until the interview to get information directly from the customer. An insurance agent setting up an appointment, for example, might ask a prospective customer his or her age, the spouse's age, their number of dependents, occupations, present insurance coverage, and so forth.

Asking the Right Questions

It should be readily apparent that customers buy products for their own reasons, not those of the salesperson or the company he or she represents. The salesperson must ask questions of the customer to determine product interest and priorities in regard to features and benefits sought. Additionally, questions are a way of showing interest in the customer and as such are a means of building rapport with the customer.

Remembering that feedback is the sole goal of the salesperson in asking questions, we can divide questions into four general categories. These are opening questions, probing questions, clarifying questions, and reinforcing questions.

Opening questions set the stage for the sales presentation by building customer rapport and presenting the purpose of the sales call. If it is a first sales call, the salesperson may tie the question to pictures, certificates, or awards the customer has on display in his or her office. For example, "I see from those pictures you must be quite a hunter. Where do you usually hunt around here?" Another opening question for a first call is one tied to a current happening in the news. As an example, "Will the new government regulations have much of an effect on your business?"

When the salesperson has called upon the customer before, the questions are usually much more specific. For example, "What did your son have to say after his great game last week against Middleburg High?" Another way of phrasing an opening question to an established customer is to tie it to a product or service. A salesperson in the publishing business described how he tied asking an opening question to an offer of a service.

> When I was in the publishing business, I used to walk through the door with a reprint of an article. Laying the article in front of my prospect, I would say, "Hi, John. I saw this in the office this morning and I thought of you. Take a look. Have you seen this? What do you think of this?"

In addition to building rapport, opening questions should focus on the purpose of the sales call. Indeed, a criticism that can be leveled against salespeople is that they spend too much time in general conversation and not enough on the purpose of the sales call and the products and services they have to offer. Usually questions of this type center on the goals of the customer and his or her perceptions of current priorities. For example, a salesperson might ask the following question: "Could we take a few moments and review your needs in regard to a control mechanism for your smaller environmental systems?"

Probing questions are aimed at determining what products the customer is interested in and for what uses and under what conditions. Probing questions are also asked about why this product or products is desired in an effort to learn the buying strategy of the customer. The latter is particularly important in getting the customer to buy from you rather than from a competitor's sales representative.

Questions about products, uses, and operating conditions are fairly straightforward. To illustrate:

- What products are you interested in?
- How are you going to use the product?
- Under what conditions in your assembly process is the product to be used?
- Ideally, how would you want this problem solved?

Questions about the customer's buying strategy help you develop the desired customer relationship. As examples:

- How do you decide on whether you are going to make a purchase?
- Why are you interested in this product?
- How do you measure this particular criterion?
- What caused you to bring my firm into the picture as a possible supplier?

Clarifying questions are used by the salesperson to determine whether he or she has defined customer requirements and strategy accurately. In other words, the salesperson asks, "Is this really what you want?" Other examples of clarifying questions include:

- What is your opinion of this product feature?
- Would you purchase a product that doesn't have this feature?
- Would you share your thoughts on a product that has the following features and benefits?

Reinforcing questions are aimed at getting the customer to agree that he or she is making the best decision in buying the salesperson's product. Through probing and clarifying, the salesperson has determined product requirements and buying strategy. All that is left is for the customer to agree and in effect close himself or herself. While the salesperson will use open-ended questions that can not be answered with a yes or no as well as closed questions during the course of the sales presentation, it is extremely important to use the former in asking reinforcing questions. One type of question that has been found to be effective is to ask the customer to look into the future.

- Suppose it is three years from now and your boss has asked you to look back and review the decision to buy this product. What would cause you to rate this as a good buy for you and your company?
- Suppose you take this sales proposal to your boss. What would you say to convince her that it would be in her best interest to approve the purchase?

Another type of reinforcing question is the one that asks the customer whether the salesperson should proceed to the next step in the selling process. Such a question might be:

- Shall I prepare a quote?
- Can I submit a formal proposal complete with financing plan next Tuesday?

Listening Skills

Salespeople often skip a critical element in establishing the customer relationship, namely effective listening. While the reason for listening to the customer are self-explanatory, in practice the salesperson often concentrates on making his or her presentation of persuasive information and in doing so excludes what the customer is saying. What the salesperson has to realize is that the customer, through his or her questions and answers, is attempting to focus on the features and benefits of the salesperson's product and the expected satisfaction.

There are three roadblocks to effective communication that, if not addressed by the salesperson, may lead to lost sales. The first is skepticism on the part of the customer. The customer can be skeptical of what the product can do, the salesperson, and/or the salesperson's company. Detecting skepticism from customer questions and answers, the salesperson has to emphasize proof-selling techniques and testimonials. The purpose is to get customers to evaluate your claims.

Misunderstanding is the second roadblock to effective communication. Oftentimes misunderstanding results from the customer not having the same vocabulary as the salesperson. It can also result from differences in product interest and knowledge. Usually the salesperson can recognize misunderstanding from the answers to clarifying questions and alter his or her vocabulary and the context of the sales presentation to fit the customer.

The third, and largest, stumbling block will probably be conflicting goals. Upon encountering this, a new position must be sought for both the salesperson and his or her company as a supplier. Such was the case with P&G and its immediate customer, the retailer. The product approach used by P&G salespeople was at odds with the goals of the retailer. The P&G salesperson wanted more product exposure in terms of shelf "facings" and promotional effort at the expense of competing brands. The retailer, on the other hand, wanted a wide variety of brands to offer to customers with varying needs and desires. Also, with scanner data the retailer was not dependent on P&G sales information. Realizing this fundamental conflict in goals, P&G repositioned itself by having its sales staff take a customer approach and begin working with the retailer as a marketing partner in such areas as inventory, distribution, and sales promotion.[2]

On a more specific basis, the salesperson may not listen to the customer for several reasons. This in turn reduces the value of feedback from the customer.[3]

- *Content of the feedback.* The salesperson does not pay enough attention or tunes out what the customer is saying.
- *Characteristics of the speaker (customer).* These include enunciation, organization of feedback, clarity, speed of delivery, tone, inflections, and volume.
- *Distractions present.* Among the distractions are sounds, lights, and odors.
- *Mind set of the salesperson.* Salespeople will have certain attitudes about themselves, their products, and their customers.
- *Language used by the customer.* The feedback by the customer may be imprecise, emotional, or overly technical.
- *Listening speed.* The feedback from the customer is at 125–150 words a minute, while the salesperson can comprehend about 500 words a minute. This difference produces excess thinking time and perhaps impatience on the part of the salesperson.

Salespeople who are good listeners listen to everything, even what they feel is unimportant or derogatory. Remembering that listening speed is greater than speaking speed, the good listener focuses on the speaker and refuses to be distracted. The good listener also takes notes. This helps him or her to remember what the customer has said, particularly in replaying the sales call and preparing for subsequent calls.

Patience is also important in being a good listener. A salesperson should not interrupt the customer, but wait until the customer is through talking. After listening to what the customer has to say, the salesperson can then ask for explanations. By allowing the customer to say everything on his or her mind, the salesperson shows not only attentiveness, but interest as well in the customer.

Using Nonverbal Skills

Salespeople need to be more than good listeners in order to respond to the feedback of customers. Experts tell us that good communication is 55 percent body language, 38 percent voice, and only 7 percent content. It is possible that what a customer says is not what he or she conveys nonverbally through body movements, facial expressions, gestures, and eye contact. Consider the following situations.

- *Body movements.* Abrupt body movements are usually an indication of nervousness. A customer sends a positive message by leaning toward the salesperson. Conversely, the message will tend to be negative when the customer leans backward or away.

- *Facial expressions.* A smile or grimace is not as revealing as the customer's eye contact. Maintaining eye contact conveys honesty and interest. Avoiding eye contact is usually a sign of disinterest.
- *Hands, arms, and legs.* Fiddling hands usually mean a lack of composure and nervousness. Involuntary gestures such as handling a product, pointing, or using the hands to convey size often reveal feelings about a product. Folding one's arms is a defensive gesture and so, too, is crossing one's legs. Concern can be conveyed by the hand being placed on the face.

The Customer

Customers differ in their involvement in the various steps of the buying procedure. Salespeople often find customers' job titles misleading. There is little uniformity; people with the same job title can have entirely different jobs in various companies. The large number of job titles also limits their use as a way to classify customers. Frequently, people involved in purchasing a single product have different job titles with relatively minor differences in job descriptions.

A more accurate approach is to classify customers by the extent of their involvement at various stages in the buying process. A convenient way is to divide up the buying process into five steps:

1. Identifying the need.
2. Establishing product specifications.
3. Selecting the vendor.
4. Price negotiations.
5. Approving the expenditure.

A salesperson calling on a manufacturer might expect to meet with engineering and production personnel to center on needs and specifications. The purchasing department, on the other hand, would tend to be more concerned with vendor selection and price negotiations.

A knowledge of the buying process is a necessity for industrial salespeople, who may see any number of individuals in the course of making a sale. This knowledge may also be helpful in selling consumer goods. In buying clothing, for example, the style-conscious person would be involved with needs and specifications, while the interest of casual dressers would more likely be vendor selection and the actual expenditure.

Goals in Selling and Buying

Earlier we noted that both salespeople and customers have goals. The salesperson initiates the selling situation to make a first-time sale of a product, take a customer away from the competition, or maintain a customer for the company. The customer enters into a selling situation looking for a solution to a problem, an upgrading or enhancement of an item or activity, or assistance in meeting an objective. Figure 7–1 outlines the nine different selling situations that exist.

In an initial sale, the customer has not made a purchase of the product before. Therefore there is a good chance that the customer is not aware of the product's potential to provide a solution, help upgrade, or provide assistance in meeting an objective. When such is the case, the salesperson has to create awareness of the product's features and benefits and also present the industry benchmarks for product performance.

FIGURE 7–1   Matchup of selling goals and purchasing goals in selling situations

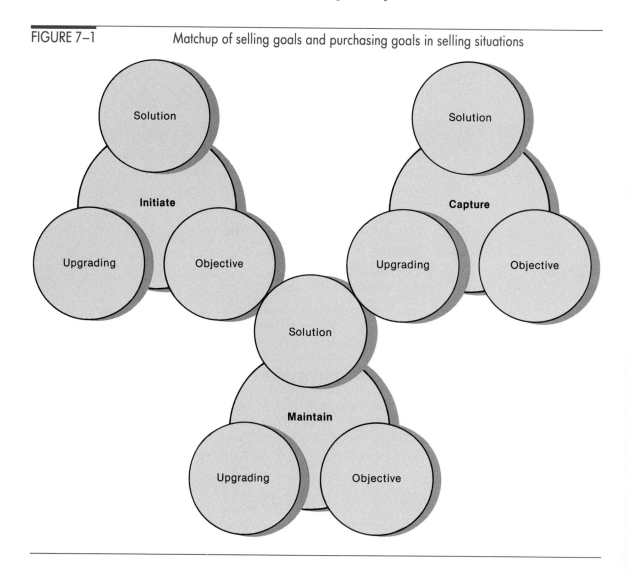

In capture selling, the salesperson must displace a competitor. The customer is knowledgeable about the product and has parameters against which to measure the product, including performance levels, quality levels, price, and service. The salesperson also has to contend with existing relationships with competitive salespeople. Superiority, not comparability, is the reason for changing to another source. Because it may not be possible to replace a competitor completely, the salesperson may ask for a portion of the business or to be next in line if problems develop with the present vendor.

In maintenance selling, the emphasis shifts from products and services to the salesperson and his or her company as a source. The salesperson builds trust and believability that instills customer confidence that his or her purchasing goals will be obtained in buying a product from this salesperson and this company. In other words, the salesperson wants the customer to look to him or her first to offer solutions, help upgrade, or provide assistance in reaching objectives.

Buying Roles and Styles

Customers will also vary according to how they visualize their role in the buying process and on their buying style. In a complex sale, a salesperson has to deal with several buying influences with different roles and possibly differing buying styles. A salesperson who is knowledgeable as to buying roles and style is able to do a better job of establishing his or her position in the selling situation and reacting to different pressures and demands of the customer relationship.

Four different buying roles can be identified. These are: (1) financial, (2) operational use, (3) supervisory use, and (4) administration.

Financial. The individual in the financial role is concerned solely with the financial aspects of the purchase. Such aspects include price, terms of sale, financing possibilities, and operational costs. It is vitally important that the salesperson identify who has the final approval for expenditures of funds. Obviously, the higher the price of the product, the higher in the organization the salesperson will have to go to secure final approval. This is because financial authority is usually related to organizational rank. When the purchase price needs board of directors' approval, the individual in the financial role is the one who will make the presentation to the board.

Operational Use. The individual in this role is chiefly concerned with the positive impact of the product on his or her job performance. More specifically, the operational-use buyer will have such questions as: "Will this product improve my performance?", "Is this product easy to work with?", and "Will I have to be retrained?" A forklift operator, an airline pilot, a secretary, and a cook for a restaurant are just a few examples of individuals who will have an operational-use role. It is important that the salesperson identify these individuals and make sure they are included in some fashion in the selling situation even if it necessitates a separate presentation.

Supervisory Use. The individual in the supervisory-use role is concerned primarily with the impact of the purchase on the area or department he or she controls. Individuals in this role have two major interests. First, does the product meet the specifications? Second, what are the benefits of the product in such terms as cost savings through less manpower, enhanced performance from workers, and ease of operation? For example, a midlevel production manager might be interested in how a salesperson's product affects scheduling of production.

Administration. The individual in the administration role is concerned with the procedures of purchasing, such as the submission of bids and information on the product. The purchasing agent typically assumes an administration role focusing on the details of purchasing, including order placement and monitoring of order progress through delivery to the customer. The influence of the individual in the administration role should never be underestimated because he or she is usually in a position to put up roadblocks for the salesperson. Particularly important is possible screening the administration buyer may accomplish. Administration-role buyers may keep salespeople from seeing those individuals in the organization who will make the purchase decision.

Another important aspect of the customer in establishing a relationship is his or her buying style. Some may be more responsive than others, while others may be more assertive, and still others more amiable. Figure 7–2 suggests that by combining buying style with buying role, the salesperson can obtain a better perspective of how a customer is likely to function in a selling situation. This in turn will help in preparing the approach, sales presentation, and particularly in anticipating objections and formulating responses to customer feedback.

Referring to Figure 7–2, likely buying styles tend to widen the differences between buying roles. Those in either a financial or administration role approach the buying decision in a structured, straightforward manner. The differences are that the former is cost conscious, while the latter wants to minimize risks from the decision. All but the financial buyer are concerned with how the decision will affect their status in the organization. Status, however, is defined differently for each buyer role. The administration buyer wants to keep from making mistakes, so he or she is prone to be conservative and will resist changes. The individual in the supervisory-use role is interested in recognition from superiors, while the operational-use buyer is interested in short-term improvements in his or her job performance.

FIGURE 7–2   Combining buying styles with buying roles

Financial	Administration
Approach: Straightforward, detailed, structured, cold, few expressions **Emphasis:** Cost details on features/benefits, product comparisons, short- and long-term results, custom-designed products, complete proposals, sales competence	**Approach:** Structured, straightforward, precise, proper, bureaucratic, conservative **Emphasis:** Features/benefits that minimize risks, tangible proof, no change, complete proposals in accepted form, guarantees
Operational use	**Supervisory use**
Approach: Imaginative, creative, expressive, open **Emphasis:** Job impact, short-term performance, service support, uses salesperson as buffer with superior	**Approach:** Responsive, personal, straightforward, short on time, own agenda **Emphasis:** Bottom line, buyer-seller relationship, options, choices, sales competence, wants credit for success

The Selling Technique

Salespeople must determine which approach to take with each customer. Success in a sales interview depends as much on selling technique as it does on product knowledge and sales preparation. Salespeople who have done a thorough job of preparing can select the selling technique that best fits a particular customer. As a result, the seller's knowledge is more evident to the customer and the likelihood of success improves.

One of the two common mistakes a salesperson can make is to assume that there are only two selling techniques: the hard sell and the soft sell. Actually, there are varying degrees of aggressiveness, with the hard sell representing the most aggressive approach and the soft sell the least aggressive approach. In the **hard sell,** the salesperson takes a forceful role, asking for the order repeatedly, pushing the customer toward a buying decision. Door-to-door selling and used car salespeople are normally thought of as hard sellers.

hard sell

aggressive sales approach

The **soft sell** is a less aggressive approach designed to develop a satisfactory relationship with the customer over a period of time through numerous sales calls. Aggressive sales tactics are not used for fear of offending customers and disrupting the buyer-seller relationship. The soft sell is low-key selling where customers never get the impression of being pushed into doing anything. Salespeople who call on their customers repeatedly tend to rely on the soft sell.

soft sell

low-key, nonthreatening sales approach

Another common mistake salespeople make is to adopt one selling technique and use it on all customers. Sellers using this approach are saying, in effect, that what worked with one customer should work with all. They forget that each customer is unique; therefore, each sales call requires a separate preparation.

Customers' involvement in the buying procedure can affect the level of aggressiveness used by salespeople. It is possible to be more aggressive with the purchasing agent, who is principally concerned with the decision of vendor selection, than with engineering personnel, who are identifying needs and determining specifications. Aggressiveness varies in relation to the degree of customer interest. The less interest customers have in products, the more aggressive the salesperson wants to be in the sales presentation.

Also, the degree of aggressiveness varies in relation to the customer's potential for repeat business. The more infrequent the sales call, the more aggressive the salesperson. Maximum aggressiveness is demonstrated in a one-call sale, in which the seller knows there is only one chance to sell the customer.

PRODUCT KNOWLEDGE VERSUS CUSTOMER KNOWLEDGE

A salesperson has the job of deciding whether to emphasize the product or the customer in preparing a sales presentation. The emphasis will change as the product passes through the stages of its life cycle. When a product is new to the market, the customer looks to the salesperson to provide the necessary information about the product's features and benefits. As the principal source of buying information, the salesperson's knowledge requirements are substantially product-oriented. The salesperson is telling the customer what the product can do, leaving it to the customer to translate this information into specific uses. The longer the product is on the market, the greater the need for the salesperson to shift his or her attention to the customer. This is because the primary concern of the customer as he or she gains knowledge of the product and becomes aware of industry benchmarks moves progressively from what the product can do, to how much it costs, to quality considerations, and finally to extras such as customer service. With this change, there is increasing competition. Products that have been on the market a considerable length of time and are readily available are called **shelf items.** Typically, the customer is thoroughly familiar with a shelf item and places orders on a routine basis.

shelf item

readily available product that has been on the market for a considerable time

The maturing of a product also means greater competition and the resulting need to differentiate through selling efforts. The shift to customer knowledge is a necessary outgrowth of product maturation and market maturation. It can be characterized as a shift from product applications to customer uses. The salesperson becomes increasingly important and the product less important.

APPROACH

The approach has two purposes: (1) getting an interview with the right person, and (2) opening the sale. If the sales representative cannot get to the right person, the quality of the opening makes little difference because the salesperson is talking to the wrong person at the wrong level. Conversely, getting to see the right person does not help much if the salesperson does a poor job of opening the interview.

Getting the Interview

Before trying to get an interview, the salesperson should double-check that the prospect is the proper person to see. Once this is established, any one of several techniques for getting an interview can be used. These include making a cold call, telephoning, getting an introduction from a third party, or writing a letter.

Selection of the specific technique depends on whether the customer is a new or an existing account and the customer's preferences. Obviously, trying to sell to someone neither the salesperson nor the company has had any prior dealing with requires a different technique than calling on a regular customer. There is no best way to approach all customers.

cold calls
unsolicited and unannounced sales calls

Cold calls are sales calls made without any prior contact with the customer. The salesperson stops in unannounced and asks to talk to the customer. It is important that the seller's identity and purpose be correctly presented; tricks, such as saying you are conducting a market survey or energy audit, create the wrong impression and are self-defeating. A potential problem in using the cold call is the amount of time the salesperson must spend waiting to see the customer. This is true even when customers set aside certain times for talking to sales personnel.

Use of the telephone to get an appointment is a good way to cut down on waiting time and travel expense. But salespeople must remember that the purpose of the call is to get an appointment, not to make a sale.

An introduction from a third party is very helpful. Sellers usually need something tangible by way of introduction from the third party, such as a business card with a notation, a letter of introduction, or a phone call to the customer.

Using a letter to get an appointment has two possible advantages: getting through to the customer and saving selling time. Many firms use standardized forms typed in a personal format. This relieves the salesperson of a disliked task, and there is a good chance that the form letter may do a better pre-conditioning job than one written by a salesperson.

PROFESSIONAL SELLING IN ACTION

Synesis Corp.

Synesis Corp., a small company with sales of less than $500,000, uses outside consultants to sell its computer-based training services. The contributions of the sales consultant are his or her ability to gain access to a qualified prospect and to be in a position to analyze the prospect's needs for the client. This is important to Synesis because once it gets a chance to bid on a project it closes the sale more than 70 percent of the time. The assistance of an outside consultant has been instrumental in getting jobs with AT&T and Independent Blue Cross of Philadelphia.

Although the number of consultants who function in a sales capacity is small, it is growing steadily, particularly in high-tech industries. Typically one-person organizations, consultants offer a wide range of marketing services. Payment is by flat fee or a commission-based payment schedule.

SOURCE: Martin Everett, "How Outsiders Can Get You Inside," *Sales & Marketing Management*, February 1990, pp. 56–57. Reprinted by permission of Sales & Marketing Management. Copyright February 1990.

Opening the Sale

Opening the sale involves creating a favorable first impression that provides a smooth transition from preparation to delivery of the sales message. First impressions do make a difference in selling. Poor impressions may result in customers not hearing much of what salespeople have to say in the remainder of the sales presentations. Asking customers to buy products is a possible opening. The advantage of such a forthright opening is that it gets customers talking about what they need or want in this product.

Above all, salespeople should not rely on personality to pave the way for the sales presentation. Good openings are based on knowing the product's benefits and their order of importance to customers.

Appearance is another way customers judge salespeople; consequently, poor appearance turns off many customers. A good appearance, on the other hand, builds customers' confidence and acceptance.

SUMMARY OF CHAPTER OBJECTIVES

1. **To explain what a salesperson must do to establish the desired customer relationship.**

The following guidelines can help establish a favorable customer relationship:

1. The salesperson must position himself or herself in relation to the customer.
2. The salesperson must ask the right questions.

3. The salesperson must be a good listener.
4. The salesperson must be in control of himself or herself as well as the selling/buying situation.
5. The salesperson must back up what he or she says.

2. To define preapproach and approach.

The preapproach is the salesperson's preparation for the sales call. The approach is opening the sale and setting the stage for the sales presentation.

3. To list and explain the advantages of preparation.

By preparing for a sales call, the salesperson can do a better job of reacting to the customer, talk about specifics with the customer, and demonstrate more confidence in the selling/buying situation.

4. To identify the critical elements in making a sales presentation.

To be the most effective, the salesperson must ask the right questions, have good listening skills, and be able to recognize nonverbal signals.

5. To classify customers in making the presentation.

Customers can be classified by level of involvement in the purchasing process, purchasing goals, buying role, and buying style.

6. To define the levels of aggressiveness in selling.

The hard sell is defined as a forceful role for the salesperson. In the soft sell, or less aggressive approach, the salesperson depends on establishing a satisfactory relationship with the customer.

7. To explain the effect of the product life cycle on the product/customer knowledge mix.

As a product moves through its life cycle, product knowledge becomes progressively less important and customer knowledge progressively more important. The salesperson moves from product applications to customer uses.

REVIEW QUESTIONS

1. Describe how the preapproach differs from the approach.
2. How can the salesperson become more effective through preparation?
3. Comment on this statement: Preparation gives a salesperson confidence.

4. Most products have a number of good features. Why should the salesperson limit a presentation to just a few?

5. Identify sales situations where cold calling is an essential aspect of selling.

6. Assume you are an insurance salesperson. Describe the husband and the wife in terms of buying role and buying style.

7. Develop a list of opening questions for selling a new line of ice cream to a buyer for a supermarket chain.

8. Define each of the different buying roles a customer might occupy.

9. Why might nonverbal signals be more important than verbal ones?

10. Differentiate between a hard sell and a soft sell.

DISCUSSION QUESTIONS AND EXERCISES

1. Select a product with which you are familiar and identify the primary benefits you would present to a potential buyer.

2. Suppose you are a buyer in the housewares department of a large department store. A salesperson you have not seen before calls on you with a new line of cookware. Should the salesperson stress product knowledge or customer knowledge?

3. For the following products, identify who in a family would be more interested in each of the stages of the buying process.
   a. Family automobile.
   b. Automobile tires.
   c. Life insurance.
   d. Set of dishes.

4. Select a product such as an appliance or furniture, and develop a list of probing questions.

5. Pair off with a fellow student and practice giving and noticing nonverbal signals. What have you learned from this exercise?

SALES DIALOG

Sam Giaconelli has worked for the Watson Company for over 12 years. The Watson Company produces and markets an extensive line of light industrial equipment such as conveyor belts and industrial supplies. He was recently transferred to northeastern Ohio where his three biggest accounts are General Motors in Lordstown, Ohio, Ford in Euclid, Ohio, and Chrysler in Twinsburg, Ohio. He and his new sales manager, Peter Haas, are having a cup of coffee and discussing a rather disastrous sales call on the General Motors assembly plant at Lordstown, Ohio.

HAAS: What went wrong, Sam, couldn't you get in to see a purchasing agent?

GIACONELLI: It is the first time for me ever, but the guard said that you have to have an appointment. I have been making sales calls for 12 years, and all you normally have to do is see to it that you know the office hours for Purchasing.

HAAS: They buy a lot from us. I really am surprised that when you talked to Purchasing over the phone at the gate they wouldn't see you.

GIACONELLI: The secretary in Purchasing told me that there was no record of my name, and their policy was appointments in advance for all new sellers. The guard also told me the same thing when I got off the line.

HAAS: Didn't you explain that GM has been doing business with us for at least five years?

GIACONELLI: We really don't do business with Purchasing in my experience. We go through maintenance and plant engineering.

HAAS: Did your old territory have any auto plants in it, Sam?

GIACONELLI: No, but one plant is a lot like any other, at least for our products.

HAAS: Have you had any problems with Ford and Chrysler?

GIACONELLI: I haven't called on them yet. I have tried to get into all the companies in Western Pennsylvania and the Youngstown-Warren area before tackling other companies.

What do you think the results of this sales dialog will be?

CASE 7–1 STRONGVILLE INDUSTRIES

Joan Dreyfus is developing a sales training program for Precision Tools, a division of Strongville Industries that markets a line of highly sophisticated machine tools. She has been with Precision Tools for six years as a salesperson, sales manager, and now an assistant to the vice president of sales.

In making a preliminary plan, she outlines the major tasks for a salesperson of a technical product line.

1. Determine the customer's type of business and the way they compete.
2. Determine the customer's position in the organization.
3. Determine the customer's primary interests—quality, price, consistency, or delivery.
4. Determine exact need—replacement, new purchase, and so forth.
5. Determine capabilities.
6. Determine authority to purchase.
7. Determine follow-up.

Questions

1. Has Dreyfus included all of the major points in making a sales call on a prospect? If not, what would you include?
2. Should Dreyfus include handling objections as a major sales task?
3. How would you emphasize customers' participation?

CASE 7–2 TEMPERATURE APPLIANCE CORPORATION

For the past 50 years, Temperature Appliance Corporation has been a quality leader in kitchen appliances. Last month it purchased a company that makes microwave ovens. The ovens are to be marketed under the TEMPCO label and sold through the same distributors that already handle TEMPCO ovens, ranges, refrigerators, and waste disposals. The competitive advantages of the microwave are price (the price is 20 percent below market competitors at each price level), sound construction (no leakage), and trouble-free performance (consumer rating service puts the TEMPCO oven at the top in this category). The competitive disadvantages are poor market representations by the previous company, lack of consumer recognition, and no dealer plan.

Susan Herschfield and Allen Thomas, two new sales representatives, have been assigned the job of developing a presentation for the new TEMPCO microwave ovens. This presentation is to be made at the next national sales meeting.

Herschfield and Thomas discussed what they should cover in the presentation and decided to skip the preparation phase because no new customer is involved. They will devote their time to supplying other sales reps with product features and the differences between the TEMPCO microwave oven and that of the competition.

Questions

1. Do you agree with Susan and Allen that preparation (preapproach) is not necessary as part of their presentation? Explain your answer.

2. What should be the mix of product knowledge and customer knowledge?

3. Undoubtedly, all the distributors now carry a competitor's line of microwave ovens. What possible benefits to distributors can you see in replacing or adding the TEMPCO product?

PART FOUR

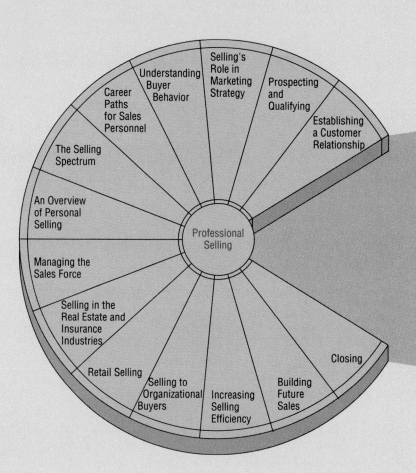

Selling's Role in Marketing Strategy

Understanding Buyer Behavior

Prospecting and Qualifying

Career Paths for Sales Personnel

Establishing a Customer Relationship

The Selling Spectrum

An Overview of Personal Selling

Professional Selling

Managing the Sales Force

Selling in the Real Estate and Insurance Industries

Closing

Retail Selling

Selling to Organizational Buyers

Increasing Selling Efficiency

Building Future Sales

Making the Sales Presentation

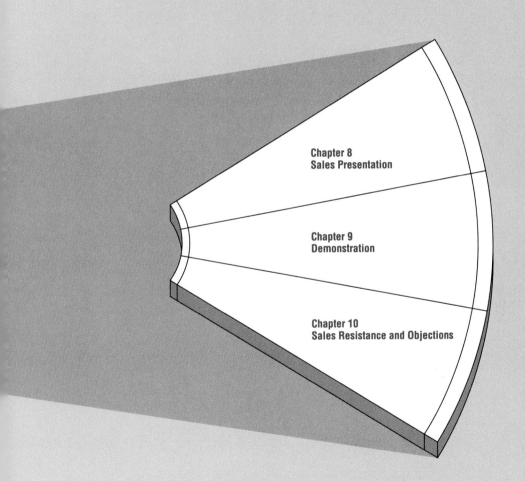

Chapter 8
Sales Presentation

Chapter 9
Demonstration

Chapter 10
Sales Resistance and Objections

CHAPTER 8

Sales Presentation

CHAPTER OBJECTIVES

1. To define sales presentation.

2. To define empathy as it relates to the sales presentation.

3. To explain the two salesperson-oriented approaches to the sales presentation.

4. To explain the two customer-oriented approaches to the sales presentation.

5. To define balanced selling.

6. To describe a canned sales presentation.

7. To list and explain sales tactics that increase the effectiveness of sales presentations.

SALES CAREER PROFILE

ANACIA PEREZ
International Paper Company

Anacia Perez is a senior account manager for White Papers Group of the International Paper Company. Perez, who is based in New York City, holds a bachelor's degree in psychology from Hunter College. She is currently studying for an MBA at Fordham University. Her interests are real estate, traveling, and fishing.

When asked why she entered sales, Perez observed, "I selected a career in selling as a stepping-stone to corporate management. At International Paper, sales is viewed as a necessary element in developing employees and I found it was by far the best way to learn the workings of the paper industry.

"I selected International Paper primarily because it's a major corporation. I came from a small publishing company. I felt working at a large company would give me mobility. My publishing background provided the connection with the paper industry."

Perez thinks that International Paper was picked as one of America's 100 top sales companies for three specific reasons: "One, I think we make good products. Two, we have an excellent customer base. And, three, salespeople at International Paper are allowed the freedom to develop their own styles and to manage their accounts."

Perez was originally hired as a customer service representative. After shifting to field sales in 1980, her progress has been rapid. She was promoted from a sales representative to a senior sales rep; then to senior account executive; and finally, to her current position.

Perez describes her sales training at International Paper: "My training program in customer service can best be described as the sink or swim school of training. My sales training, however, was substantially better. Although I was given account responsibility immediately, I was sent to courses that included business presentations, effective negotiating, selling skills, and so on. Throughout my International Paper selling career, the company has offered continuing sales courses in which we are all expected to participate."

Perez goes on to describe her current job: "The part of my job that I enjoy the most is being in the field with my accounts. I particularly enjoy working with my customer sales force in developing a new piece of business. I also enjoy giving presentations.

"My relationship with my sales peers must be, and is, a good one. In many cases, our business overlaps and we must work closely together to ensure that all of us are saying the same thing.

"My relationship with my customers must undoubtedly be a strong one. They must be able to rely on me as their paper professional. Their respect, trust, and confidence in me are essential.

"My relationship with sales management is also an integral part of my job. By participating with me on account calls as I select them, they support our customer-supplier relationships. And their leadership support basically keeps our efforts on track with the company's objective."

Describing the approach she uses in a sales presentation, Perez said, "According to the information in your chapter, my approach to selling is what you consider the balanced approach. I certainly agree that to be successful, salespeople must combine a salesperson-oriented approach by creating the awareness, the interest, the desire, and the action. However, I do balance that approach by considering the customer's interests and needs."

Discussing the best presentation she has ever made, Perez comments, "It was the presentation in which I introduced a new product to my customer sales force. The product was one that I knew customers needed and were most anxious for. International Paper produced promotional material illustrating the excellent printing properties of this new grade of paper. The theme of the printed promotion was magic. I knew that informing my customers of the product availability and simply handing out the promotional material would probably meet their needs. However, I wanted to accomplish more. Since I deal with commodity paper, one of the most important things for me to accomplish in selling is to be able to differentiate myself from my competition. This particular promotion gave me that opportunity while, at the same time, satisfying my customers' needs.

"I invited the salespeople to a local restaurant. With the help of the president of the company, all the salespeople were in attendance. When conducting presentations, I usually rely on visuals. In this case, I used slides. They not only made the point but they served as a cue for me since I never use a script or a canned presentation.

"Since the theme of the promotion piece was magic, I asked a professional magician to teach me six magic tricks all related to paper. I did the presentation in full tuxedo, including a top hat and cane. I even called on one of the salespeople to be my assistant during the magic tricks. Needless to say, I had their undivided attention.

"I consider this my best presentation because I was able to cover all the features and benefits of the product, and gave the customers the information they needed from their perspective. By differentiating myself from my competition, I ended up gaining additional overall business from these salespeople.

"Have I ever had a presentation that flopped? No, I cannot say that I have, and that's primarily because I'm always prepared and I practice before I conduct a presentation. I also know my customers well. I know what will come across and what will not. I always try to set the right environment and my product knowledge allows me to tackle questions. But, most of all, I don't think I've had a flop because I like what I do."

Effective presentations are the key to successful selling at Federal Express. The firm's salespeople use what they call the "5 percent rule." This rule is based on the principle that you never know how big your opportunities are until you see the right people and ask the right questions. What the rule says in effect is that when calling upon an individual, let's say the head of manufacturing, he or she knows 95 percent of what is important in manufacturing, but only about 5 percent of what is important in any other department. Thus, a sales rep cannot learn all there is to learn about a company's business needs from just one contact.

As a case in point, Bill Razzouk, Vice President of U.S. Sales, and Alan Meismer, a field sales rep from Chicago, called on an account where Federal Express was doing all of the customer's air express business; this amounted to about $250,000 a year. When asked about ground shipments, the customer contact did not know anything about them. After talking to other managers, the value of ground shipments was estimated to be over $8 million. Within two weeks Meismer was able to convert $1 million worth of ground shipments to air and within a year this figure rose to $2.5 million.[1]

SELECTING A SALES PRESENTATION APPROACH

The sales presentation is the sales message delivered by the salesperson to the customer. The sales presentation is typically divided into three parts: introduction, presenting reasons to buy, and close. Martin Shafiroff, a managing director of Shearson-Lehman Brothers-American Express, feels that salespeople spend too much time presenting reasons to buy and not enough time requesting an order. The approach he uses with success is to concentrate on requesting the order and, while the customer is considering his or her decision, reinforce with reasons why a favorable purchase decision should be made.[2]

While we normally think of the customer as one individual, more and more sales presentations have to be made to groups of individuals such as a buying committee, buying center, or husband-and-wife team. Because results measure how good a sales presentation is, it follows that group buying has made it even more imperative for the salesperson to select an approach that is effective and stimulates interest on the part of the customer.

empathy
ability to understand customer's viewpoint

How successful the sales presentation is depends on the salesperson's ability to understand how the customer views his or her own business and where the salesperson's products fit into this picture. This trait called **empathy** allows the salesperson to focus his or her efforts on maximizing the advantages of direct, two-way communication. Without empathy, the salesperson in delivering the sales message is comparable to an advertisement. Both hit the target, but neither scores a bull's eye. The reason is that the focus is on what the seller wants to happen rather than what a customer wants to happen from purchasing and using a product.

The salesperson with empathy asks three questions in planning his or her sales presentation. These are:

1. What products do I have that benefit the customer?
2. What specific benefits will the customer be especially interested in?
3. What reactions can be expected from the customer and what modifications will I need to make?

APPROACHES TO THE SALES PRESENTATION

The various approaches to selling are either salesperson-oriented or customer-oriented. The salesperson-oriented approaches involve a formula. The customer-oriented approaches are need satisfaction and interaction. Balanced selling is a proposed approach combining the advantages of both of these orientations.

Salesperson-Oriented Approaches

AIDA

standardized learning approach of awareness, interest, desire, and action

A basic selling formula is the standardized learning approach, **AIDA.** The sales presentation is a cumulative process starting with awareness and ending when the customer takes some buying action (see Figure 8–1). The pattern of this structured approach is, first, awareness, followed in turn by interest, desire, and action.

In applying the AIDA formula, salespeople first create awareness. There are a number of ways to do this. One of the most common is to translate a product into specific benefits for the customer. Another way is to begin with questions to learn the customer's primary interests. Once this is done, the task is to translate awareness into interest and then to convert interest into desire. Some look on this third step as getting customers to acknowledge that the product answers some conscious need or want. Salespeople who have developed sufficient customer desire for the product can then ask for the order and get buyers' action. Assuming the goals of the previous steps have been accomplished, the strength of product desire is enough to cause customers to make the purchase.

Two other steps can be added to this selling formula. One, to be inserted between desire and action, is called *conviction.* Conviction is intensified desire for the product, particularly in light of the asking price. The job of the salesperson is to convince the customer that the benefits of the product make it superior to that of the competition and worth the asking price.

The other step, called *satisfaction,* is confirmation of the correctness of the purchasing decision after the action has taken place. The salesperson has the job of making sure the customer is getting what is expected from the

---

FIGURE 8–1   The AIDA learning process in promotion

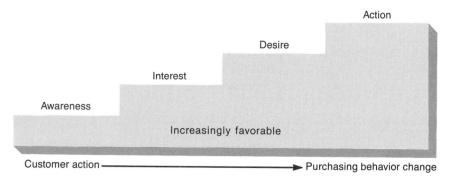

product. An important part of this involves showing the customer how to use the product, so that he or she obtains expected satisfaction.

Those who favor the formula approach feel it gives salespeople a logical framework for presenting all possible sales ideas. Sellers often base highly structured or *canned* presentations (to be discussed later) on a selling formula. Successful utilization of a selling formula depends on whether salespeople can lead customers through the various steps. The question is, can they lead customers from awareness to interest, desire, and, finally, buying action?

An obvious objection to the selling formula is that it concentrates on salespersons' actions without any regard for customers' interests. Another objection is that the selling formula tends to treat all customers alike, which removes the advantage sellers have in being able to adjust to individual differences. Further, the effect of communication is not always the same, and salespeople cannot be sure customers will respond in the sequence indicated by the standardized learning approach.

Stimulus-Response

stimulus-response approach

assumes that specific actions by a salesperson stimulate a customer to buy

The **stimulus-response approach** to the sales presentation assumes that what a salesperson says triggers a predictable response from the buyer, which leads to buying action. Like the AIDA formula, the stimulus-response approach lends itself to a scripted sales presentation. More often than not, the stimulus is emotional in nature. Fear, for example, can be used to sell life and health insurance, security systems, as well as pest control programs. Other common emotional stimuli are prestige, earning or saving money, scarcity (there are only a few left), and price.

Some examples of stimuli and expected responses are as follows:

Stimulus . . . A check from an insurance company doesn't replace a loved one, but it does help with all the troublesome bills.

Expected Response . . . Buy insurance to offset the fear of financial burdens as the result of death.

Stimulus . . . A lot of teachers find that their retirement plans don't meet their needs when there is a major age difference between spouses. The reduction in benefits when the wife is considerably younger than the husband can be as much as 40 percent.

Expected Response . . . Buy insurance on the husband so that it will provide benefits for the widow rather than serve as a retirement policy.

Stimulus . . . Have you seen the damage a termite can do to a house?

Expected Response . . . Buy a pest control program that includes an inspection.

The stimulus-response approach is based on the assumption that all customers will buy a product for the same reason. This is untrue in that different customers or the same customer in different selling situations will tend to react differently to the same stimulus. The stimulus-response approach also takes away all of the salesperson's flexibility. A response other than the expected one disrupts the sales presentation. These two drawbacks, plus the obvious lack of customer orientation, severely limits the appropriateness of this approach.

Need Satisfaction

need-satisfaction approach

customer-oriented sales approach based on customer's needs

One of the customer-oriented approaches is the **need-satisfaction approach.** Figure 8–2 pictures the sales presentation as having three parts. Participation by the customer is greatest at the beginning of the sales presentation and gradually diminishes as the salesperson determines needs, gets recognition of these needs, and presents a solution. In the first part, the salesperson queries the customer to determine specific needs, using questions designed to get the customer talking. With the technique called bottom-line selling, three questions are asked.[3] The first question is: What has worked for you (the customer) in the past? It is designed to determine what has been successful and how the customer defines success. The second question is: What hasn't worked in the past? And the third question is: What do you (the customer) want to achieve in the next few years? After identifying the customer's needs, the salesperson attempts to get the customer to recognize these needs, a step that often involves making the customer conscious of them. Finally, the salesperson shows the customer how the product being offered can solve those needs. By first finding out and making sure of the customer's needs, the salesperson does not waste time talking about all the features of a product. Instead, the salesperson picks out those that have the greatest impact on the customer. (This process can also be part of the preapproach, as noted in Chapter 7.)

FIGURE 8–2   Need-satisfaction approach

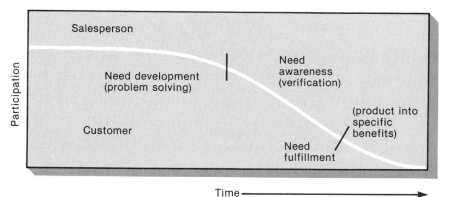

As an example illustrating the need-satisfaction approach to the sales presentation, suppose a new car salesperson approaches a customer on the showroom floor, and the following conversation takes place:

SALESPERSON: Do you have any particular car in mind?

CUSTOMER: I sure like this four-door model, but I'm afraid it's not big enough.

SALESPERSON: Are you afraid there is not enough legroom?

CUSTOMER: No, I want something to use every day in my work. I am a finish carpenter and have driven a pickup truck, camper, and sedan. Right now I am driving a pickup, but I don't like it.

SALESPERSON: Why don't you like your truck, may I ask?

CUSTOMER: Well, it's still a truck. No matter what you add to it, it still handles like a truck. When I had the sedan, I liked to drive it, but it just wasn't big enough for all my tools. I gave the sedan to my wife, and she is still driving it. Another thing, pickups and campers invite theft. I have had my pickup broken into several times, while the sedan parked next to it was not touched.

SALESPERSON: Let me see if I have this right. You need space to store your tools, but you like the luxury and handling of an automobile. Is that right?

CUSTOMER: Now I would say you are almost right. I want something nice to drive and, at the same time, something I can use.

SALESPERSON: Let's go over here and take a look at our best station wagon. Here, let me open the front door. Notice the room. This car also gets good gas mileage.

CUSTOMER: Those seats are good-looking.

SALESPERSON: Come back here; I'll open the tailgate. Notice the well between the seats. There is a lot of room down there, and the cover can be locked up. In addition, there is a small storage compartment over one of the back wheels that can be locked, too.

CUSTOMER: You know, this is exactly what I have been looking for. Let me take a look at that sticker price.

The emphasis in need satisfaction is on the salesperson and what he or she does. It is customer-oriented principally because of the early determination of customers' needs; however, needs are the only customer aspect considered.[4]

Interaction

The interactive approach gives customers a more active role than any of the others. The basis for success with this approach is the match of the salesperson's and the customer's personalities. Research has shown that the more closely the salesperson's and customer's personalities align, the more likely it is that a sale will take place.

Using an interactive approach, salespeople operate in the way their customers want them to operate. For example, a sales rep may be strictly an information source in one selling situation, while in another he or she may be part of the decision process. Partnership selling as practiced by P&G and Scott Paper, among others, is based on an interactive approach.

Balanced Selling

None of the preceding approaches completely answers the question of how salespeople can go about making their best sales presentation. Each approach has certain advantages and disadvantages. Salesperson-oriented approaches place too great an emphasis on the salesperson and what he or she does, as opposed to the customer. Yet these approaches offer this important advice to salespeople:

1. The sales presentation is a series of building blocks aimed at favorable buyer action (selling formula).
2. The actions of the salesperson can trigger appropriate responses from the customer (stimulus-response).

balanced selling

sales approach that balances customer and salesperson orientations in selling

Borrowing the strong points of the salesperson-oriented approach and combining them with the customer orientation of need satisfaction and interaction results in a new approach called **balanced selling.** In balanced selling, the sales presentation mixes customer orientation and salesperson control. The stage of the interview determines the customer's participation.

Salespeople keep these three things in mind when using the balanced-selling approach:

1. It is the salesperson's job to fit the company's product line to the needs or wants of the customer, rather than vice versa.
2. It is the salesperson's job to control the sales interview by means of the sales presentation.
3. It is the salesperson's job to differentiate between his or her products and those of competitors in terms of primary interest to the customer. For example, if the customer is primarily interested in quality, then comparisons should be between products in terms of quality.

Customer orientation in the sales presentation should not be confused with participation. *Participation,* or customers' active involvement in sales presentations, is used as a tool by salespeople to orient themselves to customers and to achieve the desired interaction. In the beginning stages of the presentation, salespeople ask questions to determine the customer's needs or wants or to see if they have the customer's attention and interest. It is a mistake to think that simply getting customers to talk is customer orientation.

Customers usually participate more in the early stages of the sales presentation than in later ones. One reason for this is that customers' answers

PROFESSIONAL SELLING IN ACTION

Scott Paper Reorganizes Its Sales Force

Scott Paper operates in one of the nation's most intensively competitive markets where every inch of retail shelf space is battled for, tooth and nail. To cope with these challenges, Scott Paper restructured its sales force, instituted a performance program for salespeople, and reinforced its product line with Softkins, a cleansing towel, and Viva Designer Collection, a complete set of paper dinnerware. The most important changes have been in the restructured sales force and the emphasis on quality sales performance.

Instead of a geographic territory and compensation based on how well the region performed, Scott salespeople are now assigned to customers and all their operations regardless of geographic location. With this national account strategy, compensation is based on how profitable these customers are to Scott. This restructuring, called "Stakeholder Alignment," has allowed salespeople to become partners with their customers in thinking about customer profit needs, what their strategy is, what they want to do with their shelf space, and what their plans are for the future.

The performance for salespeople specifies the role or mission of the salesperson and shows how each salesperson can develop his own goals and standards. The emphasis has shifted from sales volume to profit from sales.

SOURCE: "Excellence," *Sales & Marketing Management,* June 1989, p. 43. Reprinted by permission of Sales & Marketing Management. Copyright June 1989.

to questions tend to be longer at first. For example, a salesperson asks the customer to go into detail about problems to facilitate the identification of needs. In the later stages of the sales presentation, the customer may only have to give yes or no answers or indicate a preference.

The salesperson's interaction with each customer should be based on a thorough knowledge of that customer. Much of the information about customers becomes available to salespeople while they prepare their sales presentations (the preapproach discussed in Chapter 7). The rest of the information has to be developed during the course of the sales presentation. In large part, how much empathy the salesperson has with the customer's point of view determines how successful he or she is in obtaining specific and timely information about each customer.

CANNED AND VARIABLE SALES PRESENTATIONS

canned sales presentation
memorized or highly structured sales presentation

A great deal of controversy surrounds the question of how much structure is too much in the sales presentation. At one extreme are those who hold that **canned sales presentations,** or highly structured, scripted presentations, are best. They feel that canned presentations give them a degree of control over the selling situation that they cannot obtain in any other way. With this approach, sellers do not miss any points or make any unethical commitments.

A well-organized canned presentation anticipates and answers stumbling blocks such as customer objectives. New salespeople often favor canned presentations that give them confidence. Certainly sales training and supervision are easier when canned presentations are taught to salespeople.

Other sales personnel believe that the distinctiveness of each selling situation makes canned presentations useless because the salesperson reacts in mechanical terms, the presentations are developed for only one selling situation, or they are too generalized. Not only do they take away from much of the seller's inherent flexibility, but uniform presentations cannot be used when calls are made on the same customer again and again. Although it is difficult to develop presentations for each item in the product line, customers recognize canned presentations because they usually sound memorized and lack distinctiveness.

Which presentation method is best? The answer to this question often depends on whether industrial or consumer salespeople are involved. Figure 8–3 shows the mean rankings for tailored, partially structured, and canned sales presentations on a 1-to-5 scale. Industrial salespeople prefer the first two approaches significantly more than their consumer goods counterparts. By contrast, more consumer sales personnel said that a canned approach is significantly important, perhaps because they will not be calling on the same customer.

GUIDELINES FOR SALES PRESENTATIONS

Balanced selling, through interaction, mixes equal parts of customer orientation and control by the salesperson. Interaction, the basic ingredient in the selling situation, is affected by how much and how valuable the customer's participation is, how credible the salesperson appears to the customer, and how effective the salesperson is in making the sales presentation. Regardless of which basic approach is used, a successful salesperson sells what the customer wants to buy.

Customer Participation

Customer participation tells sellers what they need to know—not only the customer's needs or wants but also other characteristics, such as personality traits that affect interaction. Later in the sales interview, customer participation provides cues that signal the salesperson's progress in making the sale.

Salespeople encourage participation from customers through questions framed to obtain information, particularly early in the sales presentation. Questions designed to determine their needs or wants should allow the customers to think logically about the subject. Later questions should keep the customers on the subject of those needs and wants. Although all questions

---

FIGURE 8–3   Relative rankings of various sales presentation formats

	Mean Rankings (1-to-5 scale)	
Presentation	Industrial Salespeople	Consumer Salespeople
Tailored sales: Make a sales presentation that is specifically tailored to each prospect.	4.33	4.03
Partially standardized sales: Make a sales presentation that is slightly different for each prospect.	3.66	3.33
Standardized sales: Make the same sales presentation to all prospects.	1.68	2.11

Source: Adopted from Robert E. Hite and Joseph A. Bellizzi, "Differences in the Importance of Selling Techniques between Consumer and Industrial Salespeople," *Journal of Personal Selling & Sales Management,* November 1985, p. 25.

---

should focus on getting the appropriate response, some are designed to get customers talking. Still others help vent customers' dissatisfaction with the present state of affairs. This is common, for example, in insurance selling.

Salespeople sometimes have trouble developing questions to ascertain the needed information. While shifting from seeking information to showing how the product can satisfy the customers' needs or wants, salespeople can ask questions to check the progress being made. Depending on customers' reactions, salespersons may make some sort of adjustment in the sales presentation. Techniques in asking questions are discussed in Chapter 7.

Credibility

For the sales presentation to be persuasive, the salesperson must have credibility or trustworthiness in the customer's mind. Credibility is a result of:

- Recognition as an expert in the field. (I know what I am talking about in terms of end uses, your problems, your business.)
- Establishment of a strong relationship with the customer. (Our interests are the same.)

Age, experience, and similar social background are important factors in establishing credibility. Age and experience can indicate the salesperson's expertise to the customer, who feels that "she has been in this business for a long time, and she should know what she is talking about." Door-to-door salespeople experience more success, for example, in middle-income neigh-borhoods because they match those customers more closely on a social basis than they do in either high-income or low-income neighborhoods.

Knowledge about customers can help salespeople achieve interaction and indicate expertise. One way to demonstrate competence is for salespeople to use the same terms their customers do; in other words, salespeople and customers should speak the same language.

Because sales assignments based on matching the salesperson's and cus-tomer's characteristics are desirable but often impractical, salespeople should be matched to a variety of customers. The basis for these matches should be what the salesperson and each customer have in common, particularly in regard to customer characteristics that affect the sale. The most important of the customer's characteristics are needs and wants. The success a sales-person has in convincing a customer that they have common interests depends on:

- The orientation of the salesperson to the customer.
- The ability of the salesperson to interact with the customer.

The salesperson must use what he or she knows about a customer to persuade the customer that their interests are the same. The job is much easier if the customer knows that the buyer-seller relationship will continue over a period of time. In a one-time sale, such as that of a new house, the salesperson who emphasizes after-sale service is more persuasive.

In overcoming the customer's idea that salespeople say anything to get a sale, the salesperson should use knowledge and sales tactics to interact with the customer and convince the customer this is not so.

Tactics in Sales Presentations

Salespeople can increase their effectiveness in making sales presentations in several ways. Each sales representative should develop an inventory of sales tactics that fit particular selling situations or that apply regardless of product or customer. Some suggested tactics are:

1. *Identify and confirm the customer's needs before attempting to supply product information.* A salesperson can get so anxious to show the customer the product that he or she entirely forgets about the customer's needs. Accord-ing to sales folklore, in attempting to show the cleaning power of a product, a vacuum-cleaner salesperson threw dirt all over a living room rug, only to discover that the house had no electricity! The customer orientation in bal-anced selling dictates putting needs before product information. Remember that selling is essentially supplying what the customer wants, not telling customers about products.

A SALES MANAGEMENT NOTE

Dealing with Prospect Stress

Prospect stress can be a barrier to developing an effective buyer-seller relationship. What often happens is that the sales rep experiences stress because he or she knows that the customer is not likely to listen as closely as desired and is less likely to be responsive to the sales presentation. Sensing stress in the sales rep, the customer experiences his or her own stress and becomes more resistant to the sales presentation and taking buying action. This in turn causes the sales rep to push even harder as stress continues to grow for both parties.

There are several causes of customer stress. One is a distrust by the customer of salespeople in general. It may also be possible that the customer feeling dominated by a salesperson will develop defensive reactions in the form of stress. Yet another reason for stress is that many people may feel uncomfortable in making a decision, particularly one that involves a change.

In dealing with stress the salesperson must:

1. Clearly establish what he or she wants to accomplish (sales call objective).
2. Put the customer at ease by using the subtle clues he or she provides.
3. Establish trust in the eyes of the customer.
4. Make sure he or she is moving at the customer's pace and not attempting to force the issue.
5. Speak unhurriedly to create calmness in the customer as a listener.

SOURCE: Kevin J. Corcoran, "Dealing with the Uptight Prospect," *Sales & Marketing Management,* October 1989, pp. 109–10. Reprinted by permission of Sales & Marketing Management. Copyright October 1989.

2. *Listen carefully to what the customer says and how it is said.* Salespeople should always be good listeners, because this allows interacting with customers. The manner in which customers say things and their involuntary reactions are also important. These signals can indicate that the customer is willing to buy or that he or she has a serious objection to one or more aspects of the sales presentation.

3. *Give the customer a clear view of product benefits.* Customers should not be expected to blindly accept the salesperson's claim of product benefit. They must understand the product's features and benefits and be able to talk about them in their own words. This understanding acts to reinforce the reasons for purchasing the particular product and moves the customer closer to the salesperson's sales goal.

4. *Give the product information that is most desirable to the customer first and the least desirable information last.* For a customer who is extremely cost conscious, for example, the best approach would be to talk first about the operational savings in using the product.

5. *Use two-sided arguments that present the side favoring the product first.* What is presented first to customers tend to dominate their thinking. There is also a good chance that customers will commit themselves to the first argument before hearing the other one.

6. *Make any effort to sell other products in your line*. Concentrate especially on those that enhance the value of the product being purchased. These would include accessories, supplies, and replacements.

7. *Review how the product satisfies the customer's needs or wants*. Sales personnel must reinforce the product benefits to a customer. This review often acts as a form of closing (see Chapter 10).

Team Selling and Group Selling

team selling
more than one sales rep
calls on a customer

Interaction is a significant problem when more than two people are involved in the selling situation. In **team selling,** more than one salesperson calls on a customer, and there is limited opportunity to interact individually with the customer. Sales presentations in this situation are usually highly structured and rely extensively on audiovisual aids. Each salesperson may or may not play a role in the presentation. The only real opportunities a salesperson may have for interaction in team selling could come at the end of the presentation and during breaks.

Team presentations may also be made to groups of customers from the same organization or different organizations. In this case, salespeople should pair off with customers at every opportunity. Even though customer feedback does not allow immediate adjustment in the sales presentation, it helps in planning subsequent presentations. Moreover, pairing off emphasizes the customer's importance as an individual rather than just as a member of a group.

group selling
salesperson makes
presentation to more than
one customer

In **group selling,** a salesperson makes a presentation to more than one customer. This is most likely in an industrial situation. Instead of seeing each interested person individually and making sales presentations to every one, the salesperson makes a single presentation to a group of customers.

Industrial salespeople are not the only ones who make presentations to a group. Insurance agents, stockbrokers, and real estate agents are just a few examples of salespeople who regularly sell to groups rather than single customers.

The problem for the salesperson in group selling is interaction, whether the group is 2 or 20. The salesperson not only must try to get some interaction with each member of the group but also must realize that the members of the group are interacting with one another. To help this interaction, the salesperson should classify the members of the group as to their roles in the specific purchase decision and how each impacts the buying process.

How successful the salesperson is in interacting depends on how well prepared he or she is before starting the presentation. Selling to a group requires significant planning. The one sales tactic that is of vital importance in this situation is structuring the meeting to get the participation of all the members of the buying group and not letting anyone feel ignored. This tactic is also very difficult. Suppose a salesperson has just finished a sales presentation on a new component part for a lawn mower. The sales manager, who is a member of the buying committee for the Beautiful Lawn Mower Co., asks the first question.

SALES MANAGER: How can we justify adding more cost to the mower when we are meeting a lot of sales resistance on the basis of our price right now?

SALESPERSON: What you say is true, but before I answer your question, may I ask the design engineer, production manager, and purchasing agent each a question?

The salesperson then proceeds to ask the design engineer whether the new component would prolong the life of the mower and make servicing easier, the production manager whether the new component would facilitate assembly of the mower, and the purchasing agent whether the component could be ordered in large enough quantities to take advantage of the discount.

Thus, by encouraging the participation of the other members of the group, the salesperson has them answer the questions posed by the sales manager and, in effect, sell themselves. The goal of the sales representative is to get recognition from the group that the higher cost of the component may be offset by longer product life and easier servicing and that a better product warranty may increase sales even at a higher price.

SUMMARY OF CHAPTER OBJECTIVES

1. To define sales presentation.

The sales presentation is the sales message delivered by a salesperson to a customer. Typically, we think of it as having three parts—introduction, presenting reasons to buy, and close.

2. To define empathy as it relates to the sales presentation.

The success of the sales presentation depends on the salesperson's ability to understand the customer's viewpoint. This trait, called *empathy,* allows the salesperson to focus on how the customer views his or her own business and how the salesperson's product fits into the picture.

3. To explain the two salesperson-oriented approaches to the sales presentation.

A basic selling formula is the standardized learning approach where the sales presentation is viewed as a cumulative process beginning with awareness and followed in turn by interest, desire, and action. The stimulus-response approach assumes that what a salesperson says triggers a predictable response from the customer.

4. To explain the two customer-oriented approaches to the sales presentation.

With the need-satisfaction approach, the salesperson uses a sales presentation approach that has three parts—need development, need awareness, and need fulfillment. The customer participation decreases as the salesperson moves through the sales presentation. In using the interactive approach, a matchup of the personalities of the salesperson and the customer, salespeople operate in the way their customers want them to operate.

5. To define balanced selling.

Balanced selling mixes the strong points of the salesperson-oriented approaches with the strong points of the customer-oriented approaches to achieve a balance between the two parties.

6. To describe a canned sales presentation.

Canned sales presentations are highly structured, scripted sales presentations that possess little or no flexibility.

7. To list and explain sales tactics that increase the effectiveness of sales presentations.

1. Identify and confirm customer's needs first.
2. Listen carefully to the customer.
3. Give the customer a clear view of product benefits.
4. Give the most desirable information first.
5. Use two-sided arguments and present the favorable side first.
6. Make an effort to make add-on sales.
7. Review how the product provides customer satisfaction.

REVIEW QUESTIONS

1. Relate the standardized learning approach, AIDA, to personal selling.
2. Explain the need-satisfaction approach to selling.
3. How can salespeople tell when they are nearing a sale?
4. One suggested sales tactic is to present the most desirable product information first. What is meant by the term *desirable?*
5. A salesperson has to establish credibility with the customer. What does this entail, and how should the salesperson go about this job?
6. Differentiate between team selling and group selling.
7. Explain the differences between participation in the need-satisfaction approach and balanced selling.

8. What are the differences between customer participation in the selling process and interaction?

9. Explain why interaction is much more complex in selling to groups.

10. Under which conditions would a salesperson-oriented approach be best in making a sales presentation?

DISCUSSION QUESTIONS AND EXERCISES

1. Defend the statement: The sales presentation is crucial if the salesperson is to be able to sell.

2. In selling the following products, what would be a good stimulus and the expected response?
   a. Foreign sports car (selling price $40,000).
   b. Super-deluxe washing machine.
   c. Retirement investment program.
   d. Vacation home in Florida ($110,000–$150,000).

3. You sell swimming pools installed in the backyards of homes. Make up a list of questions to determine the needs or wants of customers.

4. In planning a team presentation to a buying committee, how would you plan to get maximum interaction?

5. How does the idea of balanced selling differ from need satisfaction and interaction?

SALES DIALOG

It is a pleasant spring morning in Hartford, Connecticut. Ed Mathews of A. H. Harris Company, a Foxboro, Massachusetts, industrial equipment distributor, is sitting in the office of Allan Sayer, the procurement director of Anex Industries. Mathews and Sayer are discussing Harris's latest product, a forklift truck.

MATHEWS: I think I have just the solution to your placement problem. Let me show you some photos of our forklift, Al. I know you will be impressed.

SAYER: Yes, someone obviously did a first-class photography job. But you know that the only thing that impresses a procurement director is performance.

MATHEWS: We have you covered on that count, Al. This forklift has less down time than any of its competitors. I know that is a big thing with your plant people. In fact, it came up consistently when I talked to your first-shift supervisors the other morning. They want trucks that are reliable . . . and the Z-42 sure does that.

SAYER: Oh, so you already checked this out with the production people. That is good to know. What about price?

MATHEWS: The Z-42's purchase price falls in about the mid-range in this marketplace. But this chart shows that over its lifetime, our product has the lowest cost per hour. The Z-42 lasts longer and requires less maintenance. Al, you have been in this field a long time, and you know that the lifetime cost per hour is what counts when buying equipment like this, right?

SAYER: Well . . . yes. . . . When did you say you could deliver those Z-42's . . . that is, if I decide to order them?

What do you think the results of this sales dialog will be?

CASE 8–1   PLASTIC FORMS, INC.

It has taken Arnold Cznerak over two months to get an appointment to sell a plastic replica of a picnic table that holds a bottle of ketchup, a jar of pickles or relish, and paper napkins. The potential customer is one of the nation's largest food processors, who would use the picnic table holder as part of a summer promotion.

Cznerak is the 73-year-old president of Plastic Forms, Inc., an injection molding firm. He has always handled the firm's outside contacts. Cznerak is proud of his abilities as a salesperson and says he has been selling for over 50 years. Plastic Forms is a very successful company which has parts contracts with the major auto companies and most of the firms making vacuum sweepers. The miniature picnic table is an attempt to diversify into other areas that are less subject to the ups and downs characterizing the automobile industry.

Cznerak made an appointment with Ronald Crise, the sales promotion manager with Tablegood Products. He began his presentation by mentioning that at a cost of $2.75, his picnic table holder was a low-cost, effective summer promotion. Having purchased bottles of Tablegood's ketchup and relish, he demonstrated how they would fit in the holder. He also placed paper napkins in the holder so that Crise could actually see the promotional deal as it would be displayed in a grocery supermarket. The following is part of the conversation that developed:

CZNERAK: You can see that the picnic table has a great appearance, and our price to you of $2.75 allows you to package the whole deal very competitively. This picnic table— or one like it—sells at K-mart for about $5.

CRISE: I like the idea, and the holders fit our bottles so there is no problem there. However, the company policy is that our product must be sold in our bottles, not special bottles or containers. Restaurants that use our products must keep it in the original package.

CZNERAK: I went to the grocery store personally to get your products . . .

CRISE: (interrupting) Suppose we want to include two other products with the holder?

CZNERAK: That's easy—we can custom-fit any products you want to the holder. I might be able to cut the price to $2.65 with a minimum order of 100,000.

CRISE: Oh, we wouldn't want that many. Our most successful promotion has been around 50,000 units. I would like to test it out with about 5,000 units using ketchup and pickles.

CZNERAK: Injection molding is a very competitive business and we need volume. If I tell you our price is $2.25, would you agree to a larger order?

The discussion continued with Crise emphasizing a smaller order and Cznerak lowering his unit price. Finally Crise ended the interview by saying he would get back to Cznerak.

Questions

1. List the features of the product and show how they benefit Tablegood Products.
2. How would you solve the dilemma over order quantity?
3. Do you feel that Cznerak made a good sales presentation? Why or why not?

CASE 8–2 COSMOPOLITAN TRAVEL, INC.

Carol Brumley had worked for Cosmopolitan Travel in Washington, D.C., for two and a half years. She had built up a solid base of satisfied clients; most were businesspeople who traveled for their firms. However, Brumley typically got their business when they needed tickets for personal or family trips. She was also adding to her list of clients on a steady, methodical basis. In short, she was pleased with how things were going in her short career in the travel business.

Late one Tuesday, Brumley had just hung up the telephone when Roger Vanderbilt walked into the office. He took a seat next to her desk.

VANDERBILT: Hi, Carol! How are you today? I happened to be downtown when I remembered that I needed some tickets for a trip next week. Rather than call I thought I'd just stop in and pick them up.

BRUMLEY: Great. Where do you want to go and when?

VANDERBILT: New Orleans, and I have to be there in time for a dinner engagement at 7 P.M. on Wednesday.

BRUMLEY: All right, how about returning?

VANDERBILT: Anytime after 5 P.M. on Thursday would be fine, but I'd prefer a direct flight.

Brumley excused herself while she put the necessary information into the computer terminal setting on her desk. After a few moments she had two flights that satisfied Vanderbilt, so she had the computer print up the ticket. After putting the sale on his credit card, Brumley gave him the ticket and leaned back in her chair.

BRUMLEY: What are you doing for Thanksgiving?

VANDERBILT: We're going to drive up to Philadelphia to see my wife's sister and her husband. They have lived there for two years already, and we have yet to visit them; it's embarrassing.

BRUMLEY: Sounds like you'll need some diversion. Why don't you and the family fly up to New York for one full day, see a play, visit some museums, have a nice dinner, and return to Philadelphia the next night?

VANDERBILT: You sure know how to spend my money! Frankly, my wife was thinking the same thing. But getting to New York costs a bunch for the five of us. On top of that, we'll need a hotel and food. I don't see how I could swing it.

BRUMLEY: Let's look at Amtrak. They have some great family fares, especially if you can go on the weekend. And there's a hotel called the Piccadilly that has a family weekend special. It's not too far from the Whitney Museum.

VANDERBILT: What do you think the whole thing would cost?

BRUMLEY: Let me do this. I'll do some investigating and call you in a day or two at your office. I'll have a complete tentative budget, food, cabs, tickets, everything. How does that sound?

VANDERBILT: OK to me, but tell me first and not Mary or the kids.

BRUMLEY: Fair enough. I'll need some information about your daughters. What are their ages and do they have any special interests? Have they been to New York before? Does your wife have any special interests? I know she gets there on business every so often, but have you and she gone there just for fun, together?

VANDERBILT: Let me talk this over with Mary and the girls and call you tomorrow with some of those answers. Maybe this is a pretty good idea. We could use a day in the Big Apple away from our normal routine.

BRUMLEY: I'll wait until you call. Do you need any other tickets?

VANDERBILT: Not right now, thanks. I'll talk to you tomorrow.

Questions

1. What type of approach is Brumley using with Vanderbilt?
2. Would you have done anything different if you were Brumley?
3. Was Brumley too aggressive?
4. Would a canned or standard presentation work in this business?

CHAPTER 9

Demonstrations

CHAPTER OBJECTIVES

1. To explain how demonstrations can be used in sales presentations.

2. To outline the reasons for using demonstrations.

3. To identify and discuss the different types of sales aids.

4. To list some general guidelines for demonstrating a product or service.

SALES CAREER PROFILE

JOHN STRANGE
Pfizer Laboratories

John Strange, the Orlando, Florida, district manager for Pfizer Laboratories, supervises 10 sales representatives. He has been with Pfizer since 1972. Strange holds a bachelor's degree in business administration from Georgia State University. His hobbies include running, reading, and waterskiing.

Why did John Strange pick Pfizer? "I feel that Pfizer had a unique situation that appealed to me. The sales aspect, number one; and, number two, the financial reward that was directly correlated to my ability to be successful in sales. Also, the opportunities for advancement were great—again, correlated to my success as a salesperson and directly related as well to my leadership potential and abilities.

"I think Pfizer Incorporated was picked as one of the top 100 U.S. sales firms because of its people orientation. By that I mean that Pfizer Labs Division and Pfizer Incorporated really operate as the Pfizer family. That attitude has become pervasive throughout the corporation, in all divisions. There is a real sense within our organization that management is working with each representative to help the organization as a whole achieve its goals.

"I also feel that Pfizer Inc. and Pfizer Labs do an exceptional job in selecting highly qualified people to fill positions. Our extensive screening and interviewing process yields good results in terms of the quality of people that we hire. I also believe that Pfizer Labs, as a division, has an excellent marketing department. When you hire good people and they're well trained and your sales policies and principles are sound, good things usually happen."

Strange described how his sales representatives work: "Their job requires a series and a succession of calls. They usually work on a four-week itinerary in a sales territory, calling on our high-prescribing, primary-care physicians. By primary care, I mean family practitioners and general internists, and also internal medicine specialties such as cardiologists and rheumatologists. It takes some time to establish credibility, sincerity, and so forth. But our representatives usually establish a sense of professionalism in a reasonably timely fashion. Their professionalism is supported by some of the things that we do with the medical community to enhance rapport, such as bringing in visiting professors from prestigious medical schools to lecture in various medical fields.

"At Pfizer Labs, we promote pharmaceuticals which are available only by prescription from a physician. We do not obtain a clear sale in the physician's office—our salespeople do not leave with a signed contract. Our selling basically involves getting a commitment from the physician to prescribe one of our products for his or her patients. Therefore, when our salespeople make a sale or a sale presentation to a physician, they try their best to obtain a strong verbal commitment."

When asked how pharmaceutical representatives can demonstrate their product,

Strange remarked, "We demonstrate it, in a sense, through samples. Most physicians, probably 90 percent of them, like to have pharmaceutical samples in their offices to give to their patients for trial. Typically, the physician gives the patient a starter sample for one to two weeks of therapy to see how that patient tolerates the drug, if the patient has any unusual reactions, and if the drug is effective for that patient. It's also a nice service to the patients who receive a free trial usage of that medication.

"Pfizer Labs supplies demonstration supports to the sales force. We carry visual aids that are prepared by our marketing department. We have a glossy visual aid, usually oriented to one of four diseases. The visual aid binder is the basis on which the representative builds his or her presentation. Within it, we frequently insert reprints from medical journals, such as the *American Journal of Medicine on Circulation*. These reprints demonstrate to physicians the efficacy and safety of our product for selected groups of patients.

"Our average time in a one-on-one presentation with a physician in an office probably runs around 10 minutes. Our objective is to present four products in a 10-minute time frame. The representative must be very succinct, concise, and to the point, while presenting as many benefits as possible for each product. At the same time, the representative must attempt to gain some commitment from the doctor to prescribe these products for patients. The crux of our presentation is built around visual aids, such as reprints from medical journals. Occasionally we use the sample pills or tablets themselves. We also have supports such as booklets for patients relating to a disease state that we might give to the physician.

"There's one final demonstration support which is somewhat unique to the medical field: the third-party endorsement. I have mentioned the visiting professors that come into the area to lecture to local physicians. What they'll do is talk about the diagnosis of a given disease state, and the therapeutic alternatives for that particular disease. As one of six or seven medications available in the treatment of arthritis, for example, our product may be mentioned, but only within the context of many other medications.

"These presentations serve several purposes: The local physicians receive the continuing medical education credits they need to remain board certified. Second, the presentations enhance the rapport we have in the medical community. And, third, they provide a platform upon which we then can, at a later time, build an excellent sales presentation."

"**M**arketing boils down to educating people." Ned Steinberger believes this is the key to his success in building a business. Beginning with six hand-built prototypes of a new guitar design in 1979, his annual sales have climbed to $2 million.

Steinberger learned at a trade show that demonstration of the product was absolutely necessary to open people's eyes to the capabilities of his radically new guitar design. A musician playing at the trade show used a Steinberger guitar and, in the vernacular of the trade, "knocked people out." As a result, the first business generated for the Steinberger guitar appeared on his doorstep the day after the show.

A key selling point of the new guitar is that it can be slammed into the floor and subsequently picked up and played, still in tune and wholly undamaged. By contrast, conventional guitars are extremely fragile instruments. For example, wood guitars go in and out of tune in relation to changes in atmospheric pressure, temperature, and humidity.

Hap Kuffner, who, with partner Stan Jay, owned a music store specializing in esoteric instruments, toured trade shows in 1981 using the torture-test demonstration as a sure-fire closer. With this and his great enthusiasm, Kuffner generated more orders than the small company could fill. Another plus for Steinberger was an award from the Industrial Design Society of America.

With recognition and acceptance no longer a problem, Steinberger tackled the price problem. The price of $2,000 clearly put the product out of reach of many consumers who might otherwise be very interested. One solution he developed was another line of guitars at a lower price.

The Steinberger guitar is very different from what people expect in such an instrument. The consumer has to learn how to use it properly and keep it adjusted all the time. Educating people—consumers, sales personnel, dealers, and the salespeople behind the counter—continues to receive the major share of attention at Steinberger's.[1] Demonstration plays a key role in this effort.

DEMONSTRATIONS SUPPLEMENT SALES PRESENTATIONS

demonstration
illustration of how customers can use a product and/or service and benefit from it

Demonstrations, actual illustrations of a product or service, are important parts of a sales presentation in almost every conceivable selling situation. They give salespeople an opportunity to appeal to customers through all applicable senses. Obviously customers cannot smell or taste a machine, but they can see it and operate it while listening to a discussion of its benefits. Selling cookware presents a unique opportunity for a salesperson to appeal to all five senses by making the sales presentation the preparation and eating of a meal. This also affords ample opportunities for the salesperson to talk about product benefits.

Sales presentations are not simply conversations between customers and salespeople. If they were, salespeople could be pictured as attempting to intereact with customers who cannot see, feel, smell, or taste. Salespeople in such situations could not hope to be as effective as those who make use of as many of the customer's senses as possible, particularly sight. Today's salespeople are equipped with a vast array of selling tools ranging from a simple presentation using slides or transparencies to a remote portable terminal that connects salespeople to computers at their home offices.

Several questions concerning demonstrations arise. These include:

- How demonstration can help sell.
- Which sales aids are available.
- How to make sure demonstrations are successful.

WHY USE DEMONSTRATIONS?

Almost every sales presentation can benefit from a demonstration. Ron Shoel is the assistant vice president for corporate sales at Beloit Corporation, a maker of custom paper manufacturing machinery. Shoel notes, "It's almost impossible to show a customer any type of complex equipment without using slides."[2] The positive benefits derived from using demonstrations are apparent in selling to individual customers as well as to groups. In fact, demonstrations are a must in team selling, where customer involvement is difficult to obtain.

Demonstrations help reveal the benefits of a product or service, especially when such benefits are intangible. For example, the only way to show the ride capabilities of an automobile is to have the customer drive the car over a bumpy road and actually experience the ride. In similar fashion, a visual aid can dramatize the "facts and figures" relative to the use of a product.

Another reason for using demonstration is the uniqueness it gives the sales presentation. A demonstration allows a salesperson to show his or her concern with the special needs or wants of particular customers. By using a demonstration, the salesperson anticipates the inevitable response from a customer that, although a product or service may work for others, the customer's problems are different. For example, a visual showing figures pertaining to the specific customer is tangible evidence of the tailoring of the product or service to the customer.

Demonstrations are also helpful in showing how to use a product. For potential customers to see value in a product, they have to see it in use, see the output from the product, and be convinced that they can use the product successfully. As an example, compare the selling impact of kitchen knives in an attractive display case with the impact of a demonstration in which potential customers are allowed to cut various food products with the knives.

Another advantage of demonstrations is the impression they can have on potential customers. Demonstrations are tangible evidence of the efforts of salespeople and their companies. This is very important in marketing to resellers. At trade shows, for example, exhibiters use audiovisual aids extensively to show not only the product in operation but also the future advertising planned for the product. IBM, for example, invests many thousands of dollars in visual presentations shown at conferences for various user groups.

Repeated demonstrations also give salespeople confidence during the sales presentation. Finally, demonstrations provide uniformity in the content of the sales presentation. Individualization is still practical through selection of what is included in the demonstration and what each salesperson emphasizes in the sales presentation.

Sales presentations that include a demonstration, as opposed to those that do not, have four distinct competitive advantages:

1. A better and more attentive customer audience.
2. A more consistent sales presentation.

3. A clearer understanding of the product benefits.
4. A higher level of quality and flexibility in the sales presentation.

Improved Customer Involvement

Experts tell us that nearly 90 percent of our understanding comes through what we see with our eyes, compared to only about 9 percent through our ears. This means that we can improve the chances of creating understanding by a multiple of 10 if we include demonstration as part of the sales presentation.

Suppose, as an example, that a salesperson is attempting to sell a product with multiple uses. The salesperson knows that although a particular customer is interested in the versatility of the product, certain applications are more important than others. If the salesperson just explains everything the product can do, confusion will result; the customer will not remember many of the uses by the end of the presentation. In other words, the customer misses the principal selling point—the versatility of the product.

When the salesperson demonstrates how the machine does each of the jobs, the customer gets a much better idea of its many pluses. More importantly, rather than merely being asked to believe, the customer sees a demonstration of what the product can actually do. A demonstration increases the credibility of both the sales presentation and the salesperson.

Demonstration often includes letting the customer operate the product. Trying out the product increases the customer's conviction and intensifies his or her desire for the item. Conviction is important because the customer must feel that a product is worth the asking price.

Products are often demonstrated several times during the course of a sales presentation. There are several advantages to this approach:

1. Repetition helps the customer remember the many uses of the product, particularly those in which interest is high.
2. Appeals are made to the sense of sight.
3. Appeals are made to the sense of touch.
4. The customer takes an active part in the sales presentation.

Appealing to All the Senses

A demonstration appeals to all the senses and increases the chances of obtaining customer understanding. For example, a flip chart or slide presentation might be combined with the actual product in a demonstration. A slide presentation might show the plant producing the item and emphasize the capabilities of the company to produce high-quality products. At the same time, the customer can examine some of the actual products produced by the company.

Combining a visual presentation with actual operation of the product is another way to appeal to all the senses. For example, in selling computer software, the visual presentation might be the steps to be followed in actually running the program. The role of the salesperson would be to talk the customer through the operation, telling why each step is necessary and making the necessary corrections.

Some sort of demonstration is a necessity in selling to a group of customers or in team selling. Just talking does not make an adequate impression in these circumstances. The fact that demonstrations hold customers' attention and enliven sales calls is important in selling to a group because individual participation is likely to be limited. In one-on-one selling, salespeople can hold the attention of customers by answering and asking questions. The opportunities for such interaction are fewer in group selling situations.

Selling teams find demonstrations valuable because they hold customers' attention longer. Generally, sales presentations by teams run longer than those delivered by individuals. The demonstration focuses customers' attention on the product, offsetting the time involved and the distraction of listening to more than one person. Demonstrations are also a good way to tie together what is said by the various members of the selling team.

In group selling, demonstrations can give each customer a part in the presentation. Having each customer handle, inspect, or, if feasible, operate the product provides the customer participation so often lacking in groups. With a selling team, demonstration provides a good opportunity for salespeople to pair off with customers. For instance, suppose a selling team makes a sales presentation of computer equipment to the administrative staff of a local hospital. One representative makes the presentation to the entire group, showing what the equipment does and how it is operated. At the conclusion of this formal part of the presentation, each salesperson pairs off with a member of the hospital staff to discuss the equipment.

A Means of Customer Orientation

Demonstrations allow the salesperson to tailor the sales presentation to individual customer needs or wants. The uniqueness the demonstration gives a sales presentation helps salespeople convince customers of their orientation to the customers' requirements.

A seller might emphasize customer orientation by using an elaborate color-slide presentation especially developed for a particular customer. In another example, the salesperson can fill out a standard form about the customer before or during the sales presentation, such as the estate planning forms used by life insurance agents. The potential size of the sale usually determines the complexity of the demonstration.

When the demonstration is of a general nature, salespeople can achieve some individualization by focusing on those product features of primary interest to the customer. Company videotapes or filmstrips usually show the

COMPANY PROFILE

Audiovisuals Are Helpful in Selling to Groups

National Revenue Corporation's 700 salespeople carry slide/audio projection units to help sell financial services packages to companies that extend credit at the wholesale and retail levels.

"Salespeople feel AV puts them in a much better position to close," insists Frank McCormick, marketing vice president. "They can sit back and make note of the audience response, then go back later and reinforce certain points." Also as a result of AV, presentations to larger groups don't require additional sales personnel. For instance, only one salesperson was needed for a recent presentation to 12 general partners of a large accounting concern. "Without AV, a sale to that large a group would have been more difficult," McCormick says. He claims that the sale, if unassisted by AV, would have required two more salespeople or two more presentations to reach the partners, four at a time. But the 13-minute AV segment, aimed at selling a cash flow management system for slow-paying accounts, conveyed the right message simultaneously to all 12 partners. By incorporating such things as charts, photographs, and a voice-over narration, it showed, McCormick says, "the concrete and mortar behind the presentation."

Presentations in National Revenue's Columbus, Ohio, headquarters are opportunities for more customizing than is usual. Sometimes an opening slide will show a dual logo to add "a nice, personalizing touch," McCormick says.

SOURCE: Abridged from Steven Mintz, "Marketers Choose Their Weapons," *Sales & Marketing Management*, January 16, 1984, p. 70. Reprinted by permission of Sales & Marketing Management. Copyright January 16, 1984.

variety of products the firm offers, but the salesperson can stop the film or video after a product feature of particular interest to the customer is presented. The representative can then make relevant comments, ask for questions, and perhaps rerun the portion dealing with that feature.

Effect on Customers

Demonstrations create a favorable impression on customers in several ways:

1. Demonstrations are tangible evidence to resellers of the efforts of salespeople and their companies. A retailer or wholesaler can see the television commercials used to sell a product.
2. Demonstrations permit potential customers to star or participate in a show of product use.
3. Demonstrations help create customer confidence in product use prior to purchase.
4. Demonstrations help create an atmosphere of honesty about what the product can and cannot do.

All of these effects are important in conveying the overall messages that salespeople seek to present. Circumstances dictate the priorities that sellers assign to each in setting up effective demonstrations.

TYPES OF SALES AIDS

sales aids

items used in a demonstration such as visual aids, audiovisual aids, and the product itself

Sales aids include the product itself, visual aids, and audiovisual aids. All of these can be used in the demonstration phase of the selling process. Sales aids not only provide emphasis by focusing on key points in the sales presentation, but also add credibility to the presentation. Customers are more likely to believe what the salesperson says if it is reinforced by a sales aid. Another important reason for using a sales aid is the impression it makes on the customer. Generally, the greater the amount of money involved in the sale and/or the higher the level of management taking part in the purchasing decision, the greater the need for a sales aid. As an illustration, one steel company reported spending nearly $4,000 on a sales presentation to a firm involving a potential sale of $140,000. A growing awareness of the impact of sales aids plus technological advances such as computer graphic systems that make slides and transparencies have broadened the acceptance of sales aids. In fact, sales and marketing applications are now the second highest component of the market for slides. Closely related executive/client presentations are the number one user of slides.[3]

Product Use

Demonstrations often make use of the actual product or service offered, but characteristics such as physical size may prevent demonstration at the customer's location. When a seller cannot demonstrate a computer in a customer's office, arrangements can be made to take the customer to a location where the computer has been installed.

plant visits

trips to the seller's facilities to check company capabilities and quality control

Plant visits, or trips to the seller's facilities, are helpful to show such product benefits as company capabilities and quality control. These visits should be more than guided tours. Customers should be allowed to see any operation they desire to see and talk with anyone they wish. In this fashion, sellers establish credibility and competency in the customer's mind about the company's capabilities and products.

At the McDonald Steel Corporation, written reports of sales calls are made available to employees in the plant. Two copies of each report are posted on employee bulletin boards and another is passed around to managers. In this way, employees are able to understand that business begins in the marketplace and that they must work to satisfy the marketplace. Also, it alerts employees to possible visits by customers and the major concerns of customers during these visits.

mobile demonstrator

unit used to demonstrate a product that is too big or complex to be carried into a prospect's office

A **mobile demonstrator** or clinic that can be moved to the site of the presentation is another way to demonstrate products too big or too complex to be carried into a customer's office. Many sales personnel believe mobile demonstrators are the best way to provide the proof of performance demanded by today's technical products buyers.

PROFESSIONAL SELLING IN ACTION

Appealing to the Sense of Taste Helped Secure a Million Dollar Loan

In 1969, at age 50, Ely Callaway bought 150 acres of arid ranch land in Temecula [California] and planted grapevines. Callaway figured that the way to make money in wine was to treat the business as fashion, not as commodity. "Farmers are poor because they give up merchandising control of their product," says Callaway. "Wine was the only agricultural product where I could retain merchandising control from start to finish."

Callaway compensated for his ignorance of the vintner's art by hiring experts. When his first harvest (Riesling, chenin blanc, sauvignon blanc, and cabernet sauvignon) was in, he sent the grapes to famous Napa Valley winemaker Robert Mondavi for crushing. The results were pleasingly dry table wines, but he had run through his initial investment of $1.5 million and needed another $1 million to expand the winery. His loan officers at the Bank of America balked—the prime rate was climbing—so Callaway took his case to the bank's top officers.

"I told them I would gamble with them," Callaway laughs. "I said, 'Appoint a panel of wine experts and I'll do the same. If they find my wine is comparable with the leading wines in northern California, you lend me the original amount agreed upon.'" If not, Callaway would have to look elsewhere. After some judicious sipping, the bank capitulated. Callaway got his $1 million.

SOURCE: *Forbes*, May 7, 1984, pp. 70–71. © 1984. "Late Bloomer" by Ellen Paris. Excerpted by permission.

Product demonstrations that take place away from the customer's location are seldom attempted on the first or even the second call. The customer has to be partially sold before an outside demonstration is arranged, particularly if considerable time and money are involved.

Visual and Audiovisual Aids

In addition to using the actual product, a variety of sales tools can be used in demonstrations. These range from simple flip charts to audiovisual equipment and computer equipment. (An ad for one type of sales tool—posters— is shown on the next page.) For instance, consider how computer terminals have been used in banking. A bank representative using a computer terminal can visually show customers the features and attributes of any bank product or service. The banker can also tailor a series of "what if" scenarios to a customer's specific needs. As the customer looks on, projections on the value of investments or periodic loan payments based on varying assumptions appear on the screen.[4]

In some cases, audiovisual aids provide most of the sales presentation; this leaves the salesperson free to personalize the presentation. Some insurance companies use comprehensive brochures to describe their products.

HOW TO MAKE IT BIG AT YOUR NEXT PRESENTATION.

As a presenter, you aim to inform, persuade, impress, dramatize, *communicate*. And our aim is to help you. With the Varitronics PosterPrinter, you can enlarge your 8½" x 11" documents up to 23" x 33."

In only 70 seconds, you can create professional-looking flip charts and other poster-size presentation materials—all in dazzling colors! It's easier

For more information, call **1-800-637-5461.** In Minnesota, 1-612-542-1580. Or mail coupon to: Varitronic Systems, Inc., P.O. Box 234, Minneapolis, MN 55440.

NAME/TITLE_____

BUSINESS PHONE (_____)_____

COMPANY_____

BUSINESS ADDRESS_____

CITY_____STATE_____ZIP_____

VARITRONICS
© Varitronic Systems, Inc. 1989

than using a copier, and it is just as quick. It's economical too. The PosterPrinter is also great for creating all kinds of custom-designed signs, posters, exhibits and point-of-purchase displays in seconds. All at a price that will make a big hit with your accountant. For full details, simply call us toll-free: **1-800-637-5461.** Or send us the coupon.

Source: Reproduced with permission of Varitronics Systems, Inc., Minneapolis, MN 55440.

Having visual aids tell the complete sales story has three advantages:

- The sales presentation is organized and all important factors are included.
- The sales presentation captures and holds the customer's attention.
- The sales presentation allows the salesperson to concentrate on sizing up the customer and determining how to interact with the person rather than worrying about what to say next.

HOW TO DEMONSTRATE A PRODUCT OR SERVICE

Demonstrations do not automatically make a sales presentation. Figure 9–1 presents a generalized format for making better sales presentations through demonstrations. It emphasizes the importance of consulting with the customer to determine his or her purchasing goals. Jon C. Logue, executive vice president, sales and marketing, at Salem Mills, advises salespeople to: "Listen—keep your antennae up to find out customers' needs."[5] The presentation and demonstration can then highlight the benefits most relevant to the buyer and proceed to a recommended purchasing action.

FIGURE 9–1   A format for sales presentation using demonstration

All benefits of product, company, and salesperson	CONSULT with customer, ask questions about purchasing goals
Benefits of critical interest to customer	PERSONALIZE by focusing on those benefits that provide satisfaction relative to purchasing goals
Reinforcement of benefits critical to customer	RECOMMEND how customer can satisfy purchasing goals

Some general guidelines for producing effective demonstrations that have a positive impact on sales presentations are as follows:

1. *Package each demonstration so that it tells a value story.* It should show you how you are presenting the best value in terms of product, price, and service.

2. *Make advance preparations.* Mistakes can be disastrous to the sales presentation, so make sure you know what you are doing. Go over your demonstration again and again until you get it perfect. Make sure everything works.

3. *Personalize your demonstration.* Avoid relying too heavily on visual aids, which may make the sales presentation too slick and impersonal. Do not read the visuals word for word. Go over each sales point in the customer's own words.

4. *Position yourself so the customer can see what is going on in the demonstration.* You should have nothing to hide, so do not turn your back or in any way cover up the demonstration.

5. *Make sure the customer sees what you want him or her to see in the demonstration.* Double-check each sales point by either asking a question or giving a more detailed explanation to avoid any misunderstanding on the part of the customer.

6. *Do not talk too fast or rush through your presentation,* since this makes it difficult for the customer to follow the buildup in the sales presentation. These presentation faults also give the customer fewer opportunities to ask questions and participate in the sales presentation.

7. *If possible, get agreement on the major points brought out by the visual aids.*

8. *Try to get the customer into the demonstration.* This is a good way to get the necessary interaction with the customer. It is best to ensure that the customer not only hears and sees but also touches. Salespeople have found, for example, that getting their customers to write down certain words or make computations is helpful in developing interaction.

9. *Make demonstrations as short as possible.* The customer is liable to become bored or confused by a demonstration that is too long.

SUMMARY OF CHAPTER OBJECTIVES

1. To explain how demonstrations can be used in sales presentations.

Sales presentations that use demonstrations allow salespeople to appeal to more than just the customer's sense of hearing. The primary emphasis in demonstrations is on the customer's sense of sight, but touch, smell, and taste may be involved as well.

2. To outline the reasons for using demonstrations.

A number of reasons exist for using demonstrations in almost every sales presentation. The first is that better customer involvement is possible because the salesperson is appealing to more than one sense. Demonstrations tend to increase the credibility of both the sales presentation and the salesperson. They are a necessity when the benefits of the product are essentially intangible in nature. Second, demonstrations are a big help in special selling situations because they hold the customer's attention better than a strictly verbal message. Demonstrations also provide the possibility of getting individual customers involved in the sales presentation. Third, demonstrations provide an opportunity for tailoring the sales presentations to individual customers. Other reasons include showing customers how to use the product, impressing customers, building confidence in the salesperson, and providing uniformity to the sales presentation.

3. To identify and discuss the different types of sales aids.

Sales aids include the product itself, visual aids, and audiovisual aids. Most salespeople prefer to use the product itself as a sales aid in demonstrations. Mobile demonstrators offer a solution to the problem of showing large, complex products. A great variety of audiovisual equipment is now available for use by salespeople. In some instances, audiovisual aids take over the whole presentation, leaving the salesperson free to personalize the sales message.

4. To list some general guidelines for demonstrating a product or service.

Some general guidelines to make demonstrations effective include:

Tell a value story.
Prepare in advance.
Personalize the demonstration.
Position yourself so the customer can see everything.
Make sure the customer sees what you want him or her to see.
Do not talk too fast or rush through the demonstration.
Get agreement on major points.
Give the customer a part.
Keep it short.

REVIEW QUESTIONS

1. Why are demonstrations an important part of sales presentations?
2. Discuss why it is important to appeal to the customer's sense of sight.

3. If you were preparing a sales training session on demonstration, what reasons would you give sales personnel for using demonstrations as part of their sales presentations?

4. How do demonstrations make what salespeople say more believable?

5. What are the major types of sales aids?

6. How do demonstrations improve the salesperson's customer orientation?

7. Discuss why salespeople prefer to use the product itself in demonstrations.

8. What are the advantages of using audiovisual aids to provide most of a sales presentation?

9. Why are demonstrations an absolute must in selling to groups of customers?

10. With several products to sell, how can salespeople keep their demonstrations short?

DISCUSSION QUESTIONS AND EXERCISES

1. John Strange points out in his profile that a Pfizer salesperson is expected to present four products during a 10-minute interview with a physician. Discuss how demonstrations allow Pfizer reps to accomplish their objectives.

2. Pick a product you are familiar with and plan a sales presentation using a demonstration.

3. Defend the statement: The more products salespeople have to sell, the more likely they are to use some form of demonstration.

4. How would you explain the seeming contradiction between the rule that the demonstration must be personalized and the fact that the demonstration focuses the attention of the customer on the product?

5. How might you demonstrate a new product line to a nationwide sales force of several thousand people?

SALES DIALOG

Jim and Kathy Herzog, a recently married couple, had just purchased their first home in a new development near San Mateo, California. When they entered the appliance section of Carter's Department Store, Jack Bricker approached them with a smile on his face and his right hand outstretched. After introducing himself and shaking Jim's hand, they got down to business.

JIM HERZOG: We just got our state income tax refund and decided to spend it on a microwave oven for our kitchen. Do you have any?

BRICKER: We have a very nice selection right over here. What kind do you want?

KATHY HERZOG: We really don't know; I've never used one except to warm things up.

BRICKER: That's OK. Let me show you some of the models we have in stock. If you like one of these, take it home today. Otherwise, we can order one from the warehouse.

JIM HERZOG: What's this one over here? It looks darned complicated. What do all these buttons do? Are these things dangerous? I've been told they leak radiation.

BRICKER: Nah, wrong on both counts. They're simple and harmless. Look at this instruction book and see how easy they are to use. And the guarantee assures you there is no danger.

KATHY HERZOG: Why can't I turn this one on? Is it broken?

BRICKER: No, we don't have any of these plugged in. The only outlets are way across the store over there, and we'd have to have extension cords laying all over the place.

JIM HERZOG: I've also been told that if you bake biscuits in one of these they come out all white and not nicely browned.

BRICKER: Not if you get one with the browning capability. With those, the biscuits come out just like this plaster model we have inside there. Just look how realistic that biscuit thing looks.

KATHY HERZOG: Do they really look like that?

BRICKER: Take my word for it.

KATHY HERZOG: How hot do they get? I want to put it right near some plants.

BRICKER: They stay cool; they're not like regular ovens.

JIM HERZOG: Sure wish I could see one run. I'm still confused.

BRICKER: Why don't you go see one of your friends' microwaves and then come back? You'll see what I mean.

What do you think the results of this sales dialog will be?

CASE 9–1   NORWESTERS MOTORS, INC.

Dan Hodgins has spent his entire career—over 30 years—in the automobile business. At the present time he owns three General Motors dealerships and a new dealership set up to sell a top-of-the-line Japanese import. This car retails in the $35,000–$40,000 range, depending on its optional equipment. Sales at the new dealership are considerably below expectations and are a matter of increasing concern to Hodgins.

The new dealership is run by Hodgins' brother, Phil. Dan Hodgins is not known to the dealership's sales personnel. As a result, Hodgins decided to make a shopping trip to the dealership with his wife and daughter. Their supposed purpose was to purchase a car for their daughter's 21st birthday. They arrive at the dealership around seven in the evening, driving an expensive American-made sedan.

After arriving at the dealership, they wandered around in the front parking lot looking at new cars for about 20 minutes before being approached by a salesperson. As far as they could tell, there were no other potential customers. The salesperson did not introduce himself. Rather, he started out by asking the model of car in which Hodgins was interested. At no time did the salesperson offer to unlock any of the cars nor did he invite them into the dealership to show them the cars on the display floor. The salesperson directed all of his attention toward Hodgins, virtually ignoring his wife and daughter. He answered questions, but did not offer any additional information. Most of his answers were, "Yes," "No," or "I would have to check on that." The salesperson asked no questions of Hodgins. He told them that a demonstration ride was not possible right now. In answering questions about price, the salesperson referred to the sticker on each car. When the Hodgins family was ready to leave, the salesperson cordially thanked them for coming and wished them a good evening.

Questions

1. What major mistakes did the salesperson make during this incident?
2. How should a salesperson demonstrates a car in this price range?
3. How can an auto salesperson develop customer participation?

CASE 9–2 LAKE CHEMICAL COMPANY

Lake Chemical Company in Milwaukee recently developed a new silicon-based plastic material called LAKSIL. The advantages of LAKSIL are its durability, high resistance to extreme heat and corrosion, and low competitive cost. The principal markets for LAKSIL are industrial machinery, wheeled vehicles (cars and trucks), appliances, and electrical transmission equipment.

Despite these advantages, sales representatives for Lake Chemical Company have experienced a great deal of apathy among customers in regard to the new product. Tom Roman, a relatively new sales representative, has done the best job in selling LAKSIL; his sales account for nearly 60 percent of the total volume. However, most of his sales have been to small customers with a limited need for the product. Only a scattering of those considered prime prospects are located in Roman's territory.

In a meeting with top management, Betty Serro, the sales manager, proposed that Tom Roman be assigned exclusively to the selling of LAKSIL, regardless of sales territory. The product manager, Pete Kasko, while acknowledging that Tom Roman has done the best job so far, brought up the point that he needed at least two customer plant visits in making every sale. If the cost of these visits related to the dollars generated by the specific sale, it would be doubtful if any of the sales of LAKSIL were profitable. His counter-proposal was to develop a slide and sound presentation that could be used by all of the sales reps. He went on to add that the printed sales information on LAKSIL was fairly good, but customers have to be shown the superiority of the product.

Questions

1. If you were a member of the management team, with whom would you agree? State your reasons.
2. Contrast a plant visit with a slide presentation for selling effectiveness.
3. Suppose Tom Roman is assigned to sell LAKSIL. What rules would you set up in regard to plant visits by customers?

CHAPTER 10

Sales Resistance and Objections

CHAPTER OBJECTIVES

1. To explain the concept of sales resistance.

2. To list the reasons prospects raise objections.

3. To classify the types of objections.

4. To understand when objections should be handled.

5. To identify and discuss the various methods of handling objections.

6. To demonstrate when and how to handle price objections.

7. To outline a sequential approach to handling objections.

SALES CAREER PROFILE

JEAN McCLOSKEY KRAK
Xerox Corporation

Jean McCloskey Krak of Xerox Corporation is the senior account manager responsible for the firm's federal government accounts in Pittsburgh. Jean holds a bachelor's degree in psychology and business management from Seton Hill College and a master's degree in counseling education from Duquesne University. Her hobbies include skiing, running, aerobics, and reading. She also has a strong personal interest in alcohol rehabilitation and addiction counseling.

Why did Jean Krak choose to enter sales? "I decided in college that I needed a broader exposure to the business world than what I'd learned in textbooks. I decided sales would offer me a flexible schedule as well as an opportunity to significantly increase my income on a short-term basis. And I felt that sales was a very good place for a female to enter the business world. I enjoy working with people, and I enjoy developing interactive and communication skills.

"Xerox was the company I was most interested in because they had an aggressive and current marketing image. Their technology was sharp; I knew people who worked for Xerox. I was aware that they had very good opportunities for females and minorities, as well as a competitive starting salary.

"Some of the chief responsibilities of my job are generating new major accounts for incremental business, uncovering and qualifying office automation systems opportunities, and identifying appropriate utilization of support personnel to maximize business objectives. I'm also responsible for representing Xerox in my account interaction and providing leadership and direction to various account support resources. In addition to ensuring customer satisfaction, my goal is to achieve the Vendor of Choice status for Xerox within the federal government in Pittsburgh.

"What do I like most about my job? I really enjoy the time flexibility. If I want to have time for a particular kind of appointment, I simply plan to work at night or on a weekend. I meet with my manager once a month, and about once a week we're on the phone for an update, but other than that, I schedule my time as I wish.

"In my marketplace within major accounts, it's important to develop long-term relationships with my customers. I really enjoy my customers, and that's probably the thing I like most about my job.

"My relations with my sales peers are, first of all, supportive. We use a team approach, make a lot of team calls, and have a lot of team strategy discussions.

"My relations with my customers are very open. In general, my customers have a strong sense of loyalty toward me. My relationship with sales management is open and very positive, whether we are sharing a funny customer story or discussing current situations that have a lot of potential where I need their support.

"Why do I think Xerox was picked as a top selling company? Xerox places the strongest emphasis on employee training in the industry, and has a strong reputation for sales skills development. Xerox has a very professional image within the industry, based on customer satisfaction."

Next, Jean Krak commented about sales resistance. "One of the biggest forms of resistance that I face in the federal, state, or other government marketplace is that people really don't know their own decision-making process: the forms, procedures, what their regulations include, or what their budget includes. To work through this kind of resistance, I establish contacts with as many people in various segments and locations of an organization as possible. The purpose of this is to gain information which allows me to assist the decision maker I'm working with.

"Many times I will call Washington, D.C., about the federal government account. After finding out what the customers' process is in making decisions and what information they will need, I go back to the locals and in a very diplomatic way explain their process to them. If they are not aware of it, I then refer them to names of satisfied people, organizations that have already made a positive Xerox decision. I clarify the customers' objectives and get them to talk about any information distortions they may have. I try to link the customers' objectives with their objections. For example, if they tell me that my product doesn't have a certain kind of feature, but they've already told me that feature is not an objection, then we can rule that objection out.

"Most importantly, I really try to maintain an ongoing communication process, no matter what decision is made. Many times customers made a decision against Xerox, and later on realize that it was a bad decision. They will come back and—because I've left the door open for a positive relationship—they feel comfortable with that approach.

"When I face resistance that I can't work through, I'll bring in a manager, a service manager, product specialist, or even a peer, whoever is available and whatever the situation requires.

"One additional form of resistance that can be masked in an objection is the amount of paperwork involved to justify what they want. So when I provide an in-depth analysis of the customer's needs and solutions, along with the competitive analysis, I'm basically doing the work for the customer and wording the justification in a way that is geared toward their organization. In other words, if it's a government facility, then I word it in that way. If it's military, educational, or medical, I use that jargon in the justification. Generally, customers then put aside the objection that they don't have time for the paperwork. I've done their paperwork for them. This gives them that much more impetus to be interested and consider seriously the proposal I'm presenting."

Price objections were common for Growmark, Inc. and its dealers in the mid-1980s. The Bloomington, Illinois-based farm supply cooperative, which sells feed, fertilizers, petroleum, and other products, was hurt by a depression in the farm belt. Growmark's products were among the highest priced options available because of the company's service strategy.

Growmark's sales representatives increasingly came up against price resistance. Training sessions on handling price objections had little impact. One senior salesperson remarked, "I guess we must be too high; 30,000 farmers can't be wrong."

Growmark's management decided that an entirely new training program was needed—one that would allow its sales personnel to understand prices from both the viewpoint of the customer and the company. Rick Wills, Growmark's manager of sales and marketing training, put it this way: "By letting salespeople see what was involved in establishing prices, we felt they would then have a greater understanding and acceptance of the numbers they were given to work with."

Wills and others developed a computer-based competitive game called "Selling against Price." This simulation became the basis of a two-day seminar which pitted teams of salespeople against each other. This exercise allowed Growmark's sales personnel to see what happened when price changes were implemented. For example, most of the teams failed to pick up enough market share to offset lowered profits resulting from price cuts.

"Selling against Price" has allowed Growmark's sales personnel to better understand pricing, and to explain it to their customers. The company remains profitable despite the shakeout that has characterized the industry. Wills now tells a story about one of the graduates of his program:

"It seems that every time he talked with one of his top prospects, he got turned down. . . . So, out of frustration, the [salesperson] . . . asked him why they couldn't do business, and the farmer told him that his present supplier said he would always beat our price by two cents per gallon. At that point, the salesman pulled his rig over to the farmer's tank and started to fill it up. When the farmer came running over and said, 'What are you doing? I told you I wasn't going to buy from you!', he said, 'I know what you told me, but I'm going to give you fifty gallons of fuel and it won't cost you a cent.' Then he told him that the next time his supplier filled up his thousand-gallon tank, he should tell him that he owed him twenty bucks! The best part is, the farmer told our salesperson that if he wanted his business that bad he could have it, and he continues to be one of our best customers."[1]

Like Xerox's Jean Krak, the Growmark salesperson knew how to overcome sales resistance. Handling sales objections is a vital part of professional selling.

THE CONCEPT OF SALES RESISTANCE

sales resistance

anything the prospect does or says to prevent or delay a close

Sales resistance is anything the prospect does or says to stop, postpone, or hinder the salesperson from successfully closing a sales interview. It is a logical and expected aspect of any selling situation because people typically resist, avoid, or delay buying decisions. Professional salespeople must anticipate and deal with this response.

Objections are outward expressions of sales resistance; experienced sales personnel treat them as buying signs. In other words, sales objections are often indications that prospects are really interested in the product or service. Consider the situation facing Michael Blumenthal, CEO of Burroughs. His firm had just announced its acquisition of Sperry, a major competitor in the computer industry. The hostile takeover was denounced by the head of a Sperry users group in New England. Blumenthal's response was to immediately place a telephone call assuring her that the Sperry line would be continued, rather than be replaced by Burroughs equipment.[2] The merged companies are now called UNISYS.

The ability to identify, analyze, and correctly adjust to customer objections is often the key to successful selling. Prospects are likely to remain prospects—rather than customers—unless salespeople can adequately handle their objections.

The prospect's sales resistance is an inherent part of the sales interview. It is usually based on lack of knowledge about the product, the salesperson, or the seller's company; the conditions of the proposed sale; or any of the other factors in the personal selling process. The salesperson should treat sales resistance as a normal aspect of any sales interview, and one that can allow the presentation of a more complete sales story. If handled correctly, sales resistance can actually improve the overall likelihood of securing an eventual sale.

WHY PROSPECTS RAISE OBJECTIONS

As an integral part of the buyer's role in the sales process, objections are one aspect of the communication interface between buyer and seller. The salesperson should study in detail the reasons for the various objections raised in the normal pattern of sales work.

The numerous reasons for objections advanced by the customer include the seven discussed below.

1. *The prospect wants to avoid the sales interview.* In many cases, the prospect is actually "too busy" or too concerned with other matters to grant such an interview. A merchandiser who is in the middle of calculating a monthly open-to-buy figure would be a poor candidate for even the best sales presentation. A supermarket manager who is preparing for a periodic inspection by the regional manager is another unlikely prospect, as is a person with a migraine headache, an executive on the way to an important meeting, or a university purchasing agent awaiting budget passage by the state legislature. All prefer to avoid or delay a sales interview. In such cases, salespeople should maintain the prospect's goodwill by withdrawing courteously and, if possible, setting up a future appointment before leaving.

2. *The salesperson has failed to prospect and qualify properly.* Often the salesperson is actually responsible for customer objections because he or she has not identified a properly qualified prospect. Objections such as "I really like the car, but the monthly payments would be equal to two paychecks a month" or "While it looks like you have a fine product, we just don't use

that type of grinder in our operation" indicate that salespeople have failed to qualify their prospects.

3. *Objecting is a matter of custom.* To many customers, objections are a matter of a custom or habit. It is second nature for some people to object to any sales presentation, even if they have already decided to purchase the item. The traditional ritual associated with selling calls for at least token sales resistance. Generally, such objections do not block salespeople from eventually closing sales.

4. *The prospect resists change.* The prospect may object because the salesperson seems to be requesting a change in one's normal behavior or pattern of life. This is the situation facing Cadillac dealers as they try to market their $57,300 sports car, the Allante, to people who have traditionally bought expensive imports. Many people naturally resist change and any proposal suggesting it; therefore, they resist many sales presentations and products. Sellers must present a package of benefits that indicates to the buyer the need for change and the benefits of change.

5. *The prospect fails to recognize a need.* Some prospects do not see the need for the product or service being offered. They do not recognize how it could help in their manufacturing operations, make their lives easier, or lend status to their families. This often happens with the selling of technical industrial equipment. In most cases in which the prospect does not recognize the need, the salesperson either has failed to qualify the prospect or has made an ineffectual sales presentation.

6. *The prospect has some negative reaction.* Prospects can have negative reactions toward a salesperson, the product, the company, the industry, or certain conditions surrounding the suggested sale. Such reactions put prospects in adverse frames of mind, and the outcome is strong sales resistance. Prospects may have an unfavorable opinion of the salesperson's personal appearance, may be biased against a firm linked to a water pollution incident, or may believe that the entire industry has ignored the needs of the elderly. Any of these factors can create the negative attitudes responsible for many sales objections.

7. *The prospect lacks information.* Prospects who do not understand certain features or characteristics of the product may use objections to solicit additional data on it. In this way, they secure information about the product's qualities, how it works, the guarantee or warranty, and performance characteristics. From the seller's viewpoint, this is the most desirable objection, since it is a natural lead to an expanded sales presentation. Such an objection allows salespeople to modify, correct, expand, or improve the sales story to help buyers better understand the product and its benefits. It also opens up several additional closing opportunities.

Many of these reasons for sales objections stem from the prospect's role expectations. Sales personnel who understand the reasoning behind sales resistance can better cope with the objections they meet during their workday.

CLASSIFYING OBJECTIONS

Customer objections are varied, but, as Figure 10–1 suggests, most can be classified as one of six major types: (1) objections to delay action, (2) product objections, (3) source objections, (4) service objections, (5) price objections, and (6) objections related to the salesperson. In many cases, prospects advance two, three, or more objections during a sales presentation. It is

FIGURE 10–1   Major types of objections

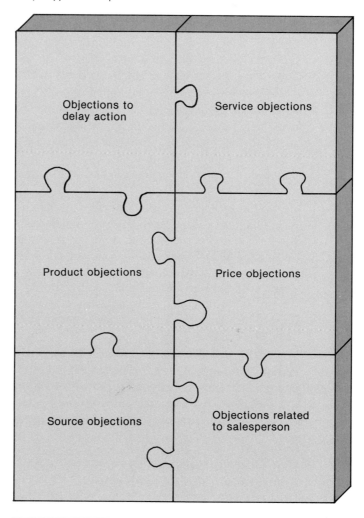

helpful for salespeople to classify each objection as it is put forth. This procedure permits the development of strong, effective answers to a limited number of objections.

We do not mean to imply, however, that every objection should be met with a canned response. Flexibility is a vital characteristic of professional salespeople, and it is maintained by those who handle objections effectively.

The initial step in handling an objection is to recognize it. The sections that follow provide illustrations to assist salespeople in properly classifying various objections.

Objections to Delay Action

Some typical objections to forestall action on the sales proposal are the following:

- Yes, I really like those new models, but I think I should talk it over with my spouse.
- I'll come back next payday.
- I'm in a hurry now, but I will come back for a test drive when I have more time.

Good salespersons anticipate that prospects may attempt to avoid action on the sales proposal. These attempts to delay the purchase decision usually mean that prospects are uncertain about the benefits to be obtained from the product.

Product Objections

Some objections concern the product itself. Prospects may be generally unwilling to buy certain products, brands, or particular items in a product line. Examples of product objections include the following:

- Yes, the new models are very attractive, but I can remember that my uncle bought one in 1988 and the car fell apart in six months.
- I agree that the Caribbean cruise would be nice, but I think I would prefer to vacation in Mexico.
- Why should I use dealership maintenance when the gas station on Jackson will do it for about 60 percent of what your service department will charge?

Product objections usually mean that prospects have failed to see the value of sales proposals. Salespeople must be able to stress the advantages of the product being offered. Furthermore, salespeople must believe in the product and be able to defend it in a realistic manner.

PROFESSIONAL SELLING IN ACTION

FrederickSEAL Deals with Prospect Delay

Field sales personnel are often frustrated by prospects that delay a buying decision by asking the rep to return in a few weeks. By that time, of course, the salesperson's travel schedule calls for him or her to be working a distant territory.

Tony Frederick, the CEO of FrederickSEAL, Inc., of Bedford, New Hampshire, hopes he has solved this problem for his sales personnel. The industrial sealing marketer divides each rep's territory into nine separate areas of equal size. Calls are often then sequenced so that the salesperson will be able to call back in a few weeks as requested.

Sales personnel work in three of their nine areas

each month. The call sequencing is as follows: Week 1: cover just one area; Week 2: work an area on the opposite side of the territory; Week 3: work an area adjacent to the first and complete unfinished calls for Week 1; and Week 4: call on key accounts in all three areas. The next month, the salesperson moves on to another three areas. All accounts are serviced, including callbacks, by the end of the quarter.

SOURCE: "In the Territory," *INC,* July 1989, p. 98. Reprinted with permission, *Inc.* magazine (July 1989). Copyright 1989 by Goldhirsh Group, Inc., 38 Commercial Wharf, Boston, MA 02110.

Source Objections

Source objections include the following examples:

- Yes, it does appear that you have a fine product, but we have been dealing with Morehead Pharmaceuticals for years.
- Your company sent me a cheap form letter when I complained about a delivery schedule last year.
- I really like the drill, but where will we be able to get replacement parts? Your firm is so small, I am worried about your parts supply system.
- Let me see . . . wasn't Allied Manufacturing the source of that toxic spill over in Jefferson County last year?

Source objections are sometimes unclear. Prospects may indicate negative impressions of firms and yet not clearly state the reasoning behind this objection or the supporting logic for it. Salespeople faced with source objections should be certain that they understand the real cause of such objections before attempting to deal with them. Probing statements such as "Tell me why you feel that way about my company" are extremely helpful in assessing the basis of source criticism.

Once salespeople understand the source objection, they can proceed to answer their prospects' objections. Professional salespersons are always positive about their companies, products, and the company's business integrity. Buyers have little respect for representatives who "pass the buck" by blaming their own firm's management or policies.

Service Objections

Service objections are numerous because many Americans honestly believe that sellers quickly forget them once the transaction has been concluded. In some cases, this admittedly has been the case. But for the vast majority of all sellers, servicing is an important and often very profitable part of their business. Good service means repeat customers for the company and the salespeople involved.

Salespeople must be able to confidently assure prospects that their service needs will be met. They must believe in the products they are selling and the servicing arrangements that support them.

Price Objections

Price objections may be the most critical questions with which salespeople deal. Typical comments in this category are:

- I can't afford to spend that much on merchandise that gives only a 33 percent return.
- We really love that house on Crescent Drive, but we just can't swing a $165,000 home for a couple of years.
- The dealer over in Jacksonville quoted a price that was $200 under your price.
- I am glad you called, Mr. Frasier, but before we get started, what is your price quotation for the lubricant? There is no use wasting each other's time unless you are competitive with Bayshore's price.

Such comments can be indicative of both uncertainty on the part of the buyer and an attempt to get a lower price. Prospects sometimes use price resistance to point out that the salesperson has failed to demonstrate product value equal to the asking price. This objection calls for an expanded sales presentation. In contrast, the price objection that a tourist raises in a Mexican marketplace suggests an interest in the item and a willingness to negotiate the price. Methods of handling price objections are further discussed later in this chapter.

Objections Related to Salespeople

Some consumers prefer not to deal with certain sales personnel or particular salespeople. The following comments are typical of this objection:

- I never deal with door-to-door salespeople.
- I don't think you represent the type of people with which we do business.
- My husband and I prefer to buy these items from mail-order companies.
- The last Universal representative who called on us tried to go over my head to get an order. Are you any different?

In dealing with these objections, sales personnel are forced to sell themselves before they can hope to close the sale. Reliability and a reputation for honest dealings are probably the most important ingredients in successfully handling this objection.

WHEN TO HANDLE OBJECTIONS

Objections can be considered at various times during the sales interview. Proper timing depends on the objection, the prospect's personality, and the environmental conditions surrounding the sale. The typical points at which objections should be handled are shown in Figure 10–2. In short, there is no one correct time to handle an objection.

A salesperson might choose to ignore an objection such as "I am not sure this is the best color for a new car." The prospect has indicated that he or she is thinking about the purchase decision, and the objection concerns a relatively minor point. The salesperson may reason that once the agreement to purchase has been secured, the matter of color can be decided. Minor objections are sometimes ignored, since a response may tend to confuse the sales presentation and make the objection appear more important than it really is. If a salesperson ignores an objection that is important to a prospect, it most certainly will be raised again later in the interview.

FIGURE 10–2   Typical points for handling objections

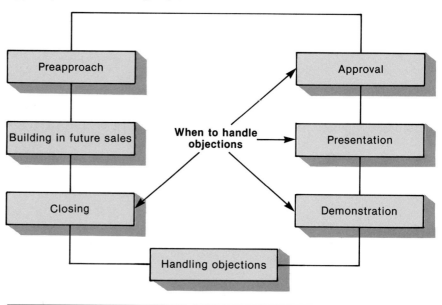

Strong objections should be dealt with immediately to maintain the salesperson's credibility. Prompt handling of an objection shows that the salesperson is sincere in his or her effort to meet the prospect's needs. In some cases, a direct response can handle the objection; the salesperson offers information, data, or arguments counter to the objection raised by the prospect. Other situations call for an indirect approach whereby the seller initially offers affirmative agreement and then proceeds to present the counterviewpoint. This approach, which is typically called the "Yes, but . . ." approach, is discussed in the next section.

Some objections are handled by delaying the response to the prospect. Typical remarks with which the salesperson can delay response are:

- That is a good question, but I'll cover it a little later in the presentation.
- Right . . . we'll come to that in just a minute.
- Yes, I can show you how the machine will work in that set of circumstances, but first let me demonstrate . . .

Such responses illustrate how objections can be postponed until a later, more advantageous point in the sales interview. Delaying objections has the advantage of letting the salesperson set the tempo of the interview, responding to objections at the most opportune time.

Timing responses to buyer objections is an important part of the technique of countering sales resistance. Correct timing comes from field experience and constant practice; all good salespeople know when to handle a particular objection, for each type of customer, in a given set of circumstances.

METHODS OF HANDLING OBJECTIONS

Literally dozens of methods for handling objections have been developed by sales personnel over the years, and more are being created every day in response to particular incidents. Sales personnel should practice the responses that have proved effective in answering the objections they typically encounter. While no list of these methods can be all-inclusive, Figure 10–3 outlines the most common methods of handling objections: (1) rebuttal, (2) the "Yes, but . . ." approach, (3) counterquestions, (4) testimonials, (5) restating the objection, (6) positive conversion, and (7) warranties and guarantees.

Rebuttal

rebuttal
immediate response that counters an objection with additional information

The **rebuttal** approach, also known as the denial method, is useful in answering direct questions that call for an immediate response. A rebuttal should be used only when the seller believes the prospect's objection is serious and important enough to merit an immediate response. There is no reason to risk a direct confrontation with the prospect over a minor objection that may later

FIGURE 10–3   Methods of handling objections

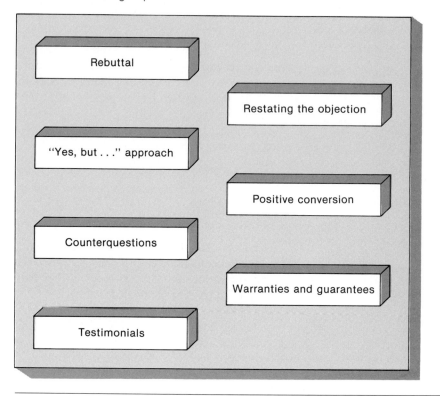

be forgotten or adequately handled by the rest of the presentation. In making a rebuttal, it is important to use a positive tone of voice. An argumentative rebuttal may give the appearance of high-pressure selling and, consequently, lead to increased sales resistance.

PROSPECT: Yes, Mr. Henderson, your company does offer some beautiful shirts, but my question is, Why should I switch from the Maddox line that I now carry in the store? After all, they also make a fine shirt.

SALESPERSON: I am glad you asked that question, Mr. Swerle. The answer is simple—we provide a markup of 52 percent while the Maddox line gives you only 47 percent. As a retailer you know that you must get the maximum possible return for each foot of shelf space. We give you a 5 percent greater return than the line you now carry . . . and profit is the bottom line in your business, isn't it?

In the example above, the salesperson welcomed the objection, then went on to counter it with a specific reason why the prospect should switch lines.

The objection was handled immediately and in a positive tone that stressed a benefit for the prospect.

The "Yes, but . . ." Approach

In the **"Yes, but . . ." approach,** the salesperson in effect agrees with the prospect's objection but then counters it with additional information:

> Yes, I agree that our economy is not in the best shape, but home ownership is just about the only tax shelter left these days.

This approach has the advantage of putting both prospect and seller on the same line of thought. The salesperson indicates initial agreement with the prospect's opinion and reasoning. As an indirect response to objections, the "Yes, but . . ." approach avoids the adversary position that sometimes characterizes the rebuttal technique.

Counterquestions

A simple "Why?" is often an effective way of dealing with objections. In effect, the seller reverses roles with the prospect. A **counterquestion** puts the prospect in the position of justifying why he or she objects to a certain point in the sales presentation. Consider the following example:

PROSPECT: What you say about your product may be true, but I am just not sure that your chemicals could hold up under the heat generated by our particular operation.

SALESPERSON: Why do you feel that way, Mr. Carpenter? I've shown you the lab reports that indicate the durability of our product.

PROSPECT: Yes, I know you have, Mr. Blake. I guess what really worries me is that the last time we bought something from your company, the order was two weeks late.

In the example, the seller's use of the why question forced the prospect to identify his real concern—the delivery schedule. Thus the prospect's original objection to the product's durability was a defense mechanism to avoid a discussion of an earlier experience with the seller. Now that the problem has been uncovered, the sales representative can proceed to deal with the prospect's true misgivings.

Testimonials

Testimonials from satisfied users or independent evaluators are often a good way to refute an objection raised by a prospect. If the buyer can be shown that people with similar circumstances (or an independent evaluator) are favorably impressed with a product, the objections usually tend to fade or diminish in importance. Here is an example of how a testimonial can be used in handling an objection:

PROSPECT: The house has everything we want . . . and it is beautifully land-scaped. But we are concerned about the school system. I am just not sure that it is as good as the one at Quarry Point.

SALESPERSON: That was the same thing that concerned Mrs. Foraker, who bought that tri-level over on the next block. Before she made an offer on the house, she investigated the school system in the area and found that it is rated in the top 15 percent in those statewide student assessment tests. She told me just the other day that her children were extremely happy in their new school. If you would like to visit the school, I'd be glad to drive you over there.

PROSPECT: No, that won't be necessary. But I am glad to hear about the high standing of the school system.

Restating the Objection

restating the objection
handling an objection by shifting the emphasis to a more favorable posture

One of the simplest techniques for handling objections is **restating the objection.** This approach has several distinct advantages. First, the salesperson can soften a prospect's criticism by rephrasing the question and shifting the emphasis to a more favorable posture. Consider these comments:

PROSPECT: I like the style, but I certainly object to seeing myself every time I walk down the street. Look at those dresses . . . they're all the same style.

SALESPERSON: Do you mean that you would prefer to look at something more traditional? I agree that this style is certainly popular this year . . . everyone is wearing it . . . but I will be glad to show you what we have in our "classics" department.

PROSPECT: Well, I guess I really am interested in this type of dress.

This salesperson, by rephrasing the objection, has switched the prospect to a more favorable attitude about the dress.

A second advantage of restating the objection is that the salesperson can sometimes make the objection seem unjustified to the prospect.

PROSPECT: I think your company has the worst customer service arrangement in our industry.

SALESPERSON: Did you say we had the *worst* customer service arrangement in our industry?

PROSPECT: Well, maybe it isn't the *worst,* but I have had some problems with your customer service people. For instance, last August . . .

On hearing the objection restated with the emphasis on the word *worst,* the prospect begins to modify the criticism and to specify actual reservations

---

Avi Ruimi and Avi Fattal Respond to an Objection

Cardboard sun protectors for windshields have been widely used in Israel for years. But they were unknown in Southern California until Avi Ruimi and Avi Fattal immigrated there from Israel. The two entrepreneurs negotiated a royalty agreement with the owners of the copyright for the shades and went into business. They developed their own cardboard design shaped like sunglasses.

The Israeli duo thought that an excellent market would be corporations that could use the shades for advertising or as premiums. However, corportions were unmoved by their sales proposals. So Ruimi and Fattal decided to respond to such objections by building consumer demand first. They concentrated on selling the shades to workers in a single business center. To build consumer demand, they cut the price of the shades in

half and sold thousands to individual consumers.

Corporate buyers began to see the shades everywhere. Gradually, the merits of putting corporate logos on the shades became obvious. Orders poured in from firms such as McDonnell Douglas Corporation, Honda Motor Company, BankAmerica Corporation, and Goodyear Tire & Rubber Company. Today, corporate orders account for 18 percent of total unit sales. It is clear that Ruimi and Fattal have successfully countered corporate buyers' initial sales objection.

SOURCE: "Using Consumer Demand to Persuade Buyers," *Sales & Marketing Management,* August 1986, pp. 60–61. Reprinted by permission of Sales & Marketing Management. Copyright August 1986.

---

about the selling firm. This step allows the salesperson to answer the prospect's doubts and improves the likelihood of a purchase.

Positive Conversion

positive conversion
transforms an objection into a reason for buying

Positive conversion—sometimes referred to as the boomerang technique—takes an objection and offers it as a reason for buying. The following sequence of remarks is illustrative:

PROSPECT: This is a tremendous piece of property. The lakefront is absolutely beautiful . . . but I am afraid real estate prices have made it a luxury we cannot afford now.

SALESPERSON: That is just the reason you should buy this property now. Real estate prices have been rising over 5 percent a year in this area. You can't afford not to buy the lot now . . . it certainly isn't going to get any cheaper.

The positive conversion method has to be implemented carefully, but in the hands of an experienced salesperson it can be an extremely effective approach to dealing with an objection. As illustrated above, positive conversion is particularly useful in countering price and expense objections.

Warranties and Guarantees

warranties and guarantees

assurances that a product will perform satisfactorily

Warranties and guarantees can be useful in answering questions about the serviceability of products. Examples are:

- I really like the sports car, but I wonder if it will hold up during our Minnesota winters.
- The merchandise meets our needs, but suppose a customer has some trouble with it. What do we do then?

A warranty or guarantee is an excellent weapon to use in combating objections about product quality, durability, performance, or service policies. Resolving the prospect's doubts stimulates a positive sales environment.

THE PRICE OBJECTION

As noted earlier, price objections are often the most critical questions with which salespeople must deal. But sales personnel must be certain that they are dealing with a price objection rather than a prospect's comment about price that is really a product- or service-related objection. Retail salespeople often encounter remarks such as, "That seems like a lot to pay for a cotton dress." In this situation, the prospect wants to be assured of the item's quality and value and is not offering a price objection per se.

flexible price policy

salesperson may negotiate a specific price with the buyer

one-price policy

sets a specific figure and does not allow the salesperson to negotiate price

Price objections can suggest uncertainty on the buyer's part or an attempt to get a lower price. In earlier days, many firms had **flexible price policies** which left the company's sales agents relatively free to negotiate specific prices with buyers. Today, manufacturing firms usually have a **one-price policy,** such as is common in retailing, and most salespeople do not have the authority to negotiate price. Any price concessions are usually under the control of the sales manager rather than field sales personnel.

Salespeople should be able to explain their company's price and justify it in relation to value received by the buyer. Sellers should treat a price objection as a sign that the prospect has not yet accepted the sales proposal. Renewed selling effort is required to show that the price level is justified for the product package offered. Certainly, salespeople should never apologize for the product's price. If they really believe in what they are selling, they also believe that the product is worth the asking price.

Price objections can be minimized, or in any event dealt with, in many other ways. Some of these techniques are:[3]

1. *Respond immediately to a price objection.* Give the prospect the information he or she seeks—now! Postponing the response arouses suspicion and causes the customer to lose confidence in the salesperson.

2. *Identify the customer's needs before citing prices.* A salesperson should not quote a whole list of prices, such as "We have this bike for $250, this model for $325, this 10-speed for $375, and, finally, this great mountain

bike for $450." This type of approach invites price objection, since the seller has failed to identify the customer's needs first.

3. *Quote a price with a supporting statement.* In other words, do not say, "It is $21,000." Say, "It is $21,000 and has a full 5 year/50,000 mile guarantee."

4. *Break the price quotation into small units.* Quote the product's price in weekly or monthly payments, cost per mile or work hour, or some similar quantity. Most good salespeople never state the total price without also citing the price per unit.

5. *Relate the price to an investment or profit.* For example, "The cost of this display unit is $4,000, and it will give you a return of $5,200 during the first year of use alone." A comparison of this nature allows the prospect to see the real value of the item.

Regardless of the technique or combination of methods used to handle price objection, it is important to handle them promptly. To do otherwise is to court failure in this most critical area.

A SYSTEMATIC APPROACH TO HANDLING OBJECTIONS

Salespeople need a systematic approach to handling objections. The eight-step sequence outlined below suggests a format to follow in handling objections. The actual selection of steps varies with each particular situation, but the sequential arrangement is essentially the same. The steps are:

1. *Anticipate the objection.* Effective salespeople are prepared to handle all questions and anticipate objections. Remember that objections are a natural part of the selling sequence.

2. *Prevent objections.* This step is best handled by preparing a complete sales presentation that considers nearly all the prospect's possible questions.

3. *Classify the objection.* Regardless of the exact wording, most objections fall into certain categories. Classification of objections is a tremendous aid in answering doubts and questions.

4. *Control the sales interview.* Salespeople who cannot adequately handle objections soon lose control of sales interviews. Unanswered objections tend to encourage other objections. To control a sales interview, salespeople must deal with objections efficiently and as promptly as possible. They must express a positive approach to sales interviews and avoid potential disagreements with prospects.

5. *Handle the objection.* Numerous techniques for dealing with objections are available to salespeople. A given set of selling circumstances dictates the techniques that might be used. If the first attempt at handling an objection is unsuccessful, sellers should turn to alternative approaches.

6. *Secure agreement from the prospect*. Salespeople should secure the prospect's agreement that the objection has been dealt with properly. A simple "Does that answer your question?" can be useful.

7. *Attempt a trial close*. Trial closes are discussed in detail in Chapter 11. They are low-keyed closes that can be helpful in determining the prospect's readiness to buy.

8. *Continue the presentation*. Assuming the prospect's objection has been answered but the individual is not yet ready to buy, the next logical step is to continue the sales presentation. This allows salespeople to put forth additional selling arguments and provides an opportunity for closing the sale.

The above steps are a rational progression in handling sales objections. Their effective implementation goes a long way toward removing the obstacles to a successful sale.

SUMMARY OF CHAPTER OBJECTIVES

1. To explain the concept of sales resistance.

Sales resistance is anything the prospect does or says to stop, postpone, or hinder the salesperson from successfully closing the sales interview. Sales resistance usually takes the form of objections raised during the course of the sales presentation. This is a logical and expected aspect of any selling situation.

2. To list the reasons prospects raise objections.

Prospects raise objections for several reasons:

1. The prospect wants to avoid the sales interview.
2. The salesperson has failed to prospect and qualify properly.
3. Objections are a matter of custom.
4. The prospect resists change.
5. The need is not recognized.
6. The prospect has a negative reaction.
7. Information is lacking.

3. To classify the types of objections.

Types of objections include:

1. Objections to delay action.
2. Product objections.
3. Source objections.
4. Service objections.
5. Price objections.
6. Objections related to salespeople.

4. To understand when objections should be handled.

Objections can be handled at various times during the sales interview. Proper timing of this effort depends on the objection, the prospect's personality, and the environmental conditions surrounding the sale.

5. To identify and discuss the various methods of handling objections.

The most common methods of handling objections are:

1. Rebuttal (immediate response to an objection that counters it with additional information).
2. The "Yes, but . . ." approach (seller notes agreement with a prospect's objection, then counters it with more information).
3. Counterquestions (asking "why" in response to an objection).
4. Testimonials (closing method that tells the prospect about the satisfaction of earlier buyers).
5. Restating the objection (method of handling an objection that shifts the emphasis to a more favorable posture).
6. Positive conversion (transforms an objection into a reason for buying).
7. Warranties and guarantees (assurances that a product will perform satisfactorily).

6. To demonstrate when and how to handle price objections.

Price objections usually suggest uncertainty on the part of the buyer or an attempt to get a lower price. A salesperson's response to a price objection is to demonstrate the value provided by the product. Studies have shown a relationship between price and consumer's perception of the product's quality. Techniques for minimizing price objections include:

1. Respond immediately to a price objection.
2. Identify the customer's needs before citing prices.
3. Quote a price with a supporting statement.
4. Break the price quotation into small units.
5. Relate the price to an investment or profit.

7. To outline a sequential approach to handling objections.

An eight-step approach to handling objections is as follows:

1. Anticipate the objection.
2. Prevent objections.
3. Classify the objection.
4. Control the sales interview.
5. Handle the objection.
6. Secure agreement.
7. Attempt a trial close.
8. Continue the presentation.

REVIEW QUESTIONS

1. List and explain the reasons prospects raise objections during a sales interview.
2. Why is it helpful for salespeople to classify each objection as it is put forth?
3. Identify and discuss the six major classifications of objections.
4. Match the objections in the left-hand column with the types of objection in the list at the right.

   _____ 1. I don't have time to look at the coats now, but I'll stop back later.   *a.* Objections to delay action.

   _____ 2. Why should I switch my business after a 15-year relationship with Oregon Products, Inc.?   *b.* Product objections.

   _____ 3. Quite frankly, I prefer to do business with the fellow from Consolidated—Larry Henly!   *c.* Source objections.

   _____ 4. I can't believe you'd want $10.50 per dozen for that item.   *d.* Service objections.

   _____ 5. I hear that rust is a serious problem with this model.   *e.* Price objections.

   _____ 6. Do you mean that if something goes wrong with the clock, I have to ship it back to the factory?   *f.* Objections to the salesperson.

5. Why is there no one correct time to deal with an objection?
6. Describe the seven common methods of handling objections.
7. Consider the following objections facing a steel salesperson:
   a. You folks produce good steel, but I have some real reservations about your delivery schedule.
   b. Is it true that the Pollution Control Board has sought an injunction against your plant in Center City?
   c. Are you sure this is the right steel for this operation?
   Cite at least two methods that could be used to handle these objections.
8. Why are price objections the most critical questions with which the salesperson must deal?
9. List and discuss five methods for minimizing price objections.
10. This chapter outlines a systematic approach to handling objections. Discuss this procedure for dealing with sales resistance.

DISCUSSION QUESTIONS AND EXERCISES

1. Describe your two most recent purchases. Did you offer any sales resistance? How did the salesperson handle your objections?
2. Consider the following statement: Salespeople never win arguments with prospects. Discuss this observation.
3. Assume that you are a real estate agent. How would you handle the following objections?

       a. Yes, I think we want to buy your listing on Oakmont. However, I think I will buy it through another real estate office . . . an old friend, Hal Stapleton, sells for Penn-Jersey Realty.

       b. The location and price are right, but this is the dirtiest house we have seen . . . and most of the rooms need to be painted.

       c. I am pretty sure we will act on that listing in Fairmont Acres, but I want to be very sure before I make an offer, since I hear that your firm is very strict about forfeiting deposits.

4. Comment on the following viewpoint: You only get what you pay for these days.

5. One of the authors once heard a salesperson remark, "How can you sell a product that has a significant price disadvantage? They (prospects) love it until it comes down to the price. That is where we lose them." How would you reply to this discouraged salesperson?

SALES DIALOG

It is a pleasant day in Tulsa, Oklahoma. Sid Vassey, a sales representative for Green Thumb Landscaping, is explaining a monthly lawn-care program to Billy Simmons.

VASSEY: Our crew will cut your grass each week, weed the flower beds, and fertilize as required. Since you travel a lot, this program will mean that you can spend the weekend relaxing with your family instead of taking care of your yard.

SIMMONS: Yes, that would be nice, but what about the price?

VASSEY: And did I mention that we also prune your shrubs as needed?

SIMMONS: No, but how much will all of this cost?

VASSEY: Before I get to that, let me show you a list of some of your neighbors who use our service.

SIMMONS: Let's hear about the price first!

VASSEY: Of course . . . the price is $150 per month and this includes our famous Green Thumb guarantee. If you do not like any of the work, we will have a crew back here to correct the situation within 24 hours.

SIMMONS: One hundred and fifty dollars a month, umm . . .

What do you think the results of this sales dialog will be?

CASE 10–1 PACIFIC PHARMACEUTICALS, LTD.

After graduation from a state college in Colorado the previous spring, Howard Jennings accepted a position as a marketing representative for Pacific Pharmaceuticals, Ltd. Following a two-month training session at Pacific's San Francisco headquarters, he was assigned a territory in Los Angeles.

As this case begins, Jennings is entering the office of Dr. Joan Tilghman, a family physician.

JENNINGS: Good morning, Dr. Tilghman. I am Howard Jennings with Pacific Pharmaceuticals. I know how busy you are, so I am glad you could take a few minutes to see me.

TILGHMAN: Nice to meet you, Mr. Jennings. How long have you been with Pacific?

JENNINGS: Just since July. I graduated from college last spring. In fact, you are my first sales call.

TILGHMAN: Oh, that is interesting! Well, tell me what new products does Pacific have that would be appropriate for my practice?

JENNINGS: As a matter of fact, we have a new pain reliever that might interest you. Here is a brochure on it. What do you think?

TILGHMAN: Yes, I heard about this one. It looks like something I would be interested in. And I have certainly prescribed a lot of Pacific products over the years. But I see that there are a couple of side effects. What can you tell me about these effects?

JENNINGS: Not too much really . . . but I would be glad to have one of our in-house specialists call you and answer any questions.

TILGHMAN: Well, I don't have time for a lot of phone calls. I also heard this item is going to sell for a 50 percent premium over its competition. I always try to keep the cost of prescriptions as low as possible for my patients. Many of them don't have prescription coverage, you know.

JENNINGS: I am sorry about the higher cost, but you know how expensive it is to develop a new product today.

Questions

1. Evaluate Jennings' first sales call. How could he have improved his efforts?
2. Analyze the reasons for Tilghman's sales resistance.
3. Which types of objections did Tilghman raise?
4. Did Jennings handle the objections adequately? Discuss.

CASE 10–2   JERSEY PRODUCTS, INC.

Jersey Products, Inc. is a large producer and distributor of commercial chemicals located in an industrial city in northern New Jersey. Last year, about 65 percent of its sales volume came from the New York metropolitan area.

Fred Lindsey, Jersey's director of purchasing, has been with the firm for seven years. Before that he was in the purchasing department of a major steel company in Pittsburgh.

One day last January, Lindsey had granted an appointment to Carl Burlchek, a sales representative for a well-known office equipment manufacturer. Lindsey and Burlchek had never met before, and Jersey had never bought equipment from Burlchek's company. About 20 minutes before the scheduled 10:30 appointment, Lindsey received a long-distance call from Burlchek in which the conversation went as follows:

BURLCHEK: Mr Lindsey, I'm sorry that I will not be able to make the appointment I set up last week. I am having car problems here in Trenton . . . and I won't be able to get the car out of the garage before 2 P.M. It just cut out yesterday morning.

LINDSEY: Oh, that is a shame.

BURLCHEK: I am sorry we won't have a chance to meet, since I have to be in Cape May tomorrow morning. But could we set up an appointment next month, when I'll be in your area?

LINDSEY: Yes, that would be OK with me. Let me transfer you back to my secretary, who can get you on the appointment book.

BURLCHEK: That's great.

LINDSEY: However, if you run into any more car trouble, please give me a little bit more notice. This upsets my entire schedule today.

BURLCHEK: Don't worry about this happening again . . . I am scheduled for a new company car in two more weeks.

Consequently, another meeting was scheduled between the two men in late February. At the appointed time, Burlchek enters the purchasing director's office.

BURLCHEK: Good morning, Mr. Lindsey, I am glad we finally have a chance to meet. Let me apologize for missing that appointment last month.

LINDSEY: That's OK. Now, let me see, as I recall you wanted to tell me about that new line of desks your company has brought out.

BURLCHEK: Yes, I do! We've had sensational success with these desks. It seems that just about everyone is ordering them . . . We think that they will end up with 35 to 50 percent of the market. The company did some very careful research on matching desks to the physical characteristics of the individuals who use them. As a result, we came up with three common sizes or types of users. We call these our Alpha, Beta, and Delta user profiles. Our studies show that people using the right size desk are more productive. Let me show you how these desks work.

Burlchek shows Lindsey booklets and graphic displays of the new product. After an extensive sales presentation, during which Lindsey sits and listens quietly, Burlchek concludes:

BURLCHEK: Great idea, huh? Like I said, we think it will revolutionize the industry.

LINDSEY: Maybe.

BURLCHEK: Mr. Lindsey, we would like to have you come down to Philadelphia . . . at our expense . . . to look at the new desks. I'm sure that once you see them, you will agree that they are just the thing for those brand new sales offices you are going to be opening.

LINDSEY: Well, I don't think I'll have a chance to get down to Philadelphia for another month or so. Besides, I kind of like the padded stuff offered by Conover Designs. In fact, their representative was in here to see me last month . . . same day you had that car trouble.

Questions

1. What is the reason for Lindsey's reaction to the new product?
2. What type of objection(s) has he raised?
3. If you were Burlchek, how would you proceed?

PART FIVE

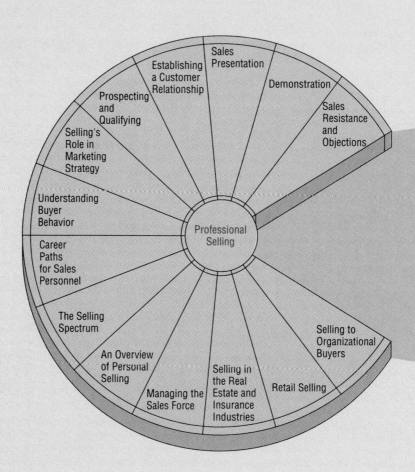

Professional
Selling

Sales
Presentation

Establishing
a Customer
Relationship

Demonstration

Prospecting
and
Qualifying

Sales
Resistance
and
Objections

Selling's
Role in
Marketing
Strategy

Understanding
Buyer
Behavior

Career
Paths
for Sales
Personnel

The Selling
Spectrum

Selling to
Organizational
Buyers

An Overview
of Personal
Selling

Selling in
the Real
Estate and
Insurance
Industries

Retail Selling

Managing the
Sales Force

Securing Sales Today and Tomorrow

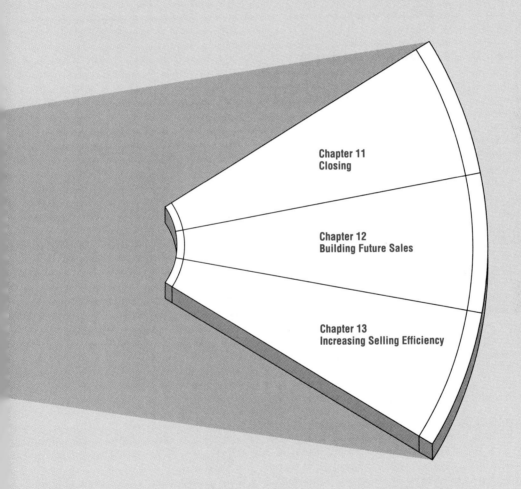

Chapter 11
Closing

Chapter 12
Building Future Sales

Chapter 13
Increasing Selling Efficiency

CHAPTER 11

Closing

CHAPTER OBJECTIVES

1. To define the concept of closing.

2. To list and explain the causes of closing failures.

3. To determine when to close a sale.

4. To outline and define the basic closing techniques available to salespersons.

5. To describe the primary postsale activities that a salesperson should employ.

SALES CAREER PROFILE

DANIEL D. KING
Nekoosa Papers, Inc.

Daniel D. King is the general sales manager for Nekoosa Papers, Inc. of Port Edwards, Wisconsin. King holds a bachelor of science degree in business and an MBA from Loyola University of Chicago. His hobbies include woodworking, golf, racquetball, running, and watching the stock market.

King describes how he became involved in sales: "While going to school I didn't really feel that I was interested in a career in production, nor did I feel that I had the skills or the temperament to get into the financial end of business. I did want a career in management, so it seemed that the sales avenue was best.

"I was living in Chicago when I was hired by Nekoosa Papers in 1972. With my wife, I moved to Wisconsin Rapids, where we set up temporary housing while I went through a six-month training program. This program involved working a series of appointments throughout the company so that I would be exposed to various facets of the organization. A great deal of time was spent in the mill learning the process involved in making paper.

"After that six-month period, I was transferred to our Chicago sales office, where I became a consumer salesman. I called on agencies, printers, any potential user of Nekoosa Papers, and yet I didn't have any direct sales responsibility. Our papers are sold through distributors or wholesalers (we call them merchants), and so the idea was to go out and make calls, show the Nekoosa line, and then tell prospects where it could be purchased.

"After that indoctrination, I became a field sales representative and received account responsibility calling on existing merchants and large direct customers. I covered many cities in the Midwest and moved around in the territories for approximately six years.

"At the end of six years, there was a retirement in our sales management group in Port Edwards, Wisconsin, and I was selected to become the product sales manager for business forms and converting papers. During the next six and a half years, my responsibility was to sell the roll products from our northern mills in Wisconsin and the southern mill in Arkansas. Then, in 1984, I was promoted to general sales manager."

When asked what he liked most about his job, King replied, "Without question, what I like are the people with whom I work, for whom I work, and to whom I sell. We're in a very good industry, a very clean industry, lots of really nice people.

"One of the things that I benefited from was the fact that I have moved from the field sales position to Port Edwards management rather quickly and at a rather young age. I moved into a position to make some changes while the comments and concerns of my fellow field salespeople were still fresh in my mind. I would say that I've developed a reputation of being fair and honest and open with salespeople who work for me, with my peers, and with my customers.

"I believe that supporting the field sales personnel is extremely important. Field sales want and need accurate and timely information. This allows them to enter the market-place more fully equipped. As a group, they also need periodic recognition. A letter to a salesperson, with a copy to the vice president, saying that I am proud of their efforts, and delighted with their performance during the last three or four months, goes a long way toward boosting that person and getting him or her going. Our company, like most mills, pays strictly on salary with no bonus, no stock options, no incentives to the field sales representatives, so we need to find people who are self-starters, with a management objective somewhere along the line, and we need to keep them motivated."

King went on to discuss why he thought Nekoosa was picked as one of the best companies to sell for in the United States: "I think that some of the reasons would be the quality of the product, the integrity of the company, and the reputation for service in the field."

Next, King described closing a sale: "Our particular business is such that we don't normally walk out of a customer location with an order. Our intent is to develop programs; but even in the development of those programs, we get into closing situations—closing the program itself, for example.

"As I interview young sales candidates, I emphasize to them the importance of being extremely cognizant of the customer, and trying to anticipate the customer's needs. A successful salesperson can see from the motions or hear from the way a person says something whether or not they are asking for more information, more time, more help, or even more pressure. And it's also extremely important that a salesperson never leave a situation where a customer is unhappy, confused, or just not fully informed.

"The most effective sales closing technique is the direct approach, just simply asking the prospect for the order. I don't like to beat around the bush. A lot of the others—alternative decisions, summary of affirmative agreements, and so forth—can come out of the direct approach. Simply ask the question! 'May I have an order?'"

As for postsales activities, King replied, "I think number one is showing appreciation. Sometimes a simple 'thank you' can mean a lot. Make it clear, and then get on to something else. Knowing when to get up and leave after showing appreciation is very important.

"I often tell our young salespeople that I'm not nearly as interested in an order as I am in a program. It does not bother me if a salesperson works on a customer for months without an order. When they finally get the program established, then the orders follow naturally. In short, I am one of those who really believes in forgoing today's highs for the long-term good of the program."

Like Daniel King, Joyce Nardone understands the importance of closing the overall sales process. Nardone is a 24-year-old sales manager with the Facsimile Division of Amfax America in Needham, Massachusetts. She recalls a sales situation in which a prospect considered the purchase of a fax machine for several weeks. Nardone had provided a demonstration model, but the prospect still could not decide among the six machines he had examined.

Finally, Nardone resorted to some classic sales lore and a direct closing technique. She told the prospect: "I wish you'd seen my machine first or last.

People don't usually buy from the middle salesperson. But I have the best product. Why don't you buy it?" Nardone's approach jarred the prospect out of his indecisiveness, and she closed the sale.[1] Nardone understood that the best presentation and demonstration in the world are meaningless if the salesperson can not close the sale.

CLOSING—A DEFINITION

closing

point at which the salesperson secures the desired agreement from the prospect

President Harry S Truman was fond of the saying, "The buck stops here!" So it is with the closing phase of the sales process. Closing a sale that is mutually beneficial to both the buyer and the seller is a salesperson's ultimate goal; in fact, it is the only reason for his or her role. **Closing** is defined as that point in the sales presentation at which the salesperson secures the desired agreement from the prospect.

Although the other aspects of the sales process—prospecting and qualifying, preapproach and approach, presentation, demonstration, handling objections, and building future sales—are all important, the actual process of closing is the salesperson's primary objective. Salespeople who cannot close cannot sell. Unless salespeople can sell the product or service to a prospect to the mutual satisfaction of both, the sales process cannot be completed. Closing is both the climax of the sales interview and the acid test of how well salespeople can sell. Over the long run, success in closing also determines the salesperson's level of income and material success.

THE CAUSES OF CLOSING FAILURES

No salesperson concludes every sales interview successfully. A survey conducted by Sales & Marketing Executives of Los Angeles, a professional sales organization, concluded that only 2 percent of sales are closed on the first call. Subsequent calls increased the close rate: 3 percent of sales were closed on the second call; 4 percent on the third call; 10 percent on the fourth call; and 81 percent on the fifth call.[2] The "100 percent effective" salesperson has not been found in any industry.

While closing failures are sales failures, they are to be expected and should not discourage salespeople from trying again. Missed sales should be treated as learning experiences to be carefully analyzed and studied to improve future sales performance. Every salesperson should devote some time to assessing the effectiveness of each sale attempted. Such an effort pays dividends in the future.

The next section discusses four of the causes of closing failures: (1) fear, (2) improper attitude, (3) verbal overkill, and (4) failure to ask for an order.

Fear—The Sales Killer

Fear of failure is a leading reason why salespeople are sometimes unable to close sales. Sales personnel operate in a fiercely competitive environment that requires tremendous personal drive and initiative. Enthusiasm is a major asset for any salesperson. It must be sustained if the salesperson is to remain effective.

A sales turndown dampens enthusiasm and the desire to try again with the next prospect. Generally, the best way to cope with this fear is to become an expert in the field and to know more than any customer could possibly learn about the firm's products or services. Fear of sales failure is inappropriate in the demanding field of professional selling.

Markita Andrews set a record when she sold 32,000 boxes of Girl Scout cookies. She later went on to write a book entitled *How to Sell More Cookies, Condos, Cadillacs, Computers . . . and Everything Else.* Andrews thinks that self-confidence is an important part of successful selling:

> If you know you want to sell something, you can gain confidence by learning absolutely everything you can about the product. You won't remember how shy you might be deep inside if you're having a good time with a customer, teaching him . . . [or her] . . . something, answering all the questions, and heading fullblast toward the sale. A good thing to remember is that you often can hide your fears behind what you know.[3]

Improper Attitude

Closely related to fear of failure is an improper attitude, which the salesperson reveals in his or her attempts to close, speech patterns, and personal mannerisms. Some salespeople have so little confidence in their presentations that they dread the closing stage; they fear failure because they have failed in earlier steps of the sales process. Maintaining a proper attitude is another key to successful selling.

Other salespeople may appear too aggressive or overly eager to close. Buyers interpret this approach as high-pressure selling or evidence of the salesperson's inexperience, overconfidence, doubts about the product, conceit, or disrespect. This interpretation is unimportant, since the end result is the same: a missed sale.

In attempting to close a sale, salespeople must be confident of both their products and their sales presentations. Sellers who exhibit positive, respectful, sincere, and helpful attitudes toward prospects are likely to secure each prospect's confidence and trust.

Verbal Overkill

Another danger in completing a sale is verbal overkill by the salesperson. Verbal overkill is characteristic of the salesperson who continues to extol the virtues of the product long after the prospect is ready to purchase. In some cases, the guilty salesperson simply lacks confidence in his or her ability to close; in others, the prospect's apparent willingness to close is not perceived. Both are costly mistakes.

Verbal overkill is a real danger. The salesperson must watch for cues indicating that the time is right to close and then must be confident enough to do so. Various closing cues are discussed later in this chapter.

Failure to Ask for the Order

Salespeople often tell the tale of a seller who had been trying to sell product X to ABC Corporation with numerous sales calls over a prolonged period of time. One day the representative was surprised when ABC's purchasing director signed an order for several months' supply of product X. The dazed salesperson, who had kept going through patience and persistence, overcame shock to ask why the purchasing director had finally decided to buy, after so many sales calls. The buyer's answer typically was "Today is the first time you ever asked me to give you an order."

True or not, the story illustrates the fact that the eventual completion of a sales interview comes when the salesperson asks the prospect for the order. The number of salespeople who never attempt to close amazes trained observers. Some salespeople—a loose application of the term—do not appear to know that they are supposed to close; others seem to forget about this most crucial step. Completion of a sale requires the salesperson to initiate and conclude the closing process. Few buyers ring up their own sales or voluntarily draw up and sign purchase orders. Even prospects actually seeking to buy an item rarely proceed with the purchase unless salespeople initiate the closing.

WHEN TO CLOSE A SALE

Old-timers believed there was one best moment for a closing in a sales interview. The effective salesperson, it was believed, could spot this moment and then close effectively. This way of thinking has long since been discounted in professional selling.

Current thought is that there are several good moments to close the sale. Although a close would be totally inappropriate at some points, the correct point could occur at any time during the sales presentation. Consider the following remarks by customers:

- *Customer entering a retail store:* Hi, Jack. Listen, I want to get one of the new razors they have been advertising on TV.
- *Purchasing director to a sales representative entering her office:* I'm sure glad you were able to stop back here this week. Lance, we've evaluated those samples you left with us, and our technical people say they are just what we need in the shop. And the price is right, too!

FIGURE 11–1   Closing opportunities exist at various points in the sales process

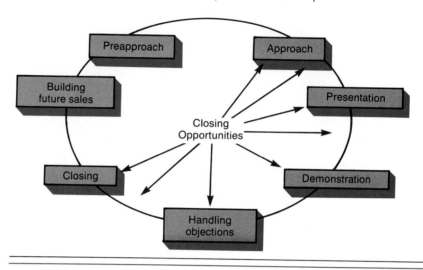

• *Prospect to a real estate agent:* Duane and I just love the house over on Linden Street. It has everything we have been looking for these past several months.

In the above situations, a salesperson would be foolish to do anything other than to attempt an immediate close. The customers have clearly indicated their acceptance of the products and their willingness to buy. All that is needed is some effort on the part of the salesperson to close. In such cases, the close can occur very early in the selling process—perhaps during or right after the approach.

It is up to salespeople to identify the exact points of the sales interview at which customers might be amenable to a closing technique. Figure 11–1 shows likely points for such closing opportunities.

Closing Cues

closing cues

verbal statements and physical actions (or signals) that suggest a buyer may be ready to purchase the product

Closing cues are comments and body language that suggest buyers may be ready to purchase products. Good salespeople study their prospects carefully for these signals to indicate when they should attempt closing. A salesperson who can correctly perceive such cues has a significant advantage over one who attempts to close indiscriminately throughout the selling process. The customer sees the former salesperson as being helpful and the latter as resorting to high-pressure tactics.

The ability to spot closing cues comes from experience and practice.

Acquiring this skill takes time. Nevertheless, all successful sales personnel have it, and the effort is well worthwhile.

Closing cues can be classified as either verbal or physical. *Verbal cues* include the following observations or questions:

- Yes, I agree that your plan really solves our marketing problem.
- Did you say 30 days is the same as cash?
- When could you deliver the refrigerator?

Physical cues are actions, such as:

- The prospect nods in agreement to a sales presentation.
- The prospect puts on a coat and admires its fit in the mirror.
- The prospect begins to carefully study an insurance policy.

The meaning of both verbal and physical cues should be obvious to salespeople. When the customer expresses an apparent interest in the product, the correct moment for a closing attempt has arrived. Other examples of closing cues include such verbal cues as:

- What other colors do you have available?
- I have always wanted a Saab.
- Can we pay for this over three years instead of two?
- What is the approximate installation time for the machine?
- This is a beautiful piece of property.
- Your company has always been fair to us in the past.
- Do you have this particular model in stock?
- Where would I get replacement parts?
- Let me taste one of your new snacks.
- I really feel great in this dress.
- I need the table for a bridge party tomorrow evening.
- The base price is great, but how much do the accessories cost?
- You say it has a two-year guarantee?
- Well, I'd have to rearrange the shop somewhat differently.
- How would I contact your service department?

Of course, there are many more verbal closing cues. The preceding examples show that verbal cues are usually in the form of a question or a positive expression about the product or service. Other physical cues include these actions:

- The prospect begins to reexamine the merchandise very carefully.
- The prospect begins to read the contract, agreement, or application.
- The prospect begins to use or sample the product.

- The prospect smiles on hearing the contract terms.
- The prospect tenses up and watches the demonstration intently.
- The customer steps back and admires the sofa.
- The purchasing agent begins to check competitive prices in other catalogs.

Physical cues to closing opportunities are numerous and varied. A good salesperson carefully watches the prospect's activities and behavior to spot these signals.

Trial Closes

trial close

closing attempt used to determine prospect's disposition to the product and the sales presentation

Another method of assessing when to close the sale is the **trial close,** an attempt to determine the prospect's attitude toward the product and the sales presentation. The salesperson may hope to consummate the sale as a result of a trial close, but the expectations of doing so are not high. Therefore, it is best to view a trial close as a probe to determine the buyer's current state of buying intention.

A trial close should be indirect and low-key. The salesperson wants to leave plenty of opportunity to continue the presentation and make additional closing attempts. If the seller were to say, "This car is an excellent buy at $16,000. When do you want to pick it up?" early in the interview, he or she might lose credibility with the customer and ruin any future chance for the transaction. Instead, the seller might say, "How would you like to handle the financing?" or "Do you like the blue or green best?" In both cases, sufficient opportunity remains to pick up the conversation and to close at a later point in the presentation. The buyer was not asked to say yes or no to the actual purchase. If the response was "I think I would prefer to handle the financing through my credit union. In fact, they have cleared me for a loan up to . . ." or "I think the blue one is the better choice," then the salesperson might launch into a final closing technique. The trial close has shown that the prospect is sincerely interested in making such a purchase and has made some tentative choices regarding the product.

Not all trial closes are verbal; some are based on a movement. The salesperson might pick up an order book, walk toward the cash register, or start to wrap the purchase. Some salespeople have mastered the art of the silent trail close. They simply stop talking and gaze intently at the buyer, hoping to hear of a decision to purchase the item. If the buyer does not respond as hoped, the salesperson breaks the silence by picking up the sales story again.

Regardless of the method used, the trial close is an excellent way of determining where a buyer stands in regard to a proposed purchase. All successful salespeople realize its value and practice it in virtually every presentation they make.

FINAL CLOSING TECHNIQUES

The first step in a successful close is for the salesperson to be alert to possible closing cues. The second is to attempt one or more trial closes during the course of the interview. In most cases, a final closing technique is used only after these earlier steps have been accomplished. The exception to this generalization occurs when the prospect is presold before actually entering the sales interview. In this case, the salesperson tries to close during or immediately after the approach segment of the normal selling sequence.

Salespeople do not expect to close every sale or to conclude most sales with just one closing technique. Fortunately, they can use a variety of closing methods. The salesperson's task is to select the technique that is most appropriate for a particular sales interview. Typically, each salesperson relies on two or three techniques that are practiced extensively until the individual is comfortable with them.

Consider the closes used by legendary car salesperson Joe Girard. Girard is listed in the *Guinness Book of World Records* for selling 1,425 trucks and automobiles during a single year. He has since relinquished his position at Merollis Chevrolet in East Detroit, Michigan, to his son. Girard now heads his own firm, which promotes his talents for sales meetings and markets films and cassette tapes used in sales training activities. He has also published books about selling.

His former colleagues frequently recall the dynamic closing techniques Girard used. Humorless prospects often burst into laughter when Girard stripped the proverbial shirt off his back. When one prospect failed to respond, Girard even took off his trousers and completed the sale dressed only in his underwear. Associates also recall Girard throwing his sports coat across a puddle for a woman who had resisted his sales presentation and was leaving the dealership. As usual, Girard eventually ended up with the sale.[4] Like other successful salespeople, Joe Girard knew the importance of an effective closing technique.

The exact titles of the different approaches vary, depending on the source consulted. This text uses the following terminology:

1. Assumptive close.
2. Direct approach.
3. Alternative decisions.
4. Summary and affirmative agreement.
5. Balance sheet approach.
6. Emotional close.
7. "If I can show you . . ." close.
8. Extra inducement close.
9. SRO method.
10. Silence as a closing technique.

These 10 approaches are the primary closing techniques used today. Effective salespeople continually strive to refine and perfect those methods that apply to their own sales interviews.

Assumptive Close

assumptive close technique

closing technique that assumes that the prospect has decided to purchase the item

In the **assumptive close technique,** sellers assume that buyers have decided to purchase the product or service offered. The salesperson could sign the contract, pass it to the prospect with a pen, pick up the phone and start to arrange delivery details, or start to ring up the purchase. This technique occasionally results in some voided cash register tapes.

An assumptive close works best where the sales interview has concentrated on or been narrowed down to just one product and the salesperson is reasonably confident of the prospect's willingness to buy. The technique then is to get the buyer to actually commit to the purchase—usually by his or her inaction. An assumptive close forces the prospect who has not decided to buy to interrupt the salesperson and indicate an unwillingness to conclude the purchase. People who do desire the product are reluctant to interrupt.

Direct Approach

direct approach

closing method in which the salesperson simply asks the prospect for the order

An obvious way to close a sale is simply to ask the prospect for the order. This is known as a **direct approach,** and it should be used only when (1) the seller is reasonably confident of the outcome, or (2) several other closes have failed and the direct approach may be the last chance to conclude the purchase. Illustrations of the use of the direct approach include:

- Well, I guess that about covers the details, Arnold. How many do you want to order for shipment next week?
- I know that you are busy, Mrs. Abrovnik, so if it is all right with you I'll start to get this order written up.
- It looks as if you prefer the Probe—I'll get some temporary license tags for you. You have certainly made a wise selection.

By resisting the direct approach, the buyer is forced to clarify his or her position on the matter. This gives the seller a starting point for picking up the sales presentation again or a chance to answer possible objections. Eventually, it allows the salesperson to try another closing technique.

Alternative Decisions

alternative decisions

closing technique in which the prospect is asked to make a choice between alternatives equally favorable to the seller

The elementary technique that proposes **alternative decisions** is one of the most commonly used approaches to closing. The alternative decision technique asks the prospect to make a choice between alternatives equally favorable to the seller. The decision may concern a major point (as with an automobile model)—Do you prefer the Civic or the Prelude?—or a minor point—Which color would you like for the living room draperies?

The alternative decision technique can actually pose a choice: "Will that be on VISA or MasterCard?" Or it can raise a related question: "Will two dozen be enough?"

By requesting the buyer to make an alternative decision, the salesperson has forced the basic purchase decision. The buyer affirms a particular choice in response to the preceding questions:

- I think I'd like to have the Civic.
- Green would probably look best in the living room.
- VISA, I guess.
- No, we're having company, so you'd better give me three dozen.

This choice commits the person to the actual purchase. If the person fails to make a choice, he or she usually identifies doubts about the product or gives some reasons for not concluding the sale at this point. In both cases, this provides sellers with an opportunity to expand the original sales interview by suggesting other models or additional uses of the product.

Summary and Affirmative Agreement

summary and affirmative agreement method
close whereby the seller summarizes the features, benefits, and advantages of the product and seeks agreement from the prospect

Although the **summary and affirmative agreement method** is sometimes divided into two separate techniques, it is logical to combine them into a uniform approach that is particularly useful when:

1. The product under discussion has many separate and difficult-to-remember features.
2. The customer seems to be impressed with particular features of the item.
3. The buyer may be forced to justify a purchase decision to a third party, like higher management or his or her spouse.

In this technique, the salesperson closes by summarizing the major features, benefits, and advantages of the product. The seller pauses at each point and seeks agreement from the prospect, with comments such as:

- I think you said that this feature would really help your loading operation.
- Didn't you say that guaranteed insurability was very important to you?
- The Hyundai is certainly in the price range you mentioned earlier.
- This is the exact thing you said you were looking for in a uniformed security service! Isn't that correct?

The summary and affirmative agreement technique has the dual advantages of reinforcing the key selling points in a sales presentation and at the same time building a series of acceptances about the need for, and importance of, these features. It is an extremely effective approach, particularly when the summary ends with some more direct closing technique.

Balance Sheet Approach

balance sheet close

close that presents negative features as well as benefits of the product

One way to close a sale that stresses logic and analytical decision making is the **balance sheet close,** sometimes known as the T-account, the two-sided, or the advantage/disadvantage close. Essentially, this approach presents the negative factors of a product, as well as its benefits. The method can be used separately or with a summary of the major product characteristics.

Sellers may actually draw up balance sheets for products, such as the following:

Assets	Liabilities
• Most comprehensive warranty in the industry. • 15 percent lower operating costs. • A complete service facility only 10 minutes away.	• The initial price is 3 percent higher than that of the competition.

When the salesperson starts by listing a liability or disadvantage of the product, the buyer is likely to appreciate the fact that the seller is acknowledging that the product is not perfect. The balance sheet approach establishes the salesperson's credibility in the mind of the prospect. If the salesperson is handling a reliable product, it should be possible to list many more advantages than disadvantages. The objectivity of this technique appeals to many buyers.

After listing assets and liabilities, the salesperson concludes with a statement such as:

> There it is in black and white, Frank! While our initial price is a little higher, a 15 percent savings in operating costs more than make up for the difference during the first year you use the machine. Then, when you consider that we have the best warranty in the industry, and the ready availability of our service facility, I don't see how you can make any other choice. Do you?

Emotional Close

emotional close

use of fear, pride, romance, or the need for peer group acceptance as a closing technique

An **emotional close** seeks to motivate the prospect to buy through appeal to such factors as fear, pride, romance, or the need for peer group acceptance. Insurance agents may attempt to close by stressing the need for the breadwinner to provide financial protection for the family should he or she die or become disabled. An emotional close can be a very potent weapon in the hands of a qualified salesperson.

For the most part, emotional closes are used only when several other approaches have failed or when the salesperson believes the prospect is particularly susceptible to this technique. Avoid emotional closes in situations where there is a high repeat-sale potential. This type of close relies on stimulating an impulsive purchase on the part of the prospect and should be carefully considered before being used in closes where long-term seller-buyer relationships exist or are sought. Continued reliance on this technique may injure this relationship.

"If I Can Show You . . ." Close

"If I can show you . . ." approach

closing technique that identifies the prospect's primary need and then offers a solution

In the **"If I can show you . . ." approach,** the salesperson begins by identifying the prospect's primary buying motive, then arguing that his or her product or service meets this need. An example would be: "Dr. Lane, if I can show you a product that eliminates the side effect that concerns you, and still does the job for the patient, would you be willing to prescribe it for your patients?" This approach provides a powerful close for the salesperson who has done a good job of identifying a prospect's concerns and needs. It is tough to say no to something you have said you needed.

The "If I can show you . . ." close is effective only if the seller has correctly assessed what the prospect wants a specific product to do. Many salespeople have been embarrassed in using this close after failing to identify the buyer's needs correctly. If the salesperson is not satisfied that this has not been accomplished, then he or she should switch to another closing technique immediately.

Extra Inducement Close

extra inducement close

use of a clincher—a selling point held in reserve—as a close

clincher

extra inducement to buy, such as rebates, lay-away options, price discounts, or reduced delivery charges

All good salespeople hold at least one selling point in reserve. These **extra inducement closes** are known in sales terminology as **clinchers.** The salesperson holds back one or more clinchers to assist the close or to help pick up the thread of conversation should the close fail.

Clinchers typically take the form of an extra inducement to buy the item. This may be a rebate, a lay-away option, a quantity price discount, a waiver of delivery charges, or a special servicing capability. Special inducements of this nature can have a significant impact on the sales interview. When the salesperson has offered a "special favor" to the buyer, many prospects feel obligated to close the sale.

The disadvantages associated with this technique are:

1. The clincher may encourage the customer to seek additional favors from the seller.
2. Special inducements must be applied uniformly to all buyers. Discriminatory behavior is unethical at least, and often illegal.

PROFESSIONAL SELLING IN ACTION

Closing the Founder of U.S. Steel

Joseph P. Day, the great New York auctioneer, sold the Empire Building to Judge Elbert Gary, founder of U.S. Steel, by overcoming fear.

Judge Gary wanted to buy a building, but nothing Day showed pleased Judge Gary. Day sensed that, deep down in his heart, Judge Gary wanted to buy the building where U.S. Steel had always rented offices. He also sensed the obstacle was Gary's fear of what other officers would think—officers who wanted "something modern." But Gary never said this in words.

Instead he found objections to the Empire Building—old-fashioned woodwork, poor location, etc. Day knew these arguments did not originate with Judge Gary. Day also knew he would have to help his prospect overcome these objections. So he said quietly, "Judge, where was your office when you first came to New York?"

Judge Gary paused. "In this very building."

Then the salesperson asked, "Where was U.S. Steel formed?"

"Right here, in this very office," he replied.

Both remained silent. At last, Judge Gary spoke. "Nearly all of my junior officers want to leave this building. But it's our home. We were born here. We've grown up here. And here is where we are going to stay."

Day had helped Judge Gary articulate his defense. Inside half an hour the deal was closed. The shrewd Day let the Judge sell himself. He helped the prospect overcome fears of others' opinions so he could decide to buy.

SOURCE: From the book by Charles B. Roth and Roy Alexander, *Secrets of Closing Sales,* 5th ed. © 1983 by Prentice-Hall, Inc. Published by Prentice-Hall, Inc., Englewood Cliffs, NJ 07632.

SRO Method

standing room only (SRO) method

closing technique in which the prospect is told that the purchase should be concluded now, since the merchandise will probably not be available later

A technique known by several names has lately been designated the **standing room only (SRO) method.** With this method the salesperson tells the prospect that the purchase should be concluded at the present time because the merchandise probably will not be available later. The real estate agent might say:

> This is the last lot in Acorn Acres. We had two people look at it yesterday, and a couple more are supposed to come out this evening. I am sure we will sell it by tomorrow morning, so if you want it, now is the time to act!

An automobile salesperson might apply the SRO technique this way:

> As you know, this is a limited-production sports car, and this is the last one we'll get until January. I'd suggest you move pretty fast on it, since our other sales rep has a professor up at the college who is interested. In fact, Professor Maxwell is supposed to come down here this afternoon.

The SRO technique works only when the availability of a product is limited or some future event may change the terms of the deal. Automobile, real estate, or many industrial supply sales personnel might say, "You'd better buy it now because we expect the price to increase next month." These salespeople use an impending event that threatens the current sales terms as a closing device.

A SALES MANAGEMENT NOTE

And Now, a Computer-Assisted Close

A California firm—the Human Edge Software Corporation—has designed a new program for use with the IBM®PC. The . . . software package is called "The Sales Edge." The salesperson notes his or her agreement or disagreement with 80 statements. Then the user does the same for 50 adjectives used to describe the prospect.

The output is an 8–10 page report on how to best handle the prospect along with specific closing strategies that best match the potential customer.

SOURCE: "Selling Psych-Out Software," *Newsweek*, January 16, 1984, p. 52.

Another modification of the SRO technique is to ask for a deposit to hold the item being considered. Rarely do customers ever forfeit their deposits and decide not to buy the product.

Silence as a Closing Technique

We discussed *silence* earlier as a method of attempting a trial close. It can also be used as a final closing technique, but silence should be used sparingly in this way. It is an aggressive close, and the salesperson may find it difficult to continue the presentation should this close fail.

The only essential difference between using silence as a trial close and as a final close is the amount of time involved. During a trial close, the silence is just a brief pause in the conversation, while it is a longer, more definite break when used as a final closing technique.

Another Closing

Some interviews between salesperson and prospect are not intended to result in a closed sale. Neither the seller nor the buyer may expect to complete the transaction at the end of an interview. For example, an IBM or UNISYS sales representative may work with a prospect for many months before a sale is actually completed, and other high-value items requiring capital expenditures are sold in a similar fashion.

In some cases, a salesperson-prospect discussion may be entirely designed to:

1. Discover who the salesperson should contact in a company about a particular item.
2. Secure an opportunity to make a sales presentation at a later date. Insurance agents typically set up presentations when both husband and wife are available.

3. Obtain an interview with the technical or operating personnel who actually use the product.

4. Set up a time to conduct a product demonstration for the prospect.

Accordingly, the preceding closing techniques are also applicable to buyer-seller interfaces. A sales representative has successfully closed in these situations if he or she has determined the correct buying contact, set up another appointment with a prospect or other interested parties (such as a company's technical personnel), or confirmed a time for a product demonstration. The same closing techniques and procedures are applicable.

POSTSALE ACTIVITIES

The sales process does not end when the buyer signs the contract or says, "I'll take it." Once the buyer agrees to the purchase, the salesperson must proceed with the concluding details of the sale: fill out the appropriate forms, arrange payment terms, and consult the buyer about delivery. The key to success at this stage is to be efficient, polite, and reassuring. Too many salespeople linger with the buyer after a sale has been completed. Most buyers appreciate those who conclude their business carefully, yet quickly, and then leave. The sales adage "Get in, get the sale, get out, and get on to the next prospect" holds true.

Postsale activities are necessary to buyer satisfaction and enhance the salesperson's likelihood of securing future business. Sales managers suggest the following guidelines for postsale activities.

1. *Show appreciation*. Salespeople should let customers know that their orders are appreciated. Sellers must avoid excessive expression of satisfaction (perhaps glee) at the successful completion of the sale. The proper attitude is restraint and dignity, since there has been an exchange that is mutually beneficial to both parties. A simple thank you or "We really appreciate the business, Jim" is appropriate.

2. *Reassure the customer*. During the time between the purchase agreement and the end of the interview, the salesperson should reassure the customer that the buying decision was correct. The following remarks are examples of how this might be done:

I know you will really enjoy wearing this sweater. Lisa, this was a good decision on your part.

Wait until you see the first efficiency rating after our system is installed.

Karen, the air-conditioning option you chose will surely make your driver happier this summer.

3. *Solicit sales leads*. Sales representatives must always be alert for sales leads. However, they must avoid any suggestion of high-pressure tactics in

seeking these leads. A simple request is adequate: "Jack, do you know anyone else in your area who might be interested in this type of policy?"

4. *A future sale versus a lost sale.* Not all sales interviews conclude with a closed sales agreement. In these cases, it is essential that salespeople build toward future sales rather than writing the interview off as a lost sale. Salespeople must strive to keep the prospect's door open to future sales presentations by thanking the person for their time and maintaining goodwill.

SUMMARY OF CHAPTER OBJECTIVES

1. To define the concept of closing.

Closing can be defined as the point in the sales presentation at which the salesperson secures the desired agreement from the prospect. Closing the sale is the goal of every salesperson.

2. To list and explain the causes of closing failures.

The causes of closing failures include:

1. Fear.
2. Improper attitude.
3. Verbal overkill.
4. Failure to ask for the order.

Missed sales should be treated as learning experiences to be analyzed and studied to improve future sales performance. They should not discourage salespeople in future sales presentations.

3. To determine when to close a sale.

There are several points in the sales process when salespeople might attempt to close, rather than only one best time. Sellers should watch the prospect for verbal or physical closing cues that suggest a readiness to purchase the product. Then they should try a trial close, an attempt at closing to determine the prospect's readiness to buy.

4. To outline and define the basic closing techniques available to salespersons.

The basic closing techniques are:
1. Assumptive close: Salesperson assumes that the prospect has decided to buy.
2. Direct approach: Salesperson simply asks for the order.
3. Alternative decisions: Prospect is asked to make a choice between alternatives equally favorable to the seller.

4. Summary and affirmative agreement: Salesperson summarizes the features, benefits, and advantages of the product and seeks agreement from the prospect.

5. Balance sheet approach: Salesperson presents the negative features as well as the benefits of the product.

6. Emotional close: Use of fear, pride, romance, or the need for peer group acceptance as a closing technique.

7. "If I can show you . . ." close: Salesperson first identifies the prospect's primary need, then offers a solution.

8. Extra inducement close: Salesperson uses a clincher—a sales point held in reserve—as a close.

9. SRO method: Salesperson tells the prospect that the purchase should be concluded now, since the merchandise will probably not be available later.

10. Silence: Dramatic close in which the salesperson simply stops talking and waits for the prospect to respond.

5. To describe the primary postsale activities that a salesperson should employ.

The manner in which sellers handle postsale activities is also important, because repeat-sale potential can depend on it. After a successful close, salespeople should (1) show their appreciation for the business, (2) reassure the customer about the decision, and (3) solicit sales leads. If the salesperson is unable to close, he or she should be sure to maintain the option of a possible future sale.

REVIEW QUESTIONS

1. Explain the following statement: A salesperson who cannot close cannot sell.
2. List and discuss the various reasons why salespeople fail to close some sales.
3. Cite some examples of closing cues for which a salesperson should watch.
4. When is the appropriate time to close a sale?
5. Identify and explain each of the closing techniques discussed in the chapter.
6. Match the remarks by sellers in the left column with the correct closing technique in the list on the right.

   a. There you are, Homer. While the policy doesn't contain the dread disease clause, it has all of the other five features you said were important to you. That is better than our competition . . . and our policy is cheaper.   _____ 1. Extra inducement close.

   b. Would you prefer to use VISA or MasterCard?   _____ 2. Alternative decision.

c. I know you want to get back to the loading dock, Earl, so why don't I get this order written up for you?

_____ 3. Balance sheet approach.

d. Marcia, if I can have your order today, we will be able to give you a special barbecue set absolutely free!

_____ 4. SRO method.

e. Mr. Lambrowski, this is the last floor model we have. If you like the set, I would suggest you give us a deposit; these floor model sales never last more than a couple of hours.

_____ 5. Direct approach.

7. Which closing techniques would probably be used by the following sales personnel?
   a. Life insurance.
   b. Home remodeling.
   c. Office furniture.
   d. Cemetery lots.

8. Describe your two most recent purchases. Which closing technique did the salesperson use in each?

9. Identify and describe two or three situations (other than an actual sales transaction) in which you might be required to use a closing technique.

10. What should the salesperson do after closing a sale? What should the seller do if he or she has failed to close the sale?

DISCUSSION QUESTIONS AND EXERCISES

1. One of the authors has had a salesperson tell him, "How do I close? Well, I just keep coming at them until they buy. I close by never quitting on a prospect until I have sold the person." Evaluate this salesperson's approach.

2. Assume you are a sales representative for a carpet-cleaning franchise. The prospect has just said, "Yes, I definitely want to get your people in here to clean this carpeting, but I really think I should consult my husband about the price, and he is on a business trip." How would you handle this objection, and then proceed to close?

3. A salesperson in one automobile dealership has a blanket authorization to negotiate up to a $500 discount from the original price quotation for any model. In a sales interview, a prospect says she will purchase the automobile if the seller reduces the original quotation by $300. The salesperson replies:

   Well, I don't know whether I can go that far. Let me check with my sales manager. (He returns to the prospect five minutes later.) This is your lucky day. The sales manager says we can cut it by $300 provided this special discount is kept just between the three of us. Let me write that up right now.

   Evaluate this closing technique. Are any ethical considerations involved?

4. Practice the various closing techniques. One method would be for a friend to pretend to be a prospect for a product, while you assume the role of the salesperson. Then reverse the prospect and seller roles and try another product.

5. Develop 20 to 30 closing statements and write each on a 3″ × 5″ card. Write the closing technique that the statement represents on the opposite side of the card. Shuffle the cards and practice identifying each close.

SALES DIALOG

Maureen Finney is a sales representative for Federal Carpets. She has been showing carpet samples to Les and Adrian Smith, who want to redecorate their Atlanta home.

FINNEY: As you can see, Federal offers a wide variety of styles, textures, and price ranges. I am sure you have spotted one that really appeals to you.

LES SMITH: They all look alike to me. What do you think, Adrian?

ADRIAN SMITH: Well, I sort of like numbers 202 and 353 . . . but 286 is nice also.

FINNEY: (Pauses for several seconds to see if Adrian Smith settles on a particular sample. She does not.) Based on the wallpaper you selected, I would suggest number 353. It is a perfect match.

ADRIAN SMITH: Yes, but I have always been partial to the texture of 202. (Les Smith nods in agreement.)

FINNEY: I see what you mean. Let me get out my order book.

What do you think the results of this sales dialog will be?

CASE 11–1   BADGER LAKE ESTATES (A)

Foster-Johnson, Inc., is a developer of a vacation-home resort community on a large lake in northern Wisconsin. Badger Lake Estates has over 600 lots priced at $30,000 and up. The development provides an 18-hole golf course; large clubhouse with dining room and cocktail lounge; extensive recreational facilities such as shuffleboard, tennis, and racquetball courts; and snowmobile and horse-riding trails for residents. Skiing is available just 10 miles away.

Badger Lake Estates has a quality image because of its location advantage, the variety of recreation available, and a sales contract that specifies only second homes in the $80,000 and above category may be constructed on the property. Approximately 30 percent of the lots have already been purchased, and on nearly half of these either construction is under way or there are finished residences. Foster-Johnson, Inc. has a subsidiary operation—Northern Wisconsin Construction Company—that builds a majority of the homes at Badger Lake.

The developer's promotional program starts with advertisements in Milwaukee, Chicago, and Minneapolis newspapers which feature mail coupons for additional information. Because over 80 percent of lot sales come from these three metropolitan areas, Foster-Johnson has a sales office in each city.

On receiving a newspaper coupon, the sales office mails out an attractive packet of sales information the same day. One week later, a sales representative calls the prospect. If the prospect appears to be a potentially qualified buyer, the salesperson seeks an appointment to discuss the property. If the appointment is refused, the sales office mails a stamped, self-addressed postcard saying that Foster-Johnson will be happy to supply additional information about the development at any time. All the prospect has to do is check the appropriate box and return the card.

When prospects approve the representative's call, the sales office arranges an appointment at which both husband and wife are present. On arrival the salesperson immediately confirms their interest in a vacation home and their ability to purchase such property. If satisfied on this count, the representative begins an extensive presentation using slides to highlight various features of Badger Lake Estates. The prospects are also given an expensive, well-illustrated booklet on the development.

Brian Sullivan, a sales representative in the Chicago area, has just finished such a presentation at the home of Dr. and Mrs. Raymond Albright. Albright is an orthodontist in an exclusive Chicago suburb.

SULLIVAN: You both appear to be very interested in establishing a vacation home in Wisconsin. Is that correct?

MRS. ALBRIGHT: Yes, I think we would be interested. Ray and I have always liked that section of Wisconsin. In fact, we spent a week there last summer.

DR. ALBRIGHT: The lakes in that area are certainly an attraction for someone who likes to fish like I do.

SULLIVAN: Great! I am glad to learn that you like our location. We think it is one of the most beautiful spots in the entire country. Now I guess the only thing we need to decide is when you can tour the property. Of course, we pay for lodging and meals. Would next weekend suit your schedule, or would you prefer to come up the following weekend?

Questions

1. What type of closing technique has Sullivan used?
2. Why didn't Sullivan attempt to close an actual lot sale at this time?
3. What is your assessment of Foster-Johnson's promotional strategy?

CASE 11-2 BADGER LAKE ESTATES (B)

It is 9:30 A.M. on a Saturday morning, and Dr. and Mrs. Raymond Albright have just arrived at the sales office of Badger Lake Estates. They are greeted by Hal Skorski.

SKORSKI: I trust that the accommodations Brian Sullivan and I arranged for you over at the Brookside Inn were OK?

DR. ALBRIGHT: Yes, they were fine. We had a very nice room.

SKORSKI: Good! Well, I know you want to see the many fine lots available here at Badger Lake. But maybe we should look at this map first . . . so I can point out where we will be going as well as the development's proximity to the other lakes and communities in the area.

Skorski points out the various places of interest on a large wall map and discusses them. Then he says:

SKORSKI: Let's get started. It is a beautiful autumn day, and I know you will enjoy the pleasant drive. The property has all the features of the best fall color tour.

After two hours of touring the property, the Albrights indicate some interest in a wooded corner lot. Skorski invites them to examine the lot.

SKORSKI: I can see by your faces that you agree with me that this may be one of the most beautiful lots in Badger Lake Estates. This is just the type of prestige location that is right for people like you.

DR. ALBRIGHT: What do you think, Susan?

MRS. ALBRIGHT: I love it! The entire development is just lovely, but this is the best pick as far as I'm concerned. But maybe we should look at some other developments in the area.

Questions

1. How should Skorski respond to Mrs. Albright's comment?
2. Suggest two or three closes that Skorski might use in this situation.
3. Assume the Albrights decline to buy the property at this time. What should Skorski do in this case?

CHAPTER 12

Building Future Sales

CHAPTER OBJECTIVES

1. To explain why building future sales is the link between today's business and tomorrow's business.

2. To identify the major sales-building activities.

3. To list the primary ways of maintaining current sales volume.

4. To outline the general approaches to expanding sales volume.

SALES CAREER PROFILE

ROBERT J. MELNYK
Allstate Insurance

Robert J. Melnyk is a senior account agent with Allstate Insurance in Renton, Washington. He holds an associate of arts degree from Tacoma Community College. Melnyk served in the Vietnam-era Air Force and was trained as an aircraft mechanic. His interests include model trains, woodworking, and restoring cars.

Asked how he selected a career in selling, Melnyk responded, "Well, I'm not sure I really selected a career in selling. I think it kind of selected me. Allstate was a company that I knew of from the time I was a kid. When I came back from Vietnam, I immediately went to Allstate and bought my car insurance. Then one day while making a change in my automobile insurance, I happened to talk to my agent about the difficulties of finding a job in the aircraft industry. The agent mentioned that he really enjoyed his career with Allstate and suggested that it might be a possibility for me. At the time, I did not give his comments serious consideration; but the more I thought about it, the more I thought that it might be something to investigate.

"Looking back at it, my main intent was to get a job—not a career, but a job. So, I called my Allstate agent and asked about applying for employment. He put me in contact with the right people, and I filled out an application. I was rejected for employment because I did not have the appropriate sales skills. I had not had any sales jobs or sales experience at the time. But once I was rejected, I wanted the job even more. Therefore, I asked whom I should contact next.

"I talked to the next level of management. Basically, I think they liked the fact that I was aggressive, that I wasn't going to take no for an answer. As a result, I was eventually hired and started something that changed my entire life.

"I was sent to the Allstate Training School in Menlo Park, California. I learned the basic skills of selling life insurance. Life insurance turned out to be the product that our company was emphasizing most at the time.

"Once you get out into the field, your training really begins and you can expand upon the things you learned in training school. I had a good manager at the time. He took an interest in me and gave me a little bit of extra help that kind of pushed me along. As a new salesperson, it's very easy to get discouraged from time to time. You go out, you make a few instant sales, they feel really good, and then you experience rejection a few weeks later. A lot of people cannot handle this, and it leads to the demise of a lot of salespeople's careers. In my situation, the manager that I had at the time held my hand a little bit, led me through it, and put things in the proper perspective.

"One of the main reasons that I feel so good about helping other agents today—especially new agents—is the fact that I knew [that] when I went into this profession,

I needed some help. It's kind of a payback system. Anything I can do to help my fellow Allstate agents is only going to come back to me.

"Today, insurance sales is no longer a job to me. It is my career. I think most of what I like about my job is the fact that in 15 years I've seen the insurance industry change a lot. Our company has changed with the industry and with the times. The products we have available to sell have changed. The level of expertise needed to sell these products has increased drastically over the years. So you are always learning something . . . there are new things happening around you every day, and it's very exciting. I look forward to the next 10 or 15 years. There will be tremendous opportunities."

Melnyk continued, "Currently, I am involved in a new program with Allstate. It is called NOA (neighborhood office program). Essentially, NOA is designed to give the Allstate agent a bigger share of the market. What I hope to do is expand my local business. In the last few months I've hired several people; I have an office manager; I have a solicitor and several other people. NOA has put me in a position to go after the bigger sales in commercial and life insurance."

Asked if he knew that Allstate was considered one of the top 100 U.S. firms to sell for, Melnyk replied, "Yes, I knew that. It doesn't surprise me. You have a good product to sell, good work atmosphere, and excellent benefits. You never have to worry about whether or not your retirement plan is going to be any good when you get ready to retire. The company is well managed and has everything going for it. That is one of the things that really motivates me."

When asked, "How important is customer goodwill in your business?", Melnyk responded, "Well, if you sell properly, you have established customer goodwill. Professional salespeople won't oversell. But what they will do is have the customers arrive at a level of satisfaction that will last long after the sales call is made. That's goodwill. It turns into referrals, multiple accounts, and long-term relationships that do not depend upon the lowest price in town."

Answering a final question about how he builds future sales, Melnyk responded, "Hard work—there's no substitute for hard work. You've got to get up every morning, and you have to go out and get at it. You have to have the tenacity of a bulldog. Sales is, to a certain degree, a numbers game. As long as you're talking to people about buying your product, you're going to be all right. I know salespeople that have gone out over the years and done relatively well in the short term because they have sold insurance to their relatives and to their friends, and as soon as they ran out of those people, they ran out of prospects. The bottom line is, the work is hard and the rewards are good. In fact, the rewards in sales are perhaps better than in most other careers."

David B. Sheldon is in a tough business. As vice president and group executive of sales and marketing for Ball Corp.'s Packaging Products Group, Sheldon competes in an industry where suppliers are experiencing high raw material prices and lower selling prices. The Colorado-based division of Ball has a 10 percent market share, but it has seen dollar volume drop, while unit sales have gone up.

Not only is the competition fierce, but purchasers have changed the marketplace in other ways. Adolph Coors was once Ball's biggest customer, but now it handles most of its own packaging needs. Anheuser-Busch also makes some of its own containers. Further complicating the situation is the fact that Coca-Cola and PepsiCo have purchased some of their bottling franchises.

Special delivery requests are commonplace for Sheldon. A customer once asked Ball to send a shipment with special labels to a designated market. Under normal circumstances, this request would take two weeks to fulfill, but Ball did it within 24 hours.

Speedy responses to special requests allows Ball to compete effectively. Sheldon also thinks it is a good way to avoid price pressures even if the costs cannot be passed on to the buyer. He remarks, "In our business, relationships enable you to retain an account, but they're not going to help you get much of a price increase."

Sheldon also builds future sales by training everyone in his organization to assist in the sales effort. Sheldon puts it this way: "Sometimes a plant person is more responsive to customers' problems than someone in sales. Once a . . . [salesperson] . . . establishes a relationship with a customer, we get people from all levels of our company to talk to their counterparts at the account."[1] Clearly, building future sales is everyone's job at Ball's Packaging Products Group.

COMPONENTS OF FUTURE SALES

This chapter discusses the last step in the sales process—building future sales. This step is really the first step, the fundamental step in creating a customer. It is the connecting link between today's business and tomorrow's business. Therefore, building a successful business means developing customers who continue to buy your products. This is particularly important for resellers, such as distributors and retailers, who must rely on the goodwill and loyalty of customers.

Many interrelated activities are involved in creating customers for the company. These activities fall into two categories: (1) maintaining current sales volume, and (2) expanding current sales volume.

MAINTAINING CURRENT SALES VOLUME

Too often, salespeople feel their job ends when they close the sale. Once an order is obtained, they move on to the next prospect. Any order follow-up or customer service is minimal.

Not following up is a shortsighted attitude toward selling because it fails to consider the importance of developing and maintaining a customer for the firm. Experienced salespeople recognize that to continually increase their sales volume they must first build a solid foundation of sales to current customers. In the insurance industry, they say that your present customers are your best customers. Sales to new customers are additions to sales volume. Without a base, sales to new customers only replace those lost in the normal course of events, and sales volume remains the same. Furthermore, according to Forum, a Boston-based consulting company, it costs five times more to find new customers than to keep old ones.[2]

Building future sales must be balanced against the return it produces. Salespeople must allocate their time in relation to the profitability of an account. For example, the sales job has changed for Hoover Universal salespeople. They now spend more time servicing their most profitable accounts by participating actively in design and engineering discussions with production people. Previously, they merely haggled over prices and took orders for car and truck seats. Now salespeople and customers exchange technical information and know-how.[3]

There are many ways salespeople can maintain established accounts and convert new customers into established ones. These include building goodwill; handling complaints; processing requests for rush delivery; and handling other special requests. All of these efforts involve convincing customers that their purchases are wise ones. A general model for building future sales is shown in Figure 12–1. The model outlines the components of the two primary sources of future sales: maintaining current sales volume and expanding current sales volume.

Successful selling involves doing something for customers. Sellers must make sure that their customers obtain the visualized benefits from the purchase of a product or service. This means more than taking orders; it means ensuring that customers recognize that they are better off with the product or service than without it. Customers also have to realize that their salespeople and their companies are responsible for the increased satisfaction.

Professional salespeople develop a formalized system to monitor customers. This might be an attachment to the customer's sales profile or a separate file to remind the seller of:

- Progress in processing orders and delivery dates.
- Matters requiring special attention, such as a priority order.
- Adjustments and settling complaints and inquiries.
- Times and nature of customer contacts.

Building Goodwill

Building goodwill among customers is a simple matter. All that is necessary is to attend to the customers' interests. This is the marketing concept in action, but putting the marketing concept into action is easier said than done.

One-time buyers who do not become repeat customers often comment on the lack of follow-up and interest on the part of the salespeople who originally sold them a product or service. Whether this is true or not is

---

FIGURE 12–1  Building future sales

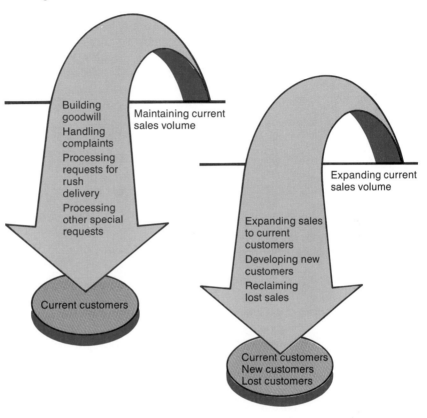

Building goodwill

Handling complaints

Processing requests for rush delivery

Processing other special requests

Maintaining current sales volume

Current customers

Expanding sales to current customers

Developing new customers

Reclaiming lost sales

Expanding current sales volume

Current customers
New customers
Lost customers

---

irrelevant. The fact is that these consumers perceived indifference on the part of the sales personnel with whom they dealt. This phenomenon is called the **indifference trap.** Indifference to new customers is particularly harmful. New customers have usually moved their business from someone else, probably because they were not satisfied with their previous supplier. Now they want to know if a new supplier is any better. Imagine what indifference can do in this situation!

What can salespeople do to protect themselves from falling into the indifference trap? First, they can keep in touch with customers and serve as liaisons between the customer and the company in settling problems, obtaining answers to questions, and making adjustments. Second, salespeople can recognize that customers—new or old—are a company's most important asset. Salespeople can also help customers by reinforcing their purchasing decisions.

Scheduling Calls

tickler file

system for reminding a salesperson to follow up on certain details with customers

Keeping in touch with customers is primarily a matter of scheduling. With proper planning, a salesperson can visit new customers and established accounts on a regular, recurring basis. To assist in this planning, it is helpful for a salesperson to maintain a **tickler file**—a reminder of things to be done. Some salespeople keep warranty cards and call their customers just before the warranty expires to ask them to bring their purchase in for a final check. Some appliance salespeople accompany the service people when they install the new appliance. Others use calendars on which they mark the dates of sales or sales reports. Whichever method is used, all professional sales representatives see their customers regularly. They have learned from experience that the best way to get repeat business is to stay in touch with customers.

How often should a customer be visited? For some types of selling, even the most important customers require a visit only once every several weeks, although telephone contact should be more frequent. In other cases, customers should be seen weekly or even more often. Sometimes a representative visits very large accounts every day of every week and may even maintain an office on the customer's premises.

callback schedule

schedule outlining the frequency of salespeople's calls on different categories of customers

Different customers also require different frequencies of salespeople's calls, or **callback schedules.** How often each customer should be visited depends on the importance of the customer, special problems, the relative newness of the account, and other similar factors. Salespeople commonly divide their accounts into categories so that each customer in a given category has the same callback frequency. They might contact all customers in category 1 every week, all those in category 2 once a month, and the remaining customers at least once every six months. Chapter 13 describes account classification in greater detail.

Recognizing the Customer's Importance

The second aspect of avoiding indifference and building goodwill is recognizing that customers are a firm's most valuable asset. This is more than a mental attitude; it is a prescription for action. Most firms carefully protect expensive laboratory or production equipment with regular maintenance routines to ensure that necessary maintenance is performed as required. Yet many customers are serviced on a time-available basis—if there is time, they get serviced; if not enough time is available, they do not.

This attitude prevails when sales personnel view customer service narrowly, seeing it as little more than reasonable delivery time and accurate order fulfillment. Nevertheless, to customers, service involves any form of contact with a supplier, whether or not salespeople are personally involved. Professional salespeople involve themselves enough with such activities to ensure that their customers are always served adequately.

Many large manufacturers have adopted these service criteria:

- Adoption of statistical process controls to guarantee the quality of parts.
- Ability to deliver parts as scheduled.
- Capacity to enter orders into the customer's information system at the time of shipping.
- Evidence of continuing productivity improvements to offset cost increases or to lower prices.

Figure 12–2 outlines a program for developing a continuing relationship with a customer. This model also shows what the customer should be able to expect from a salesperson, and vice versa. The model also outlines the steps necessary to building a continuing relationship between seller and buyer.

Customer service plays an important role in minimizing postpurchase dissonance (see Chapter 4). For many products, service after the sale is a

FIGURE 12–2   Program for developing continuing relationships with customers

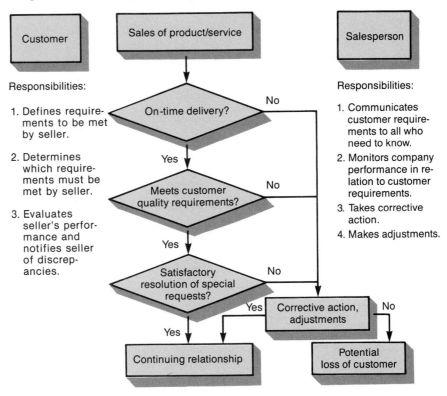

major part of the purchase decision. If the service is good, the decision is viewed favorably; if it is bad, the buyer regrets the purchase.

Salespeople can minimize dissonance. A telephone call to see if the customer is pleased goes a long way in this regard. The clothing salesperson who compliments the customer on her appearance performs the same service. And the car salesperson who chats with the customer during the car's first service trip also makes the customer feel good about the purchase decision.

One of the most difficult aspects of ensuring repeat business is handling complaints. When something is wrong, the complaint might be serious enough to affect the customer's purchase decision the next time the product is needed. Salespeople involved in building long-term relationships with customers must be able to handle complaints.

The best way to handle complaints is to avoid them. Any complaint represents a failure of the product or the company to fulfill the customer's expectations. This situation can arise in one of two ways: the performance of the product or firm is poor, or the expectations of the customer are too high.

The salesperson's presentation plays a major role in the development of the customer's expectations for the product or firm. Therefore, it is not only ill-advised to give the customer impossible expectations, it is ethically wrong.

A salesperson with integrity—by definition, a professional salesperson—establishes with a customer valid expectations for usage of a product or service. For example, a salesperson for a lawn service company must make sure that customers understand that a proper spraying of their lawns is only part of proper lawn care. To ensure lush lawns, customers must water and mow their lawns. Integrity in selling also makes good sense from a pure business standpoint. If customers' expectations are too high, the product cannot possibly meet them, and customers will be unhappy with the purchase. Customers whose expectations are met, however, are satisfied with the purchase and more inclined to buy the product again. Salespeople must remember that customers' expectations are formed at the time purchases are made, not afterward. It is up to sellers to see that customers' expectations are consistent with the performance of the product. Telling customers that there was a misunderstanding after a complaint has been registered does little good and may, in fact, add to the problem.

If the reason for the complaint is a valid one and the product does not perform to reasonable expectations, something has gone wrong in the product's manufacture. It is imperative that the firm make amends to satisfy its customers.

All too often, inexperienced salespeople are willing to have the firm reimburse customers for the extra costs incurred or to replace the defective product with a new one. This is a fast, easy solution—easy, that is, for salespeople. The firm incurs extra costs, the customer often has to wait for the delivery of the new item, and somebody in production probably is reprimanded. It would be much better if a salesperson could rectify the situation with the product already in hand. This may mean showing how the defective part can be made to work with a small readjustment, or it may mean making a quick repair on the spot. If these solutions are not possible, the customer should be given a new item or rework charges should be paid; these should be offered only if the other possibilities fail.

Processing Rush Delivery Requests

When normal delivery time will not meet a customer's needs, sales representatives can request a rush delivery. This often means that the product has to be specially handled in production and packaging; the company must also use a speedier and more costly mode of transportation to expedite delivery. All of this costs money, and someone has to pay the bill.

The ultimate example of a rush delivery request is for a just-in-time (JIT) inventory program where the purchases are not inventoried by the customer, but are scheduled to arrive just prior to use in the production process. Sellers are usually happy to absorb the increased costs, since JIT often results in the vendor being designated the only provider of this particular item. Such an arrangement is called sole sourcing and is described later in the chapter.

If the customer requests rush delivery and offers to pay the extra charges, the salesperson has little trouble handling the request. It is only necessary to see that the proper paperwork is done and that everyone in the firm understands the importance of speedy delivery and expeditious handling. Some additional handling charges may be incurred, but normally these are minimal and can easily be absorbed.

When the customer requests special delivery and handling and suggests that the salesperson's firm absorb the cost difference, however, a decision must be made. Should the deal be accepted and the additional costs absorbed? If the answer is yes, all of the firm's customers are paying for the extra delivery service because the firm's costs are going to increase, and ultimately these increases lead to higher prices. If the extra costs are not absorbed and the customer pays the bill, there is a risk of losing the customer. Acceptance of the deal depends on several factors. Is this the first time the customer has asked for special consideration, or is it standard practice? How important is the customer to the firm? Is there a possibility of getting special consideration from the customer on a later occasion? Will the customer recall the extra service, or will it be expected in the future? Answers to these and similar questions determine whether or not the charges should be absorbed.

In general, it is best if all customers receive the same service and delivery. If special service is required, the customer should reimburse the firm for the extra costs incurred. In the short run, this may be a very difficult course to pursue, especially when a very good customer starts to apply pressure. In the long run, however, it works because each customer realizes that the salesperson is treating every customer fairly and respects him or her for it.

Handling Other Special Requests

Customers can make many requests for special treatment besides expeditious delivery. They might ask for special packaging, tighter quality control, extra product tests, design changes from the standard specifications, and other exceptions to the normal processing of the product. They may request particular financing arrangements, discounts, or payment terms.

Special requests should be handled virtually the same way as rush delivery requests. The same considerations apply, and the same problems result if the customers' unreasonable demands are met too easily. But special requests have an additional dimension that does not affect rush delivery requests. Requests for rush delivery are so common that a salesperson quickly learns from experience which requests are reasonable and which are not, approximately how much each rush delivery will cost, and how the people in the firm will react to the request. This is not the case for other special requests. These requests may be totally new to the salesperson, or the salesperson may not be familiar with the effects the special treatment can have on the firm's normal operations. Accordingly, the salesperson is in a precarious position in negotiating with the customer.

To help in this regard, many companies insist that all salespeople spend some part of their sales training working in the plant. Each salesperson becomes acquainted with the effects special requests can have on the operation of the production facility. Without this experience, the salesperson may make unreasonable requests; this accounts for some of the antagonism that sometimes exists between production and sales forces.

The salesperson who recognizes the possible effects of each special request on the firm's operations is in a better position to consider the request on its individual merits. This knowledge also makes it easier to negotiate a fair arrangement with the customer and to distinguish between bargaining points and the supplier requirements.

Many companies have assigned production workers to sales and/or service activities for short periods of time. At General Motors Corporation, for example, production workers regularly work with dealers' service departments for short periods. At McDonald Steel Corporation, production workers accompany salespeople in making sales calls. In addition, all employees of McDonald Steel are kept informed of all customer contacts and what took place at these contacts.

Ill feelings can also develop between sales and service. For one foreign automobile manufacturer, sales and service organizations in the United States are two separate and distinct entities. This arrangement has led to numerous problems for dealers and car buyers seeking service. Better cooperation between sales and service results from not only giving sales training to service representatives, but also making sure each unit understands its vital role in creating customers for the firm.

EXPANDING CURRENT SALES VOLUME

Successful salespeople are able to maintain their current sales volume, but it is not enough to simply maintain current levels of sales. Successful salespeople increase their sales volume year after year. In fact, this growth in sales often distinguishes mediocre from outstanding salespeople.

The three ways of expanding sales volume are (1) expanding sales to current customers, (2) developing new customers, and (3) reclaiming lost sales.

Expanding Sales to Current Customers

The best prospects for increased sales are current customers. When salespeople have successfully built goodwill, customers who are satisfied with their purchases are the most likely prospects for additional sales. New prospects have to be found, sold, and cultivated, whereas all this has already been accomplished with satisfied customers. It is much simpler to look to current customers for increased sales than it is to look for new customers. The factors that encouraged customers to buy originally should still be in effect.

One of the two methods of increasing sales to current customers is to obtain a larger share of the customer's business. If the customer divides up the business among three suppliers, a salesperson should try to get more than one third—perhaps 40 percent. The other method is to increase the sales of the customer's end products, thus increasing demand for the salesperson's products.

Obtaining Larger Shares. When a firm provides only a portion of a customer's total needs, the most obvious way to increase sales is to increase its share of the currently available business. To do this, the salesperson must convince the customer that there are more benefits from doing business with his or her firm than with a competitor. The best way to convince a customer of this is to actually provide better service and products. The promise of greater benefits is then a fact that the customer readily recognizes.

sole source
situation where a buyer buys from only one vendor

Ultimate success in this area occurs when the customer makes the supplier the **sole source,** or only provider, of a product. Many buying firms are reluctant to grant a supplier this privilege, since it may result in a reduced level of service and performance. Some suppliers become complacent without competition. This accounts for the marketing axiom that the toughest position for a supplier is to be a sole source. The firm in this situation must work hard to maintain its position.

The discussion up to this point has been based on the assumption that each customer's total needs for a product are fixed and cannot be increased.

In the next section, we look at how suppliers can help their customers increase their total sales. Another way of increasing a need for a particular product is to show customers new uses for the product in their current operations. During the past several years, the amounts of aluminum and plastics used in American cars have increased. These industries have increased their share of the automobile companies' business by replacing other materials. Alert salespeople recognize this possibility and are constantly looking for opportunities to increase the use of the products and services they offer.

Increasing the Customer's Level of Sales. Firms that sell their products through distributors, wholesalers, retailers, and other agents can increase sales by increasing their customers' sales. Anything the supplying firm can do to help its customers boost their sales automatically increases its own sales. Suppliers have increased customer sales by training the customer's sales force to use better selling techniques and providing product information; supporting the customer's advertising, both financially and creatively; and showing customers new uses for the product.

resale programs
marketing program designed to increase customers' sales volume

Salespeople who deal in commodities, such as plastics, steel, and chemicals, often include in their respective marketing packages programs for increasing customer sales. These **resale programs** are as much a part of service to customers as on-time delivery and quality assurance. When there is little difference between competitive products except price, these resale programs help to distinguish one firm from another.

Developing New Customers

Existing customers are an ideal source of sales leads, because satisfied customers share their pleasure at having made the right decision with friends and acquaintances. Many customers provide the names of other good prospects. For example, each new customer may provide the names of two or three other prospects.

Finally, professional salespeople go beyond using customers as a source of sales leads; they ask existing customers to help them sell the product. They ask if other prospects may see the product in operation at the customer's plant, if the customer would write a brief letter recommending the product, or if the customer would endorse the product in advertisements. Activities of this sort use customers as salespeople, and this is one of the most effective means of promoting a product. Few sources are more credible than satisfied customers.

Reclaiming Lost Sales

Since sales to established accounts are the foundation of successful selling, losing business from existing customers is detrimental to long-term success. Business is usually lost because something has happened to upset the status quo. Either the products or services have deteriorated in quality, or

COMPANY PROFILE   # Quality in the Eyes of Customers

In companies that accept the concept of customer-perceived quality, formal customer-feedback channels guage buyers' satisfaction. AMP, an electrical connector supplier, measures how long it takes to process reports and proposal requests from the company's sales and applications engineers, monitors the number of proposal quotations, and has scheduled a customer satisfaction measurement system. As a result, 44 percent fewer returns were caused by product defects and the number of returns generated by shipping or clerical errors dropped 47 percent.

SOURCE: Katie Bernard, "Marketers Discover What Quality Really Means," *Business Marketing*, April 1987, pp. 58–59, 62, 64, 66, 70, 72.

competitors have introduced better products, increased services, or lowered prices to encourage customers to switch their business. In either case, salespeople have not done their jobs if the loss of business comes as a surprise.

As their firms' principal contacts with the market, salespeople must alert their firms to changes in the market that could adversely affect sales. When unexpected changes in competitors' offerings catch a firm by surprise, it may take years to regain an advantage the firm once enjoyed. The same is true for changes in the firm's operations. It is easy for a firm to become complacent and fail to notice slight changes in the quality of its products or services. Customers notice, however, and, even more important, so do competitors. If the deterioration continues long enough, it may become so bad that reconstruction is almost impossible. All of this can be avoided if the firm's sales force continually monitors the market to determine if conditions are changing, and, if so, how they are changing.

SUMMARY OF CHAPTER OBJECTIVES

1. **To explain why building future sales is the link between today's business and tomorrow's business.**

   Building future sales is usually considered the last step in the sales process. It is also the first stage in creating a long-term customer, the key to any successful enterprise. Therefore, building future sales is the connecting link between today's business and tomorrow's business.

2. **To identify the major sales-building activities.**

   The two general categories of sales-building activities are maintaining current sales volume and expanding current sales volume. The existing volume is the sales base of the firm, while increases in this base represent the organization's growth.

3. To list the primary ways of maintaining current sales volume.

Salespeople must maintain established accounts and convert new customers into established ones. Some of the approaches used to achieve this goal are: building goodwill; handling complaints; processing requests for rush delivery; and handling other special requests.

4. To outline the general approaches to expanding sales volume.

Sales volume can be expanded in the following ways: expand sales to current customers; develop new customers; and reclaim lost sales. Sales to current customers can be increased by either obtaining a larger share of the customer's business or boosting the sales of the customer's products. New customers can result from the sales leads of existing customers. Reclaiming lost sales to existing customers is a difficult task because it often means that something has gone wrong. To get the business back, the salesperson must learn what went wrong, see that it is corrected, and then convince the customer that steps have been taken to ensure that the same problem does not recur. Another possible reason for lost sales is that a competitor has changed some aspect of its product offering. Here, also, the salesperson must learn what change has taken place and what must be done to reclaim the lost business.

REVIEW QUESTIONS

1. Is building future sales the last step or the first step in selling? Explain.
2. Discuss the concept of the indifference trap.
3. Which factors ought to be taken into account in the development of a customer callback schedule?
4. How can customers' complaints be avoided? Are there things a salesperson can do to help in this regard?
5. How are rush delivery requests and special requests alike? How are they different?
6. Should a salesperson always try to meet a customer's requested delivery date? Explain.
7. Why are current customers the best source for increases in a salesperson's current level of sales?
8. List and briefly describe the two basic ways of increasing sales to current customers.
9. Explain what a resale program is and why it may be used.
10. Can a salesperson learn from sales that are lost? Explain.

DISCUSSION QUESTIONS AND EXERCISES

1. Ask a salesperson you know to show you the various sales reports he or she regularly completes. How can this information be used to build future sales?

2. Satisfied customers are a company's best salespeople. Show how this sales axiom could be used by the owner of a local restaurant.

3. Automobile salespeople know that a call to a new car buyer a short time after the delivery of the car goes a long way toward building a lasting relationship. List five different ways that a car salesperson could develop a tickler file useful for this purpose.

4. The dangers of a sole-source arrangement to the buyer are quite obvious, but the dangers to the seller are not quite as obvious. What are some of the dangers to the seller in a sole-source arrangement?

5. Interview a local firm that has a resale program. How does it work? How does it build future sales?

SALES DIALOG

Jim Lacey has called on Valley Corporation of Bakersfield, California, for over 12 years. During this time he has had to deal with numerous purchasing and engineering people. For the last two years, he has dealt with Omar Watson in purchasing and Clint Brown in production engineering.

LACEY: Valley Corporation is my best customer, and I appreciate your business. But your new policy that no supplier can have more than 40 percent of your business really hurts our relationship.

WATSON: I have to agree with you that your company has done a good job for us over the years. Yet we also feel that any firm with a major portion of the business tends to get careless.

BROWN: From an engineering standpoint, Jim, your company is competitive but not outstanding. We constantly have to prod you for improvements.

LACEY: Let me answer Clint first. We have given Valley on-time delivery of quality parts. Your own inspection people rate us satisfactory. We have done everything you ask.

WATSON: If I may interrupt, that is exactly the point, Jim. You only react to our demands because we are a volume purchaser. You never give us anything new to consider.

BROWN: We are starting a statistical quality-control program. This was fought by your company, but our purchasing power won the day. We want suppliers to constantly work for our business.

LACEY: Statistical quality control only adds to our costs. If we didn't have the volume, we would have to increase our prices.

WATSON: Jim, that sort of pricing went out several years ago. No one can get away with it today. I suggest your company get more competitive in line with other suppliers.

LACEY: That's not true. We have been your major source for what, at least 20 years. The ring bolt was a real plus for your operation.

BROWN: Jim, the ring bolt was new five years ago. Our design department made certain changes in it two years ago, and now we buy most of it from Proviso Corporation.

WATSON: My bosses are of the opinion that we should drop your company completely, Jim. It is only our insistence to preserve old loyalties that permits us to consider your company as a preferred supplier. I think you are misled if you think we will have you as the supplier with 40 percent. You probably will have no more than 15 percent of our business. Right now you are getting 80 percent.

What do you think the results of this sales dialog will be?

CASE 12–1   WESTERN INDUSTRIES

Pete Stokoff has been a sales representative for Western Industries for over 10 years. In eight of these years, he has made his quota and his evaluations have been consistently good. But nothing prepared Stokoff for the problems he is now having with his biggest account, NAL Products. Kevin Stacy, head of purchasing for NAL, told Stokoff that Western's products are not meeting specifications: NAL is not able to find out the status of orders placed; deliveries, if not late, are usually filled with back orders; and billing terms are consistently off. As a result, NAL is considering dropping Western from its list of qualified sources. NAL has all but made the final decision to do no more business with Western.

Stokoff feels that NAL, and particularly Stacy, is being unfair. Over the years he has put a lot of effort into handling the account. He has always been available to remedy situations that have gone astray and always given NAL a little more than standard practice in terms of favors.

Unfortunately, in discussing the situation over the phone with Cindy Watterson, the assistant buyer, Stokoff got mad and said it was not his fault. Why should he suffer for mistakes made by the factory people in distribution, or bean counters in finance? he stormed. Then he told her that business is business and things happen that cannot be helped.

Questions
1. How would you evaluate Stokoff's conduct in losing an account?
2. Once salespersons know they are losing an account, how should they handle themselves?
3. How does a salesperson gain respect from a customer he or she is about to lose?

CASE 12–2   GLENRIDGE COMPANY

Bud Coley of Glenridge Company is about to receive a call from Dick Phillips, purchasing agent for Holsten Crankshaft, Inc. Phillips wants to know how soon he can get 35 grinding wheels made to special specifications. He needs them as soon as possible.

Holsten Crankshaft, headquarted in Boston, is a company that finish-machines crankshaft forgings for several truck engine manufacturers. They do considerable grinding in the course of their operations. Although most of the grinding wheels Holsten uses are of standard sizes and materials, some require special processing.

For years Phillips has purchased all of Holsten's grinding wheels from Einhorn Abrasives Company. This company has served Phillips well over that period, and its prices have remained very competitive. Accordingly, Coley had never been able to get any business from Phillips, even though he was sure that Glenridge could serve Phillips as well as Einhorn Abrasives does. Coley reasoned that if Phillips gave some business to Glenridge he would be far less susceptible to the problems inherent in a sole-source arrangement. But Phillips had always been concerned about Glenridge's ability to serve him and had elected instead to give all of his business to Einhorn Abrasives.

In this particular case, Phillips called Einhorn Abrasives first, but it was unable to get the 35 grinding wheels to Phillips in less than three weeks, which was totally inadequate for his needs. If he does not get the wheels within a week, the production line is going to shut down, so he decides to call Glenridge and see what it can do. The phone conversation goes like this:

COLEY: Glenridge Company, Bud Coley speaking. May I help you?

PHILLIPS: I certainly hope so! This is Dick Phillips at Holsten Crankshaft, and I've got a problem I need some help with.

COLEY: Oh, hello, Mr. Phillips. It's been awhile since I've seen you. How have you been?

PHILLIPS: Fine, thank you, and it's nice to talk to you again.

COLEY: What's the problem?

PHILLIPS: Do you remember that special grinding wheel we use to finish-grind the flange on the Black Motor 6 shaft?

COLEY: Yes, we have a blueprint of it in our files. I gave you a quote on that item a few months ago, as I recall.

PHILLIPS: That's the one; I need 35 of those as soon as possible. How soon could you get them to me?

COLEY: Hmm. Let me put you on hold a minute and see if we have the necessary material in stock and how soon we could break into our production cycle. Hold on.

After a pause, Coley resumes:

COLEY: I checked with our production control people, and they say that if you approve and are willing to pay for a special setup, we could ship the wheels in three days. Air freight should get the wheels to you in about one or two days. But that assumes that I have a purchase order in hand, so you would have to add however long it would take you to get me a purchase order.

PHILLIPS: How much extra do you think the special setup will be?

COLEY: I'm just guessing, but I am quite sure that it won't be more than $1,000.

PHILLIPS: Go ahead. Make the wheels, and send me the bill. If this is typical of the kind of service you provide, I think I'd like to reconsider our past purchasing policies concerning your company.

COLEY: But I can't go ahead without a purchase order.

PHILLIPS: Look! I'm authorizing you to start making those things. If you want me to clear this with your boss or his boss or the president or anybody else, put him on the phone!

COLEY: My boss is out of town, and I'm sure the president doesn't want me to concern him with this problem.

PHILLIPS: Well, then go ahead, for goodness sake!

Questions

1. What should Coley do?

2. Would you pass on the cost of the special setup, or would you absorb the cost? Why?

3. Should Coley agree to this request but make it conditional upon the receipt of more business in the future, or should he just fulfill this request without any conditions attached?

CHAPTER 13

Increasing Selling Efficiency

CHAPTER OBJECTIVES

1. To relate selling effectiveness and efficiency to self-management.

2. To outline the concept of time management.

3. To explain account classification.

4. To discuss the importance of proper routing.

5. To describe the primary paperwork requirements of professional selling.

6. To discuss the role of self-motivation and personal attitude in selling.

SALES CAREER PROFILE

GIL SPEARS
Meredith Corporation

Gil Spears is the director of advertising for *Successful Farming* magazine, based in Des Moines, Iowa, part of Meredith Corporation's magazine group. The branch managers in the Chicago, New York, Detroit, and Des Moines sales offices report to Spears. In addition, such functions as sales promotion and mail order report to Spears.

Spears, a graduate of the University of Cincinnati, says he still has time for reading, hiking, and bicycling. Spears also helps raise scholarship funds for minority students and he counsels minority students at both the high school and college levels on the availability of opportunities in sales and marketing.

Spears held several sales-related jobs prior to joining Meredith Corporation. He describes how he came to *Successful Farming* and his early years with the magazine: "The people I met during the interview process were important in my decision to join Meredith Corporation. One of the things that impressed me most was the fact that many of my peers had been with the company for such a long period of time.

"I also liked their program for training, as well as the opportunity they offered me in terms of salary and other compensation. I felt it would be a challenge to sell advertising, as this would be my first experience selling a product that was completely intangible.

"I started out as a sales executive traveling the Iowa, Nebraska, and Kansas territory. After approximately three years, I was promoted to Des Moines branch manager where I had the same territorial responsibility, but also supervised another person. From that position, I was promoted to Chicago branch manager. I was responsible for hiring and training the sales staff there. After three years in that position, I was promoted to my current position as director of advertising for the entire magazine."

Asked what he liked most about his job, Spears replied, "Obviously, I like the thrill that comes with landing the sale, but I also like to help other salespeople develop their selling skills, and I derive pleasure from the joy that comes when they realize the success of their efforts."

Spears continued, "I think I have excellent relations with my sales peers. They respect me as a true professional, as an experienced seller who gets results time after time, who can be relied upon as a good team player.

"I also think the relationship I have with our customers is a good one. They see me as a person who is concerned about solving their problems, who is familiar with their needs, their marketing objectives, their products, and as someone who tries to marry those needs to the qualities and opportunities our magazine has for them."

Spears was questioned about the kind of support Meredith gives field sales personnel. "The support we give our field sales personnel is almost unlimited. For example, the editorial group stands ready to aid in informing the customer about the product. And as we are involved in farming, many of our customers want to know what our editors think of the current farming trends. We are the leading magazine in our field.

"Each seller has a manager who works right along with the salesperson in making sales calls, training the person in the management of time, learning the product and also in helping them solve the problems the customer may have.

"We have an administrative services unit which helps the sales staff in servicing the product. A sales promotion department advertises to the trade. We have brochures and other advertising support. An advertising agency creates programs to promote our product. In addition, a research department constantly performs research involving the product, its various uses, and how it ties into the customers' needs."

Spears did not know that Meredith Corporation had been picked as one of the top 100 U.S. firms to sell for, but he thinks he knows why it was picked. "One, it's a part of the business philosophy of the Meredith Corporation that profit is a requirement. We are quite up front and forward about the fact that we exist to make a profit.

"Next, it is the idea at Meredith that we are a high-quality, low-cost producer. We strive to bring our products and services to the marketplace at competitive prices without sacrificing margins or quality.

"Another philosophy is that we want to excel in those markets in which we operate. To be a dominant force, we are concerned about share marketing.

"Another philosophy at Meredith is that people are our most important asset. An individual is permitted to have his or her own style; at the same time, the company expects results. The compensation program is good. We have a sensitive management team. The company bends over backward to create a pleasant working environment."

Spears was then asked: "How do you maximize your selling time?" He responded, "I maximize my selling time by taking care of organizational planning. In other words, do all the advance preparation you can do regarding the needs of the customer, target markets, your short-term as well as long-term plans and proposals to the customer. This approach gives you the maximum amount of time in front of your customer for the selling process itself."

Asked how salespeople can become more efficient at their job, Spears commented, "All the time not spent in front of the customer should be spent planning for being in front of the customer. The maximum amount of time should be given to those customers who offer the most potential."

Finally, Spears was asked about the importance of attitude. "Your attitude is readily transferred to the customer. For example, if you are enthusiastic, your customer will be enthusiastic. It is up to you to make something happen. Your attitude about yourself, your product, your customer must be proper and positive; otherwise, you are going to transmit the wrong image to the customer."

I t is the end of the workday for the local Frito-Lay sales representative. But, instead of spending an hour or more completing sales reports, the salesperson plugs a hand-held computer into a modem at his or her home, or into a mini-computer at the local sales office. The required sales reports are immediately transmitted to Frito-Lay headquarters in Dallas. The report is then combined with those of other Frito-Lay salespeople, analyzed, and a summary report is on President Robert Beeby's desk within 24 hours.

This information system shortens the amount of time Frito-Lay representatives must spend on paperwork. More time is freed for selling. The system has also made sales management more efficient. Vice President Charles Feld remembers the paperwork system that existed before: "If something went wrong in Cleveland, the . . . [salespeople] . . . there would know it right away, but it took us in Dallas four or five months to find out."

By contrast, Robert Beeby comments on the new computer-based system: "I can get anything I want. Our distribution costs are the lowest ever, and sales are going up 10% to 12% a year without the addition of a single . . . [salesperson]." Sales management can respond promptly to marketplace developments. For example, Frito-Lay quickly moved to nationwide distribution of its low-fat snacks line when the sales force's computer reports showed no cannibalization of the company's other products.[1]

SALES EFFECTIVENESS AND EFFICIENCY

sales effectiveness
output measure of a person's selling effort

sales efficiency
input measure of how well people are carrying out their assigned sales tasks

Selling effectiveness and efficiency can be thought of in many ways. Regardless of the measure used, however, it all comes down to dollars of profitable sales obtained from a given level of time and money spent on the sales effort. In our example above, Robert Beeby of Frito-Lay was pleased with a 10–12% sales increase from the same-sized sales force. Although both effectiveness and efficiency are vitally important, self-management values effectiveness over efficiency. **Sales effectiveness** is concerned with what you should be doing in terms of selling effort. **Sales efficiency** refers to how well you carry out your selling duties.

One of the two ways to increase selling efficiency is to increase the dollars of profitable sales derived from a certain level of selling effort. To do this, a salesperson increases the effectiveness of those valuable moments spent actually selling.

The other way to increase selling efficiency is by reducing the time and money spent to get each dollar of profitable sales. To do this, a salesperson must minimize selling costs.

THE SELF-MANAGEMENT CONCEPT

self-management
combination of time management and self-motivation

Whether a salesperson is trying to increase the effectiveness of selling time or to reduce the cost of selling, self-management is the key. Selling activities can be managed in a manner similar to any other business activity.

Self-management is a combination of time management and self-motivation. Self-management is important to the salesperson for several reasons.

- Unlike other jobs, a salesperson's success and growth as a professional are due almost entirely to his or her own efforts.

- For the most part, salespeople work on their own with only arm's-length supervision.
- Without self-management, an individual salesperson finds it difficult to develop self-discipline and self-motivation.

Self-management is also important to the salesperson's employer for the following reasons.

- Effective and efficient salespeople upgrade the overall sales performance of the company.
- The opportunities for incentives other than the traditional financial reward tied to sales volume greatly increase.
- Efficiency and effectiveness can at least partially offset the steadily increasing cost of supporting a salesperson in the field.

SALES CALLS AND SALES EXPENSES

Obviously, there are considerable differences between salespeople in their utilization of time. One reason is the nature of the sales job itself. Generally speaking, the greater the emphasis on customer relations, the fewer the sales calls made in a working day. A developmental salesperson such as a sales engineer, for example, will make fewer sales calls than a missionary or trade salesperson who, in turn, makes fewer calls than a service representative.

Another reason for differences in time usage is the geographical areas covered by salespeople. Usually salespeople can make more calls in areas where customers are concentrated than where customers are distant from one another. Still another reason is the difference in individual productivity. One salesperson may be better organized and waste less time than another salesperson working under similar conditions. As a result of these productivity differences, some salespeople make not only more sales calls but also more effective sales calls during a day.

As a measurement of selling efforts, sales calls have a dramatic impact on selling costs. More sales calls translate into a lower cost per call. This generalization usually holds true even though extra expenses accrue from making additional calls. Consider the example in Figure 13–1.

Selling costs also vary widely depending on the geographical area the salesperson covers. It costs more, for example, to support a salesperson in an urban area than in a rural area. Then, too, a salesperson's costs in New York, Boston, Chicago, or Washington, D.C., are considerably more than if the same salesperson were working in Little Rock, Dayton, Wichita, or Des Moines.

FIGURE 13–1	Impact of sales calls on selling costs		

	Calls per Day		
	Six	Seven	Eight
Salary	$40,000	$40,000	$40,000
Auto expense	12,000	12,500	13,000
Entertainment expense	3,000	3,200	3,500
Total	$55,000	$55,700	$56,500
Cost/call*	$38.35	$33.29	$29.55
Savings	—	$ 5.06	$ 8.80

*Based on 239 working days a year.

THE VALUE OF TIME

time management
study and effective use
of time

Salespeople need to carefully consider their use of time because time equals money. The study of effective use of time is referred to as **time management.** The following statistics illustrate its importance. A salesperson who works 239 days a year and 8 hours a day has 1,912 hours available during the year. At various earning levels, the value of a salesperson's time is:

Earnings Level	Per Working Hour
$25,000	$13.08
30,000	15.69
35,000	18.31
40,000	20.92
50,000	26.15
60,000	31.38

Looking at it in another way, a salesperson on a 5 percent commission has to sell over $261 worth of products every working hour to equal a salary of $25,000 for the year. For a salary at the $50,000 level, hourly sales production has to be over $523, or an additional $262 per working hour.

Salespeople spend about one third of their time in actual selling situations. Therefore, a salesperson making $25,000 a year is paid $8,250 for face-to-face selling and the remainder for driving, waiting, and other nonproductive activities. Looking only at the time spent in face-to-face selling, the appropriate hourly figures in the preceding table would have to be tripled. This means a salesperson making $25,000 a year is paid $39.24 for every hour productively spent with customers. Clearly, as much time as possible must be spent with the customer, and those hours spent with customers must be as productive as possible.

ANALYSIS OF SELLING ACTIVITIES

For a salesperson to make the most efficient use of available time, the first step is to determine how the working day is spent. Figure 13–2 shows the summary results of a recent survey on how salespeople spend their time. As noted above, only a third of the available time goes into actual face-to-face selling.

A salesperson needs to make a detailed analysis of his or her own activities. This can be done by dividing up what goes on during the normal working day into productive and nonproductive activities. Some of the specific activities that could be included under *productive* are:

- Making sales presentations.
- Handling customers' complaints and problems.

FIGURE 13–2   How salespeople spend their time

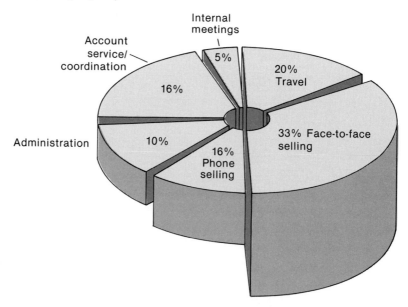

Source: Adapted from William A. O'Connell and William Keenan, Jr., "The Shape of Things to Come," *Sales & Marketing Management,* January 1990, p. 39. Reprinted by permission of Sales & Marketing Management. Copyright January 1990.

- Checking the customer's want list.
- Taking inventory of the customer's stock.
- Setting up promotional displays.
- Making telephone calls to maintain customer contact and to make appointments.
- Making collections and adjustment of customer accounts.
- Checking with other company personnel on customer requirements and delivery schedules.
- Preparing for demonstrations.
- Maintaining contact with existing customers.
- Developing customer sales plans and selling aids.
- Studying product literature.

The latter two activities are often considered extra job requirements to be completed outside normal working hours. Completing company reports, such as the call report, is a nonproductive activity that many companies expect the salesperson to do on personal time.

Some of the activities that fall under the heading of *nonproductive* are:

- Driving an automobile or traveling to the customer's place of business or residence.
- Waiting to see a customer.
- Calling on someone who is not a customer or lacks purchasing influence.
- Engaging in general conversation.
- Conducting a broken interview.
- Calling on customers who are unavailable.
- Completing paperwork.

After identifying and categorizing the different types of activities, the next step is to determine how long the salesperson should record how each working day is spent. While it is not possible to give an exact answer to this question, it would seem reasonable that a salesperson who does a lot of repetitive selling to the same group of customers should maintain a record for two complete trips through his or her territory. For a salesperson who does substantial development work and has to make numerous cold calls, the time period for analysis must be longer to capture the work pattern.

In reviewing their activities, salespeople should:

1. Eliminate those activities that need not be done at all.
2. Set activity priorities based on sales rather than urgency.
3. Determine ways of increasing productivity in important activities (shorten time involved, group similar activities together, set deadlines, standardize).
4. Develop daily and weekly schedules.

5. Set up a procedure to prepare for the next day's calls.
    a. Review customers' specific needs and wants, plus the character-
        istics of the sales situation.
    b. Plan objectives for sales calls by reviewing customer sales plans.
    c. Prepare sales presentations and walk through demonstrations.
    d. Develop a call sequence.
6. Make a concerted effort to increase selling time. As an example,
    reducing the time spent at lunch by 30 minutes, taking care of personal
    business outside of working hours, and shifting paperwork to after-
    business hours can save at least four hours a week.

By concentrating their attention on the problem, salespeople can make
changes in their approach to selling. One common change is to lengthen the
working day and spend more hours on the job. Salespeople in highly con-
gested urban areas, for example, may start their days earlier to get ahead of
the traffic or come home later after the traffic has lessened. Waiting time in
the morning might be used to review customers' sales plans; and time spent
waiting for traffic to lessen in the evening can be used to complete company
reports. Salespersons whose customers are spread out over a wide geographic
area start to travel at times other than when customers are open for business.
It is not unusual to find salespeople leaving home on Sunday afternoon rather
than Monday morning.

Although working longer hours helps salespeople become successful, it
is not the objective of time management. Time management is aimed at more
efficient use of time. After analysis of the typical working day, regardless
of its length, salespeople will undoubtedly find that they waste a great amount
of time. Although there are several obvious changes that can be made, earnest
efforts to reduce nonproductive time are based on four practical ideas: (1)
not all hours in the working day offer the same potential for productive
efforts; (2) all customers are not alike—some offer a better chance for sales
than others; (3) there can be more efficient coverage of the salesperson's
assigned territory; and (4) better ways can be developed to take care of the
paperwork.

VARYING POTENTIAL OF TIME

One of the most important ideas in time management is that not all hours of
the day have the same sales potential. Buyers may be available only during
certain hours, or the very nature of the customer's business may make it
better to visit during certain hours. For instance, a salesperson calling on a
doctor would want to avoid, if at all possible, the hours set aside for seeing
patients.

PROFESSIONAL SELLING IN ACTION

Computer-Based Planning Helps Win Marketing Award

Marc S. Clausen, account manager and laser printing specialist for the Xerox Corp. in West Des Moines, Iowa, was named "Marketer of the Year." AMA's Iowa Chapter honored Clausen for his unique marketing approach that revolved around his personal computer.

When Clausen joined Xerox, he was No. 288 in sales in the nation. By designing a computer program to identify various markets by priority and record client activity, he jumped to No. 1 . . . and more than quad-rupled his quota.

Because of his impressive performance, Clausen developed a three-day training seminar for Xerox's top management that summarized the basic elements of his personal computer program. They are:

A prospect management system that finds, adds, deletes, and changes prospect information; index-es prospect databases; and prints out a master file listing of prospects.

An activity reporting system that adds accomplished activities and prints out a weekly report.

A daily time management system that keeps track of activities, lists them according to priority, and deletes completed activities.

A reference account management system that adds reference accounts to the file, searches by refer-ence type, and displays a master list.

A sample generation system that automatically prints customized or generic mailing sample sets.

A letter master correspondence system that writes letters and prints out mass mailings and envelopes.

Clausen's computer program also has a callback tick-ler system to help him keep in touch with prospects.

SOURCE: Reprinted from "Marketer Uses His Computer to Become a Sales Champion," *Marketing News*, May 11, 1984, p. 10. Copyright 1984.

Knowing which hours are more valuable permits salespeople to allocate activities accordingly. The more important tasks, namely selling activities, are allocated to valuable time periods, and the less important or nonproductive tasks to less important hours. Even though this sounds good, it may not work out in practice. One obstacle is that some companies limit the hours sales-people can see buyers; for example, from 1 P.M. to 4 P.M. on Monday through Wednesday.

In such situations, salespeople should make appointments and call in advance to check on appointments and the availability of buyers. If a buyer does not make appointments, the salesperson has to use his or her imagination to get in to see the buyer. The buyer might be invited to breakfast or dinner occasionally rather than the overworked lunch. Another approach might be to have the buyer visit the seller's facilities.

Also, salespeople should take a traffic count of other salespeople during the time set aside by the customer. There is a good chance that there are fewer salespeople on certain days and at certain times, thus increasing the chances of spending time with the customer.

ACCOUNT CLASSIFICATION

Not all customers buy the same amount or have the same potential to buy. Sellers should practice selective selling and concentrate on accounts with the highest potential. The proportion of unprofitable accounts is usually surprisingly high. One company, for example, classified 76 percent of its customers as unprofitable and switched them to catalog buying.

The approach salespeople take to screen customers depends on the makeup of the territory. For existing customers, company sales records are the primary source of information. Additionally, salespeople should determine the share they are receiving of each customer's business. For new customers, the evaluation has to be based on potential alone, using the same standards applied to existing customers. If an existing customer who purchases $500 or more a month is a major account, a new customer with this potential should be rated similarly until proven otherwise.

account classification

categorization of accounts by their relative sales potential

The categorization of customers on the basis of their sales potential is called **account classification.** A two-way classification scheme (good/poor, major/minor) is simple and easy to understand. However, the following three-way classification scheme may be more suited to many sales territories. Salespeople usually classify customers according to their purchase volume, potential, and the type of products purchased.

A Accounts. These are existing and potential customers who are or will be the best customers of the firm. They buy a wide variety of products or in great volume.

B Accounts. These existing customers are not now good customers of the firm but they have the potential to be. Sometimes, they are customers who split their purchases among several suppliers or buy only part of the seller's product line. This in effect reduces their purchases below the minimum for an A account.

C Accounts. These new or existing customers do not—or are not likely to— buy enough merchandise to be profitable.

Selective Selling

After classifying their customers, salespeople should give priority to making calls on the better customers. Not only should they be worked first, but A accounts should also be seen more frequently than B or C accounts.

Selective selling as a means to more efficient utilization of time and, in turn, greater profitability contradicts many traditional selling philosophies. One is that the way to increase sales is to make more calls. Companies that adopt this philosophy fail to recognize that the salespeople should not make calls just to increase the probability of a sale. Sellers should direct their efforts toward those customers that are clearly profitable and will continue to be so.

The other traditional viewpoint is that all customers should be worked the same. The basis for this idea is that the business was built on customer loyalty and any changes would disrupt this relationship. What is overlooked is that only a small proportion of customers are profitable and the firm owes its major selling efforts to these customers.

national accounts
firm's biggest customers

A common approach to selective selling is the designation of important customers as **national accounts.** National accounts are assigned to a separate sales force or sales manager. Special promotions, product designs, and discount structures may help meet these customers' individual needs. The national account manager's responsibility is to coordinate all activities between the selling firm and the national account, even though the national account may have divisional or subsidiary business units in many diverse parts of the country or even the world.

ROUTING

routing
process of minimizing travel time for sales personnel

Routing refers to plans to reduce travel time between sales calls in covering an assigned sales territory. One of the easiest ways for salespeople to waste time is to spend more time than is necessary in getting from one customer to another. Excessive mileage also adds to selling costs.

Firms now use computers to plan the most efficient routing for salespeople calling on customers in different locations. Computers arrange all the locations in every possible combination to determine the shortest route. To illustrate, for 10 locations, the possible combinations number 181,440. Possible route combinations become astronomical as the locations increase.[2]

Sales call patterns can be broadly defined as either (1) routine or regular, or (2) variable or irregular. With a routine call pattern, there is very little turnover in assigned customers. Salespeople see the same customers on a regular basis. In fact, customers learn to expect the sales call, and this can be an advantage. Once a routing plan is set up, the salesperson can use it over and over again.

Sellers who make calls on an irregular basis have a greater problem. Routing plans are built around the call and the customer's location. Salespeople route calls on the way to, and back from, the customer, as well as make calls on customers in the same town as the primary call.

Routing helps salespeople use time more efficiently by focusing on customer locations and the time distance between customers. Locating customers on a map often reveals some obvious routing patterns. It is not unusual to

A SALES MANAGEMENT NOTE

Crathern & Smith Inc.

Perhaps the most interesting response to rising T&E costs comes from Crathern & Smith Inc., a manufacturer of corrugating machines and packaging equipment. It uses videos in place of face-to-face sales calls.

James R. Cuozzo, marketing manager of the Huntington Valley, Pa., firm, says that he and his staff put together four or five videos per year showing their equipment in action. They run 10 to 20 minutes, depending on the piece of equipment, include voice-over narration and music, and, except for editing, are put together entirely in-house.

"We don't make a sales call now until the customer has gotten some preliminary price quotations and has viewed the tape," Cuozzo says. In fact, he adds, "In most cases we avoid having to make a trip altogether, and the customer comes to us, or to look at one of our existing customer installations, at his own expense."

The costs, Cuozzo says, are minimal. "There was an initial investment of about $5,000 in video equipment, and each film costs about $500 to shoot and edit and another $6 per copy."

The savings, on the other hand, are pretty remarkable. His four-man sales force does about two-thirds less traveling than before, saving the company an estimated $30,000 to $40,000 per year in travel and lodging costs alone. In addition, or perhaps more important, it has cut the company's sales cycle from nine months to approximately 90 days.

"The only problem it has created, " Cuozzo says, "is that our production department has been having a hell of a time keeping up with orders."

SOURCE: "Video Sales Call," *Sales & Marketing Management*, May 1989, p. 53. Reprinted by permission of Sales & Marketing Management. Copyright May 1989.

---

find customers clustered near each other. This cluster provides a convenient division of the sales territory. Another way to develop a routing plan is to key it to the customer that the salesperson wants to call on that particular day.

The next job is to gather information on the amount of time it takes to get from one customer to another in each of these divisions. In some cases, several times should be included to reflect the time of day a salesperson travels.

Frequently, a conflict arises between account classification and efficiency in routing. The most efficient call pattern includes customers who should not receive the same frequency of sales calls. Since account classification is more important, the best approach to the problem would be to have separate routing plans for each account classification. Another approach might be to increase the number of calls made in a day and cover these customers or some portion of them on trips to A accounts.

Time restrictions on seeing a customer, account classification, and routing information should all be kept as part of the customer's sales records. Although these records add to the paperwork for salespeople, they are essential to time management.

REDUCING TRAVEL COSTS

The possibilities of reducing selling costs—particularly travel—without a loss of selling effectiveness are frequently overlooked by salespeople. Substituting phone contacts for personal visits produces significant cost reductions. Corporate travel departments and contracted agencies negotiate airfare and hotel discounts. Some sales forces use vouchers to secure discounted automobile maintenance and repair services.

HANDLING PAPERWORK

Completing paperwork, primarily the preparation of reports for management, is part of the sales job. All salespeople complain that paperwork is the least desirable aspect of a selling career, but reports are necessary in today's sales environment. Of course, sound self-management also adds to the paperwork.

Paperwork for salespeople falls into two categories. One category includes those reports, notably the call report, required by the company. The other category includes those records needed by salespeople for effective self-management of their territories. The most basic of these is the customer sales plan.

Call Reports

call report
summary of a salesperson's daily or weekly activities

Although a **call report** is nothing more than a summary of a salesperson's activities on a day-to-day or week-by-week basis, each company designs its own forms to provide specific information. These forms provide a history of contact with a customer. These logs can be used for planning purposes and can be helpful if problems develop in regard to product specifications or delivery and price discrepancies. Professional salespeople take care in completing call reports that serve as the basis of their own and their firms' future sales actions.

Other Reports

In addition to the call report, salespeople may fill out reports on account status, exceptions, dealer inventory, loss of business, new accounts, and dealer termination. As might be imagined, these reports are completed on an irregular basis as the occasion demands. A regular report required in several companies is an estimate of future sales by customer.

Customer Sales Plan

A customer sales plan such as that in Figure 13–3 may or may not be required by the company. In any case, professional salespersons should keep such plans for at least their key customers. These plans are basic to any customer

| FIGURE 13–3 | Model customer sales plan |

Customer:

Address:

Telephone:

Contacts:

Name	Availability	Preferences/dislikes	Interests	Birthday
____	____	____	____	____
____	____	____	____	____
____	____	____	____	____
____	____	____	____	____
____	____	____	____	____

Estimated sales potential:

Products	Potential	Current sales
____	____	____
____	____	____
____	____	____
____	____	____

Date: _____

file. The market plan in Figure 13–3 highlights the areas of potential sales opportunity as well as pertinent information about key customer contacts.

Time Management Records

Salespeople usually maintain time management cards for every customer, containing respective account classifications plus information on the travel times between customers. A variety of time management systems are available in the marketplace. For example, IBM uses an outside source for its time management system. New marketing representatives and systems engineers spend two days learning the system during their training program.

Information on the time management card might include:

1. Customer restrictions on times for sales calls.
2. Best times for seeing customers.
3. Length of sales interviews with customers.
4. Delays experienced in calling on customers.

Which routing sheets salespersons use depend on whether the pattern of territory coverage is regular or irregular. With a regular route, salespeople set up daily routings and follow them until a change is indicated. Salespeople following an irregular pattern fill out routing sheets during preparation for the next day's work.

Efficiency in Paperwork

Doing paperwork is unproductive in comparison to time spent with customers. It is burdensome to salespeople, yet nearly every firm requires some paperwork of salespeople. Paperwork can also increase the efficiency of salespeople.

The following suggestions may help sales personnel handle paperwork efficiently.

1. *Think positively about paperwork.* Salespeople remember that much of the paperwork increases their efficiency and enhances sales careers.

2. *Do paperwork now.* Salespeople should not allow paperwork to accumulate. Right after a sales interview or while waiting for the next interview, take notes of what happened during the previous sales interview. Dictation tapes can be mailed periodically to the home office.

3. *Set aside a block of unproductive time for working on reports and records.*Interruptions can drag out any project and cause salespeople to spend more time than is necessary on report writing. Unproductive time is the best time for scheduling paperwork. A sales rep in Los Angeles, for example, completes the day's paperwork before starting for home and in this way misses much of the heavy freeway traffic.

4. *Set priorities on paperwork.* The due date for a particular report is one type of priority. Another is the relative importance of the paperwork to the salesperson's performance. For example, it is not logical to spend a lot of time with a report that has no due date and neglect planning for the next sales day.

SELF-MOTIVATION

The second way to increase selling efficiency is to make selling time more effective. To do this, a salesperson must concentrate on personal characteristics such as attitude, appearance, health, and selling skills. Chapters 6 through 12 discussed selling skills. The remainder of this chapter discusses those personal qualities required for a successful professional selling career.

Whether we are talking about maintaining self-image, improving appearance, or working harder, the single overriding characteristic for success in selling is self-motivation. Although the financial rewards from a successful selling career can be considerable, the truly successful salesperson needs more. Studies have shown that the key feature of the sales personality is ego drive.[3] The ego-driven individual needs sales success in an intensely personal way as a powerful means for enhancing self-esteem. They get a real feeling of satisfaction from a sales victory. Their motivation comes from within. The truly self-motivated salesperson develops the proper attitude, good listening habits, and a sound mind and body.

PROPER ATTITUDE

Attitude is an important determinant of a salesperson's success. Numerous sources have attempted to describe the proper attitude for sales achievement. One of the best is Edwin P. Hoyt's book, *America's Top Salesmen;* in it he lists the characteristics of successful people:

1. Hard working.
2. Self-confident.
3. Self-disciplined.
4. Persevering.
5. Flexible.
6. Goals other than money.
7. Respect for buyer's good sense.
8. Willingness to learn from others.
9. Ability to handle big money.
10. Perfectionist.[4]

Hoyt's list provides an excellent set of guidelines for developing the proper attitude in selling.

Listening

Professional salespeople realize that to serve customers they must listen to what customers are saying. They assume that almost half of each sales interview is spent in listening. Therefore, salespeople must be good listeners and be able to respond to what customers are saying. Nothing disrupts effective communication more than salespeople thinking about what they are going to say rather than listening to what customers are saying. Figure 13–4 lists the keys to effective listening.

FIGURE 13–4   Ten keys to effective listening

Keys to effective listening	The bad listener	The good listener
Find areas of interest.	Tunes out dry subjects.	Looks for opportunities; asks "What's in it for me?"
Judge content, not delivery.	Tunes out if delivery is poor.	Judges content; skips over delivery errors.
Hold your fire.	Tends to enter into arguments.	Doesn't judge until comprehension is complete.
Listen for ideas.	Listens for facts.	Listens for central themes.
Be flexible.	Takes intensive notes using only one system.	Takes fewer notes. Uses 4–5 different systems, depending on the speaker.
Work at listening.	Shows no energy output; fakes attention.	Works hard, exhibits active body state.
Resist distractions.	Distracted easily.	Fights or avoids distractions, tolerates bad habits, knows how to concentrate.
Exercise your mind.	Resists difficult expository material, seeks light, recreational material.	Uses heavier material as exercise for the mind.
Keep your mind open.	Reacts to emotional words.	Interprets color words; does not get hung up on them.
Capitalize on the fact that thought is faster than speech.	Tends to daydream with slow speakers.	Challenges, anticipates, mentally summarizes, weighs the evidence; listens between the lines to tone of voice.

Source: Reprinted from *Your Personal Listening Profile,* booklet by Sperry Corporation.

SOUND MIND AND BODY

Centuries ago the ancient Greeks praised a sound mind and a sound body. Only recently have Americans come to realize the importance that good health has on success in any field, not just those requiring physical exertion.

Physical fitness results in better appearance, higher energy levels, and a better attitude. Being physically fit allows salespeople to accomplish more than they would otherwise.

SUMMARY OF CHAPTER OBJECTIVES

1. To relate selling effectiveness and efficiency to self-management.

Sales personnel can improve their selling effectiveness and efficiency by increasing their sales from a given level of selling effort or by reducing the time and money spent to get each dollar of profitable sales. Self-management is the key to increasing selling effectiveness and efficiency with emphasis on the former.

2. To outline the concept of time management.

Time management and self-motivation are the two primary aspects of self-management. Just how important time management is can be seen by looking at selling costs per call, a calculation of the hourly value of a salesperson's time, and the observation that a salesperson may not spend more than a third of his or her available time with customers.

Important ingredients of time management are analysis of selling activities into productive and unproductive tasks and realization of the varying potential of time periods throughout the working day. Tools used in time management include account classification, routing, cost reduction, and paperwork management.

3. To explain account classification.

Account classification refers to the categorization of customers on the basis of their sales potential. A commonly used classification scheme divides accounts into three categories—A, B, C—depending upon their purchase volume, potential, and the type of products.

4. To discuss the importance of proper routing.

Routing refers to the process of minimizing travel time for sales personnel. Routing can follow regular or irregular call patterns. A regular call pattern is used if there is little turnover in assigned customers. By contrast, irregular routing is based upon the call and the customer's location.

Proper routing reduces travel time for salespeople, thus allowing them to spend more time in face-to-face selling or other productive activities. Effective routing also reduces selling costs such as automobile and travel expenses.

5. **To describe the primary paperwork requirements of professional selling.**

   Paperwork for sales personnel can be classified into two groups: reports required by the company and those necessary for effective sales management of the territory. The call report is the best example of the first group, while the customer sales plan illustrates the second category.

6. **To discuss the role of self-motivation and personal attitude in selling.**

   Truly successful salespeople are self-motivated. They develop the proper attitude, good listening habits, and sound minds and bodies. A concern for the customer and a concern for the sale are the basics of the proper sales attitude. The key to understanding customers is listening, a skill that can be learned. Keeping physically fit helps salespeople by giving them better appearances, higher energy levels, and better attitudes.

REVIEW QUESTIONS

1. Differentiate between sales effectiveness and sales efficiency.
2. What is self-management and why is it important to salespeople and their employees?
3. What is time management and why is it important in professional selling?
4. How do salespeople spend their time?
5. For a salesperson who regularly calls on hardware stores in a three-state area selling a line of tools, list some of the possible productive and unproductive selling activities.
6. How can sales personnel reduce their nonproductive time?
7. Explain the value of account classification to time management.
8. Explain the conflict between account classification and routing efficiency.
9. What are the two types of paperwork for a salesperson?
10. What should be included in time management records?

DISCUSSION QUESTIONS AND EXERCISES

1. Who is the most efficient person you know? Why do you consider this person to be efficient? Why do you think the person you selected possesses this quality?
2. Take a typical day at school and divide it up, showing the varying potentials for studying and attending class.
3. If a salesperson receives a 2 percent commission on sales, how much will he or she have to sell every hour to make $35,000 during the year? $50,000?

4. Criticize the statement: The more calls, the more sales.

5. Assess your own self-motivation to succeed in sales. Support your conclusion with factual data or anecdotal evidence.

SALES DIALOG

Sitting next to the fireplace and sipping a cup of coffee, George Douglas was getting edgy. Nancy Hyer had called a few moments earlier to say that she didn't realize that her first sales call that evening was on the other side of Providence and that she would be about 45 minutes later than she had expected. What concerned George most was whether they would be able to finish their business before the fifth game of the World Series began.

When Nancy arrived at 7:45 P.M., George couldn't help but notice that she looked as if she had been "thrown together." Her shoes needed polish, her hair needed brushing, and when she opened her briefcase, several papers fell out.

HYER: Hi, George, sorry I'm late, but I was way on the other side of town. I've been running around since the middle of the afternoon.

DOUGLAS: That's OK. Where's my policy?

HYER: It's right here someplace. Let me see if I can find it. Isn't this briefcase a mess? You ought to see my apartment! By the way, I'm sorry about the late premium notice. I hope we didn't rush you too much. Here's your policy. Take a look at it to make sure that everything's all right.

DOUGLAS: Ummmmm. I thought we were going to increase the coverage on the beach house. Didn't I call you about that?

HYER: Now that you mention it, you did. I must have forgotten to tell my secretary.

DOUGLAS: Also, we were going to increase the liability coverage.

HYER: Right again! I don't know what's the matter with me. I'll tell you what, I'll get this fixed tomorrow afternoon at the office and run it by here tomorrow night. Will you be home? You know, I seem to keep losing things or not telling my secretary about things she needs to know! I must be working too hard. How do you do it, George? You always seem so relaxed.

What do you think the results of this sales dialog will be?

CASE 13–1   DELUXE FOOD PRODUCTS

Janet Robinson, a veteran of seven years with Deluxe, was recently promoted from sales representative to marketing manager for the East Coast Division. Her new office is in Towson, Maryland. Janet is extremely happy with the promotion and the significant pay increase. However, she does feel it had taken too long.

Meeting with other marketing managers for the first time, she expressed the opinion that the delay in getting the promotion was because she was a woman in a man's world. Dick Vermell disagreed with this and told her it had taken him 10 years and Bob George 8 years to get promoted. Other marketing managers joined in the conversation and all felt that too much time was spent at the sales representative level. Another problem was the difficulty in hiring college graduates when opportunities for advancement were slow in coming.

The next day Janet made an appointment for lunch with the vice president of marketing. At the lunch she related what she saw as a problem, namely slow advancement. His reply was that maybe a maximum should be placed on the number of years an individual should remain in the job of sales representative. If the individual was not promoted at the end of so many years, he or she would be released.

Questions

1. Do you feel the suggestion of the vice president would have a positive motivational effect on the sales force?
2. How would you change his suggestion?
3. In what ways would you defend the concept of selling as a career without the need for advancement?

CASE 13–2 MID-AMERICA SUPPLY COMPANY

The Mid-America Supply Company, located in Chicago, Illinois, is a wholesaler of hardware products in an eight-state area. Thirty salespersons call on retail dealers in Illinois, Indiana, Iowa, Kentucky, Michigan, Minnesota, Missouri, and Wisconsin.

Salespeople see each of their accounts once a month on a regular schedule. No distinctions are made between accounts on the basis of sales volume.

For the last two months, an outside consulting firm has been studying how all 30 sales representatives spend their time. Exhibit 1 shows the average results for the eight salespeople with the highest sales volume and the eight with the lowest.

EXHIBIT 1   How sales reps spend their time

	Average working day (percent)	
Activity	Best salespeople	Worst salespeople
Essential:		
Face-to-face selling	28%	18%
Checking want list	20	14
Setting up displays	10	9
Helping with advertising	5	2
Handling adjustments	3	2
Handling billing and credit	3	5
Total	69%	50%
Nonessential:		
Driving	13%	18%
Waiting for interviews	7	12
Broken interviews	3	6
General conversation	2	10
Completing records	6	4
Total	31%	50%

Questions

1. What conclusions can be reached from the results of the study?

2. How would you go about setting up a training program in time management?

3. How would you introduce the subject of account classification to top management of Mid-America Supply Company?

PART SIX

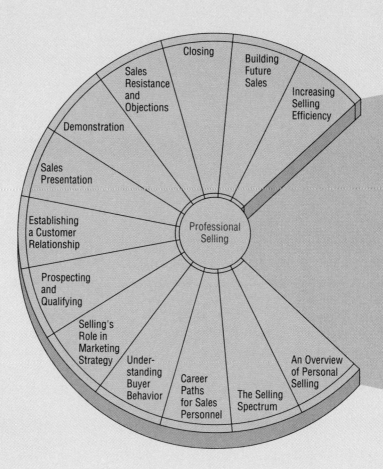

Additional Dimensions of Selling

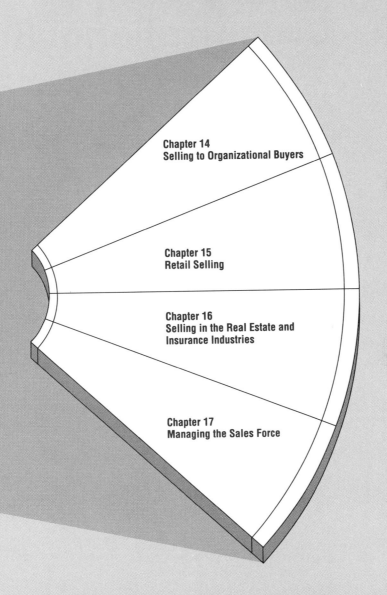

Chapter 14
Selling to Organizational Buyers

Chapter 15
Retail Selling

Chapter 16
Selling in the Real Estate and
Insurance Industries

Chapter 17
Managing the Sales Force

CHAPTER 14

Selling to Organizational Buyers

CHAPTER OBJECTIVES

1. To identify the different types of organizational buyers and explain how they differ from individual consumers.

2. To set up a classification system for industrial products.

3. To identify the characteristics of industrial demand.

4. To discuss the size and role of government purchasing.

5. To explain the buying motivation of resellers.

6. To outline the different buying situations.

7. To list and discuss the latest concepts in organizational buying.

SALES CAREER PROFILE

PAUL BASSA, JR.
Air Products and Chemicals, Inc.

Paul Bassa, Jr., is the brand manager at Air Products and Chemicals, Inc.'s industrial gas facility in Buffalo, New York. A graduate of the United States Air Force Academy, Bassa also holds a master's degree in human resources management from Pepperdine University. Bassa's personal interests include music, stereo equipment, sports, and photography.

Bassa explained his decision to enter sales: "I selected sales as a career to satisfy my enthusiasm for challenges and competition. The thrill of making the sale and the satisfaction of a happy customer are positive emotional events that can be enjoyed repeatedly. Developing strategies to implement programs to solve customers' operational problems is also a day-to-day occurrence providing mental and physical stimulation. But the most rewarding aspect of sales is the involvement with people."

Bassa described how he was hired by Air Products. "I had four interviews with Air Products sales managers from Houston, Detroit, and Pittsburgh. After a second interview in Pittsburgh, I was offered a sales engineering position in the Pittsburgh sales district.

"I selected Air Products because of the positive and professional attributes of the interviewers, the type of sales position available, the growth opportunities presented to me during the interview, and the leadership position the company enjoys in its industry."

Bassa thinks that Air Products was selected as one of the nation's top 100 sales companies because the company is well managed, provides strong support for its sales force, and is committed to giving its customers the best goods and services. "Our marketing and sales philosophies have proved very successful, as demonstrated by Air Products' growth and success during the early 1980s when the economy was severely depressed."

After a stint as a sales engineer in Pittsburgh, Bassa was promoted to his current position. "I like interacting with other people and selling a variety of applications to industry while working for a company that has a reputation for quality.

"My function is to ensure that existing customers receive our products in a timely, professional, and safe manner. I attempt to answer customers' questions, to coordinate interactions of customers with other Air Products' agencies, to respond to customer complaints and problems, to inform customers of new technologies and activities within Air Products, and to be aware of customer developments that might require action by Air Products.

"I keep sales management informed of activities within my area of responsibility such as customer changes, customer expansions and new ventures, sales strategies, and progress in the development of new accounts."

Regarding future career plans, Bassa remarks, "Air Products spends a good deal of time helping employees realize their full potential and follow their career paths. I can move into a district manager's position or one of several positions available in the corporate offices."

Bassa was asked to describe the products he sells and to classify them according to the system in Chapter 14. "We supply industrial and specialty gas products which can be described as operating supplies because the gases are normally consumed during the production or manufacturing process. Industrial gases are used for various applications including propulsion, reducing, inerting, and freezing. As an example, hydrogen can be used in some manufacturing atmospheres to reduce the oxygen content. The gases are consumed and customers must reorder on a continuing basis."

In describing the buying situations he faces in his job, Bassa commented, "An Air Products salesperson experiences repeat purchase, replacement purchase, and new purchase situations. Normally, a purchase order or supply agreement obligates the buyer to Air Products and Air Products to the buyer.

"As a result of the competitive nature of the industrial gas business, we sometimes attempt to replace an existing gas from another supplier with either the same gas, a superior process using the same gas, or a different gas. In other instances, we attempt to replace existing processes and equipment with gas applications that will improve the manufacturing or operating process and/or the end product.

"Finally, diversification and new applications are the methods Air Products uses to maintain and increase its market share. Surveys and application/process studies determine a potential customer base, as well as the potential for new applications."

Differentiating between industrial selling and other types of selling, Bassa commented, "Both the salesperson and the customer spend a greater amount of time reviewing and fully comprehending the gas application and its effect. The gas application normally becomes an integral part of the customer's manufacturing process.

"Selling to an industrial customer frequently includes meetings and discussions with purchasing, engineering, and manufacturing. Each of these departments must be familiar with Air Products, the recommended gas application, the projected economics, the timing to implement, the expected impact, and the potential benefits.

"Perhaps the most important aspect of the industrial gas sale is the postsales follow-up. An industrial gas salesperson must work with the customer to assess at least four items: (1) the effect of the gas application on the operation; (2) the effect of the gas application on manufacturing personnel; (3) the type and method of implementing modifications required, if any; and (4) the cost-effectiveness of the gas application."

The sales challenge for Pall Industrial Hydraulic, a maker of filter systems, is to convince key buying influences, such as project engineers who may routinely replace $5,000 pumps once a month, that Pall filter systems can extend the normal life of their equipment by a multiple of 10 to 100. To meet this challenge, Pall has organized a missionary marketing effort. The sales team includes 4 field marketing specialists, 7 regional sales managers, 28 independent distributor organizations, and 250 distributor salespeople. Selling efforts are keyed to 31 industrial markets divided into smaller segments for prospecting and product development purposes.[1]

INDUSTRIAL BUYERS

Selling to industrial buyers is indeed different from selling to individual consumers. The buying motives of industrial buyers differ and so do the ways the purchasing task is carried out. Industrial buying is typically grouped with buying by governmental units and resellers and called organizational buying. This chapter takes a close look at various organizational buyers.

Industrial buyers purchase products and services to:

1. Become part of another product.
2. Produce another product.
3. Facilitate the operation of an organization.

A packager of soft drinks, for example, buys fructose, corn syrup, and/or sugar to be used as a sweetener. The purchaser also buys containers for the soft drinks, packaging machinery, and trucks to deliver the products to retail outlets. In addition, there is a need for paper in various forms, computers, copying machines, office furniture, legal services, and supplies such as pencils, paper clips, and staples. All of this can be considered industrial demand. It adds up to an annual market of over $500 billion.[2]

Intended use determines whether a product is an industrial or consumer product. While it is obvious that packaging machinery is an industrial product, sugar can be industrial or consumer depending on purchasing intentions. Individual consumers buy sugar to use in cooking and to place on the table as a sweetener for meals. In this case, it is a consumer product. The biggest use of sugar, however, is as an industrial sweetener for a wide array of products. About 75 percent of the sugar consumed in the United States is purchased by processors for inclusion in other products.

Another example of a product that can be an industrial or consumer product is an automobile. An automobile may be purchased by an individual consumer for personal or family use or by a business organization for its sales personnel. The difference is the intended use of the product.

Industrial Products

To better understand the products industrial buyers purchase, they are classified into six general categories. These categories cover a range of items from complex mechanical installations to jet engines to paper clips.

machinery and equipment

used to manufacture other products

Machinery and Equipment. In the plant such items as grinders, screw machines, robots, and stamping mills manufacture other products without becoming part of the final products themselves. **Machinery and equipment** of a more administrative nature include computers and postage meters. When the machinery or equipment has a high unit price and is carried as an asset on the balance sheet, it is considered major equipment. An example of major equipment is a steel mill's overhead crane with a price tag of nearly $1 million.

Machinery and equipment classified as accessory items are lower priced and have shorter life spans than major items. Chain saws, spray guns, staplers, and shelving are examples of accessory equipment.

Machinery and equipment can be single purpose or multipurpose. A single-purpose machine or piece of equipment is designed to perform one specific task. In many underground mining operations, machinery or equipment is specifically designed to do one job in one particular location. Multipurpose machinery and equipment are used with little or no modification in a number of operations. Power wrenches, chain hoists, forklifts, personal computers, and cash registers are examples of multipurpose equipment.

raw materials
unprocessed natural products

Raw Materials. **Raw materials** are unprocessed products that come from mines, forests, wells, fisheries, and farms. The only processing necessary is that required for transporting and storage. Examples of raw material that go into other products include iron ore, bauxite, and copper. Raw materials are typically graded using universally recognized standards.

processed materials
partially completed items that will become part of a finished good after further processing

Processed Materials. **Processed materials,** such as strip steel, receive some processing but require even more before becoming part of a finished product. Usually, processed materials lose their identity as part of the finished product. The wide range of applications for a processed material makes competition intense. Consider, for example, the competitive battle between steel and plastics in automobiles, as well as paper, plastics, and tinplate (tin-coated steel) in packaging.

component parts
products inserted intact into the final product

Component Parts. Products inserted intact into the final product are **component parts.** Examples include batteries, transistors, ball bearings, and pumps. A component is added to the total product package for two possible reasons; one is that the component is essential to the functioning of the total package. Semiconductors and batteries are added because they are essential as integral parts of the total package.

Another reason for adding a component is that it enhances the total product package. A technical enhancement might be a control mechanism that automatically adjusts the feed of paper into a machine. Many of the extras added to an automobile are marketing enhancements. These include radios, dashboard digital displays, locking systems, and power assists.

operating supplies
products used up in the production process, such as lubricants or office supplies

Operating Supplies. **Operating supplies** are products that lose their usefulness or are used up in the production process or the administrative operation of any organization. Normally, supplies have a low per-unit cost and, rather than build up inventories, reorders are placed on a routine basis. Lubricants, cleaning solvents, abrasives, coatings, and protective clothing such as gloves are all production supplies. Gloves, for example, are worn by auto assembly workers. In some parts of the plant, a worker needs a new pair each day. Administrative supplies include paper, pencils, paper clips, fuel, and maintenance products.

Industrial Services.   Two types of industrial services exist: physical and advisory. Examples of physical services include welding, electroplating, and the rebuilding of electrical motors. Advisory services include the x-raying of castings for flaws, geological surveys, location studies, and management consulting. Outside service contractors often provide professional specialization at a lower cost than could be done in-house. Then, too, industrial buyers might not want to get involved in particular operations and prefer purchasing them from outside service organizations.

Characteristics of Industrial Demand

Often called the market behind the market, the industrial market is not only immense in dollars spent but also indicates the economic health of the nation. One of the major differences between industrial buyers and individual consumers is the critical nature of the industrial purchasing decision. A poor decision made by an individual consumer results in the realization that money was spent unwisely and causes unhappiness with the purchase. On the other hand, the wrong decision by an industrial purchaser may translate into many thousands of dollars lost in production downtime, increased product costs, and faulty product performance. The industrial buyer might even lose his or her job. So industrial purchasing personnel must be professional and, as a rule, highly trained for their jobs. Consequently, they are quite knowledgeable about what they purchase and are inclined to make their buying decisions on the basis of cost and quality.

derived demand

purchasing process where industrial demand is triggered by the demand for a consumer product

Salespeople in industrial markets are aware that demand for what they are selling is derived rather than direct. **Derived demand** means that the purchasing process is triggered by the demand for the output of the purchaser. For example, Figure 14–1 might suggest that a manufacturer of tank cars will buy steel castings, machinery, and other industrial products only if there is demand for tank cars. The entire process is initiated by the individual consumer demanding a product that contains an ingredient shipped by tank car or is packaged with a material made up of some ingredient shipped by tank car.

Industrial demand can be compared to an earthquake. At the center of the quake is the purchasing by individual consumers. The tremors going off in all directions are the derived demands for industrial products brought about by the demand for consumer products.

Because industrial demand is derived, it is subject to violent swings. For example, a stamping plant of General Motors Corporation may consume 3,000 tons of cold-rolled steel a day when the assembly plants it serves are operating at full capacity. When the demand for cars falls, so does the demand

FIGURE 14–1   Hypothetical example of actual and possible flows of industrial demand

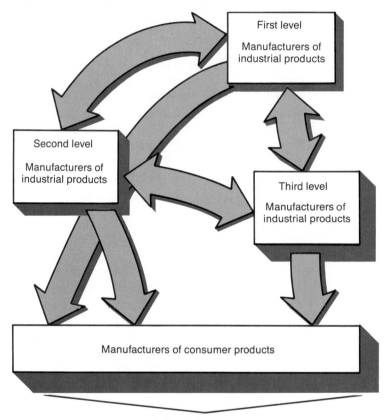

inelasticity of demand
product demand that is
not influenced by price
fluctuations

for steel. In fact, if demand for new cars falls far enough, the stamping plants as well as the assembly plants cease production entirely until the excess inventories of new cars are sold off.

Price changes have little effect on demand for industrial products. One of the biggest reasons for this **inelasticity of demand** is its derived nature. For example, if the price of steel is reduced, auto manufacturers are not going to buy more steel. What makes an automobile manufacturer buy more steel is increased requirements brought on by increased sales of new cars or increased use of steel in each car. Using the same reasoning, an increase in the price of steel does not mean a lesser quantity of steel is purchased.

As a rule, industrial prices are adjusted by taking small changes in one direction so demand for the industrial products in question often run counter to what is normally expected from a price change. Suppose, for example, the price is increased for a basic material used in the manufacture of a finished product. If the material can be stored and further price increases are likely, industrial buyers may increase the amount ordered. In this case, demand increases with an increase in price. If the price of the basic material drops, the industrial buyer reduces purchases as much as possible because the price will probably go even lower.

reciprocity
practice of extending purchasing preference to suppliers who are also customers

The practice of reciprocity is also found in industrial purchasing. **Reciprocity,** or trade relations as it is sometimes called, is the practice of extending purchasing preference to those suppliers who are also customers. In an oversimplified example, an industrial buyer buys only from suppliers who purchase his or her products or products of another division of the company. Although the practice can be an illegal restraint of competition and is discouraged by the Federal Trade Commission, industrial buyers can select suppliers who are also customers if it does not harm competition.

SPEAR
Supplier Performance Evaluation and Review

JIT
Just-in-time inventory that integrates supplier shipments with customers' production scheduling

The adoption of supplier performance evaluation and review (**SPEAR**) and just-in-time inventory (**JIT**) policies by industrial consumers has had a far-ranging effect on industrial marketing. Supplier salespeople must now be prepared to discuss such concepts as statistical process control and quality assurance with almost every buyer. Throughout all sectors of the industrial market, companies such as the Packard Electric Division of General Motors Corporation are placing increasing emphasis on the quality of products purchased from suppliers. Also gaining widespread attention is JIT. It appears as if no one wants to carry an inventory. Consequently, suppliers must integrate their shipments with the production scheduling of customers.

GOVERNMENT BUYERS

Government units at the federal, state, and local levels make up the governmental market. Indeed, governmental buyers are the single biggest customer in the United States. The range of products purchased by the government is vast; anywhere from bathroom tissue to light bulbs to missiles to gigantic computer systems. At the federal level, the General Services Administration is the principal purchaser of civilian items, while the Defense Department buys military products.

There are two reasons for government purchases. The first is to maintain the operation of the governmental units. A city government, for example, must buy fire engines, police cars, and snowplows. These in turn require governmental purchasing of land and buildings, buses, and surfacing materials. As a result, sellers must appreciate that the public sector is not profit driven, so buying motivations are more diverse than those of the private sector.

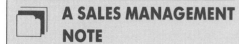

A SALES MANAGEMENT NOTE

DOD Specs for Oatmeal Cookies

The Department of Defense (DOD) has issued 15 pages worth of specifications for the purchase of oatmeal cookies by the Armed Services. The cookies are required to:

- Be wholly intact.
- Be free of any cracks.
- Not be browned on top.
- Weigh exactly 13.7 grams.

Critics have pointed out that such specifications are unneeded and do little to add to the nation's defense capability.

SOURCE: "In the News," *Arkansas Gazette*, June 2, 1989, p. 1A.

Pros and Cons of Selling to the Federal Government

Selling to the federal government is potentially attractive for a variety of reasons. Some of the benefits include:

1. The immense size of the total market and a significant growth rate.
2. The wide variety of products purchased.
3. The evident stability of purchasing patterns.
4. The availability of complete information.

Obstacles and dangers in selling to the federal government also exist. These include:

1. The differences in purchasing from unit to unit.
2. The transfer of much of the risk to the seller.
3. The apparent hesitancy to deal with new vendors.
4. The difference from commercial practices in packaging, shipping, and costing.[3]

Purchasing Procedures

For government purchases over a certain dollar figure, the usual procedure is for bids to be taken from approved suppliers. Exceptions to this are permitted if the project involves not only considerable research and development but also considerable risk to the supplier. In open-bid buying, salespeople must make sure their firms are on the list of approved suppliers for the product in question. Salespeople must also communicate the specifications accurately to their firms for preparation of bids. Finally, salespeople should counsel their firms on whether the government gives any nonprice considerations or whether it follows a strict low price policy.

In negotiated contracts, salespeople act as coordinators in getting the technical people from their firms together with those from government. Salespeople usually wind up with the responsibility of developing proposals submitted to the government.

Legal Constraints on Purchasing

Government purchasing is made even more complex by the legal constraints on buyers. For example, a certain proportion of purchases must be awarded to minority enterprises. Some states such as Ohio accord purchasing preference to products of state firms. Firms that are classified as small businesses also may receive preferential treatment.

RESELLER BUYERS

resellers

organizations that purchase products solely for resale or rental to others

Resellers are defined as organizations that purchase products solely for resale or rental to others. Their purpose in reselling or renting is to make a profit over and above the costs of the purchased products and the reseller's marketing functions. Resellers do not buy products they cannot resell profitably. The two major resellers are wholesalers or distributors and retailers.

Normally, wholesalers and distributors are positioned between manufacturers and retailers or customers. Their basic job is to facilitate exchange of products. Since their primary concern is whether the product will sell, salespeople calling on wholesalers may find it necessary to work with the wholesaler's staff in developing demand. For example, a factory representative may call on the customers of an industrial distributor, or a detailer for a drug company may call on physicians for drugs sold by prescription in a drugstore or retail outlet.

Retailers resell to individual consumers. Similar to wholesalers, they buy in hopes of profitable resale and can use the help of missionary sales efforts. In selling to retailers, sellers emphasize the support that will be given in promoting the product. A salesperson, for example, shows the retailer the following information about the product:

1. The results of performance tests for the product.
2. Improvements made in the product since its introduction.
3. The availability of technical help to assist the selling process.
4. The results of market tests and/or special campaigns.

In selling canned vegetables, for example, a can is often split in half to show a cross section of the product. Manufacturers of electric razors, appliances, and cosmetics frequently hold sales clinics in retail stores to bolster sales.

In their promotional efforts to support the product, salespeople inform retailers about:

1. The major promotions and dollar size of the promotion budget.
2. Examples of advertisements and commercials to be run.
3. The dates advertising is to appear or trade promotions, such as a coupon or allowance, are to be provided.
4. The opportunities provided for co-op advertising with the reseller.

BUYING SITUATIONS

vendor analysis

quantitative assessment of suppliers using factors such as quality, price, delivery, and service

Figure 14–2 illustrates the three different industrial buying situations and four levels of complexity. Repeat purchasing involves buying the same product over and over again. Purchasing management is thoroughly familiar with the product and various suppliers for the product. Evaluation focuses on those suppliers, and takes the form of vendor analysis. **Vendor analysis** is a quantitative assessment of suppliers using such factors as product quality, price,

FIGURE 14–2   Industrial purchasing situation and complexity

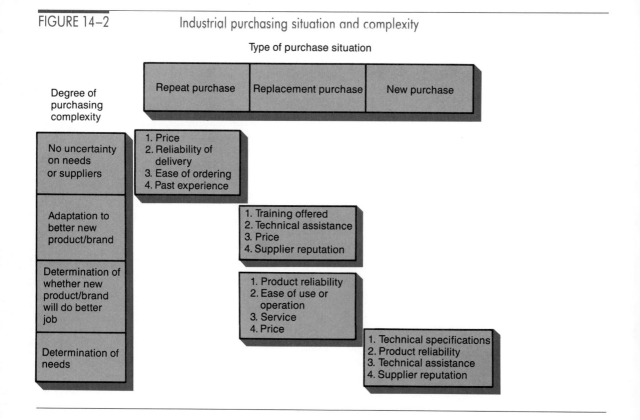

delivery, and service. Figure 14–2 shows that price, reliability of delivery, ease of ordering, and past experiences with suppliers are among the important considerations.

Occasionally, repeat purchasing involves adaptation to a new brand of product of proven superiority. Figure 14–3 points out that in such a situation, the principal purchasing considerations are training offered by the supplier, quality assurance by the supplier, price, and service.

replacement purchasing
purchasing which considers new products of proven superiority or potential superiority

Normally a more difficult and complex buying task, **replacement purchasing** considers new products of proven superiority or potential superiority. Buyers require a great deal more information than when they are involved in repeat purchasing. The emphasis in buying considerations shifts from supplier to product, particularly in cost-benefit analysis.

value analysis
process whereby each product part is related to the function it performs so that costs can be cut with no loss in quality or performance

One way to do this is to conduct a value analysis of the product. In **value analysis,** the cost of each identifiable part of a product is related to the function performed by that part with a view toward cost reduction without a compensating loss in quality and performance. As an example, such an analysis might result in the substitution of a lower-cost material (plastic) for

FIGURE 14–3 Possible repeat purchase complexity

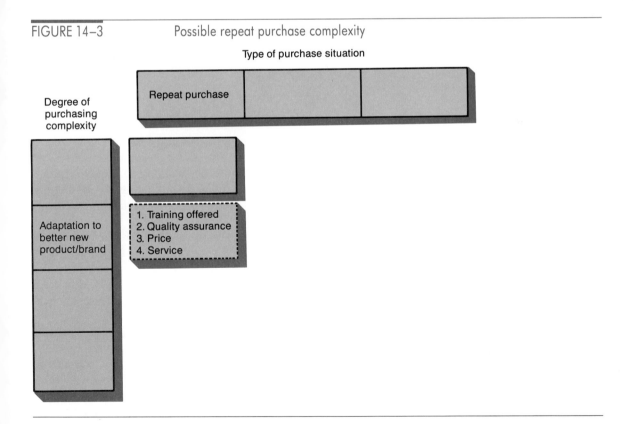

Type of purchase situation

Degree of purchasing complexity

Repeat purchase

Adaptation to better new product/brand

1. Training offered
2. Quality assurance
3. Price
4. Service

FIGURE 14–4   Possible replacement purchase complexity

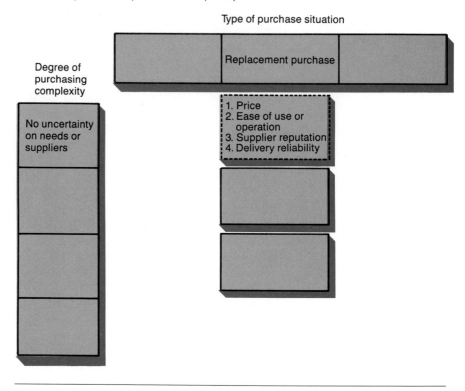

a higher-priced material (steel) with no loss in physical properties. Steei service centers are practicing value analysis by working to reduce end-use manufacturers' in-process inventories to absolute minimums. This cuts the buyer's cost of possession and provides preproduction processing at lower cost.[4]

When there is no uncertainty about needs or suppliers, but the purchasing situation involves more detail than normally encountered with a repeat purchase, it can be labeled a replacement purchase. Figure 14–4 notes that the purchasing motivation shifts toward the supplier's price, reputation, and delivery reliability. The major product consideration is ease of use or operation.

new purchases

purchasing situation where the emphasis is on developing specifications for a product

New purchases are the most difficult purchasing situations. The emphasis is on developing specifications to define the needs satisfied by the product. In working with an individual account, salespeople must be able to reconcile the needs and wants of the various interested parties and decision makers. Although the salesperson works almost exclusively with members of the purchasing department in repeat situations, new purchases require the

COMPANY PROFILE

Total Account Management Means Sales

Brian L. Merriman, vice president of sales for Konica Business Machines, credits total account management for their successful penetration of the U.S. copier market. Concentrating on major accounts, Konica sales personnel endeavor to establish a high level of credibility at the onset by bending sales cycles to fit customers' buying cycles and delivering in-depth marketing and product presentations. Once sold, the emphasis shifts to service and maintenance.

On a local basis, sales representatives deal with the customer on a day-to-day basis. Regional management coordinates installation, service, and volume tracking.

SOURCE: Brian L. Merriman, "Konica Uses Total Account Management to Capture a Larger Share of Copier Market," *Marketing News*, May 23, 1986, pp. 14–15.

salesperson to work with decision makers and influencing agents in engineering, production, marketing, and finance.

Engineering, for example, is concerned with (1) enhancement of the product from a technical standpoint (will the new product, as part of or in addition to our final product, make it function better?); (2) regulations governing the product, such as those involving safety; and (3) servicing of the product. Production personnel, on the other hand, direct their attention to such areas as the efficiency and effectiveness of production, the capital-labor mix of production, maintenance of the product if it is an item of machinery, and make-or-buy considerations.

Marketing and sales personnel concentrate on whether the product enhances the position of the buyer's product in the marketplace. They are interested in whether it will help in the sale of their product. Marketing and salespeople are also interested in the cost impact on the final product's price. They do not want something that will make the price of the product uncompetitive. Likewise, they want components and/or materials that reduce costs to provide a pricing edge. A manufacturer of portable chain saws utilizes the decision rule of "$1 a pound" in an effort to combine two vital purchasing considerations—cost and weight. Quite often, marketers and salespeople are interested in the image of the product in the marketplace. If so, the specification of product needs should reflect this image.

The interests of finance people concern payment timing, the depreciation of the product, and the availability of funds to pay for the product. The interests of top management, other than those already mentioned, focus on the product's contribution to the output of the firm. Their question concerns the kind of product they want to offer to the marketplace.

In new purchase situations, where salespeople can expect different parts of the customer firm to have product interests, they may want to

FIGURE 14–5   Chart used in identifying purchasing interests

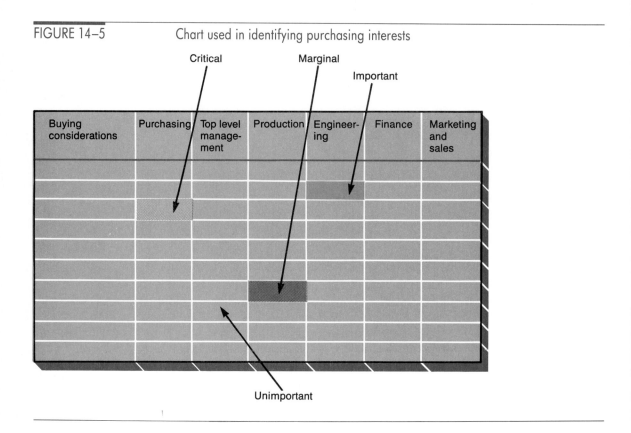

develop a chart such as that shown in Figure 14–5. Here the interests are identified by their relative importance to the purchasing decision. Four levels of importance might be used—critical, important, marginal, and unimportant.

Supply Management

In an effort to improve their purchasing operations, many firms have started to pay more attention to purchasing and its profit impact on the firm. Better purchasing performance translates into the need for professionalism in selling. Throughout the text, we have emphasized the need for customer sales plans. Nowhere is this more important than in organizational markets.

To minimize supply vulnerability and maximize potential buying power, firms have developed supply strategies. One of the important parts of any supply strategy is a classification of purchased items. One classification scheme uses two criteria to classify purchased items into four categories.

FIGURE 14–6   Classification of purchased items in terms of profit impact and supply risk

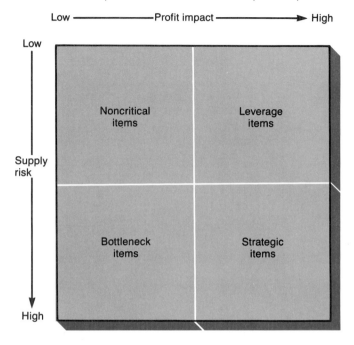

Source: Based on Peter Kraljic, "Purchasing Must Become Supply Management," *Harvard Business Review*, September–October 1983, pp. 109–17.

The first criterion, profit impact, is defined by the volume purchased, percentage of total purchasing costs, or impact on product quality or business growth. The other criterion, supply risk, is assessed in availability, number of suppliers, competitive demand, make-or-buy opportunities, storage risks, and substitution possibilities.[5]

The four categories in Figure 14–6 are labeled strategic, bottleneck, leverage, and noncritical. Each category requires a different matchup of selling and purchasing strategies. For example, in purchasing items classified as strategic, buyers require more information than they would in buying other items and use more analytical techniques because of the high profitability impact. It is also very probable that the decision is made at a higher level in the organization. Conversely, noncritical items require less risk assessment and information. The decision can be made at a much lower level in the organization.

Obviously, the salesperson's job is to supply much of the information required by the buyer. Salespeople must also be aware of the analytical techniques purchasers use.

VENDOR ANALYSIS

Vendor analysis is increasingly becoming a part of purchasing situations for all items. As stated earlier, it is the quantitative assessment of supplier variables in relation to a specific product. It is a common way of evaluating the salesperson's firm as a supplier of a product. Salespeople selling to industrial accounts constantly have to deal with vendor analysis.

For example, assume a purchaser evaluates suppliers according to three variables: price, reliability of delivery (on-time, shortages, and so forth), and product reliability (whether there are defects). The next step is to weigh all the variables. One of the two ways to do this is to weigh all the variables on a 1 to 10 scale. Another way is to assign portions of a number such as 10, or possibly 100, to each variable. Using either approach, purchasers develop and total scores for each supplier.

To illustrate how this might work in actual practice, suppose there are three suppliers for a particular item. The information on these three performance variables is as follows:

	Competitor		
	A	B	C
Price per unit	$2.68	$2.80	$3.05
Delivery— % made when promised	85%	95%	90%
Quality— % rejections	20%	15%	4%

Vendor analysis converts this information into some form of weighting system. Let's take price as our first example. We can readily see that Competitor A has the lowest price. Therefore, if Competitor A gets a 10, we have to give Competitor C a 7.6 and give a 9.6 to Competitor B when comparing their higher prices to that of the lowest price competitor.

Competitor B has done the best job at delivery, getting 95 percent of deliveries to the buyer's place of business as promised. Awarding a 10 to Competitor B, the delivery performance of Competitor C is 9.5, and competitor A's is 8.9. Competitor C has the best record for quality with only 4 percent rejections. Giving a 10 to that firm, Competitor A gets a score of 8.3 while Competitor B has a score of 8.8. Summarizing what has been done, we have the following scores.

	Competitor		
	A	B	C
Price	10.0	9.6	7.6
Delivery	8.9	10.0	9.5
Quality	8.3	8.8	10.0
Total	27.2	28.4	27.1

Treating each variable as the same weight on a 10 to 1 scale, we see that the highest overall performance as a supplier goes to Competitor B and that Competitors A and C have almost identical performances. However, if we assign relative weights to each performance variable, a somewhat different evaluation of supplier performance results. Competitor B is still doing the best job for the buying firm, but the difference between Competitor C and Competitor A is greater.

	Competitor		
	A	B	C
Price (5)	50.0	48.0	38.0
Delivery (2)	17.8	20.0	19.0
Quality (3)	24.9	26.4	30.0
Total (10)	92.7 or 9.27	94.4 or 9.44	87.0 or 8.7

It is obvious that salespeople can do a much more effective job if they know how a buyer is evaluating suppliers. In the previous example, the salesperson for Competitor C needs to concentrate on showing, if possible, that the buyer is not actually paying more for the product. Perhaps better terms of sales could be offered or the supplier could reduce the need for large inventories of product, which in turn reduces supplier costs and the total cost of possession.

MATERIALS REQUIREMENT PLANNING

materials requirement planning (MRP)

computerized system that provides the purchasing department with requisitions for a particular purchasing situation

Materials requirement planning (MRP) is another important concept in industrial buying situations. MRP is a computerized system that provides requisitions to the purchasing department in time for placement with suppliers. It gives "real need" dates that are used in setting up a just-in-time inventory policy. By providing a means of faster communication with suppliers, MRP ties the supplier to the movement of items through the production process. MRP cuts costs by keeping the inventory with suppliers for a longer time and thus reducing inventory costs as well as eliminating shortages and improving on-time delivery. In short, MRP is a master schedule of production that integrates supplier resource products with the flow of the total product through the plant from one machine or subassembly line to the next. Suppliers usually need to tie into the customer's computer network to implement this concept.

BUYING CENTERS

buying centers

all the people involved in the purchasing decision process

A **buying center** refers to all the people involved in the purchasing decision process. As noted earlier, a number of individuals within an organization are involved in the buying process. Lateral involvement consists of functional areas (production, engineering, marketing, and so on), separate departments, and divisions. Vertical involvement is the level of organization exerting influence and communicating within the buying center. The six levels of authority are:

- Ownership.
- Top management (chief executive officer, chief operating officer).
- Policy-level management (functional vice presidents).
- Upper-level operating management.
- Lower-level operating management.
- Production work.[6]

The composition and size of the buying center depends on the purchased item and the firm doing the buying. The two aspects that seem to have the greatest effect on shaping the buying center are the degree of formality in the organization and the purchasing situation. The more people involved in the buying center, the more important and complex the purchase. Buying firms that are more formalized have larger buying centers. The role of the purchasing manager in the communication network is partially a function of the individual's informal role in that job.

SUMMARY OF CHAPTER OBJECTIVES

1. **To identify the different types of organizational buyers and explain how they differ from individual consumers.**

   Organizational buyers, whether they are industrial buyers, government buyers, or resellers, differ from individual consumers in their buying motives and the ways they carry out the purchasing task. Organizational buyers undertake purchasing from the standpoint of the firm. In industrial buying, products are purchased to (1) become part of another product, (2) produce another product, or (3) facilitate the operation of an organization.

2. **To set up a classification system for industrial products.**

   Industrial products can be classified as either: (1) machinery and equipment, (2) raw material, (3) processed material, (4) component parts, (5) supplies, or (6) services.

3. **To identify the characteristics of industrial demand.**

   Industrial buying situations are based on motives such as cost and quality and involve knowledgeable buyers. Demand for industrial products is derived from that of consumer products which often causes violent swings in the amount demanded. Price changes have little effect because of the inelasticity of demand. Reciprocity is also prevalent. New concepts such as SPEAR and JIT are having a decisive impact on industrial purchasing.

4. To discuss the size and role of government purchasing.

Government buyers at all levels are the largest customer in the United States. Governmental purchasing maintains the operation of governmental units and translates social objectives.

5. To explain the buying motivation of resellers.

Resellers buy products to resell or rent. Their motivation in buying is to purchase products that return a profit over and above the cost of purchases and the marketing functions performed.

6. To outline the different buying situations.

In industrial buying, the three purchasing situations—repeat purchase, replacement purchase, and new purchase—each call for a different mix of purchasing considerations. Development of supply strategies has led to a classification of purchased items and, in turn, purchasing requirements.

7. To list and discuss the latest concepts in organizational buying.

Salespeople calling on industrial accounts need to be aware that buying operations use vendor analysis to evaluate their firm's supply performance, MRP to tie in suppliers with their operation, and the buying center concept where a number of people are involved in the purchasing function.

REVIEW QUESTIONS

1. What motivations dominate organizational buying?
2. Outline the various types of industrial products.
3. What determines whether a piece of machinery is classified as major or accessory?
4. Contrast component parts and processed materials.
5. What are the classifications of industrial demand?
6. Describe a situation where reciprocity is legal.
7. How are government buyers and resellers different from other organizational buyers?
8. Differentiate among the different buying situations.
9. Distinguish between value analysis and vendor analysis.
10. What is a buying center?

DISCUSSION QUESTIONS AND EXERCISES

1. Interview salespeople selling different industrial products and look for similarities and differences.
2. Visit the purchasing department of a manufacturer, and write a report on how it operates.
3. Why do you think the industrial market is called the market behind the market?
4. One of the major obstacles in selling industrial products is the practice of spreading out purchases so that the risk is somewhat lessened. Develop a sales presentation that has as its purpose increasing a firm's share of the total purchase volume.
5. Select a particular industrial product and show the various product interests of members of its buying center.

SALES DIALOG

Sam Wylie, a senior sales representative for the Balderstrom Company of Pittsburgh, Pennsylvania, has come to his boss, Jack Parsons, with a problem. It seems that more and more of his customers are introducing new purchasing tools. First it was value analysis, then vendor analysis, and now MRP. Wylie feels insecure because he does not know how to handle these analytical techniques.

WYLIE: Jack, I am not smart enough to deal with MRP or, for that matter, value analysis, and vendor analysis.

PARSONS: Sam, you have been with us for 20 years and have seen a lot of changes. Some blow over and are forgotten while others stay. You don't hear as much about value analysis as you used to, and I don't think vendor analysis is all that common.

WYLIE: I think that purchasing agents use these tools to maintain a kind of superiority over salespeople. I, for one, think we have the best product at a competitive price. All the fuss in the world doesn't change that.

PARSONS: You are so right. Purchasing agents with all the tools still have only one interest and that is price.

WYLIE: It still bothers me that I cannot talk to purchasing agents about these tools.

PARSONS: Maybe we ought to provide you with some information on each of the tools so you can at least talk with them. I don't think you need to be an expert.

WYLIE: I am worried by my lack of knowledge, but what you suggest is not the answer. It seems to me that we should poll our customers and find out what they are really doing, and then instruct our technical experts to help us in the field.

What do you think the results of this sales dialog will be?

CASE 14–1   TONKIN MANUFACTURING COMPANY

Tonkin Manufacturing Company, located in Kanas City, Missouri, is a manufacturer of components for material handling and earthmoving equipment. Sales this year are expected to reach $30 million.

The company has few customers, so the 10-member sales force can spend a lot of time with each account. Almost every customer is considering the implementation of some form of MRP. Tonkin's entire sales force has spent 16 classroom hours learning about MRP.

At a quarterly sales meeting, all the salespeople voiced the need for their company to adopt a leadership role in helping customers to get MRP off the ground. It is their opinion that providing this service to customers would give Tonkin a big edge over competition. While such a presale service would not be cheap and would take countless hours, the results could be tremendous.

Questions

1. Almost all of Tonkin's customers are bigger than Tonkin. Will a proposal to help them with a program seem presumptuous on the part of Tonkin?

2. Would it be better to train two production people as technical specialists and let them provide sales assistance as needed to the sales force?

CASE 14–2 MARION STEEL CASTINGS CORPORATION

Marion Steel Castings Corporation is the sole source for stainless steel maintenance covers purchased by Ohio Tank Car. Ohio Tank Car is a leading manufacturer of tank cars; they are regarded as the best in the industry. The purchasing policy of Ohio Tank Car is to pay more for quality so that all the facets of purchasing and production flow smoothly. Poor quality to Ohio Tank Car inhibits standard operating conditions by introducing repair, replacement, and possibly substitution.

Beginning with an upsurge in demand for corn syrup cars, Ohio Tank Car has tripled its need for covers. Marion Steel Castings Corporation has responded poorly to this surge in demand. The pressure to meet tight delivery schedules has resulted in Marion sacrificing quality for shipments. The following costs have been absorbed by Ohio Tank Car:

$5,120—Repair of cracks, leaks, and other quality problems for the last year.

$46,920—Production of 75 stainless covers to make up for the covers returned to Marion. This is some $12,000 more than the cost of such covers from Marion.

$4,243—Cost of a new pattern for covers from another source, Conway Industries, for 100 covers.

In addition, Ohio Tank Car has had to contend with the paperwork in returning covers, special tests of quality, and complaints from their customers about quality.

Questions

1. If you were the salesperson calling on Ohio Tank Car for Marion, how would you go about answering their complaints?

2. Do you feel that Marion should probably recognize that they cannot be the sole supplier for Ohio Tank Car? The sales projection for corn syrup cars is that 70 covers a week will be needed over the next two years.

CHAPTER 15

Retail Selling

CHAPTER OBJECTIVES

1. To explain how retail selling differs from other types of personal selling.

2. To identify the primary requirements of retail selling.

3. To outline the retail selling process.

4. To list and describe the basic purchasing decisions in a retail setting.

5. To differentiate among trading up, substitute selling, and suggestion selling.

SALES CAREER PROFILE

JEANETTE STEBBINS
Pfizer Labs

Jeanette Stebbins is a pharmaceutical sales representative in the Seattle district for Pfizer Labs. Stebbins holds nursing degrees from the University of Washington and Seattle Pacific University. Her hobbies and interests include gardening, piano, sailing, skiing, and snowmobiling.

Stebbins came to Pfizer in an interesting way. "I was working as a headhunter (recruiter) at the time this position opened up with Pfizer Labs. One of my candidates did not show up for the interview, so I decided to interview for the position myself. I was approved by the personnel manager and was then interviewed by the district manager. Finally, I went to California for an interview with the regional manager."

Stebbins decided that she liked the sales field. She comments about her job at Pfizer: "It offers unlimited financial remuneration due to the commission scale. It allows me continuous opportunity for growth and development, comparable to managing my own business, and allows me a lot of flexibility.

"I am an extroverted and expressive person who enjoys communicating and working with people. I would not like a career where I would be doing the same thing every day. I truly do enjoy the challenge that a sales career offers."

Stebbins continues, "Pfizer is a *Fortune* 500 firm, and one of the top pharmaceutical companies in the world. It has a tremendous research and development program. In the seven years I have been here, Pfizer has continuously developed and marketed products that are the top in their field. We are highly respected in the pharmaceutical industry. Pfizer is a very competitive company, but we also have a lot of integrity."

Asked about the initial training provided by Pfizer, Stebbins responded, "The training is a three-week program in New York City that is very intense and stressful. But the program gave us ample preparation and knowledge to present the products to the doctors with confidence. At the end of the three weeks, we had a test over everything we had learned. One of the most stressful parts of the training in New York was role-playing, practicing presentations before members of the training department and being critiqued on our presentations. Some of us had never had any formal sales experience."

Stebbins was asked what she liked most about her job. "I thoroughly enjoy the contact I have with people each day. I find physicians to be very professional. On the whole, they are respectful and considerate. They are very knowledgeable and challenging to work with. I have developed some meaningful friendships over the years.

"A lot of what we are doing is continuing medical information. Pfizer Labs is on the cutting edge of a lot of medical knowledge, particularly in areas like cardiovascular and arthritic drugs. We are able to relay this information to physicians and really make an impact on the lives of their patients.

"After seven years, I have developed a rapport with most of the physicians in my territory. Many of them consider me a part of the medical team, and use me as a resource for continuing medical educational symposiums."

When asked where she would go next in her sales career, Stebbins replied, "There are many opportunities for career advancement with Pfizer. I have been offered promotions over the years. Recently I declined a promotion to cardiology specialist. It is an honor to be considered for a promotion, and I appreciate the opportunities that have been given to me. At any time that I am interested in a promotion, Pfizer management has said that I would be one of the first they would consider. At present, I am very satisfied and challenged in my current territory, but I will consider the possibility of accepting a promotion at a later time."

Stebbins was asked to comment on some topics specifically related to Chapter 15 of *Professional Selling*. She was first asked to discuss the unique nature of pharmaceutical sales. "Pharmaceutical sales is a unique type of selling because you do not actually sell a product. You are trying to persuade a physician to write the prescription, and then the patient actually buys the product. You are working with a very special, intelligent individual who has had extensive training and background in his or her field. Everything you tell the physician must be accurate because it can have an impact on the patient. I believe that a pharmaceutical sales rep is really involved in the education of the physician. There are many times when we are able to make an impact in an area that would not otherwise have been made because the physician does not have the time to attend continuing medical education programs or read the medical journals. So we are actually updating the physician on new data and medical knowledge. We are not really 'detail' people, but we have a great responsibility to do everything we can to be knowledgeable and credible, and to present information that can really have an impact. A pharmaceutical sales rep is a valuable person to the physician, the community, and the patient. We are also very involved in continuing medical education programs for patients. We are truly part of the medical team."

The final question asked was: "Why is professionalism so important in pharmaceutical sales?" Stebbins answered, "We do not make a cold call and have that person sign a sales contract and never see the individual again. We continually see that same person month after month, year after year. We have a very important responsibility, and we are truly a member of the medical community. We need to conduct ourselves well and present an image that is truly professional."

Jeanette Stebbins' products are sold through retailers that are considered part of the medical profession. Other retailers have different conceptualizations of their businesses. Consider the case of Tres Mariposas. "We're a sales and marketing organization that happens to sell through a store," says Charles Napier, citing the key role of salespeople in sparking Tres Mariposas, an El Paso, Texas, fashion specialty shop, to sales of $2.25 million from $200,000 in just 11 years.

When a customer enters a store in search of sportswear, fashion jewelry, or furs, a "customer service specialist" greets her and offers her a glass of cola or wine. Casual chat is the rule; there is no hint of a possible purchase for at least five minutes as the pair makes its way up the grand stairway amid cascading fountains and aisles of apparel.

Salespeople, who have contests to test their knowledge of every item in the store, are drilled in the art of selling to upscale consumers, and if they survive the rigors of Napier's coaching, they gradually build their own clientele. "If you don't make people accountable, what you have is a clerk, and I don't want clerks," he says, noting that his seven salespeople can expect to earn from $15,000 to $75,000 a year. "If someone says, 'Can I help you?' she doesn't work for me long."

Beginners are guaranteed $5 an hour, but the key to Napier's system is an incremental commission structure that encourages the ambitious to sell more and the fainthearted to look for other work. Thus a salesperson earns 5% on her first $100,000 of sales, 6% on the next $100,000 of sales, and so on. If she exceeds her sales target for three consecutive quarters, she may request an increase in her draw, but if she falls short for just one quarter, the draw is reduced.

Rather than leaning on counters to while away the time, salespeople are expected to call at least three customers a day to tell them about newly arrived merchandise. Napier goes over call sheets with the salespeople weekly to see if they've met their objectives. "Every person has her personal trade book," he says. "It's just like the guy selling drill bits." [1]

RETAIL SELLING AND ITS ROLE IN OUR ECONOMIC STRUCTURE

retail selling
sale of products and services to individual consumers for their own or others' personal use

Retail selling is the sale of products and services to individual consumers for their own or another's personal use. Retail selling can be done in department stores, drugstores, automobile and truck dealerships, discount stores, boutiques, tire stores, and restaurants. Some retail selling, however, is done outside retail establishments. Examples are selling life insurance in a prospect's home, door-to-door selling, and selling over the telephone. Earlier chapters described the sales process in which the seller goes to the customer. This chapter discusses only in-store retail selling. When the customer comes to a store, the seller's task is considerably different. These differences require changes in the sales approach.

Retail selling is treated in a separate chapter because it occupies a unique and vital position in our economy. The importance of retail selling is apparent in light of its role in the overall economic structure, its financial importance in our free enterprise system, and the vast numbers of people employed full-time as well as part-time in retail selling.

The marketing system in a free enterprise economy such as ours distributes the output of production to consumers. Without an efficient marketing system, these products might never reach consumers or might be too expensive for them to buy.

standard of living
quantity and quality of goods and services consumers can provide with their resources

The country's **standard of living** refers to the quantity and quality of goods and services that average consumers can purchase with their financial resources. The standard of living of each family or household rises with an increase in income or a decrease in the cost of the items consumed. An efficient marketing system can increase the standard of living by minimizing the costs of distributing goods and services and making them readily available to consumers.

Retailing is crucial to marketing because it is the final step in the marketing process for many products. As such, retailing has a direct effect on the level of the standard of living in a society. A sage has said, "In a product's long journey from the producer to the customer, the last two feet are the most important." The last two feet is the distance across the sales counter.

THE RETAIL SALESPERSON'S JOB

Generalizations about the duties and responsibilities of retail salespeople are difficult to make. Retail salespeople have different responsibilities because they sell widely different products and services. In spite of the differences in the duties of retail salespeople, two things are expected of all—they must have a complete knowledge of all the products carried in inventory and be able to interact with a wide variety of consumers. Figure 15–1 points out that these two job dimensions distinguish between retail sales clerks and professional retail salespeople. In more concise terms, their job is to keep consumers coming back and to turn consumers into customers.

Certain characteristics are common to all in-store retail selling. The most distinctive feature is that consumers come to the store, instead of salespeople seeking them out. Consumers who enter a retail store usually are looking for something specific that they desire or for something new; they are further

FIGURE 15–1   Critical dimensions of retail selling

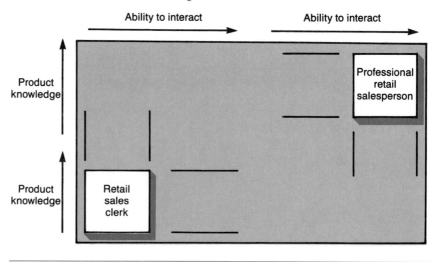

along in the buying process than consumers in other selling situations. Retail salespeople merely help consumers complete the buying process, which began before they ever entered the store. Other sales personnel have to start the buying process by showing consumers they have unsatisfied needs which a certain product or service can help satisfy.

Retail salespeople face two major problems. First, they are unable to select consumers because consumers do the selecting. Salespeople, therefore, must sell to a large variety of consumers; this is more difficult than selling to consumers with similar purchasing goals and buying habits. When salespeople sell to consumers who are alike, experience accumulates as sales situations occur over and over. They learn much from previous successes and failures. Although this also happens with a large variety of consumers, the learning process takes much longer and is more difficult.

Second, when consumers select the store and the salesperson, the burden of attracting consumers falls on the store's advertising, displays, physical characteristics, and, most importantly, its salespeople. Research has shown that a retail store's image and its patronage appeal are primarily determined by the personality of its salesclerks. In a sense, the personality of the store and its major differentiation from other stores cannot be separated from the personality and professionalism of the salespeople in the store. Nowhere is this more obvious than in a restaurant.

REQUIREMENTS FOR THE RETAIL SALESPERSON

A number of changes have occurred in retailing. Stores are more attractive inside and out, have more consumer-oriented merchandise, are better located, and offer more services. Unfortunately, the situation in regard to retail salespeople has not changed appreciably. With notable exceptions, retailers have been reluctant to upgrade sales personnel. Too many retail salespeople consider themselves clerks or order takers instead of selling professionals capable of affecting the buying decision of their customers.

The difference between an order taker and a sales initiator is that the latter is appealing and informative, whereas the former usually lacks these qualities. For example, well-dressed shoe sellers who pay special attention to their own footwear and have good merchandise knowledge are more likely to be effective than sales personnel who lack these qualities.

The following sections suggest answers to the question, Which personal qualities and skills do I need to become an effective salesperson?

Pride

The primary requirement for professional retail selling is pride—the belief in oneself, in the merchandise, and in the store. Without this pride, the sales presentation is unconvincing, transparent, and uninspiring; with it, the sales presentation is dynamic, convincing, and informative.

Knowledge

The second basic requirement is knowledge of the store, the merchandise, and, most importantly, the consumer. Effective retail salespeople must know a great deal about the store to serve consumers properly. They must be well acquainted with such information as:

- How the store handles refunds, exchanges, and sales adjustments.
- Where other departments are located and which merchandise each carries.
- Procedures for credit sales, delivery, installation, and other special customer services.
- Advertisements the store is currently running and any special promotions in the department.
- When the store is normally open and what the hours are during special seasons.
- Whether any future special promotions are planned and when they will be held.

Consumers also expect salespeople to have extensive knowledge about the merchandise they sell. A salesperson, for example, may be asked if a garment is washable, guaranteed not to shrink or fade, or appropriate for formal occasions; some consumers ask salespeople for their opinions and preferences. Other consumers might want to know how the store's merchandise compares with that of the competition. A seller unable to answer such questions loses sales.

Retail salespeople must also have enough knowledge about consumers to be able to understand and interact with them. In retail sales, as in other selling, salespeople must be able to ascertain not only a consumer's needs and wants but also how they can be satisfied. Several factors affect salespersons' ability to communicate effectively with consumers. For instance, because in-store retail salespeople face an endless variety of customers, what they can learn about each customer is limited. They must be good listeners, since they know nothing about the consumers until they meet in the store; in short, sellers must learn as much as possible very quickly during the sales encounter. Although one way to learn is by observing consumers' dress and mannerisms, asking questions and listening attentively are most important. Consumers tell a lot about themselves; however, salespeople must listen to what they say and be constantly alert to nonverbal cues.

One way to personalize selling and increase sales is for retail salespeople to keep a file of regular customers. One salesperson in a women's apparel shop keeps track of two kinds of information in her customer book. One section contains the lifestyles, sizes, and color preferences for a limited number of customers. When new merchandise arrives at the store she checks her customer list to see if it matches up with any of the customers. If it does, she places a phone call or sends a note. In a second situation, she keeps

PROFESSIONAL SELLING IN ACTION

Ricart Ford

Fred Ricart claims to be the biggest car dealer in the world. His Columbus, Ohio, Ford dealership employs 127 salespeople, and sells over 24,000 vehicles a year. Ricart stars in his own TV commercials, often strumming a six-string guitar and singing off-key versions of songs written by his 10-year-old daughter.

While Ricart will admit to being a showman on television, his sales operation is all business. Ricart Ford covers 77 acres and includes $30 million of inventory. Ricart offers customers such amenities as a child care center, a 24-hour service center, and optional videos of repair work for those who do not trust mechanics. In fact, Ricart Ford even has a $23,000 diagnostic van complete with a technician dressed in coat and tie available for on-site repairs.

Ricart explains his approach to the retail car business this way: "We've made this a big Disneyland complex. You don't see someone silly on TV and then come in and see come snub-nosed salesman. We want to make it fun."

SOURCE: Jennifer C. Kent, "In Ohio, One Zany Dealer Sells 24,000 Fords a Year," *Arkansas Gazette*, June 11, 1989, pp. 1F, 3F.

track of this year's and last year's daily and weekly sales totals. These figures and the resulting comparisons motivate her to keep doing better.[2]

Service Organization

As professionals, salespeople must have a sincere desire to serve consumers. Professional selling is not persuading people to buy things they do not want or need. Rather, professional selling in a retailing environment is interacting with consumers, with the goal of maximizing satisfaction. Only by adopting this orientation can salespeople expect to be successful in the competitive retailing arena.

PURCHASING DECISIONS

general decision
situation where consumers know which item they want to buy, but are unclear about specific details

specific decision
situation where consumers know both the product and the brand they wish to buy

Before looking at the steps retail salespeople go through in the selling process, it is necessary to understand consumers' purchasing decisions and where they make which decisions. Figure 15–2 outlines this process. Of the four decisions, two are made outside the store and two inside the store. With a **general decision,** consumers have an idea of the products they wish to buy, but are unclear of specifics. For example, a woman might decide that she needs a new outfit for a party but has nothing specific in mind. Visits to a hardware store, paint store, and gift shop are also usually preceded by a general decision.

In making a **specific decision,** consumers have a good idea of the product and the brand they want to buy. Visits to a retailer are limited to those stores

FIGURE 15–2   Purchasing decisions for individual consumers

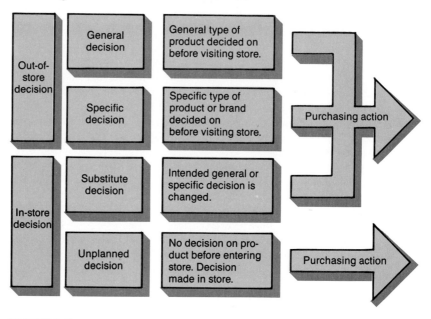

that handle the specific brand of the product desired. Specific decisions are often reached on automobiles and appliances.

substitute decision

a change in a general or specific decision

Once inside a retail establishment, a **substitute decision** may change a general or specific decision made earlier. There are several reasons consumers make substitute decisions:

- Other products and/or brands on display catch consumers' attention.
- Other products and/or brands are on sale.
- Other products and/or brands are not immediately available.
- Other products and/or brands are presented as a better fit with purchasing goals.

unplanned decision

situation where consumers make on-the-spot purchase decisions without benefit of prior planning

add-on purchase

an additional unplanned purchase

Obviously, retail salespeople can be of major importance in substitute decisions. They are also very important in the other in-store decision—the unplanned decision. **Unplanned decisions** are made in the retail establishment with no planning prior to the store visit. Unplanned decisions are not impulse purchases. The consumer makes a decision in the store. One category of unplanned decision is the add-on purchase. An **add-on purchase** is something extra or additional to what was planned prior to entering the store. A shirt, tie, or belt to go along with the planned purchase of a suit are good examples of add-ons.

THE RETAIL SELLING PROCESS

Similar to other forms of selling, the retail selling process involves a series of steps. Although such a structure is helpful in describing the process, in practice, the selling process is a smooth flow and some steps are not always required.

The basic steps in the retail selling process are: (1) approaching the consumer, (2) determining his or her needs and wants, (3) presenting the merchandise, (4) meeting objections, (5) closing the sale, and (6) selling by suggestion. Note that the process for retail selling differs very little from the more general sales process described earlier.

Approaching Customers

Many retail sales are made or lost in the first few seconds after customers arrive in a department. If customers are treated warmly and salespeople exhibit a helpful, courteous attitude, the process starts off well. But if sellers neglect consumers by treating them indifferently or discourteously, sales may be lost. Salespeople should act as if consumers are guests, to be attended to and pleased. Both the salesperson's personal appearance and that of the department are important in the approach stage.

What the salesperson says in approaching and greeting customers can be a critical factor. Undoubtedly, "May I help you?" is the most overworked and ineffective approach used today. Everyone knows the standard response to this: "No, thank you," or "I am just looking." Once the customer says this, the salesperson must either leave or risk offending the customer by staying around. In either case, things have started out poorly; other approaches are much better.

Among the phrases that can be used are, "May I help you look for your size?", or "Which color did you have in mind?" These phrases are offers of assistance which customers cannot reject. Retail salespeople using these approaches are offering assistance without making consumers ask.

Three other approaches—"Have you seen our ad in today's paper?", "Would you like to see what just came in?", and "Have you seen our sale merchandise?"—are better still. All show that the sellers have the interests of consumers in mind and that they are willing and able to provide useful information. Most consumers appreciate this kind of assistance.

Another possible approach is to talk to the children that accompany their parents. For example, the salesperson might say, "Good morning, I see you are helping your mother (or father) shop today. Maybe you both would be interested in some items I have on special."[3]

Determining Customers' Needs and Wants

To tailor sales presentations to the consumers' needs and wants, expressed as their purchasing goals, sellers must learn as much as possible about each patron. As noted before, this is one of the most difficult tasks for retail salespeople because of the variety of consumers they serve. But this does not make it any less important.

To learn consumers' needs and wants, salespeople must be adept at observing consumers. What kind of clothes is the consumer wearing? What is the first thing the consumer looked at or picked up? Are children along? Is the consumer in a hurry or just browsing? Does the consumer appear happy or sulky? Is the consumer shopping alone or with friends or family? Is the purchasing decision likely to be made jointly by a husband and wife, or parent and child? By simply observing the consumer's clothing, facial expression, mannerisms, and shopping group, sellers can answer these questions.

Retail salespeople can also ascertain consumers' needs by asking leading questions. What is the consumer going to do with the merchandise? Do his or her tastes seem to be different from that of the salesperson? Will the consumer need the merchandise soon, or can he or she wait? Many questions can only be answered by asking the consumer directly. Beginning salespeople often mistakenly assume things about their customers. If they see a woman with a little girl looking at a child's dress, they assume it is for the child, whereas it might be a gift. Or they assume that because they like green, customers also like green. If there is any doubt, salespeople should ask appropriate questions.

To get to know consumers, retail salespeople must learn to listen. The key to good listening is concentration on what the consumer is really saying. This can be a help in understanding consumers' needs and wants, and identifying their purchasing goals.

Presenting Merchandise

Product demonstrations can be vital to retail sales presentations. The merchandise should always be demonstrated if requested because it is immediately available and ready for presentation. Consumers experience a product through merchandise demonstrations. They can taste a new flavored vitamin pill; see how a coat looks on them; get the feel of a golf club; smell an expensive French perfume; touch a satin bedsheet; and drive a car. In each case, the effect handling the merchandise has on a consumer's senses is one of the primary reasons for purchasing the item.

From a salesperson's point of view, demonstration is vital because it puts the consumer one step closer to purchase and becoming a customer. It converts a looker into a buyer. Demonstration can also help salespeople persuade consumers to trade up or to buy substitute merchandise when the merchandise sought is not carried by the store.

trading up

situation where a consumer buys additional or more expensive items than originally planned

Consumers **trade up** when they buy more expensive merchandise or more merchandise than they had intended to purchase. Demonstrations show consumers the advantages of trading up by allowing them to see and experience the difference between the merchandise they intended to buy and more expensive merchandise. Conventional wisdom says that most retail sales presentations should feature a medium-priced item. This allows consumers to adjust their original purchase intention as they see fit.

substitute selling

situation where a seller attempts to sell something other than what the customer requested

Substitute selling encourages consumers to purchase merchandise that is different from what they requested. Usually sellers use this tactic when the store does not carry the requested merchandise. Retail salespeople might also suggest other merchandise such as another brand of the same item because the substitute merchandise is more suited to the consumer's needs or wants.

Both trading up and selling substitute merchandise can be dangerous selling techniques, however. Consumers may become dissatisfied with the alternative merchandise and blame the seller. These approaches should be used only if a salesperson honestly feels that the alternative merchandise will produce a more satisfied customer. If the salesperson does not feel this way, it is better to give consumers what they originally wanted, even if this means sending them someplace else to get it.

Avoiding and Handling Objections

To inexperienced personnel, probably the most frightening aspect of retail selling is consumer objections. Beginners have a natural tendency to believe that consumers raise objections because they do not want to buy the merchandise they are considering. This is not the case at all. Consumers who do not want to buy or who do not see what they want usually leave and do not stand around to discuss the matter. Consumers who raise objections are still very interested in the merchandise, but they have doubts about the advisability of buying it. They may be concerned about its cost, some of its characteristics, or whether to buy now or sometime in the future. Occasionally, a consumer might object to the store itself. Normally this involves the store's reputation, a service policy regarding delivery or installation, or the store's pricing policy.

The best way to handle objections is to answer them in advance. Salespeople should anticipate objections and provide the necessary information before consumers can raise any objections. For example, a consumer may be concerned about the high price of the merchandise and/or the delivery charges. The salesperson, however, describes and demonstrates the exceptionally high quality of the article and explains the reason for a delivery charge during the sales presentation. In this way, the potential objection is answered before the consumer even mentions the price.

Even the best salespeople must face objections, nonetheless, because they are not always able to anticipate all the consumer's concerns beforehand.

When this happens, professional salespeople depend on a variety of techniques for handling objections. These techniques are the same for retail sales as for any other sales process. It does not matter which approach is used in handling objections, as long as salespeople remember that consumers who raise objections still want to buy. The problem is that they just need help in convincing themselves.

Closing the Sale

Closing the sale is as important in retail selling as it is in other types of selling. Without a close, there is no sale.

The various approaches to closing sales described in Chapter 11 are applicable in retail situations. All salespeople must decide when to close and how to do it. The closing of a retail sale is the same as in any other sale, but the timing of the closing is distinctly different in retail selling. If retail consumers are slower to purchase than most other buyers, then it logically follows that they are also closer to closing. A retail sale may take less than a minute, or it may take much longer. Since a retail sale can occur very quickly and it is impossible to predict in advance how long it will take, retail salespeople must always be ready to close, from the very moment they start the sales process. Too often sales are lost because salespeople fail to close soon enough; it is far better to try to close too soon than too late. Usually it is advisable to try to close several times in each sales presentation.

There are certain dangers in trying to close too early. The salesperson may appear to be overly aggressive. Alternatively, the consumer may feel the salesperson is rushing the sale to be able to serve other customers. Both of these dangers actually relate to how the closing is made rather than to when it is made. If sellers take care not to make consumers feel pushed, it is possible to try to close half a dozen times or more in a single sale. The danger of closing too early is that goods may be returned. A customer who has not purchased the right product will return it. This involves not only the possibility of a lost sale, but also a used product that cannot be resold. After the sale is completed, of course, salespeople should thank customers for shopping at the store. They should also make sure that customers feel welcome to discuss other aspects of the product, take care of problems, and make future purchases at their store.

Selling by Suggestion

After a retail sale has been closed, but before the sales ticket is written up and the merchandise delivered, there is an opportunity for the retail salesperson to encourage additional purchases. This opportunity, which is unavailable to almost any other seller, is the chance to sell by suggestion.

When retail salespeople encourage customers to make one or more add-on purchases, or to buy larger quantities of the same merchandise, they are

suggestion selling

retail salesperson's effort to sell add-on purchases or larger quantities

using **suggestion selling.** Two forms of suggestion selling, trading up and selling substitutes, have already been described. In addition to these two there are others, such as:

1. *Suggesting complementary items*. Examples of this are suggesting a tie to go with a shirt or a blouse to go with slacks.
2. *Suggesting merchandise never before available*. If a consumer is buying deodorant, the salesperson may show the soap and shampoo available in the same line.
3. *Suggesting seasonal merchandise* such as suntan lotion for the summer, electric hand warmers for the winter, or door wreaths for Christmas.
4. *Suggesting sale merchandise*. Often retail customers are unaware of a special promotion another department is running, and a suggestion is all that is needed to encourage them to look at the items. Many customers appreciate such attempts to "save them money."

Incorrect suggestion selling can offend customers and make salespeople appear overly aggressive and forceful. This does not mean that suggestion selling should be avoided, but that it should be done properly. The best approach to use in suggestion selling is very similar to that used to close a sale. Salespeople must sincerely want to help customers by offering additional information the customer might not have thought of or known about. Note how different the following two approaches are in suggesting that the customer buy an additional shirt. An inept salesperson might say, "Can I talk you into one more of these?", while a professional salesperson would say, "For the remainder of this month, you can buy two of these shirts for only $68, a savings of $10!" In the first case, the customer is asked to do the salesperson a favor; in the second, the salesperson offers to do one for the customer. Obviously, the latter is the better approach.

Retail salespeople can take three steps to improve their ability to sell by suggestion. First, they can develop a list of other items related to every item sold in the department. Every time an item is sold, the seller automatically thinks of related items and suggests one to the customer. Second, salespeople can make sure they know about all the special promotions in the department, as well as in the store. And third, retail sales personnel can make all sales suggestions specific instead of general. Instead of saying, "Will there be anything else?", for example, they can say, "Let me show you these new silk ties we just received."

If retail salespeople are aware of the needs of customers and consciously try to assist them, suggestion selling can not only increase sales but also contribute to the reputation of the store. If, on the other hand, they apply the selling by suggestion technique in an offensive manner, or if they try to sell customers things they neither want nor need, suggestion selling can give the store a bad image.

THE FUTURE OF RETAIL SELLING

Personal selling has been written off as a merchandising tool many times. Today people can buy life insurance, magazines, books, handkerchiefs, golf balls, hot soup, and a host of other things without the assistance of salespeople. Mechanical troubles in automobiles are diagnosed by testing machines instead of mechanics. Bank machines give cash advances and credit deposits to accounts. Art is sold through the mail, and people join clubs to buy books and records.

Yet to conclude that retail selling will soon pass away is to disregard equally significant changes in today's consumers. They are better educated, can afford more things, and are more willing to be different; they want better quality, and, most of all, are clamoring to be treated as individuals. Taking these and other factors into account, we conclude that (1) effective personal selling is critical for many retail stores, and (2) the best form of differentiation a retail store may have is the quality of its sales personnel.

SUMMARY OF CHAPTER OBJECTIVES

1. **To explain how retail selling differs from other types of personal selling.**

   Retail selling occupies a unique position in our modern economy because it is the critical link between product and consumption. In-store retail selling differs from all other selling, including the retail selling done outside of stores, in two respects: retail consumers come to the salesperson, and they are nearer a purchasing decision than are other consumers. Balancing these distinct advantages is the fact that retail salespeople must deal with a larger variety of consumers.

2. **To identify the primary requirements of retail selling.**

   The critical dimensions of retail selling are knowledge of products and ability to interact with a wide variety of consumers. Too many retail salespersons consider themselves to be clerks or order takers, rather than professional sales personnel. Pride, knowledge, and the desire to serve consumers are vital ingredients in successful retail selling.

3. **To outline the retail selling process.**

   The retail selling process has six distinguishable steps: (1) approaching the customer, (2) determining the customer's needs and wants, (3) presenting the merchandise, (4) answering objections, (5) closing, and (6) selling by suggestion. Although retail selling resembles the traditional sales process, some special problems and opportunities are inherent in the retail selling process.

4. **To list and describe the basic purchasing decisions in a retail setting.**

Retail buying decisions can be classified by where they are made—outside the store or inside the store. Out-of-store decisions can be subclassified into general decisions (general type of product) and specific decisions (the specific type of product or brand). In-store decisions consist of substitute decisions (when the general or specific decision is changed) and unplanned decisions (when no product decision is made prior to entering the store).

5. **To differentiate among trading up, substitute selling, and suggestion selling.**

Trading up and substitute selling are two types of suggestion selling. Trading up refers to the purchase of more expensive merchandise than originally planned. Sellers sometimes use demonstrations to allow consumers to experience the more costly merchandise. By contrast, substitute selling encourages consumers to buy merchandise that is different from what they requested. Sellers use this tactic when the requested item is unavailable, or to better solve the buyer's needs.

REVIEW QUESTIONS

1. Explain the role of retailing in the marketing of products and services.
2. How does in-store retail selling differ from other selling? Do these differences affect the way retail sales personnel perform their jobs? If so, how?
3. What skills are required for successful retail selling?
4. What are two major disadvantages of retail selling when compared to other selling?
5. Select a product line and describe the four possible decisions a consumer might make.
6. List and briefly describe the six major steps in the retail selling process.
7. What are some things a retail salesperson should look for, or questions that should be asked, to determine the needs and wants of a consumer shopping for a new set of golf clubs? For a new car?
8. What is the best approach to use in a retail setting?
9. Describe four different types of suggestion selling, and show how each can be used by a salesperson selling paint and wallpaper.
10. What is the best way for retailers to differentiate themselves from competition?

DISCUSSION QUESTIONS AND EXERCISES

1. Visit several local bicycle dealers and tell them you are shopping for a new 18-speed mountain bike. (Other products may be substituted.) Observe the sales techniques used by each salesperson and later prepare a brief written summary of each encounter. Pay special attention to the sales techniques and potential pitfalls discussed in this chapter. Rate each salesperson on overall retail sales effectiveness. Compare your

experiences and ratings with those of other class members. How many sales personnel received high marks, and how many received low marks? Can you draw any conclusions from this experience?

2. Make a log of your contacts with retail sales personnel. At the end of a month, prepare a report on which salesperson impressed you the most and which impressed you the least, and why.

3. Select one member of the class to act as a consumer shopping in a large department store. Other members of the class are to assume the roles of retail salespeople. In turn, have the "shopper" enter each "salesperson's" department. Each seller must greet the consumer without using the phrase "May I help you?" and may not repeat an approach already used. Continue until the list of approaches is exhausted—or, more likely, quit when the class is exhausted.

4. Is suggestion selling an unethical practice used by retail sales personnel to simply increase sales, or is it a service that most customers appreciate? Explain.

5. List three businesses in which retail selling is likely to become more important in the future and three businesses in which it is likely to become less important.

SALES DIALOG

Tom Schultz is the assistant manager of The Clothes Horse, a men's clothing store in the Los Angeles area. The Clothes Horse carries upscale brands and features custom made suits priced at $900 and up. Recently, Schultz attempted to fit 50-year-old Harold Summers, a local attorney and long-time customer.

SCHULTZ: Harold, it looks like you will need the 48 . . . let's try this jacket on for size.

SUMMERS: Yea . . . you are right, the old 46s just don't do the job anymore. Even my new fitness campaign doesn't seem to help.

(Summers tries on the coat and looks at the fit in the mirror. He continues.)

You know it just doesn't look right . . . it buttons tight across the middle, and the collar raises up.

SCHULTZ: Well, we could let the back seam out a bit and pull down the collar.

SUMMERS: You did that with the last suit I bought from you . . . and I still didn't think it looked good.

SCHULTZ: Harold, let me propose another option. How about one of our custom-made suits?

SUMMERS: But didn't I see where they cost $900 and up?

SCHULTZ: Yes, they do, but we could tailor a suit to fit you perfectly. We all know that our body measurements shift as you get older . . . sometimes off-the-rack suits just don't do the job.

SUMMERS: Maybe so . . . but I have never paid $900 for a suit before.

SCHULTZ: Look, Harold, the suit you are holding costs $525 and you don't think it will look the way you want it to look. So for only $375 more, you can have a perfect fit. What do you think?

What do you think the results of this sales dialog will be?

CASE 15–1 WARMGLOW WOOD STOVES

Kip Ward, a graduate of the local college with a degree in philosophy, had recently opened a store specializing in the sale of energy-saving devices. His primary merchandise was a line of well-known, high-quality wood stoves. Accordingly, he had chosen the name Warmglow Wood Stoves for his store.

He had found an ideal location in a mall which had opened in a converted old factory. The mall's unique character resulted from a large number of massive exposed beams in the ceiling and brick floors underfoot. Ward was confident that his business would be a resounding success. This pleased him because he felt he was also contributing to the solution of the nation's energy problem.

One day Ward was sitting behind the counter reading a textbook entitled *Professional Selling* he had borrowed from a friend of his in the business school. He was particularly interested in the chapter on retail selling. As he sat there, he noticed a young couple come in the door and walk over to the wood stoves.

WARD: May I help you?

YOUNG MAN: Yes, I hope so. We've been doing some reading about the cost savings associated with using a wood stove; we think we might want one installed in our home.

YOUNG WOMAN: I also understand that they're very cozy. We keep our thermostat down quite low, and it gets a bit chilly at times. I was hoping that the wood stove could help in this regard also.

WARD: It well might help you on both counts. Where would you put the stove? Do you have a good central location?

YOUNG WOMAN: Not really. Our fireplace is in the family room, which is located to one side and to the back of the house. Also, it is separated from the rest of the house by the breakfast room.

WARD: I'm not sure that a wood stove will work very well for you then. They seem to work better when they are centrally located. Maybe you ought to look at some other ways of solving your problem. Does your house have storm windows?

YOUNG MAN: No, do you sell those also?

WARD: No, I don't, but they might help as much or more than the stove. How about a blower for your fireplace? I sell those. Or how about some insulated draperies for your windows? Those could help too. I also sell caulking to seal your windows and insulating plates to put behind your plugs and electrical outlets. And I sell . . .

YOUNG MAN: Hold it! I'm confused. How about this? Why don't you come out to our house, look it over, and then tell us what you would advise us to buy?

WARD: I'm really not qualified to do that, but there are people available at the power company who are. Why don't you call them?

YOUNG WOMAN: Maybe that's the best idea. Let's do that.

Questions

1. Review the retail selling process used by Kip Ward. Cite instances of good retail selling techniques and instances of bad techniques.
2. How might Kip have handled the situation differently?

3. Would you have tried to sell the young couple the wood stove?

4. Has Kip learned anything about services or merchandise that he might add to his current offering?

CASE 15–2   THE TAILOR HOUSE

The Tailor House is an exclusive ladies' shop in University Park, Virginia, home of the University of South Virginia. Clientele at the Tailor House range from high school students who live in University Park to wealthy matrons from the surrounding area.

Many of the store's clerks attend the university. These clerks work for modest wages but receive considerable discounts on the merchandise they buy. All are well-dressed with a good sense of what the clientele expects from a store like the Tailor House. Other clerks are middle-aged women from the community who have worked in the store for several years. One of these women, Mary Beth Grant, has worked for the Tailor House for seven years. She purchases most of her clothes there and makes sure that her friends at the country club know that she does. She is also the assistant manager of the store.

One day Grant was straightening a pile of sweaters on a sale table when Beth Perreault, the 15-year-old daughter of one of the professors at the university, walked in with a package under her arm. She approached Grant and opened the package.

GRANT: May I help you?

PERREAULT: Yes, I hope so. I purchased this sweater here three weeks ago and have worn it twice since I bought it. Earlier this week I hand-washed the sweater and look what happened. There are yellow streaks all over the white. I would like to exchange it for another sweater.

GRANT: But you're only supposed to dry clean that brand of sweater. I'm quite sure that washing these sweaters will damage them.

PERREAULT: But it says right here on the label that the sweater may be either dry cleaned or washed by hand.

GRANT: Oh, it does, doesn't it? Still, I think you better get it dry cleaned first.

Beth left the store a little angry and a little hurt. She had saved a long time to buy a $75 sweater from her meager earnings as a babysitter and snack shop clerk at the faculty club pool. She had bought the sweater at the Tailor House because her parents had always told her she was better off buying a few high-quality items than several low-quality pieces. Now she was afraid she would be stuck with a sweater she couldn't wear.

She went straight to the dry cleaners and gave them the sweater to clean. Three days later she picked it up and saw that the streaks were still there. She was upset. She went home and asked her mother to go with her to the Tailor House to talk to Grant since she had felt intimidated the first time.

Mrs. Perreault and Beth walked into the Tailor House and asked for Grant. They were told that this was her day off and were asked if anyone else could help them. Another clerk, Terry Meyers, a student at the university, came over to them to see if she could be of assistance. Mrs. Perreault told Terry what had happened and showed her the streaks in the sweater.

MEYERS: What cleaners did you take this to?

BETH PERREAULT: Sam's in the mall. Why?

MEYERS: Remind me never to take any of my things to Sam's!

MRS. PERREAULT: What does that have to do with anything? I'm getting mad! Clearly there is something wrong with the sweater. Why don't you give Beth either her money back or another sweater?

MEYERS: I'm sorry. I didn't mean to make you angry. But I can't make exchanges. Only Mrs. Grant or the manager can do that. You'll have to come back tomorrow.

MRS. PERREAULT: This is the poorest excuse for service I've ever run into!

The next day Beth and her mother successfully exchanged the sweater for another. Although no angry words were exchanged, the atmosphere was clearly icy.

Questions

1. Should Grant have handled the situation differently? How about Meyers?

2. Was there anything in the store's policies that you would change?

3. Would you buy a sweater at the Tailor House knowing Perreault's experience? Do you think Beth and her mother told their friends about their experience?

CHAPTER 16

Selling in the Real Estate and Insurance Industries

CHAPTER OBJECTIVES

1. To describe professional selling as it relates to real estate and insurance.

2. To explain the concept of listings as it applies to the sales job of the real estate agent/broker.

3. To describe the selling task of matching customers with real estate.

4. To define professional requirements for real estate salespeople.

5. To describe insurance selling.

6. To define professionalism for insurance salespeople.

SALES CAREER PROFILE

JOAN J. HARDING
U.S. Home Corporation

$\mathbf{J}$oan Harding of Howell, New Jersey, sells new homes in an adult community for U.S. Home Corporation. Harding graduated from Kean College with a BS in education and a major in art. She has also taken real estate courses at Fairleigh Dickenson University. Her current hobbies include astrology, reading, computers, and telecommunications.

Why is an art major selling real estate? Harding explains, "When my ex-husband got out of the service we had three children, a very small income, and nowhere to live. If it were not for a very sympathetic real estate broker, I do not know what we would have done. He found us something we could afford to rent until the mortgage came through. At the time I decided that as soon as I could start working I would not teach but make my career in real estate. I thought that helping others find the right homes was an important thing to do. I do not think of my career as selling; I think of it as helping."

Harding, who had earlier retail sales experience, began her career in real estate brokerage by listing homes and packaging land for a developer. She continues, "I then took a position selling new homes for a small builder, and I built them from the foundation to completion. I was a staff of one doing everything. The compensation was terrible but the education was invaluable!

"When I started with U.S. Home Corporation, it was a small local building company, and I was hired as the sales manager. As the company grew, I worked my way up to become the director of marketing with the responsibility for a department of 26 people. I was in charge of all the customer contact from the initial planning stage, advertising, equipping the sales offices, staffing them, obtaining the mortgage commitments, right on through to the closing of titles on homes."

When a reorganization of U.S. Home eliminated Harding's position, she decided to stay with the firm as a sales representative because "the compensation package for salespeople was excellent. Plus, I like new homes, the planning and design of the communities, and seeing the prospective buyer getting excited over the homes and communities."

Harding obviously shares her new home excitement with her clients. She reports that her customers are her greatest source of new sales. In fact, 80 to 90 percent of the homes Harding sells are referrals.

When asked what makes home selling unique, Harding replied, "It is a very emotional time for buyers. Something in their lives has triggered a need to change. It is an important change, one of the biggest in their lifetimes. It may be a happy event such as a new job with more money or the increasing size of their family, or it could be a need for a change due to a tragedy such as loss of income or a family member. Retirement also brings on a very emotional condition as the prospective buyers are about to give up everything that in their minds has made them useful, important persons. The salesperson must be a good and sympathetic friend. It is a close relationship for anywhere from three months to a year depending on delivery time."

Regarding emerging trends in real estate selling, Harding commented, "The product may change because of the shortages of land in commuting range and the sad state of our public transportation system. I think a lot of neighborhood renovation will take place if the roads and public transportation are not modernized. The emotional needs of the buyer do not change—families will still want space, good schools, trees, and a nice neighborhood. The single person will still need conveniences and company, and as much space and convenience as possible. I would not predict a long-range trend, for we are still in a position to change directions. Do we rebuild the cities with the conveniences of utility systems in existence, or improve transportation and develop more rural areas? We shall have to watch to see which route the politicians take, and how much power the ecology groups have; then we can develop our strategy accordingly. In the meantime the communities that emphasize services for home owners are my top pick."

Harding also thinks that we may see a spurt in condo sales. "This type of ownership is important for the growing number of buyers that do not have the time or do not want to spend the time on maintenance. Our society right now is being deluged with messages to keep fit, be beautiful, and have fun 'because you owe it to yourself.' The divorce rate is high and the number of children shrinking. If this continues for many more years we will have a buyer who is more interested in condo living with fitness centers and a high degree of maintenance services, close to his or her work center. Condos with parks near the cities and major area towns will be the spots to be selling."

T oday's salesperson in either real estate or insurance faces formidable challenges. Markets, product offerings, and organizational structures are undergoing rapid and significant changes. The result is that historical characterizations of either type of selling have all but disappeared. The marketplace for real estate or insurance has become more complex and more competitive. Cathy Schneider, an agent with Better Homes and Gardens in Plymouth, Michigan, believes that to successfully sell real estate today, an individual must:

1. Maintain an adequate inventory of listings for each prospect. Agents who have no homes to show have nothing to sell. At the other extreme, agents with too many homes cannot give clients the necessary attention or treat all sellers fairly.

2. Counsel sellers on how to properly prepare their homes for showing. Don't be afraid to make suggestions on cleaning, repairs, and even redecorating.

3. Gauge customers, and be prepared to work with them on their level. The days when a buyer dropped into an office and said, "I would like this particular piece of property," are gone forever. Today an agent must search out customers and ask the right questions to be in a position to develop a relationship.

4. Be persistent, and don't give up too quickly. Selling real estate is a tough job and one where the agent has to fit into someone else's time schedule.

PROFESSIONAL SELLING IN ACTION

Realty-TV

What's new in selling real estate? The answer is Realty-TV. Realty-TV allows prospective buyers to view photos of different houses and neighborhoods complete with phone numbers and addresses of the appropriate real estate agent in their own homes. So far its use in 50 or so national markets has boosted sales and sharply increased name recognition for real estate companies. According to Jim Murray, senior vice president of marketing for Weichert Realtors, a Morristown, New Jersey, realtor, "name awareness has significantly advanced and so too the number of prospects directly attributable to the program."

Weichert Realtors has introduced an interactive program that airs on Sunday mornings. Seeing a house he or she finds attractive, a viewer can dial an 800 number along with a three-digit code number that corresponds to the particular house. A computer voice can provide an estimate of monthly mortgage payments based on whatever down payment is made and directions to the "open houses." In addition the caller's phone number is automatically registered and the caller is questioned about receiving additional information. With more than 1,000 calls per show, this monitoring device has proven valuable in providing leads.

SOURCE: "House Hunting—At Home," *Sales & Marketing Management* August 1989, p. 20. Reprinted by permission of Sales & Marketing Management. Copyright August 1989.

Agents who honestly feel that the deal can benefit both buyer and seller should keep working until the deal is consummated.

5. Work with all parties to get a closing. Today it is getting more and more difficult to coordinate all the parties to a close. Lending institutions, appraisers, title companies, buyers and sellers all have to be in agreement to close.

6. Follow up every sale.

7. Take advantage of every opportunity to view new properties.

THE IMPORTANCE OF REAL ESTATE AND INSURANCE SELLING

Real estate and insurance selling require special consideration for several reasons. Real estate was the first industry outside of retailing to accept women as professionals in selling; and today, women outnumber men in full-time selling positions. A female owner/broker founded the first real estate board in 1892, and the names of three women appeared on the membership rolls of the National Association of Realtors in 1912.[1] On the other hand, relatively few women have entered insurance selling, a situation major insurance companies are correcting with organized recruiting efforts.

Professionalism is of major importance in real estate and insurance selling. Unlike other salespeople, real estate agents are licensed by each state. States

GRI
Graduate Realtors®
Institute

regulate all the activities of those engaged in real estate selling, including the distribution of commissions and educational requirements. In addition, real estate agencies commonly require their salespeople to maintain memberships in local boards and state associations. Each of these has codes of conduct salespeople must follow in selling real estate. The designation **GRI** (Graduate Realtors® Institute) signifies educational achievement in the field of real estate selling.

CLU
Chartered Life
Underwriter

CPCU
Chartered Property
Casualty Underwriter

Today life insurance agents must be registered representatives to sell mutual funds. This requires passing the NASD Series 6 exam. In life and health insurance fields, agents have the opportunity to obtain the professional designation of Chartered Life Underwriter (**CLU**). This designation is based on strict ethical, experience, and education requirements. The American Institute for Property and Liability Underwriters has developed an education program that leads to the Chartered Property Casualty Underwriter (**CPCU**) designation.

Finally, the structures of both industries are undergoing fundamental changes that affect selling. Typically localized businesses, the real estate industry has experienced dramatic changes with the development of national franchise and financial service networks. The increasing demand for services of a real estate agency has permitted specialization in selling for some of the larger firms. Meanwhile, the changes in the insurance industry seem almost in direct conflict with each other. For example, life insurance companies are adding property and casualty insurance to broaden their respective customer bases. But within some of these same companies, salespeople are becoming more specialized. Thus, a salesperson in an agency might handle only product liability insurance. Mergers are another structural change for both real estate and insurance. For example, Metropolitan Life, which owns Century 21, has started selling insurance to home owners through realty offices with a fair amount of success.

Another change is that the small firm, while still the most numerous, employs only one in every 10 salespeople in real estate. A salesperson in real estate will be much more likely to work for a firm employing 50 or more salespeople (see Figure 16–1).

THE UNIQUE NATURE OF REAL ESTATE SELLING

listings
an inventory of homes
for sale

Real estate selling differs from other selling in a number of ways. First, and perhaps the most obvious difference, is that real estate selling is actually two jobs in one. The real estate salesperson must not only go through the selling process common to any product, but he or she must also obtain **listings** or build an inventory of homes to sell. They have an ethical obligation to serve competently both buyers and sellers. Many real estate salespeople consider obtaining listings the more important aspects of the job. They point out that they cannot sell what they do not have.

FIGURE 16–1   Comparisons of size of firm and sales force

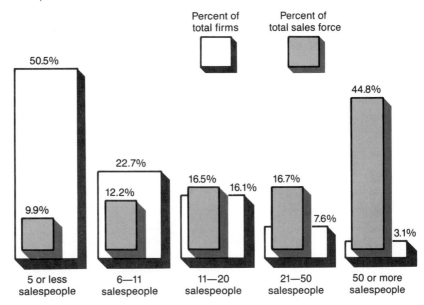

Source: National Association of Realtors®.

A second difference is the degree of competition within a firm. Real estate salespeople from the same firm compete with one another to sell a particular piece of property. The use of sales territories makes little sense in selling real estate, although salespeople tend to specialize in certain neighborhoods or types of property.

Third, prospecting also differs in real estate selling. Referrals are of utmost importance, and prospective customers see the firm's signs on property in which they may be interested. A third source of prospective customers is **walk-ins.** Regardless of the source, these potential customers are further along in the buying process because they have more of a need than those one would expect to find in most other selling situations, with the exception of retail buying. The emphasis must therefore be on helping consumers clearly define their housing needs rather than selling them a listing. Whatever prospecting method is used, the principal job is to get consumers to think of a salesperson when they think of real estate.

Generally speaking, prospective home buyers have little knowledge of construction or how to determine a home's value. Since they do not know what to look for, their attention shifts to the neighborhood in which the house is located. In fact, the top three reasons for buying a particular house are location, location, location! This buying motive tends to be emotional and beyond the control of the salesperson. As a consequence, salespeople need

walk-ins

potential real estate customers who walk in to the firm's office without prior contact by the agent to know a great deal about housing and to be able to show consumers what to look for in a house besides location. A good way to do this is to develop a list of strong and weak points about each house as well as about each neighborhood.

Consumers may also become confused by all the details and complexities involved in buying and financing, and look to the real estate salesperson for advice and up-to-date information. Consequently, salespeople must help in handling all the paperwork and guiding customers through the necessary procedures. The complexity of buying a house places added emphasis on the salesperson's reputation.

Frequently, salespeople have to deal with multiple buying influences and decision makers. Usually their respective roles, however, are much clearer than those involved in the purchasing of a house. There is a family unit itself, with the husband and wife playing dominant decision roles. The impact of children on the decision can vary widely from situation to situation. Complicating the buying process still further is the fact that friends, relatives, and business acquaintances can and do play influencing roles.

As a result, real estate salespeople continually talk about having to have everything "right" to sell a house. As an illustration, a real estate broker related an experience he had in getting the right environment to close a sale a few years ago.

> One young couple must have looked at a certain house five times, each time taking about an hour. I have been in the business over 20 years, and I could tell they were in love with the house and the neighborhood. Yet there was something holding them back from closing the deal, and it wasn't price. I finally asked them whether they would like their parents to see the house. They agreed it might be a good idea, so the next Sunday after church the couple, their parents, and grandparents went through the house without me. On Monday we closed the deal.

Finally, the amount of money involved in purchasing a house makes the amount of risk seem overwhelming to some customers. In such situations salespeople must step in as the primary source of additional information and not let customers rely on past experiences. It is also important that salespeople supply rational motives for buying the house (see Figure 16–2).

TASKS IN REAL ESTATE SELLING

As noted earlier, the selling of real estate is actually two jobs in one. The first job is acquiring listings, which is considered the most basic task in the industry. The second job is matching up customers with properties.

FIGURE 16–2   Characteristics of real estate customers and selling rules

Customer   Salesperson

Lacks knowledge about
real estate
- Establish advisor role
- Highlight strong points
- Develop rational motives
  for purchasing

Confused by complexities
of purchase
- Handle the details
- Simplify by showing the
  procedure step-by-step
- Match mortgage money
  sources and payment plans
  to customer's needs

May be exposed to
multiple buying influences
and decision makers
- Do not ignore any
  possible influence
- Give each influencer and
  decision maker reasons
  for purchasing

Perceives high amount of
risk
- Establish credibility
- Be primary source of
  information

A SALES MANAGEMENT NOTE

Another Type of Real Estate Selling

The skills required to sell manufacturing/assembly or warehouse/distribution space are not substantially different from those required in selling office or residential space. However, some specialized knowledge is relevant.

1. Analyze your market to look for imbalances and major events that indicate opportunities.

2. Know your prospect's needs and wants. Manufacturing/assembly prospects typically have specific requirements while warehouse/distribution prospects with a less complex basic function have less specific needs.

3. Determine prospect's requirements in terms of location, utilities, and building characteristics.
   - Where does the prospect need to be for the suppliers, customers, employees, and transportation systems?
   - What kind of power and water supply is needed, how much, and what are the relative costs for various locations?

- What type of building is needed? Type of construction, loading facilities, clear height, column spacing, power and sprinkler system may all bear on the decision.

4. Determine transaction "stumblers" and "breakers." Stumblers can be resolved with knowledge of the market and selling skills, knowledge of the prospect, and knowledge of the brokerage business.

5. Determine who actually makes the decision. The safest course is to simply ask the question, "Who is involved in the decision?"

SOURCE: John P. Anderson, "Learn to Talk and Sell Industrial," pp. 48–52. Adapted from the April 1988 issue produced by *Real Estate Today®* by permission of the NATIONAL ASSOCIATION OF REALTORS.® Copyright 1988. All rights reserved.

Obtaining Listings

The job of obtaining a listing involves getting the owners of the property to believe that the salesperson and/or the firm represents the best means of selling the property. The more credibility the salesperson has with the customer, the more likely the customer is to take the advice of the salesperson, and the better the listing. A good listing usually means a quicker sale and a satisfied customer.

There are three selling jobs in getting a listing. First, the salesperson must sell the need for his or her services. This usually includes information about the property, about other sales, and why it is good business to deal with a realtor. Second, the salesperson must sell the consumer on his or her abilities, usually through a recap of his or her experience and what he or she has done for other clients. Third, the salesperson must sell his or her company.[2]

In offering a firm's services to sellers, salespeople must show what can be expected. These services normally include:

1. Collecting data on all the features of the property.
2. Knowing current financial information.
3. Printing and dissemination of information on the property.
4. Showing the property.
5. Arranging advertising.
6. Obtaining loan commitments.
7. Closing the sale once it is made.

Usually the question of price enters into any listing negotiation. This can be a problem if the property owners have in mind a price that the market will not support. When this happens, the salesperson has to sell the property owners his or her market knowledge. A **market analysis** is invaluable to salespeople in convincing property owners to accept a more competitive but lower-than-hoped-for price.

market analysis
a valuation of real estate based on current market condition

A market analysis includes:

1. Competitive advantages of the property (location, extras, loan, and the like).
2. Drawbacks to the property.
3. Area market conditions.
4. Reasons for selling (such as moving or buying another house).
5. Requirements of the seller (time limitations, financial needs, and so forth).

Matching Customers and Real Estate

This part of the selling job in real estate is very similar to selling other products. The salesperson is involved in showing the house to qualified buyers, uncovering basic information about buyers and determining readiness to buy, arranging and coordinating advertising, and handling the negotiations between buyers and sellers.

showing
a sales presentation in the real estate industry

Actually, the word **showing** the house is a poor one because the salesperson wants to make sure prospects are thoroughly familiar with the house and are aware of all the features of the house. Therefore, the salesperson must know the house thoroughly by going through it as many times as necessary with the present owners. It is essential that the house be shown only when it is in good condition. The salesperson also needs to collect information about the house independently. Much of this information probably appears on the market analysis form.

open house
property that is open to inspection by all interested parties

A common and practical way of showing a home is through an **open house.** An open house is when a property is open to inspection by all interested parties. Often, newspaper ads and signs placed in strategic locations announce the event. One disadvantage of the open house is the lack of opportunity to screen prospects. Another disadvantage is that when several groups of prospects are scattered throughout the house, the salesperson cannot make his or her presentation to each group. An open house, however, does give the property exposure to a large part of the market. Some real estate people look on this technique as simply a form of prospecting.

Making an appointment to show the house has many advantages over the open house. When people respond to an ad or sign, it is advisable if at all possible to have them meet you at your office. The salesperson can screen the prospects beforehand, prepare, concentrate his or her attention on just one group, and develop two-way communication with the prospects. While driving to the house, the salesperson may gain a great deal of information about the prospects, particularly the purchasing roles of each member of the family.

To make the most profitable use of time, salespeople should first find out as much as they can about prospective buyers. The following list of questions might prove useful in separating lookers from buyers.[3]

- What are the buyers' names?
- What is their current housing situation?
- What do they want and what do they need?
- What features do they like in a house?
- What do they dislike in a house?
- What other features are important?
- Outside of the house itself, what features are important to them? (Examples: location, schools, shopping.)
- What isn't important to them?

Next, the salesperson needs to determine the prospects' readiness to buy a home. This can be determined by using three factors: motivation, financial ability, and urgency.[4] Motivation can be defined as the strength of the prospective buyer's need to make a purchase. A big difference exists between needing to buy a house for one reason or another and wanting to buy a house. With the latter, potential buyers have an interest in purchasing a home and are collecting information on what's available. It is also very possible that they do not have a clearly defined purchasing goal. Financial ability refers to affordability or the amount of money the buyers have to work with, the maximum monthly payment they can afford, and available financing. Urgency is the time pressure faced by the buyers. The question is whether the prospective buyers have to have a house within any time limits or simply when something appropriate appears on the market.

Another responsibility of real estate salespeople is to oversee when, where, and how often advertisements are placed. Salespeople often write the property descriptions that appear in the advertisements.

Most experienced real estate salespeople believe that salespersons experiencing trouble in closing have done a poor job in pricing and market analysis. In other words, the property is either priced too high in relation to its market value as revealed by market analysis, or the salesperson has failed to match the buyer with the house.

Legally, real estate salespeople are bound to report all offers to sellers. However, salespeople can discourage buyers from making offers that are unreasonable. They should clearly emphasize to buyers that as agents of the seller, they are representing the seller's interests.

EDUCATION REQUIREMENTS

Licensing and professional designations for salespeople in real estate are closely allied to courses offered by accredited and approved institutions of higher learning and professional organizations. In Ohio, for example, Real Estate Principles and Practices and Real Estate Law are prerequisites to sitting for the real estate salesperson's examination. Salespersons must complete two additional courses, Real Estate Finance and Real Estate Appraisal, prior to taking the real estate broker's examination. After taking these four courses plus Real Estate Brokerage and a course labeled Special Topics (e.g., condominiums and cooperatives, commercial estate, investment analysis), salespeople are eligible for the Graduate Realtors® Institute comprehensive examination.[5]

NATIONAL FRANCHISE NETWORKS

national realty network
a group of local real estate offices (often franchised) linked by name, advertising, and computer listings

A widespread, recent change in the selling of real estate is the development of **national realty networks.** Some of the more familiar franchise operations are Century 21, Coldwell Banker, and Better Homes and Gardens. While each franchise has a different method of operation, the two major advantages of being a member of a national franchise network are referrals and national recognition.

Local real estate firms have always had national systems for referrals, but national franchises have formalized and improved the system. In some cases, consumers can see pictures of homes in another city minutes after making the request at a local franchise.

National franchise networks provide all the advantages of national recognition to what has always been a very local business. Traditionally, real estate firms have built reputations over the years in their local areas. Being a member of a national organization without losing local identity provides the firm several unique advantages.

This new dimension to the real estate business permits consumers to move from city to city or suburb to suburb and still be associated with the same organization. In one location, a member of the franchise network can sell the present residence and provide information about homes in a new location. In the area where the consumer intends to relocate, another member of the franchise network supplies information on homes and makes arrangements to help the consumer in purchasing a home. This advantage takes on even more significance with today's highly mobile population. Uniformity in clothing—such as Century 21's gold blazers—signs, forms, and various marketing tools all help to develop consumer recognition, familiarity, and trust.

Most national franchisers offer sales training programs to local members of their network. These sales training programs are helpful in teaching the basics of selling real estate.

Last, but certainly not least, is the advantage a member of a national franchise network has in advertising. Actually, this advantage is two-fold. First, advertising has a significant impact on consumer recognition. The names of several national real estate networks are as well-known today as many consumer products on store shelves. Second, local real estate firms can benefit from advertisements by paying only a shared cost rather than the total cost.

THE UNIQUE NATURE OF INSURANCE SELLING

Although national sales organizations are relatively new to real estate, the insurance industry has relied on them for much of its history. Insurance selling includes not only life insurance but a vast array of plans such as property and casualty, health, product liability, and retirement funds. The insurance industry also has two different types of salespersons or agents. One is an employee of the insurance company, who is typically found in the life and health insurance business and with large property and casualty firms such as State Farm and Allstate. The other is the independent agent who is principally a seller of property and casualty coverage.

Another complication in insurance selling is that the approach differs depending on the product. Customers buy property and casualty insurance because they are required to have insurance on their cars as well as their homes. Consequently, the selling of this insurance is service-oriented.

On the other hand, the need for life insurance or retirement plans is less obvious. Salespeople in this situation are more likely to be, and in fact have to be, creative in their selling efforts. The necessary change from service to creative selling has proved troublesome when independent agents or companies have added various types of insurance to their product lines.

The insurance salesperson must also acquire an ever-increasing amount of product knowledge just to keep pace with a varied list of product offerings. Insurance companies are developing dozens of new products ranging from savings plans with fixed interest rates to intricate term riders, variable annuities, and mutual funds.

INSURANCE AS AN INTANGIBLE

Regardless of the type of insurance, the biggest difference between insurance selling and other forms of selling can be traced to the fact that insurance is an intangible. Because insurance is intangible, salespeople should keep these points in mind when making presentations:

1. The form of insurance proposed must reduce uncertainty.
2. The form of insurance must fit the purchasing goal.
3. The salesperson must establish credibility in servicing the form of insurance.
4. The salesperson must reduce complexity through simplification.

Uncertainty over insurance arises from three sources, all related to the salesperson. The first is the question of whether the proposed insurance will reduce uncertainty. Typically, questions involve adequacy: Does the policy provide adequate protection in case of death, accident, or destruction of property?

A second source of uncertainty is whether the salesperson and his or her firm can identify the consumer's purchasing goal. Questions concerning the amount of liability for driving a car, the reimbursement of medical costs, or the building of an estate can be overwhelming to consumers. To reduce this uncertainty, salespeople must build confidence.

One of two possible ways to build confidence is to concentrate on the reputation of the firm by citing statistics on past performance. In this approach, salespeople are not concerned with customers' specific problems; instead, they utilize such selling techniques as:

1. Showing the approach to be taken in identifying consumer needs and wants.
2. Showing the record of performance for both the salesperson and the company.

A second way to build confidence is to focus on the specific purchasing goals of consumers. In life insurance, this might involve a review of present insurance coverage plus study and development of a financial needs program. With such an approach, an agent goes through a series of sales interviews and continually builds confidence in the consumer. For example, in selling a group retirement policy to a manufacturer, the salesperson must show that the program gives complete and adequate coverage at the lowest possible cost.

Finally, the consumer may be uncertain about the salesperson and his or her abilities to deliver. The perception a salesperson has of himself or herself can be a key factor in reducing uncertainty. Some salespeople separate their professional strengths from the insurance product. Others combine experience in insurance with professionalism in selling, placing emphasis on the latter.

Insurance today is very complex. To reduce the resulting confusion for the consumer, it is necessary that the salesperson simplify as much as possible and talk in terms the consumer will understand.

Professionalism in Insurance Selling

Professional certifications are available to sellers of life and health insurance, as well as those handling property and liability. This indication of professionalism is designated by the titles Chartered Life Underwriter (CLU) and Chartered Property Casualty Underwriter (CPCU), bestowed on men and women by The American College and the American Institute for Property and Liability Underwriters, respectively. The CLU and the CPCU are awarded on the basis of individuals fulfilling specified educational, ethical, and experience requirements.

Candidates for the CLU must be of good moral character, hold a high school diploma or equivalent, and have three years of relevant experience. In addition, they must pass a series of 15 two-hour examinations encompassing the following subject areas:[6]

1. Economic security and individual life insurance.
2. Life insurance law and mathematics.
3. Group insurance and social insurance.
4. Economics and modern management.
5. Accounting and finance.
6. Investments and family financial management.
7. Income taxation.
8. Pension planning.
9. Business insurance.
10. Estate planning and taxation.
11. Legal environment of business.
12. Advanced pension planning.
13. Advanced estate planning.
14. Accounting and business valuation.
15. Risk management of property—liability exposures.

The admission requirements of the American Institute for the CPCU designation are basically the same as for the CLU, namely good moral character, high school education, and three years' experience in the field. The curriculum includes eight subject areas:[7]

1. Principles of risk management and insurance.
2. Personal risk management and insurance.

COMPANY PROFILE

Great Southern Life: Sophisticated Equipment Can Support the Professional Insurance Salesperson

Selling universal life insurance to potential policyholders requires radical departures from the marketing tools traditional to the insurance industry.

Conventional rate books, for example, cannot illustrate the flexibility of universal life insurance policies, their ability to be tailored and retailored as a policyholder's needs and goals change, or the current and constantly changing interest rates offered on the savings portion of the policy.

Marketing Tools

Thus, as increasing numbers of companies decide to offer universal life, they concurrently face the need for new marketing tools. This translates into two typical problems:

Each client requires an individual proposal to be written; and

How can the agent selling the policy illustrate and write these individual proposals?

Great Southern Life introduced its universal life insurance policy early in 1981. Confronting the mar-

keting problems, the company simultaneously began providing portable point-of-sale computer terminals to its general agents.

Within a year, 80 percent of the general agents were using the terminals. And "Lifetime Life," Great Southern's universal life policy, had become the sales leader among the company's life insurance products.

These developments occurred at the same time that Great Southern increased the number of its general agents by 30 percent and expanded its marketing base for universal life throughout its operating territory.

"Results . . . were fantastic in terms of premium income and growth of our agency force," said Raymond H. Stallings, senior executive vice president at Great Southern. "It isn't just the policy. It's the fact that we have a support program, the computer program, that works with the policy. They can't be separated."

SOURCE: Abridged from "Point of Sale Computer Terminals Support Universal Life Sales for Great Southern," *National Underwriter—Life and Health Insurance Edition,* August 21, 1982, p. 28. Copyright 1982. Used with permission.

3. Commercial property risk management and insurance.

4. Insurance company operations.

5. The legal environment of insurance.

6. Management.

7. Economics.

8. Insurance issues and professional ethics.

Although nearly 1,800 companies sell life insurance today, the largest seem to dominate the industry by writing most of the policies in force today. Salespeople are indispensable in selling life insurance, given the vast number of companies and their respective product offerings. As an example, suppose that each of the 1,800 companies average 20 seemingly different policies. This means a total of 36,000 different options, an impossible buying task for consumers to sort through and make a decision without the assistance of salespeople. Major companies acknowledge the vital role of the salesperson by focusing on him or her in their advertising.

The job of life insurance salespeople has become more difficult because of higher social security payments, employee benefits from businesses, new tax laws, and the increasing unpredictability of the future. Almost every business has a plan for its employees. Increases or other changes are made through group plans rather than individual plans.

While competitive presssures prevent raising the price of life insurance policies, salespeople have to sell more life insurance to keep pace with the growth of salaries and future expectations. Further complications are that salespeople make a limited number of sales in a year, thereby forcing a higher value of insurance per sale, and a reduction in sales of group policies because of the lower premiums. Interestingly enough, it now takes considerably more than a million dollars in life insurance sales to qualify for the prestigious Million Dollar Round Table.

SUMMARY OF CHAPTER OBJECTIVES

1. **To describe professional selling as it relates to real estate and insurance.**

   Special attention is given to real estate and insurance selling for several reasons. One is the early acceptance of women as selling professionals in real estate licensing. Another is the regulation of both real estate and insurance salespeople. Still another is the structural changes in both industries that have affected the jobs of both types of sales professionals.

2. **To explain the concept of listings as it applies to the sales job of the real estate agent/broker.**

   The job of the real estate salesperson differs from other selling jobs in that he or she has to build a product inventory of houses and in effect serve both buyers and sellers. Obtaining a listing of houses involves selling owners of property on the idea that the real estate agent/broker represents the best means of selling the property in question.

3. **To describe the selling task of matching customers with real estate.**

   This job involves showing houses, uncovering basic information about buyers and their readiness to buy, arranging and coordinating advertising, as well as handling negotiations.

4. **To define professional requirements for real estate salespeople.**

   Licensing and professional designation for real estate salespeople are closely allied to institutions of higher learning (universities) and professional organizations (local and state real estate boards).

5. **To describe insurance selling.**

   In selling insurance, not all agents sell the same plan or plans, nor do all have the same arrangement with the parent company. More creative selling is required with life insurance and retirement plans than with either property or casualty insurance. Insurance is both complex and intangible. This means the salesperson must reduce uncertainties, simplify, help with specific problems of customers, and build confidence.

6. **To define professionalism for insurance salespeople.**

   Registration to sell mutual funds is required of sellers of life insurance. In addition, professional certifications are available to sellers of life and health insurance as well as those handling property and liability insurance.

REVIEW QUESTIONS

1. Explain how real estate agents sell homes.
2. In which ways does matching consumers with pieces of real estate differ from other selling situations?
3. How do consumers for real estate differ from consumers for other products?
4. Give the reasons real estate firms have traditionally been local firms.
5. Discuss the reasons that consumers interested in any type of insurance may feel uncertain in purchasing it.
6. Why should an insurance agent become either a CLU or CPCU?
7. Describe the two basic types of insurance salespeople?
8. Are there any advantages to a life insurance agent's adding homeowner's coverage and auto insurance to his or her product offerings?
9. Contrast selling life insurance with selling real estate insurance.
10. Explain why every real estate salesperson must obtain listings.

DISCUSSION QUESTIONS AND EXERCISES

1. Discuss why relatively few women sell insurance.
2. Imagine that you are trying to convince a homeowner that you and your real estate firm can do a better selling job than they can themselves. List the reasons.
3. Visit a local real estate association office and find out the requirements for obtaining a license and membership in the assocation.

4. Visit the offices of an independent insurance agent and an insurance company. Identify the unique characteristics of each type.

5. Develop a selling plan for talking about insurance to a professional (someone like an engineer or college professor) who works for a large institution and who is covered by social security and extensive employee benefits.

SALES DIALOG

Herb Crawford turned his car into the driveway of the Adams' house in Waterbury, Connecticut. Beth and Larry Adams had moved from their house four and a half months before. The lawn had been mowed recently, but the bushes needed trimming and there were seven old newspapers lying on the front porch. As Herb turned the key in the lock and opened the door, he stood aside to allow Joe and Nancy Klein to enter the house. Nancy and Joe were very interested in the multiple listing service.

CRAWFORD: Sorry it's so cold in here; I'll turn the heat up a bit.

NANCY KLEIN: Boy, it sure looks empty without any rugs or furniture or drapes.

JOE KLEIN: Is this hole in the living room wall for the TV antenna? Can it be fixed?

CRAWFORD: Sure, no problem. You should have seen this place when the Adamses lived here. They had it decorated very nicely. They were both kind of artsy. Had things kind of modern.

NANCY KLEIN: (calling from the kitchen): Doesn't the water work?

CRAWFORD: (laughing and bumping Joe in the ribs) Of course! (in a low voice to Joe) Women don't seem to understand mechanical gadgets. . . . Let me run downstairs and turn the water on.

JOE KLEIN: Nancy, did it say in the listing that the Adamses were taking the dining room fixture with them? There's a big hole in the ceiling.

CRAWFORD: (emerging from the basement): Well, what do you think? Isn't this the little, rose-covered cottage you've always wanted?

What do you think the results of this sales dialog will be?

CASE 16–1   GREENVALE REAL ESTATE INC.

Janet Remy has been in the real estate business for 25 years. After leaving college, she joined her father's firm and worked there until five years ago, when she left to form her own firm, Greenvale Real Estate, in a suburb of Atlanta.

During the last two years, gross commissions have tripled for Greenvale. The business that Remy started with just herself and a secretary has grown to 10 full-time salespeople and 4 part-timers. The suburb is still growing at a rapid rate, and the prospects for the real estate business look good.

In the past month, Janet Remy has received an offer to join a national real estate network. The other two major real estate firms in this suburb are already members of national networks. In the meantime, Janet's father has announced his intention to retire.

It is his wish that Janet buy him out and merge the two operations.

In discussing the various possibilities with other real estate people in suburbs around Atlanta, Remy discovers a great deal of interest in forming a local group of firms under common ownership. This ownership group, which Remy might head up as president, could include some 15 agencies.

Questions

1. Outline the various alternatives for Remy.

2. List the advantages for each alternative.

3. If you were Remy, what would be your decision and why?

CASE 16–2   JOHN PENDERGAST, INDEPENDENT AGENT

John Pendergast, an independent agent, has been selling property and casualty insurance for 40 years in a small community of 25,000 people. The makeup of the community has been steadily changing for the last 10 years from a rural-based economy with a scattering of large estates and a population of 8,000 to a suburb of Charlotte, North Carolina, some 10 miles away. As this change has been taking place, John's business has fallen off rapidly in the last three years.

Reviewing his list of customers with his son, who has recently joined him in business, they find that the number of new accounts (new business written in each year) represents only 10 percent of total business for each of the last five years. Further, there has been considerable turnover in new accounts, making it rare for one to last as many as three years. John's son, Ray, feels that most of the newcomers are professionals or executives with national firms.

Questions

1. What do you feel are the reasons for the downturn in business for John Pendergast?

2. What sort of program would you suggest to attract new customers?

3. Several life insurance companies have approached the Pendergasts with the idea of taking on their line of life insurance. What should be their reaction?

CHAPTER 17

Managing the Sales Force

CHAPTER OBJECTIVES

1. To explain how sales managers differ from salespeople.

2. To outline the components of a sales system.

3. To differentiate among the primary organizational structures used for sales forces.

4. To explain turnover rate and show how it impacts recruitment and selection.

5. To differentiate between initial and continuous sales training.

6. To identify the primary determinants of a sales climate.

SALES CAREER PROFILE

STEVE MARTIN
Pfizer Laboratories

Steve Martin is the Pfizer Labs district manager for Washington and Alaska. Martin, who has 12 representatives reporting to him, holds a bachelor's degree from California State University, Fullerton, and a master's degree from Pepperdine University. His interests include camping and hiking with his family, as well as participating in marathons and triathalons.

Martin was hired by Pfizer after a four-year stint as a Marine Corps. public affairs officer. Asked how he picked Pfizer, Martin replied, "I would say that it was a combination of reasons. One was location. They had a sales position located in Northern California. The other one—probably more important—was selling for what I considered to be a higher caliber of customer, that is, to physicians and pharmacists."

Asked if he knew Pfizer was one of the top U.S. firms to sell for, Martin responded, "No, I wasn't aware of that, but I'm not surprised because Pfizer is an excellent company to sell for, and it's been very progressive, creative, and profitable.

"I think the primary reason it was picked is its professionalism. It has a tremendous research and development program, so we are constantly coming out with new, different, and better products. It has a tremendous support element in its marketing program. Pfizer is one of the leaders in the industry. The training program the sales representatives and managers go through is extremely extensive. I know a number of companies emulate Pfizer's training program. The overall combination of research and development, marketing, and training is a tremendous asset in attracting very highly qualified candidates to Pfizer. We closely scrutinize the people we hire to ensure that they can make it through the training program. These are top-notch college graduates from a variety of backgrounds."

Steve Martin has held a variety of positions with Pfizer Labs: professional sales representative, district hospital representative, assistant to the Chicago regional manager, and now district manager. Asked where he would go next in his career, Martin responded, "There are a variety of steps one can take from district manager. Pfizer is not only domestic, so there is the international route. But the next most common step for sales managers is to regional manager. There are seven in the country. Regional sales managers usually have between 8 and 10 district managers working under them."

Asked what he liked best about his current job, the district manager replied, "I would say the daily challenge. You are constantly challenged regarding new and different techniques of selling, as well as managing, motivating, and creatively stimulating people to perform."

When asked about the most important part of his job as a Pfizer sales manager, Martin continued, "The most important aspect of my job is the ability to make others produce.

Pfizer puts together the yearly quotas, and it's our responsibility to meet or exceed them. Probably the most important thing I do is try to tap in to individuals, find out their needs, and assess the best way for them to meet assigned goals and reach their full potential."

Finally, the authors asked Martin about his leadership style and how he motivates and supervises his sales force. "I went through a sales program once that categorized me as an 'Amiable Expressive.' For the most part, that's my leadership style. I'm considered by many to be very energetic, very enthusiastic, a 'full of energy' leader. The Marine Corps helped. Since I've been with Pfizer, my style has been to put a lot of responsibility on the individuals who report to me. I essentially try to choose a strong team of mature individuals. I give them their goals and their responsibilities, but it's their territories, their business, so I only try to ensure that they live up to their own expectations.

"I consider myself a very flexible leader. I allow a lot of give and take, a lot of opinions. I don't believe there is only one way. I think that there must be a variety of different ways and we try them. Being somewhat expressive, I'm really big into high energy levels and high intensity. In other words, I feel that certain things are contagious, and one thing is a high energy level. If people get fired up and excited about what they are doing, they tend to do well. I feel very strongly that people should be having fun at what they are doing.

"I supervise the field force through a variety of means. I work with my field sales force at least once a month. I see individuals. We have parties, we have picnics, and we have dinners. I see my people on a regular basis; I talk to them at least once a week on the phone. Everybody sends me mail on a weekly basis. I am someone who can help them reach their full potential, maybe point out things that are missing, things that could be of help to them in the future, things that would make their overall performance or standings better.

"I think the whole issue of leadership boils down to one key element, and that is communication. My leadership style, my motivation, and my supervision work on communication. I take as much time and effort as I possibly can to better educate myself in the area of communication, not only various leadership styles but social styles and behavioral styles. I try to be able to read individuals as well as I can, and I feel that the better I can stay in communication with the people I work with the more successful I will be.

"The greatest pleasure I get from this position is seeing others do well. I realize that in any type of sales, there are rewards, there are accolades, there are promotions, and there are financial incentives. But for me, the greatest reward that I get from this position is seeing others meet their goals and expectations. When I see them do well, I feel good and ultimately I do well also. It's almost like being a coach. I love to see everybody perform at their best, come in winners, and when they are happy, it just tickles me to death."

The sales climate at upscale Infiniti dealers is not like that of most other car dealers. Infiniti salespeople do not describe their sales victories as "slam dunks" of customers. Instead, potential buyers are treated to a Japanese style soft sell. Sales personnel serve them tea or coffee on Noritake china. Customers can consider their purchases alone in specially designed "contemplation areas."

Nissan also wants its Infiniti dealers to have the sound of running water in their show room. Floors are carpeted with sound-absorbing hemp. The contemplation areas are shoji-screened. Everything is done to highlight the low-pressure nature of the dealership.

The Zen-like sales climate is communicated through a training program which is mandatory for all Infiniti dealership employees. Everyone from salespersons to mechanics spends an average of eight days learning the Infiniti style of selling. Jim Benson, a Brooklyn, New York, Infiniti salesperson, describes the difference this way: "Used to be we worked on the premise that if a guy comes in, he's going to be driving someone's new car in 72 hours, so you do whatever you have to do to get the deposit. Now, I've got people out there two months, and I still haven't asked for the order."

Nissan's management is confident that they have created the right sales climate to sell expensive automobiles in the 1990s. Infiniti's general manager, William Bruce, comments, " . . . if we stay the course with this selling approach, we've got a sure home run down the road."[1]

The sales climate is just one aspect of sales management. This final chapter looks at the complete spectrum of activities required in the management of sales personnel.

SELECTING SALES MANAGERS

The primary reason for the difficulty firms face in selecting a sales manager is the major difference between selling skills and management skills. Not all good salespeople make good managers. Similarly, not all good managers are good salespeople. Promoting a poor sales performer to sales manager is difficult, however, because the sales force lacks respect for the new manager. For this reason, most successful sales managers were successful salespeople.

The danger of promoting successful salespeople who lack management skills is that they often become disillusioned and quit. They did not realize the real difference between a sales job and a sales manager's job.

Selling is action: doing, traveling, and constantly testing your own individual abilities. In many respects, salespeople are in control of their own destinies. On the other hand, successful managers must delegate and work through others. They coach and counsel; in so doing, they de-emphasize their own egos and support the egos of others. For those who want to be leaders and to see others develop and mature due to their efforts, sales management is an exciting career.

How then do you know whether you should accept that initial promotion into sales management? This chapter can help you answer that question.

TRAITS OF AN EFFECTIVE SALES MANAGER

In a classic study, Aptitude Testing for Industry, a Los Angeles-based testing firm, followed the career paths of 97 successful salespeople. Two out of three of the star performers ended up in sales management. This study also showed that those who went into management differed from those who stayed in sales in several ways:

1. Almost five times as many of those in management had college degrees.
2. Those who went into management were more mentally alert, particularly in their ability to use and interpret numerical data.
3. Those in management were more confident, assertive, and persistent.
4. Those who went into management could make tougher decisions, because they were more objective.
5. Those in management had a stronger urge to lead, to take charge.[2]

Although it is interesting to note the specific traits of effective sales managers, it is also important to look at the tasks they perform. This is the only way salespeople can decide if sales management is appropriate for them.

SALES MANAGEMENT AND MARKETING STRATEGY

As noted earlier, sales strategy must fit with the firm's overall marketing strategy. To understand how sales strategy flows directly from marketing strategy and, in turn, how the manager's tasks are a function of the sales strategy, study the diagram in Figure 17–1.

Home plate is the end-all in baseball. Here is where everything begins and ends. So it is with the customer in marketing; to make a sale, all four bases need to be crossed. By analyzing the needs and wants of customers, market researchers try to match their resources to the risks and opportunities in the competitive environment. This is called the marketing strategy; it is the responsibility of the chief marketing executive. If the strategy is sound, the firm makes it to first base.

sales system

policies and practices related to the management of a sales force

At this point, the chief sales executive determines the role to be played by the sales force and puts together a **sales system** to support them. This role (or desired behavior) is encouraged by the combination of policies and practices related to selection, training, and compensation. If the sales system is sound, the firm makes it to second.

sales climate

situation wherein the sales force attempts to match its behavior with that desired by the firm

It is up to the field sales manager to develop a **sales climate** wherein the sales force wants to and can match its behavior with that desired by the firm. The field sales manager does this by performing the dual role of leader and supervisor. If actual behavior matches desired behavior, the firm is on third, ready to score.

At this point, it is entirely up to the individual salesperson. As it is often said, "Nothing happens until the sale is made." So it is in baseball. The only way to score is to cross home plate. We wrote the previous 16 chapters of this book to help readers get from third to home.

With this baseball framework in mind, the tasks of sales management become clearer, particularly as they fit into the firm's marketing strategy.

FIGURE 17–1   Framework for sales and marketing strategy

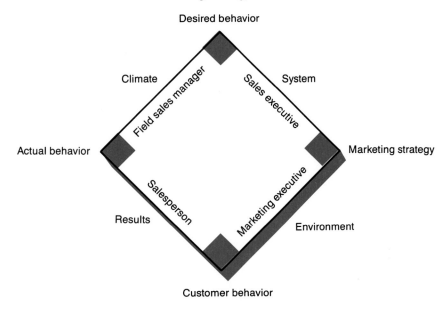

Source: Derek A. Newton, *Sales Force Management: Text and Cases* (Homewood, Ill.: Business Publications/Richard D. Irwin, 1982), p. 4.

THE SALES SYSTEM

There are several elements to the sales system. When properly designed, each element does its part to support the sales force in its marketing strategy role. Typically, a sales system consists of policies and practices related to:

1. Organization and deployment.
2. Selection and recruitment.
3. Training and development.
4. Compensation and expenses.
5. Forecasts, budgets, and quotas.
6. Performance evaluation.

In large organizations, the development and the overseeing of these policies and practices are the responsibility of the chief sales executive. In this case, field sales management is responsible for implementing these policies and the establishment of the proper sales climate. In small organizations, both the sales system and the sales climate may be the responsibility of the sales manager.

Organization and Deployment

Several questions face the sales executive trying to decide how to organize and deploy the sales force:

- Where should the sales organization fit in the firm?
- How should the sales force be organized (by product, by customer, by territory)?
- How large should each territory be?

In many cases, the sales force is simply part of the marketing organization of the firm. The chief sales executive reports to the chief marketing executive. The marketing executive, in turn, reports to the chief operating officer, who is either the president in a small firm or a division or business unit manager in a large, multidivision firm. Figure 17–2 illustrates a large organization.

In some large organizations, a number of divisions or business units share a sales force. The salespeople sell the products of all the divisions or business units for which they are responsible (see Figure 17–3). Marketing is a part of each division's organizational structure. Which of these two basic alternatives is chosen depends primarily on whether each division serves the same or different markets.

pooled sales force
situation in which salespeople sell all of their firms' products to each account they serve

If several divisions serve the same customers and markets but produce different products or services, then a **pooled sales force** is typically the

---

FIGURE 17–2   A line marketing organization

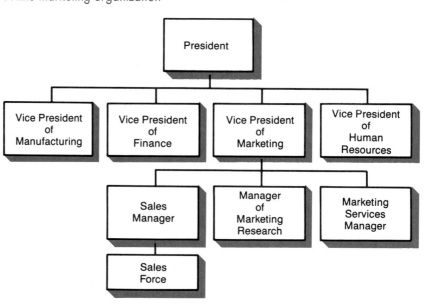

choice. Each salesperson sells the product of each of the various divisions to each account they service. If each division had its own sales force, the customer would find several salespeople from the same firm servicing their business. So the pooled sales force is more efficient in this case. Since the sales force is not part of any one division and marketing is, it becomes difficult to coordinate sales and marketing strategies with a pooled sales force.

Westinghouse Electric Corporation uses a pooled sales force, but the salespeople only handle products of divisions serving the same basic markets with similar marketing strategies. In so doing, Westinghouse hopes to get the benefits of both organizational formats.

The second major question facing sales executives relates to organizing the sales force itself. Should it be deployed by customer, by product, or by territory? When an intimate knowledge of the customer's individual needs is important in making the sale, then organizing by customer is recommended. Some computer manufacturers use different sales forces for retailers, banks, and manufacturers. Customer-based sales forces learn their customers' business and how their firm's product can help their customers succeed. Since the sales force often sells a variety of products, considerable sales training time is devoted to product knowledge.

Some products or services are so complex, however, that salespeople need to focus their energies on understanding the product and how it can benefit a variety of customers. Customers look to salespeople as product experts. They expect detailed product information as a part of their purchase decision. Here it makes sense to organize the sales force by product. For

FIGURE 17–3   A pooled sales force organization

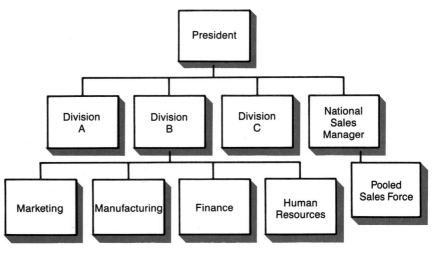

example, a manufacturer of medical equipment might have one sales force for CAT scanners, another for surgical equipment, and another for laboratory equipment.

When there is no compelling reason to organize the sales force by either product or customer, managers set up territories along geographic lines. The primary advantage of assigning salespeople to geographic territories is that it minimizes travel. This is important for two reasons. First, travel is a significant, ever-increasing portion of selling costs and requires close control. Second, excessive travel demands are one of the primary aspects of some selling jobs. Minimizing travel thus saves money and reduces sales force turnover.

Finally, the sales executive must decide on the size of each territory or, if organized by product or customer, the number of accounts assigned to each salesperson. The goal is to develop territories or customer assignments in which each salesperson can realistically serve each assigned customer. This depends on the minimal size for a profitable account, call frequency, the length of the typical sales call, and a host of other factors. Even beyond this attempt to equalize the workload across salespeople, the sales executive may also want to equalize territory sales' potential across salespeople. This approach gives each salesperson equal earning potential, and allows the sales executive to make performance comparisons among sales personnel.

Selection and Recruitment

Once the organization and deployment of the sales force has been developed, the next series of decisions relate to the selection and recruitment of the sales force. The major questions to be answered are:

- How many salespeople do we need?
- What is our turnover rate? What will our replacement needs be?
- Where will we find prospects for our sales positions?
- What kind of people do we need?
- How will we know whether a recruit has the proper traits? How will we measure those traits?

turnover rate

percentage of the sales force lost each year to resignation, discharge, retirement, and other reasons

The number of salespeople needed is largely determined by the number of territories. How many salespeople need to be hired each year will depend on the **turnover rate,** which is the percentage of the sales force lost each year due to resignation, discharge, retirement, and other miscellaneous reasons. The turnover rate varies greatly from one industry to another. Clearly, the higher the turnover rate, the more salespeople that must be recruited and hired each year.

A variety of sources are available for finding prospects for sales jobs. The most obvious source is the company's other employees. Although many departments in a company can yield sales prospects, certain areas of the firm are natural sources. Customer service, inside sales, billing, and other departments that come into direct contact with customers can often provide excellent salespeople.

Other popular sources for sales candidates are trade schools, colleges, and universities. More and more companies are finding the selling task to be so complex that to succeed their salespeople need the intelligence and drive required to get a college education. This is particularly true for high-technology products and products requiring close customer follow-up after the sale.

Employment agencies and classified advertisments allow prospects from a variety of careers and organizations to learn of a firm's sales openings. Some agencies specialize in filling sales and marketing positions. The advantage of using an employment agency over a classified advertisement is that the agency screens the candidates so only qualified candidates interview with the hiring firm. The disadvantage is the cost involved, which can equal up to three months of the starting salary.

While a logical source of salespeople is other companies, there are dangers associated with hiring another firm's salespeople. First, they have already been trained, and if the training was inappropriate to the hiring firm's needs, they may be difficult to "untrain." Second, it may start a personnel war in which retaliation results in the loss of salespeople. No one wins when two companies start raiding one another. Third, there are ethical considerations involved in hiring salespeople from a competitor, particularly if the salesperson brings some of the competitor's customers along or if the newly hired salesperson divulges trade secrets of the competitor. Fourth, hiring experienced salespeople can raise selling expenses significantly.

Picking the Right Salespeople. The key to sales success is matching the salesperson to the customer's needs.[3] To match the salesperson to the job, the company must determine what the selling environment involves. Is a sale expected on the first call? Is organizational ability important or must the salesperson be a stickler for details? Is the product technically complex? Does the selling involve dealing with engineers and laboratory personnel? Only by developing a detailed description of the selling environment can a company begin to write the specifications for sales candidates.

Once the specifications have been decided on, the company must still find ways to determine whether a particular candidate possesses these skills or not. The two most useful tools for this purpose are tests and personal interviews.

A great many tests measure personal traits related to sales success. But the test should be chosen only after determining the job specifications. Plus, "testing should not be the instrument of decision," according to Robert Guion, author of a book on personnel testing. "It should be used as a flag that either agrees with or contradicts your impressions about a person."[4] In other words, it all comes down to the interview.

Interviews are important, because the person making the hiring decision sees the candidate as the customer will. Only in this case, the product the candidate is selling is himself or herself. That's why an earlier chapter in this book advised readers to sell themselves in the interviewing process. It may well be the most important sales call in your entire sales career.

Training and Development

The principal objective of any sales training program is to develop selling proficiency, particularly in increased sales production and establishment of long-term customer relationships. The sales training program at Dow is outlined in Figure 17–4. The specific objectives of training depend on the type of training, which can be classified as either initial or continuous.[5]

initial sales training
preparation and orientation of new sales personnel

Initial sales training involves the preparation and orientation of new sales personnel. The emphasis in initial training is on forming proper selling habits so that the salesperson can assume a field position as quickly as possible. The preparation necessary depends on several factors, such as the recruiting source, technical complexities in the product and market, the amount of typical buyer knowledge, the organizational status of purchasing influences, the financial strength of the firm, and the attitude of sales management. For example, when Diasonics—a medical imaging firm—decided to increase the size of its ultrasound sales force, it concentrated on getting individuals with capital equipment sales experience, rather than those with technical backgrounds. Diasonics' management reasoned that they could provide the necessary product knowledge and application training, so it was more important to pick salespeople who could understand the influences on the targeted buyer. The Diasonics experience illustrates the close relationship that often exists between recruiting and training.[6]

continuous sales training
refreshing, improving, and updating of the selling skills and marketing knowledge of experienced personnel

Continuous sales training involves refreshing, improving, and updating the selling skills and marketing knowledge of experienced personnel. Continuous training also helps to remotivate experienced sales personnel. The changes taking place in all markets necessitate the retraining of experienced sales representatives so that they have the latest sales techniques and products as well as market knowledge at their command.

Companies gain several major benefits by adopting good sales training programs. The primary benefit is that sales productivity improves through better seller-buyer relationships. For example, Massachusetts Mutual Life Insurance Company was able to increase the sales of new representatives 15 percent by introducing interaction video training.[7]

Another advantage of sales training is that it can reduce the turnover rate. A well-trained salesperson is better able to cope with the demands of the job and less likely to seek other employment. Because sales training builds morale among the field force, it helps to establish a positive attitude, which also helps reduce turnover.

COMPANY PROFILE

Avis's Training Experiment

When's the best time to start training your new hires? An Avis study's answer: The sooner the better.

Avis split a group of just hired customer representatives into two sections: One went immediately into the company's two-week training program; the other was given the training several months later—Avis's usual practice.

Says vice president Russ James, "The first group had half the turnover of the second group." Most of those who quit did so before the training could begin. Says James, "Now we bring employees into training when they're at their highest level of motivation—when they start."

SOURCE: Reprinted from "Training People to Stay Put," *Sales & Marketing Management*, May 1989 p. 90. Reprinted by permission of Sales & Marketing Management. Copyright May 1989.

Sales training also improves the efficiency of sales management and reduces the cost of supervision. A well-trained salesperson is self-motivated and requires less direction, control, and supervision from sales management.

The typical company spends thousands of dollars on developing a field sales representative. The costs of sales training must be considered in evaluating the potential benefits of such efforts.

The costs of initial and continuous sales training are really different in nature. Initial sales training involves considerable out-of-pocket costs, whereas the primary costs of continuous training are indirect ones such as the time sales personnel are out of the field. One survey of 1,554 companies found that the median time spent training experienced salespeople was 8½ days annually.[8]

Sales training is costly when considered as an expense item, but in relation to its results, most firms consider it to be an extremely profitable expenditure of company funds. The key factor is developing the most efficient sales training program possible with company resources and personnel.

Compensation and Expenses

Although nonsales employees rank compensation as the third most important motivator, a research study has found that salespeople rank money as the best and first reward. Money was ranked even higher by salespeople with a mortgage. The study concludes that "money isn't everything, but there isn't much else worth mentioning."[9]

With money assuming that much importance to the sales force, it is clear why sales executives devote as much time and attention as they do to the design and administration of the sales compensation plan. The fact that the third chapter of this book has an extensive discussion of compensation systems is further evidence of the importance of compensation in the field of selling.

FIGURE 17–4   Components of Dow's sales training program—sales representatives' training

	Orientation session (3 weeks)	Customer service center (3 months)	Resource awareness session (1 week)	Product department project (3 months)
Orientation	• Expectations of you • Field sales career • Organization of Dow • Benefits • Compensation philosophy • Housing/relocation • Strategic orientation • Goal setting • QSPP • Top management interface • CDP panel • Performance management cycle	• CSC operation	• Plant tour • Top management interface • Quality	
Dow resources	• CFS • Legal issues • Customer service center • Market research • Role of TS&D • Business information center	• Interaction with various resources • CSC order entry • Order team (CSC, production representative, scheduler, CFS)	• Communications • Legal/antitrust • Direct marketing services • Public issues • Marketing information dept. • Corporate account executive	• Work with market research • Work with product department • Use BIC • Work with field sales
Customer/ market knowledge	• Product group presentations	• Customer interaction via telephone calls • Work with distributors		• Customer interaction • Conduct a market research project • Develop understanding of business network • Develop understanding of competitors • Business analysis
Selling skills	• CSTS • Competitive pricing • Field sales roundtable	• Reinforce CSTS	• Competitive pricing	• Joint sales calls

SOURCE: Reprinted with permission of Dow Chemical.

Selling skills session (2 weeks)	Field sales project (3-6 months)	Product department	Field sales seminar (1 week)
• Top management interface	• Practical experience	• Department structure • Department personnel • Objectives, goals, and plans of department • Department values	• Top management interface
• Legal contracts and distribution	• Resource utilization	• Introduction to TS&D • Introduction to manufacturing • Introduction to support staff • Work with marketing staff	
• Distribution channels	• Customer interface • Work with distributors	• Distributor channels • Customer base • Industry trends • Competition	
• Competitive pricing • Precall planning • PSS III • Post-call followup • Purchasing project • Joint calls • Negotiations	• PSS III reinforcement • Selling skill application • Joint calls with DSMs, field sellers	• PSS III reinforcement	• Negotiating to "Yes" response • Competitive situations

FIGURE 17–4   *(concluded)*

	Orientation session (3 weeks)	Customer service center (3 months)	Resource awareness session (1 week)	Product department project (3 months)
Business skills	• Computer training (as needed)	• Computer skill reinforcement • Order entry/order flow	• Aggressive corporation	• Reinforce telephone skills • Reinforce computer training
Product knowledge	• Chemistry of Dow	• Product training		• Product training
Personal skills	• Safety • Commentary drive • Articulate listening • Understanding social styles • Presentation skills • Time management • Writing skills • Dictation • Using secretary as a resource • Expense accounts • Traveling safety • "Up with Life" • Valuing diversity • "Citizens against Crime"	• Interpersonal skills • Letter writing • Report writing • Demonstrate problem solving skills • Use organizational skills • Creativity • Listening skills	• Presentations • Working with Midland management • Safety • Decision making • Skill review	• Report writing • Analytical skills • Planning • Organizing • Evaluating • Decision making • Listening skills
Performance Appraisal	• Performance evaluation process • Mentor feedback	• Monitored by direct supervision • JPR • Mentor feedback	• Mentor feedback	• Monitored by direct supervision • JPR • Mentor feedback

Most problems associated with compensation plans arise when sales executives fail to realize that in spite of their importance, salespeople require rewards in addition to money. Personal recognition, promotion, challenge, and a healthy working environment all serve to reward and motivate salespeople. An overreliance on compensation is simply a failure to manage well.

Forecasts, Budgets, and Quotas

Forecasts, budgets, and quotas are all part of the sales system. Accordingly, the design of the sales system must make provisions for:

Selling skills session (2 weeks)	Field sales project (3-6 months)	Product department	Field sales seminar (1 week)
• Value • Territory management	• Introduction to territory analysis	• Understand depart-ment computer system	
	• Product training	• Features/benefits • Learn product technol-ogy/specifications • Read literature • End uses • Competitive products	
• Safety • Presentations • Customer entertain-ment • Real estate decisions • Stress management • Advanced driver train-ing	• Safety • Time management • Budget management • Planning • Territory management • Call scheduling		• Safety • Versatile salesperson
• Mentor feedback	• Supervision by DSM • JPR • Mentor feedback	• Done by department	

- The responsibility for, timing of, and techniques used in the development of sales forecasts.
- The responsibility for, and timing of, sales budgets.
- The responsibility for, timing of, techniques used, and personnel involved in quota setting.

Forecasts. Those closest to the customer should forecast sales, for it is the customer's behavior that sales forecasting attempts to predict. So even though sophisticated procedures may be employed, and even though many people may have a part, and even though large databases and consulting firms may be used, it still all comes down to answering three simple questions:

1. Which customers will buy?
2. How much will they buy?
3. When will they buy?

Salespeople and sales managers are the best source of answers to these questions.

All financial planning in a firm begins with a sales forecast. Whether the firm is preparing its next annual operating plan or trying to decide whether to introduce a proposed new product or to build a new plant or buy a piece of equipment, the first information needed is level of sales. Only then can the rest of the analysis be completed.

For this reason, it is so important that sales forecasting becomes a major part of the sales system. Everyone from the salesperson in the field to the chief marketing executive needs to have input to ensure utmost accuracy.

Budgets. One major assumption in all sales forecasts is the amount to be spent on marketing. Clearly, the more that is spent on advertising, sales force compensation and incentives, and product design and development, the higher sales will be. But it is also true that at some point, more dollars spent on marketing do not result in sufficient new sales to justify the additional marketing expenditures. Economists call this the point of diminishing returns. The sales budget should be set here. Beyond this point, dollars spent may generate sales, but they are not profitable.

sales quotas
performance standards based on expected sales volumes

Sales Quotas. To motivate the sales force to make the sales forecast within budget, most firms establish **sales quotas** for the sales force. If companies use incentive compensation, the quotas determine the compensation level. But even with straight salary, management looks at quotas when making employee evaluation decisions related to promotions, annual salary increases, and territory assignments. Sales quotas can also be used in retail selling. Nordstrom, the Seattle-based retailer, uses "sales per hour" to pay commissions and bonuses.[10]

Because sales quotas play a large role in the salesperson's career, they should be set jointly between the sales manager and the salesperson. If the salesperson has no part in the establishment of the quota, there is less chance that the quota can become a meaningful motivator. The quota may be judged too high or too low, but in either case, it fails to properly motivate. In one case, sales goals are too easy to reach; and in the other case, the salesperson believes the sales goals are too high to reach and unfair. Sales quotas are an important motivational tool for sales managers if they are properly set.

Performance Evaluation

All well-managed organizations conduct periodic performance evaluations. So too with managing a sales force; salespeople need to know how they are doing.

Salespeople have an advantage over many other employees because they have several clear measures that tell them how well they are doing. The most frequently used indicator is sales volume, but many others are also available. Selling expenses, sales calls conducted, new accounts opened, share of business from a given customer, and number of complaints handled are just some of the quantitative measures a salesperson can use to personally judge performance. The salesperson also needs to know that management is aware of the level of performance achieved.

There are also nonquantified ways to evaluate salespeople. Is the salesperson a cooperative team player? Does the salesperson complete reports on time and properly? Answers to these questions are critical to the salesperson's future with the firm. Only through an employee performance appraisal system can salespeople learn management's reaction to their efforts. Managers can specify areas for improvement and note areas for praise.

Unfortunately, a number of sales performance appraisal systems are difficult for the average field sales manager to use. In other instances, some appraisal systems have failed to treat all sales employees fairly. Because of these problems, many companies are shifting their appraisal systems in the following directions:[11]

- From a focus on personality traits to a focus on job-related behaviors and results.
- From an emphasis on rehashing past mistakes to an emphasis on future actions.
- From viewing performance appraisal as an annual ritual to viewing it as a continuous process.
- From a focus on evaluation to a focus on development.
- From one-way appraisals to two-way discussions.

THE SALES CLIMATE

The primary task of the field sales manager is to establish a sales climate in which the actual behavior of the sales force matches the behavior of the sales system it is designed to encourage.[12] The field sales manager has a number of managerial techniques at his or her disposal to establish the proper sales climate.

supervision

planning, directing, controlling, and evaluating of salespeople

The climate is typically established by the field sales manager and is largely dependent on his or her supervisory and leadership skills.[13] **Supervision** is planning, directing, controlling, and evaluating salespeople.

COMPANY PROFILE

Leadership Development at GE

Sales and marketing managers at General Electric Corp. are evaluated not only by the people who report to them but also by their peers as part of the company's management development program.

According to James P. Baughman, manager of corporate management development at GE, a manager's peers and subordinates are asked to fill out an evaluation questionnaire whenever the manager is scheduled for a corporate training session. The questionnaire asks about the individual's personal effectiveness in a variety of management and technical areas. The results are processed as part of the training program.

"The individual then gets feedback from the training staff in three different ways," says Baughman. "First, he [or she] gets his [or her] individual results, that is, where he [or she] has done well or poorly in areas such as delegation, interpersonal relationships, and other areas. Second, he or she sees the results in comparison to other managers in that particular training class. And third, because we've built a database around these questionnaires over the years, we can see how a particular sales manager's results stack up against how other sales managers did at the same stage in their careers."

At the beginning of each day of training at the corporate center, managers get feedback on results in those areas for which they'll be receiving training. That feed-

back comes in the form of individual counseling on ways in which a manager can improve results and a certain amount of customizing the group training effort to address specific problem areas. "That way," Baughman says, "the individual gets what amounts to a personal plan of action for leadership development."

The important thing to note about General Electric's evaluation process, however, is that it is not part of the company's formal performance evaluation program. "We do it in a developmental context and not in an appraisal context. The results don't go to the individual's boss and don't affect performance reviews or compensation," Baughman says.

Managers can see how far they've gone in correcting their shortcomings, and how effective their training has been, by initiating the evaluation questionnaire themselves six months or a year down the road and comparing results.

And how do managers like the idea of being evaluated by their workers and peers? "They love it," Baughman says, "as long as the results stay outside the chain of command."

SOURCE: Reprinted from "How It's Done at GE," *Sales & Marketing Management*, March 1989, p. 26. Reprinted by permission of Sales & Marketing Management. Copyright March 1989.

---

leadership
personal style by which one supervises

Leadership is the way one supervises; it is a personal style designed to get others to follow.

Supervision

Much of the task of supervising depends on the sales system within which the sales manager must operate. Many planning activities depend on the sales forecasting system, the budgeting system, and the manner in which quotas are set. Similarly, evaluation activities largely depend on the evaluation system. Finally, controlling activities depend on the reporting relationships designed into the sales organization and on the compensation system. However, directing sales force activities is not nearly as much a function of the sales system as it is of the sales manager's supervisory skills and style.

In directing a sales force, a sales manager must act as coach, counselor, motivator, and administrator. As coach, the sales manager must personally help salespeople improve their selling skills. This objective can be accomplished through training, counseling, and constructive evaluation.

Often, members of the sales force have problems related to their careers, their families, their personal lives, or their finances. Even though it can be argued that these problems are not, and should not be, the concern of the company, the professional sales manager understands that anything that has the potential for adversely affecting the behavior of a salesperson is a problem that must be addressed. While most sales managers are not trained to deal with serious personal problems, anyone can listen sympathetically (maybe even empathetically), ask questions to further appreciate the nature and seriousness of the situation, and try to offer suggestions as one human being to another.

One problem that frequently arises in the field of selling is that of motivation. Even though Chapter 13 addressed the importance of self-motivation, and even though the compensation system's sales incentives and nonfinancial rewards are designed to act as motivators, all salespeople need pep talks now and then. Professional managers relish their roles as motivators.

Finally, professional sales managers are administrators. The sales manager should see that the sales office runs smoothly, reports are finished on time, performance appraisals are completed periodically, and so forth. These may be the least exciting parts of the sales manager's job but, similar to the importance of reports to salespeople, they must be done and done well.

Leadership

There are many ways to lead. When one thinks of leaders, people such as General George Patton, President George Bush, and Winston Churchill quickly come to mind. But so do names like Casey Stengel, Lee Iacocca, and Walt Disney. Some lead by example, some by intimidation, some by persuasion, and others by sheer force of intellect. The only consistent characteristic is that great leaders all have the ability to get others to follow.

Some say that great leaders are born, and others say that they are made by the demands of the situation. In either case, to lead one must (1) understand and agree with the organization's goals and (2) intimately know those who are to be led.

SUMMARY OF CHAPTER OBJECTIVES

1. **To explain how sales managers differ from salespeople.**

   Selling skills differ from managerial skills. Selling is action-oriented and dependent upon one's personal efforts. By contrast, sales management must delegate and work through others. While the skills differ, most sales managers were also successful salespeople. It is important for sales personnel to respect management, an objective that can best be accomplished by promoting successful salespersons to sales management slots.

2. To outline the components of a sales system.

A sales system refers to the combination of policies and practices related to the management of a sales force. The primary components of a sales system are policies and practices related to organization and deployment; selection and recruitment; training and development; compensation and expenses; forecasts, budgets, and quotas; and, performance evaluations.

3. To differentiate among the primary organizational structures used for sales forces.

Sales forces can be organized by product, customer, or geographical territory. Customer-based organizations are used when specific knowledge of buyers' needs are important. For instance, some computer manufacturers use customer-based organizations to sell to retailers, banks, and manufacturers. If detailed product knowledge is important in the sales situation, a product-based organization may be used. In other words, separate sales forces are set up for different product groups. Finally, territories can also be set up on a geographical basis. This approach minimizes travel, thus saving money and reducing turnover.

4. To explain turnover rate and show how it impacts recruitment and selection.

Turnover rate is the percentage of the sales force lost each year due to resignation, discharge, retirement, and other miscellaneous reasons. Turnover rates vary from industry to industry and company to company. The higher the turnover rate, the more salespeople that must be recruited and hired each year.

5. To differentiate between initial and continuous sales training.

Sales training can be classified as either initial or continuous. Initial sales training involves the preparation and orientation of new sales personnel. By contrast, continuous sales training involves refreshing, improving, and updating the selling skills and marketing knowledge of experienced personnel.

6. To identify the primary determinants of a sales climate.

A sales climate refers to a situation wherein the sales force attempts to match its behavior with that desired by the firm. The actual climate that is established depends largely on the sales manager's supervisory and leadership skills. Supervision refers to the planning, directing, controlling, and evaluation of salespeople. By contrast, leadership refers to the way one supervises; it is a personal style designed to get others to follow.

REVIEW QUESTIONS

1. Do good salespeople always make good sales managers?
2. According to research done by Aptitude Testing for Industry, how do sales managers differ from salespeople?
3. What is a sales system? How does it operate?
4. What is meant by a pooled sales force?
5. When should the following approaches be used to organize a sales force?
   a. Customer-based organization.
   b. Product-based organization.
   c. Geographical organization.
6. Which primary factors determine the size of a sales territory or the number of accounts assigned to a salesperson?
7. Identify various sources of sales recruits.
8. Outline the benefits and costs associated with sales training programs. What do you conclude from this analysis?
9. Why do you believe salespeople rate money as a more important motivator than do nonsalespeople?
10. What determines a firm's sales climate?

DISCUSSION QUESTIONS AND EXERCISES

1. Contact several firms in your area, and determine what training is given to salespeople who are about to become sales managers.
2. Draw the organizational chart of the marketing side of a local firm. Note where the sales force fits. Why is the sales force organized as it is?
3. Talk with several firms in your area that hire salespeople directly from the local schools. Determine what traits they are seeking in their salespeople and why.
4. Contact a recent graduate of your college who has entered a sales career, and ask him or her to describe the sales training he or she has received.
5. Find three different definitions of leadership. Cite one person who exemplifies each kind of leadership, and state why you believe the person you selected is a good example.

SALES DIALOG

Peter Haughton, an applicant for the position of Associate Dean for Development (a fund-raising position) at Mid-Texas State University, walked into Dean Atwater's office for his interview. The Search Committee had selected Haughton as one of five finalists. Each of the finalists would be interviewed by the dean and the Search Committee before they made a final decision.

Haughton was currently the head of development for a small, private Texas school. Because the job represented quite a promotion, he was eager to impress the dean and the committee.

After Dean Atwater and Haughton exchanged the usual pleasantries, Atwater got down to business.

ATWATER: Tell me, Peter, why do you wish to leave your current job? Isn't Stanley College a good place to work?

HAUGHTON: It certainly is. The people are nice, it's an exciting small school, and it's a great little town to raise kids. But this would be a big promotion for me, and I feel the move would be perfect for my career at this time.

ATWATER: Fair enough. But tell me what you don't like about your current job; there must be some things wrong with it.

HAUGHTON: Sure there is. As with everything else, nothing's perfect. To begin with, the salary isn't very good, and I have a small baby now, so our expenses are going up. Second, the development effort at Stanley isn't very successful, and I can't seem to turn it around. In fact, it's a pretty bad situation.

ATWATER: How's that?

HAUGHTON: Well, the alumni aren't very loyal. It seems that nearly everyone I approach for a contribution turns me down; it gets disheartening.

ATWATER: What participation rate does Stanley get?

HAUGHTON: Only about 20 percent of the alumni contribute at all. Plus, the average gift is only about $75.

ATWATER: That's really not that bad for a school like Stanley; maybe you expect too much.

HAUGHTON: Maybe I do. But I see these people making a good living, and they don't give anything back to their alma mater. I don't understand people like that. They just plain make me mad.

ATWATER: But I've heard that you've brought in a few reasonably large gifts. That had to make you proud and happy.

HAUGHTON: Well, it did—to an extent. But when I think about how little I'm getting paid and how little those rich alums give, it really gets discouraging.

ATWATER: Why do you think it'll be much different here?

HAUGHTON: When I go to our professional meetings, I hear about the greater information bases the large universities have. And then I read about the gifts in the hundreds of thousands of dollars. It simply sounds as if it'll be a lot more fun!

What do you think the results of this sales dialog will be?

CASE 17–1 PORTLAND MUTUAL INSURANCE COMPANY

Oregon-based Portland Mutual Insurance Company offers a variety of insurance coverages and financial packages. A sales force of 88 representatives is spread across the United States. These representatives report through a comprehensive field sales management organization headed by district and zone sales directors.

Portland Mutual is judged to have one of the best initial sales training plans available in the insurance industry. Beginning sales personnel are trained for a full year in a series of classroom, on-the-job, and office assignments. Management has always been justly proud of the quality standards maintained in its initial sales training program.

Robert C. Bowman, Portland's president, is discussing sales training with the company's newly appointed national sales manager, Ann McNeil.

BOWMAN: We have always been proud of our training of new sales representatives, but you know, there is one aspect we consistently neglected.

McNEIL: What is that, Bob?

BOWMAN: Continuous training for our experienced sales personnel! What do we do for these people? I'll tell you . . . very, very little! The district sales managers work with them about two weeks each year to identify trouble spots, and we hold a national sales meeting each July. I have always thought that insufficient product knowledge is one of our company's problems. Most of these people came on board long before we offered Keogh Plans, mutual funds, tax deferred annuities, and the like. Most of them were trained to sell life insurance—period! I just don't think spending a couple of hours at a national sales meeting is enough to cover the complicated new financial packages we are offering. Also, very little is done to introduce new selling techniques or market information.

McNEIL: Yes, I agree that we don't do much to help the professional development of our experienced salespeople. Let me start working on next year's sales meeting; maybe I will be able to come up with an improved format to meet our continuous sales training needs.

BOWMAN: Good idea. . . . Why don't you get back to me on this in two weeks?

Questions

1. Identify the various deficiencies in the continuous training plan of Portland Mutual Insurance Company.

2. Can a continuous training program be based on an annual sales meeting and an occasional visit by the district sales manager? Explain.

3. What format would you use for the next Portland Mutual sales meeting? Prepare a brief outline for McNeil's report on this subject.

CASE 17–2 THOMPSON SUPPLIES, INC.

Thompson Supplies of Virginia Beach, Virginia, distributes a complete line of plumbing supplies. Their products range from tubs, shower enclosures, toilets, and sinks to pipes, fittings, and supplies. Virtually everything required by a commercial or residential plumber is represented in the line. In some instances, Thompson represents several manufacturers but for most products they carry only one manufacturer's line. In most cases, their manufacturers are the high-quality, higher-priced end of the business.

Thompson has five distribution locations in the southeastern part of the United States. According to its growth projections, Thompson expects to add two more locations over the next two years.

Thompson has a highly motivated and talented sales force that is the envy of its competitors. Because the firm is growing rapidly, Thompson will have to add 10 to 15 new salespeople over the next two years.

College recruiting has been successful in the past. Several of the firm's top salespeople joined Thompson right after graduation. But competition for good sales prospects from college is getting tougher. They estimate that their recruiting effort only resulted in one hire out of 10 candidates interviewed.

Feelings are mixed about continuing the college recruiting programs. Even though the net cost is about $35,000 per salesperson hired, the starting salary of a college person is lower than more experienced salespeople, and the college recruit is easier to train in Thompson's way of doing business. Because of increasing competition and the lack of interest in the plumbing business as a career, however, the cost per hire is expected to continue to increase.

The vice president of sales, Bill Tilden, feels the company ought to start raiding the sales forces of competitive firms. The Thompson salespeople know who the good salespeople are in the field and could be helpful in identifying prospects. Tilden also believes that an executive recruiting firm should be used to find salespeople with competitive firms.

The president of the company, Fred Thompson, thinks people from other departments within Thompson are an underutilized source. Only three members of the current sales force came from within Thompson, and they all came from the customer service department. The problem with taking personnel from customer service is two-fold. First, none of these people have finished college, while nearly all of the Thompson sales force has done so. Secondly, good customer service people are difficult to find, and Thompson's reputation over the years has been largely based on its excellent customer serivce.

Both Thompson and Tilden feel a complete review of their sales recruiting program is in order.

Questions

1. Should the college recruiting program be discontinued? Why?

2. If it is discontinued, where should Thompson focus its recruiting efforts?

3. If it is continued, how can the college recruiting program be improved? Develop a complete outline for an improved college recruiting program for Thompson Supplies.

APPENDIX A

Comprehensive Sales Dialog

Stan Noe, a sales representative for Chicagoland Painting Contractors, is inspecting the freshly painted home of Ed and Marcia Stone of Schaumburg, Illinois. Noe is the account representative in charge of the exterior painting job that the Stones hired Chicagoland to do.

MRS. STONE: I think it looks great, and the color you suggested for the trim is perfect.

NOE: Great . . . glad to hear it.

MRS. STONE: Yes, we are very happy with the job your crew did. They were very polite and efficient. And of course, it didn't hurt that your price was $200 lower than the bid I got from Jones and Zimmer, the other firm that looked at this job.

prospecting

NOE: Chicagoland prides itself on doing a quality job at a reasonable price. In fact, I was wondering if you know anyone else in the neighborhood who might be considering some painting work?

MRS. STONE: No, I don't think so, but Ed's cousin over in Barrington might. Their name is Fox, and they live at 1815 Lincoln Place. Every time I talk to Barbara, she tells me how much she wants Les to paint their house.

NOE: Thanks for the tip . . . one of Chicagoland's crew could sure make the summer more pleasant for Mr. Fox, I'll bet.

A few hours later, Noe had completed his inspections and is back at the office. He looks up Fox's number in Barrington and dials it.

FOX: Hello.

NOE: Hello, Mr. Fox, this is Stan Noe with Chicagoland Painting Contractors. The . . .

FOX: Listen, I really don't have time for a sales pitch. I've got a tee time reserved in 25 minutes.

approach

NOE: I know you are in hurry, but your cousin-in-law, Marcia Stone, suggested I give you a call.

FOX: What about?

trial close

NOE: Well, I understand you might be in need of some exterior painting this summer.

FOX: Yeah, I suppose the place is looking a little ragged. My wife seems to remind me of it everytime I am headed for the golf course. But my brother is going to be visiting this summer from California, and he said he would help me paint it.

NOE: I'll bet you guys would rather spend your time playing golf, huh?

FOX: That's for sure.

NOE: I know the feeling. It is tough to work hard all year and spend your vacation painting a house. So why don't you let me come over sometime and give you a free estimate? The Stones were delighted with the price I gave them.

FOX: OK, let's do it Monday evening . . . but I have to run now.

NOE: Fine. How about six on Monday?

FOX: That will be fine. Good-bye.

At 6 P.M. Monday evening, Noe arrives at the Fox residence in Barrington. Barbara Fox has just pulled into the driveway after delivering her son to Little League practice.

NOE: Hello, Mrs. Fox, I'm Stan Noe with Chicagoland Painting.

MRS. FOX: Oh, good. I'm very anxious to learn what it would cost to paint the old homestead.

NOE: Well, let me look the job over, and I will get right back to you. But first, you might tell me exactly what you want done and the colors you are considering.

MRS. FOX: Sure. I think . . . (Barbara Fox proceeds to outline the painting job for Noe).

Half an hour later, Noe is seated in the living room with Lester and Barbara Fox.

presentation

NOE: Well, I think your choice of colors is beautiful, Mrs. Fox. I think they will go together perfectly, and they'll fit in with your neighborhood. But of course, you realize that it will take a little more paint to do your home than the Stones', since you have quite a bit more area to cover.

MRS. FOX: Yes, our home is larger.

trial close

NOE: Here is the estimate that I have developed (handing it to the Foxes). I could have a crew start Thursday if you would like.

MRS. FOX: Boy, that is quite a bit more than you charged Les's cousin.

handling objections

NOE: Yes, but your home will require a day more than the job at the Stones. By the way, did I mention our guarantee?

MR. FOX: It sure would be a lot cheaper if my brother and I painted it. That is a lot of money . . .

demonstration

NOE: You will be getting a quality job with the best guarantee in the state. And more important, you can spend your time on the golf course rather than on a ladder. Did you have a chance to see your cousin's home after we painted it?

MR. FOX: Yes, it was a very good job.

MRS. FOX: Les, we both know the house needs to be painted. But I think you would be happier letting professionals do the job, so you can enjoy your brother while he is here.

NOE: Since the painting will take three days, would you folks rather have the crew start on Thursday, or wait until next Monday so we would not have to split the job over the weekend?

MR. FOX: Well, a partially painted house over the weekend doesn't bother me, what about you, Barbara?

MRS. FOX: No, it doesn't bother me. Get a crew in here on Thursday. Where do you want us to sign?

Noe completes the paperwork and thanks the Foxes for their purchase. He then assures them that he will check the job while it is in progress and will inspect their house after the painting is completed. Noe leaves his business card with the Foxes and tells them to call him if they have any questions about the work the Chicagoland paint crew does.

Eight days later, Noe is standing outside the Fox residence in Barrington. He has just inspected the painting job with Barbara and Lester Fox.

NOE: Well, I am glad you both liked the job. Here is a copy of our guarantee for your files.

MRS. FOX: Yes, I think our home is a real showcase now. I am delighted.

MR. FOX: I think I'll call my brother in California. I know he'll be happy we hired you guys (laughing).

NOE: Yes, I am sure he will. May I ask a favor of you folks?

MR. FOX: Sure.

building future sales

NOE: Do you know anyone else in your neighborhood who might be considering some painting work?

Questions

1. If you were Noe's sales manager, how would you rate his performance in this sales dialog? Discuss.
2. Identify Noe's strongest point and weakest point in the course of the dialog.
3. How would you have handled his weak points differently?
4. What does this comprehensive sales dialog illustrate about the nature of professional selling? Comment.

APPENDIX B

Directory of PC-Based Sales and Marketing Applications Software

S&MM's sixth annual directory lists in sequence: (1) vendor's name; (2) title of software package; (3) explanation of functions; (4) required memory; (5) price; (6) necessary computer models/operating systems; (7) network compatibility; (8) availability/cost of demo disk; (9) number of units sold/age of package; (10) accessibility/cost of in-person training; (11) availability/cost of telephone assistance program.

Once you've chosen the software packages that fit your company's needs, you can find out how to buy or test them by checking the Vendor Directory. In your selection process, consider the following:

First, when you call the vendor, ask for demo disks or evaluation copies, which will show you how the software works and often allow you to enter your own data.

Second, ask for the names of at least three customers, preferably those in sales or marketing. By talking to them, you will get a better idea of the software's overall performance.

(Note: The descriptive information contained here is provided by the vendors; therefore *Sales & Marketing Management* has no way of guaranteeing the accuracy of this information.)

This directory was researched by Thayer Taylor, Bristol Voss, and Barbara Guthrie.

SOURCE: *Sales & Marketing Management,* December 1989, pp. 57–99. (Note: some sections have been omitted.) Reprinted by permission of Sales & Marketing Management. Copyright December 1989.

VENDOR	PACKAGE	DESCRIPTION	MEM.	PRICE	HARDWARE/SYS.	NETWK.	DEMO/$	#/AGE	TRAIN.	PHONE

ACCOUNT MANAGEMENT

VENDOR	PACKAGE	DESCRIPTION	MEM.	PRICE	HARDWARE/SYS.	NETWK.	DEMO/$	#/AGE	TRAIN.	PHONE
Automated Micro	Norma AIM: Account Information Manager†	For account-oriented salespeople; tickler, notecards, report writing, labels, letter merge, auto-dial.	512K	$159	IBM PC and comp.; DOS 2.0 +	No	Yes/$15	New	No	Yes/free
Brock Control Systems	Brock Activity Manager Series (BAM)†	Integrated system supports telemarketing, customer support/analysis, sales and marketing; customized individual applications.	2MB	$6,300	AT&T, NCR Tower, IBM PC-RT, Compaq 386	All major	No	300 + / 4 years	Yes/on-site, fees	Yes/free, unlimited
Caddylak Systems	Make Contact	Electronic master file for client tracking; mailings/labels, auto-dial, reports, form letters.	512K	$59.95	IBM PC and comp.; DOS 2.0 +	No	No	1,000/ 2 years	No/tutorial	Yes/free, unlimited
Caddylak Systems	Sales Magic†	Controls, plans, organizes sales activities; tracks prospects and customers; monitors contracts, sales records; reports.	320K	$99.95	IBM PC and comp.; DOS 2.0 +	No	No	2,000-3,000/ 2 years	No/tutorial	Yes/free, unlimited
Champaigne Systems	PC Dossier†	Tracks, sorts, and profiles clients; mass mailings; follow-up calls.	128K	$245	IBM PC and comp.; DOS 2.2 +	No	No/guarantee	2,500/ 3.5 years	Yes/on-site, fees	Yes/free, unlimited
Chang Laboratories	C•A•T III	Relational database for business contacts; tracks clients, activities, time; word processor; automated letters and forms.	512K (hard disk)	$399.95	Mac, MOS	All MAC comp.	Yes/$15	15,000/ 2 years	Yes/on-site fees	Yes/90 days free, $75/year
Computer Strategies	Organizing for Successful Selling	For individual salespeople to organize all client and account data.	128K	$49.95	IBM PC and comp.; MS DOS	No	No	500 + / 3-5 years	No/manual	Yes/free, unlimited
DAC Software	Lucid 3-D†	3-D spreadsheet with graphics for account managers.	256K	$99.95	IBM PC and comp.; DOS 2.0 +	No	No	30,000/ 1 year	No	Yes/contract
Datanetics	dataTRAC†	Relational database for direct mail, telemarketing, lead tracking, account management.	512K (hard disk)	$3,495-$15,995	IBM PC-XT, -AT, PS/2 and comp.; Super DOS	All major	No	30 + / 2 years	Yes/on-site, fees	Yes/6 months free
EMIS Software	EMIS I†	Sales and marketing software for account and prospect management; letters, sales reports, envelopes, mail merge.	512K (hard disk)	$695 & up	IBM PC and comp.; DOS 3.1 +	Novell, 3Com, PCNet, Banyan	Yes/ free; evaluation/$50	1,250 + / 2 years	Yes/on-off-site, fees	Yes/contract
Esprit Software Technology	SELLSTAR!-AT†	Sales productivity using artificial intelligence; account territory management and strategy.	640K	$495	IBM PC and comp.; DOS 2.1 +	No	Yes/free	100 + / 2 years	No	Yes/90 days free
Information Managers	Contact and Facts Address Book	Keeps track of people, addresses, notes; electronic Rolodex.	512K	$39.95	IBM PC and comp.; DOS 2.1 +	No	Yes/free	400 + / 3 years	No	Yes/free, unlimited
JEB Systems	Marketing Management System/Plus†	Marketing and sales automation, direct marketing, lead tracking, telemarketing, lead analysis, sales forecasting, sales analysis.	256K	$995-$15,000	Digital PC-, MS DOS	All major	No/dial-in	1,300/ 9 years	Yes/on-site, fee	Yes/maintenance agreement
Laptop Express	Quota Maker†	Sales prospecting and marketing system; tickler, labels, Rolodex, Word Perfect.	512K	$495	IBM PC and comp.; DOS 2.0 +	No	Yes/free	375/ 6 years	Yes/off-site, fee	Yes/free, unlimited
Lowell Corp.	Prosell†	Automated time/account management.	640K	$795	IBM PC and comp.; laptops; MS DOS 3.0 +	Banyan, Novell, 3Com	Yes/free	30/1 year	Yes/on-site, fees	Yes/contract
Management Software	PC Briefcase Client & Business Activity Manager	Maintains thousands of client information records; to-do lists, calendar, auto-dialer, tickler file, mailing lists, quota tracking; T&E system.	256K	$55	IBM PC and comp.; MS DOS	All major	Yes/$20	550/1 year	No/manual	Yes/free, unlimited
Management Software	PC Briefcase Executive Reports	Analyzes information and prepares comparative reports on clients.	256K	$295	IBM PC and comp.; MS DOS	All major	No	75-90/ 1 year	No	Yes/free, unlimited
Management Software	PC Briefcase Marketing Assistant	Maintains product and service descriptions, creates quotes, pricing plans, graphic presentations; seven geographic maps.	256K	$55	IBM PC and comp.; MS DOS	All major	Yes/$20	400 + / 1 year	No	Yes/free, unlimited
Management Software	PC Briefcase Reference Source	Database of corporate and federal addresses, phone numbers; U.S. geographic and demographic data by state, zip, area codes; data sorts, labels, calculator.	256K	$55	IBM PC and comp.; MS DOS	All major	Yes/free	425/1 year	No	Yes/free, unlimited
MarketWare	SNIPER	Sales tool targets competitors and desired accounts in high dollar value selling situations.	640K	$8,000 & up	IBM PC and comp.	All major	No	New	Yes/on-site, fees	Yes/free, unlimited
Odesta Corp.	Double Helix†	Relational database to create customized applications including inquiry/order, list/account management, time & billing, lead tracking, sales management.	1MB	$595	Mac +, SE, II	No	Yes/$10	50,000 + / 5 years	Yes/on-off-site	Yes/free, unlimited
Pearl Communications	PCI Sales Management System†	Customer tracking/support, quote generation, forecasting.	256K	$695-$1,295	IBM PC and comp.; MS DOS 2.0 +	Novell	Yes/free	8 + / 4 years	Yes/on-site, fee; off-site, free	Yes/90 days free
Remote Control	Bridgit	Complete sales organization support, telemarketing, order entry, accounting.	640K	$265-$650	IBM PC and comp.; PC DOS 3.3 +	Novell, 3Com, IBM Token Ring	Yes/$29	New	Yes/to dealers, free	Yes/6 months free, then contract

VENDOR	PACKAGE	DESCRIPTION	MEM.	PRICE	HARDWARE/SYS.	NETWK.	DEMO/$	#/AGE	TRAIN.	PHONE
Richmond Software	The Maximizer Contact Management Software†	Organize/manage unlimited number of clients/prospects; complete recordkeeping.	640K (hard disk)	$195-$495	IBM PC and comp.; laptops; MS-, PC DOS 3.0	LAN	Yes/$12	10,000 + / 2 years	No	Yes/free, unlimited
Sage Worldwide	accuSPACE Key Account Manager†	Organizes field sales information; customer/product/history data.	684K	$8,471 & down	IBM PC and comp.; DOS	No	Yes/free	New	Yes/on-site fees	Yes/contract
Sales & Marketing Systems	SalesCTRL 2†	Integrated package: prospect database with territory account/sales force/promotion analysis; remote transmission of account updates, letter writer.	512K (hard disk)	$695-2,795	IBM PC-AT, XT and comp.; DOS 2.1 +	Novell, 3Com	Yes/$13	1,500/ 4 years	Yes/on-site, fees	Yes/90 days free, then contract
SalesFacs	SalesFacs Prospector/ Quote Log/ Personal Selling	Account/contact management, lead tracking, potential analysis, quotation tracking, direct mail, personal correspondence.	640K	$950 & up	IBM PC, laptops and comp.; PC-, MS DOS	All major	Yes/$25	85/2 years	Yes/on-site, phone fees	Yes/180 days free
Saratoga Systems	Sales Productivity System†	Customized account/sales information system with unique displays.	640K	$1,250 & up;	MS DOS 1.5 +	LAN	Yes/free	100 + / 2 years	Yes/on-site, fees	Yes/contract
Scherrer Resources	Sales Ally†	Customer/prospect tracking system, database management, word processing, auto-dial, telemarketing, account management, order entry.	256K	$395	IBM PC and comp.; MS DOS 2.0 +	Novell	Yes/$10	5,000 + / 3 years	Yes/on-site, off-site, fees	Yes/free, unlimited
Scott Computing Systems	Scott Customer Manager†	Account data management, lead/prospect tracking, call reporting, contact records, user-defined customer profiles.	640K	$995	IBM PC, PS/2 and comp.; MS-, PC DOS 3.0 +	No	No	500 + / 9 years	No/ manual	Yes/30 days free
SimplSoft Products	Client Manager†	Organizes business/personal contacts, prints follow-up reports/labels/index cards, searches all files for first/last name.	256K	$69.95	IBM PC and comp.; DOS 2.1 +	All major	No	300/1 year	Yes/on-site, fees	Yes/free, unlimited
SNAP Software	SNAP†	Direct marketing, lead tracking, telemarketing, account/sales management, forecasting.	512K	$2,000/ user	IBM PC and comp.; MS DOS	All major	Yes/free	800/ 5 years	Yes/on-site fees	Yes/contract
Softek Design	A4†	Integrated, customizable programs: accounting, sales tracking, account/prospect/client/vendor history, word processing, graphing, spreadsheet, labels, etc.	1200K (hard disk)	$2,000-$10,000	Mac +, SE, II, laptops; MOS	AppleShare, PSN, Tops, Novell	Yes/$30	105/1 year	Yes/on-site, fee; HQ, free	Yes/14 months free
System Vision Corp.	Sales Vision Field Sales†	Field sales account management system, keeps contact logs, calendar, makes reports.	640K (hard disk)	$295	IBM PC and comp.; DOS	No	Yes/free	1,000/ 5 years	Yes/on-site, fee	Yes/30 days free
Target Microsystems	RIFLESHOT†	Account management, call scheduling, database marketing, direct/bulk mail, telemarketing, forecasting, call reports.	640K (hard disk)	$495-$1,995	IBM PC-XT and comp.; DOS 2.0 +	Novell	Yes/free	20 + / 1.5 years	Yes/on-site, fees	Yes/free, unlimited

CHARTS

VENDOR	PACKAGE	DESCRIPTION	MEM.	PRICE	HARDWARE/SYS.	NETWK.	DEMO/$	#/AGE	TRAIN.	PHONE
Banner Blue	Org Plus	Automatically draws, positioning text and spaces; calculates budgets, salaries; generates reports and charts.	320K	$79.95	IBM PC-XT, -AT, PS/2 or comp.; DOS 2.0 +	Novell, PC LAN, 3Com, Banyan, PCNET	No	10,000 + / 5 years	No	Yes/free, unlimited
Banner Blue	Org Plus Advanced	Automatically draws, positioning text and spaces; generates reports and charts; sideways printing; choice of fonts.	384K	$129.95	IBM PC-XT, -AT, PS/2 or comp.; DOS 2.0 +	Novell, PC LAN, 3Com, Banyan, PCNET	No	10,000 + / 5 years	No	Yes/free, unlimited
Caddylak Systems	Chart Creator	Twelve different charts, import/export data.	320K	$99.95	IBM PC and comp.; DOS 2.0 +	No	No	2,000/ 1.5 years	No	Yes/free, unlimited
Caddylak Systems	Form Designer with Fill-in Feature	Creates forms, charts, worksheets; automatically fills out data; database.	512K	$149.95	IBM PC and comp.; DOS 2.0 +	No	No	9,000/ 3 years	No	Yes/free, unlimited

ELECTRONIC MAIL

VENDOR	PACKAGE	DESCRIPTION	MEM.	PRICE	HARDWARE/SYS.	NETWK.	DEMO/$	#/AGE	TRAIN.	PHONE
Coker Electronics	†POST E-Mail	Menu-driven electronic mail links field laptops and branch office desktops with HQ; forms, fax, LAN options available.	256K	$129-$495	IBM PC and comp., DOS 2.0 +	LAN	No/guarantee	1,000 + / 2 years	Yes/on-site, fees	Yes/120 days free
Cross Information	CROSS + POINT	Electronic mail with scheduling and phone pad.	120K	$49-$395	IBM PC and comp., DOS	LAN	Yes/$9.95	500-1,000/ 4 years	Yes/on-site, fees	Yes/free, unlimited
Datanetics	Bulletin Board	Sends messages anyone can read.	512K	$295-$1,195	IBM PC-XT, -AT, PS/2 and comp.; Super DOS	All major	No	New	Yes/on-site, fees	Yes/6 months free
Datanetics	dataMAIL	Electronic mail system, must have password to read mail.	512K	$395-$1,695	IBM PC-XT, -AT, PS/2 and comp.; Super DOS	All major	No	New	Yes/on-site, fees	Yes/6 months free
1st Desk	1stBBS	Remote database and bulletin board system.	512K	$195	Mac	No	No	New	No	Yes/free, unlimited
Galacticomm	The Major BBS†	A bulletin board system used by sales/marketing professionals for E-mail.	512K	$59-$1,844	IBM PC; DOS 3.0 +	Novell, 10-Net	No	2,000/ 3 years	No	Yes/included

VENDOR	PACKAGE	DESCRIPTION	MEM.	PRICE	HARDWARE/SYS.	NETWK.	DEMO/$	#/AGE	TRAIN.	PHONE
LEADtrack Services	LEADpass†	E-mail package includes voice mail, automated attendant, call routing.	640K	$995-$1,500	IBM PC and comp.; MS-, PC DOS	Novell	Yes/free	New	No	Yes/60 days free, then contract
McDonnell Douglas Applied Communications Systems	PC OnTyme Plus	Message management system to create, send, receive, file E-mail.	320K	$150/each	IBM PC-XT, -AT, PS/2, Compaq 386 and comp.; DOS 2.2 +	TYMNET	No/video	New	Yes/on-site, off-site, fees	Yes/free, unlimited
3X USA	Mail-Server†	Communication software for outside sales force using laptops to check mailbox/send reports.	384K	$195	IBM PC and comp.; DOS 2.0 +	All major	Yes/free	350/1 year	No	Yes/free, unlimited

FIELD SALES/REPRESENTATIVES

VENDOR	PACKAGE	DESCRIPTION	MEM.	PRICE	HARDWARE/SYS.	NETWK.	DEMO/$	#/AGE	TRAIN.	PHONE
Beacon Data Systems	REP$ II	Sales analysis and tracking for manufacturers' sales reps.	640K	$1,995	IBM PC and comp., MS DOS	LAN	Yes/$35	200 + / 5 years	Yes/on-site, fees	Yes/1 year free, then contract
Free World Marketing	PRIMO†	Personal information manager designed for field salespeople; pop-up calendar, auto-dialer, integrated word processing, management reports, territory analysis.	256K (hard disk)	$295	IBM PC; DOS 2.0 +	All major	Yes/$25	New	Yes/on-site, fees	Yes/90 days free, then contract
Generation Four	MBA:Clients†	Database functions include: key word search, letters, mailing lists, contact files, open source codes.	1MB (hard disk)	$189	Mac +	All major	Yes/$10	New	No	Yes/on-line, free
GPS CUSTOM Software	GPS CUSTOM with Sales & Marketing CUSTOMware†	Fully customizable; features include: lead tracking, management and statistical reporting, telemarketing, order entry, proposal and contract generation.	512K	$295-$995	IBM PC and comp.; MS DOS 3.0 +	All major	No	1,000 + / 2 years	Yes/on-off-site, fees	Yes/contract
Harris Publ.	Selectory	Database of manufacturing firms for managers and salespeople to identify qualified prospects.	512K (hard disk)	$249-$695	IBM PC-XT and comp.; MS-, PC DOS 2.0 +	All major	Yes/$10	2,500/4 years	No	Yes/free, unlimited
IDSC Rental Co.	marketrieve PLUS†	Lead tracking (especially multiple contacts at same company); market analysis, forecasting, direct marketing, telemarketing, field sales and management.	1MB (hard disk)	$1,595 and up	IBM PC and comp.; MS-, PC DOS	LAN	Yes/free	85/1 year	Yes/on-site, fees	Yes/contract (incl. updates)
Market Power	SALES WIZARD 5.62	For individual or field sales reps; customer/prospect tracking and history; direct mail, mail merge; integrated word processor with calendar, calculator.	320K	$249	IBM PC and comp.; DOS 3.0 +	LAN, Novell, 3Com	Yes/free	1,000 + / 3 years	Yes/on-site, fees	Yes/30 days free
Norman R. Sutherland	Find-A-Rep†	Database program helps sales managers define/identify the best manufacturing rep for their products.	384K	$195 and up	IBM PC and comp.; DOS 2.0 +	All major	Yes/$20	100/1 year	No	Yes/free, unlimited
The Pipeline Software Co.	PIPELINE†	Sales/marketing modules for: productivity, lead tracking, lead management, telemarketing, customer service; database download to remote rep laptops.	640K	$16,000	IBM PC and comp.; DOS 3.1 +	LAN	Yes/$25	4 + /1 year	Yes/on-off-site, fees	Yes/contract
Profit Management Systems	Outcome†	Field sales/marketing system with lead tracking, account/territory management, sales forecasting, scheduling.	256K	$500-$1,500/user	IBM PC and comp.; DOS 2.1 +	All major	No	8,000 + / 2.5 years	Yes/on-site, included	Yes/contract
The Salmon System	The Salmon Sales Management System†	For sales managers and reps: activity/productivity reports, account/call history, follow-ups, analysis, word processing.	640K (hard disk)	$1,000 and up	IBM PC and comp.; DOS	All major	Yes/$10	350/4 years	Yes/on-site, included	Yes/contract
Software Complement	Client/MAC†	For sales reps; tickler files, contact history notes, time tracking, mail merging, letterwriting.	1MB	$125	Mac	Mac comp.	Yes/$25	150/3 years	No	Yes/free, unlimited
TeleVell	TeleSell-Salesperson Module†	Call management, notes, scheduling, product/competition information, mail-list management, travel directions; fully customizable reports.	640K	$695-$2,190	IBM PC and comp.; PC DOS 3.0 +	3Com, MSNet, Novell	No/video, $45	300 + / 2 years	Yes/on-off-site, fees	Yes/free, unlimited

FLEET CAR MANAGEMENT

VENDOR	PACKAGE	DESCRIPTION	MEM.	PRICE	HARDWARE/SYS.	NETWK.	DEMO/$	#/AGE	TRAIN.	PHONE
Fleet Technologies	Integrated Fleet Administration System based on Paradox 3.0†	Tracks information on fleets/employees including mileage, accidents, reordering cycle.	640K	$1,995-$2,995	IBM PC and comp.; DOS 2.0 +	All major	Yes/$5	New	Yes/on-site, fee	Yes/90 days free, contract

GRAPHICS

VENDOR	PACKAGE	DESCRIPTION	MEM.	PRICE	HARDWARE/SYS.	NETWK.	DEMO/$	#/AGE	TRAIN.	PHONE
Adobe Systems	Adobe Illustrator 88	Draw from scratch or use basic shapes, scale objects and patterns, blend colors; various typefaces.	1MB	$495	Mac +, SE, II, MOS 4.2 +	All major	No	New	Yes/on-off-site, fees	Yes/contract

VENDOR	PACKAGE	DESCRIPTION	MEM.	PRICE	HARDWARE/SYS.	NETWK.	DEMO/$	#/AGE	TRAIN.	PHONE
Advanced Graphics Software	SlideWrite Plus	Creates presentation charts and graphs; scientific graphic features.	390K	$445	IBM PC and comp., DOS	All DOS networks	Yes/free	10,000 + / 4 years	Yes/on-off-site, fees	Yes/free, unlimited
Ashton-Tate	DRAW APPLAUSE 1.1	Charts, graphs, diagrams, free-form drawings, library of 125 images, color slides, overhead transparencies, color or monocrome prints.	640K	$495	IBM PC-XT, -AT, PS/2 or comp.	All major	Yes/$4.95	New	Yes/on-off-site, fees	Yes/90 days free
Ashton-Tate	RapidFile 1.2	File manager for data, reports, form letters, mailing labels, monochrome or color graphics.	256K	$295	IBM PC-XT, -AT, PS/2 or comp.	All major	Yes/$4.95	50,000 + / 1 year	Yes/on-off-site, fees	Yes/90 days free
Broderbund Software	Drawing Table	Professional drawing tools, illustrations, maps, diagrams, fliers, posters, logos, letterheads.	1MB	$129.95	Mac +, SE, II	No	No	New	No	Yes/free, unlimited
Execucom Systems	Impressionist Business Graphics	Graphics system for new to advanced users; produces analytical and boardroom presentations.	512K	$895	IBM PC or comp.; MS DOS	All major	Yes/free	2,000/ 3 years	No	Yes/free
Frame Technology	FrameMaker 1.3-X	Professional publishing software provides word-processing graphics; layout tools for creating documents, complex technical manuals, reports.	16MB	$2,500	SUN, HP; Sony Tektronix, Apple NCR.	No	Yes/free	8,500/ 4 years	Yes/included	Yes/included
HyperGraphics Training Systems	HotAUTHOR†	Uses text, graphics, animation to illustrate a product or marketing concept; interactive Q&A capabilities.	256K	$2,500 +	IBM PC and comp.; DOS 2.0 +	PCNET	Yes/free	25 + / 3 years	Yes/off-site, fees	Yes/free, unlimited
HyperGraphics Training Systems	StoryBOOK	Uses text, graphics, animation to illustrate a product or marketing concept.	256K	$275	IBM PC and comp.; DOS 2.0 +	PCNET	Yes/free	8/3 years	Yes/off-site, fees	Yes/free, unlimited
Information Dimensions	BASIS/Images	Provides image storage and retrieval; text to image applications.	Any memory	$40,000-$100,000	Any IBM, MAC, DEC, Unisys, Control Data, Wang	All major	Yes/free	1,600/ 1.5 years	Yes/on-off-site, free	Yes/free, unlimited
Informix Software	SmartWare II†	Package includes modules for database, spreadsheet, business graphics, word processing; customizable.	512K	$249-$699	IBM PC-XT, -AT, PS/2 and 100% comp.; DOS, UNIX	3Com, LAN, Novell, Netware, Starlan, Vine	Yes/free	150,000/ 5 years	Yes/off-site, fees	Yes/free, unlimited
Interactive Market Systems	FloChart	Graphics package esp. for media schedules.	640K	$1,500	IBM PC-XT, -AT and comp.; DOS 3.1 +	All major	No	100 + / 2.5 years	Yes/on-off-site, fees	Yes/free, unlimited
Management Science Assoc.	PC Maris†	Data retrieval and display system; tabular or graphic display feeds into spreadsheet programs.	512K (color monitor)	$3,000 and up	IBM PC-XT, -AT, PS/2 and comp.; DOS 3.0 +	No	Yes/free	100 + / 2 years	No/ manual	Yes/free, unlimited
Marketing Graphics	PicturePak [4 editions]	Electronic clip art: Executive and Management, Finance and Administration, Sales & Marketing, and Federal Government; thematic words, images, logos, seals, symbols, borders, backgrounds.	$128K	$145/ each	IBM PC, Mac, PS/2 and comp.; DOS	All major	Yes/free	New	No	Yes/free, unlimited
MicroMaps Software	MacAtlas	Comprehensive collection of clip-art map templates of the entire world, USA by state, and all 50 states by county; can customize, colorize, or modify maps by adding fill patterns, graphic objects, text, numbers, etc.	128K-1MB	$79-$676	Mac(requires comp. graphics programs)	All Mac	Yes/free	3,000/ 2 years	No/ manual	No
New England Software	GB-STST	Statistical analysis and data-management package with fully integrated graphs.	512K	$299.95	IBM PC and comp.; MS-, PC DOS 2.0 +	All major	Yes/off-site only	100,000 + / 1 year	No	Yes/free, unlimited
New England Software	Graph-in-the Box 2.2	Presentation/business graphics by analyzing numbers from other programs while they are on the screen.	256K	$139.95	IBM PC and comp.; MS-, PC DOS 2.0 +	All major	Yes/off-site only	100,000 + / 3 years	No	Yes/free, unlimited
PictureWare	PicturePower†	Integrated system incorporates photographic quality images with text and database.	640K	$1,995-$2,900	IBM PC-XT, -AT, PS/2 and comp.; DOS 3.1 +	Netware	Yes/$25	3,200/ 3.5 years	Yes/on-off-site, fees	Yes/free, unlimited
Silicon Beach Software	Super-Card	Gives users full screen graphic, drawing, painting power.	1MB (color monitor)	$199	Mac +, SE, II; Mac 6.02 +	No	No	25,000/ 1 year	No/ phone only	Yes/free, unlimited
STSC Inc.	STATGRAPHICS Statistical Graphics System†	Designed for market researchers, package integrates graphics with wide range of research procedures.	512K	$895	IBM PC and comp.; MS-, PC DOS 2.0 +	No	No	20,000 + / 4 years	Yes/on-site, fees	Yes/contract
SYSTAT	FASTAT	Intermediate package with scatterplot brushing tools and three-dimensional full-color graphics for presentations and reports.	1MB	$195	Mac +, SE, SE30, II, IIx	No	Yes/free	600/1 year	Yes/HQ free	Yes/free, unlimited
Visual Business Systems	Visual Business No.5/Output Manager	Creates true three-dimensional charts; puts chart on high resolution film recorder and thermal printers.	1MB	$395	Mac II	All Mac	Yes/free	2,000/ 1 year	Yes/off-site, fees	Yes/30 days free
Xerox Desktop Software	Xerox Graph	Analytical and graphing package allows data manipulation/analysis, graph generation with curve-fitting and other devices.	1MB (hard disk)	$295	IBM 286, 386	No	No	New	No	Yes/60 days free

VENDOR	PACKAGE	DESCRIPTION	MEM.	PRICE	HARDWARE/SYS.	NETWK.	DEMO/$	#/AGE	TRAIN.	PHONE
Zenographics	Pixie 1.01	Window-space charting and drawing package; library of symbols, import/export capabilities.	640K	$195	IBM PC-AT, -XT and comp.	No	Yes/free	10,000 + / 2 years	No	Yes/free
Z-Soft	Paintbrush Plus	Bit-map graphic editor with full page, 300DPI editor; scanner/laser printer support.	640K	$149	IBM PC and comp.; PC MS DOS 2.0 +	All major	Yes/free	250,000/ 3 years	Yes/on-site, fee	Yes/free unlimited
Z-Soft	Publisher's Paintbrush	Bit-map graphic editor, full-page editing, zoom and advertising features.	1.5MB	$285	IBM PC and comp.; PC MS DOS 2.0 +	All major	Yes/free	100,000 + / 2 years	Yes/on-site, fee	Yes/free unlimited

HIRING & TRAINING

VENDOR	PACKAGE	DESCRIPTION	MEM.	PRICE	HARDWARE/SYS.	NETWK.	DEMO/$	#/AGE	TRAIN.	PHONE
Addison-Wesley Publ.	Marketing Tool Kit	Teaches marketing principles to trainees or students.	128K	$25.75	IBM PC-XT and comp., DOS 2.0 +	No	No	3,000 + / 4 years	No	Yes/free
Automated Micro	KIA Product Learning System†	Trains salespeople about product via interactive questions, customized.	256K	$3,000 and up	IBM PCs and comp., DOS	No	Yes/free	15/2 years	Yes/fees	Yes/free
Courseware	SOLD!	Face-to-face selling program; teaches skills; database keeps track of appointments.	128K	$39.75	IBM PCs and comp., DOS	No	Yes/free	2,000/ 5 years	No	Yes/free, unlimited
Custom Databanks	Executive Search System	Merges names and addresses of 2,000 search firms with letters; firms classed by industry, location, job category, salaries; updated six times/year.	384K	$75-$300	IBM PC and comp., DOS 2.0 +	No	No	1,000 + / 3 years	No	Yes/free, unlimited
Experience in Software	The Art of Negotiating	Negotiation preparation and training for closing the sale. Plans scenarios and produces reports on all aspects of sale.	256K	$195	IBM PC; DOS 2.0 +	No	No	5,000/ 5 years	No	Yes/free, unlimited
The InMar Group	TrainingMate†	Interactive customized training.	†	$10,000-$50,000	IBM PC and comp., Mac	All major	No	10/3 years	No	Yes/free, unlimited
Leadership Development	The Competency Builder†	For product/marketing training of sales reps, dealers, distributors.	260K	$2,500-$25,000	IBM PC and comp.; DOS	All major	Yes/free	3,000 + / 2 year	Yes/included	Yes/included
Leadership Development	Sales Advisor†	Teaches how to chart the course of a sale, maintain control, handle objections, trigger a prospect's buying impulse, size people up.	256K	$195	IBM PC and comp.; DOS	All major	No	1,000/ 1 year	No/ manual	Yes/free, unlimited
Lincoln Systems	ISP: Interactive Statistical Program	Program for teaching statistical marketing research; includes high-resolution graphics.	384K	$40-$150	IBM PC and comp., DOS 2.0 +	All major	Yes/free	2,500 + / 3 years	Yes/contract	Yes/free, unlimited
Management Software	PC Briefcase Instructional Seminars	Interactive program teaches and reviews selling skills; account management.	256K	$95	IBM PC and comp.; MS DOS	All major	No	600-800/ 1 year	No	Yes/free, unlimited
MarketWorks	The Marketing Mentor	Teaches marketing planning.	640K	$49	IBM PC-XT, -AT, 386, PS/2 and comp.; MS DOS 2.0 +	No	No	1,000/ 1 year	No	Yes/free, unlimited
Neuralytic Systems	Dr. Shrink	Assesses client's personality; analyzes the public vs. private self (including secrets/sexual fantasies); recommends how to communicate with/persuade the person.	164K	$49.95	IBM PC and comp.; DOS	No	No	42,000/ 2 years	No	Yes/free, unlimited
Neuralytic Systems	Quality Personnel Screen	Employment screening: 105-question test (via computer or paper/pencil) measures honesty, substance abuse, agreeableness, extroversion, etc.	256K	$498.95	IBM PC-XT, -AT and comp.; DOS 2.0 +	No	No	New	No	Yes/free, unlimited
Profiles Int'l.	The Profile†	Program gives managers personality assessment and description of employees/salespeople.	256K	$65 and down	IBM PC and comp.; MS DOS 2.1 +	All major	Yes/free	500 + / 3 years	No	Yes/free, unlimited
Profiles Int'l.	Sales Selection Analyst†	Identifies a sales candidate's ability to develop rapport, identify client needs, present the product, solve objections, close sales.	246K	$69.95 and up	IBM PC and comp.; MS DOS 2.0 +	All major	Yes/free	500 + /3 years	Yes/tutorial	Yes/free, unlimited
The Scientific Press	Applying Marketing Management PC Simulations	Exercises illustrating positioning, strategy, competitive strategy, new product development, lifecycle forecasting.	256K	$15.00	IBM PC-XT, -AT, PS/2 and comp.	No	No	100 + /3 years	No	Yes/free, unlimited
The Scientific Press	ENTERPRISE, an Integrating Management Exercise	Integrated marketing/management simulation teaches marketing concepts.	256K	$22.50	IBM PC-XT, -AT, PS/2 and comp.	No	No	New	No	Yes/free, unlimited
The Scientific Press	Marketing Analysis & Decision Making	Text and cases with Lotus 1-2-3-based self-study for new product development, test marketing, product modifications, marketing mix management.	256K (need Lotus)	$48.75	IBM PC-XT, -AT, PS/2 and comp.	No	No	50 + /2 years	No	Yes/free, unlimited
The Scientific Press	Marketing Management: Analytic Exercises with Lotus	Lotus 1-2-3 based exercises teaching marketing concepts in a variety of situations.	256K (need Lotus)	$27.50	IBM PC-XT, -AT, PS/2 and comp.	No	No	New	No	Yes/free, unlimited

VENDOR	PACKAGE	DESCRIPTION	MEM.	PRICE	HARDWARE/SYS.	NETWK.	DEMO/$	#/AGE	TRAIN.	PHONE
The Scientific Press	Markstrat 2	Marketing strategy simulation for training strategy and techniques; for individuals or sales teams.	256K	$27.50	IBM PC-XT, -AT, PS/2 and comp.	No	No	500 + /12 years	No	Yes/free, unlimited
Spinnaker Software	Putting the One Minute Manager to Work	Teaches how to identify goals and establish performance criteria; follow-up system gives feedback on answers.	128K	$99.95	IBM PC and comp.; MS DOS 2.1 +	No	Yes/free	12,000/3 years	No	Yes/free, unlimited
Strategic Management Group	Business Learning System	Training for marketing, operations, strategic planning, finance.	256K	$475	IBM PC and comp.; DOS 2.0 +	No	Yes/$10	7,500/2 years	Yes/on-site, fee	Yes/free, unlimited
Strategic Management Group	Business School	Learning tool simulation of management techniques.	512K	$59.95	IBM PC-AT, -XT and comp.; DOS 2.0 +	No	No	25,000/6 years	No	Yes/free, unlimited
Strategic Management Group	Business Simulator and Business Strategist	Simulates strategy situations in five different industries.	256K-512K (2 disk drives)	$69.95-299.95	IBM PC-XT, -AT, PS/2 and comp.; MS-, PC DOS 2.0 +	No	Yes/$5	1,500-10,000/3-7 years	No	Yes/free, unlimited
Strategic Management Group	Business Week's Business Advantage†	Learning tool simulation of running all aspects of a large corporation.	384K	$69.95	IBM PC, Mac and comp.; DOS 2.0 +	No	Yes/free	12,500/2 years	No	Yes/free, unlimited
Strategic Management Group	Strategic Management Game Individual Learning Game	Simulates competition among four different companies with three products each in three markets.	256K (2 disk drives)	$99.95	IBM PC-XT, -AT, PS/2 and comp.; MS-, PC DOS 2.0 +	No	Yes/$5	5,000/8 years	No	Yes/free, unlimited
Strat X * Int'l.	MA	User is "in charge" of a simulated marketing department, must devise strategies.	256K	$245 and up	IBM PC-AT, -XT and comp.; DOS 2.0	No	Yes/free	2,000 + /1 year	No	Yes/free, unlimited
SYSTAT	MYSTAT	Teaches/simplifies business statistics and forecasting routines.	1MB	$195	Mac + , SE, SE30, II, IIx	No	Yes/free	60,000/3 years	Yes/HQ, free	Yes/free, unlimited

INQUIRY/ORDER

VENDOR	PACKAGE	DESCRIPTION	MEM.	PRICE	HARDWARE/SYS.	NETWK.	DEMO/$	#/AGE	TRAIN.	PHONE
Applied Software Technology	VersaForm XL	Programmable relational database, order entry, tracking, contact lists, accounting.	512K	$245-$495	IBM PC and comp., MS DOS	All major	No	35,000 + /8 years	No	Yes/30 days free, then contract
Inquiry Intelligence Systems	IQ System†	Inquiry management program for marketing directors and sales managers.	640K	$1,295	IBM PC-AT, -XT and comp.; DOS 3.0 +	All major	No/video	120/4 years	No/video	Yes/30 days free
International Software Technology	MOMe	Handles mail order, inventory control, order processing, list management, fulfillment, reporting.	384K	$1,995-$2,995	IBM PC-AT, -XT, PS/2 and comp,; PC-, MS DOS 2.0	All major	Yes/free	350/5 years	Yes/on-site, fee	Yes/contract
Merle Systems	OrderOne	Order entry/tracking, sales analysis, import/export; add-on features available.	640K (2MB hard disk)	$3,500	IBM PC and comp.; MS-, PC DOS 3.1 +	Novell	Yes/$100	500 + /4 years	Yes/on-off-site, fees	Yes/90 days free
Software Institute	Close Call†	Customer referral program designed to locate closest dealers.	512K (hard disk)	$395	IBM PC-AT or 100% comp.; DOS 2.0 +	All major	No	New	No	Yes/free, unlimited
Turnkey Data Solutions	Electronic Sales Assistant†	Automation of sales forms for orders, expenses, weekly revenue, price inquiry; inputs information into E-mail or host.	128K	$295	IBM PC and comp.; MS-, PC DOS 3.0 +	Unix	Yes/$90	2,000 + / 3 years	Yes/on-site, fee	Yes/90 days free

LEAD TRACKING

VENDOR	PACKAGE	DESCRIPTION	MEM.	PRICE	HARDWARE/SYS.	NETWK.	DEMO/$	#/AGE	TRAIN.	PHONE
A la Carte Int'l.	MARKETEM-PLATES	Customer tracking and order processing.	512K	$1,000 and up	IBM PC-XT, -AT, and comp., DOS 2.0 +	No	No	100 + / 5 years	Yes/on-site, fees	Yes/contract
Argonaut Systems	PLAN†	Tracks prospects and customers, orders; forecasts future sales.	512K	$89	IBM PC and comp.,	No	Yes/$5	New	No	Yes/free, unlimited
Arlington Software & Systems	PCAT: Professional Contact and Tracking System	Lead tracking for sales and marketing managers.	384K	$1,295-$6,400	IBM PC and comp., MS DOS	Novell, IBM Token Ring, Banyon, 3-COM	Yes/$12	3,500 + /8 years	No/manual and tutorial	Yes/free, unlimited
Automated Business Designs	ADVANTAGE†	Prospect history, notes, automatic mailing, telemarketing, management reports, follow-up reminder.	64K	$2,000 and up	IBM PC and comp., MS DOS	No	No	50 + / 3 years	Yes/on-site, fees	Yes/contract
Bartel Software	TOTALL MANAGER†	Customized market plans, lead tracking, letters, telemarketing scripts, expense tracking, client billing, report writer, order processing.	640K	$395-$2,295	IBM PC and comp., DOS 3.0 +	All major	Yes/$5	1,000 + / 3 years	Yes/on-off-site, fees	Yes/30 days free
Bits and Bytes	Lead Tracker	Lead tracking and organizing.	256K	$129	IBM PC and comp., MS DOS	No	Yes/free	100/1 year	Yes/on-site, fees	Yes/free, unlimited
Breakthrough Prod.	Market Master Manager†	Manages and automatically follows up leads for sales forces.	1MB (hard disk)	$595-$1,995	Mac + , SE, II, MOS	All major	Yes/$10	100/ 1.5 years	No	Yes/1 year free
Breakthrough Prod.	Market Master Results Analyst†	Manages and automatically follows up leads for individual salesperson.	1MB (hard disk)	$295-$395	Mac + , SE, II, MOS	Mac comp.	Yes/$10	500/ 3 years	No	Yes/1 year free
Bricker-Evans	Tangibility	Analyzes lead programs before and after implementation; marketing communications.	640K	$495	IBM PC and comp., DOS	No	No	20 + / 1.5 years	No	Yes/free, unlimited

VENDOR	PACKAGE	DESCRIPTION	MEM.	PRICE	HARDWARE/SYS.	NETWK.	DEMO/$	#/AGE	TRAIN.	PHONE
CATT Systems	PROMOTRAK†	Lead and manager tracking system for present and past accounts, reports, follow-ups, activities, expenses; direct mail.	†	$1,500-$6,000	†	UNIX, IBM	No	45/5 years	Yes/on-site, included	Yes/free, unlimited
Commercial Micro	Sales Busters†	Client and prospect tracking, tickler, calendar, built-in backup, import/export capabilities, scripts, reports.	640K (hard disk)	$395-$795	IBM PC and comp., DOS 3.3 +	LAN	Yes/$15	500 + / 7 years	No	Yes/free, unlimited
Computer Innovations	Branch-Out†	Sales support system for distributors: pricing, bidding negotiations, comparative tracking.	512K	$1,995	IBM PC and comp., DOS, Unix	Novell	No	New	Yes/on-site, fees	Yes/$60 per hour, or contract
Computer Innovations	S-DOT†	Sales tracking, lead control profiles, forecasting, marketing research and analysis.	256K	$500-$3,500	IBM PC-AT, 386 and comp., DOS, Unix	Novell	No	25/4 years	Yes/on-site, fees	Yes/$60 per hour, or contract
Computer Masters	Client Master	Database marketing tool, mini word processor, auto-dialer, client tracking.	256K	$199	IBM PC and comp., MS DOS	All major	Yes/$10	50,000/ 2.5 years	No/ manual	Yes/free, unlimited
Datamatics Management Services	Professional Marketing System†	60 different modules for market response tracking, lead tracking, customer service analysis.	400K	$2,195	IBM PC and comp.; MS DOS 3.1 +	Novell, PT, ARC, Ethernet	No/free 30-day trial	30/5 years	Yes/on-site, fees	Yes/90 days free, then contract
EIGHTY/20 Software	EIGHTY/20 Advanced†	Client tracking and sorting; word processor for letters, mass mailings; telemarketing scripts; expense reporting.	640K	$495-$1,495	IBM PC and comp.; MS DOS 2.0 +	All major	Yes/$10	1,000/ 2 years	Yes/on-site, fees	Yes/free, unlimited
EMIS Software	EMIS II†	Lead tracking and account management; custom letters, mail merge, unlimited database, spreadsheets.	512K	$1,995 and up	IBM PC and comp.; DOS 3.1 +	Novell, 3Com, PCNet, Banyan	Yes/free; evaluation/$50	1,500 + / 6 years	Yes/on-site, fees	Yes/contract
Esprit Software Technology	SELLSTAR!-PM†	Sales productivity for prospect management, lead tracking, telemarketing.	512K	$195	IBM PCs and comp.; DOS 2.1 +	No	No	New	No	Yes/90 days free
ETS Systems	Call Focus	Tracks sales calls with follow-up tickler.	640K	$3,500	IBM PC-XT and comp., DOS 2.0 +	No	No	20/2 years	Yes/on-site, fees	Yes/60 days free, then contract
1st Desk Systems	1stFILE†	Esp. for sales teams and marketers in lead tracking, follow-up, order entry; mailing labels and lists.	512K	$95	Mac	All major	No	25,000/ 5 years	No	Yes/free, unlimited
1st Desk Systems	1stTEAM†	Lead tracking, follow-up, order entry for sales teams.	512K	$495	Mac	All major	No	1,000/ 4 years	No	Yes/free, unlimited
Free World Marketing	ProMotion IQ†	Query and reporting module for promotion; produces reports, analyzes data, creates graphs, exports data to ASCII and Lotus files.	256K	$300	IBM PC; DOS 2.0 +	All major	Yes/$25	250/ 3 years	Yes/on-site, fees	Yes/90 days free, then contract
GoldData Computer Services	Sales Prospect Tracking System	Lead tracking and telemarketing with mail merge, letter, label, back-end reporting capabilities.	192K	$124.95	IBM PC and comp.; MS DOS 2.0 +	Novell	Yes/$10	$400/ 4 years	Yes/on-site, fees	Yes/free, unlimited
High Caliber Systems	peopleBASE†	Sales management system analyzes by lead source, salesperson; phone/mail follow-up of customers and prospects.	640K	$129-$1,000	IBM PC-XT, -AT and comp.; MS-, PC DOS	All major	Yes/$10	4,000/ 3 years	Yes/on-site, fees	Yes/free, unlimited
Hill Street Publ.	LeadChaser†	Comprehensive package tracks sales leads.	512K	$49.95	IBM PC and comp.; MS DOS 2.0 +	No	Yes/$5	20/2 years	No	Yes/free
HMS Computer Co.	Prospect Tracking System†	Track prospects through buying cycle; generates mailings and demographic reports.	640K; 1MB (MAC)	$395-$595	IBM PC and comp., Mac + ; DOS	All major	Yes/$29	150/ 2 years	Yes/on-site, fees	Yes/free, unlimited
Innovative microSystems	MarketExpert	Sorts, segments, analyzes customers and prospects for targeted direct mail or telemarketing lists.	640K	$1,500	IBM PC-XT, -AT, PS/2; MS-, PC DOS	Token ring, PC network	Yes/free	5/1 year	Yes/included	Yes/free, unlimited
Inter Active Micro	The Front Office†	Marketing and sales system for prospect and lead tracking, telemarketing, call reporting, job and commission cost tracking, performance evaluation.	640K	$198-$295	IBM PC-XT, -AT and comp.; DOS 2.1 +	All major	Yes/$15	50 + / 5 years	Yes/off-site, fees	Yes/1 year free, then contract
JKL Marketing	Sales/Marketing Solution System†	Integrated sales/marketing databases; prospect management, telemarketing, sales call reporting, product registration, market research.	512K	$895 & up	IBM PC & comp., DOS	Unix/Xenix	Yes/free	500/ 5 years	Yes/off-site, fee	Yes/free, unlimited
LEADtrack Services	LEADtrack†	Sales, marketing, lead tracking, inquiry fulfillment package for all industries and levels of salesperson.	640K	$2,250	IBM PC and comp.; MS-, PC DOS	Novell	Yes/$10	200/ 5 years	Yes/on-site, fees	Yes/60 days free, then contract
Logic Design Corp.	ELECTRONIC Client Management System†	Keeps track of sales leads; telemarketing, direct mail, follow-up, auto-dialer, mass mailings.	256K	$195	IBM PC and comp.; DOS 3.0 +	Novell	Yes/$10	1,000/ 5 years	Yes/on-site, fee	Yes/90 days, free
M&T Publ.	Time and Task Management†	Tracks clients, follow-up/pending dates; organizes time, hours, activities, budgets.	256K	$49.95	IBM PC and comp.; MS-, PC DOS	No	No	1,000-2,000/ 3 years	No	Yes/free, unlimited

VENDOR	PACKAGE	DESCRIPTION	MEM.	PRICE	HARDWARE/SYS.	NETWK.	DEMO/$	#/AGE	TRAIN.	PHONE
Market Power	THE SALES MANAGER S.62†	Customer/prospect tracking, tickler files, reports, appointment schedule, sales transaction analysis, expense tracking, to-do list, word processor.	320K	$795-$1,995	IBM PC and comp.; DOS 2.0 +	LAN, Novell, 3Com	Yes/free	3,000 + / 6 years	Yes/on-site, fees	Yes/con-tract
MICOR Systems	ProTrakAR System†	Tracks and categorizes calls and correspondence to clients; prints envelopes, letters, labels, lists.	1MB	$395	Mac + 5.0 +	All major	Yes/$15	New	No	Yes/3 months free
MZ Group	Fortune 500 Prospector†	Prospecting database with current information on top industrial and service companies and executives in U.S.; can rank, segment, analyze; print reports, mailing labels; auto-matic tickler; graphics.	512K	$299	IBM PC-XT, -AT, PS/2 or 100% comp.; DOS 2.0 +	All major	Yes/free	New	No	Yes/free, unlimited
MZ Group	Instant Prospects Los Angeles & Chronicle 100†	Two packages with extensive in-formation on top Los Angeles and San Francisco companies including key executive contact, sales, SIC codes, telephone numbers.	512K (hard disk)	$299	IBM PC-XT, -AT, PS/2 or 100% comp.; DOS 2.0 +	All major	Yes/free	New	No	Yes/free, unlimited
Nelson Business Systems	Client Tracking System†	Organizes/tracks clients and pros-pects, features individual notepads for each record/letter file, labels, internal dial.	512K	$495-$1,095	IBM PC and comp.; MS-, PC DOS	Novell	Yes/$10	24/1 year	No	Yes/30 days free, then contract
Pace Computer	SalesBaase/PC	Sales management package with calendar and mail merge, tracks sales leads, analyzes data, forecasts.	640K	$495	IBM PC-AT and comp.; MS DOS	No	Yes/$10	300/ 4 years	No	Yes/free, unlimited
Planning Works	Sales Manager System†	Forms for lead tracking, record-keeping, reports, market analysis; created by sales managers.	256K	$495	IBM PC and comp., laptops; MS DOS 2.0 +	All major	Yes/$15	150 + / 6 years	Yes/on-site, fees	Yes/con-tract
Prism Systems	LEADMARK†	Customized lead tracking per unique requirements; access to pro-duct/competition summaries.	512K (hard disk)	$950-$3,995	IBM PC-AT, -XT, PS/2 and comp.; MS-, PC DOS 2.0 +	All major	Yes/free	New	Yes/on-site, fees	Yes/fees
Sales Executive	Sales Executive	Package for lead tracking, telemar-keting, client managment, sales productivity, direct mail.	512K	$395-$1,595	IBM PC and comp.; MS-, PC DOS	All major	Yes/free	4,000/ 3 years	Yes/on-off-site, fees	Yes/free, unlimited
Sales Productivity Group	Sales Producer	Prospect tracking, sales information reporting system includes profiling, follow-up, sales order entry.	384K	$495-$695	IBM PC and comp.; MS DOS	All major	Yes/$20	450/ 3 years	Yes/on-off-site, fees	Yes/90 days free
Softworks	MARKIS	Lead qualification, tracking, prompting system.	256K	$389	IBM PC-XT, -AT, and comp.; DOS 2.1 +	All major	Yes/free	1,000 + /4 years	No/ manual	Yes/free, unlimited
Stanford Business Systems	STAT: Sales Tracking and Analysis Tool†	For salespeople/managers: lead tracking, sales productivity/ analysis.	1MB	$795-$895	Mac	Mac comp.	Yes/$35	New	Yes/on-site fee	Yes/30 days free
SUCCESSware	Lead Prioritizer†	Helps newer sales personnel get up to higher level; aids others in select-ing/prioritizing/evaluating leads.	256K	$109	IBM PC-XT, -AT, PS/2 and comp.; MS-, PC DOS 2.1 +	All major	No/30-day guarantee	2,500/ 1 year	No	Yes/free, unlimited
Sysmark Information Systems	The Professional Sales Manager†	Package determines purchasing trends, evaluates advertising, auto-mates direct mail, qualifies/assigns lead, supports telemarketing, evalu-ates sales productivity/potential (up to 1,000 users).	640K	$6,995 and up	IBM PC and comp.; PICK	No	Yes/free	5 + /1 year	Yes/on-site, fee	Yes/free, unlimited
Target Microsystems	BULLSEYE†	Automates inquiry processing, makes follow-up assignments, mea-sures ad paybacks, tracks each salesperson's effectiveness.	640K (hard disk)	$495-$1,995	IBM PC-XT and comp.; DOS 2.0 +	Novell	Yes/free	20 + / 1.5 years	Yes/on-off-site, fees	Yes/free, unlimited
Technical Sales & Marketing Assoc.	Sales Source Manager†	Sales lead tracking/management program.	512K	$495	IBM PC-XT, -AT, PS/2 or comp;. PC-, MS DOS	No	Yes/free	50 + / 1 year	Yes/on-off-site, fees	Yes/free, unlimited
Tronsoft	Capital Ideas†	Complete detailed databases of 200 venture capital companies in U.S. and Canada; generates quali-fied leads.	512K	$295	Mac	No	No	New	No	Yes/free, unlimited
Tronsoft	Franchise Finder†	Complete detailed databases of franchise companies in U.S. and Canada; qualifies leads by industry and other criteria.	512K	$99	Mac	No	No	New	No	Yes/free, unlimited
XYCAD Group	FollowUp†	Generic sales package designed to track clients; handles sales-related correspondence and reports.	384K	$249.95-$895.95	IBM PC-AT, -XT and comp.; MS-, PC DOS 2.0 +	Novell	Yes/$5 & up	5,000/ 4 years	No/tuto-rial	Yes/one-year free

MAPPING-GEOGRAPHIC

VENDOR	PACKAGE	DESCRIPTION	MEM.	PRICE	HARDWARE/SYS.	NETWK.	DEMO/$	#/AGE	TRAIN.	PHONE
Geographic Data Technology	GeoSpread-Sheet	Spreadsheet integrated with com-puterized map for spatial analysis; county, zip code, census track in-formation for site analysis, thematic mapping, territory planning.	640K (hard disk)	$595 -2,490	IBM PC and comp.; DOS 3.1 +	No	Yes/$35	New	Yes/on-off-site, fees	Yes/90 days free, then contract
Geographic Data Technology	MatchMaker/ GDT†	Address-to-coordinate matching system gives geographic location (longitude and latitude) for analysis and territory assignment.	640K (hard disk)	$10,000	IBM PC and comp.; DOS 3.1 +	No	No	15/3 years	Yes/on-off-site, fees	Yes/1 year free, then contract

VENDOR	PACKAGE	DESCRIPTION	MEM.	PRICE	HARDWARE/SYS.	NETWK.	DEMO/$	#/AGE	TRAIN.	PHONE
Geosoft Corp.	MapBuilder†	Thematic maps display customer locations, sales territories, other demographic information.	512K	$250-$400	IBM PC and comp.; DOS 2.1 +	No	Yes/free	100 +/ 4 years	No	Yes/90 days free
GEOVISION	GEOSystem: Windows on the World and GEODisk†	User can customize to own geographic and desktop map systems; can display and manipulate large quantities of vector geographic data.	640K	$595	IBM PC and comp.; MS-, PC DOS 3.2 +	All major	Yes/free for requests on letterhead	1,200 +/ 2 years	Yes/contract	Yes/contract
GEOVISION	TIGERTOOLS	Uses U.S. Census Bureau Tiger (topologically integrated geographic encoding and referencing) files to process, classify, catalogue data.	1MB	$495 - $1,495	IBM PC-XT, -AT, PS/2 and comp.; MS-, PC DOS	All major	No	New	Yes/contract	Yes/contract
Map Information Services	MapInfo†	Mapping system analysis, displays, maps, and geographic data; performs dBase searches, address matches; shades and colors boundries; other add-ons available.	640K	$750	IBM PC-XT, -AT, and comp.; PC-, MS DOS 3.0 +	Novell	Yes/free	2,000 +/ 3 years	Yes/onsite, fees; offsite free	Yes/90 days free, then contract
National Planning Data	MapAnalyst†	Package analyzes and presents demographic data, U.S.G.S. roads and highways.	512K (hard disk)	$495	IBM PCs and comp.; MS-, PC DOS 3.1 +	All major	No	550 +/ 6 years	Yes/HQ only, free	Yes/free, unlimited
Odesta Corp.	GeoQuery	Automatically creates maps for presentation/analysis of address-based data; used for territory/site planning, direct mail, account management, sales analysis, zip code tracking, presentations.	1MB	$349	Mac +, SE, II	No	Yes/$5	3,000/ 1.5 years	No	Yes/free, unlimited
Select Micro Systems	MapMaker 4.0	Business-mapping packager for thematic mapping creates map with legends for geographic analysis.	512K	$395	Mac 512K +, SE, II	Mac comp.	Yes/$10	4,000 +/ 3 years	No	Yes/free, unlimited
Street Map Software	StreetSmart†	Package designed to help plan route direction; with or without TIGER maps.	640K	$349	IBM PC and comp.; MS DOS	Novell	Yes/free	100 +/ 2 years	No	Yes/free, unlimited

MARKET ANALYSIS

VENDOR	PACKAGE	DESCRIPTION	MEM.	PRICE	HARDWARE/SYS.	NETWK.	DEMO/$	#/AGE	TRAIN.	PHONE
Application Consulting Group	ACG Window†	Marketing and sales analysis of internal and syndicated data, reporting, graphics and statistics, esp., for consumer packaged goods co.s.	640K	$15,000-$25,000	IBM PC, PS/2 and comp., DOS	LAN, Novell	No	20/2 years	Yes/included	Yes/contract
Business Research & Surveys	TABULIZER†	Survey analysis, cross-tabulation, reporting, data entry and generation.	256K	$495	IBM PC and comp., MS DOS	All major	Yes/$20	400 +/ 6 years	Yes/onsite, fees	Yes/free, unlimited
CACI	Market America†	Demographic information available geographically; analyzes trade areas, sites, product mix; database.	640K	$57,000	IBM PC-AT, 286, 386, DOS 3.30	No	Yes/free	75/ 1.5 years	Yes/2 days onsite, free	Yes/free, unlimited
Claritas Corp.	COMPASS†	Market analysis and mapping; integrates clients and third-party database.	640K	$15,000	IBM PC and comp., DOS 3.0 +	No	Yes/free	200-300/ 2 years	Yes/onsite, offsite, free	Yes/free, unlimited
Donnelly Marketing Information Services	CONQUEST	Marketing system with access to demographic data on consumer businesses.	640K	$9,000	IBM PC, PS/2 and comp.; DOS 2.1 +	No	No	200 +/ 3 years	Yes/offsite, free; onsite, fees	Yes/free, unlimited
Donnelly Marketing Information Services	CONQUEST BusinessLINE	Marketing system with access to demographic and geographic database of over 7 million businesses.	640K	$24,000	IBM PC, PS/2 and comp.; DOS 2.1 +	No	No	New	Yes/offsite, free; onsite, fees	Yes/free, unlimited
France Int'l.	GoldSpread	Integrated package with spreadsheets, data management, graphics; compatible with Lotus 1-2-3.	512K	$39.95	IBM PC, Mac +, SE, II and comp.; DOS	No	Yes/$5	10,000 +/ 2 years	No	Yes/free, unlimited
France Int'l.	GoldSpread Statistical	Lotus 1-2-3 compatible spreadsheet with full range of statistical commands and functions.	512K	$79.95	IBM PC, Mac +, SE, II and comp.; DOS	No	Yes/$5	10,000 +/ 1 year	No	Yes/free, unlimited
Information Resources/Javelin Products Group	EXPRESS Marketing Management System†	Product, brand, marketing, performance, sales analysis.	640K	$50,000-$150,000	IBM PC and comp.; MS DOS	All major	Yes/free	50/2 years	Yes/included	Yes/free, unlimited
Information Resources/Javelin Products Group	Javelin PLUS†	Modeling and analysis program combines spreadsheet and database; creates reports and graphs.	512K	$395-$995	IBM PC and comp.; MS DOS 2.1 +	3Com, 3Plus, Novell Advanced, Token Ring	Yes/free	50,000/ 4 years	Yes/onsite, offsite, fees	Yes/free, unlimited
Lotus Development Corp.	Lotus 1-2-3 Release 2.2†	Analytical spreadsheet, customization of fields, publishing capabilities.	320K	$495	IBM PC or Lotus comp.; DOS 2.0 +	All major	Yes/free	New	Yes/offsite, fees	Yes/free, unlimited
Management Science Assoc.	EASY†	Cross-tabulation program analyzes survey results.	512K	$2,500 & up	IBM PC and comp.; DOS 3.0 +	No	No	50/2 years	Yes/onsite for installation, free	Yes/free, unlimited
Marketing Data Research	Master Tab†	Tabulates survey questionnaire data into finished tables; displays most-frequently-used statistical measures.	128K	$250	IBM PC-XT, -AT and comp.; MS-, PC DOS 2.0 +	No	Yes/$40	600 +/ 5 years	No/ manual	Yes/free, unlimited

VENDOR	PACKAGE	DESCRIPTION	MEM.	PRICE	HARDWARE/SYS.	NETWK.	DEMO/$	#/AGE	TRAIN.	PHONE
MaxThink	MaxThink†	Outlines commands for analytical, managerial, creative thinking; graphs the results.	300K	$89	IBM PC and comp.; DOS 2.0 +	Novell	Yes/$6	20,000/ 5 years	No/cassette	Yes/free, unlimited
MediaMark Research	MEMRI†	Series of programs for analyzing survey data, cross-tabulation, and rating.	640K	$10,000	IBM PC and comp.; DOS	No	No	200/ 3.5 years	Yes/on-off-site, free	Yes/free, unlimited
Microtab	Microtab Cross Tabulation Software†	Questionnaire cross-tabulation package; summarizing reports and statistics; handles unlimited numbers of cases and variables.	256K (hard disk)	$495	IBM PC and comp.; DOS 2.0 +	All major	Yes/$50	800 + / 7 years	Yes/on-site, fees	Yes/free, unlimited
Minitab	MINITAB Statistical Software†	Descriptive statistics, regression, ANOVA, discriminant analysis, principal component analysis, tabulation, distribution, time series analysis; interface with Lotus.	640K (hard disk)	$695	IBM PC and comp.; DOS 2.0 +	All major	No/free trial	20,000 + / 17 years	Yes/on-site, fees	Yes/free, unlimited
National Demographics and Lifestyles	OASYS (Opportunity Analysis System)†	Marketing decision support system with detailed demographic/lifestyle profiles of geographic areas by zip code; reporting and mapping.	640K	$5,000-$35,000	IBM PC and comp.; DOS 3.0 +	No	Yes/$25	15/1 year	Yes/off-site, free	Yes/free, unlimited
Oxicron Systems	Oxiscan	Marketing system for analyzing single-source scanner data or integrated databases.	512K	$995	IBM PC-XT, -AT, PS/2 and comp.; DOS 2.1 +	No	Yes/$75	New	Yes/on-site, fees	Yes/30 days free
Oxicron Systems	Oxistas	Analyze single-source scanner data.	512K	$395	IBM PC-XT, -AT, PS/2 and comp.; DOS 2.1 +	No	Yes/$75	New	Yes/on-site, fees	Yes/30 days free
Pilot Executive Software	Time Intelligence	Data management/analysis for sales/marketing information; time series manipulation, integrated modeling, multidimensional consolidation, color graphs, reports.	640K	$100,000	IBM PC, 286, 386; MS DOS	3Com, Novell	No	8/1 year	Yes/on-site free	Yes/free, unlimited
P-STAT	P-STAT	Statistical analysis, survey displays, data/file management, report writing, data display.	640K	$695	IBM PC-AT, -XT, PS/2 and comp.; DOS	PC NET	Yes/$125	1,000/ 4 years	No/ manual	Yes/contract
Quest Management Systems	INCITE†	Market/sales planning tool uses competitive information to support operating, tactical, strategic decisions; database with text, image, numeric data.	640K (2MB hard disk)	$10,000/ site	IBM PC-AT, PS/2 model 50 or better; DOS	LAN	Yes/$25	5/1 year	Yes/included	Yes/contract
SAMI Div. of Arbitron	Decision Master†	Customized SAMI information, competitive market data, manipulation, presentation.	640K	$25,000-$50,000	IBM PC and comp; DOS	All major	No	175-200/ 2.5 years	Yes/included	Yes/included
SAMI Div. of Arbitron	Supermarket Solutions†	Demographic database of 28,600 grocery stores analyzing demographic factors and individual store facts.	20MB	$8-$15/store	IBM PC and comp; DOS	All major	No	35 + / 2 years	Yes/included	Yes/included
SDG Decision Systems	Sensitivity	Automatically performs sensitivity analysis on spreadsheet variables.	640K	$175	IBM PC, Mac II, and comp.; DOS	No	No	1,000 + / 4 years	No	Yes/free, unlimited
Select Micro Systems	ExStatix†	General-purpose statistics with graphics program including full descriptive regression analysis.	512K	$349	Mac 512K +, SE, II	Mac comp.	Yes/$10	1,000 + / 1 year	No	Yes/free, unlimited

MARKETING MANAGEMENT

VENDOR	PACKAGE	DESCRIPTION	MEM.	PRICE	HARDWARE/SYS.	NETWK.	DEMO/$	#/AGE	TRAIN.	PHONE
Interactive Systems	OmniTrac†	Maintenance program for salespeople and managers generating call lists, management reports, mailing lists; does multi-product forecasting and tracking.	640K (hard disk)	$1,200	IBM PC-AT, -XT and comp.; DOS 3.0	PCNET, Novell	Yes/free	180/ 5 years	Yes/on-site, fees	Yes/fees
Management Science Assoc.	Profile Marketing Work-station†	Customer/prospect information file integrates mapping, cross-tabulation, household selection, word processing, spreadsheets, graphics.	640K	$10,000-$20,000	IBM PC and comp.; DOS 3.2 +	Novell	Yes/free	50/1 year	Yes/included	Yes/free, unlimited
Maryland Interactive Technologies	The Business Disc	Sophisticated simulation leads user through the steps of planning and managing a small business.	512K (laser disk)	$2,995	IBM PC and comp.; MS DOS	No	No/2-week loan	150/ 2 years	No	Yes/free, unlimited
Realty Systems	REAL/Easy Analysis	Sales/marketing management tool; esp. for real estate industry.	640K (hard disk)	$795	IBM PC and comp.; DOS 3.1 +	Novell	Yes/$39.50	1,200/ 11 years	Yes/on-site, fees	Yes/30 days free
The Sachs Group	THE MARKET PLANNING†	Customized integration of functions: forecasting, database management, cross-tabulation, mapping, graphing, communications; esp. for medical sales reps/managers.	640K (20MB hard disk)	$30,000	IBM PC-AT, PS/2 and comp.; DOS 3.0 +	All major	No	175 + / 3 years	Yes/included	Yes/free, unlimited
SUCCESSware	Executives Market Decision Kit†	Helps managers target markets, price products, select ad programs, prioritize sales leads.	256K	$299	IBM PC-XT, -AT, PS/2 and comp.; MS-, PC DOS 2.1 +	All major	No/30-day guarantee	300 + / 1 year	No	Yes/free, unlimited
Technology Development	SalesMaker	Marketing management, sales management, automatic fulfillment, telephone sales, planning, reporting	640K	$3,995	IBM PC and comp.; MS-, PC DOS 3.0 +	All major	No	110/1 year	Yes/on-site included	Yes/1 year free, then contract

VENDOR	PACKAGE	DESCRIPTION	MEM.	PRICE	HARDWARE/SYS.	NETWK.	DEMO/$	#/AGE	TRAIN.	PHONE
MEETING PLANNING										
ACEware Systems	Conference Coordinator	Registration management providing invoices, confirmations, name tags, mailing labels, reports, financial statistics.	640K	$995 - $1,895	IBM PC-AT and comp., MS DOS	All major	Yes/$25	50/5 years	Yes/off-site, one day free	Yes/one year, free
Administrative Headquarters	Trip Mate†	Simultaneously tracks and registers up to 96 groups of people in 9 cities by hotel, room, arrival, and departure details.	640K	$1,995-$3,495 & up	IBM PC and comp.; DOS	All major	Yes/$15	14/1 year	Yes/on-off-site, fees	Yes/60 days free, then contract
Applied Econometrics	MOST†	Automates convention sales and marketing, call tracer, tickler, account data, call reports, recommended for IACVB members.	640K	$6,000 (IACVB members)	IBM PC; DOS	LAN	Yes/free	10/1 year	Yes/on-off-site, fees	Yes/fees
The Association Store	Lil Badger System†	Badge making, housing reports, airline manifest, conference bookkeeping, preregistration, custom fonts and logos.	256K	$295-$595	IBM PC and comp.; DOS	LAN	Yes/$25	50 + / 4 years	No/on screen	Yes/free, unlimited
Aztech	Central*Ware†	Customized demographic database, labels, rosters,	640K	$695	IBM PC and comp.; DOS	Novell	Yes/free	50/6 years	Yes/included	Yes/free, unlimited
Aztech	Conference*Ware†	Unlimited tracking of conferences, events, fees, participants, payment history, hotels; produces badges, tickets, reports, bills.	640K	$1,995 & up	IBM PC and comp.; DOS	Novell, ICHost	Yes/free	25/3 years	Yes/included	Yes/free, unlimited
Aztech	Note*Ware†	Equivalent to Post-it notes; esp. for meeting planners.	640K	$695	IBM PC and comp.; DOS	Novell	Yes/free	15/ 1.5 years	Yes/included	Yes/free, unlimited
CME Assoc.	Complete Meeting Manager	Tracks attendees; prints name tags, diplomas, mailing lists.	512K	$2,995	IBM PC and comp.; DOS 2.0 +	IBM PCLAN, Novell	No/evaluation, $200	30 + / 2 years	No/ manual	Yes/1 year free
Computer Solutions & Development	ConEx Conference Express†	Financial details of registration: payments, sessions per conference.	540K	$1,995-$4,995	IBM PC and comp.; DOS	Novell	Yes/free	36/ 2.5 years	Yes/on-site fees	Yes/contract
Computer Solutions & Development	MemEx Member Express†	Organizes accounting, billing, mailing labels, form letters.	540K	$1,995-$4,995	IBM PC and comp.; DOS	Novell	Yes/free	48/3 years	Yes/on-site fees	Yes/contract
Convention Central	DecoWest†	Maintains data for convention attendance: hotels, air/ground arrangements, events; detailed reports for suppliers.	512K	$3,500	IBM PC and comp.; DOS	No	No	New	No/ manual	Yes/3 months free
Dynamic Software Systems	DSS/Exact	Prospective client and lead tracking; convention management, registration, speakers' bureau database; integrated accounting applications.	1MB	$1,000-$2,500	Wang VS under PACE	LAN	No	New	Yes/on-site, free	Yes/free, unlimited
ETS Center	Name Processor†	Database for handling names/addresses for mailing lists and meetings; prints labels, badges, logos.	256K	$149	IBM PC and comp.; DOS	Novell	Yes/free	2,000 + / 5 years	No	Yes/free, unlimited
G.G. Tauber	Badgepro	Makes badges, customizes logos; three fonts, six points sizes.	640K (½MB printer)	$395	IBM PC and comp.; DOS	All major	Yes/free 10-day trial	36/1 year	No	Yes/free, unlimited
International Conference Management	Event Manager Series†	Registers individuals for unlimited events and sessions; tracks attendees, speakers, exhibitors, vendors, hotels, rates, room types, and reservations; accounting.	640K (hard disk)	$2,995-$5,995	IBM PC and comp.; DOS	Token Ring, Novell, 3Com	Yes/free	5/1 year	Yes/on-off-site, fees	Yes/free until up and running
K/M Data Systems	K/M Registrar + †	Registers participants' activities, fees, and show income; produces 15 reports and bills; modules for academic applications.	520K	$995-$1,995	IBM PC and comp.; MS DOS	Novell; IBM Token Ring	Yes/$14.95	50 + / 5 years	Yes/on-site, fee	Yes/free
Marketech Int'l.	MSSP: Meeting Site Select Program	Optimizes expenses in selecting travel arrangements, meeting sites, food, lodging.	132K	$265	IBM PC and comp.; MS DOS	No	Yes/$10	300/ 2 years	No	No
Mastr.Soft	Conference Auto-Ministrator†	Tracks conferences, hotels, attendees, speakers; billing.	640K	$2,495	IBM PC and comp.; MS DOS	No	Yes/$55	50/6 years	Yes/on-off-site, fees	Yes/contract
Peopleware	ListPro	Mailing list and professional credit tracking system for past registrants; transcripts, direct mail labels, letters.	512K (hard disk)	$745-$1,495	IBM PC and comp.	All major	Yes/$50	300/ 8 years	Yes/on-off-site fees	Yes/contract
Peopleware	MeetingPro II†	Integrated registration management system for seminars and conferences; report generator, lists, letters, typeset quality badges.	512K (hard disk)	$995-$3,995	IBM PC and comp.	All major	Yes/$50	400/ 8 years	Yes/on-off-site fees	Yes/contract
Peopleware	NameTags Plus†	On-site and premeeting system produces typeset quality badges, certificates, table tents; exports to word-processing systems for personalized confirmations.	512K (hard disk)	$245-$445	IBM PC and comp.	All major	Yes/$50	125/1 year	No	Yes/contract
Peopleware	Speaker Scheduling System†	Integrated speaker/instructor/event scheduling system; database with speaker bios, fees, evaluations.	512K (hard disk)	$745-$1,495	IBM PC and comp.	All major	Yes/$50	New	No/tutorial	Yes/contract
Phoenix Solutions	MeetingTrak†	Meeting registration tracks registrants, sessions, events; creates name tags; mail-merge; financial reports.	480K	$1,995/ user	IBM PC and comp.	Novell, 3Com, Ethernet, Token Ring	Yes/free	700/ 5 years	Yes/on-off-site, fees	Yes/free, unlimited

VENDOR	PACKAGE	DESCRIPTION	MEM.	PRICE	HARDWARE/SYS.	NETWK.	DEMO/$	#/AGE	TRAIN.	PHONE
System Dynamics	CRIS: Conference Registration Information System†	For small and medium-sized conferences (up to 5,000 participants); program generates participant reports, tracks fees, breaks participation into categories.	256K	$700	IBM PC and comp.; MS-, PC DOS 2.0 +	No	No/30-day guarantee	180 + / 5 years	No/tutorial	Yes/free, unlimited
Topitzes and Assoc.	E-2/Tag	Prints name tags, certificates, table tents, overheads for presentations.	128K	$99	Mac IIe, IIc and comp.	No	Yes/free for 20 days	150/ 3 years	Yes/ phone only	Yes/½ hour free
Topitzes and Assoc.	PC/Nametag I, II & III†	Name-tag and database registration software; stores/sorts on 18 fields; generates typeset quality name tags and certificates; mailing labels, reports, import/export.	256K-384K	$299-$599	IBM PC, Mac and comp.; DOS	No	Yes/free for 20 days	1,670 + / 4 years	Yes/ phone only	Yes/½ hour free
Travaco Management Systems	Meeting Manager Plus	Consolidates/tracks: arrivals/departures, accommodations, transportation, food/beverages, programs, recreation/entertainment; on-site computer reports, electronic notepads, and spreadsheet capabilities.	640K	$5,995	IBM PC and comp.; DOS 3.0 +	All major	No	23/2 years	Yes/off-site, included	Yes/included

PERSONAL MANAGEMENT

VENDOR	PACKAGE	DESCRIPTION	MEM.	PRICE	HARDWARE/SYS.	NETWK.	DEMO/$	#/AGE	TRAIN.	PHONE
Abend Assoc.	CallBack	System for salespeople/managers to track phone calls and action taken.	2MB	$695 & up	Oracle RDBMS	All major	No/$59 trial copy	75/1 year	Yes/on-site, fee	Yes/30 days free
Brightbill-Roberts	HyperPAD	Daily, monthly, yearly calendar; phone/addresses, expense tracking, graphics.	384K	$99.95	IBM PC and comp., DOS 2.1 +	All major	Yes/free	New	Yes/off-site	Yes/free, unlimited
Britz Publishing	Eight-in-One	Desktop organizer, outlines for writing, word processor, spreadsheets, database, graphics.	384K	$59	IBM PC and comp., DOS 2.1 +	No	Yes/$59	150,000/ 2 years	No/ manual	Yes/free, unlimited
Campbell Services	Reminder Plus	Time and management program, follow-up, mini database.	340K	$239	IBM PC and comp., MS DOS 2.1	No	Yes/free	5,000 + / 2 years	Yes/ phone only	Yes/free, unlimited
Campbell Services	Reminder System	Time and management program, follow-up.	256K	$99	IBM PC and comp., MS DOS 2.1 +	No	No/evaluation copy	12,000/ 5 years	Yes/ phone only	Yes/free, unlimited
DAC Software	Rolodex Live†	Memory resident personal information manager.	256K	$49.95	IBM PC and comp.; DOS 2.1 +	No	No	10,000/ 1 year	No	Yes/contract
DayFlo Software	DayFlo TRACKER	Database for text and data, modifiable forms and reports; esp. for managers.	384K	$195	IBM PC or comp.; DOS 2.1 +	All major	Yes/$20	10,000 + / 3 years	Yes/on-site, fees	Yes/unlimited
Lawco	Decision Aids	To-do list, calendar, criteria rank, alternative routines.	128K	$99.95	IBM PC and comp.; DOS 2.0 +	No	No	1,500/ 3 years	No	Yes/30 days free
People and Contacts	People and Contacts	Maintains personal calendar of contacts/schedules, telemarketing support with auto-dial, direct mail support with labels, prints rolodex cards.	384K	$197	IBM PC and comp.; DOS 2.0 +	No	No	1,000/ 3 years	No	Yes/ 1 year free
Performer Systems	PERFORMER	Integrated program for salespeople organizes/tracks time schedules, contacts, client information.	640K	$149.95-$295	IBM PC and 100% comp.	All major	Yes/$15	New	Yes/on-site, fees	Yes/30 days free
Polaris Software	Polaris PackRat	Personal information manager organizes appointments, calendar, data; telephone dialer.	512K (hard disk)	$395-$695	IBM PC, PS/2 and comp.; MS DOS, OS/2	All major	Yes/$15	3,000 + / 1 year	Yes/free tutorial or on-site, fees	Yes/free, unlimited
Popular Programs	Pop-Up DeskSet Plus	System combines two word processors, address book, schedules, financial calculator, alarm clock, phone dialer.	20K	$69.95-$129.95	IBM PC-XT, -AT and comp.; DOS 2.0 +	Novell	No	400,000/ 7 years	No	Yes/free, unlimited
Popular Programs	Pop-Up Today	Daily, weekly, monthly to-do lists; automatically sorts any field.	40K	$39.95	IBM PC-XT, -AT and comp.; DOS 2.0 +	Novell	No	20,000/ 3 years	No	Yes/free, unlimited
Spinnaker Software	Résumé Kit	Formats résumés, produces fonts for typeset look; database for contacts, calendar, full word processer.	384K	$49.95	IBM PC and comp.; DOS 2.1 +	No	Yes/free	40,000 + / 1 year	No	Yes/free, unlimited
Star Software Systems	Venture — The Entrepreneur Handbook†	Database and word processor with business plans/documents, spreadsheets, double entry general ledger, graphics.	512K	$349	IBM PC and comp.; MS DOS 3.0 +	All major	No/video $19.95	New	Yes/on-site, fees	Yes/30 days free, contract
Symmetry Corp.	Acta	Desk accessory: outlines, plans, organizes, sorts.	512K	$129	Mac +; Mac 6.0 +	All major	Yes/$5	30,000 + / 3 years	No/ manual	Yes/free, unlimited
Valor Software	Info-XL†	Combines/links/stores unlimited amounts of personal/business data; client management, research, letters.	384K	$295	IBM PC and comp.; DOS 2.0 +	No	Yes/free	5,000 + / 2 years	Yes/on-site, off-site, fees	Yes/free, unlimited

VENDOR	PACKAGE	DESCRIPTION	MEM.	PRICE	HARDWARE/SYS.	NETWK.	DEMO/$	#/AGE	TRAIN.	PHONE

PRODUCT MANAGEMENT

VENDOR	PACKAGE	DESCRIPTION	MEM.	PRICE	HARDWARE/SYS.	NETWK.	DEMO/$	#/AGE	TRAIN.	PHONE
AGS Management Systems	MULTI/CAM	Integrated systems development and product management.	640K	$4,000	IBM PC and comp., DOS 2.0 +	LAN	Yes/free	450/ 3 years	Yes/on- site, fees	Yes/free, unlimited
Apian Software	Decision Pad	Interactive worksheets help custom- ers make choices, produce data for analysis.	256K	$195	IBM PC and comp., DOS 2.0 +	All major	Yes/$10	1,000 + / 2 years	Yes/ off-site, fees	Yes/ unlimited, free
Applied Systems and Technology	TrAid-Names	Interactive program creates new products, services, business names.	512K	$159	MAC and IBM PC and comp.; MOS or MS DOS	All major	No	300 + / 2 years	No/ manual	Yes/free, unlimited
Caddylak Systems	On Schedule	Planning-and-scheduling program creates schedules, assignments, tasks for large projects.	256K	$89.95	IBM PC and comp., DOS 2.0 +	No	No	3,000/ 2 years	No/ tutorial	Yes/free, unlimited
Caddylak Systems	Take Stock†	Comprehensive inventory system tracks prices and vendor informa- tion for 3,200 items in 19 catego- ries; prints purchase orders and labels.	256K	$89.95	IBM PC and comp., DOS 2.0 +	No	No	New	No	Yes/free, unlimited
Information Resources	Apollo Space Management System	For suppliers to address merchan- dising efficiency; financial analysis; traffic flow.	1.5MB plus 640K	$35,000- $40,000	IBM PC and comp.; MS DOS	No	No	700/ 5 years	Yes/on- off-site, fees	Yes/ contract
Information Resources	Laptop Apollo	Store-level merchandising; informa- tion entry and analysis.	640K	$8,000	All major laptops	No	No	50/1 year	Yes/on- off-site, fees	Yes/ contract
Information Resources	TotalStore Apollo	Merchandising analysis and support.	640K	$10,000	IBM PC and comp.; MS DOS	No	No	200/ 2 years	Yes/on- off-site, fees	Yes/ contract
Management Con- trol Systems	PROMASTER: Project Evaluator	Systematizes gathering of market data and costs for starting a new product.	512K (hard disk)	$89	IBM PC and comp.; DOS 2.0 +	No	No	250 + / 3 years	Yes/on- site, fees	Yes/ 45 days free
MarketWare	Pegman A. I. (Automated Intelligence)	Automatically organizes regularly and irregularly shaped products into space optimized planograms; tracks and displays inventory.	640K	$9,600	IBM PC and comp.	All major	Yes/$100	New	Yes/on- site, fees	Yes/free, unlimited
MarketWare	Pegman Plus	Retail space management allows presentation quality planograms of carded, boxed, and shelved prod- ucts up to 32'.	640K	$5,600	IBM PC and comp.	All major	Yes/$60	New	No	Yes/free, unlimited
Sage Worldwide	accuSPACE Shelf Manager†	Organizes shelf space/position, calculates DPP by products/categories/square feet/return-per-linear-foot.	684K	$6,778 and down	IBM PC and comp.; DOS	No	Yes/free	100 + / 1.5 years	Yes/on- site fees	Yes/ contract
Sawtooth Software	ACA System for Adaptive Con- joint Analysis	Conjoint trade-off analysis for product development, simulates im- pact on market share of changes in product features/prices.	265K	$1,500- $3,000	IBM PC and comp.; DOS	No	Yes/free	750/ 4 years	No	Yes/free, unlimited
SPAR	SPARTRAC†	Organizes in-store factors and assesses their impact on clients'/competitors' products.	640K	$10,000 & up	IBM PC-AT and comp.; MS DOS	All major	Yes/$5	150 + / 5 years	Yes/ included	Yes/ included
TBX Inc.	FasTRACK	Traffic management system tracks 1,000 products at once.	256K (hard disk)	$995	IBM PC-XT; MS DOS	All major	Yes/$5	6 + / 2 years	No/ manual	Yes/free, unlimited
Vocam Systems	SHIPTRAC'R Autoplanner	Manages vendor deliveries, cus- tomer shipments, route planning, freight and bill audits/claims; analysis.	640K	$2,000	IBM PC-AT and comp; MS-, PC DOS 3.3	All major	Yes/$25	45 + /6 years	Yes/on- off-site, fees	Yes/free, unlimited

PROJECT MANAGEMENT

VENDOR	PACKAGE	DESCRIPTION	MEM.	PRICE	HARDWARE/SYS.	NETWK.	DEMO/$	#/AGE	TRAIN.	PHONE
AGS Management Systems	WINGS/PC	Multiuser project management and budgeting system with scheduling and cost capabilities.	640K	$3,900- $9,995	IBM PC and comp.; DOS 2.0 +	LAN	Yes/free	200/ 4 years	Yes/on- site, fees	Yes/free, unlimited
Chronos Software	WHO-WHAT- WHEN	Person, project, time management; generates reports; builds time lines; mailing list; auto-dialer.	512K	$295	IBM PC and comp.; DOS 2.0 +	No	Yes/free	35,000/ 1.5 years	Yes/on- off-site, fees	Yes/free, unlimited
Chronos Software	WHO-WHAT- WHEN ENTERPRISE	In real time: person, project, time management; generates reports; builds time lines; mailing list.	640K	$695	IBM PC and comp., DOS 3.1 +	Novell, LAN	Yes/free	New	Yes/on- off-site, fees	Yes/free, unlimited
Computer Aided Management	ViewPoint Project Man- agement Software	Project planning and scheduling, re- source and cost analysis, tracking and reporting, multiple calendars, diagrams.	512K	$2,990	IBM PC and comp DOS 2.1 + (hard disk, color monitor)	LAN, Novell, 3Com, Banyan	Yes/free	10,000/ 4 years	Yes/ off-site, 3 days free	Yes/free, unlimited
Digital Marketing	MILESTONE	Business project planning.	128K	$99	IBM PCs and comp.; DOS 2.0 +	All major	No	12,000/ 8 years	No	Yes/free, unlimited
InstaPlan	InstaPlan†	Planning tool for project manage- ment and spreadsheet; produces overheads and handouts.	640K	$99-$495	IBM PC and comp.; DOS 2.1 +	Novell	No/30-day free trial	30,000/ 3 years	Yes/on- site, fees	Yes/free, unlimited

VENDOR	PACKAGE	DESCRIPTION	MEM.	PRICE	HARDWARE/SYS.	NETWK.	DEMO/$	#/AGE	TRAIN.	PHONE
Symantec	TimeLine 3.0†	Project management program helps track time/resources; outlining, resource-driven scheduling, resource leveling and histogramme.	640K	$595	IBM PC and comp.; MS-, PC DOS 3.0 +	All major	Yes/free	150,000/ 5 years	Yes/on-site, fees	Yes/free, unlimited

SALES ANALYSIS

VENDOR	PACKAGE	DESCRIPTION	MEM.	PRICE	HARDWARE/SYS.	NETWK.	DEMO/$	#/AGE	TRAIN.	PHONE
SPAR	SPAR†	Assists sales manager in assessing incremental changes in promotional programs, analyzes/forecasts effects.	640K	$20,000 and up	IBM PC-AT and comp.; MS DOS	All major	Yes/$5	20 + / 3 years	Yes/ included	Yes/ included
Spring Systems	MktSim Marketing Simulation 2.2†	Collects data on competitors, plays "what if" with marketing mix variables for planning/forecasting, hypertext on-line documentation.	256K	$249.95	IBM PC and comp.; MS DOS, OS/2	All major	Yes/trial, $20	New	Yes/on-site, fees	Yes/free until up and running
Spring Systems	Turbo Spring Stat 3.0†	Twenty modules for complete data management from elementary statistics to multivariant procedures, time series.	385K	$39.95-$469.95	IBM PC and comp.; MS DOS, OS/2	All major	Yes/trial, $15	New	Yes/on-site, fees	Yes/free until up and running
SPSS	SPSS/PC + †	Advanced statistics, table building, time-series analysis, forecasting, graphics, mapping, conjoint/correspondence analysis.	512K	$795	IBM PC and comp.; MS-, PC DOS	All major	No	28,000/ 5 years	Yes/on-site, fees	Yes/free, unlimited
Strawberry Software	A-CROSS	Survey research/questionnaire data-analysis system works with dBase/Lotus/mainframe data.	512K (hard disk)	$995	IBM PC-XT, -AT, 386, PS/2 and comp.; MS DOS 2.0 +	All major	Yes/free	1,000 + / 2.5 years	Yes/on-site, fees	Yes/free, unlimited
TOM Software	System IV†	Tracks/analyzes sales/commissions; performs other sales/marketing functions including split commissions.	56K	$1,000 & up	IBM PC-XT, -AT, PS/2 and comp.; MS/Super DOS	Novell	No	5,000 + / 2 years	Yes/on-off-site, fees	Yes/ contract
Tronsoft	The Profit Center†	Sophisticated business analysis using real-time graphing and break-even analysis; forecasts with or without complete information.	512K	$695	Mac	No	No	New	No	Yes/free, unlimited
Zone1	Hyper-XCall	Using FORTRAN subroutines compiled with MacFortran, program creates market-models and simulations for analysis.	1MB	$99	Mac +, SE, II; Mac 4.1 +	AppleTalk	No	New	No	Yes/free, unlimited

SALES & MARKETING

VENDOR	PACKAGE	DESCRIPTION	MEM.	PRICE	HARDWARE/SYS.	NETWK.	DEMO/$	#/AGE	TRAIN.	PHONE
Advanced Marketing Systems	CAS†	Customized marketing and sales automation for medium/large co.s; prospecting, telemarketing, lead tracking, order entry, sales forecasting, account management.	640K	$2,500	DEC PC and comp.	All major	No	2,500/ 5 years	Yes/on-off-site, fees	Yes/free, unlimited
Argonaut Systems	Sales Commission Tracker†	Tracks sales commissions from direct and distributor sales, analyzes sales activity.	512K	$45	IBM PC and comp.; MS DOS	No	Yes/$5	New	No	Yes/free, unlimited
Gateway Systems	SYNERGIST†	Custom applications for all sales force automation modules; built-in database, catastrophic recovery capabilities.	512K	$1,500-$15,000	IBM PCs and laptops	No	Yes/free	60 + / 5 years	Yes/on-off-site, fees	Yes/free, unlimited
Green Light Software	Client Portrait†	Organizes client information for marketing purposes; identifies conflicts of interest.	512K	$6,950	Mac	All major Mac	Yes/$10	50-100/ 2 years	No/ manual	Yes/free, unlimited
Mel Long Assoc.	Combi-Names II	Helps manager create names for new products, services, companies.	320K	$99	IBM PC-XT, -AT, PS/2 and comp.; DOS 2.1 +	No	Yes/$10	168/ 1.5 years	No	Yes/free, unlimited
SimplSoft Products	The Unspreadsheet†	English-language calculator with 100 applications for sales/marketing management.	256K	$49.95	IBM PC and comp.; DOS 2.0 +	All major	No	15,000/ 4 years	Yes/on-off-site, fees	Yes/free, unlimited
Tronsoft	Business Power of Attorney†	Document processor with an exhaustive library of customizable business forms on topics like sales/distribution agreements, purchase agreements, employment-service-confidentiality agreements.	512K	$1,495	Mac	No	No	New	No	Yes/free, unlimited

SALES & MARKETING ANALYSIS

VENDOR	PACKAGE	DESCRIPTION	MEM.	PRICE	HARDWARE/SYS.	NETWK.	DEMO/$	#/AGE	TRAIN.	PHONE
Market Statistics	GIS: Geographic Information System†	Package can analyze information and sales data for any geography in U.S., including your own sales territories or future sites, and then easily manipulate them geographically; results can be displayed on a screen, map, or spreadsheet.	640K	$5,950-$50,000	IBM 286, 386, and comp.; DOS 3.3	All major	No	25/ 2 years	Yes/2 full days on site, free	Yes/free, unlimited

VENDOR	PACKAGE	DESCRIPTION	MEM.	PRICE	HARDWARE/SYS.	NETWK.	DEMO/$	#/AGE	TRAIN.	PHONE
Market Statistics	YMC: Your Marketing Consultant-Consumer†	Thirty nine consumer variables for all counties, metros, ADIs, DMAs or, your sales territory; sets sales goals, measures market performance.	512K	$1,000	IBM PC and comp.; DOS 2.1 +	No	No	200/ 4 years	No	Yes/free, unlimited
Market Statistics	YMC-BTB: Your Marketing Consultant-Business-to-Business†	Thirty-nine business-to-business variables for all counties, metros, ADIs, DMAs, or your sales territory; sets sales goals, measures market performance.	512K	$1,000	IBM PC and comp.; DOS 2.1 +	No	No	100/ 4 years	No	Yes/free, unlimited

SALES FORECASTING

VENDOR	PACKAGE	DESCRIPTION	MEM.	PRICE	HARDWARE/SYS.	NETWK.	DEMO/$	#/AGE	TRAIN.	PHONE
Application Consulting Group	ACG Forecast Window†	Integrated sales forecasting with automated statistical calculations, reporting, and graphics; esp. for consumer packaged goods co.s.	640K	$30,000	IBM PC, PS/2 and comp., DOS	LAN, Novell	No	4/1 year	Yes/ included	Yes/ contract
Business Forecast Systems	Forecast Pro†	Forecasting by taking historical data that is extrapolated to future.	512K	$495	IBM PC and comp., DOS	No	Yes/free	500 + / 2 years	Yes/on-off-site, fees	Yes/free, unlimited
Business Forecast Systems	Foresee	Forecasting for Lotus 1-2-3.	640K	$149.50	IBM PC and Lotus 1-2-3	No	No	New	No	Yes/free, unlimited
Free World Marketing	ForeCaster†	Forecasts projected sales for field territory reps by month, product, manufacturer.	256K	$395	IBM PC; DOS 2.0 +	All major	Yes/$25	New	Yes/on-site, fees	Yes/ 90 days free, then contract
Management Science Assoc.	Market Impact†	New product sales forecasting, concept evaluation, planning and control.	512K (1.6MB hard disk)	$10,000-$12,500	IBM PC and comp.; DOS 2.1 +	No	Yes/free	50/3 years	Yes/on-site for installation, free	Yes/free, unlimited
Market Engineering Corp.	Crystal Ball	Forecasting program uses "MonteCarlo" simulation to graphically illustrate the entire range of results for a particular situation; built-in spreadsheets.	1MB	$395	MAC +, SE, II, IIcx, IIx, SE30	MAC comp.	Yes/$10	1,000 + / 1 year	No/consulting	Yes/free, unlimited
MarketWorks	The Sales Forecaster	Produces three types of sales forecasts without Lotus 1-2-3: most likely, expected value, and risk analysis.	256K	$349	IBM PC-XT, -AT, 386, PS/2 and comp.; MS DOS 2.0 +	No	Yes/$20	New	Yes/disk	Yes/free, unlimited
Resource N	Plans 'n Totals†	Forecasting tool with budgeting, financial planning applications.	512K	$99	IRM PC and comp.; DOS 2.0 +	All major	Yes/$5	6,000/ 5 years	No/ manual	Yes/fees
Scientific Computing Assoc.	PC-UTS	Forecasting and time-series analysis using Box-Jenkins methodology.	640K (hard disk)	$745	IBM PC, Mac and comp.; DOS, OS/2	No	No	500 + / 3 years	No	Yes/free, unlimited
SmartSoftware	SmartCasts II†	Forecasting tool for sales/marketing managers with expert system graphics and data analysis; projects sales, demand, costs, revenues.	256K	$495	IBM PC and comp.; MS-, PC DOS	All major	Yes/$15	3,500 + / 5 years	Yes/off-site, fees	Yes/free, unlimited
SmartSoftware	SmartForecasts II BATCH/300†	BATCH processing for large forecasting jobs handles 300 items per file, reads/writes ASCII, DIF, Lotus, Symphony.	640K (hard disk)	$2,500	IBM PC-XT, AT and comp.	All major	No	New	Yes/off-site, fees	Yes/free, unlimited
Solar Additions	Prospect Management System†	Custom-developed for client's specifications on sales forecasting, sales management applications.	1MB	$1,500 & up	IBM, Mac; MS DOS	All major	No	14/9 years	Yes/ included	Yes/ included
SPAR	SPARCAST†	Forecasting system takes into account the effects of current events on marketing strategy.	640K	$10,000 & up	IBM PC-AT and comp.; MS DOS	All major	Yes/$5	New	Yes/ included	Yes/ included
Symantec	The Budget Express	Tailors Lotus 1-2-3 for forecasts and other planning applications.	64K	$149	IBM PC-XT, -AT, PS/2 and 100% comp.; Lotus 1-2-3	All major	Yes/free	New	No	Yes/free, unlimited
Technical Sales & Marketing Assoc.	FORECASTER†	Sales forecasting program for manufacturers or distributors/reps who sell products/services.	512K	$495	IBM PC-XT, -AT, PS/2 or comp;. PC-, MS DOS	No	Yes/free	New	Yes/on-off-site, fees	Yes/free, unlimited
TeLevell	TeleSell-Sales Manager Module†	Develops strategies, identifies trends, forecasts sales by product/customer/rep/territory/division; fully customizable reports.	640K	$595-$1,295	IBM PC and comp.; PC DOS 3.0 +	3Com, MSNet, Novell	No	40/1 year	Yes/on-off-site fees	Yes/free, unlimited
TMS Systems	Easy Caster†	Menu-driven forecasting package incorporates 10 forecasting techniques and 4 data analysis methods.	256K	$295	IBM PC and comp.; DOS 2.0 +	All major	Yes/$50	250 + / 5 years	Yes/on-site fees	Yes/ 1 year free
TMS Systems	Multi Caster†	Automatically forecasts any number of products in a spreadsheet environment; creates reports.	640K	$1,495	IBM PC-AT and comp.; DOS 3.3 +	All major	Yes/$50	New	Yes/on-site, fees	Yes/ 1 year free

VENDOR	PACKAGE	DESCRIPTION	MEM.	PRICE	HARDWARE/SYS.	NETWK.	DEMO/$	#/AGE	TRAIN.	PHONE
SALES MANAGEMENT										
Advanced Microlink Systems	Domino Sales Manager†	In/outbound calling, scripting, lead tracking, call analysis, sales projections and tracking, to-do list, word processing, reports.	640K	$995-$1,995	IBM PC, DOS 3.0 +	All major	Yes/$49	15/1 year	Yes/$75 per hour	Yes/90 days free
Bits and Bytes	Sales Manager's Companion	Tracks sales, territories, quotas, comparisons among salespeople; produces bar chart.	256K	$159	IBM PC and comp., MS DOS	No	Yes/free	1,000/1.5 years	Yes/on-site, fees	Yes/free, unlimited
Commercial Data Systems	TeleCall A/B/C†	Integrated package for salespeople selling to individual clients or to businesses.	640K	$995-$30,000	IBM PC, and comp., DOS	Unix	No	100 +/4 years	Yes/on-site, off-site, fees	Yes/$60 per hour
Computer Technology Consultants	A.S.I.S.	Prospect and customer management, history, and follow-up; forecasting and analysis, order status, expense reporting.	640K	$495 & up	IBM, DEC, micros, mainframes, and laptops; DOS, Unix, Xenix	Novell, 3Com, Banyan, IBM Token Ring	Yes/free	200/3 years	Yes/on-site, off-site, fees	Yes/3-year contract
Contact Software Int'l.	ACT!	Word processing, telemarketing, and time management for salespeople/managers; organizes daily business activities.	460K	$395	IBM PC and comp., DOS 2.0 +	Novell	Yes/video, $15	80,000/2 years	No	Yes/free, unlimited
Contact Software Int'l.	MERGE-UPDATE!	Merges files and data from other software packages without overriding or duplicating.	256K	$189	IBM PC and comp., DOS 2.0	All major	No	New	Yes/through dealer	Yes/free, unlimited
Dilg Publ.	LetterMaster ADVANCED†	Sales automation, client tracking, callbacks, word processor, letters, scripting, expense tracking, autodial.	512K-640K	$495	IBM PC and comp.	Novell	No	New	No	Yes/free, unlimited
Dun's Marketing Services	Dun's SalesSearch	Helps sales/marketing managers control sales cycle from analysis through sale.	512K (hard disk)	$495	IBM PC-AT, -XT, and comp.; MS DOS 2.0 +	No	Yes/free	100/2 years	No	Yes/free, unlimited
Envoy Systems	SalesMate†	Integrated, customized field sales force system for account and territory management; order entry, E-mail, personal information management.	640K	$500-$1,500	IBM PC-XT, -AT and comp., laptops; DOS	No	Yes/free	2,000 +/6 years	Yes/on-site, fees	Yes/free, unlimited
Esprit Software Technology	SELLSTAR!-UP†	Especially for sales management and territory analysis.	640K	$695	IBM PCs and comp., DOS 2.1 +	No	Yes/free	New	No	Yes/90 days free
ETS Systems	Sale Focus†	Sales management tool organizes and tracks incentive compensation, sales.	640K	$6,000	IBM PC-XT and comp., DOS 2.0 +	No	No	80/5 years	Yes/on-site, fees	Yes/60 days free, then contract
Evergreen Ventures	The Sales Associate	Sales package for managers and salespeople.	384K	$124.95	IBM PC and comp.; DOS 2.0 +	No	No	65/2 years	No	No
First Phase	Daily Routine	Creates agenda of follow-up activities, customer history files, call and time reports, quotation summaries, memos, mileage data, merge files.	195K	$49.95	IBM PC; MS DOS 2.0 +	No	No	200 +/2 years	No	Yes/free, unlimited
Hugh Carver Group	Sales Solution Pack†	Library of complete sales and marketing management programs; integration support.	512K	$300-$1,000	IBM PC and comp.; MS-, PC DOS, Unix, PS/2	Novell	No	20/2 years	Yes/on-site, fees	Yes/contract
Information Research	Syzygy	Operates over LAN giving managers the status of projects, salespeople; Gantt charts; to-do lists.	512K	$395-$2,995	IBM PC and comp.; DOS 3.1 +	LAN	Yes/free	200/1 year	No	Yes/30 days free
Information Resources/Javelin Products Group	EXPRESS Sales Management System†	Territory management system for sales managers.	640K	$50,000-$125,000	IBM PC and comp.; MS DOS	All major	Yes/$5	30/2 years	Yes/included	Yes/free, unlimited
The Intelligent Technology Group	ClienTrak†	Relationship management system esp. for sales and marketing productivity.	640K	$12,000 +	IBM PC-AT and comp.; DOS 2.0 +	All major	No	500 +/5 years	Yes/included	Yes/free, unlimited
John M. Roche	KNOWLEDGE Sales Process†	Using existing forms, customized program tracks customers/prospect/competition; territory analysis, direct mail, national account information.	384K	$2,000 & up	IBM PC-XT, -AT, PS/2 and 100% comp.	No	No	12 +/5 years	Yes/included	Yes/included
Julian Systems	AMS: Automated Management System†	Tracks sales by salesperson, product, history; inventory and order tracking; mail merge.	2MB	$5,000	Macintosh, MacPlus	All major	Yes/$10	New	Yes/on-site, off-site	Yes/included
KD Systems	Quorts	Order and commission tracking; esp. for manufacturers' reps.	640K	$1,500-$2,300	IBM PC/AT and comp., MS-, PC DOS 2.1 +	Alloy	Yes/$50	12/7 years	Yes/fee	Yes/12 hours free
Logic Design Corp.	Sales Management System†	Telemarketing, lead tracking, form-letter generation, customized order entry, inventory.	640K	$2,495 & up	IBM PC and comp.; DOS, Unix	Unix	No	New	Yes/on-site, fee	Yes/contract
MacServices	RetailMac†	Handles customer tracking, invoicing, mailing labels, inventory control; esp. for retail point-of-sale.	Mac Plus	$1,295	Mac Plus	All major	Yes/$35	30 +/2 years	Yes/on-site, off-site, fees	Yes/90 days free, then contract
Management Control Systems	PROMASTER: Sales Expense Manager	Tracks salespeople's expenses per person; generates expense reports by category of expense/person.	512K (hard disk)	$89	IBM PC and comp.; DOS 2.0 +	No	No	100/1 year	Yes/on-site, fees	Yes/45 days free

VENDOR	PACKAGE	DESCRIPTION	MEM.	PRICE	HARDWARE/SYS.	NETWK.	DEMO/$	#/AGE	TRAIN.	PHONE
Market Power	MATRIX Information Technology†	Completely customizable sales management package; creates sales forecasts, market analyses, reports, calendars, appointment schedules, to-do lists; direct mail applications; bar menus eliminate most typing.	300-400K	$1,000 & up	IBM PC and comp., laptops; DOS 3.0 +	LAN, Novell, 3Com	Yes/free	New	Yes/on-site, included	Yes/free, unlimited
Modatech Systems	Modatech Systems†	Portable decision support system: order entry, account/territory management, profit/distribution analysis; esp. for sales reps, managers, distributors.	1MB	$2,000-$3,500/rep	IBM PC and comp.; DOS, Unix	LAN, WAN, SNA	No	12/2 years	Yes/on-off-site, fees	Yes/free, unlimited
National Management Systems	Salesmanager's Workstation†	Fully customizable tool for national sales organizations: telemarketing/sales productivity, call history, ad-hoc reporting, budgets.	640K	$995	IBM PC and comp., laptops and comp.; MS DOS	All major	Yes/free	5,000 + / 6 years	Yes/on-off-site, fees	Yes/1 year free
Prism Systems	Prism Sales Focus†	Integrated modular system: lead tracking, direct mail, telemarketing, call reports, sales/promotion analysis, expense tracking.	512K (hard disk)	$2,995-$7,995	IBM PC-AT, -XT, PS/2 and comp.; MS PC DOS 2.0 +	All major	Yes/free	New	Yes/on-site, fees	Yes/fees
Realty Systems	REAL/Easy Office	Sales office management tool, data entry, printing.	640K (hard disk)	$395	IBM PC and comp.; DOS 3.1 +	Novell	Yes/$39.50	500/3 years	Yes/on-site, fees	Yes/30 days free
Sales Technologies	†	Integrated modules each fully customized; sales reporting, territory management, E-mail/forms, spreadsheets, sales reference.	640K	$1,000 & up	IBM PC-AT, -XT; MS DOS 2.1 +	No	No	15,000 + / 6 years	Yes/included	Yes/included
The Salinon Corp.	SALLYFORTH†	Multilevel marketing information system provides/manages historical sales, forecasting, budgets; esp. for managing multiple sales territories.	640K	$25,000	IBM 286, 386 and comp.; MS-, PC DOS 3.0 +	All major	Yes/free	New	Yes/on-site, included	Yes/free, unlimited
Spaulding	OpRep†	Lotus 1-2-3 companion tracks sales, spreadsheet-like reporting.	256K	$395	IBM PC and comp.; MS DOS 2.0 +	All major	No	100/4 years	Yes/on-site, fees	Yes/90 days free
Trendware	TRENDWARE CLIENT†	Customizable client/sales management system tracks customers, contacts, business/financial data; pop-up windows.	1MB	$195	Mac +, SE, II	No	Yes/$5	500 + / 1.5 years	No	Yes/free, unlimited
Vortex Technologies	Vortex	Comprehensive modular program for sales/marketing with: account managmnt, customer service, direct marketing, E-mail, field sales/rep management, I/O, lead tracking, market/sales analysis/management/forecasting, T&E, zips.	512K	$195-$23,595	IBM PC and comp.; MS DOS 3.0 +	Not bios	Yes/$10	New	Yes/on-off-site	Yes/3 months free
ZS Assoc.	EVALUMAP†	Customized software for sales managers to evaluate the performance of sales reps; integrated approach to performance evaluation and sales analysis.	640K	$30,000 and up	IBM PC-AT, -XT, PS/2 and comp.; MS DOS	All major	No	500/4 years	Yes/included	Yes/included

SALES PLANNING

VENDOR	PACKAGE	DESCRIPTION	MEM.	PRICE	HARDWARE/SYS.	NETWK.	DEMO/$	#/AGE	TRAIN.	PHONE
Expert Technologies	Business Plan Expert (BPE)	Step-by-step structure for analyzing products/services, clients/companies, marketing strategies, productions/operations that produce a written business plan.	256K	$195	IBM PC and comp.; DOS 2.0 +	No	Yes/$10	New	No	Yes/free, unlimited
Management Advisory Services	MAPS: Management Analysis and Planning System†	Long-range planning and diagnostic package prepares forecasts by default or specific assumptions.	512K	$495 & up	IBM PC, and comp.; DOS 2.0 +	All major	No	2,000/5 years	Yes/on-site, fees	Yes/30 days free
Management Advisory Services	Master Planner†	Five-module yearly planning system for sales and other management details.	512K	$495	IBM PC, PS/2 and comp.; DOS 2.0 +	All major	No	150/1.5 years	No	Yes/30 days free
Sales Implementation Systems	MarketFax†	Automated sales plan makes sure salespeople stay on track with predesigned plan; input any logical flow chart.	640K (hard disk)	$395-$3,595	IBM PC and comp.; MS-, PC DOS 3.0 +	LAN only	Yes/$50	4,000 + / 10 years	Yes/on-off-site fees	Yes/90 days free, contract

SALES PRESENTATIONS

VENDOR	PACKAGE	DESCRIPTION	MEM.	PRICE	HARDWARE/SYS.	NETWK.	DEMO/$	#/AGE	TRAIN.	PHONE
Aldus Corp.	Aldus Persuasion	Desktop presentations with drawing, charting, B&W or color overheads, 35mm slides, speaker notes, word processing.	1MB	$495	MAC +, SE, SE30, II, IICX (hard disk req.)	No	Yes/$5	New	Yes/manual	Yes/contract
American Intelliware Corp.	Scriptwriter†	Advanced word processing, built-in page breaks and formatting, video-audio- text synchronization, teleprompter.	1MB	$495	MAC +, SE, SE30, II, IICX	All major	Yes/$25	2.5 mil./5 years	Yes/on-site, fee	Yes/90 days free

VENDOR	PACKAGE	DESCRIPTION	MEM.	PRICE	HARDWARE/SYS.	NETWK.	DEMO/$	#/AGE	TRAIN.	PHONE
American Intelliware Corp.	Storyboard†	Desktop publishing, drawing, artificial intelligence, multimedia split-screen capability, digitized image animation.	1MB	$495	MAC +, SE, SE30, II, IICX	All major	Yes/$25	2.5 mil./ 5 years	Yes/on-site, fee	Yes/ 90 days free
Brightbill-Roberts	Show Partner	Produces self-running shows using partial screen; other advanced effects and graphics; palette shifting, animated objects; GXZ format from Lotus Freelance.	360K	$395	IBM PC and comp., DOS	All major	Yes/free	10,000/ 3 years	Yes/off-site	Yes/free, unlimited
Caddylak Systems	Great Presentations	Graphics and illustration, text and business charts, free-form drawings, slide-show presentations with animation and interaction.	256K	$99.95	IBM PC and comp., DOS 2.1 +	No	No	2,500/ 1.5 years	No	Yes/free, unlimited
CompuDoc	Interactive Electronic Media*	Interactive presentations for exhibits, trade shows, POP kiosks, product demonstrations; sales literature, direct mail.	512K	$5,000-$50,000	IBM PC and comp.	No	Yes/free	60,000 + / 1 year	No	Yes/free, unlimited
Cricket Software	Cricket Presents	Designs presentations: ruler-based text editor, drawing tools, built-in graphs and tables, 16.7 million color-palette, spell checking and thesaurus.	1MB (hard disk)	$495	MAC +, SE, II	Apple	No	New	Yes/on-site, fees	Yes/free, unlimited
General Parametrics	Desktop Presenter†	Presentation packet with fill-in-the-blank format; choice of 29 chart styles.	512K	$800	IBM PC and comp.; DOS 2.0 +	All major	No	5,000/ 4 years	Yes/on-site, fees	Yes/free, unlimited
General Parametrics	PictureIt†	Presentation package with charts, graphs, diagrams, fully scaled fonts.	256K	$695	IBM PC-XT, -AT, PS/2 and comp.; MS DOS, OS2	All major	Yes/$5	20,000/ 5 years	Yes/on-off-site, fees	Yes/free, unlimited
Informatics Group	Act III Authoring System 2.0†	Esp. for non-programmers to generate courseware or disk-based presentations incorporating graphics, sounds, animations, branching, interactive text.	640K	$495	IBM PC and comp.; DOS 2.0 +	All major	Yes/$10	600/ 1.5 years	Yes/on-site, fees	Yes/free, unlimited
InstaPlan	ShowText†	Makes overhead slides for presentations.	512K	$99	IBM PC and comp.; DOS 2.1 +	No	No/30-day free trial	50,000/ 5 years	No	Yes/free, unlimited
MacroMind Inc.	MacroMind Director	Creates multimedia presentations, videos, training courseware, simulations; combines animation, graphics, text, colors, music, and sound effects.	1MB (for B&W) 2MB (for color)	$695	Mac +, SE, SE/30, II, IIx	No	Yes/$9.95	New	Yes/on-off-site, fees	Yes/free, unlimited
Management Graphics	Easy Slider II†	Creates presentations by manipulating information, creating and coloring images/charts/slides without having to re-edit.	MAC	$49.95-$149.95	MAC II, x, cx, SE	No	Yes/$5	New	No	Yes/free, unlimited
Microsoft Corp.	PowerPoint 2.1	Professional quality color presentations; produces 35-mm slides; easy artwork and text arranging; full-featured word processor.	1MB (2 800K floppies)	$395	Mac +, SE, II 4.1 +	AppleShare Multifinder	Yes/free	New	No	Yes/free, unlimited
OWL Int'l.	Guide 2 Hypertext Authoring System	Organizes/manages free-form information, mixing text, graphics, videodisc images, sound to convey message; pop-up windows.	640K (1.5MB hard disk)	$295	Mac 512K, IBM PCs	No	Yes/$12.95	10,000 + / 3 years	Yes/on-off-site, fees	Yes/free, unlimited
Software Publ.	Harvard Graphics†	Integrated graphics program with bullet text, data, bar/line charts, free-hand drawing tools, 300 + symbols; creates slides/reports/documents.	512K (hard disk)	$495	IBM PC and comp.; MS DOS	All major	Yes/free	250,000 + / 2 years	Yes/on-site, fees	Yes/free, unlimited
Spinnaker Software	Pinstripe Presenter†	Business presentation/graphics program creates charts, graphs, drawings, 35mm slide production.	512K	$195.95	IBM PC and comp.; MS DOS 2.1 +	No	Yes/free	4,000/ 3 years	No	Yes/free, unlimited
StradeWare	PresentationPro 1.11†	Presentation graphics, creates slides/drawings.	512K (hard drive)	$295	Mac +; Apple 6.01 +	All major	No	New	Yes/ included	Yes/ included
VisionBase	Presentation Software	Presentation of photographs, videos, slides, graphs, charts.	512K (1.5MB EMS)	$4,995	IBM PC, laptops, and comp.; MS DOS	No	Yes/$25	50/4 years	Yes/on-site, fees	Yes/1 year free
Xerox Desktop Software	Xerox Presents	Desktop presentation product creates text, drawings, graphs, tables, handouts, speaker notes, slides, overheads, on-screen exhibits.	1MB (hard disk)	$495	IBM 286, 386	No	No	New	Yes/off-site, fees	Yes/60 days free
Zone1	Hyper-XRemote	Professional desktop presentation program incorporates conventional transparencies into pitch; scripting.	1MB	$65	Mac +, SE, II; Mac 6.0 +	AppleTalk	No	New	No	Yes/free, unlimited

TELEMARKETING

VENDOR	PACKAGE	DESCRIPTION	MEM.	PRICE	HARDWARE/SYS.	NETWK.	DEMO/$	#/AGE	TRAIN.	PHONE
Advanced Microlink Systems	Domino Telebusiness Manager†	In/outbound calling, scripting, lead qualifying and tracking, credit card ordering, inventory status and history, itemized client billing.	640K	$2,995-$19,995	IBM PC, DOS 3.0 +	All major	No	18/1 year	Yes/included	Yes/1 year, free
BFC Software	Telemarketing/ Sales Lead†	Tracks lead sources, salesperson efficiency, forecasting, reports, mass mailings, list sorting.	640K (hard disk)	$1,500 and up	IBM PC and Comp., DOS, RPG 2	All major	Yes/$10	12/1 year	Yes/on-off-site, fees	Yes/60 days free, then contract

VENDOR	PACKAGE	DESCRIPTION	MEM.	PRICE	HARDWARE/SYS.	NETWK.	DEMO/$	#/AGE	TRAIN.	PHONE
Concurrent Marketing Systems	T.O.P.C.A.T.†	Multiuser automates telmarketing and telesales; windowed screen presentations, scripting, database and list management, call reporting.	4MB	From $1,500/ station (1 to 33 + stations)	386 PC, Xenix, Unix	IBM Token ring	Yes/free	15/2 years	Yes/included	Yes/included
CR Complete Business Systems	TELEMATE/ TELEMAGIC	Telemarketing package; extensive notepad, recall, direct dial, order entry; interface with accounting; on-line information.	512K (hard disk)	$295-$1,995	IBM PC and comp.	Novell	Yes/ $15-$25	250/1 year	No/tutorial	Yes/30 days free
Digisoft Computers	Telescript†	Customizable telephone interviewing system, full script capabilities.	512K	$850 & up	IBM PC and comp.; MS-, PC DOS	All major	Yes/free	New	Yes/1 day free, then by hour	Yes/1 year free
Excaliber Sources	EXSELL†	Sales and telemarketing software includes word processor, tickler, reports.	384K	$395 & up	IBM PC, PS/2, and comp.; DOS 2.0 +, Xenix, Unix	All major	Yes/$15	4,000/ 6 years	Yes/on-site, fees	Yes/60 days free, then contract
Exceiver	TelePrompt†	Automated telemarketing system handles order entry, lead tracking, sales follow-up.	1MB	$995 (incl. customization)	MAC and comp.	All major	Yes/$20	10/3 years	Yes/on-site, fees	Yes/1 year free, then contract
Generation Four	MBA·TeleFel†	Sales scripts, order taking, question-answer file, literature mailing, export orders.	1MB (hard disk)	$189	MAC +	All major	Yes/$10	New	No	Yes/on-line, free
Holmes	HOLMES	Telemarketing tool keeps track of clients.	512K (hard disk)	$129	IBM PC and comp.; DOS 2.1 +	No	Yes/free	200 + / 3 years	No	Yes/90 days free
MaxSolutions	TeleMagic†	Telemarketing program with to-call list, scripts, auto-dial, recordkeeping, report and follow-up letter generation.	1MB	$495	IBM PC, MAC and comp.; MS DOS	Novell, 3Com	Yes/$29.95	40,000/ 4 years	Yes/on-, off-site, fees	Yes/6 months free, then contract
Me-Di-Co	Telemagic Autocall†	For telephone sales reps and managers to sell, prospect, analyze data/sales.	384K	$595-$1,995	IBM PC-XT, -AT and comp.; MS-, PC DOS 2.0 +	All major	Yes/$10	25,000/ 5 years	Yes/on-site, fees	Yes/1 week free
Plaid Bros. Software	Prospect†	Telemarketing, lead management program with auto-dial, word-processing, mail-merge, alarm clock, calendar, scripts, reports, import/export of ASCII data.	512K	$450	IBM PC and comp; MS DOS	Novell	Yes/$25	1,500 + / 5 years	Yes/on-, off-site, fees	Yes/1 year free
Prism Systems	TELEMARK†	Automated lead introduction, qualification, and assignment; access to product/competition summaries; custom scripting, in/outbound calls.	512K (hard disk)	$2,995-$5,995	IBM PC-AT, -XT, PS/2 and comp.; MS-, PC DOS 2.0 +	All major	Yes/free	50 + / 1 year	Yes/on-site, fees	Yes/fees
Profidex Corp.	SCAMP: Sales Control and Marketing Plannner	Telemarketing/direct mail package with auto-dialer, customized reports on prospects/territories/ branches/ regions.	512K	$695-$5,000	IBM PC; MS DOS 3.0 +	Novell, Data General	Yes/free	1050 + / 3 years	Yes/on-site, fees	Yes/30 days free, then contract
Prophecy Development Corp.	Profit Tool†	Telemarketing sales tool helps operator to make consistent sales presentations, overcome objections.	512K	$695	IBM PC and comp.; MS-, PC DOS 2.0 +	Novell	Yes/free	100 + / 4 years	Yes/on-site, fees	Yes/30 days free
QAX International Systems	InQuiry Action eXpress†	Telemarketing script processor, individualized sequence letters, labels, lead tracking, inquiry fulfillment.	640K	$895-$2,495	IBM PC-AT, -XT, PS/2, 386 and comp.; superDOS	VM386	Yes/$10 & up	36 + / 4 years	No	Yes/90 days free
Remote Control	TeleClose	Supports telemarketing/sales staff, integrated with accounting, order entry, receivables, etc.	640K	$250	IBM PC and comp.; PC DOS 3.3	Novell, 3Com, IBM Token Ring	Yes/$29	New	Yes/ dealer, free	Yes/6 months free, then contract
Remote Control	Telemagic Professional Release TEN†	Complete sales/telemarketing support including: tickler files, call reports, contact lists, auto-dialer, scripting, form letters, labels, word processor; also avail in Network, Xenix, Unix, Macintosh versions.	512K	$495-$30,000	IBM PC and comp.; PC DOS 2.1 +	Novell 286, 3Com, LAN	Yes/$29	30,000 + / 3 years	Yes/ dealer, free	Yes/6 months free, then contract
Remote Control	TeleMate	Telemarketing package integrated with various sales/marketing functions.	640K	$265-$695	IBM PC and comp.; PC DOS 3.3	Novell, 3Com, IBM Token Ring	Yes/$29	200 + / 1.5 years	Yes/ dealer, free	Yes/6 months free, then contract
SaleMaker Software	SaleMaker Plus†	Integrated system for telemarketing, direct marketing, client management, follow-up letters, sales reports.	640K (hard disk)	$695-$2,495	IBM PC and comp.; DOS 2.0 +	LAN, Novell	Yes/$49	5,000 + / 4 years	Yes/off-site, fees	Yes/30 days free
Sales & Marketing Systems	Telemarketing CTRL†	Scripts with branching and logic; instant access to product/competitor/ objection information.	512K (hard disk)	$495-1,995	IBM PC-AT, XT and comp.; DOS 2.0 +	Novell, 3Com	Yes/$13	30 + / 1 year	Yes/on-site, fees	Yes/free, unlimited
Sawtooth Software	Ci2 CATI System for Computer Aided Telephone Interviewing	Interactive interviewing/call management system, quota control, call disposition, monitoring, random/ auto-dialing, etc.	265K & up	$5,000-$20,000	IBM PC and comp.; DOS	LAN	Yes/free	80/3 years	No	Yes/free, unlimited
Software Science, The Research Group	TELEVIEW II†	Telephone interview system creates surveys, 1,000-questions questionnaires, automatically coded answers; reflexively finds next "logical" question.	256K	$99	IBM PC and comp.; MS-, PC DOS	All major	No	100/ 9 years	No/tutorial	Yes/free, unlimited

VENDOR	PACKAGE	DESCRIPTION	MEM.	PRICE	HARDWARE/SYS.	NETWK.	DEMO/$	#/AGE	TRAIN.	PHONE
System Vision Corp.	Sales Vision Telemarketing†	Telemarketing/account management with scripts and support for direct mail.	640K	$495-1,995	IBM PC and comp.; DOS	All major, special LAN program	Yes/free	1,000/5 years	Yes/on-site, fee	Yes/30 days free
Telemarketing	Telemarketing Services†	Used for lead list management, market coverage, scripting, productivity.	640K	$3,000	IBM PC and comp.; MS-, PC DOS 2.0 +	All major	No	42/10 years	Yes/on-off-site, fees	Yes/free, unlimited
Tess	TeleMac†	Telemarketing, inside sales, prospecting, mail-merge, reports.	1MB	$99	Mac	Mac II, CX, SE	No	New	No	Yes/free, unlimited
Travis DataTrak	TelePro†	Multiuser telemarketing/direct-mail package, also analyzes results.	512K	$1,199-$15,000	IBM PC and comp.; MS-, PC DOS 3.1 +	LAN	Yes/free	300 + /4 years	Yes/on-site, fees	Yes/contract
Tribase Systems	TAPIT†	Telemarketing and management tool.	10K (hard disk)	$449	IBM PC and comp.; MS DOS	No	Yes/$10	400 + /1.5 years	No	Yes/free, limited

TERRITORY MANAGEMENT

VENDOR	PACKAGE	DESCRIPTION	MEM.	PRICE	HARDWARE/SYS.	NETWK.	DEMO/$	#/AGE	TRAIN.	PHONE
Dynacomp	Customer Profile†	Tracks current and prospective customers, assigns sales reps to territories.	128K	$59.95	IBM PCs and comp., TRS-80, SP/M; DOS 2.0 +	No	No	2,000 + /3 years	No	Yes/30 days free
Dynacomp	Sales Assistant	Lead, sale, product tracking; assigns sales reps to territories; campaign scheduling, mailings.	128K	$59.95	IBM PCs and comp.; DOS 2.0 +	No	No	1,000/1 year	No	Yes/30 days free
Geosoft Corp.	MapBuilder†	Thematic maps display customer locations, sales territories, other demographic information.	512K	$250-$400	IBM PCs and comp.; DOS 2.1 +	No	Yes/free	100 + /4 years	No	Yes/90 days free
Metron	TERRALIGN	Creates optimal territory alignment that balances sales potential and other attributes; color map interface with digital road network computes/minimizes travel time.	640K (2MB hard disk)	$10,000 & up	IBM PC-AT and comp.; MS-DOS 3.1 +	No	Yes/$25	New	Yes/free	Yes/free, unlimited
Sammamish Data Systems	Sales Territory Manager†	Interactively allows user to define/modify new/existing sales/franchise territories.	640K	$2,995	IBM PC-AT, 386 and comp.; MS DOS 3.0 +	All major	Yes/$25	45 + /2 years	Yes/included	Yes/included
Sudor Corp.	Territory Management System†	Call reporting/analysis, to-do lists, forecasts, customer/prospect profiles, contact lists, covers 24 territories.	128K	$350	IBM PC and comp.; DOS 2.0 +	No	Yes/$10	35/8 years	No	Yes/free, unlimited
TTG	Territory Planner†	Geographic information/mapping system for sales analysis combines maps with spreadsheet logic.	640K	$1,995	IBM PC-AT; MS-, PC DOS 3.2 +	No	No	50/1 year	Yes/on-site fee	Yes/30 days free
TTG	Territory Planner Plus†	Combines mapping and spreadsheet function for territory design/analysis; high-resolution graphics; esp. for companies with large geographically located sales forces.	640K (hard disk)	$2,995	IBM PC-AT; MS-, PC DOS 3.2 +	No	No	10/2 years	Yes/on-site fee	Yes/30 days free
ZS Assoc.	MAPS IV†	Customized software for sales territory alignment; integrates company data with U.S. geography.	640K	$35,000 & up	IBM PC-AT, -XT, PS/2 and comp.; MS DOS	All major	No	75/6 years	Yes/included	Yes/included

TRADE SHOW MARKETING

VENDOR	PACKAGE	DESCRIPTION	MEM.	PRICE	HARDWARE/SYS.	NETWK.	DEMO/$	#/AGE	TRAIN.	PHONE
Free World Marketing	FreeLink†	Instantly reads badges from most major trade shows; stores names and addresses.	256K	$295	IBM PC; DOS 2.0 +	All major	Yes/$25	1,200/2.5 years	Yes/on-site, fees	Yes/90 days free, then contract
Free World Marketing	ProMotion†	Electronically reads information from trade show badges; mass mailings sorted by categories.	256K	$595	IBM PC; DOS 2.0 +	All major	Yes/$25	600/4 years	Yes/on-site, fees	Yes/90 days free, then contract
Inquiry Plus	Inquiry Management Software†	Tracks inquiries; creates letters and labels; electronic transfer of leads from trade shows.	560K (hard disk)	$1,500	IBM PC and comp.; DOS 2.0 +	All major	Yes/$89.95	200 + /5 years	No/free tutorial	Yes/90 days free

TRAVEL & ENTERTAINMENT

VENDOR	PACKAGE	DESCRIPTION	MEM.	PRICE	HARDWARE/SYS.	NETWK.	DEMO/$	#/AGE	TRAIN.	PHONE
C&H Enterprises	Frequent Flyer Award Trakker†	Tracks mileage according to airline programs, maximizes mileage strategy.	256K	$39	IBM PC, PS/2, MAC and comp., DOS 2.0 +	No	No	400/1 year	No	Yes/free, unlimited
CP Software	Sales Express†	Keeps track of clients; reports on expenses and commitments; mailings, labels, addresses (incl. international).	512K	$69	MAC, MAC 4.5	Topps, 3Com, Appleshare	Yes/$20	New	No	Yes/free, unlimited
Danart Corp.	EXPEN$E MA$TER: The Expense Report Processor†	Automatically creates all T&E reports required from entries.	363K	$69.95	IBM PC and comp.; DOS 2.0	All major	No	4,000 + /2 years	Yes/on-site, fees	Yes/free, unlimited
Danart Corp.	EXPEN$E MA$TER: Review and Consolidate†	Consolidates and analyzes expense reports created by the expense report processor.	640K (hard disk)	$69.95	IBM PC and comp.; DOS 2.0	All major	No	New	Yes/on-site, fees	Yes/free, unlimited

VENDOR	PACKAGE	DESCRIPTION	MEM.	PRICE	HARDWARE/SYS.	NETWK.	DEMO/$	#/AGE	TRAIN.	PHONE
Generation Four	MBA›TraveLog†	Travel and expense planner and log; fleet vehicle management, custom letters, mail merge; stores and prints itinerary.	1MB (hard disk)	$189	MAC+	All major	Yes/$10	New	No	Yes/on-line, free
Para-Tech Division of Paramount Technologies	Expense Easy†	Business and travel expense system.	512K	$79.95	IBM PC and comp.; MS-, PC DOS	All major	Yes/$5	2,000/ 1.5 years	No/ manual	Yes/free, unlimited
Quantic Corp.	Quadrant†	Processes expense reports, audits them against company travel policies/ procedures, summarizes.	640K	$495- $1,395	IBM PC and comp.; MS-, PC DOS 3.1+	No	Yes/$15	New	No	Yes/free, unlimited
Quantic Corp.	Touch 'n Go†	Tracks/reports T&E expenses for business travelers.	256K	$139	IBM PC and comp.; MS-, PC DOS 2.1+	No	No	1.000/ 2 years	No	Yes/free, unlimited
Robert B. Fields	ON THE GO EXPENSE REPORTS	Prepares business expense reports.	256K	$29.95	IBM PC and comp.; MS-, PC DOS 2.0+	All major	No	500+/ 5years	No	Yes/free, unlimited
TravelTrak	TravelTrak†	Tracks business travel expenses incl. mileage, hotel, T&E; prints statements.	256K	$395	IBM PC-AT, -XT, PS/2 and comp.; DOS 2.0+	No	Yes/$10	4/2 years	No	Yes/free, unlimited

ZIP CODE TRACKING

VENDOR	PACKAGE	DESCRIPTION	MEM.	PRICE	HARDWARE/SYS.	NETWK.	DEMO/$	#/AGE	TRAIN.	PHONE
Geographic Data Technology	Handshake/ GDT†	Customer referral package identifying customers' nearest dealer/distributor by zip code/locality.	360K (hard disk)	$495	IBM PC and comp.; DOS 3.1+	No	Yes/$35	New	No	Yes/90 days free, then contract
Hawthorne Software	PINMAP	Multicolored "push-pin"-style maps for plotting data by city or zip code; computer shows, slides, presentations.	5MB	$750	IBM PC-XT, -AT, PS/2 and comp.; MS DOS 3.2+	No	Yes/free	New	No	Yes/free, unlimited

†Customizable program
‡Free to American Marketing Assn. members

VENDOR DIRECTORY

Information has been supplied by the vendors; contacts given where applicable.

À La Carte Int'l., 1080 Riker St., Suite 14, Salinas, CA 93901-2236 (408-753-0882).

Abacus Concepts, Inc., 1984 Bonita Ave., Berkeley, CA 94704 (415-540-1949). Will Scoggin

Abend Assoc., Inc., 265 Winn St., Suite 305, Burlington, MA 01803 (617-273-5383). Shelley Orenstein

ACEware Systems, 1828 Erickson, Manhattan, KS 66502 (913-537-2937). Chuck Havilcek

ACRS Division M/A/R/C, Inc., 7850 N. Beltline Rd., Irving, TX 75063 (214-506-3400). Bill Jurgensen

Addison-Wesley Publishing, Co., Jacob Way, Reading, MA 01867 (617-944-3700). Order Dept.

Administrative Headquarters, 15520 Rockfield Blvd., Suite G, Irvine, CA 92718 (714-855-6792). Fred Young

Adobe Systems, Inc., 1585 Charleston Rd., P.O. Box 7900, Mountain View, CA 94039-7900 (415-961-4400 or 800-344-8335). Lavon Collins, Paul Towner.

Advanced Graphics Software, 333 W. Maude Ave., Suite 105, Sunnyvale, CA 94086 (408-749-8620). Order Processing

Advanced Marketing Systems Corp., 2 Lowell Research Center, Lowell, MA 01852 (508-454-6472). Paul Sullivan

Advanced Microlink Systems, Inc., 3600 Clayton Rd., Concord, CA 94521 (415-674-1600). Mike Finnicum

AGS Management Systems, Inc., 880 First Ave., King of Prussia, PA 19406 (215-265-1550).

Aldus Corp., 411 First Ave. South, Suite 200, Seattle, WA 98104 (206-622-5500). Customer Relations

American Intelliware Corp., P.O. Box 6980, Torrance, CA 90504 (213-533-4040).

Apian Software, P.O. Box 1224, Menlo Park, CA 94026 (415-851-8496 or 800-237-4565).

Application Consulting Group, Inc., 16 South St., Morristown, NJ 07960 (201-898-0012). James Cloniger

Applied Econometrics, Inc., 450 W. St., Amherst, MA 01002 (413-253-9342). Norman Cournoyer, Sabina Cournoyer, Christopher L. Wall

Applied Software Technology, 591 W. Hamilton Ave., Suite 20, Campbell, CA 95008 (408-370-2662 or 800-370-2662). Sales

Applied Systems and Technology, Inc., 227M Hallenbeck Rd., Cleveland, NY 13042 (315-675-8584).

Argonaut Systems, 15466 Los Gatos Blvd. Box 109-314, Los Gatos, CA 95030 (408-867-5029). David Arnold

Arlington Software & Systems Corp., 21 Daniels St., Arlington, MA 02174 (617-641-0290). Peter Brajer

Ashton-Tate, 20101 Hamilton Ave., Torrance, CA 90502-1319 (213-329-8000). Tracie Owens

The Association Store, Ltd., 8828 Monard Dr., Silver Springs, MD 20910 (301-588-3345 or 800-222-2977). Toni Lofthouse

Automated Business Designs, 1011 E. Touhy, Des Plaines, IL 60018 (312-827-6644). Terri Roeslmeier

Automated Micro, P.O. Box 3689, Santa Clara, CA 95055 (408-245-0350). Jim Lemezis

Aztech Corp., Artery Plaza West, 4733 Bethesda Ave., Bethesda, MD 20814 (301-907-333). Manny Flecker

Banner Blue, P.O. Box 7865, Fremont, CA 94537 (415-794-6850).

Bardsley & Haslacher, Inc., 1250 Aviation Ave., Suite 200E, San Jose, CA 95110 (408-293-6840). Leonard Nole

Bartel Software, 942 E. 7145 South, Suite A-101, Midvale, UT 84047 (801-566-5544 or 800-777-6368).

Beacon Data Systems, 220 Dogwood Ave., Melbourne Beach, FL 32951 (407-725-3594). Gary Kronengold

Beaumont Organization, Ltd., 220 White Plains Rd., Tarrytown, NY 10591 (914-332-5070). David Zietland

BFC Software, Inc., 799 Roosevelt Rd., Bldg. 6, Suite 108, Glen Ellyn, IL 60137 (312-790-8383). Lyle Castle

Bits and Bytes, Inc., 1650 Oakland Blvd. #105, Walnut Creek, CA 94596 (415-945-0987). Wilma Ram

BMDP Statistical Software, Inc., 1440 Sepulveda Blvd., Suite 316, Los Angeles, CA 90025 (213-479-7799). Eric Wiltshire

Breakthrough Productions, 10659 Caminito Cascara, San Diego, CA 92108 (619-281-6174). Marla Robinson

Bretton-Clark, 516 Fifth Ave., Suite 507, New York, NY 10036 (212-575-1568 or 201-766-6081). Steve Herman

Bricker-Evans, 2350 Mission College Blvd., Suite 450, Santa Clara, CA 95054 (408-970-0362). Mark Evans

Brightbill-Roberts & Co., 120 E. Washington St., Suite 421, Syracuse, NY 13202 (315-474-3400 or 800-444-3490). Stephanie Hubbard

Britz Publ. Co., P.O. Box 1156, Madison, MS 39130 (601-853-1394).

Brock Control Systems, Inc., 2859 Paces Ferry Rd., Suite 100, Atlanta, GA 30339 (404-431-1200 or 800-221-0775). Stephanie Zehna

Broderbund Software, Inc., 17 Paul Dr., San Rafael, CA 94903-2101 (800-521-6263). Customer Service

Business Forecast Systems, 68 Leonard St., Belmont, MA 02178 (617-484-5050). Sales Dept.

Business Research & Surveys, 50 Greenwood Ave., West Orange, NJ 07052 (201-731-7800). Jill Herman

C&H Enterprises, 19818 Ventura Blvd., Suite 343, Woodland Hills, CA 91634 (818-703-8944). Sales Dept.

CACI, 3040 Williams Dr., Fairfax, VA 22031 (703-698-4641).

Caddylak Systems, Inc., 131 Heartland Blvd., Brentwood, NY 11717 (800-523-8060). Customer Service

Campbell Services, 21700 Northwestern Hwy., Suite 1070, Southfield, MI 48075 (313-559-5955).

CATT Systems, 7929 Liberty Rd., Baltimore, MD 21207 (301-655-8858). Al Ruppel, Sheldon Schwartz.

CGA, Inc. Marketing Management Group, 140 Main St., Los Altos, CA 94022 (415-948-1300). Phil Graves

Champaigne Systems, Inc., 1140 W. Washington Blvd., Suite 200, Oak Park, IL 60301 (312-386-0062). David Kesler

Chang Laboratories, 3350 Scott Blvd., Santa Clara, CA 95054 (408-727-8096). Gary Chappell

Chronos Software, Inc., 555 De Haro St., Suite 240, San Francisco, CA 94107 (800-777-7907). Terry Peckham

CISIA, c/o Elizabeth Berry, 100 Bank St., 3H, New York, NY 10014 (212-691-7543). Elizabeth Berry

Claritas Corp., 201 Union St., Suite 200, Alexandria, VA 22314 (703-683-8300).

CME Assoc., 3619-C Midway Dr., Suite 325, San Diego, CA 92110 (619-223-2997). Howard Groveman

Coker Electronics, 1430 Lexington Ave., San Mateo, CA 94402 (415-573-5515). Mark Coker

Commercial Data Systems Corp., 1000 South Pioneer Dr., Atlanta, GA 30082 (404-799-1000). Kerrie Tucker

Commercial Micro, Inc., P.O. Box 1998 Rosewell, GA 30077-1998 (404-992-2701). Judy Bryant

CompuDoc, Inc., 1090 King George Post Rd., Suite 808, Edison, NJ 08837 (201-417-1799). Robert Sinnott

Computer Aided Management, Inc., 1318 Redwood Way, Suite 210, Petaluma, CA 94954 (707-795-4100 or 800-635-5621). Sales Dept.

Computer Innovations, 11 E. Adams, Suite 900, Chicago, IL 60603 (312-663-5930). Jean Franz

Computer Masters, 6505 S. Sepulveda Blvd., Los Angeles, CA 90045 (800-MASTER-1). Bob Seaman

Computer Solutions & Development, Inc., 4550 Montgomery Ave., Suite 850 North, Bethesda, MD 20814 (301-951-5505). Charlie Morenus

Computer Strategies, Inc., P.O. Box 88039, Atlanta, GA 30338 (800-225-7072). Joan

Computer Technology Consultants Inc., 2845 Eastern Blvd., York, PA 17402 (800-832-ASIS). Jeanne Gleeson

Computerease Software, Inc., 654 Metacom Ave., Warren, RI 02885 (401-245-1523 or 800-221-6841). Carol Berg

Computers for Marketing Corp., 547 Howard St., San Francisco, CA 94105 (415-777-0470). Josephine McIver

Concurrent Marketing Systems, Inc., 4807 Bethesda Ave., Suite 216, Bethesda, MD 20814 (301-657-0199)

Contact Software Int'l., 9208 W. Royal Lane, Irving, TX 75063 (214-929-4749 or 800-627-3958). Sales Dept.

Convention Central, Inc., P.O. Box 8837, Honolulu, HI 96830-0837 (808-737-2001). Robert Ahlstrom

Courseware, Inc., 10075 Carroll Canyon Rd., San Diego, CA 92131 (619-578-1700). Nanci Dalzell

CP Software, 1501 Adams Ave., Milpitas, CA 95035 (408-262-5185). Dan Cordoba

CR Complete Business Systems, Inc., 18141 Beach Blvd., Suite 385, Huntington Beach, CA 92648 (714-841-5868 or 800-266-5868). Bob Drohan

Creative Research Systems, 15 Lone Oak Center, Petaluma, CA 94952 (707-765-1001). Lisa Bacon

Cricket Software, 45 Valley Stream Pkway., Malvern, PA 19355 (215-251-9890).

Cross Information Co., 1881 9th St., Suite 311, Boulder, CO 80302 (303-444-7799). Mike Brough

Crunch Software Corp. 5335 College Ave., Suite 27, Oakland, CA 94610 (415-420-8660).

Custom Databanks, 127 E. 59th St., New York, NY 10022 (212-888-1650). Sales Dept.

DAC Software, 17950 Preston Rd., Dallas, TX 75252 (214-248-0205). Sales Dept.

Danart Corp., P.O. Box 267, San Rafael, CA 94915 (415-454-9100 or 800-635-7272). Sales Dept.

Data Resources, 24 Hartwell Ave., Lexington, MA 02173 (800-541-9914). Gene Guill

DATAMAP, Inc., 6436 City W. Pkway., Suite 105, Eden Prairie, MN 55344 (612-941-0900 or 800-533-7742). Grant I. Warfield

Datamatics Management Services, Inc., 330 New Brunswick Ave., Fords, NJ 08863 (201-738-9600).

Datanetics, 114 N. Beatty St., Pittsburgh, PA 15206-3002 (412-363-DATA). Jerry Lisovich

DayFlo Software, 18013 Sky Park Circle, Suite E, Irvine, CA 92714 (714-474-2901 or 800-367-5369). Sales Dept.

Derby Micro-Computer Services, P.O. Box 220566, Charlotte, NC 28222 (704-536-7721). Mike Derby

Detail Technologies, Inc., 29 Emmons Dr., Building A-2, Princeton, NJ 08540 (609-452-8228). Ron Vangi

Diamante Software, 11651 Plano Rd., Suite 160, Dallas, TX 75243 (214-556-0923 or 800-223-2165). Chris Dikmen

Digisoft Computers, Inc., 245 E. 92nd St., New York, NY 10128 (212-289-0991). Sales Dept.

Digital Marketing Corp., P.O. Box 2010, Walnut Creek, CA 94595 (415-947-1000). Bob Baker

Dilg Publ., 1200 Corland Rd. East, Suite 303, Arlington, TX 76011 (817-338-9181). Bob Dilg

Donnelly Marketing Information Services/Dun's Marketing Services, 70 Seaview Ave., P.O. Box 10250, Stamford, CT 06904 (203-353-7208). Jeff Knebel

Dun's Marketing Services, 3 Sylvan Way, Parsippany, NJ 07054 (201-605-6000). John Bagnasco

Dynacomp., Inc., P.O. Box 18129, Rochester, NY 14618 (716-671-6160). Fred Ruckdeschel

Dynamic Software Systems, 1900 L St. NW, Suite 500, Washington, DC 20036 (202-857-0181). Donna M. Gruntz

ECF System Development, 31955 10th Ave., South Laguna, CA 92677 (714-499-5135). Ed Fredian

EIGHTY/20 Software, P.O. Box 682, Hutchinson, MN 55350 (800-635-8020). Sales Dept.

EMIS Software, Inc., 901 NE Loop 410, Suite 526, San Antonio, TX 78209 (512-822-8499 or 800-822-3647). Mike Horridge

Enter Active Services, 8 Mitman Lane, Perkosie, PA 18944 (215-657-1515). Joel Feingold

Envoy Systems Corp., 1432 Main St., Waltham, MA 02154 (617-890-1444). Lynne Anderson Daly

Esprit Software Technology, P.O. Box 726, Hollis, NH 03049 (603-465-3378). Sales Dept.

ETS Center, 849 Seven Gables Circle SE, Palm Bay, FL 32909 (800-833-4777). Dora Rexrode, L.O. Rexrode

ETS Systems, Inc., 1048 Ridgewood Dr., Highland Park, IL 60035 (312-433-1188).

Evergreen Systems, P.O. Box 445, Voorhees, NJ 08043 (609 753-0758). Miriam Bernstein

Excaliber Sources, P.O. Box 467220, Atlanta, GA 30346 (404-956-8373). Sales Dept.

Exceiver Corp., 14688 County Rd. 79, Elk River, MN 55330 (612-441-8166). Randy Thomas

Execucom Systems Corp., 9442 Capital of Texas Hway. North, Austin, TX 78759 (512-346-4980 or 800-456-2222). Heidi Thomas

Experience in Software, 2039 Shattuck Ave., Berkeley, CA 94704 (415-644-0694 or 800-678-7008). Sales Dept.

Expert Technologies Corp., 3618 Burlington, Houston, TX 77006 (713-526-0909 or 800-327-8752). Kate McCusker

1st Desk Systems, Inc., 7 Industrial Park Rd., Medway, MA 02053 (508-533-2203 or 800-522-2286). Ned Hinds

First Phase, Inc., P.O. Box 4504, Greensboro, NC 27404 (919-855-8858). Pat Maggerd

Fleet Technologies, Inc., 50 Scott Adam Rd., Suite 201, Hunt Valley, MD 21030 (301-683-0166). Amy Koren

Frame Technology, 1010 Rincon Circle, San Jose, CA 95131 (408-433-3311 or 800-U4-FRAME). Steve Klann

France Int'l., Ltd., 11767 Bonita Ave., Owings Mills, MD 21117 (301-581-4117). Ralph France

Free World Marketing, 444 N. Newport Blvd., Newport Beach, CA 92663 (714-722-6414 or 800-642-4844). David Raney

G.G. Tauber Company, Inc., 4940 Wyaconda Rd., Rockville, MD 20852 (301-881-3567 or 800-638-6667). Deborah Paris

G. Temple Assoc., Ltd., 27777 Franklin Rd., Suite 700, Southfield, MI 48034 (313-353-9750). Duane Temple

Galacticomm, Inc., 4101 Southwest 47th Ave., Fort Lauderdale, FL 33314 (305-583-5990). Dave Ellich

Gateway Systems Corp., 2400 Science Pkway., Okemos, MI 48864 (517-349-7740). Charles Warzecha

General Parametrics, 1250 Ninth St., Berkeley, CA 94710 (415-524-3950 or 800-223-0999). Sales Dept., Bertina Tribuzi

Generation Four, Inc., 3232 San Mateo NE, Suite 199, Alburquerque, NM 87110 (505-294-3210). John Zoltai

Geographic Data Technology, 13 Dartmouth College Hwy., Lyme, NH 03768 (603-795-2183). Account Executives

Geosoft Corp., 38 Park St., Vernon, CT 06066 (203-875-7782). Bruce Johnson

GEOVISION, Inc., 270 Scientific Dr., Norcross, GA 30092 (404-448-8224). K.S. Shain

GoldData Computer Services, 2 Bryn Mawr Ave., Suite 200, Bryn Mawr, PA 19010 (215-525-1036 or 800-432-3267).

GPS CUSTOM Software Company, 2700 NE Loop 410, Suite 440, San Antonio, TX 78217 (512-344-5511). Sales Dept.

Green Light Software, 79 W. Monroe, Suite 1320, Chicago, IL 60603-4969 (312-782-6496). Daniel Kegan

Group 1 Software, 6404 Ivy Lane, Suite 500, Greenbelt, MD 20770-1400 (301-982-2000 or 800-368-5806). Leslie Vogel

H&D Leasing, 3012 Wallace St., Clovis, NM 88101 (505-762-3324).

Harris Publishing, 2057 Aurora Rd., Twinsburg, OH 44087 (800-888-5900).

Hawthorne Software, P.O. Box 35, Hawthorne, NJ 07507 (201-304-0014).

High Caliber Systems, 165 Madison Ave., New York, NY 10016 (212-684-5553). Al Schwendtner

Hill Street Publ., P.O. Box 616, Champaign, IL 61824-0616 (217-352-0003). Mary Auth

HMS Computer Co., 2401 Pilot Knob Rd., Suite 108, Mendota Heights, MN 55120 (612-452-5928). Bob Nobel

Holmes, Inc., 3518 SE 21st St., Topeka, KS 66605 (913-232-8222). Jim Springer, Jr.

Hugh Carver Group, Inc., 7 Deerport Dr., Suite E, Monmouth Junction, NJ 08852 (201-274-3400). Todd C. Scofield

HyperGraphics Training Systems, 308 North Carroll Blvd., Denton, TX 76201 (817-565-0004 or 800-438-6537).

IDSC Rental Co., Inc., 350 Harvey Rd., Manchester, NH 03103 (603-645-6677 or 800-443-IDSC). Edward Lucia

Informatics Group, Inc., 80 Shield St., West Hartford, CT 06110 (203-953-7407). Michael Ganci

Information Dimensions, Inc., 655 Metro Place South, Dublin, OH 43017 (312-977-0077 or 800-328-2648). Dawn Haskins

Information Managers, 777 S. Wadsworth Blvd., Irongate Bldg. 4, Suite 118, Lakewood, CO 80226 (303-987-8511). David Linke

Information Research Corp., 414 E. Marketsville, Charlottesville, VA 22901 (804-979-8191 or 800-363-3542).

Information Resources, Inc., 150 N. Clinton St., Chicago, IL 60606 (312-726-1221). Beth Christopher

Information Resources, Inc., Javelin Products Group, 200 Fifth Ave., Waltham, MA 02154 (617-890-1100 or 800-JAVELIN). Chris Stockton

Information Science Assoc., 676 N. St. Claire, Suite 1880, Chicago, IL 60611 (312-787-2723). Lori Torman

Informix Software, Inc., 16011 College Blvd., Lenexa, KS 66219 (913-599-7100 or 800-438-7627).

The InMar Group, 4241 Woodcock Dr., Suite A125, San Antonio, TX 78228 (512-733-8999). Keith Horne

Innovative microSystems, Inc., 790 Holiday Dr., Pittsburgh, PA 15220 (412-922-4999). Kathy K. Shoop

Inquiry Intelligence Systems, 12842 Pennridge Dr., Bridgeton, MO 63044 (312-984-1045 or 314-298-0599). Mike Moss

Inquiry Plus, 814 Eagle Dr., Bensenville, IL 60106 (312-595-5059). Ken Corradini

InstaPlan Group, 655 Redwood Hway., Suite 311, Mill Valley, CA 94941 (415-389-1414 or 800-852-7526). Sales Dept.

The Integrator, 8513 Bardmoor Pl., Largo, FL 34647 (813-393-5310).

The Intelligent Technology Group, Inc., 115 Evergreen Heights Dr., Pittsburgh, PA 15229 (412-931-7600). Sales & Marketing Dept.

Inter Active Micro, Inc., P.O. Box 478, Bradford, NH 03221 (603-938-2127). Howard Brooks

Interactive Market Systems, 55 Fifth Ave., New York, NY 10003 (212-924-0200).

Interactive Systems, Inc., 600 Suffolk St., Lowell, MA 01854 (508-937-8500 or 800-347-3001). Maria Carvalho

International Conference Management, 7152 SW 47th St., Miami, FL 33155 (305-661-5115 or 800-327-8338). Steve Adler

International Software Technology, Inc., 1112 7th Ave., Monroe, WI 53566 (800-356-0022). John Ditter

JEB Systems, Inc., 32 Daniel Webster Hway., Suite 23, Merrimack, NH 03054 (800-821-1006). Donna Brock

JKL Marketing, 13990 Olive Street Rd., Suite 204, Chesterfield, MO 63017 (314-434-3514). Cliff Langston

John Deighton, 2103 Marston Lane, Flossmor, IL 60422 (312-798-8993). John Deighton

John M. Roche & Assoc., 205 Nelson Rd., Scarsdale, NY 10589 (914-472-5497). John Roche.

Julian Systems, Inc., 2280 Bates Ave., Suite J, Concord, CA 94520 (415-686-4400).

KD Systems, 160 Hampton Rd., Sharon, MA 02067 (617-784-4390). Norm Kelson

Key Systems, Inc., 512 Executive Park, Louisville, KY 40207 (502-897-3332). Sue Wise

Laptop Express, 1424 Larimer Sq., Suite 208, Denver, CO 80202 (303-595-9800). Robert Hamilton

Lawco Ltd., P.O. Box 2009, Mantica, CA 95336 (209-239-6006).

Leadership Development, Inc., P.O. Box 2457, Truckee, CA 95734 (916-587-6322 or 800-447-7775). Bob Toliver

LEADtrack Services, 595 Colonial Park Dr., Roswell, GA 30075 (404-587-0412 or 800-992-0412). Michael Stack

Lincoln Systems Corp., P.O. Box 391, Westford, MA 01886 (508-692-3910). Mike Harde

Logic Design Corp., 1025 S. Moorland Rd., Suite 404, Brookfield, WI 53005 (414-785-1301). Eric Hedman

Lotus Development Corp., 55 Cambridge Pkway., Cambridge, MA 02142 (617-577-8500 or 800-343-5414).

Lowell Corp., P.O. Box 158, Worcester, MA 01613 (617-756-5103 or 800-456-9355). Richard Mahan

M&T Publ., 501 Galveston Dr., Redwood City, CA 94063 (415-366-3600 or 800-533-4372; in CA: 800-356-2002).

MACE, Inc., 2313 Center Ave., Madison, WI 53704 (608-244-3331). Carl Voelz

MacroMind, Inc., 410 Townsend, Suite 408, San Francisco, CA 94107 (415-442-0200).

MacServices, 7702 Bayberry, San Antonio, TX 78240 (800-777-8094). Van Rinn

Management Advisory Services, 2401 Fourth Ave., Seattle, WA 98121 (800-325-4322). Gary Greer

Management Control Systems, 215 Spring Ridge Dr., Roswell, GA 30076 (404-642-0235). John Rilling

Management Graphics, Inc., 1401 E. 79th St., Minneapolis, MN 55425 (612-854-1220).

Management Science Assoc., Inc., 6565 Penn Ave. at Fifth, Pittsburgh, PA 15206-4490 (800-MSA-INFO). Tom Petro

Management Software, Inc., P.O. Box 35082, Minneapolis, MN 55435 (612-831-9591). Bob Sliwinski

MANYLINK Corp., P.O. Box 350, Redmond, WA 98073 (206-881-5060). Keith Goben

Map Information Services, 200 Broadway, Troy, NY 12180 (518-274-8673 or 800-FASTMAP). Bob Galo

Marc Software Int'l., Inc., 260 Sheridan Ave., Palo Alto, CA 94306 (415-326-1971). Wendy Wytyshyn

Market Action Research Software, Inc., Bradley Univ., Business Technology Center, Peoria, IL 61625 (309-677-3299). Dr. Betsy Goodnow

Market Engineering Corp., 1675 Larimer St., Suite 600, Denver, CO 80202 (303-803-0100). Sales Dept.

Market Power, Inc., Computer Innovations, 101 Providence Mine Rd., Suite 106A, Nevada City, CA 95959 (916-432-1200). Lance Bellows

Market Statistics, 633 Third Ave., New York, NY 10017 (212-984-2381). Robert Katz

Marketech Int'l., P.O. Box 366, Far Hills, NJ 07931 (201-204-0933).

Marketing Data Research, 8103 104th St. SW, Dept. M5, Tacoma, WA 98498 (206-588-4149). Tish Anderson

Marketing Graphics Inc. (MGI), 4401 Dominion Blvd., Suite 210, Glen Allen, VA 23060 (804-747-6991 or 800-368-3773). Tanya Meimaris

Marketing Information Systems, Inc., 906 University Place, Evanston, IL 60201 (312-491-3885). Sales Dept.

Marketing Metrics, 305 Rt. 17, Paramus, NJ 07652 (201-599-0790). Patrice Cross

Marketing Software, Inc., 1233 N. Mayfare Rd., Suite 317, Milwaukee, WI 53226 (414-778-3737). Mr. Rao

Marketools, Inc., P.O. Box 1178, Barrington, IL 60011 (312-381-8636). Jan Blanke

MarketWare Corp., 80 Prospect St., Cambridge, MA 02139 (617-576-1700). Bob Jablonski

MarketWorks, Inc., 19 Linda Vista, Tiburon, CA 94920 (415-924-2117 or 800-627-5389).

MAR-REL Analytics, Inc., P.O. Box 39506, Rochester, NY 14604 (716-265-1179). Robert Hertz

Maryland Interactive Technologies, 11767 Bonita Ave., Owings Mills, MD 21117 (301-581-4117). Ralph France

Mastr.Soft Corp., 24293 Telegraph Rd., Southfield, MI 48034 (313-358-3366). Dan Natelborg

MaxSolutions, 241 12th St., Del Mar, CA 92014 (619-481-0479). Rodney Palmer

MaxThink, 44 Rincon Rd., Kensington, CA 94707 (415-428-0104). Order Desk

McDonnell Douglas Applied Communication Systems, 2560 N. First St., San Jose, CA 95131 (800-435-8880). Customer Service Center

MediaMark Research, Inc., 708 Third Ave., New York, NY 10017 (212-599-0444). Erica Phillips

Me-Di-Co, 2233 Northwestern Ave., Waukegan, IL 60087 (312-249-1213). Bill Sultan

Mel Long Assoc., 715 N. 21 St., Allentown, PA 18104 (215-433-2588).

Merle Systems, Inc., 160 Mt. Vernon St., Suite D-10, Boston, MA 02125 (617-282-1846). Steve Winer

Metron, Inc., 1481 Chain Bridge Rd., McLean, VA 22101 (703-790-0538). Tom Stefanick

MICOR Systems, 8959 Hillside, Cottage Grove, MN 55016 (612-459-0154). Dan Ramler

MicroMaps Software, Inc., P.O. Box 757, Lambertville, NJ 08530 (609-397-1611 or 800-334-4291). Robert Dahl

Microsoft Corp., 16011 NE 36th Way, Box 97017, Redmond, WA 98073 (206-882-8080).

Microtab, Inc., 5825 Glenridge Dr., Suite 210A, Atlanta, GA 30350 (404-847-0605).

Minitab, Inc., 3081 Enterprise Dr., State College, PA 16801 (814-238-3280). Cheryl Ferrin

Modatech Systems, Inc., 50 Charles Lindburgh Blvd., Uniondale, NY 11803 (516-942-0339).

MZ Group, 1388 Sutter St., Suite 612, San Francisco, CA 94109 (415-885-5551). Allison Elliot

National Decision Systems, 539 Encinitas Blvd., Encinitas, CA 92124 (619-942-7000 or 800-882-6200).

National Demographics and Lifestyles, Inc., 1621 18th St., Denver, CO 80202 (303-292-5000). Bill Schneider

National Management Systems, 1945 Old Gallows Rd., Suite 206, Vienna, VA 22182 (703-827-0797). Robert Tillson

National Planning Data Corp., P.O. Box 610, Ithaca, NY 14851 (607-273-8208). Jim Spear

NCSS, 865 E. 400 North, Kaysville, UT 84037 (801-546-0445).

Nelson Business Systems, Inc., 8714 N. Otis Ave., Tampa, FL 33604 (813-935-2258).

Neuralytic Systems, 66 Bovet Rd., Suite 319, San Mateo, CA 94402 (415-573-9001).

New England Software, Greenwich Office Park #3, Greenwich, CT 06831 (203-625-0062 or 203-625-0714). Technical Support

Nielsen Marketing Research, Nielsen Plaza, Northbrook, IL 60062 (312-498-6300 ext. 2743). Molly Powers

Norman R. Sutherland & Assoc., 6290 Sunset Blvd., Suite 1126, Los Angeles, CA 90028 (213-463-5090). Norman Sutherland

Odesta Corp., 4084 Commercial Ave., Northbrook, IL 60062 (312-498-5615). Michael Demeyer

Option Technologies, Inc., 200 Carleton Ave., East Islip, NY 11730 (516-277-7000 or 800-645-2287). Ed Harms

Owl Int'l., 14218 NE 36th Way, Redmond, WA 98073-9717 (206-747-3203).

Oxicron Systems Corp., 1 Bridge Plaza, Suite 400, Fort Lee, NJ 07024 (201-592-0222). William Kester

P-STAT, Inc., 271 Wall St., P.O. Box AH, Princeton, NJ 08542 (609-924-9100). Sebbie Buhler

Pace Computer Inc., 6266 Peachtree St., Commerce, CA 90040-4015 (213-721-6200). Brandy Wong

PaceCom Technologies, 14040 NE 8th St., Bellevue, WA 98007 (206-641-8217). Al Mattson

Pagex Systems, Inc., 77 W. Sheffield Ave., Englewood, NJ 07631 (201-871-0800). Bob Sieminski

Para-Tech Divison of Paramount Technologies Corp., Inc., 100 W. Monroe St., Chicago, IL 60603 (312-263-4946 ×710 or 800-628-2828). Rudy Allison

Parker Marketing Research, 1080 Nimitzview, Suite 201, Cincinnati, OH 45230 (513-232-1800). Michael Kosinski

Pearl Communications, Inc., P.O. Box 767937, Roswell, GA 30076 (404-640-6609). Forrest Edwards

People and Contacts, 3212 Collinsworth, Fort Worth, TX 76107 (817-332-5203). Dr. Gary Lipe

Peopleware, Inc., 1715 114th SE, Bellevue, WA 98004 (206-454-6444). B.J. Martindale

Performer Systems, Inc., 161 S. Junipero Serra, Suite B, San Gabriel, CA 91766 (818-300-8570). Ann Margaret Ng

Persimmon Software, 1901 Gemway Dr., Charlotte, NC 28216 (704-398-1309). Dr. Charles Cicciarella

Phoenix Solutions, Inc., 372 W. Ontario, Chicago, IL 60610 (312-664-6881 or 800-669-MTGS). Liz Tinsman

PictureWare, Inc., 111 N. Presidential Blvd., Bala Cynwyd, PA 19004 (215-667-0880). Jennifer Moller

Pilot Executive Software, 40 Broad St., Boston, MA 02109 (617-350-7035). Gary O'Connell

The Pipeline Software Co., 11491 Sunset Hills Rd., Reston, VA 22090 (703-471-5165).

Plaid Brothers Software, 17952 Skypark Circle, Suite K, Irvine, CA 92714 (714-261-7255). Eric Peters

Planning Works, Inc., 6665 Huntley Rd., Suite K, Columbus, OH 43229 (614-436-5300). Judy Pennybacker

Polaris Software, 613 W. Valley Pkway., Suite 323, Escondido, CA 92025 (619-743-7800 or 800-338-5943). Sales Dept.

Popular Programs, Inc., 6915 La Granada, Houston, TX 77083 (713-530-1195; for orders: 800-447-6787).

Prism Systems, Inc., P.O. Box 40968, Indianapolis, IN 46240 (317-872-4808).

Productive Access, Inc., 434 Webster Ave., Westwood NJ 07675 (201-358-1898). Ron Pinelli. Or, 21087 Carlos Rd., Yorba Linda, CA 92686 (714-970-1130). John Doyle

Profidex Corp., 80 Park Ave., Hoboken, NJ 07030 (201-420-3700).

Profiles Int'l., 2350 Airport Freeway, Suite 200, Bedford, TX 76022 (817-354-1704). Ron Brown

Profit Management Systems, 9800 4th St. North, Suite 204, St. Petersburg, FL 33702 (813-578-0190). Ronald H. Ackerman

Prophecy Development Corp., 2 Park Plaza, Boston, MA 02116 (617-451-3430). Norman Lang

Pros and Cons Inc., 6917 Arlington Rd., Suite 215, Bethesda, MD 20814 (301-951-8441). Peter Van Brunt

PRO/TEM Software, Inc., 814 Tolman Dr., Stanford, CA 94305 (415-947-1024). Bob Baker

Pulse Analytics, 152 Jeffer Court, Box 116, Ridgewood, NJ 07450 (201-447-1395). Stan Cohen

QAX International Systems Corp., 4273 Cavehill Dr., Springhill, FL 34606 (904-596-2090). Robert Quackenbush

Quantic Corp., 44 Friendly Rd., Smithtown, NY 11787 (516-361-3322). David Linker

Quark, Inc., 300 S. Jackson, Suite 100, Denver, CO 80209 (303-934-2211).

Quest Management Systems, 2301 W. Big Beaver Rd., Suite 318, Troy, MI 48084 (313-643-4555). Tom Jenks

Questar Data Systems, Inc., 2905 W. Service Rd., Eagan, MN 55121 (612-688-0089). Edward Siegal

Realty Systems, 10909 W. Bluemound Rd., Milwaukee, WI 53226 (414-258-7700). Kay Koehler

Remote Control, Inc., 514 Via de la Valle, Suite 306, Solana Beach, CA 92075 (800-992-9952). Judy Persky

Resource N, Inc., 721 Lowell St., Carlyle, MA 01741 (508-264-4450). Deanne Brownrigg

Revelation Technologies Corp., 2 Park Ave., New York, NY 10016 (212-689-1000). Customer Service

Richmond Software, Inc., 420-6400 Roberts St., Barnaby, British Columbia, Canada V5G 4C9 (604-299-2121). Greg Pelling

The Right Brain, Inc., 420 N. Fifth St., No. 970, Minneapolis, MN 55401 (612-334-5620). Kristin Jacobson

Right Soft, Inc., 4545 Samuel St., Sarasota, FL 34233 (813-923-0233 or 800-992-0244).

RightNICHE Software Co., 315 First Ave. South, Suite 2, Seattle, WA 98104 (206-583-2338). Ron Hansen

Robert B. Fields, 1810 Wright Ave., Rocky River, OH 44116 (216-356-9265). Robert Fields

Robinson Assoc., Inc., 500 S. Roberts Rd., Bryn Mawr, PA 19010-1137 (215-527-3100). Dr. Bruce Kossar, John Robinson

Round Lake Publ., 415 Main St., Ridgefield, CT 06877 (203-438-5255).

The Sachs Group, 1800 Sherman Ave., Evanston, IL 60201 (312-492-7526 or 800-366-PLAN). Janet Guptill

Sage Worldwide, Inc., 450 Park Ave. South, New York, NY 10016 (212-685-0600 or 800-542-7778). Tony Schnug

SaleMaker Software, P.O. Box 531650, Grand Prairie, TX 75053 (214-264-2626).

Sales & Marketing Systems, Inc., 1950 Old Gallows Rd., Suite 300, Vienna, VA 22182 (703-790-3222 or 800-832-0050). Henry Jordan

Sales Executive, Inc., 5505 Morehouse Dr., Suite 150, San Diego, CA 92121 (619-455-6094). Alan Kaldor

Sales Implementation Systems, 16074 Beach Blvd., Huntington Beach, CA 92647 (714-847-1134).

Sales Productivity Group, Two Brentwood Commons, Suite 150, 750 Old Hickory Blvd., Brentwood, TN 37027 (615-371-6187).

Sales Technologies, 3399 Peachtree Rd. NE, Atlanta, GA 30326 (404-841-4000). Gayle Baxter

SalesFacs, Inc., 3000 Galleria Towers, Suite 800, P.O. Box 36307, Birmingham, AL 35236 (205-985-3134). Huey J. Hall

The Salinon Corp., 7424 Greenville Ave., Suite 115, Dallas, TX 75231 (214-692-9091). Mike Carr

Salmon Systems, 2211 Fifth Ave., Seattle, WA 98121 (206-441-8100). Edith Hilliard

SAMI, Division of Arbitron, 55 Greens Farms Rd., Westport, CT 06880 (513-852-3809). Mike Maynard. Or, 800 Broadway, Cincinnati, OH 45202 (513-852-3800).

Sammamish Data Systems, 1813 130th Ave. NE, Suite 218, Bellevue, WA 98005 (206-867-1485). Michael Abraham

Saratoga Systems, Inc., 1550 S. Bascom Ave., Suite 330, Campbell, CA 95008 (408-371-9330). Al Smith

SAS Institute, Inc., SAS Circle, Box 8000, Cary, NC 27512 (919-467-8000). Software Sales

Sawtooth Software, 1007 Church St., Evanston, IL 60201 (312-866-0870). Suzanne Weiss

Scarsdale Marketing Co., Harwood Bldg., Suite 415, Scarsdale, NY 10583 (914-725-5445). Robert Wals

Scherrer Resources, Inc., 8100 Cherokee St., Philadelphia, PA 19118 (215-242-8751). Bob Cottrill

Scientific Computing Assoc., Lincoln Center, Suite 106, Lisle, IL 60532 (312-960-1698). Sue Blumenschein

The Scientific Press, 507 Seaport Court, Redwood City, CA 94063-2731 (415-366-2577 or 800-451-5409). Katharine Whipple Vestri

Scott Computing Systems, 2780 Bert Adams Rd., Atlanta, GA 30339 (800-241-7576). Peggy Stevens

SDG Decision Systems, 2440 Sand Hill Rd., Dept. SM, Menlo Park, CA 94025-6900 (415-854-9000 or 800-852-1236). Karen Bencomo

Select Media, 1111 Third Ave. South, Suite 112, Minneapolis, MN 55404 (612-339-3844 or 800-288-3844). Douglas J. Denny

Select Micro Systems, 322 Underhill Ave., Yorktown Heights, NY 10598 (914-245-4670). Daryl Scott

Significant Statistics, 3336 N. Canyon Rd., Provo, VT 84604 (801-377-4860). Richard Galbraith

Silicon Beach Software, Inc., 9770 Carroll Center Rd., Suite J, San Diego, CA 92126 (619-695-6956). Macintosh Software Dealers

SimplSoft Products, Inc., P.O. Box 13173, Boulder, CO 80308 (303-444-8771 or 800-326-2276). Sales Dept.

SKOPOS Corp., 4966 El Camino Real, Suite 216, Los Altos, CA 94022 (415-962-8590). Tony Tasca

SmartSoftware, Inc., 392 Concord Ave., Belmont, MA 02178 (617-489-2743 or 800-SMART99).

SNAP Software, Inc., 175 Canal St., Manchester, NH 03101 (603-623-5877). Debbie Watrous

The Softbridge Group, 125 Cambridge Park Dr., Cambridge, MA 02140 (800-325-6060; in MA: 800-325-5959).

Softek Design, 882 Calgary Way, Golden, CO 80401 (303-525-0606). Client Service Dept.

Software Architects, Inc., 4327 Rucker Ave., Everett, WA 98203 (206-252-6897). Robert Zollo

Software Complement, 8 Pennsylvania Ave., Matamaras, PA 18336 (717-491-2492). Karen Cohen

Software Institute, 10044 Adams Ave., Suite 410, Huntington Beach, CA 92646 (714-962-6019). Stephen McHenry

Software Publ., 1901 Landings Dr., Mountain View, CA 94039 (415-962-8910). Lizanne Haygood

Software Science, Inc.; The Research Group, 100 Valley Dr., Brisbane, CA 94005 (415-571-5019). Max Weinryb

Softworks, Inc., 7700 Old Branch Ave., Suite E206, Clinton, MD 20735 (301-856-1892 or 800-638-9254). Dave Underwood

Solar Additions, Inc., P.O. Box 241C, Rt. 40, Greenwich, NY (518-692-9673).

Sophisticated Data Research, 2251 Perimeter Park Dr., Atlanta, GA 30341 (404-451-5100).

SPAR, Inc., 580 White Plains Rd., Tarrytown, NY 10591-5106 (914-332-4100 or 800-443-2833). Pat Franko

Spaulding, 303 Research Dr., Suite 140, Norcross, GA 30092 (404-449-1634). Dick Hays

Spinnaker Software Corp., 1 Kendall Square, Cambridge, MA 02139 (617-494-1200). Catalogue Sales

Spring Systems, P.O. Box 10073, Chicago, IL 60610 (312-275-5273 or 312-ARK-LARD). John Pavasars

SPSS, 444 N. Michigan Ave., Chicago, IL 60611 (312-329-3300). Sales

Stanford Business Systems, Inc., 5250 W. Century Blvd., Suite 407, Los Angeles, CA 90045 (213-417-4940). Amin Shahidi

Star Software Systems, 363 Van Ness Way, Torrance, CA 90501 (213-533-1190 or 800-242-STAR). Sales Dept.

Statistical Innovations, Inc., 375 Concord Ave., Belmont, MA 02178 (617-489-4492). Tom Gentile

Stolzberg Research, Inc., 3 Seabrook Court, Stony Brook, NY 11790 (516-751-4277). Dr. Mark Stolzberg

StradeWare, 12600 W. Colfax Ave., Suite B110, Lakewood, CO 80215 (303-232-8282). Tara Miller

Strat*X Int'l., 222 Third St., Cambridge, MA 02142 (617-494-8282 or 800-541-9585). Michael Daitch

Strategic Management Group, Inc., 3624 Market St., University City Science Center, Philadelphia, PA 19104 (215-387-4000 or 800-445-7089). Sherrie Marafino, Nana Odoi

Strawberry Software, Inc., 42 Pleasant St., Watertown, MA 02172 (617-923-8800 or 800-4-ACROSS). Elmer Bartek

Street Map Software, 1014 Boston Circle, Schaumburg, IL 60193 (312-529-4044). Lynn Barton

STSC, Inc., 2115 E. Jefferson St., Rockville, MD 20852 (800-592-0050 or 301-984-5467). Mark Whalley

Suburban Software, 579 Franklin Tpke., Ridgewood, NJ 07450 (201-652-8085). Bill Bartlett, Pat Humes

SUCCESSware, Inc., 203 Annandale Dr., Cary, NC 27511 (919-469-0119). Robin Lee

Sudor Corp., 6251 N. Camino Esquina, Tucson, AZ 85718 (602-299-0651). John Schacht

SumQuest Software, 350 Victoria St., Toronto, Ontario, Canada M5B-2K3 (416-599-0404). Ross Macnaughton.

Surveytab, P.O. Box 369, Annapolis Junction, MD 20701 (301-498-1299). Michael Reifer

Symantec Corp., 10201 Torre Ave., Cupertino, CA 95014 (408-253-9600).

Symmetry Corp., 225 E. 1st. St., Suite 107, Mesa, AZ 85201 (800-624-2485). Stella Ramirez

Sysmark Information Systems, Inc., 49 Aspen Way, Rolling Hills Estates, CA 90274 (213-544-1974). Dave Taylor

SYSTAT, Inc., 1800 Sherman Ave., Evanston, IL 60201 (312-864-5670). Tracy Koe

System Dynamics, P.O. Box 4031, Santa Barbara, CA 93140 (805-963-9626). Gordon Feingold

System Software Assoc., Inc., 500 W. Madison, Suite 3200, Chicago, IL 60606 (312-641-2900). Sally Green

System Vision Corporation, P.O. Box 281166, San Francisco, CA 94128 (415-355-7308). Virginia Tormey

Target Microsystems, Inc., 444 Castro St., Suite 400, Mountain View, CA 94041 (415-967-3990 or 800-SELLPRO). Don Ridgeway

TARP Information Systems, 309 E. Main St., Suite 204, Salisbury, MD 21801 (301-546-2223).

TBX, Inc., 106 Woodcrest Dr., Rome, GA 30161 (404-234-4260).

Technical Sales & Marketing Assoc., P.O. Box 8655, Fountain Valley, CA 92728 (619-321-5730). Hal Horrocks

Technology Development, 48 Stiles Rd., Salem, NH 03079 (603-893-2422). Karyn Murphy

Telemarketing, Inc., 13801 86th Ave. North, Minneapolis, MN 55369 (612-420-8551). John Meegan

TeLeVell, 3175 De La Cruz Blvd., Santa Clara, CA 95954 (408-748-0111). Carl Nelson

Tess, 21075 Bank Mill Lane, Saratoga, CA 95070 (408-741-1519). Perry Lynne

3X USA, One Executive Dr., Fort Lee, NJ 07024 (201-592-6874). Matthew Simonet

TMS Systems, Inc., 3000 Tall Oaks Dr., Blacksburg, VA 24060 (703-552-5685). Mark E. Poole

TOM Software, 127 SW 156, Seattle, WA 98166 (206-246-7022)

Topitzes and Assoc., 6401 Odana Rd., Madison, WI 53719 (608-273-4300).

Travaco Management Systems, 2550 Som Center Rd., Willoughby Hills, OH 44094 (216-943-4100 or 800-435-1495).

Traveling Software, 18702 N. Creek Pkway., Bothell, WA 98011 (206-483-8088 or 800-662-2652). Marci Maule

TravelTrak, P.O. Box 4261, Greenwich, CT 06830 (203-531-0288). Joyce Wice

Travis DataTrak, 381 Elliot St., Newton, MA 02164 (617-964-8960). Andy Sumberg

Trendware Corp., P.O. Box 2285, Huntington, CT 06484 (203-926-1116).

Tribase Systems, Inc., 28 Beechwood, Summit, NJ 07901 (201-522-1212).

Tronsoft Corp., 133 Wess De La Guerra, Santa Barbara, CA 93101-3289 (805-564-3386 or 800-451-8585; in CA: 800-237-7316). Jerry Donaldson

TTG, 400 W. Cummings, Suite 3900, Woburn, MA 01801 (617-932-6500). John Kubicek

Turnkey Data Solutions, Inc., 11210 Steeplecrest Dr., #120, Houston, TX 77065 (713-894-9400). John Zysk

Useful Software of Princeton (USP), 1079 Stuart Rd., Princeton, NJ 08540 (609-921-3119). George Wilson

Valor Software, 2005 Hamilton Ave., San Jose, CA 95125 (408-559-1100). Gary Josie

Viking Software Services, Inc., 4808 E. 67th St., Suite 100, Tulsa, OK 74136 (918-491-6144). Les Robinson

VisionBase, Inc., 380 Foothill Rd., Bridgewater, NJ 08807 (201-218-0900). Kevin Moran

Vocam Systems, 10800 Lyndale Ave. South, Bloomington, MN 55420 (612-888-4890).

Vortex Technologies, Inc., 11103 San Pedro, San Antonio, TX 78216 (512-344-5511).

Walonick Assoc., 6500 Nicollet Ave. South, Minneapolis, MN 55423 (612-866-9022). Leon Storm

White Crane Systems, 6400 Atlantic Blvd., Suite 180, Norcross, GA 30071 (404-446-0660). Technical or Customer Support

WordPerfect Corp., 1555 N. Technology Way, Orem, UT 84057 (801-225-5000). Information Services Dept.

Working Computer, P.O. Box 87, San Louis Rey, CA 92068 (619-721-0501). Lisa Waggoner

World Research Systems, Ltd., P.O. Box 11099, Chicago, IL 60611 (312-527-1006).

Xerox Desktop Software, 9745 Business Park Ave., San Diego, CA 92131 (800-822-8221).

XYCAD Group, 1577 St. Clair Ave., Cleveland, OH 44114 (216-589-5788 or 800-428-8457; in Canada: 800-661-1461). Terry Stiglic, Bill Zimmerman.

Zenographics, 19712 MacArthur Blvd., Suite 100, Irvine, CA 92715-9976 (714-851-6352). Sales Office

Z-Soft, 450 Franklin Rd., Suite 100, Marrietta, GA 30067 (404-428-0008).

Zone1, Inc., 382 Nalley Dr., Suite 101, Stone Mountain, GA 30087 (404-381-8659).

ZS Assoc., 1600 Sherman Ave., Evanston, IL 60201 (312-492-3600). Annette Simon ☐

Endnotes

Chapter 1

1. Joshua Hyatt, "Sell Mates," *Inc.,* December 1989, p. 126.
2. "At Scott, a Sales Force with a Business Mentality," *Sales & Marketing Management,* June 1989, p. 43.
3. Beth Brophy, "The Birth of a Saleswoman," *U.S. News & World Report,* February 6, 1989, p. 41.
4. "The Colossus That Works," *Time,* July 11, 1983, pp. 46–47.

Chapter 2

1. Bill Kelley, "Is There Anything That Can't Be Sold by Phone?" *Sales & Marketing Management,* April 1989, pp. 60–64.
2. Mark H. McCormack, *What They Don't Teach You at Harvard Business School* (New York: Bantam Books, 1984), p. 89.
3. "How the Game Will Change in the 1990s," *Sales & Marketing Management,* June 1989, pp. 52–61.
4. "Why Sell One Nail Whan You Can Sell a Barrel Full?" *Sales & Marketing Management,* December 1989, p. 14.
5. This section based in part on Allan J. Magrath, "To Specialize or Not to Specialize?" *Sales & Marketing Management,* June 1989, pp. 62–68.
6. "Excellence," *Sales & Marketing Management,* June 1989, p. 45.
7. Thayer C. Taylor, "Computers, " *Sales & Marketing Management,* March 1989, p. 70.
8. "Computers," p. 70.
9. Louis Rukeyser, "The Territory's Face Is Changing as More Women Go into Sales," *The (Cleveland) Plain Dealer,* April 2, 1989.

Chapter 3

1. You Can Do Great Things at Dow in Sales and Marketing, Company Publication, undated, Form No. 460-103-88-B&L.
2. Mathew Shank and Cynthia Lunnemann, "Proper Pay and Reward Help Retain Sales Force," *Marketing News,* March 5, 1990, p. 7.

Chapter 4

1. Ron Zemke and Dick Schaaf, *The Service Edge* (New York: New American Library, 1989), pp. 158–59.

Chapter 5

1. Nolan D. Archibald in a Presentation, 1989 Marketing Conference, Conference Board, New York, October 31–November 1, 1989.
2. William Band, "The 'Three I's' of Customer Satisfaction Need Your Vision," *Marketing News,* October 23, 1989, p. 7.
3. "P&G Rewrites the Marketing Rules," *Fortune,* November 6, 1989, pp. 34–48.
4. "Rubbermaid—Yes, Plastic," *Business Month,* December 1988, p. 38.

Chapter 6

1. Bill Kelley, "Picking the Best from the Rest," *Sales & Marketing Management,* July 1989, pp. 28–33.
2. Kelley, "Picking the Best," pp. 28–33.
3. Cunningham is quoted in Kerry Hannon, "A Foot in the Door," *Forbes,* October 20, 1986, p. 136.
4. Todd Mason, "Radio Shack Puts on the Pin Stripes," *Business Week,* September 1, 1986, p. 66.

Chapter 7

1. Dave Scarangella, "Rep's Task Now More Complex," *Furniture/Today,* January 18, 1988, pp. 8–10.
2. Gerhard Gschwandtner, "Bottom Line Selling," *Personal Selling Power,* November/December 1988, pp. 28–29.
3. Brian Dumaine, "P&G Rewrites the Marketing Rules," *Fortune,* November 6, 1989, pp. 35–40.
4. Jack E. Hulbert, "Barriers to Effective Listening," *The Bulletin,* vol. LII (June 1989), pp. 3–5.

Chapter 8

1. Gerhard Gschwandtner, "Secrets of Sales Success at Federal Express," *Personal Selling Power,* January/February 1990, pp. 12–20.
2. Robert L. Shook, *Ten Great Salespersons* (New York: Harper & Row, 1986).
3. Information provided by James Lorenzen & Associates, Titusville, Florida.
4. For more information, see *Non-Manipulative Selling,* Tony Alessandra, Phil Wexler, and Neil Rackham, *SPIN Selling* (New York: McGraw-Hill, 1988).

Chapter 9

1. Thayer C. Taylor, "Reinventing (and Marketing) the Wheel," *Sales & Marketing Management,* September 1987, pp. 54–57.
2. "AV for Any Audience," *Sales & Marketing Management,* January 14, 1985, pp. 76–77, 79–80.
3. This data is reported in "On the Road to More Affordable Presentations," *Sales & Marketing Management,* November 1989, p. 121.
4. "New System Makes Selling Easy for Bank Officers and Tellers," *NCR ALPHA* 5, no. 4 (November 1985), pp. 6–8.
5. Logue is quoted in William Keenon, Jr., "Back on the Fast Track," *Sales & Marketing Management,* November 1989, p. 32.

Chapter 10

1. Richard Kern, "Letting Your Salespeople Set Prices (Sort Of)," *Sales & Marketing Management,* August 1989, pp. 44–45, 47–49.
2. "Burroughs Chief on the Road," *Sales & Marketing Management,* July 1986, pp. 32, 34.

3. Some of these techniques are adopted from *Seven Steps in Retail Selling Photographic Salesmen* (Jackson, Michigan: Photo Marketing Association, 1970), p. 7.

Chapter 11

1. Martin Everett, "Selling's New Breed: Smart and Fiesty," *Sales & Marketing Management,* October 1989, p. 59.
2. "The Road to Success Is Paved with Calls," *Sales & Marketing Management,* July 1989, p. 82. The original source was *The Competitive Advantage Newsletter.*
3. Markita Andrews, "How to Sell Anything," *Parade,* March 2, 1986, p. 6. The quote is from Markita Andrews with Cheryl Merser, *How to Sell More Cookies, Condos, Cadillacs, Computers . . . and Everything Else* (New York: Vintage Books, 1986).
4. Fred Kirsch, "There Never Was a Salesman Like Girard—Says Girard," *The Detroit News,* February 17, 1980, pp. 1-D, 11-D. Copyright 1980. The Evening News Association, *The Detroit News.*

Chapter 12

1. "How Ball's Sales Team Kicks the Cans of Competitors," *Sales & Marketing Management,* June 1989, pp. 41–42.
2. "Mean It When You Say Yes," *Sales & Marketing Management,* June 1989, p. 23
3. Bob Woods, "Selling Parts with Service." *Sales & Marketing Management,* July 4, 1983, p. 29. Used with permission.

Chapter 13

1. Jeremy Main, "Frito-Lay Shortens Its Business Cycle," *Fortune,* January 15, 1990, p. 11.
2. "Science & Technology," *Business Week,* June 2, 1986, pp. 93–94.
3. Jeanne and Herbert Greenberg, "The Personality of a Top Salesperson," *Nation's Business,* December 1983, pp. 30–32.
4. Murray Raphel, "The Ten Characteristics of Top Salesmen! Part II," *Direct Marketing,* December 1981, p. 75.

Chapter 14

1. Sally Scanlon, "Pall Hydraulic's Devoted Missionaries," in *Portfolio of 1983 Sales and Marketing Plans,* ed. Bob Albert (New York: Sales & Marketing Management), pp. 17–19. © 1983. Used with permission.

2. "How to Sell in the Big Time," *Sales & Marketing Management,* February 1990, p. 42.

3. This section is based on Warren H. Suss, "How to Sell to Uncle Sam," *Harvard Business Review,* November–December 1984, pp. 136–38.

4. John Fitts, "Service Centers Likely to Become More Specialized," *Purchasing World,* April 1981, pp. 77–78. Used with permission.

5. This section taken in part from Peter Kraljic, "Purchasing Must Become Supply Management," *Harvard Business Review,* September–October 1983, pp. 109–17. Used with permission.

6. This section is based on Wesley J. Johnson and Thomas V. Bonoma, "The Buying Center: Structure and Interaction Patterns," *Journal of Marketing,* Summer 1981, pp. 146–47, 152–54.

Chapter 15

1. Reprinted from "One Store Where Selling Is Still in Style," *Sales & Marketing Management, September 1989, pp. 31–32.*

2. Robert Bearson, "Retailing for Developers," *Shopping Center World,* July 1983, p. 16. Used with permission.

3. Robert Bearson, "Talking with Children Is Effective Way to Sell Parents," *Shopping Center World,* September 1982, p. 18. Used with permission.

Chapter 16

1. "Women Step Forward," *Real Estate Today*®, Anniversary Issue, 1988, pp. 52–53.

2. David Colby in "Select the Tools that Shape Success," *Real Estate Today*®, April 1988, pp. 8–14.

3. Floyd Wickman, "Pick Prospects Who Are Ripe for Purchase," *Real Estate Today*®, May 1988, pp. 30–33.

4. Wickman, "Pick Prospects Who Are Ripe for Purchase," pp. 30–33.

5. The Ohio Association of Realtors®.

6. Based on information supplied by The American College, Bryn Mawr, Pennsylvania.

7. Based on information supplied by American Institute for Property and Liability Underwriters, Malvern, Pennsylvania.

Chapter 17

1. Joshua Levine, "The Sound of No Dealers Selling," *Forbes,* February 19, 1990, pp. 122, 124.

2. "Making a Salesman a Manager," *Industry Week,* March 17, 1980, pp. 49–50.

3. Herbert M. Greenberg and Jeanne Greenberg, "Job Matching for Better Sales Performance," *Harvard Business Review,* September–October 1980, p. 311.

4. Sara Delano, "Improving the Odds for Hiring Success," *Inc.,* June 1983, pp. 145–50. Guion quote from p. 150.

5. "Taking on the Big Boys," *Sales & Marketing Management,* July 1986, p. 28.

6. Allan J. McGrath, "Eight Ways to Avoid Marketing Shock," *Sales & Marketing Management,* April 1989, p. 37.

7. William Keenan, Jr., "Are You Overspending on Training?" *Sales & Marketing Management,* January, 1990, p. 58.

8. "Nothing Matches Money as a Motivational Device for Sales," *Marketing News,* May 11, 1984, p. 3.

9. "Retailing's Golden Rules," *U.S. News & World Report,* March 12, 1990, p. 19.

10. Derek A. Newton, *Sales Force Management: Text and Cases* (Homewood, Ill.: Business Publications/Richard D. Irwin, 1982), pp. 142–43.

11. Newton, *Sales Force Management,* p. 53.

12. Newton, *Sales Force Management,* p. 56.

Glossary

account classification (p. 292) categorization of accounts by their relative sales potential

add-on purchase (p. 338) additional unplanned purchase

AIDA (p. 176) standardized learning approach of awareness, interest, desire, and action

alternative decisions (p. 248) closing technique in which the prospect is asked to make a choice between alternatives equally favorable to the seller

antitrust legislation (p. 13) laws that prohibit efforts to monopolize a marketplace

approach (p. 150) opening of a sales interview with the right person

assumptive close technique (p. 248) closing technique that assumes that the prospect has decided to purchase the item

attitudes and beliefs (p. 89) predispositions to react in certain ways in certain situations

bagmen (p. 11) textile industry sales personnel during the Industrial Revolution

balanced selling (p. 180) sales approach that balances customer and salesperson orientations in selling

balance sheet close (p. 250) close that presents negative factors as well as benefits of the products

best or most important criterion decision rule (p. 82) arrangement of relevant choice criteria in order of importance

best overall decision rule (p. 83) rating all products or brands on each criterion

bonuses (p. 58) achievement rewards not directly related to sales

buyer's market (p. 12) market characterized by a plentiful supply of goods

buying centers (p. 325) all the people involved in the purchasing decision process

cafeteria plan (p. 58) allows employees to select the mix of salary, commissions, bonuses, and fringe benefits that best suits their needs

callback schedule (p. 268) schedule outlining the frequency of salespeople's calls on different categories of customers

call report (p. 295) summary of a salesperson's daily or weekly activities

canned sales presentation (p. 181) memorized or highly structured sales presentation

career path (p. 52) series of steps employees go through in preparation for advancement

caveat emptor (p. 11) "let the buyer beware"

chain of prospects (p. 137) situation where a seller tries to get one or more additional prospects from each person interviewed

choice criteria (p. 80) features/benefits with the most importance or priority in producing customer satisfaction

clincher (p. 251) extra inducement to buy, such as rebates, lay-away options, price discounts, or reduced delivery charges

closing (p. 241) point at which the salesperson secures the desired agreement from the prospect

closing cues (p. 244) verbal statements and physical actions (or signals) that suggest a buyer may be ready to purchase the product

CLU (p. 354) Chartered Life Underwriter

cold calls (p. 163) unsolicited and unannounced sales calls

cold canvassing (p. 134) securing prospects through unsolicited contacts by the sales force

combination plan (p. 58) compensation plan that has both a set salary and a commission component

commercial travelers (p. 12) term applied to field sales personnel toward the end of the 19th century

commission plan (p. 57) pay plan that links sales reps' compensation directly to their sales productivity

communications (p. 114) sharing of information between a buyer and a seller

competitive wage (p. 57) compensation plan that is about standard for the industry

component parts (p. 312) products inserted intact into the final product

continuous sales training (p. 380) refreshing, improving, and updating of the selling skills and marketing knowledge of experienced personnel

counterquestion (p. 225) asking "why" in response to an objection

CPCU (p. 354) Chartered Property Casualty Underwriter

creative selling (p. 25) situation in which the salesperson makes prospects aware of needs or wants and convinces them that his or her services will solve the procurement problem

demonstration (p. 197) illustration of how customers can use a product and/or service and benefit from it

derived demand (p. 313) purchasing process where industrial demand is triggered by the demand for a consumer product

detailer (p. 32) a sales rep who brings basic product information to the attention of physicians

detailing (p. 32) sales situation where the salesperson actively sells to someone other than the actual buyer

developmental salesperson (p. 26) generates new customers in initiation or capture selling situations

direct approach (p. 248) closing method in which the salesperson simply asks the prospect for the order

drawing accounts (p. 58) advances against commissions earned by sales reps

driver salesperson/order taker (p. 31) sales rep who takes customer orders and provides regular and efficient service

drummers (p. 12) 19th century sales reps

emotional close (p. 250) use of fear, pride, romance, or the need for peer group acceptance as a closing technique

empathy (p. 175) ability to understand the customer's viewpoint

expense accounts (p. 58) reimbursements to cover legitimate costs of fulfilling the job requirements of selling

extensive decision making (p. 75) substantial purchasing effort over an extended period of time to make a complex evaluation of multiple alternatives

external search (p. 79) use of personal, published, seller, and experience sources in the buying decision process

extra inducement close (p. 251) use of a clincher—a selling point held in reserve—as a close

features (p. 80) characteristics of a product or service that provide benefits or value to consumers

feedback (p. 116) the receiver's response to a sales message

flexible price policy (p. 228) salesperson may negotiate a specific price with the buyer

fringe benefits (p. 58) financial rewards not directly tied to a firm's compensation plan

general decision (p. 337) situation where customers know which item they want to buy, but are unclear about specific details

Green River Ordinances (p. 13) state and local governments' restrictions on door-to-door selling

greeters (p. 12) representatives of wholesalers and manufacturers, mid-1800s

GRI (p. 354) Graduate Realtors® Institute

group selling (p. 186) salesperson makes presentation to more than one customer

guaranteed draw (p. 58) compensation plan whereby the sales rep is not liable for repayment if the draw is more than the commission earned in a given period

hard sell (p. 161) aggressive sales approach

"If I can show you . . . " approach (p. 251) closing technique that identifies the prospect's primary need and then offers a solution

implementation (p. 106) procedures necessary to carry out a plan

indifference trap (p. 267) customers' perception that salespeople do not care about their business

inelasticity of demand (p. 314) product demand that is not influenced by price fluctuations

initial sales training (p. 380) preparation and orientation of new sales personnel

interference (p. 116) distractions that occur in a communications channel. Also called noise

internal search (p. 78) study of relevant information from memory of past searches, personal experiences, and learning

JIT (p. 315) just-in-time inventory that integrates supplier shipments with customers' production scheduling

key-influence method (p. 135) prospecting method that uses people who command respect within their social, work, or professional groups

leadership (p. 388) personal style by which one supervises

limited allowance (p. 60) expense account plan that limits reimbursement to a set amount

limited decision making (p. 76) situation involving fewer alternatives and less purchasing effort than extensive decision making

list brokers (p. 137) firms that sell mailing (or prospect) lists

listings (p. 354) an inventory of homes for sale

machinery and equipment (p. 311) used to manufacture other products

maintenance selling (p. 26) situation in which the salesperson is responsible for maintaining or increasing sales volume from existing customers of the firm

market analysis (p. 359) a valuation of real estate based on current market conditions

marketing concept (p. 12) organizational philosophy oriented toward solving consumer problems and meeting the needs of the marketplace

marketing information system (p. 41) computer system designed to produce information relevant to marketing decisions

materials requirement planning (MRP) (p. 325) computerized system that provides the purchasing department with requisitions for a particular purchasing situation

minimum acceptance decision rule (p. 82) consumer acceptance based on a product or brand surpassing the minimum standard on any one criterion

minimum standards decision rule (p. 82) consideration of all products or brands that surpass a minimum standard on each evaluation criterion

missionary salesperson (p. 33) a sales rep who concentrates on the customers of resellers

mobile demonstrator (p. 202) unit used to demonstrate a product that is too big or complex to be carried into a prospect's office

national accounts (p. 293) firm's biggest customers

national account selling (p. 41) assignment of nationwide accounts to just a single salesperson or team

national realty network (p. 361) a group of local real estate offices (often franchised) linked together by name, advertising, and computer listings

need-satisfaction approach (p. 178) customer-oriented sales approach based on customers' needs

new purchases (p. 320) purchasing situation where the emphasis is on developing specifications for a product

one-price policy (p. 228) sets a specific figure and does not allow the salesperson to negotiate price

open house (p. 359) property that is open to inspection by all interested parties

operating supplies (p. 312) products used up in the production process, such as lubricants or office supplies

order receiver (p. 25) a sales administrator or trade salesperson who routinely processes a customer's order

peddlers (p. 12) self-employed salespeople in colonial times

periodic allowance (p. 59) expense account plan that sets the reimbursement at a given level for a time period

personal selling (p. 8) interpersonal persuasive process designed to influence someone's decision

planning (p. 105) selecting the actions necessary to attain desired future sales states

plant visits (p. 202) trips to the seller's facilities to check company capabilities and quality control

point system (p. 58) pay plan that awards points or credits for achievement; the total is then converted to a compensation payment

pooled sales force (p. 376) situation in which salespeople sell all of their firms' products to each account they serve

positive conversion (p. 227) transforms an objection into a reason for buying

postpurchase dissonance (p. 85) doubt related to a relatively nonrevocable decision

preapproach (p. 150) preparation for a sales call

processed materials (p. 312) partially completed items that will become part of a finished good after further processing

prospect (p. 127) sales lead that the salesperson or other party has identified as needing or desiring the product or service

pull strategy (p. 111) promotional strategy emphasizing advertising

purchase involvement (p. 75) amount of effort or interest a consumer puts into the decision-making process

push strategy (p. 111) promotional strategy emphasizing personal selling

qualified prospect (p. 130) customer who has the ability and/or the authority to purchase the good or service

qualifying (p. 130) determining a prospect's ability and authority to buy a product

raw materials (p. 312) unprocessed natural products

rebuttal (p. 223) immediate response that counters an objection with additional information

reciprocity (p. 315) practice of extending purchasing preference to suppliers who are also customers

referral (p. 133) prospecting method in which the customer introduces and recommends the seller to prospects

replacement purchasing (p. 319) purchasing which considers new products of proven superiority or potential superiority

repurchase (p. 150) continued purchases at the present level or increases in purchase volume

resale programs (p. 274) marketing program designed to increase customers' sales volume

resellers (p. 317) organizations that purchase products solely for resale or rental to others

restating the objection (p. 226) handling an objection by shifting the emphasis to a more favorable posture

retail selling (p. 333) sale of products and services to individual consumers for their own or others' personal use

Robinson-Patman Act (p. 13) prohibition against charging different prices to different customers unless costs differ

routine decision making (p. 76) purchase that incurs little or no purchasing effort

routing (p. 293) process of minimizing travel time for sales personnel

sales administrator (p. 27) the customer contact within the supplier's organization

sales aids (p. 202) items used in a demonstration such as visual aids, audiovisual aids, and the product itself

sales climate (p. 374) situation wherein the sales force attempts to match its behavior with that desired by the firm

sales effectiveness (p. 285) output measure of a person's selling effort

sales efficiency (p. 285) input measure of how well people are carrying out their assigned sales tasks

sales engineer (p. 26) salesperson with technical qualifications regarding the product

sales lead (p. 127) prospective customer the salesperson has identified as needing or desiring a product or service

sales plan (p. 104) contains the sales goal for a given customer as well as sales strategies, analysis of the customer, and specific actions to be taken

sales presentation (p. 175) step in the sales process where the salesperson delivers a specific customer

sales quotas (p. 386) performance standards based on expected sales volumes

sales resistance (p. 215) anything the prospect does or says to prevent or delay a close

sales system (p. 374) policies and practices related to the management of a sales force

selectivity (p. 86) screening process that affects exposure, perception, and retention

selectivity profile (p. 86) likely reactions of the consumer to the products or services, salesperson, and the vendor company

self-management (p. 285) combination of time management and self-motivation

seller's market (p. 12) market characterized by a relative scarcity of goods

service representative (p. 30) salesperson whose primary duty is to provide after-sale customer service

service selling (p. 25) situation in which the salesperson assists customer in completing a transaction without influencing the nature of the transaction

shelf item (p. 162) readily available product that has been on the market for a considerable time

showing (p. 359) sales presentation in the real estate industry

silent close or silent trial close (p. 253) closing technique in which the salesperson stops talking and waits for the buyer to respond

soft sell (p. 161) low-key, nonthreatening sales approach

sole source (p. 273) situation where a buyer buys from only one vendor

SPEAR (p. 315) supplier performance evaluation and review

specialist selling (p. 28) division of a sales force into groups that specialize in certain customers

specific decision (p. 337) situation where consumers know both the product and the brand they wish to buy

spotters (p. 135) people who make specialized surveys or canvasses to assess prospects' needs

standing room only (SRO) method (p. 252) closing technique in which the prospect is told that the purchase should be concluded now, since the merchandise probably will not be available later

standard of living (p. 333) quantity and quality of goods and services consumers can provide with their resources

stimulus-response approach (p. 177) assumes that specific actions by a salesperson stimulate a customer to buy

straight salary plan (p. 57) compensation plan that pays sales reps a given amount at specified times

strategic plans (p. 101) broad, long-range plans designed to reach major objectives

substitute decision (p. 338) a change in a general or specific decision

substitute selling (p. 341) situation where a seller attempts to sell something other than what the customer requested

suggestion selling (p. 343) retail salesperson's effort to sell add-on purchases or larger quantities

summary and affirmative agreement method (p. 249) close whereby the seller summarizes the features, benefits, and advantages of the product and seeks agreement from the prospect

supervision (p. 387) planning, directing, controlling, and evaluating of salespeople

systems selling (p. 38) marketing of a product line or service that satisfies an identifiable need

team selling (p. 186) more than one sales rep calls on a customer

technical specialist (p. 31) sales rep who deals with the technical details of a buyer-seller relationship

testimonials (p. 225) closing method that tells the prospect about the satisfaction of earlier buyers

tickler file (p. 268) system for reminding a salesperson to follow up on certain details with customers

time management (p. 287) study and effective use of time

traders (p. 11) sales personnel who operated in ancient societies

trade salespeople (p. 26) salespeople who sell to retailers

trading up (p. 341) situation where a consumer buys additional or more expensive items than originally planned

trial close (p. 246) closing attempt used to determine prospect's disposition to the product and the sales presentation

turnover rate (p. 378) percentage of the sales force lost each year to resignation, discharge, retirement, and other reasons

unlimited expense account (p. 59) reimbursement plan that pays all legitimate expenses

unplanned decision (p. 338) situation where consumers make on-the-spot purchase decisions without benefit of prior planning

value analysis (p. 319) process whereby each product part is related to the function it performs so that costs can be cut with no loss in quality or performance

vendor analysis (p. 318) quantitative assessment of suppliers using factors such as quality, price, delivery, and service

walk-ins (p. 355) potential real estate customers who walk in to the firm's office without prior contact by the agent

warranties and guarantees (p. 228) assurances that a product will perform satisfactorily

Wheeler-Lea Act (p. 13) ban on deceptive promotional practices

"Yes, but . . . " approach (p. 225) seller notes agreement with a prospect's objection, then counters with more information

Index